W9-BSC-858

BERKSHIRE ENCYCLOPEDIA OF

Extreme Sports

BERKSHIRE PUBLISHING GROUP

BERKSHIRE ENCYCLOPEDIA OF
Extreme
Sports

Douglas Booth & Holly Thorpe, Editors

Published by:
Berkshire Publishing Group LLC
314 Main Street
Great Barrington, Massachusetts 01230
www.berkshirepublishing.com

Printed in the United States of America

Library of Congress Cataloging-in-Publication Data
Berkshire encyclopedia of extreme sports/Douglas Booth and Holly Thorpe, editors.
    p. cm.
Includes bibliographical references and index.
ISBN 978-0-9770159-5-5 (alk. paper)
    1. Extreme sports—Encyclopedias.   I. Booth, Douglas.   II. Thorpe, Holly.
GV749.7B47 2007
796.04'6003—dc22   2007008290

Editorial and Production Staff

Project Directors
David Levinson
Karen Christensen

Project Coordinators
Scott Eldridge II and Cassie Lynch

Editorial Staff
Marcy Ross, Jennifer Frederick,
Liz Steffey, and Erin Connor

Editorial Interns
Jake Makler and Ashley Winseck

Photo Coordinators
Joseph DiStefano and Scott Eldridge II

Copyeditors
Mike Nichols and Dan Spinella

Designers
Joseph DiStefano and Gabriel Every

Composition Artist
Brad Walrod/High Text Graphics, Inc.

Proofreader
Mary Bagg

**Information Management
and Programming**
Trevor Young

Indexer
Peggy Holloway

Printers
Thomson-Shore, Inc.

Contents

List of Entries

Introduction

Taking risks with one's life in sport competitions is nothing new in the human experience. Gladiatorial competitions in ancient Rome and jousts in medieval Europe are two examples of sports that fit the modern definition of extreme. Extreme sports in their modern form are a recent development and the list of pursuits and sports categorized as "extreme" is long and growing as is the number of athletes and spectators. Extreme sports now form a distinct sector within the larger sports industry, although exactly where it fits is not at all clear.

Extreme sports have diffused around the world at a phenomenal rate and far faster than established sports. Extreme sports have benefited from a historically unique conjuncture of mass communications, corporate sponsors, entertainment industries, political aspirations of cities, and a growing affluent and young population.

Extreme sports are about taking risks, pushing the limits, breaking the rules, and—at least sometimes—about having fun. They are also a major cultural, commercial, and media phenomenon whose importance far transcends the relatively few active participants. Culturally, extreme sports are seen as representing values such as fierce individualism, civil disobedience, the quest for human potential, taking control of one's own life, and intimate engagements with the environment. Commercially, *extreme* is the password for corporations and advertisers to access young people, especially men, in the thirteen-to-thirty-four-year-old demographic. Whereas the median age of the baseball demographic is the mid-forties, the X Games and Gravity Games are primarily watched by twelve- to seventeen-year-olds. The media, notably ESPN, sponsors and broadcasters of the Summer X Games and Winter X Games, has played a critical role in the diffusion and popularization of the extreme sports.

Extreme sports do not constitute a single category of physical activity. Some are indeed very free while others are codified and commercialized. Most are legal but a few, like buildering, are illegal. Like the sports themselves, extreme sports athletes also defy ready classification. Most are middle-class men or boys and most are young and white. But extreme sports increasingly attract participants from different social classes and age groups, as well as females and minority groups.

Extreme sports are both similar to and dissimilar from established sports. They are similar in that athletes are willing to take risks while also maintaining a concern for personal safety, people participate to a significant degree to have fun, and athletes and sports officials are willing to rationalize and institutionalize activities in order to enhance the growth and spread of their sports. Extreme and established sports are also alike in that many specific sports are now global activities and many sports are contested at international sport competitions which are televised to international audiences. They are dissimilar in that extreme sports are much more likely to be individual rather than team sports, the primary objectives tend to be meeting personal challenges and testing oneself, extreme sports often involve close interaction with the Earth's natural features and forces, and many extreme athletes reject mainstream sports values.

At the center of the rapid global diffusion of extreme sports sits the cable television network ESPN. It broadcast the first Summer X Games in mid-1995. Staged at Newport (Rhode Island), Middletown (Rhode Island), and Mount Snow (Vermont), the inaugural games featured twenty-seven events in nine categories: bungee jumping, eco-challenge, in-line skating, skateboarding, skysurfing, sport climbing, street luge, biking, and water sports. Twelve months later X Games II attracted around 200,000 spectators, and early in 1997 ESPN staged the first Winter X Games at Snow Summit Mountain Resort (California). The initial Winter X Games were televised in 198 countries and territories in twenty-one languages. The X Games have witnessed exponential growth in terms of participants and television audiences in the decade since the first games. Among the target

About the Design

The design of the book reflects the unpredictability and daring of the subject we're covering. With a sporting genre known for flips, dips, and all things extreme, our design echoes this theme with "extreme numbering." The mirrored page numbers (on right-hand pages) may appear at first to be a typographical error, but like sports, design can take an extreme spin!

demographic of boys and men, the Summer and Winter X Games are a staple of the global sporting culture. Like the corporate sponsors of established sports, those involved with the X Games view their associations as a means to convey cultural credibility. Although corporate sponsors of extreme sports highlight risk taking and individualism, in contrast to sponsors of established sports who emphasize teamwork and cooperation, both continue to underscore traditional notions of masculinity. Corporate interests have successfully transformed living on the edge into an aspirational consumer product: wearing North Face gear, drinking Mountain Dew, talking on an X Games mobile phone are about appearance and the passive consumption of risk.

The *Berkshire Encyclopedia of Extreme Sports* provides the first international survey of extreme sports; it is a state-of-the-art summary of where extreme sports are today, where they have come from, and how they are likely to grow and change in the years ahead. The encyclopedia provides 114 articles written by sixty-nine sports experts and athletes covering more than fifty sports, biographies on more than thirty athletes, essays on nine extreme sports venues, and seventeen social issues.

The idea for this volume devoted to extreme sports emerged during the Berkshire Encyclopedia of World Sport project published last year. The team at Berkshire Publishing realized that extreme sports, as a relatively new but fast growing and truly global domain in the world of sports, required an entire volume of its own to fully cover the topic. They also realized that as the world of sport evolves, examining extreme sports will provide further and new insights into how sport grows and spreads.

As a collection, these articles describe and explain extreme sports and provide biographies of leading athletes. A number of articles also discuss issues in extreme sports such as gender and violence and place the growing phenomenon of extreme sports and the concept of extreme in their wider contexts of sports, human physical activity, commercialization, and the human experience in general.

Douglas Booth and Holly Thorpe

Acknowledgements

This project began in June 2005, while several of us were attending the American Library Association meeting in Chicago in 95-degree heat and humidity. Our lead publication at the meeting was the *Berkshire Encyclopedia of World Sport* and one evening riding back from dinner, we came up with the idea of a separate work on extreme sports. Perhaps it was the heat and navigating Chicago streets that brought the topic to mind. In the fall we began to plan the project with a short schedule, and that led us to Doug Booth and Holly Thorpe, who accepted our invitation to edit the book and then cleared their decks to get the project off to a quick start; they stayed engaged throughout, quickly reviewing articles, suggesting additional contributors, and writing several articles themselves. Doug and Holly went to great lengths to find a group of expert contributors who themselves worked with us to produce original articles on a wide range of topics, some of which have hardly been heard of, let alone studied and written about.

Our project coordinator Cassie Lynch worked closely with them to get the project up and going and moving forward steadily, and when she left for graduate school, Scott Eldridge took it to completion. Thanks also to other members of the BPG editorial team—Marcy Ross, Erin Connor, Jenn Frederick, Liz Steffey—who took time from their own projects to assist with manuscript proofing, sidebar editing, and photo preparation. Thanks also to interns Ashley Winseck and Jake Mackler for helping process articles and research photographs. Mike Nichols and Dan Spinella copyedited the articles, which required them to figure out how the new language of "extreme" fits into the Berkshire style.

I want also to acknowledge the stellar performance of our out-of-house production team who worked very hard to make the book attractive and engaging as well as informative: Joe DiStefano for his page and cover designs, Brad Walrod for composition, Mary Bagg for proofreading, and Peggy Holloway for the index. Also deserving of thanks is Trevor Young, our information and technology specialist, for helping streamline the processes that go into collecting all the information you see before you.

David Levinson

Reader's Guide

Contributors

Alaniz, Jose Angel Pablo
University of Texas-Pan American
Eisenberg, Arlo
Julio, Jon
Khris, Taig

Appleby, Karen M.
Idaho State University
Boudering: North America

Bach, Alice R.
University of Copenhagen
Crandal, Louise

Barbour, Karen
University of Waikato
Outrigger Canoe Racing

Beal, Becky
University of the Pacific
Skateboarding

Beaven, Martyn
Physiology of Risk

Bell, Martha
University of Otago
Adventure Racing

Bennett, Richard
thesurfermind.com
Kite Surfing

Bonini, Gherardo
European University Institute
de Gayardon, Patrick
Deegan, Brian
Motocross
Valeruz, Toni

Booth, Douglas
University of Waikato
Baumgartner, Felix
Hamilton, Laird
Meaning of Extreme, The
Noll, Greg
Open Water Swimming
Surfing

Bourgard, Dane
University of Western Ontario
Wakeskating

Brown, David
The University of Exeter
Body and Extreme Sport, The

Butryn, Ted
San Jose State University
Foley, Mick
Professional Wrestling

Charlston, Jeffery A.
University of Maryland
Ferreras Rodriquez, Pipin
Free Diving
Scuba Diving
Streeter, Tanya

Cooper, Jason
University of Calgary
BASE Jumping

Crawford, Russ
University of Nebraska, Lincoln
Media and Extreme Sport
X Games

Crawford, Scott A. G. M.
Eastern Illinois University
Knievel, Evel

Cumo, Christopher M.
Independent Scholar
Strength

de Loca, Paul J.
North American Society
    for Sport History
Ice Yachting

Dickson, Geoff
AUT University
Hawk, Tony
Mullen, Rodney

Edwardes, Dan
Urbanfreeflow.com
Parkour

Erickson, Bruce
York University
Rock Climbing

Findley, Carolyn
Auburn University, Montgomery
Psychology of Risk

Fisher, Kevin
University of Otago
Big Wave Contests
Dogtown and Z-boys
Dora, Miki

Ford, Nick
The University of Exeter
Body and Extreme Sport, The

Forss, Matthew
Northern Michigan University
Ultramarathon

Gill, Nicholas
University of Waikato
Physiology of Risk

Goksoyr, Matti
Norwegian School of Sport Science
Ski Jumping

Gullion, Laurie
University of New Hampshire
Whitewater Kayaking and Canoeing

Hansen, Peter
Worcester Polytechnic Institute
Hillary, Sir Edmund and
Tenzig Norgay

Hattery, Angela J.
Wake Forest University
Violence

Hynes-Hunter,
Joanne Margaret
California Polytechnic
State University
Gladiator Competitions
Jousting

Johnson, Jay
University of Toronto
Initiation/Hazing

Jutel, Annemarie
Otago Polytechnic
Triathlon

Kochetkova, Tatjana
Louis Bolk Institute
Spirituality

Kusz, Kyle
University of Rhode Island
BMX (Bicycle Motocross)
Hoffman, Mat
Mirra, Dave
Nyquist, Ryan
Whiteness and Extreme Sport

Laurendeau, Jason
University of Calgary
BASE Jumping
Skydiving/Skysurfing

Levinson, David
Berkshire Publishing Group
Vine Jumping

Lewis, Jan
Central Queensland University
Carmichael, Ricky

Lundy, Audrey
Northern Michigan University
Waterskiing

Masucci, Matt
San Jose State University
Mountain Bike Racing
Stamstad, John
Ultimate Fighting

McConnell, Robin
The Grove, KeriKeri
Bungee Jumping
Hackett, A. J.
Leadership and Extreme Sport
Queenstown

Mead, Melissa
Ohio Northern University
Jet Skiing
Wakeboarding

Miller, Jaclyn
Ithaca College
da Silva, Fabiola

Moloney, Nick
Offshore Challenges Sailing Team
Round-the-World Yacht Racing

Oliver, Jon
Eastern Illinois University
In-line Skating/Rollerblading

Palmer, Catherine
Flinders University
Commercialization

Paraschak, Vicky
University of Windsor
Iditarod

Pike, Elizabeth C. J.
University College, Chichester
Injury

Platchias, Dimitris
University of Glasgow
Agon Motif
Pankration

Popovic, Megan
University of Western Canada
Bonifay, Parks

Quercetani, Roberto
Long Distance Racing and
Pedestrianism

Reynier, Veronique
Universite Joseph Fourier
France

Robinson, Tom
Hanze University of Groningen
Cave Diving

Schimmel, Kimberly S.
Kent State University
Caving

Self, Don
Auburn University Montgomery
Psychology of Risk

Skott, Beth
Ballooning
Extreme Ironing
Shaw, Phil (Steam)

Smith, Earl
Wake Forest University
Violence

Staurowsky, Ellen J.
Ithaca College
Barrel Jumping
Coleman, Bessie
da Silva, Fabiola
Muldowney, Shirley
Wing Walking

Stranger, Mark
University of Tasmania
Sociology of Risk

Sturm, Damion
University of Waikato
Motorvehicle Sports

Thorpe, Holly
University of Waikato
Alaska
Dakides, Tara
Extreme Media
Gender
Haakonsen, Terje
Kelly, Craig
Meaning of Extreme, The
Snowboarding
Whistler
White, Shaun

van Hilvoorde, Ivo
Vrije Universiteit
Bouldering
Buildering

Vassort, Claire
Independent Scholar
Hang Gliding

Vermeir, Kevin
Université Joseph Fourier
France
Skiing

Wachs, Faye Linda
California State Polytechnic
University, Pomona
Venice Beach

Wassong, Stephan
Liverpool Hope University
Climbing
Playgrounds

Weigel, Dana
Ohio Northern University
Belle, David
Foucan, Sébastian

Wheaton, Belinda
University of Surrey Roehampton
Jaws
Windsurfing

About the Editors

Douglas Booth (PhD, Macquarie) and Holly Thorpe (BPhEd[Hons], Otago) teach courses on the culture of sport and the social psychology of sport respectively in the Department of Sport and Leisure Studies at the University of Waikato, New Zealand. Their research includes the historical, political, sociological, and theoretical dimensions of sport. Douglas and Holly are members of several scholarly associations including the North American Society for Sport History and the North American Society for the Sociology of Sport. They have both won academic awards for their work, which has appeared in a cross section of peer-refereed academic journals including *Australian Studies*, *Journal of Contemporary History*, *International Journal of the History of Sport*, *Sociology of Sport Journal*, *Sport and Society*, and *Waikato Journal of Education*. Both have written articles on sport for specialist encyclopedias, newspapers, and niche sports magazines.

Douglas and Holly are cultural insiders, immersed in surfing and snowboarding respectively; they write about the extreme versions of these pursuits in the *Berkshire Encyclopedia of Extreme Sports*. As well as travelling internationally in pursuit of waves and powder, they have competed in various surfing and snowboarding competitions, and remain active participants in these two fields.

Disclaimer

The *Berkshire Encyclopedia of Extreme Sports* is not designed to be a "how-to" manual for the sports and activities described within. All forms of extreme sports are inherently dangerous. Get professional instruction before attempting any of the activities described in the *Berkshire Encyclopedia of Extreme Sports*. Any advice that is given by authors or entries in the *Berkshire Encyclopedia of Extreme Sports* is purely informational and should not be misconstrued as professional instruction. Participating in extreme sports without proper training and instruction could result in serious injury, or possibly death, and all activities should be considered dangerous.

BERKSHIRE ENCYCLOPEDIA OF

Extreme Sports

Adventure Racing

Wilderness environments provide a unique setting for the challenges of speed, efficiency, and endurance in a long-distance race. For more than twenty years individuals and teams have competed on remote and risky backcountry race courses. Now global in their occurrence and known as "adventure races," such competitions are almost all team-based to achieve the elements central to adventure: navigation en route, shared decision making, and responsibility for all members of the team.

Essence of Adventure

The essence of adventure racing is the exploration of wilderness at a pace designed to withstand the rigors of harsh terrain. Adventure comes from encountering the unanticipated and the unfamiliar, testing all the skills and experience of expedition members. Pressures of time, sleep loss, and performance under duress are usually anathema to adventurers, who prefer to move at a rate responsive to contingencies in weather, landscape, equipment, and group fitness. Aiming to reach a specific destination in a prescribed time spoils the purpose of the trip.

Adventure racing challenges the skills, knowledge, and reflexes of even the best wilderness travelers. From the starting gun, teams must determine an optimal route while on the run. They must vary their modes of travel, demonstrating skill in a range of outdoor pursuit disciplines, while equipping themselves for all possible eventualities and still racing without stopping. They have little planning time, at most a few hours the night before the race begins. The first team to reach the finish line intact, having passed through a series of designated checkpoints, often each with its own time limit, wins the race. Adventure races take days to complete, and teams race through the night.

Adventure racing's difficulty lies deeply embedded in its essential contradiction. A wilderness journey does not adhere to deadlines. Nor is exploration fruitful with a stopwatch running. Remote routes are meticulously planned and then pursued for their safety and ease, not for their obstacles. Expedition parties stop regularly, whether to take shelter in a storm, rest at nightfall, or retreat in the event of an injury. Fellow travelers always share local area knowledge and warnings of dangers ahead, along with a few yarns.

Turning Adventure into Sport

Turning adventure into a sport places participants at new levels of risk and forces new tests of endurance and courage under pressure. In this relatively new type of race, teams strive to preserve expedition values while also moving at a fast pace with the minimum of sleep in hostile conditions such that they rely on human relationships as much as human strength. Some people have raced together as teams for years on the adventure racing circuit; racers even talk of the joys of spending a week with friends. The greatest challenge for the majority of teams, however, lies in the combination of personalities and levels of commitment of team members in the face of extreme difficulty and discomfort.

Similar challenges exist for elite-level athletes turning to the adventure race to extend their capacity. They learn to eat, hydrate, navigate, adjust clothing, and check on team morale while moving at the fastest pace achievable and then to stop for a quick sleep. They also learn to appreciate a sunrise, a snowfall, a peak ascent, or a lake traverse whenever it occurs in the midst of their race. Athletes find that physical skill, strength, speed, endurance, conditioning, nutrition, and motivation are as much a part of a 500-kilometer race as they are a part of a 25-kilometer race.

Original Adventure Races

Adventure racing started as a form of extreme multisport competition. Modeled on the triathlon, three outdoor pursuits were incorporated into one race such that racers were required to hike, bike, and paddle through the wilderness. The roots of adventure racing are also evident in endurance feats in which competitors are literally trail running through woods, canyons, desert, rain forest, and tundra, carrying a mountain bike when the terrain is too difficult to cycle, carrying paddles ready to travel on waterways, and carrying mountaineering equipment to and from passes. As it grew into an off-track event, adventure racing involved wilderness orienteering and thereby embraced another little-known twenty-four-hour sport named "rogaine." Not until later was the original concept elaborated into an adventure experience package.

The French took this concept to New Zealand in 1989. Gérard Fusil, an adventure sports journalist, kept secret for many months his plan to showcase a French expedition race in an international landscape. The Raid Gauloises, also known as the Grand Traverse, was as flamboyant as its reputation, involving racers on foot and horseback forging across dramatic scenery. It found its wilderness in the Southern Alps and its spectators in the readers of *New Zealand Adventure* magazine, the cover of which it dominated. This race put New Zealand on the world stage as the wildest, most remote region for the teams who galloped across its stark, alpine high country.

New Zealanders worked with the advance group of French entrepreneurs who arrived to design the unusual trekking race in the Southern Hemisphere. The following years New Zealanders served as race logistics crew, safety marshals, and race plan consultants. New Zealand teams also raced in the Raid Gauloises, winning first, second, and third place. This race introduced to international observers the central elements of adventure racing: coed teams of five members traveling under human or animal power only, making all decisions autonomously, traveling self-sufficiently, totally immersed in the natural environment. Although they raced the clock nonstop for however many days it took, the theme for racers was more of a grand contest between humans and nature.

Rules of the Race

Adventure races cross a wide variety of terrain, involve athletes of different skills and styles. There are six basic rules for adventure race participants focused mostly on respect for the sport and the area where the races take place. These rules form the United States Adventure Racing Association's Adventure Racer Code of Ethics:

1. I will practice minimum impact travelling.
2. I will respect the land, and inhabitants, in which I travel.
3. I will not litter.
4. I will practice good sportsmanship.
5. I will lend aid to those in need during competition.
6. I will abide by the rules and regulations of the event.

Source: United States Adventure Racing Association. (n.d.). Retrieved June 29, 2006, from http://www.usara.com/home.aspx

Two years later New Zealanders established their own international classic. The Southern Traverse followed the Grand Traverse. In 1991 Geoff Hunt became race director, using his experience of working on the original Raid and working as a wilderness raft guide. The new race was situated only a little south of the route of the Raid, also traversing the Southern Alps and covering more than 400 kilometers of ground. Although the Raid moved to other countries, the Southern Traverse is still held annually in New Zealand. By the late 1990s international teams arrived to compete against the predominantly New Zealand–based teams. Recently the race was held in the northwest of South Island, and racers were sent through some of the deepest caves in the Southern Hemisphere.

The internationally known races were said to start with these original ventures; however, races obviously were held in many countries—as early as 1980 in New Zealand and 1983 in Alaska. Most likely other countries held similar multisport challenges in their backcountry.

It is difficult to say which race came first. However, it is not as difficult to say which is the best known of the adventure races. The Eco-Challenge was first held in 1995 in the Utah canyon lands. Its second year, staged in British Columbia, Canada, produced such a rugged course that only fourteen teams of seventy contestants overcame the terrain to finish the race. The Eco-Challenge solidified its reputation. The winning team, Team Eco-Internet, was made up of New Zealanders.

Eco Ethic

The Eco-Challenge is unique for three reasons. As a result of the vision of its creator, Mark Burnett, it has grown in size, scope, and spectacle into a small industry. Unlike the French and New Zealand approach, Burnett's U.S. event sought media sponsorship at the outset from the Discovery Channel and has been televised from its first year. British-born Burnett's own experience racing in two Raid Gauloises races had convinced him of the potential for human interest in the fate of racers.

Burnett also linked the first Eco-Challenge to a lifestyle brand that he had designed some years earlier to align adventure tourism and traveling spectatorship with adventure racing. He knew that the global growth of this small industry would attract, and depend upon, vicarious thrill seekers along with the physical thrill seekers. He then developed

Adventure racing often involves travel through spectacular land and waterscapes such as this one. Source: istock/David Penner.

a race management headquarters and held training camps across states during the 1990s to give potential competitors the wide range of outdoor pursuit skills needed to compete in an adventure race.

More important to the sport, though, Burnett inscribed into his race's ethos a commitment to environmental responsibility and cultural awareness. From the beginning he required each team to comply with a minimum-impact code of camping. Community service and other cultural projects must also take place prior to or following every race, no matter its location in the world.

Mark Burnett wanted to promote a lifestyle that does not exploit the beautiful locations in which races are held but rather contributes to their preservation. Racers are encouraged to see cultural differences and learn from them instead of focusing on their personal lives and race aspirations. Competitors might construct canoes from local materials in the style of the indigenous people, for example, and paddle them to the next transition point. Later the boats would be given to the villagers in appreciation to enhance the retention of traditional fishing customs. Constructing the team's own form of transport in the middle of a race would be one of the many surprises designed to test competitors' tolerance for obstacles and ensure that they give their attention to the people living in the environment surrounding them.

Other adventure races have adopted the eco ethic as well. A race may donate its proceeds to benefit a local program such as wildlife rehabilitation or a person needing lifesaving medical treatment. Personal excess or waste is not part of the eco ethic. All teams must practice minimum impact as their code of ethics. In the mountaineering adage, they must "pack out what they pack in" to the wilderness. Even race management crews are reminded by the United States Adventure Racing Association (USARA) on its webpage that after their race they must "clean up race site, leave no trace of your event."

Racing Green

Many racers describe adventure racing as more than a competition, as a lifestyle linking green values of sustainability and personal responsibility with physical self-sufficiency. Treating racing as a privilege and not a conquest is fundamental. Many race organizations encourage racers to maintain an ethical commitment to nonexploitation of the Earth's resources beyond racing when they purchase food, clothing, and gear for their everyday lives as much as for their expeditions.

Teams are generally made up of four or five people.

All the top international races stipulate mixed-sex teams; regulations require at least one woman. Local or national races make their own stipulations; some even allow "soloists" and two-member teams. Team members must begin by developing a level of cardiovascular fitness and endurance so that they can compete in short races of six hours to start with. Short races are often run on tracks, and equipment is provided. Longer races require mandatory equipment, which is purchased by the team. Eventually, if the team travels to international races, members will research ways of buying their equipment after they arrive in the country of the race.

As they race together, team members start to experiment with the right equipment, clothing, footwear, and food. Their goal is to find ways to carry what they need without hindering their ability to travel quickly and safely. They will refine their refueling systems and means of accommodating their bodily needs en route. They will train for longer races by going into the local wilderness as often as possible to race the clock. After they can race during the daytime, they will practice racing at night and then racing through the night. After they can keep a steady pace for twenty-four hours, they have begun to experience adventure racing.

Prepared for Emergencies

Teams carry first-aid kits and act as their own medical advisors. Dehydration, overheating, and chilling are constantly monitored and alleviated by rehydration and a change of clothing. Chafing, blisters, bleeding, and infection are common consequences of long-distance racing. Joint injuries and tissue damage can present an emergency as well. Even so, sometimes team members carry an injured teammate until he or she is able to race again. The most severe risk to a person's health is posed by diarrhea. Sudden gastrointestinal illness on the trail is usually irreversible and weakens the team member to the extent that he or she cannot finish the race.

Adventure racing's emphasis on team responsibility defines winning: No team can finish the race without all of its members together. Accidents and injuries that eliminate a member, therefore, jeopardize the entire team's goals. A team's ability to keep every member focused and safe enhances its chances of getting through each checkpoint to the finish line.

To make the preparation as difficult as possible, a course is typically kept secret from competitors. Although prerace materials might describe the terrain and hint at distances, racers try to plan for a course that they cannot study in advance. Teams work on the principle that they should train in areas most similar to the climate and topography of the terrain in which they will be competing so that they come to know what to expect. A big international race is typically 500 kilometers in length. A shorter race can be from 60 to 200 kilometers. Races for first-time racers will provide as much information and support as possible to make adventure racing a positive experience.

Whether first-time racers or veteran racers, all teams race with a respect for their environment and their fellow competitors. Teams are advised when to depart from a track and when traveling off-track is not allowed because the natural vegetation is too fragile to be crossed. Biodegradable food waste and human waste are not left behind. All teams are responsible for carrying their waste. Attention is therefore necessary before and during races to ensure that errors are not made, from planning menus and optimized eating and drinking systems to eliminating packaging ahead of time, reducing the weight of equipment, and planning proper hygiene practices for toileting and washing.

Trail running, bush bashing, vertical ascending, rappelling, Tyrolean traversing, and river running, among many varieties of modes of travel for four or five days, take their toll on judgment as much as on stamina. Because adventure races are unpredictable by design, problem solving could cost the team a lot of time, depending on how clearly roles are designated and how well individuals' skills and knowledge complement each other. Whereas hunger and fatigue can be managed, the most debilitating effects of constant racing are the consequences of sleep deprivation, performance stress, and psychological distress. Racers tell of suffering hallucinations, panic attacks, mood changes, and loss of appetite and even falling asleep while racing. Grueling physical demands can affect the ability of team members to communicate with each other, observe safety standards, abide by group decisions, and avoid conflict. When teams can find what is called "team synergy," then team members begin to trust each other. Different team members may even contribute to group leadership at different times, forcing a meal or navigation stop, dealing with an emergency, reversing a poor decision, encouraging a slower member, or refocusing a team's attention. The metaphor for racing takes form when teams find their own rhythm.

New Quest

When adventure racing began in the 1980s, creators were often wilderness enthusiasts and endurance racers themselves. It was easier then to abide by a not-for-profit philosophy. Many races were run across public land in the conservation estate, and high technology had not affected outdoor equipment design. By the 1990s the spirit of exploration had given way to the quest for marketing and media coverage, team sponsorship, high-tech equipment, flawless safety systems and logistics management, and top prize money. Race organizers began to promote, and manage contacts for, their events using the Internet. By the end of the 1990s races posted day-by-day accounts on websites, along with team rankings, team profiles, journalists' reports, and photographs.

Now racing associations use the Internet to disseminate race calendars, registration requirements, association information, membership benefits, online purchase details, web links to adventure racing clubs worldwide, adventure racing books, adventure racing training information, and adventure racing team blogs. World championship events and global positioning systems, although mostly disallowed, are both indications of how globalization and its digitally connected environment have influenced the adventure world.

Alongside this new digital environment, adventure racers continue to run one step at a time in a distinctly nondigital world of sweat, effort, maps, ropes, and energy bars, battling only their own deepest resistance to pushing themselves to the ultimate in physical feats. Racers talk about a loss of ego and new appreciation for simplicity emerging from the intensity of adventure racing. In the end racers and race organizers know that something more powerful than sporting prowess emerges when the worries of ordinary life are shed and the body and the wilderness meld to allow for new possibilities in human will and achievement.

Martha Bell

Further Reading
Bell, M. (2003). Another kind of life: Adventure racing and epic expeditions. In R. E. Rinehart & S. Sydnor (Eds.), *To the extreme: Alternative sports, inside and out* (pp. 219–253). Albany: State University of New York Press.

Cotter, J. (2003). Eco (ego?) challenge: British Columbia, 1996. In R. E. Rinehart & S. Sydnor (Eds.), *To the extreme: Alternative sports, inside and out* (pp. 207–217). Albany: State University of New York Press.

Marais, J., & de Speville, L. (2004). *Adventure racing.* Champaign, IL: Human Kinetics.

Paterson, D. (1999). *Adventure racing: Guide to survival.* Wellington, NZ: Sporting Endeavours.

Agon Motif

The ancient Greek word *agon* is the root of the English word *agony*, and it means a fight or a contest in physical, psychological, or ideological context. *Agones* were ancient Greek endurance contests in which combatants demonstrated their skill through strenuous competitive games or activities. *Agonizomai* or *agonizesthai* means "to struggle" or "to strive." For the Greeks agon was a never-ending struggle to perceive clearly and judge the things around us. The Greeks used the word *agon* to refer to the war between the Greeks and the Persians, to a trial for justice, and even to the life of married partners. Soldiers strive to attain victory in warfare, athletes strive to attain victory in athletic games, and all of us are in a perpetual struggle between two sides in sport, morality, learning, fighting, and so forth. For the Greeks, in pretty much all aspects of life, whereas victory was the goal, the essence was the struggle.

Usage of Agon

In a collection of essays published in 1968, Jean-Pierre Vernant, Marcel Detiene, and Jacqueline de Romilly spoke of Greek warfare as an agon, a contest like a tournament with ceremonies and rules. However, according to the story of the *mantis*—the Greek word for prophet or seer—Tisamenos, it is unlikely that the term *agon* was in general use for "battle" before the Persian invasions. When Tisamenos asked the Delphic oracle about a child, Pythia predicted that he would win five *agones*. Thus, he trained for the pentathlon and almost won at the Olympics. In fact, he had lost only in wrestling. The Lacedaemonians (Spartans) then realized that the oracle meant five battles and persuaded Tisamenos to become their seer. He then helped the Lacedaemonians win five victories, beginning with the battle of Plataia in 479 BCE. W. K. Pritchett claims that the extension of the word *agon* from *agora* (a place of congregation, marketplace) in Homer to either an athletic or a military contest seems to have developed more or less simultaneously. According to Peter Krentz, the earliest text to use the term *agon* in the sense of "battle," Aeschylus's *Eumenides*, dates to 458 BCE.

The usage of *agon* is by no means restricted to athletic or physical activities. Isocrates, for instance, uses *agon* and *agonizesthai* when he discusses his educational principles. In a speech to Nicocles written about 370 BCE, Isocrates writes: "no athlete is so called upon to train his body as is a king to train his soul; for not all the public festivals in the world offer a prize (epathlon) comparable to those for which you who are kings strive (*agonizesthai*) every day of your lives" (Norlin, 1980 §11). The Socratic dialectic is also said to have been in essence a competitive practice. According to the German philosopher Friedrich Nietzsche, Plato's Socrates invented another type of agon, a new contest that was a mental form of wrestling or fighting. Further, in ancient Greece even poetry was an agonistic event. The ancient Greek poet Hesiod is reputed to have traveled around Greece winning prizes for his hymns. And according to many commentators, the Pythian Games at Delphi started out as poetry competitions, and athletic competitions followed. Finally, in ancient Greek drama (both in comedy and tragedy), *agon* refers to a formal debate (contest) that takes place between two characters, usually with the chorus acting as the judge. The typical agon in Greek tragedy consisted of two set speeches, each followed by two—rarely three—lines from the chorus. However, according to some commentators, it is an exaggeration to say that this kind of agon was a traditional part of the drama with fixed rules. Tragedy began as a choral dance, and any such kind of agon was not likely until the introduction of the second actor.

Historical Background: Early Period

In *Paul and the Agon Motif*, Victor Pfitzner talks interchangeably about the "*agon motif*" and the "*agon* image" or "athletic imagery." According to most commentators, the concept of *agon* originated in ancient Greece. The idea of developed competitive contests is typically Greek. According to Pfitzner, physical training in the sense of culture of the body played no important independent role in the other ancient cultures. Wherever such training was practiced it was primarily for military purposes. For the ancient Greeks the spirit of contention and competition was one of the ma-

The Temple of Olympian Zeus, also known as the Olympeion, is an ancient temple, now in ruins, in the center of Athens, Greece. Source: Istock/David Pedre.

jor sources of impetus urging them on to activity and self-assertion. Pfitzner writes, "It is thus understandable why the word 'agon,' apart from being used to designate the *agones* [contests in athletics, riding, and music], found such a wide use in the thought and language of the Greeks. It was used not only for the united struggle of the people in war, but also for every kind of contest in civil life . . . not only in the field of athletics was the victor celebrated. Feats in every field of endeavor were acclaimed, so that the entire civic life of a Greek became, as it were, an Agon" (Pfitzner 1967, 16–17).

The oldest myths of Greek literature are about contests between the gods. Rivalry between the gods can be found both in the Homeric epics, especially in the *Iliad*, and in Hesiod. The latter pictures the contest for power between the god Zeus and the representative and champion of mortals, Prometheus, in the form of an agon. The athletic contests—*agones*—stood under the protection of a deity to whose honor and service the whole assembly was dedicated. The *agones* had a holy nature. Athletics, especially to the ancient Greeks, were far more than just games. They represented important ritual and one of the fundamental forces of civilization. Jakob Burckhardt (1963) introduced the term *agon* to describe the ancient Greek culture. Since then Greek athletics have been viewed as a natural fulfillment of the *agon*. They represent the need to compete and win acclaim as an individual. In line with Nietzsche, both Burckhardt and Poliakof (1988) have argued for the importance of *agon* to ancient Greek civilization.

Pfitzner says the Pre-Socratic philosophers mark the beginning of a philosophical picture of *agon*. In the writings of the Pre-Socratics, we find not only that wisdom alone is of value to the state but also that the emphasis is on the exercise of the soul over the exercise of the body. The Pre-Socratic philosopher Heraclitus had already suggested the Cynic-Stoic picture of the agon of the sage in his struggle to subject his impulses to the law of reason. Democritus defines the struggle against the passions as a matter of exercise and discipline. Plato, in line with the Pre-Socratics, saw the athletic contests of his time reach an exaggerated importance and tried to lead sports to serve their original (according to him) purpose, that is, as a preparation for war. In the Platonic dialogue "Gorgias," Socrates says that he seeks for the truth, trying to live and die as a virtuous man. He sees the whole life of a philosopher striving to live and die seeking for the truth as an agon. In both Platonic and Stoic thought, the word *agon* means a battle or a struggle between reason or the rational part of the soul and the desires and passions. A difference exists, however, as to what the end or the aim of such a struggle is. According to Plato, the soul struggles to gain a vision of the eternal ideas (universals) of justice and knowledge, whereas according to the Stoic tradition, the agon has as its end *apatheia* (freedom from the violent feelings) and *ataraxia* (freedom from disturbance). In other words, the goal according to the Stoic tradition is peacefulness of the mind.

Lastly, Aristotle makes frequent use of the athletic imagery in his *Nichomachean Ethics*. The goal of the agon of reason over the impulses and desires, according to Aristotle, is to achieve *eudemonia* or *eudaimonia*. *Eudaimonia*, for Aristotle, is the opposite of *kakodaimonie* (*kako* = bad, evil; *daimon* = soul). *Eudaimonia* (*eu* = good; *daimon* = soul) is the "truthful" happiness for a person. This state of mind is to be found between the extremes of exaggeration and *ellepsis*. As the expert in wrestling avoids overtraining or undertraining, the pursuit of *eudemonia* always aims at the middle ground between two extremes. Finally, sports, alongside art, philosophy, and music, were an integral aspect of the philosophy of *kalokagathia*, which was based on the ideals of beauty and value (*kalós kai agathós* = beautiful and good).

Later Period: The Moral Athlete

Plato and the Pre-Socratics saw the athletic contests of their time reach an exaggerated importance. In a similar spirit, the Cynic-Stoic tradition argued for the superiority of exercise of the soul against the exercise of the body. The Cynic-Stoic tradition first developed a complete picture of the agon of the sage or the philosopher. And according to Pfitzner, Paul was dependent on the Cynic-Stoic diatribe to elucidate his Christian concept of *agon*. The task of the philosopher is portrayed by the Cynic-Stoic tradition as an agon against pleasure and pain, and the ideal of *kalokagathia* receives a decidedly ethical interpretation. The wise man's struggle for virtue while using his reason and self-control was the true agon (also found in Paul). The hero Hercules is used as a great example of a moral athlete. According to Epictetus, every person is to be used in the exercise of self-discipline, even the one who is reviled because he exercises "my dispassionateness, my gentleness." The goal of the moral agon became peace of mind and satisfaction, which replaced glory. The sage wasn't the object of adulation like the athlete.

Philo of Alexandria, a Hellenistic philosopher, proposes that the true *agon* of life that is of intrinsically holy nature is the struggle for virtue against passions and vices. Philo mocks the efforts of the athletes and all kinds of athletic activities. According to him, superior physical strength and prowess can be observed even in animals, and, further, physical injury, which is normally punishable, is rewarded in the arena. However, we must note that according to Norman Gardiner (1930), in ancient Greece, as opposed to the Roman Empire, contests were intimately related to the concept of arête (excellence, virtue, honor). Xenophon, for instance, writes that honor is the object of agonal effort "and herein precisely lies the difference between a man and other animals, in this outstretching after honor" (Morford and Clark 1976, 180).

Philo argues that whereas athletes are interested only in the improvement of the body, the philosopher is engaged in the *agon* of life or, in other words, in the *agon* of virtue. Philo uses both the athletic and the military imagery. Above all he was a faithful Jew. Pfitzner tells us that the agonist for Philo is a fighter for God. God has replaced in Philo the judges and the *athlothetes* (organizers of athletic competitions) of the ancient Olympic Games. God is the *athlothetis*, he is the one who prepared the world as an arena and the one who awards the prizes and crowns all toils.

Jewish and Christian religious authorities have used athletic metaphors and imagery to enhance their rhetorical devices. According to Paul, for instance, life is like a contest (*agon*), and the prize (*epathlon*) offered to the athlete of life is that he or she will go to heaven. The *agon* motif of this era finds its expression in Paul's phrase "to fight as a soldier." As soldiers must strive to attain victory in warfare, so the evangelist must strive to proclaim the gospel, notwithstanding the difficulty. As with Philo's view of the agon, Paul's fighter is an agonist of God who is ready to yield the honor to God and who has his *epathlon* granted by God rather than claiming it for himself (as opposed to what the Cynic-Stoic tradition held). When Paul was imprisoned, just before his execution, he wrote in his final letter: "I have fought the good fight; I have finished the course; I have kept the faith. From now on, there is stored up for me the crown of righteousness, which the Lord, the righteous judge, will give to me on that day; and not to me only, but also to all those who have loved his appearing" (2 Tim. 4:7–8). However, we must note that the central characteristic of the concept of agon we find in both Philo and Paul, namely, that the agon is a pious one, is found also in the Cynics.

An underlying similarity clearly exists between the contemporary athlete and the moral athlete. The contemporary athlete, apart from the physical dimension of his or her agon, is a moral athlete. Athletes today are in a perpetual agon or struggle for virtue against passions and vices, too. The latter may refer to drugs, steroids, or to an unhealthy way of life in general. No one likes the athlete who fails to pass an antidoping test. Whether or not an athlete uses drugs is a serious matter, central to the discussions after a race or a game. We admire athletes who manage to win in this agon for virtue, and we have contempt for those who don't.

An illustrative case is the 100-meter British Olympic medalist Linford Christie. In 1999 at the routine antidoping test at a meet in Dortmund, Germany, he was found guilty of using the banned drug nandrolone. A leak of the story to the news media resulted in the cancellation of the £100,000 contract with his sponsor, Puma. Although the British Athletic Federation found him to be not guilty, the International Association of Athletics Federations (IAAF) overruled and confirmed the suspension. Christie, who was once Britain's favorite athlete and captain of the British Olympic team, was absent from the team in London's successful bid for the 2012 Olympic Games, even though he states he attempted to get involved. It appears that agon cannot be divorced from arête. Without arête agon may degenerate into shameless self-aggrandizement based on win-at-all-cost attitude. Above all, we want our athletes to be moral athletes. As Paul puts it in his final letter, we want them to fight the good fight.

Agon Motif, Play, and Education

Johan Huizinga (1950) contrasts agon and play. He notes that the ancient Greeks made a verbal distinction between contest (agon) and play. Most importantly, according to them, agon involved the element of "seriousness." Contests of every description played an enormous part in ancient Greek culture, and "nonseriousness" was not a rule explicitly expressed in the word *agon*. Nevertheless, Huizinga suggests that we should group agon with play. The central claim of Huizinga's influential *Homo Ludens: A Study of the Play Element in Culture* is that an underlying identity exists between play and contest or agon. Play, for Huizinga, is never synonymous with any single, isolated feature of play but rather is a notion that refers to a generic human propensity (hence the label "homo ludens"). He says the agon in ancient Greek life or the contest anywhere else in the world bears all the formal characteristics of play and, as to its function, belongs almost wholly to the sphere of the festival, which is playsphere. According to Huizinga, we cannot separate

the contest as a cultural function from the complex "play-festival-rite." He mentions that Plato uses *paignion* (play or game) for the armed ritual dances and says that the fact that the majority of Greek contests were fought out in deadly earnest is no reason for separating the agon from play or for denying the play character of the former. We can see this by contrasting the ancient Olympic Games (the playsphere festivals, according to Huizinga) to the institutionalized barbarism in the gladiator contests of the Roman Empire, which, according to Gardiner (1930), were brutalized events catering to the cravings of a detached society that found the ancient Greek events unappealing.

Play needs to be taken seriously. Huizinga observes that not only agon but also play involve the element of seriousness as well as rules and limitations. Huizinga says that seriousness is one of the most important characteristics of real play. Lastly, following Schiller's *On the Aesthetic Education of Man*, he sees play as serving nothing other than itself—not any set of external needs or desires. According to him, both play and agon are largely devoid of purpose. That is, the action begins and ends in itself, and the outcome does not contribute to the necessary life processes of the group. To Huizinga the popular Dutch saying to the effect that "it is not the marbles that matter, but the game" expresses this notion clearly enough.

According to the sociologist Roger Caillois (1961), games are playful activities. Although influenced by Huizinga's ideas, Caillois used the term *agon* in a more restricted sense to refer only to one of the four basic types of game. Agon applies to games based on skill as opposed to those based on chance (*alea*), imitation (mimicry), or vertigo (*ilinx* = whirlpool). The concept of alea appears to be unlike the concept of agon in that it represents an emphasis on destiny or fate and the denial of merit of skill as basis of a contest. However, as Caillois observes, an underlying similarity exists between agon and *alea*, namely, they both provide a kind of equality often denied in real life. In both cases players can escape the real world and enter an artificial world with the same rules for everyone; in the case of agon all players have the same possibility of proving their superiority, and in the case of *alea* all players have the same probability favored by chance. We might do well here to contrast *alea* and agon to *ilinx*. The latter refers to a condition that can be attained by whirling, dancing, tumbling, spinning, and so forth. We might say that this condition can also be attained by drinking or using drugs and other forms of self-destructive behavior. It is difficult to see how some of these activities can be classified as games because they are not subject to rules

or limitations. As opposed to *alea* and agon, the pleasure in *ilinx* apparently comes from a refusal to acknowledge rules or limits on appropriate behavior.

It appears that *ilinx* is a feature of today's extreme sports. The latter are celebrated for their adrenaline-pumping thrills. Snowboarders for instance, emphasize frequently the total sense of freedom they experience. Notwithstanding, extreme sports appear to be a special kind of activities which combine agon and *ilinx*. In the case of extreme sports, it appears that the athletes can achieve ilinx while being subjects to rules or limitations. Extreme sports involve an element of seriousness as well as rules and limitations but are based on skill (as opposed to based on chance). As for the moral dimension of agon, the same considerations apply to extreme sports athletes. Above all, we want them to be moral athletes.

Edward Kuhlman (1994) argues for the intimate relation between agon and arête and shows the significant role that the conception of ancient Greek agonistic spirit can play in contemporary education. According to Kuhlman, agon involves struggle, but it doesn't imply raw aggression. One cannot define agonism solely in terms of its aggressive element as though it were bestial and barbaric. All life is a struggle, says Kuhlman. Technology attempts to deceive us that it is not. Agonism was central in the ancient Greek civilization, but today people have forgotten the basic truth and wisdom of this reality. Kuhlman says:

> I received a revelation during my school-teaching days in the 1960s when the word "bored" was ever on students' lips. I don't recall my own pretechnology generation using that word very often. Boredom is a function of excess leisure. Too much time, especially time made available by technologies that eliminate time-consuming effort, creates unhealthy moods which cannot tolerate unscheduled time. When a culture alters the natural tempo and rhythm which nature prescribes, pathological dislocations occur. Alterations in biorhythmic patterns which cause metabolic distress, sleep deprivation, and other organic disorders have been documented. Psychological maladjustment results from disharmony with the natural order created by seasonal variations and survival tasks... Anyone from the hectic, time-driven West who has visited the pastoral peoples of East Africa, notably the Maasai, cannot help but envy their unhurried, uncluttered pace and the organicity of their relationships... Exercise

and cardiovascular activity, which are normally undergone in the course of typical agonal survival, have been cavalierly brushed aside as machines now replace the natural modes of transportation and labor. Consequently, a generation of overweight, malnourished, and unconditioned, indulgent technocrats suffers from a host of diseases caused by a nonagonal culture. (Kuhlman 1994, 38–39)

Huizinga's observation still provides the classic crystallization of the idea that the agon motif is the cornerstone on which the educational edifice must be built (Huizinga 1950, 63): "From the life of the child right up to the highest achievement of civilization one of the strongest incentives to perfection, both individual and social, is the desire to be praised and honored for one's excellence. In praising another each praises himself. We want the satisfaction of having done something well. Doing something well means doing it better than others. In order to excel one must prove one's excellence: in order to merit recognition, merit must be manifest. Competition serves to give proof of superiority."

Dimitris Platchias

See also Gladiator Competitions; Meaning of Extreme, The; Psychology of Risk; Violence

Further Reading

Burckhardt, J. (1963). *History of Greek culture* (P. Hilty, Trans.). London: Constable.

Caillois, R. (1961). *Man, play and games.* New York: Free Press.

Gardiner, N. (1930). *Athletics of the ancient world.* Oxford, UK: Oxford University Press.

Huizinga, J. (1950). *Homo ludens: A study of the play element in culture.* New York: Harper & Row.

Krenz, P. (2002). Fighting by the rules: The invention of the hoplite agon. *Hesperia, 71*(1), 23–39.

Kuhlman, E. L. (1994). *Agony in education: The importance of struggle in the process of learning.* Westport, CT: Bergin Garvey.

Loy, J., & Hesketh, G. (1984). The agon motif: A prolegomenon for the study of agonetic behavior. In K. Olin (Ed.), *Contribution of sociology to the study of sport* (pp. 31–50). Jyvaskyla, Finland: University of Jyvaskyla Press.

Morford, W. R., & Clark, S. J. (1976). The agon motif. *Exercise and Sport Science Review, 4*, 163–193.

Norlin, G. (Trans.). 1980. *Isocrates.* Cambridge, MA: Harvard University Press.

Pfitzner, V. C. (1967). *Paul and the agon motif.* Leiden, Netherlands: E. J. Brill.

Poliakoff, M. B. (1987). *Combat sports in the ancient world: Competition, violence and culture.* New Haven, CT: Yale University Press.

Schiller, F. (2004). *On the aesthetic education of man* (R. Snell, Trans.). Mineola, NY: Dover Publications.

Vernant, J.-P. (1968). *Problems of the war in ancient Greece.* Paris: Mouton&Co.

Weeber, K. W. (1991). *Die unheiligen Spiele: Das antike Olympia zwischen legende und wirklichkei* [The unholy games: The antique Olympics between legend and reality]. Munich, Germany: Artemis & Winkler.

Airchair

See Waterskiing

Alaska

Alaska is the home of extreme snowboarding and offers some of the biggest and most celebrated terrain in the world. Annual snowfall averages more than 25 meters, and 1,500-meter vertical runs are plentiful.

Professional snowboarder Tina Basich describes Alaska as "so intimidating" because "unlike a ski resort, there are no boundaries or clearly marked trails and warnings about cliffs and crevasses or shallow snow. It's up to you to learn the mountain you're riding. Alaska is mother-nature at her most extreme—the weather changes quickly, snow conditions can change within one run—it's vast and steep and bigger than all of us" (Basich 2003, 72). According to Israel Valenzuela, senior editor of *Heckler* magazine, there are "cliffs that dot the landscape that are as big as the biggest ski resort in Tahoe and they are merely part of the terrain." In her autobiography Basich highlights some of the perils and pleasures of snowboarding in Alaska:

The helicopter dropped us off and we crouched down with our gear and waited for it to lift off. Right after the heli[copter] started to rise our radios exploded with the voice of the helicopter pilot, "it's gone, it's gone! The whole thing is gone!" About seven feet away from where we were standing there was a fracture line going across the entire mountain. The entire mountain had avalanched. The pressure from the heli[copter] landing had released this fracture, called a climax fracture, which means it cracked off all the snow all the way down to the dirt, rock and ice, sending the entire side of the mountain sliding all the way across the entire bowl. The avalanche had gone 3,500 feet down to the glacier below. We were all very quiet and just waited for the helicopter to come back and pick us up. It was a freaky feeling because if any of us had dropped into that bowl, it would have released and we would not have survived. (Basich 2003, 133–134)

The feeling of the untracked powder under my board as I was flying down the run was amazing. The glittering snowflakes flew in plumes off the side of my board as I made my turns. I was so small riding down this huge mountain and had to keep turning, remembering to look back every couple of seconds to see if any snow was moving with me. When I got to the bottom, I sighed with relief that I'd made it down, and what an accomplishment! I named the mountain "T-top." I looked back up at my turns and the run I had just come down and could barely believe it. I couldn't tell if I was going to cry or laugh, so I just kept smiling. (Basich 2003, 172)

The Alaskan heli-skiing phenomenon started in the mountains surrounding Valdez and Juneau during the early 1990s when local skiers and snowboarders convinced local pilots to give them a lift. Among the handful of Alaskan snowboarding pioneers were Jay Liska, Ritchie Fowler, Nick Perada, Shaun Falmer, Tom Burt, Jim Zellers, and Bonnie Leary. "There were probably only twenty people that were skiing or snowboarding in Valdez," recalls snowboarding cinematographer Mike Hatchett. "There were no guides; it was total cowboy" (Reed 2005, 116). Hatchett's film *TB2: A New Way of Thinking* (1993) documented some of the first Alaskan heli-snowboarding.

By the mid-1990s snowboarding videos were introducing Alaskan big mountain riding to the broader boarding culture. "When people saw the videos of people making sick powder turns in Alaska, they wanted that. It became a fantasy," says early professional snowboarder Jeff Fulton, but the majority of snowboarders "aren't educated enough to be out there" (Howe 1998, 134). Nevertheless, Alaska quickly became "a destination of choice" for snowboarders seeking the ultimate challenge. According to cultural commentator Jamie Brisick, Alaska is "the place to go if your dreams, board, wallet, and balls are big enough." (Howe 1998, 119)

Snowboarder jumping off a cliff at Alyeska Mountain, Alaska. Source: istock/Atan Lightstone.

King of the Hill

*Nick Perata, one of the forerunners of extreme snowboard-
ing, is planning to relaunch the international extreme
snowboarding competition, King of the Hill. Here, in an
excerpt from his website, Nick describes the event.*

Today's generation of snowboarders ha[s] surpassed
previous generations with [its] technical ability and
amplitude. With all the emphasis today on resort type
contests, these riders are limited to the size of the kicker
or half pipe to show their skills. These riders deserve the
opportunity to show off their abilities on the grandest
stage of all snowboarding.

From Valdez, Alaska … [t]he world's best athletes
will compete on the world's best stage, for the Alpine
disciplines coveted title of, "King of the Hill." I created
and organized the "King of the Hill" competition in 1992
after competing in the first extreme snowboard contest
in 1991. I realized that there was a better and safer way
to put on an extreme event. "King of the Hill" ran successfully for seven years total before the snowboard
market turned to freestyle and park riding became
more the emphasis than back country.

… With "King of the Hill" the only limits the riders
face are the limits within themselves. This unique event
encompasses all three disciplines of the sport; speed,
freestyle and extreme, via helicopter and ski plane
access.

Day One—Downhill

The first event held will be the Alaskan downhill. This
venue is 3,000–4,000 ft. vertical mountain with an average slope of 30–45°. Competitors will reach speeds in
excess of 70mph while negotiating a series of 20 specifically placed gates throughout the slope.

Day Two—Freestyle

This course is a 3,000 ft. vertical mountain with many
natural features including wind lips, waves, walls, cliffs
and natural half pipes. Each competitor will have to negotiate all natural obstacles as well as six cheese wedge
pro jumps placed throughout the 30–50° slope. Use of all
the terrain and difficulty of trick will be the main goal.

Day Three—Extreme

Extreme will take us to the biggest peaks in the Chugach.
This day will test the competitors to their limits. The
venue takes place on a 4,000–5,000 vertical ft. mountain
with the slopes ranging from 40–60°. There are steeps
cornices, cliffs, drops and all around big mountain terrain.… This is as good as it gets.

Source: Perata, N. (n.d.). King of the Hill Extreme Snowboarding Competition. Retrieved February 1, 2007, from http://www.
nickperata.com/koh.htm

Heli-skiing and heli-boarding have blossomed into a cottage industry in which diehards make the long pilgrimage
each spring, and a day of snowboarding can cost $1,000, a
cost that covers both helicopter rides and trained guides.
However, a healthy bank account is not the only requirement for snowboarding in Alaska. Courage is also required.
Certainly, experience, education, skill, and courage cannot
be feigned on top of an Alaskan peak. Cultural commentator Rob Reed (2005, 66) describes Alaska as "a place where
mythic lines and narrow escapes give way to snowboarding
legend."

Holly Thorpe

Further Reading

Basich, T. (2003). *Pretty good for a girl: The autobiography of a snowboarding
pioneer.* New York: HarperCollins.

Howe, S. (1998). *(Sick): A cultural history of snowboarding.* New York: St.
Martin's Griffin.

Reed, R. (2005). *The way of the snowboarder.* New York: Harry N.
Abrams.

Ballooning

The first hot air balloon was developed as a children's toy in China sometime between the years 100 and 200 CE. However, until late in the eighteenth century, few, if any, modifications were made that would allow for human travel. The history of the modern hot air balloon involves several inventors who worked nearly concurrently. Beginning with the invention and later perfection of the hot air balloon, it has been used for both transportation and competition. The first balloon race was held in 1906, in France. Beginning in the 1970's, hot air balloon competitions became more popular, drew larger crowds, and required the pilots to compete more tasks and more complex tasks.

A hot air balloon rises above the ground in Taos, New Mexico. Source: istock/James D. Williams.

French brothers Steven and Joseph Montgolfier are often credited with inventing the hot air balloon. Their work in a paper factory inspired them to use smoke to raise bodies into the air. The brothers started small, experimenting with small models of paper balloons powered by hot air, and then moved to larger balloon designs by early 1783. One of their first successful attempts, a spherical paper balloon, rose 300 meters and flew 1,200 meters. On 5 June 1783, they demonstrated an unpiloted balloon that rose 1,800 meters and flew 2,400 meters for ten minutes.

News of this accomplishment traveled fast and attracted a great deal of competition from new inventors as well as those who were already working on their own hot air balloons. One such inventor, French physicist, chemist, and aeronaut Jacques Alexandre César Charles, is credited with inventing the hydrogen balloon. On 27 August 1783, Charles traveled nearly 48 kilometers and ascended to 3.2 kilometers in a balloon called the *Charlière*. It was destroyed by terrified townspeople in Gonesse upon his landing. Four months later he and fellow ballooner Aine Roberts rode in a balloon that rose 500 meters and traveled 43 kilometers.

Charles Green of Great Britain agreed that gas is better than hot air in terms of balloon power and experimented with coal gas instead of hydrogen. In 1836 his coal-powered balloon, named *Royal Vauxhall*, carried twelve passengers 770 kilometers, from England to Germany. Perhaps more significant were his invention of trail ropes to assist in steering and his innovations in landing.

Another inventor, Jean François Pilâtre de Rozier, was present for the Montgolfier brothers' unpiloted demonstration in 1783. Inspired by their success, he launched an untethered balloon holding a sheep, a cockerel, and a duck. This experiment led him to become the first person to pilot a hot air-powered balloon in free flight (untethered) when he and Marquis d'Arlandes spent twenty-five minutes airborne in a Montgolfier hot air balloon on 21 November 1783. Rozier then developed a hybrid balloon that has separate chambers for a nonheated lifting gas as well as a traditional heated lifting gas. In comparing balloons powered by hot air and those powered by hydrogren, he noted that gas power allows balloons to travel higher and for longer periods of time but that hot air power allows for easier changes in altitude. His hybrid balloon had limited success, and gas balloons dominated ballooning for the next two hundred years. In the late twentieth century the Rozier hybrid was again explored, this time with more success, although the other two types still dominate the sport.

Enhancements to the basic balloon structure took place

over a relatively short period of time. The science of ballooning developed in less than two years. The Montgolfier and Rozier balloons remain among the most popular models today. Although over time better and cheaper materials, both for the balloon and the hot air, would be perfected, the basic idea of the balloon and power remains the same.

Up, Up, and Away

On 4 June 1784, French opera singer Marie Elisabeth Thible completed the first free flight by a woman. Before that four women had flown in a tethered hot air balloon. On 9 January 1793, French balloonist Jean Pierre Francois Blanchard flew for a crowd, including President George Washington in Philadelphia. This marked the first flight in the United States.

The first successful balloon trip around the world started in the Swiss Alps on 1 March 1999, and finished twenty days later in Egypt. Although Bertrand Piccard of Switzerland successfully piloted the *Breitling Orbiter III* on this trip, he and his teammates had failed before. For example, in January 1997 a fuel leak forced Piccard and Wim Verstraeten to abandon their journey shortly after it started, and one year later, nine-days loss of fuel and the lack of permission to fly over China forced Piccard, Verstraeten, and Andy Elson to land.

Uses of Balloons

People have used balloons for a variety of purposes, including military, exploratory, and scientific research.

In the United States balloons were used during the Civil War for reconnaissance by both the Union and Confederate armies. Thaddeus Lowe was instrumental in this use, presenting options directly to President Abraham Lincoln on 17 July 1861. The first U.S. military balloon, the *Union*, had limited capabilities but allowed Lowe to detect Confederate troops and telegraph their location back to Union officers. The use of balloons during the war ended in 1863 because of funding cutbacks. Balloons were also used in the Franco-Prussian War and World War I for military observations. They were used in World War II to protect London from low-level air attacks and carried bombs for the Japanese army.

In 1897 Swedish scientist S. A. Andrée led a team from Spitsbergen to the North Pole by balloon. However, after

only two days their balloon crash-landed onto the ice pack. Unequipped to handle the elements, the men did not survive the trip.

In 1803 the scientific community used balloons to measure the amount of electricity in the air. Through the mid-twentieth century balloons were used in scientific research to measure the composition of the air, to better understand the makeup of the atmosphere, and to measure the physiological reactions of humans at high altitudes.

Sport Ballooning

Balloons are also used for fun, adventure, and competition. In balloon racing speed is not necessarily the objective because all the contestants use the same wind; instead, the objective is to land as accurately as possible in a designated spot. Therefore, the term *racing* is technically a misnomer. Balloons cannot be steered except vertically; changes in altitude allow pilots to fly in airstreams moving in certain directions and at specific speeds. Generally, in competition a pilot will fly toward a designated target, throwing a marker down after he or she reaches it. Throwing a marker enables competitions to involve multiple targets. Competitors have gotten so good that the difference between first place and third or fourth can be fractions of an inch. Each task is scored separately, with points from all tasks compiled into one overall score. Competitive balloon flights begin with a debriefing meeting in which pilots are given the set of tasks and receive relevant data, such as time limits, starting time, and distance requirements. Although more than one task has become the norm in competitive ballooning, four tasks has been accepted as the maximum, and only a few competitors have successfully completed four tasks.

Many countries, states, and cities sponsor balloon festivals. The first World Air Games, organized by the Federation Aeronautique Internationale (FAI), patterned after the Olympics, and held every four years, was held in Turkey in 1997. These games included not only hot air ballooning, but also other aviation sports, including parachuting, air racing, hang gliding, and paragliding. Participation in the World Air Games is competitive, with each country selecting pilots to enter, traditionally based on national championship competitions. The second World Air Games were held in Spain in 2001. Out of the twenty-four countries that participated, France topped the medal count with twenty-seven, six of which were gold. However, Russia won twenty-two medals and

Ballooning World Records

While hot air ballooning may not seem as risky or extreme as other sports, there is still a significant amount of risk involved. The extracts below, from e.balloon.org, highlight three of the more significant hot air ballooning feats.

In 1987 Richard Branson and Per Lindstrand were the first to cross the Atlantic in a hot air balloon, rather than a helium/gas filled balloon. They flew a distance of 2,900 miles in a record breaking time of 33 hours. At the time, the envelope they used was the largest ever flown, at 2.3 million cubic feet of capacity. A year later, Per Lindstrand set yet another record, this time for highest solo flight ever recorded in a hot air balloon—65,000 feet!

The team of Richard Branson and Per Lindstrand paired up again in 1991 and became the first to cross the Pacific in a hot air balloon. They travelled 6,700 miles in 47 hours, from Japan to Canada breaking the world distance record, travelling at speeds of up to 245 mph. 4 years later, Steve Fossett became the first to complete the Transpacific balloon route by himself, travelling from Korea and landing in Canada 4 days later.

Finally, in 1999 the first around the world flight was completed by Bertrand Piccard and Brian Jones. Leaving from Switzerland and landing in Africa, they smashed all previous distance records, flying for 19 days, 21 hours and 55 minutes."

Source: The history of hot air ballooning. Retrieved January 30, 2006, from http://www.eballoon.org/history/history-of-ballooning

took home the most gold medals with eleven. The third World Air Games, set for 2005, was cancelled for organizational reasons.

The first FAI European Hot Air Balloon Championship was held in Sweden in 1976 and since 1980 has generally been held every two years. Overall, Great Britain has won the most gold medals with four, followed by Germany, France, and Austria at two each.

The annual Hot Air Balloon World Honda Grand Prix was established in 1998. This competition generally consists of multiple stages, with events in the United States, Europe, and Asia. In 2006, for example, the first round was in the United States, the second round in Luxembourg, and the third in Japan. The team with the most points from all of the stages is declared the winner.

Beth Pamela Skott

Further Reading
Bacon, J. M. (2006). *The dominion of the air: The story of aerial navigation.* Gloucester, UK: Dodo Press. (Original work published 1870)
BBAC Competitions Club. (2004). A brief explanation of competition ballooning. Retrieved August 10, 2006, from http://www.bbac.org/af-fil/comps/website/compsexplained.htm
Bernstein, J. (1925). History of air navigation. *The Congressional Digest,* 4(7), 219–221, 249.
Cowl, C. T. & Jones, M. P., et al. (Eds.) (1998). Factors associated with fatalities and injuries from hot-air balloon crashes. *JAMA,* 279, 1011–1014.
Evans, C. M. (2002). *War of the aeronauts: The history of ballooning in the Civil War.* Mechanicsburg, PA: Stackpole Books.
Hardy, J. (2005). Legacy of flight. *Aviation History,* 16(1), 74.
Karwatka, D. (2002). The Montgolfier brothers and the first hot air balloon. *TechDirection,* 62(3), 10.
Piccard, B. (1999). Around at last! *National Geographic,* 196(3), 30–51.
Thompson, A. M. (1992). How safe is Scottish hot air? *British Medical Journal,* 305(6855), 691.
West, S. (1982). Ballooning science. *Science News,* 119(15), 237–238.

Barefoot Skiing

See Waterskiing

Barrel Jumping

Long before the ESPN cable TV network debuted its X Games, men and women sought fame, fortune, and fulfillment by testing themselves against the elements of nature. In the realm of physical feats of derring-do, the mention of Niagara Falls conjures up images of the daredevils who encased themselves in barrels and attempted to "jump"

the thundering currents of the rapids that precede the falls and the 51-meter drop that follows.

Whereas one can more easily see why adventurers aspire to scale great summits, pedal long distances, climb into motorized vehicles and race like the wind, or balance precariously atop fiberglass boards to ride the surf, barrel jumping requires a different sort of comprehension. How does encasing oneself in a wooden barrel that offers no directional control become not only a possibility but even a good thing to do?

Barrel jumpers were hardly immune from suspicions that they were foolhardy or unbalanced psychologically. However, their motives warrant closer scrutiny. Although the history of Niagara Falls does include its share of eccentrics, lost souls, and those who accidentally met unpleasant fates, daredevils intent on mastering the falls did so with the intent of living to tell the tale and potentially cashing in on the notoriety.

Not exclusive to Niagara Falls, the barrel-jumping craze began during the mid-1800s and was practiced in many locations, such as lesser-known Genesee Falls, New York. However, the legend and lure of barrel jumping are most familiar within the context of Niagara Falls.

Although alien to contemporary ways of thinking, during the nineteenth century the premise of barrel jumping possessed its own kind of logic. Like other wooden vessels that are buoyant (i.e., ships, canoes, rafts, and boats), a barrel provided a means of navigating rough waters while offering some semblance of protection from the torrents that would otherwise engulf the craft and batter the rider. Wooden barrels were considered works in progress, and jumpers and their advisors would later experiment with metal barrels and plastic "spheroids" while tinkering with design elements to ensure safety.

Of course, as more than one commentator has observed, going over the falls was the easy part. Survival was a matter of what happened after the barrel landed. Would there be enough air to sustain the jumper until the barrel surfaced and was retrieved by people on shore? Would the barrel itself withstand the trip and remain intact? Buffeted about like a ball in a lottery drawing, how bruised might the jumper inside the barrel be by the time he or she was freed?

Barrel jumpers were not the only daredevils who became such a part of the commercialized tourism industry that grew up around Niagara Falls in the 1820s and has carried forward to today. The compelling nature of staged human dramas performed by tightrope walkers, self-styled "rivermen," and barrel jumpers relegated what was at one time *the* attraction in Niagara—the natural spectacle of

the falls themselves—to a position of backdrop or prop in some cases.

Niagara Falls

To better appreciate falls daredevils such as Annie Edson Taylor, the Great Blondin, and Sam Patch, another key player needs a more complete introduction: Niagara Falls itself. In 1683 Father Louis Hennepin described Niagara Falls as "the most beautiful and at the same time the most frightful cascade in the world" (McKinsey 1985, 11). Unexplored by Europeans in the seventeenth century, Niagara Falls was in the land of the Six Nations. Also known as the Iroquois Confederacy, the Six Nations include the Cayugas, Mohawks, Oneidas, Onondagas, Senecas, and Tusacaroras. Together they form what is considered the oldest living democracy on earth (Johansen 2002).

The site of numerous military battles, the Niagara frontier would eventually give way to European settlement. After the War of 1812 locals with an eye for profit and industry cultivated schemes to generate economic growth. The appeal of Niagara, however, is not merely its industrial potential but rather the meaning of Niagara in the hearts, minds, and imaginations of people across the globe. During the past two centuries Niagara has become "a lodestar for North American culture and invention: site of the first railway suspension bridge, inspiration for Nikola Tesla's discovery of the principle of alternating current, and subject of Frederic Church's most celebrated landscape; a natural wonder that has bewitched generations of scientists, authors and utopians, and stimulated innovations and social movements still casting long shadows" (Clarke 1997, 8).

Niagara Falls straddles the U.S.-Canadian border with residence in both the state of New York and the province of Ontario. Formed by the Niagara River, a product of the Ice Age, Niagara Falls is the second-largest waterfall in the world. More properly, Niagara Falls is a collection of three: the American Falls, the Bridal Veil Falls, and the Horseshoe Falls. These falls and the surrounding islands have served at various times as co-stars, supporting cast, and nemeses in the stunts performed by daredevils.

Stunts Aplenty

The first major tourist gathering at Niagara Falls was the brainchild of William Forsyth, a man of questionable reputation but singular interest in making money. The falls presented inviting possibilities for someone like Forsyth, who had an entrepreneurial bent and an attitude that the falls were there not just to be seen, but also to be exploited. Playing on the trepidation that visitors had about the power of the falls, Forsyth devised a plan to send a condemned schooner, the *Michigan*, over the falls with a cargo of live animals in 1827. It was a gruesome prospect, to say the least, but much in the style of shock television today, the scheme worked, at least from a financial perspective. Approximately fifteen thousand onlookers witnessed the event. Despite an anticlimactic finish because the *Michigan* fell apart shortly after being towed into the rapids above the falls, local merchants learned that taverns thrived and hotels filled when crowds were offered something out of the ordinary.

Within two years a group of Buffalo businessmen promoted an appearance by Sam Patch, a former millhand with a purported fondness for liquor who refined the art of leaping from great heights into bodies of water. Although he survived a 36-meter leap into the Niagara River, a short time later he met his demise while diving off a platform into the Genesee Falls. In the aftermath of his death, Patch became a mythic folk hero to the working classes, becoming immortalized in works by Herman Melville and Nathaniel Hawthorne and inspiring the expression, "What the Sam Patch is this!" (Berton 1997, 84).

Conquering the Falls

By the mid-1800s jumping the falls from a free-standing position was replaced by crossing the gorge on a tightrope. Jean Francois Gravelet, "a small, well-muscled Frenchman with flaxen hair and a goatee to match," was said to have seen the U.S. landscape artist Frederic Church's painting *Niagara* in 1858 and vowed in that moment to cross its roaring waters (Berton 1997, 90).

With arresting calm and theatrical flare, the Great Blondin, as Gravelet was known, captivated audiences, who were amazed by his courage on something as unstable as a cable strung between two points (in truth the cable had an intricate latticework of guy wires extending to the sides of the gorge). In fact, the ease with which Blondin traveled the wire actually proved a disappointment for spectators who longed for more visible signs of danger.

As with great athletes and performers of this age, Blondin's act did not meet with unified approval. Prior to his first walk across the Niagara River, an article in the *New York Times* depicted him as a fool who should be arrested to protect him from his own self-destructive tendencies (Berton 1997, 94). After his successful crossing, however, the same newspaper heralded his accomplishment as "the greatest feat of the Nineteenth century" (Berton 1997, 95).Regardless of the view, Blondin appears to have been born to perform on

The Horseshoe Falls, Niagara Falls, Canada. Source: istock.

Famous Barrel Jumpers at Niagara Falls

Niagara Falls is one of the most popular barrel-jumping sites, due less to the success of the jumpers and more to the popularity of the waterfalls themselves. The excerpts below, from the Niagara Falls Live website detail a few of the more notable barrel jumps over the falls.

24 October 1901

Annie Taylor was the first person to conquer the falls in a barrel. After climbing inside her airtight wooden barrel, the air pressure was compressed to 30 p.s.i. with a bicycle pump. Though bruised and battered, Annie made it.

25 July 1911

The infamous Bobby Leach plunged over in a steel barrel. Bobby broke both kneecaps and his jaw during his daring event. Years later while touring in New Zealand, Bobby slipped on an orange peel and died from complications due to gangrene!

11 July 1920

Englishman Charles G. Stephens equipped his wooden barrel with an anvil for ballast. Charles tied himself to the anvil for security. After the plunge, Chuck's right arm was the only item left in the barrel.

3 July 1984

The first Canadian to conquer the Falls was Karel Soucek. Karel survived the plunge, but later that year Karel was killed while recreating the drop from a platform inside the Houston Astrodome. (Karel's barrel hit the edge of the water tank.)

Source: Daredevils of Niagara Falls. (n.d.) Retrieved February 2, 2007 from http://www.niagarafallslive.com/daredevils_of_niagara_falls.htm

---

the high wire. Under the tutelage of a troupe of acrobats who had camped close by his father's home, Blondin had acquired enough skill to begin his professional career by the age of six.

Ever the showman, Blondin did not merely walk across the wire but rather traversed it in style, somersaulting, leaping, executing handstands, performing blindfolded, and hanging perilously from the wire using only one arm and one leg. On several occasions Blondin made the crossing while carrying his manager on his back and once supposedly allowed a sharpshooter on board the *Maid of the Mist* boat to put a bullet through Blondin's hat while he was en route above. Both Blondin and his accomplice knew that the shot fired was a blank and that the hole had been made in the hat prior to the start of the show. Nevertheless, the fraud went unchallenged by the local press.

Blondin was challenged in other ways, however. A Canadian rival, William Leonard Hunt, whose stage name was "Signor Guillermo Antonio Farini," pursued a slightly different path to a show business career that reveals the differences in their personalities. As a boy, Farini was described as incorrigible, impatient with the strictures of a straightlaced physician father who thought a more suitable career for his son would be in medicine. Farini, on the other

hand, wrote that he courted peril because he loved it. Farini would eventually apprentice with a traveling circus and bill himself as a strongman.

The contrasts between Blondin and Farini were not simply a matter of their paths to the high wire. Farini was much better at staging spectacles. Leaving nothing to chance, he devised promotions to assure that people would attend his performances and arranged for a take of the box office revenue. He developed relationships with the main transportation companies (railroad and steamship) and negotiated bonuses from them for his performances. And he tried, when possible, to get an upper hand on Blondin when it came to performances.

Besting Blondin, however, proved to be a near-impossible task. He dominated the high-wire scene and remained popular long after such acts were considered commonplace. Blondin was the standard with whom all others were compared. The value of being identified with Blondin led other performers to assume his name; thus, Harry Leslie referred to himself as the "American Blondin," and Professor J. F. Jenkins was the "Canadian Blondin." Notably, the only woman to cross the gorge, Marie Spelterina, could "out-Blondin Blondin" by moving along the tightrope backward and blindfolded and wearing peach baskets on her feet.

Taking the Plunge

According to official records, the first person to go over the falls in a barrel was Annie Edson Taylor, who took the plunge in 1901. That plunge would occur another fifteen times during the next one hundred years. Not all took the plunge in a barrel. Not all who took the plunge survived.

However, long before Taylor's trip, thrill seekers had congregated at the falls to plunge into the rapids and ride the crest of the waves in a barrel. Carlisle Graham, a cooper from Philadelphia, had earned the title of "Hero of Niagara" by completing four trips through the Whirlpool Rapids in a barrel he had made himself. In 1889 claims that both Graham and another stunter, Steve Brodie, had actually gone over the falls were later found to be fraudulent.

Carlisle Graham's perilous fifth trip through the rapids in 1901 fueled the imagination of Taylor, a sixty-three-year-old dance instructor in Bay City, Michigan. While reading about the Pan-American Exposition in Buffalo in the *New York World*, which was drawing massive numbers of people to see the fair and Niagara Falls, she had an epiphany. As a widow with few financial resources and mounting debt, she could ensure her future by doing what many men had done before her: She would blaze her own trail to greatness. She would be the first person to go over the falls.

In historical accounts Taylor is often depicted as a desperate woman who was willing to do almost anything to escape the grim fate that awaited women of limited means in the early part of the twentieth century. To some degree, there is reason to believe these accounts. As she grew older, and as fewer students enrolled in her dance classes, she lived an itinerant lifestyle, moving from city to city in the hopes that business would improve. She largely lived off the charity of her family. Confronted with the option of continuing to accept her family's grudging support or taking menial jobs below her station, she wrote, "I didn't want to lower my social standard, for I have always associated with the best class of people, the cultivated and refined" (Berton 1997, 192).

To assume that Taylor was a helpless, desperate woman would be a mistake, however. When writing about her life, Taylor revealed that she had the courage that a trip over the falls would require. During her life of travel, she claimed to have survived fires, ocean storms, thieves, and at least one earthquake. The thieves, by the way, walked away empty handed from their encounter with her. Thus, for all of the depictions of Taylor as a woman who aspired to be associated with the upper class, she was in fact a working-class woman who was not overwhelmed by extreme weather conditions or even the barrel of a gun.

In preparation for her trip over the falls, Taylor solicited the assistance of a local cooper, John Rosenski. Taylor, however, designed the barrel and was involved in the selection of the materials, preferring staves of Kentucky oak. When the barrel, named the "Queen of the Mist," was finished, it was 1.3 meters high and weighed 72 kilograms.

Taylor's sense of propriety affected the manner in which her trip over the falls was promoted. For example, she withheld from her manager, Frank M. "Tussie" Russell, the financial motive for the event, claiming that she wished to use the proceeds to help pay off a mortgage on a ranch in Texas. Fearing that her age was a liability, Taylor told both Russell and the newspapers that she was twenty years younger than she really was. And Taylor declined the usual public display of walking through town in costume to stir up interest prior to the jump, believing it was unbecoming for a woman of her age and station.

Taylor also created some suspicion as to whether she was serious about going over the falls when she failed to appear on October 20, the day designated for her launch. Apologizing for not showing, she attempted to jump the next Wednesday, but the jump was cancelled because of weather conditions. Risking alienating reporters and spectators who were beginning to think that the promised jump was a hoax, Taylor delivered on her promise to go over the falls on October 24.

Describing the experience, Taylor said she felt as if "all nature was being annihilated." Rescued seventeen minutes after the barrel was released into the rapids and came to rest at the base of the falls, Taylor left the barrel with the sound of the falls "like continuous thunder" still ringing in her ears (Berton 1997, 201). Weak from the experience but spared injury apart from a superficial scalp wound, Taylor accomplished what no one else had before her and few have since. Unfortunately, Taylor's ultimate goal of financial security was never realized. Her manager absconded with the barrel and set out on the lecture circuit himself to talk about the event. Despite her efforts, Taylor died in poverty, having risked her life to prevent just such a circumstance.

Adding Insult to Penury

More than one hundred years after Taylor emerged from her barrel, Kirk Jones, another person from Michigan facing unemployment and an uncertain future, devised a plan to master the falls. This time, however, the journey would be made using no flotation devices or other equipment. On 20 October 2003, Jones, wearing only the clothes on his back, jumped into the upper Niagara River just above Horseshoe Falls and plunged into the basin 51 meters below. Sustaining minor bruises to his ribs, Jones was admitted involuntarily to a psychiatric unit by authorities to determine if the act was suicidal or a stunt. Upon being released from the hospital, Jones was then arrested and charged with mischief and performing a stunt within the Niagara Parks. After pleading guilty to both charges, Jones was fined $3,000 and required to reimburse the Niagara Parks an additional $1,408 in lost revenue because an attraction was shut down at the time of his rescue.

The regulation of jumpers by law enforcement authorities has been a longstanding subplot to the story of Niagara. The publicity prior to Annie Taylor's jump was cryptic, in part, because of a concern that she would be arrested before the barrel was let into the rapids. Fred Robinson, a riverman who had been approached about assisting with the retrieval of her barrel, declined to be involved at the last minute because police had made him aware that he could be charged with manslaughter if Taylor died as a result of the stunt.

In 2003 Sarah Wood, events and public relations coordinator for the Niagara Parks Commission, explained that the parks' prohibition against stunting is intended to deter would-be thrill seekers and to protect the rescue workers called upon to save those who jump. As is the case with other extreme sports that have been limited by local statutes, individual rights of expression are weighed against the overall public good. In the case of barrel jumpers at Niagara Falls, it is difficult to know if the small number can be attributed to the daunting nature of the jump or to the effectiveness of the stunting prohibition.

Ellen J. Staurowsky

See also Meaning of Extreme, The

Further Reading

Berton, P. (1997). *Niagara: A history of the falls.* New York: Kodansha America.

Clarke, T. (1997, February 16). Roll out the barrel. *New York Times Book Review,* pp. 8–9.

Dubinsky, K. (1999). *The second greatest disappointment: Honeymooning and tourism at Niagara Falls.* New Brunswick, NJ: Rutgers University Press.

Facts about Niagara Falls. (n.d.). Retrieved August, 8, 2006, from http://www.niagarafallslive.com/Facts_about_Niagara_Falls.htm

Fink, J. (2003, May 23). Niagara-on-the-set: Hundreds of movies, TV shows have been filmed just across border. *Buffalo Business First: Western New York's Business Newspaper.* Retrieved July 7, 2006, from http://buffalo.bizjournals.com/buffalo/stories/2003/05/26/focus1.html

Kusmierz, M. (2004, October). Anna Edson Taylor (1839–1921): Bay City teacher was first person to go over Niagara Falls. *Bay-Journal.* Retrieved July 7, 2006, from http://www.bay-journal.com/bay/1he/people/fp-taylor-annie.html

Johnson, P. E. (2004). *Sam Patch: The famous jumper.* New York: Hill and Wang.

McKinsey, E. (1985). *Niagara Falls: Icon of the American sublime.* Cambridge, UK: Cambridge University Press.

Murray, J. (2000). *Queen of the mist.* Boston: Beacon Press.

Staba, D. (2003, October 22). Family stunned after man takes Niagara Falls plunge and lives. *New York Times,* p. B-1.

BASE Jumping

Although a somewhat obscure activity, BASE jumping (less commonly known as "fixed object jumping") may be the archetypal extreme sport. Jumping from a 35-meter bridge, for example, allows almost no margin for error. If a jumper's parachute hesitates (opens slowly) or, worse, malfunctions, the jump will almost certainly result in serious injury or even death. Even in cases where jumpers' equipment works as planned, BASE jumps are almost always rife with hazards, including facing challenging wind conditions, landing on rock, flying into structures or wires, or, occasionally, being arrested.

These hazards have led some people to call BASE jumping the "most serious play in the world." Almost one hundred fatalities have been documented in the relatively short history of the sport. Contextualization of this number is, of course, difficult because, as advocates of the sport point out, tens of thousands of successful jumps have been made. Despite its obscurity, and perhaps because of its status as an extreme sport, BASE jumping has been covered by a number of major television networks, including the Australian Broadcasting Corporation, the Outdoor Life Network, and the American Broadcasting Company. In addition, it has been featured in several James Bond films and other popular culture outlets.

Technical Issues

The term *BASE* is an acronym for "Building, Antenna (or Aerial), Span (i.e., bridges), Earth (i.e., cliffs and other rock formations)," the four categories of objects from which participants jump. Although not all objects neatly fall into one of these four categories, a broad classification into one of the four based on geometry and interaction with the wind can be useful for risk-assessment purposes and is therefore common. For other purposes unusual objects may be designated simply "Other." Most jumpers, for example, would require that an object be designed to be occupied in order to be classified as a building, thus excluding an object such as a grain silo from this category. Depending on the height of the object from which they are launching, jumpers may either undertake a short freefall before deploying their parachute or set up a static line—a piece of equipment that rapidly deploys their parachute as soon as they have launched.

Whether they are in freefall or under an open parachute, the most important objective of BASE jumpers, from a safety perspective, is to create distance between themselves and the hazards in the area. Often the most important of these hazards is the object from which a jumper has just launched. In this respect BASE jumping benefited from two advances in skydiving during the 1970s: tracking and the ram-air parachute. Tracking is the use of body position to generate forward speed in freefall. A skilled jumper can achieve a glide ratio of nearly 1:1, that is, the jumper can cover one foot horizontally for every foot he or she descends—even without specialized clothing. Meanwhile, ram-air parachutes (commonly called "rectangular") create a great deal more forward drive and maneuverability than do older round parachutes. Together these advances changed the face of BASE jumping.

Although BASE jumping shares some important technical elements with skydiving (the use of a parachute being the most obvious of these), a number of elements of BASE jumping differentiate it from skydiving. Whereas skydiving entails jumping from an aircraft, BASE jumping entails jumping from fixed objects such as cliffs and buildings. Meanwhile, the fact that a BASE jumper's parachute is generally not inflated as he or she leaves the "object" differentiates it from sports such as paragliding and ground launching. A standard feature of skydiving "rigs" is a reserve chute for use in case of a malfunction of the main parachute. A BASE jumping rig has no reserve parachute. Two factors motivate this choice: First, many BASE jumps are undertaken from such a low altitude that there would not be time for a reserve parachute to inflate in the case of a malfunctioning main parachute; and second, the presence of a reserve parachute would complicate a system whose reliability stems partly from its simplicity and would introduce additional failure modes.

BASE jumping generally has a far smaller margin for error than does skydiving. Experienced skydivers, for ex-

ample, generally deploy their parachutes at least 600 meters above the ground, providing for a certain amount of time to deal with hazards (such as a malfunctioning parachute or obstacles in the landing area). BASE jumping, on the other hand, is sometimes done from objects lower than 60 meters or in areas with many obstacles, including not only the object from which the jumper has just launched, but also often a hazardous landing area.

The lowest altitude from which BASE jumps can be made with any degree of safety, even by the most experienced jumpers using modern equipment, is 30–60 meters. This highlights the fact that BASE jumping is an intrinsically dangerous sport because the heights from which a parachute can be effectively used render survival unlikely if it fails. Furthermore, in many scenarios a BASE jump can become life threatening even after the parachute opens properly. Significant technical knowledge and prior training are important in mitigating these risks.

History

BASE jumping shares an early history with skydiving. The first recorded descents from a fixed object occurred around the beginning of the twentieth century, including several

A BASE jumper leaping off a cliff. Source: istock/Jason Lugo.

jumps from the Upper Suspension Bridge near Niagara Falls (the earliest of these by H. P. Peer in 1879) and a promotional jump from the Statue of Liberty by steeplejack Frederick Law in 1912. These early jumps were stunts in the sense that they were performed by a handful of people, many of them accomplished performers, who generally did one or two such jumps in a lifetime.

The first record of sports parachutists jumping from fixed objects is from the mid-1950s, with cliff jumps by a dentist in the Italian Dolomites. In 1966 Michael Pelky and Brian Schubert, both experienced skydivers, made the first jumps from El Capitan in the Yosemite valley. After a successful freefall, Pelky had difficulty maneuvering his round parachute and broke his ankle after flying into the cliff face. Schubert's parachute collapsed 15 meters from the talus below, injuring him more seriously.

In 1978 the first jumps using ram-air parachutes and modern skydiving freefall techniques to achieve separation from the object were organized by Carl Boenish. In 1981 Boenish coined the term *BASE jumping* and began issuing sequential BASE numbers to jumpers who completed one jump from each of the four object types, awarding "BASE 1" to Phil Smith. More than a thousand BASE numbers have been issued since.

BASE Jumping Community

Because of the hazardous and specialized nature of the sport, BASE jumping has attracted a small number of participants compared with other sports, with perhaps five to ten thousand jumpers worldwide. Although firm statistics have not been compiled, participants are predominantly male and urban, with an average age in the range of thirty. The largest BASE jumper populations are found in North America, eastern and western Europe, the United

Kingdom, Australia and New Zealand, South Africa, and Russia. Few jumpers come from the remainder of Asia and Africa. Anecdotal evidence suggests that BASE jumpers are, on average, of a relatively high socio-economic status. Like skydiving, BASE jumping requires a certain amount of discretionary income (for equipment, travel, etc.) and time.

The small size and broad distribution of the community are reflected in a lack of formal structure in the sport. In contrast to skydiving, BASE jumping is largely unregulated, with associations such as Cliff Jumpers Association of America and the Alliance of Backcountry Parachutists focusing on advocacy rather than regulation. Indeed, although jumpers generally adhere to a code of ethics and are outspoken in favor of responsible use of sites, most are resolutely against setting formal rules.

BASE jumping has no mandated student progression and no formal rating system. The large majority of BASE jumpers enter the sport only after having completed hundreds of skydives, most of the remainder beginning with considerable experience in some other area of aviation. Whereas many do their first jumps through an organized course offered by an experienced jumper or equipment manufacturer, others are mentored by a local jumper. Because of the high levels of technical expertise and awareness demanded of participants, many experienced jumpers are reluctant to act as mentors to neophytes whose abilities they do not know or trust.

Some evidence indicates a move toward institutionalization of the sport. In 2005, for example, a number of French BASE jumpers formed an association that is now part of the Fédération Française des Clubs Alpins (French Federation of Alpine Clubs—FFCA). This organization still does not mandate particular progression guidelines but has formally aligned itself with other alpine activities. One interesting dimension of this development is that through this association with the FFCA, affiliated BASE jumpers have access to insurance coverage for personal injury, as well as some coverage for legal fees associated with arrests in certain national parks.

The rapid dissemination of information within the community is important because techniques and equipment continue to evolve at a fast pace. Although a number of publications have arisen, from *BASE Magazine* in 1981 to *BASEline*, *Jump*, and *Fixed Object Journal* in the mid- to late 1980s, none lasted longer than five years. Web forums have largely supplanted these, with some of the most reliable sources of technical information on BASE jumping including forums on Dropzone.com, Blinc, and, more recently, the BASE Wiki.

BASE Jumping and the Law

Although popular opinion holds that BASE jumping is illegal, this is not the case in most instances. However, a minority of jumps are made from urban objects or other private property; in such cases, object access may involve trespassing. Furthermore, flight in urban areas is often tightly regulated, though the agencies responsible do not generally concern themselves with flight at the altitudes from which BASE jumps are conducted. BASE jumpers sometimes engage in elaborate acts of deception in order to gain access to high-profile "objects" from which jumping is forbidden. In the spring of 2006, for example, Jeb Ray Corliss IV, a thirty-year-old experienced BASE jumper from Malibu, California, donned an elaborate disguise to gain access to the Empire State Building in New York. Hiding his BASE rig under a "fat suit," Corliss was able to access the roof of the building posing as a tourist, although he was apprehended before he was able to jump. Corliss faced charges of criminal trespassing, reckless endangerment (the authorities argued that had he jumped, he would have been placing pedestrians below at risk), and assault (a charge stemming from resisting apprehension).

Jumps made in the backcountry from public lands are generally permitted. In some cases BASE jumping has been made illegal even there by inclusion in a broader aviation ban. Such is the case, for example, in Canada's national parks and in some of its provincial parks, where BASE jumping is prohibited under legislation against taking off or landing an aircraft. In other cases BASE jumping has been the target of specific legislation, as is the case in the national parks of the United States. A history of conflict exists between the National Park Service (NPS) and BASE jumpers, beginning with a 1978 ban on jumping in Yosemite, a park in which jumping was (briefly) permitted. The NPS argued that BASE jumping technically violates 36 CFR 2.17(a)(3) ("Delivery by air"). The NPS opposition was formalized in section 8.2.2.7 of the 2001 NPS Management Policies:

> 8.2.2.7 BASE Jumping. BASE (Buildings, Antennae, Spans, Earth forms) jumping—also known as fixed object jumping—involves an individual wearing a parachute jumping from buildings, antennae, spans (bridges), and earth forms (cliffs).

This is not an appropriate public use activity within national park areas, and is prohibited by 36 CFR 2. 17(a)(3).

There are some indications that the section will be removed in subsequent revisions.

Important Locations and Events

In a technical sense, BASE jumpers can jump almost anywhere. However, a number of locations and events serve as touchstones in the BASE jumping community.

Bridge Day

At a height of 267 meters, the New River Gorge Bridge near Fayetteville, West Virginia, is the second-highest vehicular bridge in the world. The bridge lies within the New River Gorge National River Park, and consequently jumping is forbidden almost year around. On the third Saturday in October of each year, however, BASE jumpers are invited to jump from the bridge for a six-hour window beginning at 9 A.M. The event, part of a day celebrating the bridge, was first held in 1980 and has since been held annually with the exception of Bridge Day 2001 (cancelled because of September 11, 2001). Bridge Day attracts more than 450 BASE jumpers and 200,000 spectators annually.

Bridge Day is a popular event for skydivers making their first BASE jumps. In terms of avoiding collisions with the structure from which a jumper has just launched, bridges are generally the safest object type. The bridge's height and the presence of a large number of boats to pull jumpers from the river make for a particularly safe first jump.

Twin Falls

The community of Twin Falls, Idaho, is unusual in North America because it has welcomed BASE jumpers as a part of its tourist industry. The I. B. Perrine Bridge, crossing the Snake River Canyon at a height of 148 meters, is one of the most popular destinations for BASE jumpers worldwide. Jumps can be made legally from the bridge year around, with local authorities asking only that they be informed when the day's jumping begins and ends.

The Perrine Bridge is among the safest locations in North America. The Snake River moves slowly below the bridge, and a large meadow is available as a primary landing area. The influence of the bridge on modern BASE jumping can hardly be overstated. Until the early 1990s the most experienced BASE jumpers had perhaps a hundred jumps, made over ten or more years of jumping. A few jumpers now have more than a thousand, often with 30 percent or more of those made in Twin Falls.

Norway

The fjords of southern Norway are home to a number of popular exit points visited by BASE jumpers from around the world. Sheer or even overhanging cliffs measuring 600 meters and higher, with 300 meters or more of high-angle scree below, allow for freefalls exceeding twenty seconds even without special equipment. On such long freefalls, the jumper has time to reach "terminal velocity," the speed at which the force of drag equals that of gravity and the jumper falls at a constant rate of nearly 200 kilometers per hour vertically. At one site jumpers can take advantage of camping near the cliffs, bus rides to the trail head, boat rides back, and even an annual "heli-boogie" for jumpers who wish to forgo the two-hour hike.

Moab

Moab, Utah, is a center for outdoor activities of all kinds, from mountain biking to climbing to off-road driving. Much of the land surrounding Moab is controlled by the federal Bureau of Land Management, which supports responsible BASE jumping in the area. The cliffs surrounding Moab range in height from about 60 to 180 meters, making them much more technically challenging jump locations than higher cliffs.

Kuala Lumpur, Malaysia

In recent years Malaysian authorities have courted extreme sports participants as part of a tourism-marketing strategy. State-sanctioned jumps from structures such as the 452-meter Petronas Towers in downtown Kuala Lumpur began in October of 1999 and show no signs of slowing.

Exotic Locations

For many jumpers the most rewarding jumps are those that occur from an object that is in some sense unusual. In addition to objects that simply do not fit into one of the four

BASE Jumping, Up Close and Personal

The following is author Jason Cooper's account of a BASE (Bridge, Antenna, Span, Earth) jumping training day. An experienced skydiver, Cooper was getting ready for his first BASE jump.

I had driven twenty-five hours with my brother from Calgary, Alberta, to a place near Los Angeles, California, to learn how to BASE jump. I had five hundred skydives when I headed out, and even with that background this wasn't a simple three-hour course like a person takes when they sign up to make their first skydive. Three full days, from nine in the morning to nine at night, learning how to determine the height and suitability of an exit point, how to recognize acceptable weather conditions for a jump, how to reconfigure equipment.

What to do if this or that happens on opening, and how to rig a parachute so that this or that never happens in the first place. Mock exits on a 20-foot bungee cord from under a bridge, repeated until we got it just right.

On the last day, we head out to an open field where a hot-air balloon waits for us, tethered to the ground by an 800-foot rope. I've never jumped from less than 3,000 feet. On the way up, we draw straws. I'm going first. All I can think about is that I packed the rig on my back just yesterday. Did I miss anything? I can see the headlines: "Man dies in fall from…" The next round of students is going to learn to avoid the mistake I already made. Or am about to make. No. I'm here to jump. The balloon [reaches eight hundred feet] and I step onto a plank outside the wicker basket. Breathe. "Ready when you are," says the instructor quietly. I'm terrified. I give the count: "Three, two, one…See ya."

My peripheral vision explodes as my feet leave the plank. It's all perfectly clear now—why I did this. Then, with a sudden crash, the canopy opens over my head, and the revelation becomes a vague memory.

The opening is perfect. I bring it around to a landing, and I head up again."

Jason Cooper

basic categories, many exotic locations are available to the jumper with sufficient financial resources. Examples include organized trips to Venezuela's Angel Falls, Canada's Baffin Island, and (until jumps there were prohibited in early 2004) even Mexico's Cave of the Swallows, in which the entire freefall is made underground.

Future Directions

A number of controversies are likely to shape not only the future of BASE jumping, but also the possibilities for research into this sport. In terms of the sport itself, technological and performance innovations are likely to continue to expand the possibilities of what kinds of objects BASE jumpers may choose to jump from. A recent skydiving innovation, for instance, is the "wing suit"—a suit that allows jumpers to slow their fall rate toward the Earth while covering tremendous horizontal distances (see "Skydiving" for further elaboration). Recently some BASE jumpers have employed this technology to jump from cliffs and freefall more or less diagonally just a few meters from the trees and rock, following the slope of a cliff as it descends before deploying their parachutes.

Anecdotal evidence indicates that BASE jumpers are resistant to those who are interested in investigating BASE jumping from a social-scientific perspective. Like many other risk-sport enthusiasts, BASE jumpers seem to be of the (perhaps understandable) opinion that those who do not engage in the sport cannot understand why BASE jumpers do what they do. Moreover, participants seem to be concerned that researchers will unfairly demonize the sport by citing the hazards without considering the huge number of successful jumps that have been made.

Overall, the hazards associated with the sport, together with the sometimes clandestine activities of participants, present challenges to researchers but make the sport an interesting area for the investigation of the sociological dimensions of extreme sports.

Jason Cooper and Jason Laurendeau

See also Skydiving

Further Reading

Association de Paralpinisme. (2004). Retrieved June 23, 2006, from http://www.paralpinisme.net/

BASE Wiki. (n.d.). Retrieved June 23, 2006, from http://www.basewiki.com/

Blinc. (n.d.). Retrieved June 23, 2006, from http://www.blincmagazine.com/

Bridgeday information (n.d.). *What is Bridge Day?* Retrieved June 23, 2006, from http://www.bridgeday.info

Club Alpin Francais. (n.d.). Retrieved June 23, 2006, from http://www.ffcam.fr/fr/actualites/index.php?le_num_info=231&le_num_rub=1&le_num_sous_rub=0

Dedijer, J. (2004). *BASE 66: A story of fear, fun, and freefall.* New York: iUniverse Star.

Di Giovanni, N. (n.d.). BASE jumping history. Retrieved June 23, 2006, from http://www.basicresearch.com/base_history.htm

Dropzone.com. (n.d.). Retrieved June 23, 2006, from http://www.dropzone.com/

Fensch, T. (1980). *Skydiving book.* Mountainview, CA: Anderson World.

Ferrell, J., Milovanovic, D., & Lyng, S. (2001). Edgework, media practices, and the elongation of meaning: A theoretical ethnography of the Bridge Day event. *Theoretical Criminology, 5*(2), 177–202.

Frappr. (n.d.). Retrieved June 23, 2006, from http://www.frappr.com/basejumpers

Greenwood, J. (1978). *Parachuting for sport* (2nd ed.). Blue Ridge Summit, PA: Tab Books.

Horan, M. (1979). *Index to parachuting 1900–1975.* Richmond, IN: Parachuting Resources.

Huston, J. (1972). *Out of the blue.* West Lafayette, IN: Purdue University Studies.

Jakeman, S. (1992). *Groundrush.* London: Arrow Books.

Martha, C., & Griffet, J. (2006). Sauter dans le vide: Le BASE-jump, le jeu le plus sérieux du monde [BASE-jumping: The most serious play in the world]. *Ethnologie française,* (4).

Baumgartner, Felix

Felix Baumgartner (b. 1969) is a BASE (Building, Antenna, Span, Earth) jumper, skydiver, stuntman and stunt coordinator, and free-fall camera operator. His number, "BASE 502," identifies Baumgartner as the 502nd person to have jumped from the four categories in the discipline—building, antenna, span, earth. His most acclaimed jumps include those from the Petronas Towers in Kuala Lumpur (451 meters), the statue of *Christ the Redeemer* atop Corcovado Mountain, Rio de Janeiro (29 meters), and the bridge over the Parne River near Millau, France (343 meters). Baumgartner regards the BASE jump into the Mamet Cave, Velebit National Park, Croatia, as his most dangerous. The

7.5-second jump into darkness was, he said, "everything you don't want: it's a deep hole, it's steep, and it has a nasty landing area." Equally treacherous was the jump from the statue of Christ. Baumgartner had just 1.5 seconds to open his parachute before potentially crashing on to the visitors platform and then, immediately on deploying the parachute, he had to turn sharply to clear the edge of Corcovado Mountain. Baumgartner admitted being "really scared" when "standing on top of Jesus and knowing that there was just one second between living and dying." Baumgartner performed his most publicized feat in 2003 when he glided across the English Channel wearing an aerodynamic suit and a 6-foot wing. During the flight, which began at 10,000 meters over Dover and lasted 6 minutes, 22 seconds, Baumgartner endured temperatures of minus 40° C and traveled up to 360 kilometers per hour.

Baumgartner possesses all the guile, stealth, agility, and physical skills required of successful BASE jumpers who participate in an activity that in most circumstances is illegal. Baumgartner disguised himself as a businessman and carried forged identification to access the Petronas Towers; his briefcase contained a parachute and video camera! To reach the launching platform for the statue of *Christ the Redeemer*, Baumgartner fired an arrow from a crossbow over the extended right arm of the icon; the arrow carried a fine steel cable to which he attached climbing ropes. Before jumping from the heavily guarded Parne River Bridge, Baumgartner had to climb, unsecured, up a 230-meter column in the early hours of the morning. He then hid in steel formwork under the road until first light when he received an "all clear" text message from his cameraman. But Baumgartner has not always evaded the law. Panamanian police arrested him, and his photographer, after Baumgartner jumped from a height of 108 meters on the Bridge of the Americas (which connects North with South America) in September 2004. The pair languished in prison for a week.

Born in Salzburg, Austria, where he still maintains a residence, Baumgartner trained at Porsche as a machine fitter. Conscripted into the military, he worked as a tank driver and helicopter pilot, but his commanders labeled him a "troublemaker" and declared him "unsuited for military services." Baumgartner completed his first parachute jump as a teenager in 1986; ten years later he made his first BASE jump, from the New River Gorge Bridge (Fayetteville, West Virginia) on Bridge Day. (Authorities open the bridge to BASE jumpers on one day each year.) In 1999 Baumgartner left the anonymity of Porsche to pursue a professional career in extreme aerial pursuits.

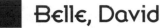
While Baumgartner describes the air as his "second home" and talks about searching for challenges, the decision to turn professional lay in an astute recognition of the commercial potential in the tripartite relationship involving extreme pursuits, the media, and sponsors. The media has an insatiable appetite for visual images of extreme pursuits that also appeal to an array of sponsors. In the case of BASE jumping, images are usually on tap because jumpers must produce them as part of the documentation required to receive official recognition of their feats. Thus Baumgartner slipped easily into the relationship. For example, he gave six hours of interviews and appeared in hundreds of newspapers and magazines after gliding across the English Channel. Not only did this coverage enhance Baumgartner's reputation, it generated maximum publicity for his primary sponsor, Red Bull—the energy drink that "gives you wings." Paradoxically, the illegality of many BASE jumps increases media and public interest. As an explanation for why he generally doesn't request authorization to jump, Baumgartner comments that "if you want to sell it to the media, it's cooler if you have no permission."

Baumgartner dismisses the label "adrenaline junkie" and rejects charges that he is "crazy" and "doesn't care about life." On the contrary, he emphasizes meticulous planning, patience, and training. "I'm not stupid," he says, "I prepare myself." Baumgartner's jump into the Mamet Cave involved months of preparation by him and his forty-strong support team, including practice leaps from a hot-air balloon and laser measurements of the cave. He used an MP3 player as a precision timer for the countdown to the jump and for opening the parachute. Baumgartner's preparations for the glide across the English Channel extended into years. They included developing an aerodynamic suit—that doubled to protect him from the cold at high altitude—and a carbon wing to achieve maximum glide in free fall. The wing passed through several prototypes to increase the gliding angle from an initial 3:1 ratio (3 meters horizontal movement for every 1 meter descent) to an eventual 7:1. Many tests in the laboratory and the field also preceded the flight. In one field test Baumgartner was strapped, with his suit and wing, to the top of a Porsche vehicle that was then driven at 320 kilometers per hour.

Patience is a Baumgartner virtue. Arriving at the launching platform on the Sentech Tower (formerly Brixton Tower) in Johannesburg, South Africa, for a rare officially sanctioned jump, Baumgartner declared the wind too strong. "It's hard to say no," he admitted, "but it saves your life. It doesn't matter how many people are there, it doesn't

matter how many camera guys are there. If the wind is like this, it's definitely a no go." (He eventually completed the jump several days later.) Similarly, training is paramount. "You have to train a lot," he stresses, "you can't do it from the very first moment. You have to train your eye to be really precise. Most of the time when I jump and open my parachute at the very last second, I look at the people on the ground. As they get bigger, at a certain point you know that it's time to pull. The altimeter is just to know the altitude when you step off the launching platform. You don't use it in free-fall."

One of a rare breed who makes a living from extreme sports, Felix Baumgartner is also a member of a coterie that has made history. Recounting his "greatest personal moment," the glide across the English Channel, Baumgartner noted that humans "shouldn't be at 10,000 meters. But there I was with wings strapped to my back, a little oxygen pipe in my mouth and a little skydiving suit. And I was flying through history."

Douglas Booth

Further Reading

Baumgartner, F. (2003). Interview with R. Wiegmann and W. Block. Volvo SportsDesign forum, Munich. June 28. Retrieved July 20, 2006, from http://www.isposportsdesign.com/english/forum/press/press releases/pressrelease9/index.html

Baumgartner, F. (2004). Interview with D. Watts. Carte blanche, *M-Net* (South Africa), February 8. Retrieved July 20, 2006, from http://www.carteblanche.co.za/display/Display.asp?Id=2421

Cave jump. (December/January 2005). *New Zealand Adventure*, 13–15.

No risk, no fun. (2006). *Ryanair Magazine*, 10. Retrieved July 20, 2006, from http://www.ryanairmagazine.com/issue_detail.asp?AR_ID=52&A_ID=6

Tomlinson, J. (2004). *Extreme sports: In search of the ultimate thrill.* London: Carlton Books.

Belle, David

In the world of *parkour*, David Belle is known as the creator; the originator. A Frenchman, Belle is credited with the invention of a sport known as free running in the United States and *parkour* elsewhere. Using the architecture around him he can scale walls, leap from roof to roof, and tumble down hills. His creative and athletic abilities and his role in founding the sport have earned him a place in this modern sport's history.

Born on 29 April 1973 in the Normandy region of France, Belle's maternal grandfather was an inspiration to him, and would inspire the *parkour* later. As a military firefighter Belle's grandfather was known for his courageous rescues and inventive use of structures to aid him in these rescues. Belle left school at the age of fifteen as he was beginning to practice what would become *parkour*. According to his personal website, he imagined himself in rescue situations and devised ways to use the things around him to escape.

Around this time Belle moved to a Parisian suburb where he began training to become a firefighter like his grandfather. A wrist injury ended that pursuit and after recovery he joined the French Marine Corps instead. While in the Corps he excelled at the gymnastic and agility portions of training, even earning several certificates of physical achievement. However, the rigidity of the military did not suit his free spirit and he eventually left to pursue other things.

After leaving the military, Belle and his childhood friend Sébastien Foucan started a group called Yamakasi. This group began practicing the sport and created the ideals behind it. Belle eventually left this group and began his own when he feared that *parkour* was losing its original purpose; he worried about the commercialization of the sport. Belle views *parkour* as showing people "what it is to move." As *parkour*'s popularity increased so did David Belle's exposure. He made several promotional videos for advertisers such as BBC1, Nissan, and Nike as well as his own which can be found across the internet. These artistic videos display Belle's unique ability to use the physical world as an obstacle course finding the most direct way to move from one point to another. Belle has stated that while *parkour* is a sport it is important to him that it be useful as well. For him *parkour* is an athletic feat, an artistic expression, and a way to move in everyday life.

Parkour, and Belle, gained more prominence when he began making appearances in films such as "L'Engrenages," "Femme Fatale," and "Crimson Rivers 2." The most widely reviewed of these being "Banlieu 13," a science-fiction action film set in the future in which Belle and fellow *parkouristes* (or *traceurs*) use their *parkour* skills to help a friend in the district. The film is mostly focused on the *parkour* aspect making it one of the first nondocumentary films about the sport.

The world of *parkour* is opening up for David Belle and his fellow athletes. He created the Parkour Worldwide Association (PAWA) and is currently on a World Tour with that group. Belle once said "We want to go where no human has ever been before" and it certainly seems that the sport he created as a teenager will take him there.

Dana M. Weigel

Further Reading

Gordon, Devin. (2006). "District" derring-do. *Newsweek, 147*(22).

Heslett, Charles. (2006, May 16). Thrilled to the 'kour. *Yorkshire Evening Post.*

Longino, Bob. (2006, June 2). French thriller works best at full speed. *Atlanta Journal-Constitution*, 3G.

Schofield, Hugh. (2002, April 19). The art of le parkour. BBC News Online. Retrieved January 31, 2007, from http://news.bbc.co.uk/2/low/entertainment/1939867.stm

Big Wave Contests

Big wave contests must be understood against the general historical backdrop of big wave surfing. Although big wave contests with prize money and media coverage are a phenomenon of modern professional surfing (from the late 1960s onward), they still reflect the association of wave size, privilege, and prestige that characterized the ritual function of big wave surfing in ancient Hawaiian and Polynesian cultures.

Brief History

In traditional Hawaiian surfing certain locations renowned for their large surf were *kapu*—forbidden to all but the *ali'i* (chiefs), whose social prestige was expressed through performances of courage and skill in big waves. Thus, an element of contest has always existed in big wave surfing. What has changed in modern big wave surfing is the superimposition of professional and commercial functions upon its previous ritual function. This superimposition was not the result of a historical evolution, but rather of the reinvention of big wave surfing after the 150-year decline of surfing from Captain Cook's arrival in Hawaii in 1778 until its revival in the first decades of the twentieth century. Tom Blake, a key pioneer in the revival of surfing, claims that big wave surfing did not revive until 1905–1908 and that few surfers of the time could handle the larger surf: twice the height of the surfer or more in size.

Big wave surfing in the twentieth century was also driven by important innovations in surfboard design, including the development of skeg or fin technology, absent on the traditional Hawaiian boards, and the application of new surfboard construction materials, moving from the heavy, solid, redwood blanks to Fiberglass-laminated balsa wood cores in the early 1950s and finally to Fiberglas-laminated polystyrene foam boards by the end of the decade. These design developments allowed lighter, more stable, more maneuverable, and more refined wave-riding equipment, which greatly aided in the exploration of larger surf.

Big Wave Contest Sites

Hawaii is the undisputed home of traditional big wave surfing, the early twentieth-century revival of its premodern form, and its modern translation through contemporary materials and professional contest formats. Another critical factor in the development of modern big wave surfing and contests was the shift of focus toward surf locations on the North Shore of Oahu during the late 1950s, which, although internationally famous today, were still unknown and unnamed until mid-decade. At that time the center of big wave surfing was still at Makaha, on the west coast of the island, also the site of the first International Surfing

Contest in 1953. However, contests during the 1950s were still preprofessional events with prizes rather than prize money. They also lacked the sort of formalized judging systems developed during the 1960s and did not make the size of the surf a prerequisite for holding the event, as do most contemporary big wave contests.

A precedent-setting big wave contest in this regard was the Duke Kahanamoku International Surfing Championship of 1969. The event was conceived by Kimo McVay, owner of Duke's Restaurant in Waikiki, as an invitation-only contest held annually in honor of the legendary Hawaiian waterman known as "the Duke," who played a large role in the twentieth-century revival of surfing. McVay's idea for the contest had been inspired by an article in *Surfer Magazine* by big wave pioneer Fred Van Dyke, who recounted a day in the early 1960s when Sunset Beach on the North Shore of Oahu was breaking triple overhead and bigger with excellent conditions, and many famous surfers from the era were in the water together, inspiring one another with their surfing and driving their performances to a higher level. "The Duke," as the event came to be known, was a significant prototype for modern big wave contests in its connection to a particular big wave break: Sunset Beach, the requirement of large surf, and its invitational nature. The first Duke Invitational in 1965 offered no prize money but was a huge success and held in 3–3.6-meter (triple overhead)

Surfing in South Africa under big wave conditions. Source: istock/Henk Badenhorst.

surf. Mike Doyle became the first person to win money at the Duke Invitational in 1969 when he walked away with $1,000 for first place.

Professionalism and Commercial Sponsorship of Contests

The Duke Invitational also drew thousands of spectators, thus providing the impetus for a series of commercially sponsored professional big wave contests. In 1970 the Smirnoff Pro Surfing Contest, inaugurated in California in 1968, moved to the North Shore of Oahu. In 1971 another North Shore location known for big surf became the site of the Hawaiian Professional Surfing Association Haleiwa Open, and 1971 also brought the addition of the Hang Ten American Pro Championship and the Pipeline Masters. This triad of events established the first viable annual pro surfing tour in Hawaii focused around the North Shore's most prestigious and consistent big wave locations: Haliewa, Sunset Beach, and Pipeline. Although sponsorship of the events would change over the years, the events were held consistently through the 1970s and would become formally integrated as the Triple Crown of Pro Surfing in 1983, offering a bonus purse to a surfer who won all three events. However, the most infamous big wave contest on the North Shore would become associated with Waimea Bay, which required at least 3-meter waves before it even started breaking and was rideable in up to 9-meter faces, measured from trough to crest. In 1974 the Smirnoff Pro (a mobile event) was held at 6-meters-plus Waimea because the rest of the North Shore was closing out in the huge swells, with waves breaking over all at once and making the waves unrideable. Hawaiian Reno Abellira took first place, and the contest set a new standard for big wave competition. However, because no one could guarantee that Waimea (and other big wave-only locations) would break at that size every winter, such events were not integrated into the regular professional surfing world tour, which had to be preorganized for specific dates and locations regardless of wave size.

Criteria for Big Wave Contests

Big wave contests such as the 1974 Smirnoff Pro also underscored the need for judging criteria different from those used in normal-sized contest conditions. Although wave size has always been one among many criteria applied in the judging

---

The Waves of Ancient Hawaii

These definitions of Hawaiian waves were published as newspaper accounts in 1869 and 1870.

That which swells and rolls in "furrows" *('aui kawahawaha)* just *makai* of the surf line *(kua'au)* is a *nalu*, a wave. A wave that breaks along its entire length is a *kai palala, nalu palala,* or *lauloa*; if it breaks on one side, that is a *nalu muku*. A wave that is sunken inward when breaking *(po'opo'o iloko ke po'i ana)* is a *nalu halehale* (cavernous wave) [called "tube" by modern surfers]; one that draws up high is a *nalu puki*; one that does not furrow or break is an *'aio,* a swell; one that sinks down just as it was about to break is a *nalu 'opu'u*. A wave that swirls and "eats away" [the sand] *(po'ai 'onaha)* is a *nalu 'a'ai* or *'ae'i*; one that rolls in diagonally *(waiho 'ao'ao mai)* is a *nalu kahela*.

Where waves meet at one place because of some rise on the sea bottom—or a mass of coral heads perhaps—is called a *pu'ao* and where they break constantly at coral heads they are called *nalu ko'aka*.

The "furrows" *(kawahawaha)* of the ocean that are stirred up by the wind become waves called *'ale*, billows or *ni'au*; a swell that blows off above *(pu'o iluna)* and breaks below *(po'i iho)* is an *'ale ni'au*. A long swell, *aio,* that breaks and spreads in *(po'i pahola mai)* is an *'ale lauloa*; long swells that break in lines [in sets] are *'ale kualono*. A swell that twists about and breaks here and breaks there in an agitated manner *(kupikipiki'o ka po'i ana)* is an *'ale wiliau,* and when many swells break agitatedly against points or capes of land they are called *'ale wiliau maka lae*.

Source: Kamakau, S. M. (1976) *The works of the people of old: Na hana a ka po'e kahiko* (pp. 12–13). Honolulu: Bishop Museum Press.

of regular events on the Pro Surfing Tour, in big wave contests wave size is elevated to the central (and in some cases overriding) criterion. The inadequacy of normal judging criteria in big wave conditions has also been underscored by certain regular pro tour events that turned into impromptu big wave competitions, such as the 1981 Bells Beach Pro in southeast Australia, which greeted many shocked and underequipped competitors with 4.5-meter surf.

Three criteria common to all contemporary big wave contests are the size of the wave, the critical nature of the maneuvers performed by the surfer, and the length of ride. However, whereas small wave contests emphasize the amount of maneuvers performed on the face of the wave, big wave contests emphasize how deep the surfer can ride in the critical section of the "tube" (curl of the wave) or just in front of the breaking wave. In this way the differential judging criteria employed for big wave contests also reflects the inherited values of traditional big wave surfing.

The rapid economic growth of the surf industry and popularization of surfing during the 1990s led to the development of a series of innovative big wave competitions, led by the Quicksilver in Memory of Eddie Aikau. In many ways "the Eddie" reproduces the spirit and structure of "the Duke." Big wave surfer George Downing conceived "the Eddie" as a contest to honor the big wave surfer, lifeguard, waterman, and Hawaiian cultural advocate who was killed while piloting a traditional Polynesian outrigger canoe between islands in 1978. "The Eddie" is held once each winter at Waimea Bay if and only if the surf is judged to be at least 6 meters in height. As a consequence the contest has been held only in 1986, 1990, 1999, 2000, 2002, and 2004. By combining surfing memorial and professional contest, sponsor Quicksilver merged the economy of prize money and corporate sponsorship with the ritual function of traditional big wave surfing. Quicksilver resuscitated the symbolism, if not the explicit ritual function, of traditional Hawaiian big wave surfing but conferred the prestige of the performances and of the icon of Eddie Aikau to its own corporate brand. "The Eddie" would provide the model and inspiration for other contemporary big wave contests such as the Men Who Ride Mountains Contest, held for the first time in 1999 at Mavericks in Halfmoon Bay, California (also sponsored by Quicksilver through 2000), the Red Bull Big Wave Challenge at Dungeons in South Africa from 1999, and the Rex Von Huben Memorial Big Wave Challenge in New Zealand at South Island big wave locations such as Block Island and Papatowai from 1999 through 2003.

Paddle-In or Tow-In?

Until the 1990s and the advent of tow-in big wave surfing, the way in which surfers caught a big wave was the same way as catching a small wave: They paddled down the face. The size of the waves that surfers could ride was limited by the steepness of the drop and the speed at which the wave was moving. If the drop of the face was too steep, surfers could get "pitched" by the lip of the wave or free fall down the face (before or after getting to their feet) because of the extreme pitch of the wave face. Wave speed was also a related limiting factor that created special problems for surfboard design: The board had to be both long and buoyant enough to allow the surfer to build up the paddling speed required to catch the wave, but the board also had to have enough rail edge to hold to the face and adequate maneuverability to negotiate the ride.

Tow-in surfing, in which a surfer is towed into the waves on jet skis at much higher than paddling speeds, was pioneered during the early 1990s by Laird Hamilton at Peahi (also known as "Jaws") on the island of Maui, Hawaii. Tow-in surfing made strides in overcoming the limitations of traditional paddle-in big wave surfing by allowing surfers to enter the waves on smaller boards and at much higher speeds, surfing faces up to 18 meters—double the size of the largest surf that can be paddled into. Tow-in surfing has provided access to big wave locations previously considered unrideable because of the speed and steepness of the waves, especially at open ocean locations such as Outside Log Cabins on Oahu, Jaws on Maui, Green Island in New Zealand, and Cortez Bank off the coast of San Diego, California.

Some paddle-in surfers feel that tow-ins have compromised the purity of big wave riding. The rivalry between paddle-in and tow-in big wave surfing was marked by the timing of the first tow-in contest at Jaws—on the same day as "the Eddie" at Waimea Bay on 12 January 2001. Some contestants had planned to enter both events and were forced to choose between the two, much to the chagrin of paddle-in traditionalists and "Eddie" organizer George Downing, who felt that his contest should take priority.

In 1997 *The Billabong Odyssey*, an annual big wave contest, introduced the concept of a non-site-specific contest running from April to March of each year with a cash prize for the biggest wave ridden and documented by still or moving images. For the first time big wave surfers were competing against one another in diverse locations and conditions. The format of the contest has provoked much debate about what constitutes wave size, and because the largest wave award has been won every year by a tow-in surfer except for the inaugural year in 1997, separate "Monster Paddle-In," "Monster Tube," "Best Overall Performance," and "Girls Best Overall Performance" awards have been added to reflect the contemporary diversity of big wave surfing traditions.

Kevin Fisher

See also Surfing

Further Reading

Blake, T., & Lynch, G. (2000). *Surfing 1922–1932.* Los Angeles: T. Adler Books.

Coleman, S. H. (2004). *Eddie would go: The story of Eddie Aikau, Hawaiian hero and pioneer of big wave surfing.* New York: St. Martin's Griffin.

Dixon, P. (2001). *Men who ride mountains: Incredible true tales of legendary surfers.* Guilford, CT: Lyons Press.

Long, J. (1999). *The big drop: Classic big wave surfing.* Nashville, TN: Falcon Press.

Lynch, G., Gault-Williams, M., & Hoopes, W. K. (2001). *Tom Blake: The uncommon journey of a pioneer waterman.* Los Angeles: Croul Family Foundation.

Noll, D., & Grabbard, A. (1992). *Da bull: Life over the edge.* Berkeley, CA: North Atlantic Books.

Van Dyke, F. (1989). *30 years of riding the world's biggest waves.* Kailua, HI: Joseph Grassadonia.

BMX (Bicycle Motocross)

BMX is the term used to describe a variety of bicycle activities, called "disciplines," all of which use specifically designed bicycles with 50-centimeter wheels to either race against other competitors, perform jumps and stunts, or execute tricks on flat terrain. BMX comes from the phrase *bicycle motocross* and was coined from the sport's derivation from motocross racing (with motorcycles). Another term that was used to describe the sport during its early days but that lost out in popularity to BMX was *pedal-cross.*

The original discipline was BMX racing. BMX racing involves competitors racing on dirt tracks that are approximately 300 meters in length and filled with sharp turns on high berms and hills of various sizes over which the competitors jump. Races involving skilled riders are usually 30–40 seconds in duration. Participants use specially designed bikes characterized by their sturdiness, durability, light weight, and, of course, 50-centimeter wheels.

The first bicycles used in BMX racing—before specific BMX bicycles were created—were Sting Rays made by Schwinn. As the sport became more popular and as organized races began appearing regularly, participants (with the help of industrious parents) made modifications to the frame, handlebars, and pedal cranks of the Sting Ray to make it more conducive to racing on dirt tracks. Not until the mid-1970s did manufacturers begin to mass produce bikes designed for BMX racing. The Mongoose was the first mass-produced BMX bicycle. In 2006 the average cost of a quality BMX bicycle was $300. Although this cost might be prohibitive for some, from its start BMX was considered a more affordable alternative to motocross racing.

Although BMX racing was the original discipline, today BMX freestyle generates more attention in the BMX media (i.e., magazines and videos) and in the mainstream media coverage of extreme or action sports. *BMX freestyle* is a blanket term referring to the disciplines of street, park, vert, trail/dirt jumping, and flatland riding. What these disciplines have in common—and what makes them different from BMX racing—is the execution of jumps, stunts, and tricks as opposed to racing.

Street riding is arguably the most creative of the disciplines because riders' skills and riding experience are bound only by their imagination. Street riding is an informal activity organized by the participants themselves. They, without the influence of adults or sporting authorities, make up the "rules." A skilled street rider is able to perceive mundane aspects of urban landscapes such as curbs, stairs, and railings as mechanisms to attempt jumps, stunts, and other trickery that require daring, athleticism, and artistry.

Park riding shares the creativity and a similar skill set but requires less imagination because it takes place in skate parks where tailor-made obstacles and terrains are provided for skateboarders and BMX freestylers to perform jumps, stunts, and other technical skills.

Vert riding most commonly takes place within a large wooden structure called a "half-pipe" or a concrete bowl where riders' skill is evidenced in the height of their jumps (which can be 3–4.5 meters in the air) and the stunt maneuvers (i.e., spins, twists, and technical skills) they can perform on the bike while in the air.

Trail riding and dirt jumping are similar to vert riding in that each centers on the rider getting "big air" by performing spectacular jumps that involve acrobatics performed while in the air. Some of these acrobatics entail the rider letting go of the handlebars, spinning the handlebars (and front wheel), or even detaching most of his or her body from the bike—all before touching back down to the ground. In one of the more spectacular acrobatic moves a rider separates from the bike seat by kicking his legs out behind him so that his entire body is parallel to the ground while maintaining contact with the bike by holding on to only the handlebars. This move is called the "Superman" because the rider at the height of his jump strikes a pose like Superman in flight.

Finally, flatland riders perform technical spins and acrobatics while riding on a flat area usually made of concrete or asphalt. Flatland riders often practice their skills in the parking lots of shopping malls and supermarkets. While attempting these maneuvers, riders try not to touch the ground with their feet as they transition from one maneuver to another.

Throughout the course of a flatland routine, a rider often transfers the weight of her body to various parts of the bike (i.e., a rider's feet may be placed on the pedals, seat, frame, pegs, and even handlebars). Flatland riding also does not involve jumps or more conventional forms of riding as the other disciplines do. Usually flatland riders pedal their bikes only a couple of rotations before they initiate their routines. Instead they often move the bike by using a single foot to rotate a wheel slightly. Flatland routines often look as if the rider were dancing with his bicycle because the routines take place in a relatively small area and the rider executes a series of spins and choreographed maneuvers with his bicycle.

There is much crossover between these disciplines and little specialization by BMX riders. Because BMX is a participant-driven sport, many people who simply love to ride and perform tricks on their bicycles grow up participating in a number of these disciplines.

Jumping on a BMX bike. Source: Istock/Arkadiusz Stachowski.

History

BMX originated in southern California in the summer of 1969 when a group of boys in Palms Park, located near Santa Monica, wanted to race their Sting Rays on dirt tracks like local motocross racers. A couple of films featuring motorcycles were inspirational in the creation and rise of BMX. The film most frequently cited is *On Any Sunday* (1971). Although the film is centered on motocross, it begins with a scene showing California teens riding and jumping their Sting Rays through dirt terrain. Bob Osborn, a BMX pioneer, credits the 1953 film *The Wild One* (starring film icon Marlon Brando), with its glamorizing of motorcycles (and their male riders), as a cultural force that led California

teens to begin to modify their bicycles to make them look more like choppers.

In 1963 the growing popularity of these modified bikes with teens in southern California led Schwinn to send bicycle engineer Al Fritz to their neighborhoods to create a new style of bicycle that would appeal to them. Fritz's trip resulted in the creation of Schwinn's Sting Ray. By 1968 the Sting Ray had 70 percent of bicycle sales in the United States.

By the early 1970s California kids and their parents were making modifications to the Sting Ray to better equip it for BMX racing. This tradition of BMX participants making innovations in bicycles continued in the creation of technologies such as pegs and gyros, which better enable BMX freestyle riders to execute their ballet-like tricks, stunts, and maneuvers. A peg is a sturdy cylinder extending from the joint made between the center of a wheel and the bicycle frame on each side of the bike. Pegs allow riders to put their feet on the joints in the middle of the front and back wheels

Taj's Weight Theory

Taj Mihelich, a BMX competitor, finds that the bicycle needs to be a certain weight for freestyle tricks. The extract below sets out his theory on the weight of bikes.

I've always liked lighter bikes than heavy "freestyle" bikes. My bike currently weighs 28.5 pounds. I think what makes BMX unique is that the bike becomes a counterweight for the rider. On a motocross bike, the rider is like a feather on a rhino; you are totally riding that bike and that is all there is to it. On the opposite side is a skateboard; they are so light (compared to the rider) that you can flip it around and do whatever with it. A BMX bike is in the "pocket" of weight that makes it a counterbalance for the rider while riding. You can throw a BMX bike around, but it also has enough mass to help throw you around. My theory with weight is that you need to find the weight that feels right to you. One pound can make a huge difference.

Source: Set ups—Taj Mihelich. (2005, July 21). Retrieved February 2, 2007 from http://www.bmxonline.com/bmx/features/article/0,15737,1085393,00.html

Scot Breithaupt, at the age of thirteen, created the first organizing body in 1970 when he created BUMS (Bicycle United Motocross Society) in Long Beach, California. Scot organized some of the first BMX races by convincing local youths to ante up a quarter each as an entrance fee to race for one of his motocross trophies. Scot had been a motocross racer himself, so he followed the motocross model for organizing the races. He says the acronym *BUMS* was a tongue-in-cheek joke between him and his fellow BMXers that noted the transient men who congregated around the park where they staged their first races. Thus, BUMS was hardly a serious attempt at creating a lasting organizing body.

The first official organizing body was the NBA (National Bicycle Association), created by Ernie Alexander and Suzanne Claspy on the West Coast in 1973. Alexander and Claspy were early promoters of BMX races, and the NBA is cited as instrumental in making BMX racing more popular nationwide.

On the East Coast, in Pompano Beach, Florida, in 1974 George Esser Sr. established the National Bicycle League (NBL) to organize and administer racing. In 1982 the NBL became the preeminent BMX organizing body when it subsumed the racers and events from the defunct NBA. In 1997 the NBL became a part of U.S.A. Cycling, which is in turn a member of Union Cycliste Internationale (UCI), which is the main organizing body for bicycling in the world. U.S.A. Cycling and UCI have worked together recently to get BMX racing included in the 2008 Olympics in Beijing, China.

Today the American Bicycling Association (ABA) is the key sanctioning body of BMX racing in the United States. The ABA invented the Direct Transfer System, which allows racers who take first in the qualifying rounds to sit out subsequent races until the final event, thus expediting races, was the first to install electronic gates for its starting line to ensure fairer starts, and created the BMX Hall of Fame to recognize the pioneers and stars of the sport and to preserve its history. The ABA is the largest sanctioning body in the world with sixty thousand members and 232 affiliated tracks in the United States, Mexico, and Canada.

rather than just on the pedals. Pegs are essential for flatland riders to perform their moves. A gyro is a mechanism that allows the handlebars to spin 360 degrees without being obstructed by hand brake wires. The gyro is invaluable to vert, dirt, park, and flatland riders.

A couple of those innovating parents became among the first entrepreneurs responsible for creating the BMX bicycle market. This model of the BMX participant as BMX entrepreneur has continued to the present through riders such as Mat Hoffman, Dave Mirra, and TJ Lavin, who have created their own BMX bikes and launched their own brands.

Organizing Bodies

Although the history of BMX, like that of skateboarding, is often written with an emphasis on the informal, participant-driven character of the sport, BMXers, following the model of motocross racing, have ironically always had organizing bodies.

History of Freestyle

BMX freestyle originated as riders attempted tricks (i.e., wheelies, endos [reverse wheelies]) during the downtime between BMX races. However, the history of BMX freestyle also parallels the history of skateboarding: BMXers often rode side by side with skateboarders in urban terrains and empty swimming pools. Freestyle originated in 1974 or 1975 in southern California. Thom Lund's no-handed wheelie, captured on film at a BMX race in 1974, is one of the first documented examples of freestyle.

John Palfryman was the first person to ride freestyle (vert) in an empty swimming pool (called "carving"). Although other youths were surely carving pools during this era, Palfryman is recognized as the first to ride above the coping of the pool and the first to execute what would later be called a "kick turn." Wes Humpton, an early BMX rider and now an oral historian of BMX, also credits Palfryman with being the first rider to "get air" out of the pool (i.e., jump his bike above the lip of the pool), an innovation responsible for the progression of the sport from freestyle trick riding to vert.

In dirt jumping Stu Thomsen was the first rider to perform a 360-degree jump, later called a "helicopter," in 1975. As evidence of how BMX riders regularly cross disciplines, Thomsen, not Palfryman, was the first rider to be filmed getting air while riding in a pool in 1977. Thus, some credit Thomsen as being the person who launched vert riding.

Debate also surrounds the question of who progressed BMX into the flatland discipline. Bob Haro, who later became a key entrepreneur in the design and manufacture of BMX bicycles, is considered by many to have been the first flatland freestyler when he performed the Rock Walk, which was captured on film. Years later Haro's frequent riding partner, John Swanguen, claimed that the Rock Walk was the only trick that he, not Haro, invented.

The first BMX freestyle show—performed by Haro and R. L. Osborn—took place on 9 February 1980, in Chandler, Arizona, at the American Bicycling Association Winternationals.

BMX participants point out that there is no organic connection between BMX freestyle and the "artistic cycling" that has existed since the beginning of cycling. They stress that the key sporting influences on BMX freestyle riding were skateboarding (especially with its emphasis on progression, individuality, and innovation) and BMX racing (from which most BMX freestyle riders came).

Ups and Downs

Since its beginning BMX has had surges and declines in popularity. After the initial wave of interest in BMX racing and freestyle subsided during the late 1970s, BMX enjoyed a short-lived boom during the early to mid-1980s. By the late 1980s BMX had, in the words of BMX freestyle rider and historian Brett Downs, "all but died out."

However, BMX would again experience a surge in popularity in the mid-1990s when it was featured in ESPN's Extreme Games (which later became the X Games). At the initial Extreme Games held in Fort Adams, Rhode Island, in 1995, BMX vert, park, and flatland riders were featured in televised coverage. Since then BMX vert riders, along with vert skateboarders, have become some of the marquee performers in the X Games franchise. Whereas BMX park riders have maintained a lesser presence at the X Games, flatland riders no longer appear in ESPN's coverage of the X Games. More recently BMX dirt jumping, with its death-defying aerial acrobatics, has garnered greater television coverage at the X Games. In an ironic twist of fate, the interest in BMX dirt jumping led to the inclusion of motocross dirt jumping—in which riders are propelled even higher into the air, thereby increasing the risk for riders and excitement for spectators—in the X Games. Thus, BMX appears to have returned the favor for its predecessor by introducing new fans to the sport.

This latest surge in interest in BMX via the popularity of the X Games not only has made millionaires of BMX riders such as Mat Hoffman, Dave Mirra, TJ Lavin, and Ryan Nyquist, but also these riders have become recognizable figures in the youth cultures of the United States, Europe, South America, and Australia. Indeed, the global presence of ESPN networks has facilitated the spread of BMX riding globally since the mid-1990s. Today more than forty countries have national sanctioning bodies for BMX racing and freestyle.

Kyle Kusz

See also Mirra, Dave; Hoffman, Mat; Skateboarding; X-Games

Further Reading

American Bicycle Association. (2005). History of BMX. Retrieved June 23, 2006, from http://www.abamx.com/ index.php?page=home_history

Downs, B. (2003). Small bikes, big men. In R. E. Rinehart & S. Sydnor (Eds.), *To the extreme: Alternative sports, inside and out.* Albany: SUNY Press.

HickokSports.com. (2004). Bicycle stunt riding: History. Retrieved April 20, 2006, from http://www.hickoksports.com/history/bikestuntriding.shtml

Kusz, K. (2003). BMX, extreme sports, and the white male backlash. In R. E. Rinehart & S. Sydnor (Eds.), *To the extreme: Alternative sports, inside and out.* Albany: SUNY Press.

Union Cycliste International. (2000). A short history of BMX. Retrieved April 20, 2006, from http://www.uci.ch/english/bmx/index.html

VintageBMX.com. (2005). The history of freestyle. Retrieved April 20, 2006, from http://www.vintagebmx.com/

Boardsailing

See Windsurfing

Body and Extreme Sport, The

The topic of the body and extreme sport is important for at least three reasons. First, the body is in many ways the source, medium, and outcome for the thrill and pleasure that are derived from participation in extreme sports. Second, the body is often put at considerable risk in extreme sports, and the reasons why people choose to take such risk is far from evident. Third, the body is powerfully socialized and shaped through the sustained acts of participating in extreme sports. Indeed, without an appreciation of the body in extreme sports one cannot understand these activities more generally. In order to develop the idea of the extreme sports body, one must first make sense of what we mean by "the body" in sociocultural terms.

In the humanities and social sciences "the body" is a complicated interaction between biology and society. The social and cultural impact of the socialized human body in modern societies is increasingly being recognized as substantial. This impact, which is often referred to as the "socialization" or "social construction of the body," suggests that we more accurately should state that we live with and through our bodies, rather than in them; in other words we *are* our bodies. Subsequently, our bodies are not merely passive containers controlled by our minds; rather, our bodies are active in their own right, behaving in ways over which we sometimes seem to have little or no conscious mental control. The body then helps to shape the mind as well as the mind shapes the body. Researchers sometimes refer to this integrated view of the simultaneously socially constructed and biological body as the "lived body." Therefore, although the body and mind can be named separately, they cannot be experienced or understood separately from each other. In other words, mind and body are a duality rather than a dualism.

As a result of these developments in thinking, during the past two decades the body has become a central theme for the disciplines of anthropology, psychology, sociology, literary criticism, history, and cultural geography, among others. Research and theory on the body have developed rapidly. However, perhaps ironically, only relatively more recently has the significance of the socialized body in sports and physical culture become fully recognized. Furthermore, within developing areas of the study of physical culture such as extreme sports, the sociocultural understandings of body remain relatively underdeveloped.

Here we will explore the body in extreme sports by drawing on a selection of the most useful perspectives from social theory of the body. Most of the ways of understanding the body in extreme sports can be condensed into three (almost irreducible) dimensions of human activity: that of practical bodies, interacting bodies, and storied bodies (by this we mean that all humans are seen to engage with their bodies in these ways through the act of living; hence, they allow for discrete analytical domains of activity).

Practical Bodies

Social practice (the carrying out of repetitive actions) is fundamental to us all if we wish to take part in any organized society. Participants in extreme sports immerse their bodies in specific practical engagements with the world. This practice leaves an indelible mark on bodies by inscribing them with experience. Perhaps the most refined perspective of the practical body is that developed by the French sociologist Pierre Bourdieu. The perspective relies on a three-way theoretical relationship between fields, habitus, and capital, which combine to provide a "logic of practice," as Bourdieu (1990) refers to it. Rather than thinking and then acting, for Bourdieu, people "feel" with their bodies and then act. This feeling is a social conditioning known as "habitus." Habitus is constantly formed and reformed through everyday practice: "The principle of this construction is the system of structured, structuring dispositions, the habitus, which is constituted in practice and is always oriented toward practical functions" (Bourdieu 1990, p. 52).

According to this viewpoint practical logics normally make complete sense only in relation to that sphere (field) of human activity that produces and gives them value (capital).

For example, the social logic of surfing revolves around surfing practices that over time inscribe or condition the body (habitus) in ways that then have a social (relating to social institutions), cultural (relating to ways of living), economic (relating to material wealth), and symbolic (relating to an association to something else of value) exchange value in what can be described as a cultural economy of groups of people who share an interest in these practices (i.e., surfers and surfing practice). In this way surfing practices produce bodies that have value which makes "real" sense only in practical relation to one another and to surfing culture.

A more specific illustration from surfing culture is worth considering here. To find good surf nearly every surfer must relearn how to "read" the weather by finding ways of checking the surf conditions, whether this is by checking surf forecasts on radio, TV, the Internet, or the Coast Guard or by reading the conditions first-hand. Most surfers must schedule these predicted good surf times around their working lives or be in a position to take holiday to coincide with the best surf. Many "hardcore" surfers pursue employment that gives them the flexibility to leave work at short notice or take extended periods of work where they can travel and surf. Added to this is another series of practical logics in terms of the actual practicing of surfing itself (negotiating crowded surf breaks, making the wave, deciding how far to push one's technical ability on a given wave, adapting to different weather conditions, etc.). These practical logical "embodied" decisions come to shape the various subcultures of surfing around the world. As mentioned, the result of this practical engagement is the creation of a form of surfing-specific habitus.

Extreme Sports Body Habitus

Through sustained practical engagement with the rules, knowledges, and physical practices of their particular sporting field, extreme sports athletes come to inscribe certain qualities into and onto their bodies that begin to define them as surfers, climbers, white water canoeists, and so forth. The physical inscriptions also begin to orientate them toward engaging with the social world in particular ways that fit in with the logics of being a surfer, a climber, a white water canoeist, and so forth. The surfing habitus is composed of a number of core dispositions that take a considerable amount of practice and time to acquire. Gabrielson's *The Complete Surfing Guide for Coaches* includes almost a compendium of practices providing insights into the composition and construction of a surfing habitus. For example, in the section on learning to surf Gabrielson comments:

Learning how to stand up on a board is not an easy thing to do. In addition, simply learning to paddle out through rough breaking waves, sit on a board outside, and then paddle into a wave takes considerable balance, strength, endurance, wave knowledge, and patience. Since these techniques take time and practice to learn, the beginner should not be expected to have success the first time out. (Gabrielson 1995, 4.1)

These qualities would seem to be fundamental to the surfing body. However, as practice inscribes itself upon the body, its possibilities increase. In practicing their way from basic technicians to accomplished surfers, beginners must learn to "feel" their way into extending their surfing technique by being thoughtful and experimental about their surfing style and in particular by seeking the experience of surf practice on different waves. Gabrielson comments:

The final way to improve style is with lots of practice in various conditions. Surf big Hawaiian waves in the winter, point breaks, quick reef breaks, beach breaks, and close beach breaks or shore breaks. Each break type will contribute its own characteristics to your overall style. (Gabrielson 1995, 4.4)

Illustrated here is implicit understanding that the experiential imprint of a particular type of wave inscribes itself onto the body, augments the habitus, and extends the body's ability to feel its way in different surf conditions. Bourdieu points out that "what is 'learned by the body' is not something that one has, like knowledge that can be brandished, but something that one is" (Bourdieu 1990, 73). Therefore, when we say that Laird Hamilton is a big wave surfer, it is more than merely a nickname or label; we are referring to valued cultural experiences that are inscribed into his body; they are who he is; if those experiences were removed from his body he would not be the same person.

Extreme Physical Capital

Just as the practices in different extreme sports vary, so does the type of extreme sporting body that results from them. Some marked points of distinction are manifest and result in different proportions of capital in relation to their field of activity (i.e., the field of surfing or the field of climbing, etc.). These forms of distinction and physical capital also differentiate the extreme sporting body within its own field

A man training in an ashta-vakrasana (hand stand) yoga posture. Source: istock/Andray Plis.

of activity. The varied fields of surfing, for example, produce different bodies with different capital value resulting from using different boards, styles of surfing, techniques of surfing, styles of talk and dress, training methods, diet, and so forth. Therefore, the surfing bodies of Laird Hamilton, Lisa Anderson, and Kelly Slater all possess quite different forms of habitus, but each converts well into physical capital within his or her respective parts of the field of surfing.

Interacting Bodies

The second fundamental observation of the extreme sporting body is that it constantly and significantly interacts with other bodies, selves, objects, and its environment. As such the extreme sports body can also be said to be an "interacting" body in the sense that "human interaction is mediated by the use of symbols, by interpretation, or by ascertaining the meaning of one another's actions" (Blumer 1962, 180). The U.S. interactionist sociologist Erving Goffman used this idea to explain the construction of embodied identity. He distinguished between social (virtual) identity and self (actual) identity. These identities are mutually interdependent because the identity that an extreme sportsperson thinks he or she has (self or actual identity) will normally form the basis of his or her social performance, which will

then be judged by others and as a result their social (or virtual) identity assigned. The feedback that a person receives about how others perceive him or her to be in such situations will have significant effects on self (actual) identity. Any small disjunctures between actual and virtual identities can lead to embarrassment for the person but are normally repairable and do not affect self-identity in the long term.

An example of this idea in surfing is when a surfer has a bad day when the surf is up, for instance, just not catching enough waves or being able to perform maneuvers up to that person's standard. This situation is repairable with a subsequent successful session. However, if social (virtual) identity is judged by others to be generally unsatisfactory, for example, if the same surfer consistently misses waves, drops in, or wipes out on moves, then the surfer can become stigmatized and his or her social identity will undergo a gradual shift (becoming a "spoiled" identity) that can then damage and forcibly alter the self (actual) identity as a "competent surfer."

The Performing Extreme Sports Body

The key point about identity management in extreme sports is not only that it is dynamic but also that it centrally involves the successful management or "performance" of one's body and its movement in, and through, extreme sports spaces, places, and times. This is because the nature of extreme sports makes the body so immediately visible and therefore classifiable by others. Dyck and Archetti conclude, "Just as the self is embodied in performance, so is any performance an embodiment of selves" (Dyck and Archetti 2003, 10). Therefore, these performances provide both opportunities and constraints on bodily actions and signals in given circumstances that give rise for the need of body management of factors, including "bodily appearance and personal acts, dress, bearing, movement, and position, sound level, physical gestures such as waving or saluting, facial decorations and broad emotion expression" (Goffman 1963, 33), to name a few.

Rather like Donnelly and Young's (1988) study of rock climbers and rugby players, most extreme sports bodies require identity confirmation from key others within the particular subculture as part of the construction of a positive subcultural identity. In surfing, for example, it will include demonstrating and having validated such embodied aspects as good balance, timing, a technical repertoire, "guts," a practical sense of surf etiquette, surf technologies, and surf culture.

Extreme Sports Body Idiom

All of these and other performances of bodily management represent aspects of bodily behavior that have a ritualized idiom attached to them. Consequently, extreme sportspeople tend to have an understanding of a shared set of meanings in specific sports that is attached to bodily behavior in their particular domain. "Body idiom" refers to the way in which these meanings are shared by both performer and valued observer of the behavior. Body idiom serves as ritualized, normalized forms of self-expression that can be seen in many extreme sports but are perhaps most obviously developed and differentiated in the surfing subculture, as Kampion illustrates:

> Modern surfing has rich history, a unique system of rituals, distinctive language and symbolic elements, tribal hierarchies, and other unique lifestyle characteristics all of which have been broadly imitated and emulated around the world. Witness the "shaka" hand gesture (extended pinky and thumb), praying for surf, rules of the road at surf spots, hierarchical protocols at all notable beaches, honour-

ing of subcultural elders, related lifestyle clothing industry, and a specialized language that gives esoteric meanings to common terms such as "green room," "stoke," "shack," "A-frame," "rip," "session," and "strapped." (Kampion 2003, 59)

The tension here is that cross-cultural body idioms can differ, and this leads to a problem of communication when it is encountered. In line with this perspective, the globalized subculture of surfing has many embodied interactional variations that need to be accommodated by traveling surfers, as Kampion again testifies:

> At significant surf spots, the structure, rules, and strength of the local hierarchy control activity within the territory. All surfers know this. Every time we venture into new surf spot and test a new territory, we enter into a "force field" of hierarchy. This field might be highly organized or it could be extremely anarchic; either way, you can bet there's an organizing paradigm, and every newcomer has to "get with it." (Kampion 2003, 59)

Personal and Possessional Territories of the Extreme Sports Body

Goffman introduces the idea of "territories of the self" (Goffman 1971, 28–44), which helps illuminate how the relationship between individuals' performing bodies and social space is fundamental to successful social interaction. Although a number of subcategories are contained within this idea, two that are particularly worthy of highlighting are personal space and possessional territory. Personal space is the "space surrounding an individual" (Goffman 1971, 29). Goffman contends that in most social settings our bodily space may not be violated indiscriminately and that culture dictates when, where, and how others might enter this personal space. Surfing provides an illustration of this: The space that is occupied by a surfer in the water is seen as his or her personal space; violating that space (and perhaps even colliding with an individual) is often not only seen as an accident but, more seriously, as an infringement of that person's identity.

Possessional territory is all those objects "that can be identified with the self and arrayed around the body wherever it is" (Goffman 1971, 38). In surfing a good example is the surfboard. During the totally absorbed experience of riding a wave, the surfboard almost seems to disappear, becoming an extension of the body. In a sense the surfer and board become a hybrid machination, and a form of cyborgification could be said to be occurring. When board designers make different boards they effectively evolve the potential for new interactions with the surf environment. An example of this is the development of what Kampion refers to as "surfing's ultimate speciality product—the big wave gun" (Kampion 2003, 51). When these objects were combined with the introduction of jet skis to tow surfers onto giant waves that were previously moving too fast to catch, the combination of these objects facilitated interaction with waves hitherto unsurfable by a single surfer and a standard surfboard. Therefore, as Booth has noted, as surfboards are developed by surfing subcultures, so new cultural practices, interactions, and, as we shall see, stories can be forged from using them.

Finally, perhaps the most fundamental example of personal and possessional territory in surfing is the "liminal" space that fleetingly "belongs" to surfers who have just committed to a breaking wave. Here, the space around the surfing body and specifically the line they are taking on the wave becomes "theirs" for the short period of the ride on that part of the wave. If others drop in on this space, almost invariably some form of interpersonal conflict ensues.

Storied Bodies

A third fundamental observation of the body in extreme sports is that it becomes storied. Cobley reflects the widely held view that "wherever there are humans there appear to be stories" (Cobley 2001, 2). The U.S. sociologist Arthur Frank suggests that the stimulus for storytelling and the stories people tell about themselves are not merely cognitive, intellectual social phenomenon, but rather the outcome of the two-way infolding and outfolding of experience onto and from the body. In other words, the lived body "speaks" to us directly through our socialized sensations. As we have illustrated, these sensations will in a large part have been socialized through prolonged practice and interaction within extreme sport's cultures. We then "story" these socialized sensations.

The storied body perspective has been drawn upon in a growing range of qualitative sociological studies of the body in sports and physical culture. In particular Sparkes and Smith (2002) develop the view that the process of "storying"

takes place within certain social limitations based around the "storying" resources (or narrative resources) that persons are able to construct from their situatedness in time, culture, and society. For example, a novice surfer may lack the appropriate narrative resources to describe the embodied sensations from his or her first experience of surfing, whereas later in his or her surfing career, after a long period of immersion in the subculture, the same surfer will be likely to have accumulated a more wide-ranging vernacular to express the sensations generated by surfing and surfed bodies. As time goes by the identities of extreme sports athletes become substantially constructed and maintained by the stories they are able to tell about their embodied experiences.

However, as indicated, these stories are intimately connected to the subcultural social group of which they are a part (e.g., freestyle climbing, big wave surfing, white water canoeing, BASE [building, antenna, span, Earth] jumping, etc.), because within these groups such body-generated stories become told and over time consolidated through repetition. These stories then take on a different existence as circulated as shared stories or "public" narratives, which initiates into the culture then draw on in order to make sense of their own experiences.

Undoubtedly the storied or "narrative" body represents an important perspective for the analysis of the extreme sports body because of what it can illuminate about the body-self-society relationship of both individuals and groups. That said, it is unlikely that extreme sporting bodies will always make it easy for coherent stories to be told about them. Indeed, there is a growing recognition that "coherence is not an inherent feature of the narratives told, but is artfully crafted in the telling, drawing from the available meanings, structures and linkages that comprise stories in specific cultural contexts" (Smith and Sparkes 2002, 167).

Therefore, the extreme sports body, when storied, is likely to be a changeable representation of self-identity that will reflect the current state of the body in a person's perception of it (in surfing, for example, whether a surfer is young, old, healthy, ill, injured, fit, novitiate, intermediate, experienced, feeling "amped," "stoked," etc.). It will also be influenced by the linguistic resources (language, vernacular, idiom, plots, sequences) that the teller has at his or her disposal. Clearly, some people craft their stories more artfully than others.

We can also situate the storied extreme sports body in a much broader social context. In an increasingly biographically sensitive Western culture, the telling of personal stories has become important and so has the way such stories are told. The more formalized the telling of these stories becomes, the more they evolve into considered acts of representation where the degree of separation between the body and the story increases considerably with each new motive for, and act of, retelling. For example, the story of a "perfect day" in the surf is likely to alter dramatically as it becomes retold by the same surfer in a different time and location and to different people. Such a story is likely to be further transformed when related as reported speech by other surfers. The story might become a written representation on a website blog, a surfer's journal, or a written biography. The experience might become reported by a newspaper or even thematized into a documentary or a movie. Each of these is a representation of the original body sensation-producing experience; each will add a style or genre of its own, and each will alter the original representation of the embodied experience.

Therefore, the perspective of the storied body can inform on the experiences of persons but also on how experience is represented through everyday face-to-face interaction, the media, publishing, and film industries, the Internet, and consumer industries seeking to capture, package, and sell the experience of extreme sports through their products. Ultimately, most of these genres have more to tell us about representations of experience than experience itself.

Extreme Sports Bodies and Their Emotions

Burkitt appears to present a consensus view when he states, "There is no such thing as the 'mind' considered as something separate from the body and its spatio-temporally located practices" (Burkitt 1999, 147). This view of the body-mind complex is sometimes referred to as a "holistic ecological view." Perhaps nowhere in society is such a view more clearly exposed than with extreme sports. Extreme sports bodies are clearly a mixture of the practically inscribed, the interactively adept, and the coherently storied (at least most of the time), with all of these taking place within specific environmentally (and increasingly technologically) contingent circumstances (be it riding waves, jumping out of planes or off buildings, climbing cliff faces, etc.). However, something elemental remains missing, something that binds the physically biological and the socially constructed. One convincing viewpoint forwarded by Elias and Dunning (1986) is that the emotions provide a bridge between not just body and mind but also between biology and society. They comment:

> In advanced industrial societies, leisure activities form an enclave for the socially approved arousal of moderate excitement behaviour in public. One cannot understand the specific character and the specific functions which leisure has in these soci-

Key to Success: Junk Food?

Dean Karnazes ran fifty marathons in fifty days. He does two hundred miles just for fun. The extract below details a secret to his success: eating junk food and lots of it.

You wouldn't believe the stuff Karnazes consumes on a run. He carries a cell phone and regularly orders an extra-large Hawaiian pizza. The delivery car waits for him at an intersection, and when he gets there he grabs the pie. The trick: Roll it up for easy scarfing. He'll chase the pizza with cheesecake, cinnamon buns, chocolate éclairs, and all-natural cookies. The high-fat pig-out fuels Karnazes' long jaunts, which can burn more than 9,000 calories a day. What he needs is massive amounts of energy, and fat contains roughly twice as many calories per gram as carbohydrates. When he's not in the midst of some record-breaking exploit, Karnazes maintains a monkish diet, eating grilled salmon five nights a week. He strictly avoids processed sugars and fried foods. He even tries to steer clear of too much fruit because it contains a lot of sugar. He believes this approach—which nutritionists call a slow-carb diet—has reshaped him, lowering his body fat and building lean muscle. It also makes him look forward to running a race, because he can eat whatever he wants.

Source: Davis, J. (2007. January). The perfect human. *Wired.* Retrieved February 1, 2007, from www.wired.com/wired/archive/15.01/ultraman.html

eties if one is not aware that, in general, the public and even the private level of emotional control has become high by comparison with that of less highly differentiated societies. (Elias and Dunning 1986, 65)

In spite of their foresight on this topic, as Duquin notes, "Emotion is a relatively new area of research in sociology" (Duquin 2000, 477) and even more so in our understanding of embodied physical cultures such as extreme sports. One of the few writers to begin to tackle the issue of the emotions and the body in extreme sports is the French sociologist Le Breton, who comments:

Certain physical or sports activities are developed in the passionate search for emotion, sensation and physical contact with the world and they provide intense moments of pleasure and a sense of fusion with the world. (Le Breton 2000, 8)

While remaining aware of the dimensions of practice, interaction, story, and the linkages provided by the emotions, further research into the body and extreme sports is likely to provide insights into the limits and possibilities of human embodiment. However, in order to achieve this, future research will need to address one of the most difficult and enduring dichotomies in human thought: the mind-body dualism.

Beyond the Mind-Body Dualism

Western scholarship faces particular challenges in articulating the intensely embodied character of extreme sports because of its traditional dualism of the mind-body split. Other entries of this encyclopedia refer, for instance, to the physiology and peak experiences associated with extreme sports, perspectives that privilege the body and mind. This entry has sought to briefly review four perspectives (practical, interacting, storied, and emotional bodies) that afford the possibility of a more integrated grasp of the place of the body in extreme sports.

Other perspectives include the notions of Affect theory (Evers 2006), "sensuous geographies" (Rodaway 1994; Lewis 2001), with their concern with the senses of touch and kinesthetics; the parallels with embodiment in contemporary dance studies (Flynn 1987; Morris 1996: Zarilli

2004); the notion of postmodern aesthetic sensation rather than interpretation (Featherstone 1991; Stranger 1999); and the broad area of what has been termed "nonrepresentational theory" (Thrift 1997). All of these perspectives seek to go beyond the straightjacket of text and representation to explore ways of understanding the simultaneously social and biological nature of embodiment. Collectively these perspectives express avenues for further research into extreme sports.

David H. K. Brown and Nick J. Ford

See also Hamilton, Laird; Meaning of Extreme, The; Surfing

Further Reading

Allen Collinson, J., & Hockey, J. (2001). Runners' tales: Autoethnography, injury and narrative. *Auto/Biography*, 9(1–2), 95–106.

Blumer, H. (1962). Society as symbolic interaction. In A. Rose, (Ed.), *Human behaviour and social process: An interactionist approach*. Boston: Houghton Mifflin

Booth, D. (1999). Surfing: The cultural and technological determinants. *Culture, Sport, Society*, 2(1), 36–55.

Booth, D. (2003). Expression sessions: Surfing, style and prestige. In R. E. Rinehart & S. Sydnor (Eds.), *To the extreme: Alternative sports, inside and out* (pp. 315–336). New York: State University of New York.

Bourdieu, P. (1990). *The logic of practice*. Cambridge, UK: Polity Press.

Bourdieu, P. (1998). *Practical reason: On the theory of action*. Stanford, CA: Stanford University Press.

Burkitt, I. (1999). *Bodies of thought: Embodiment, identity and modernity*. London: Sage.

Butryn, T. (2003). Posthuman podiums: Cyborg narratives of elite track and field athletes. *Sociology of Sport Journal*, 20(1), 17–39.

Cobley, P. (2001). *Narrative*. London: Routledge.

Donnelly, P., & Young, K. (1988). The construction and confirmation of identity in sport subcultures. *Sociology of Sport Journal*, 18, 48–65.

Duquin, M. (2000). Sport and emotions. In J. Coakley & E. Dunning (Eds.), *Handbook of sports studies* (pp. 477–489). London: Sage.

Dyck, N. & Arcehtti, E. P. (Eds.). (2003). *Sport, dnce and embodied identities*. Oxford, Berg.

Elias, N., & Dunning, E. (1986). *The quest for excitement: Sport and leisure in the civilising process*. Oxford, UK: Basil Blackwell.

Evers, C. (2006). How to Surf. In *Journal of sport & social issues*, 30(3), 229–243.

Featherstone, M. (1991). *Consumer culture and postmodernism*. London: Sage.

Frank, A. (1991). For a sociology of the body: An analytical review. In M. Featherstone, B. Hepworth, & B. Turner (Eds.), *The body: Social process and cultural theory* (pp. 36–102). London: Sage.

Frank, A. (1995). *The wounded storyteller*. Chicago: University of Chicago Press.

Flynn, P. J. (1987). Waves of semiosis: Surfing's iconic progression. *American Journal of Semiotics*, 5(3), 397–418.

Ford, N., & Brown. D. H. K. (2006). *Surfing and social theory: Experience, embodiment and narrative of the dream glide*. London: Routledge.

Gabrielson, S. (1995). The complete surfing guide for coaches. Retrieved January 13, 2005, from http://www.surfcoachbook.com

Goffman, E. (1963). Stigma: Notes on the management of spoiled identity. New York: Prentice-Hall.

Goffman, E. (1971). Relations in public: Microstudies of the public order. London: Allen Lane.

Jenkins, B. (1997). Laird Hamilton: 20th century man. The Australian Surfer's Journal, 1(1), 84–121.

Kampion, D. (2003). The way of the surfer: Living it 1935 to tomorrow. New York: Harry N. Abrams.

Le Breton, D. (2000). Playing symbolically with death in extreme sports. Body and Society 6(1), 1–11.

Lewis, N. (2001). The climbing body, nature and the experience of modernity. In P. Macnaghten & J. Urry (Eds.), Bodies of nature (pp. 58–80). London: Sage.

Morris, G. (1996). Moving words: Re-writing dance. London: Routledge.

Rodaway, P. (1994). Sensuous geographies: Body, sense and place. London: Routledge.

Shilling, C. (2003). The body and social theory (2nd ed.). London: Sage.

Shilling, C. (2005). The body in culture, technology and society. London: Sage.

Smith, B., & Sparkes, A. C. (2002). Men, sport, spinal cord injury and the construction of coherence: Narrative practice in action. Qualitative Research, 2(2), 143–171.

Sparkes, A. C. (2004). Bodies, narratives, selves and autobiography: The example of Lance Armstrong. Journal of Sport & Social Issues, 28(4), 397–428.

Sparkes, A. C., & Partington, S. (2003). Narrative practice and its potential contribution to sport psychology: The example of flow. The Sport Psychologist, 17, 292–317.

Sparkes, A. C., & Silvennoinen, M. (1999). Talking bodies: Men's narratives of the body and sport. Jyvaskyla, Finland: University of Jyvaskyla.

Sparkes, A. C., & Smith, B. (2002). Sport, spinal cord injury, embodied masculinities and the dilemmas of narrative identity. Men and Masculinities, 4(3), 258–285.

Stranger, M. (1999). The aesthetics of risk: A study of surfing. International Review for the Sociology of Sport, 34(4), 265–276.

Thrift, N. (1997). The still point: Resistance, expressive embodiment and dance. In S. Pile & M. Keith (Eds.), Geographies of resistance (pp. 124–151). London: Routledge.

Turner, B. S. (1984). The body and society. Oxford, UK: Blackwell.

Zarilli, P. (2004). Toward a phenomenological model of the actor's embodied modes of experience. Theatre Journal, 56, 653–666.

Bonifay, Parks

Parks Bonifay (b. 1981) is one of wakeboarding's greatest freeriders. Born in White Haven, Florida, Bonifay attributes much of his success to his initial development in waterskiing. At the age of six months he was listed in the *Guinness Book of World Records* as the world's youngest water skier. His mother operates the Bonifay Ski School, and both Parks and his younger brother Shane grew up performing at the Cypress Gardens theme park. Parks's early years sparked his love for performing in front of crowds, and he attributes his powerful cutting (edging) skills to his background in slalom waterskiing.

Since becoming a competitor in wakeboarding in 1994, Bonifay has had much success while maintaining the respect of those within the wakeboard community. In addition to being voted "Best Wakeboarder" by *Wakeboard* magazine, Bonifay has won many titles in the last decade, such as the X Games (1996, 1999), Pro Wakeboard Tour Season Champion (1996, 1998, 2001, 2003, 2004), Wakeboard World Champion (2004), Vans Wakeboarding Pro Champion (2004), the Gravity Games (2000, 2003), and Wakeboard National Champion (1997, 2001). He was the first rider to land a ten-eighty on a wakeboard (a jump in which the rider spins 1,080 degrees in the air before his board touches the water). He is known for having an aggressive riding style and for performing larger jumps than his competitors. Tony Smith, editor at large of *Alliance Wakeboard Magazine*, says on EXPN.com: "He's old school power and new school creativity all rolled into one."

Bonifay lives in Orlando, Florida, which is the hub of the wakeboarding community. Brother Shane is also a professional wakeboarder and one of the top ten riders on the professional tour. The Bonifay brothers maintain a close friendship, despite being competitors on the wakeboard circuit. Shane said in an interview with Kidzworld.com, that his relationship with his brother is friendly. "Me and Parks are pretty tight and I don't hold any grudges because he's doing better. The whole tour is a blast. We're all just a bunch of young guys and we always hang out and party together." Shane possesses a more fluid riding style than Parks and attributes his style to his passion for inline skating and skateboarding. The brothers have joined with friends in the wakeboarding industry to develop a film company, Pointless Productions. The company produces extreme wakeboard movies and is based in Orlando.

Parks Bonifay is sponsored by several companies, including Spy, Fox, DVS, Mastercraft, Red Bull, Hyperlite, Pointless, and OG. He has appeared in many wakeboard films and was highlighted in Liquid Force's video *Relentless*. The wakeboarding company Hyperlite produced the first Parks signature board in 2003. The board was designed by Bonifay with technology specifically for aggressive riding. A Parks Bonifay trading card and two action figures also are sold. In his spare time Bonifay enjoys spinning records, surfing, and snowboarding.

Megan Popovic

See also Wakeboarding

Further Reading

Parks Bonifay. (2003). Retrieved January 31, 2007, from http://expn.go.com/athletes/bios/BONIFAY_PARKS.html

Wakeboarding: Boarding brothers. (n.d.) Retrieved January 31, 2007, from http://www.kidzworld.com/site/p1112.htm

Wampler, P. (2001). Parks Bonifay takes the tour. Retrieved November 29, 2006, from http://www.wakeboarder.com/display.phtml?a=56

Bouldering

Bouldering literally means climbing boulders. But what boulders should be climbed? The term *bouldering* encompasses the safest as well as the most extreme and dangerous ways of climbing. One definition states that bouldering is done on relatively small rocks that can be traversed without too much risk of harm if the climber falls. While doing this type of climbing, the climber does not make use of ropes and cannot climb higher than a few meters. In fact, climbing higher than 7 meters is often considered free soloing or free climbing. However, since many climbers still prefer to call free climbing an extreme variant of bouldering, and since it involves many similar techniques, this article will cover both ends of the continuum between absolute safety and extreme risk.

Human Urge to Boulder

Bouldering is one of the fastest growing variants of climbing. Some reasons explaining this popularity are that it can be done safely, there are rocks for every age and level of climbing, it can be simple and cheap, and not much equipment is required. The popularity of climbing can also be viewed from an anthropological and historical perspective. Why have all human beings, of all ages, and at all times found it joyful to climb and to boulder? When mountaineers are asked why they climbs a mountain, they will often reply: "Because it is there." This answer refers to both the "purposelessness" of the activity (that is, there is no reason beyond the climbing itself) and to the human urge to climb, to "conquer" a mountain, a piece of rock, or a glacier just because it is there and "asks" to be climbed.

The human urge to climb starts at a young age with the playful urge to keep the feet off the ground. Babies show a certain instinct to hang on to objects in their environment. Before they fully understand the concept of "falling down," they try to master the ability to climb. Games of not touching the floor give the child some feeling of magic. Climbing ropes and ladders and swinging from one apparatus to another remain some of the more popular kinds of games that are part of physical education.

When adult boulderers are asked to reflect on their passion, they often refer to a special or "pure" experience with nature. Bouldering is called the purest form of climbing or even the "essence of climbing." This description not only refers to the experience in nature itself, but also to the climbing techniques and particularly the unaided grips that are basic to all forms of climbing. To put it in sport psychological terminology: Bouldering ideally results in some kind of *flow experience*, in which the body takes over and knows what to do and where to go.

Although boulderers can be very competitive and are always comparing their achievements with those of others, the activity itself is very much an individual experience; it is usually bouldering alone that is the attraction. As female boulderer Bobbi Bensman describes it: "Climbing with others is great, but you can go bouldering solo—no partner, no gear, just you and the rock, and a pair of boots. I love the purity of the sport" (Bensman 1999, 8).

History and Evolution

Although bouldering became an international sport around the early 1970s, the origin of bouldering itself can be dated much earlier. Climbing boulders continues a long tradition of climbing, in particular gymnastic climbing. Ropes, ladders, masts, and poles have been used in physical education for centuries. Some of the early-nineteenth-century handbooks of the European pioneers of physical education contain illustrations of equipment similar to modern indoor climbing walls. Friedrich Jahn organized climbing competitions within his famous Turnplatze at the beginning of the nineteenth century. Rope climbing was even an athletic event at the Olympics between 1896 and 1932.

Some climbers will argue that the history of "artificial climbing" is unlike that of bouldering, which is all about the direct experience with unspoiled nature. Within the

A man bouldering showing close up of his bare fingers gripping a hold. Source: istock/Matt Theilen.

history and evolution of bouldering, several phases can be distinguished in which the "natural" and "artificial" play different roles.

Bouldering on actual rocks, without the use of special gear, can be considered the first phase. Although initially not necessarily meant as a playful activity, this way of climbing probably is as old as human existence. Phase two, climbing on artificial walls, also has a history going back more than two centuries, but it didn't become really popular worldwide until the late twentieth century.

A third phase within the evolution of bouldering can be distinguished with the modern manufacturer of artificial boulders that are then introduced into public spaces. Realistic looking rocks of different sizes and levels of challenge are now made suitable for bouldering in suburban environments. For experienced boulderers indoor climbing is often considered a good way of practicing.

One can even define a fourth phase, namely climbing on buildings—"buildering"—which has become an extreme sport activity in itself.

Equipment, Ethos, and Technique

The question of what equipment you need to boulder depends on the definition of the activity. Boulderers usually need climbing shoes, chalk, a chalk bag, and a crash pad that functions as a cushion when the climber falls. Some protection can also be provided by a spotter—a person who accompanies and assists the boulderer. Sherman (1997) mentions "the four essentials," including a toothbrush to clean chalk and dirt from holds and a carpet patch to wipe the shoes.

Some purists of the sport not only refrain from taking any safety measures, but also resist using modern shoes or chalk. The use of ropes is a controversial within the bouldering community. According to John Gill, who is one of the main pioneers of bouldering and who began practicing and promoting bouldering in the mid-1950s, a defining characteristic of contemporary bouldering is that ropes are not to be used. Although bouldering has become in some ways very much a "grown-up" sport (including grades of difficulty, measurements of performance, and lists of elite practitioners), there are still several controversial aspects to it. Chipping holds within the rocks is even more controversial than the use of ropes. Doing so can fundamentally change the rock as an existing problem. (Boulder routes are perceived immediately as puzzles or "problems" to be solved.)

Another controversial "trick" is the use of "cheater stones," placed on the ground to allow a climber to reach the first hold of a problem. Although climbing is often described as an individual experience, climbers can be fanatical about what they consider as the cheating of other climbers. The ban of "cheater stones" is however no fixed rule, and if it was, it would in the first place favor taller climbers. Many climbers agree with Bensman (1999), who states that being taller (and therefore being better able to reach the first hold) has not much to do with being a more talented climber.

It is evident that free climbing involves taking more risks, or, as one climber puts it, being "prepared to risk dying." The risks the climber experiences when climbing big rocks without ropes give the achievement a more outstanding and spectacular character. The knowledge that making a mistake can result in death requires an outstanding and well-suited psychological state of mind.

Climbing technique itself, however, does not so much depend on the height, but rather on the texture and difficulty of the rocks. Every rock, and every climbing area, has its own character and specific difficulties and challenges. Only the highly experienced climbers can explain what the particularities and differences are when climbing in famous boulder places, like Fontainebleau (France), Yosemite (U.S.), the Buttermilks (U.S.), Stanage (U.K.), Dover Island (Canada), Peak District (U.K.), or Hueco Tanks (U.S.).

It is impossible to discuss all the climbing techniques here, but what follows is a review of at least a few:

Crimping is an essential technique to grab the rock with the fingers bent. It is a technique that requires much strength in both the arms and hands. A few other hand techniques are the pinch grip and the open-handed grip.

The ways in which the hands, fingers, legs, or feet are able to carry the weight of the climber can vary and will of course depend on available holds and grips. Eventually, the coordination of the whole body is crucial. One technique in which the whole body is directly involved is called a dyno, one of the most spectacular, free aerial moves. A dyno is a specific technique that enables the climber to get to a hold that is beyond his or her reach. Using the power of the legs, the climber "jumps" to the next hold. With the so-called double dyno it is even possible that both arms and legs come off the wall at the same time.

Since leg muscles are usually stronger than the muscles of the arms, it is important to have the legs do most of the heavy work. Some footwork techniques are smearing (putting the rubber of the foot sole against the rock to create friction), edging (putting the edge of the boot onto a rock ledge), or heel-hooking (raising your foot over your head, and using it as a claw). Again, the experienced climber will know many more of the technical nuances that are required to solve specific problems. Some of the more demanding techniques will also require specific, and sometimes lengthy, hand training. Given the enormous amount of weight that boulderers carry with only a few fingers or a single hand, it is not hard to explain why the most common lesions are on the arms and hands, in particular on the flexor pulley system of the fingers. Climbers with much dedication to climbing and, surprisingly enough, those with the most ability, are most at risk.

Levels and Qualities of Climbing

There are several grading systems that are used to indicate the difficulty of a climb. The most widely known systems are the V-grade system (ranging from V0 to V16) created by John Sherman, and the Fontainebleau system, ranging from 1 to 8+. There is always a human element in these systems of grading, so they are dynamic, and there can be variance in the grading of a specific climb.

The inexperienced climber might think that bouldering has much to do with strength and will climb accordingly, that means in a relatively static way, searching at each position with one arm or one leg for the next hold. This technique will do for an easy climb, but the harder climbs require complex coordination, anticipation, flexible strategies, and thinking. The elite boulderer becomes more or less one with the boulder, while solving the problem presented by the climb.

An elite climber needs the right balance of strength, agility, and flexibility, combined with certain mental abilities that enable the climber to stay cool under extreme circumstances (in particular when free soloing). Good climbers are characterized by well-developed muscular endurance and great strength (especially of the high upper body) related to body mass. Although many good climbers are often small and have low body mass, research indicates that the variance in climbing performance can largely be explained by trainable variables. That means that an elite climber must not necessarily possess specific anthropometric characteristics in order to excel.

Not all requirements for becoming a good boulderer are the results of training. Watching and listening to the climbers themselves are good ways to get acquainted with some of the special and complex talents that are needed to climb the difficult rocks. The documentary *Stone Monkey*, for example, gives a nice portrait of British top climber Johnny Dawes. When talking about climbing the Indian Face (one of the most dangerous climbs in Great Britain), Dawes emphasizes the intense memory of the climb. "I can still feel the movements, the rocks are still under my hand." According to Dawes, "You don't get it by thinking, you get it by being instinctive." Dawes compares climbing with dancing. When you dance you enjoy the music, with rock climbing you enjoy the rocks and the wind. Dawes, and other top climbers, may indeed be considered "Nureyevs of the rock." In some respect climbing a rock is like performing. Boulderers are composers and performers at the same time.

Ivo van Hilvoorde

See also Bouldering: North America; Buildering

Further Reading

Ament, P. (1998). *John Gill: Master of rock.* Mechanicsburg, PA: Stackpole Books.

Ament, P. (2002). *Wizards of rock: A history of free climbing in America.* Berkeley, CA: Wilderness Press.

Bensman, B. (1999). *Bouldering with Bobbi Bensman.* Mechanicsburg, PA: Stackpole Books.

Dawes, J. (Director). (2006). *Stone monkey. Portrait of a rock climber* (film). Alan Hughes Productions Ltd.

Horan, B. (2000). *Best of boulder bouldering.* Helena, MT: Falcon Guide.

Hörst, E. J. (2002). *Training for climbing. The definitive guide to improving your climbing performance.* Guilford, CT: Globe Pequot Press.

Jensen, M. (1984). *Bouldering, buildering and climbing in the San Francisco Bay region.* Yuma, CA: M&M Publishing.

Mermier, C. M., Janot, J. M., Parker, D. L., & Swan, J. G. (2000). Physiological and anthropometric determinants of sport climbing performance. *British Journal of Sports Medicine, 34*(5), 359–365.

Montchausse, J., Montchausse, F., & Godoffe, J. (2001). *Fontainebleau climbs: The finest bouldering and circuits.* London: Baton Wicks.

Owen, C. (2004). *Urban rock: Stoney Point bouldering & top roping.* Winnipeg, Canada: Hignell Book Printing.

Sheel, A. W. (2004). Physiology of sport rock climbing. *British Journal of Sports Medicine, 38* (3), 355–359.

Sherman, J. (1994). *Stone crusade. A historical guide to bouldering in America.* Golden, CO: American Alpine Club.

Sherman, J. (1997). *How to rock climb series: Better bouldering.* Conifer, CO: Chockstone Press.

Sherman, J., Head, M., Crump, J., & Head, D. (1991). *Hueco Tanks: A climbers and boulderers guide.* Evergreen, CO: Chockstone Press.

Sottile, J. (1994). *Jackson Hole: A sport climbing and bouldering guide.* Pingora Press

Watts, P. B. (2004). Physiology of difficult rock climbing. *European Journal of Applied Physiology, 91* (4), 361–372.

Wright, D. M., Royle, T. J., & Marshall, T. (2001). Indoor rock climbing: Who gets injured? *British Journal of Sports Medicine, 35*(3), 181–185.

Bouldering: North America

Bouldering, like other forms of climbing, can be defined as an extreme form of sport. Bouldering is a type of rock climbing in which the athlete performs short, powerful, gymnastic-type movements on rocks or cliff bands 7–8 meters high (Donelly 2003), and it has become increasingly popular in the United States, with climbers scaling the granite rock outcroppings in the Northeast, to the sandstone arches and boulders in the Southwest. While bouldering was once used as a means to gain strength for other types of climbing, it is now a unique and distinctive form of the sport with its own subculture. Unless performed in a competitive setting, bouldering requires no rulebook, no formal venue, and no judge or official. This lack of formality earns bouldering its definition as "extreme."

The sport of bouldering is often described in relation to other types of rock climbing such as sport climbing, traditional climbing, and mountaineering. These four forms of the same activity (i.e., rock climbing), however, are much different in terms of technique, subculture, and safety. While sport climbing, traditional climbing, and mountaineering often require the use of ropes and other safety measures such as carabineers, pitons, caming devices, bolts, hangers, belay devices, harnesses, and quick draws, the sport of bouldering involves none of these items. Bouldering is a sport in which no fixed safety gear is necessary except for a crash pad (a large mattress-like pad that cushions a fall) and the use of

Splash Out

Where to climb when you're away from the hills? There are many urban solutions, but in Alabama, the popularity of "water bouldering" is taking off.

Since not every climber has the money or time to fly to Mallorca we all learn to cope with our local provisions. In New York City people climb in Central Park, in Los Angeles they climb on plastic in the sewers, and during Alabama's sweltering off-season we go shallow water bouldering in Little River Canyon.

As with all summertime bouldering in the Deep South, water bouldering does not lend itself to particularly difficult climbing. When pulling onto rock from the water there are a few added challenges: no chalk, no climbing shoes, and the looming wet sloper on the horizon. Because of these factors, it is easier for a water boulderer to desire movement on a classic line rather than a big number.

When the boulderer, someone intrinsically preoccupied with the summit, has just as much fun falling as he or she does climbing, then the true spirit behind the sport will blossom. It is the same spirit we seek everyday we go climbing on hard ground, a spirit much easier to find in the shallow waters of Little River Canyon. A spirit of happy faces, content fingers, and a refreshingly new recreation.

Source: Payne, L., Splash out. Retrieved 2 February 2007 from http://www.modump.com/articles.php?subaction=showfull&id=1101856594&archive=&start_from=&ucat=3&

a "spotter" (a fellow boulderer who uses his or her hands to break the fall of a climber).

John Gill and the History of North American Bouldering

The period between 1950 and 1970 is commonly referred to as the Golden Age of North American bouldering. At this time rock climbers began to seek out new forms of training for other methods of climbing. Specifically, it was rock climber John Gill's passion for this new technique of climbing that triggered the development of bouldering in the 1950s. Gill was a gymnast who suggested that gymnastics training, specifically his work on the still rings, inspired his interest in bouldering. In a 1992 interview with *Flash Training Magazine* (that was later published as an article on the website TrainingForClimbing.com), Gill commented that he was "introduced to gymnastics and began working the apparatus for the sake of learning artistic gymnastic moves—which appealed to both my aesthetic nature and the hidden athlete in me—and also as conditioning for rock climbing" (Horst n.d., 1).

Intrigued by the unique power and balance required in this new activity, Gill began to seek out new boulder "problems," that is, specific routes across boulders, that would test his strength and that of others. In the 1950s and 1960s, Gill and renowned climbing partners Yvon Chouinard and Rich Goldstone began bouldering in the northwestern part of the United States, specifically setting up boulder problems in Grand Teton National Park in Wyoming (Sherman 1999). Throughout his bouldering career Gill continued to set and complete groundbreaking boulder problems in areas such as the Needles in South Dakota, Yosemite National Park in California, and Estes Park in Colorado. At this time, however, bouldering was still viewed as peripheral to rock climbing. Bouldering was unique and interesting, but few considered it a legitimate form of rock climbing. In the 1970s bouldering gradually became more accepted within the rock-climbing subculture, especially in northwestern area of the United States (Sherman, 1999).

Difficulty Ratings in the Sport of Bouldering

In the 1970s the sport of bouldering started to shift from an obscure hobby for a few climbers, to a genuine sport. John Gill and a handful of other climbers had established problems on different boulders across the United States. New climbers began to seek out the boulder problems attempted by Gill and to repeat his routes. What they found was that bouldering was much more difficult than it was originally given credit as being. Each boulder problem had been assigned a grade that distinguished its level of difficulty. Gill, a college mathematics professor at Southern Colorado State College (now Colorado State University at Pueblo), devised a simple rating system that determined the difficulty of the boulder problems attempted by him and his colleagues. This rating system consisted of three general difficulty levels: B1 (easiest level of difficulty), B2 (medium level difficulty), B3 (hardest level of difficulty). According to Gill, this rating of difficulty was used in order to challenge other climbers to attempt boulder problems and, in essence, improve their climbing ability. However, this system proved vague and, therefore, faulty in the eyes of many, especially those who sought competitive ends in the climbing world. According to Gill: "My idea was to promote this new sport by challenging climbers to improve their technical skills to the point they were capable of 'bouldering level' difficulty, but discourage the degeneration of bouldering itself into a numbers-chase. Unfortunately, my system was a bit too abstract and went against the grain of normal competitive structures, where a simple open progression of numbers or letters signifies progress (Gill 2006, 2).

Currently, the most popular rating system used among North American boulderers is called the V-grade system, which was conceived by innovative boulderer John Sherman. This rating system ranges from V0 (least difficult) to V16 (most difficult). Much like many climbing grades, bouldering grades are often subjective—until several people have attempted the problem and a general consensus concerning its difficulty appears to emerge. Unlike Gill's original bouldering grades, which depicted boulder "problems" as easy, medium, and/or hard, the V-grade system provides a more specific description of the difficulty level. However, it should be noted that grades of boulder problems are always subjective. In the words of John Sherman, one must "view ratings merely as a rough indication of but one component of a problem's overall make-up" (Sherman 1999, xxxvii).

The Bouldering Subculture

The subculture of bouldering lends itself to the sport's classification as "extreme." Like many other extreme sports, the bouldering subculture can be considered "fringe" in many ways. The current demographic of boulderers welcomes and promotes a hedonistic group of young athletes. These athletes have often been introduced to rock climbing in indoor gyms and commonly participate in bouldering competitions. In many cases this emphasis on standard competitive ends sets boulderers apart from traditional climbers and mountaineers, forms of climbing that have no competitive venues (although, competition is highly prevalent in both of these sports). Interestingly, athletes such as John Gill originally coveted bouldering for its connection to the elements of na-

ture and for its physical aesthetics and mental skillfulness. Ironically, current bouldering is prized more for accessibility, physical difficulty, and competitive reward. It should be noted, however, that not all boulderers compete and many still enjoy bouldering for the simple pleasure of testing one's skill in a natural setting.

Bouldering versus Traditional Climbing, Sport Climbing, and Mountaineering

While the lack of technical safety gear may appear to put the climber in physical peril, this is often not the case. Bouldering, as stated earlier, is performed on short rocks or cliff bands and involves dynamic, powerful movements that require a combination of muscular power, balance, and

A woman bouldering on the Peabody boulders in Bishop, CA. Source: istock/Erik Harrison.

flexibility. Sport climbers, traditional climbers, and mountaineers often perform their sports 50 meters or more off the ground, making safety equipment essential. Boulderers do not need this same type of equipment for protection and very rarely do boulderers sustain severe injuries as a result of participating in the sport. While bouldering differs from other forms of climbing in the ways already described, many consider bouldering a distilled form of rock climbing because many of the hardest physical aspects of the sport (e.g., muscular strength and power, balance, and flexibility) are involved in problems.

The Future of Bouldering

In recent years bouldering areas have been developed in almost every state in the United States. The United States, of course, is not the only place where bouldering is popular. New and challenging boulder problems are being established all over the world. Many of the hardest boulder problems have been established in countries such as France, Spain, England, and the Czech Republic. Boulderers such as Frederick Nicole (France) and Bernd Zangerl (Austria) are legendary in the sport for establishing some of the most difficult boulder problems. In the United States young boulderers/rock climbers such as Chris Sharma and David Graham have pushed the envelope in this sport and established and repeated some of the most challenging contemporary boulder problems. This form of rock climbing that was once used as a training regimen is now one of the most popular forms of rock climbing.

Bouldering as a competitive pursuit is also becoming more and more popular. In recent years the United States has experienced an upsurge in bouldering competitions. In North America organizations such as the American Bouldering Series (ABS) and the Junior Competition Climbing Association (JCCA) provide competitive bouldering and climbing contests. Nevertheless, bouldering is still a sport that can be experienced in the lap of nature and as a noncompetitive, individual pursuit.

Karen M. Appleby

See also Bouldering

Further Reading

Ament, P., & Gill, J. (1998). *John Gill: Master of rock.* Mechanicsburg, PA: Stackpole Books.

Donelly, P. (2003). The great divide: Sport climbing versus adventure climbing. In R. Rinehart & S. Sydnor (Eds.), *To the extreme: Alterna-*

tive sports inside and out (pp. 291–304). Albany: State University of New York Press.

Gill, J. (2006). Reactions and ratings. Retrieved May 27, 2006, from www.johngill.net

Horst, E. (n.d.). John Gill—The father of training for climbing. Retrieved May 27, 2006, from http://www.trainingforclimbing.com/html2/johngill-interview.shtml

Sherman, J. (1999). *Stone crusade: A historical guide to bouldering in America.* Golden, CO: American Alpine Club.

Buildering

Buildering, also known as "urban climbing," is the activity of climbing human-made structures designed for purposes other than climbing. For some people buildering means nothing more than bouldering on buildings. However, climbing on buildings is usually illegal (trespassing). Nonetheless, much that can be said about bouldering also can be said about buildering. Builderers and boulderers use similar equipment (climbing shoes, chalk, crash pads), and buildering can be executed either with safety or with high risk. Both activities involve climbing with technical expertise, mastering the environment, having outstanding body strength and body control, and playing with gravity or, in some cases, playing with life and death. Reaching a top (of either a skyscraper or a mountain) can be (but is not necessarily) of importance for builderers and boulderers.

Builderers and boulderers have similar philosophies with respect to freedom, individuality, and nonconformism. The "family resemblances" of both activities are also evident in their ethics. In his book on bouldering and buildering, Jensen (1984) includes a section on ethics in which he urges participants to take responsibility for their actions. He also warns against the use of chalk and the destruction of property, which might throw a negative light on the climbing community. Changing the rock or the building is discouraged because of the damage it causes and because it is contrary to the ethics of climbing.

Buildering concentrates on making playful and athletic use of the environment, not changing the environment for athletic, competitive, or other purposes. Builderers embrace the city as a "natural environment." Climbing on human-made structures involves reconceptualizing the urban environment as a sporting space. The city becomes a playground, a gymnastic arena in which the architecture does not speak in aesthetic or functional terms but rather in terms of climbing *affordances*. The climber reads the incongruities of the building in terms of climbability, opportunities, and techniques. The building "tells" the climber where and how to climb. Dedicated builderers talk about the city as an "urban jungle."

However, important differences between bouldering and buildering exist. Buildering is not just an illegal variant of bouldering. Buildering has its own history and stories of outstanding performances. In terms of media attention and achievements, buildering can easily compete with all other ways of climbing.

History of Roof Climbing

A person whose pastime is climbing the outside of buildings is also called a "stegophilist." Translated from Greek, this term literally means someone who is infatuated with roofs. In fact, the early pioneers of buildering called themselves "roof climbers." Although there are obvious similarities with climbers of rock, climbers of buildings are often more affiliated with other adventurous activities in cities such as urban exploration and *parkour* (a discipline in which participants attempt to pass obstacles using skills such as jumping and climbing). These modern activities toy with the borders between extreme sports and crime, between traditional gymnastics and fearless risk, between rebellion and extreme self-control.

A strong link exists between the origin of buildering and the city of Cambridge, England. In 1899 Geoffrey Winthrop Young (1876–1958), an English writer and mountaineer, published *The Roof Climber's Guide to Trinity*, in which he described all the possible climbing routes on the roofs of Cambridge. He also wrote *Wall and Roof Climbing* (1905), which included an appendix on haystack climbing.

Under the pseudonym "Whipplesnaith," Howard Noel Symington and others wrote *The Night Climbers of Cambridge*, which was first published in 1937 (and reprinted in 1952 and 1953). This book has become a collector's item, not in the least because it serves as a great guidebook to the ancient buildings in Cambridge. It contains some photographs of nocturnal climbing as well as diagrams; one, for example, explains an escape from the roof of the department store Marks & Spencer.

The following passage explains both the attraction of buildering and the reason for the relative absence (at that time) of literature on the subject.

> It may lop off many a would-be climber who cannot risk being sent down, and keep many an adventurous spirit from the roof-tops, drain-pipes and chimneys, but this official disapproval is the sap which gives roof-climbing its sweetness. Without it, it would tend to deteriorate into a set of gymnastic exercises. Modesty drives the roof climber to operate by night; the proctorial frown makes him an outlaw. And outlaws keep no histories. (Whipplesnaith 1937)

The book stresses important differences between roof climbing and mountaineering. Most of the roof climbers did not belong to a mountaineering club, and most of the regular mountaineers were not roof climbers, facts which the authors commented upon:

"Underground" Buildering

The sport of buildering—climbing of man-made structures—often takes place under the radar, with underground buildering groups keeping track of the best times and places to climb. With the proliferation of the Internet, these tips circulate faster, and easier, but not without increasing the risk of exposure. It is illegal to climb most private and public structures, so buildering tends to take place under the cover of darkness. Here is how one website—www.urbanclimbing.dk—describes climbing a building in the Danish city of Aarhus: "The financial centre is an excellent urban spot, with good possibilities for long traverse routes. The sizes of the holds vary between small and medium, which makes climbing relatively difficult and challenging. The best time to climb is after closing time and in weekends— then the suits will have left the building."

Source: Where to climb. Retrieved February 5, 2007, from http://www.urbanclimbing.dk/main.html

**A man practicing climbing
on a rock-wall building.
Source: istock.**

Until they have tried themselves on buildings, they assume roof-climbing to be as straightforward as a rope in a gymnasium, a travesty in all ways of the true sport. On the other hand, the greatest roof-climber we know has never climbed a mountain. The two sports are quite distinct, appealing to the same instincts without helping or interfering with each other. (Whipplesnaith 1937)

It is interesting, notwithstanding the differences between mountaineering ("the true sport") and buildering ("a travesty"), that the ethos of both ways of climbing is similar and as old as the game itself. *The Night Climbers of Cambridge* warned against leaving boot scratches and damaging stonework, "which is not consistent with the night climber's ideal of leaving no trace where he has been. The use of the rope in climbing is a controversial matter. A rope is not necessary, but is an asset. It should be regarded as an additional safeguard" (Whipplesnaith 1937).

The community of modern builderers recognizes its predecessors of urban climbing. On the other hand, much has changed since roof climbing of the early twentieth century. Some of the important changes involve the international organization of the climbing community (mainly via the Internet) and the increase of competitiveness and the athleticism and abilities of elite builderers.

Extreme Performances

The early roof climbers did not consider their night climbing activities a competitive sport. The following quote suggests that the pioneer builderers had quite moderate ambitions.

Mountaineers have always some bigger mountain they hope to climb, some steeper rock face they hope to assault. However, in Cambridge, with the exception of several dangerous or difficult buildings that few climbers attempt, there is no graded list of climbs, no classification of climbs according to their degree of severity . . . A moderate degree of fitness is advisable. A man who can pull on a horizontal bar until his chin is level with his hands should be able to manage the severest climbs (Whipplesnaith 1937).

Today builderers no longer perform in small groups or in anonymity. The Internet enables builderers to communicate with each other and exchange accomplishments, pictures, movies, and stories. Meanwhile, buildering also has classifications and competitions. Buildering nowadays involves the climbing of extremely high, difficult, and dangerous buildings for which a moderate degree of fitness does not suffice anymore.

On January 2006 a group of climbers from Germany, Turkey, and the Netherlands met for the first world buildering championships in Cologne, Germany. However, Luk described the "informal atmosphere" as "charming" and devoid of professionalism. This characterization suggests that buildering remains a subcultural activity. Indeed, buildering is one of the few "sports" in which a world championship is not required to determine who is the best athlete.

The French urban climber Alain Robert (b. 1962) more or less sets the standards for elite performance and defines the upper limits of buildering. Without using ropes or other safety devices, Robert has climbed more than seventy skyscrapers and monuments all over the world. The documentary *Alain Robert Is Spiderman* has appeared at many festivals around the world. Robert writes on his website, "Spiderman is my nickname, but I have no supernatural powers. When I climb skyscrapers, there's no special effect. No safety net!" (www.alainrobert.com).

Robert has had two severe accidents. He was in a coma for five days after a fall of 15 meters. After this fall doctors considered him 60 percent disabled. Asked what motivates his climbing, Robert said, "Calculated risk. Mastering my fear" (www.alainrobert.com). As the night climbers of Cambridge already knew: "The fear of heights is the easiest of all fears to cure, though one of the most troublesome while it exists" (Whipplesnaith 1937).

No doubt climbers such as Robert have outstanding capabilities, but should he be considered an athlete like others? Is buildering a "true sport" or a "travesty"? After Robert has climbed a skyscraper, there is usually no prize, no ceremony. Some elite climbers do have sponsors and get paid for their climbing, but often they are arrested for trespass.

Whether builderers are adrenaline addicts, gathering in an illegal underground scene, or whether their climbing should indeed be considered sport is open to debate. However, one thing is certain: Urban authorities will continue to frown on the activity. However, for many urban climbers official disapproval is merely the bonus that separates buildering from other climbing activities. This means that buildering will probably remain an underground activity instead of a sport.

Ivo van Hilvoorde

See also Bouldering; Climbing; Meaning of Extreme, The

Further Reading

Alain Robert: Spiderman. (2006). Retrieved January 31, 2007, from http://www.alainrobert.com

Borden, I. (2001). *Skating, space and the city: Architecture and the body.* Oxford: Berg Publishers.

Jensen, M. (1984). *Bouldering, buildering, and climbing in the San Francisco Bay region.* Danville, VA: M&M Publishing.

Luk, F. (2006). *The new (a)social climbers. How a young wave of builderers are reinterpreting the structures that surrounds us.* Retrieved August 10, 2006, from http://www.ubyssey.bc.ca

Whipplesnaith (Noel Howard Syminton). (1937). *The night climbers of Cambridge.* London: Chatto and Windus.

Young, G. W. (1899). *The roof climbers guide to Trinity.* Cambridge, UK: W.P. Spalding.

Young, G. W. (1905). *Wall and roof climbing.* Spottiswode, UK: Eton College.

Bungee Jumping

People have always exhibited an interest in aerial activity and the engagement of the body with gravity. People have engaged in high diving, parachuting, trapeze artistry, ballooning, mountaineering, and high-wire walking. Bungee jumping builds on this legacy. Bungee jumping is leaping from a high point with an elastic cord fastened to one's body or a body harness, the cord stretching and contracting with the jumper's weight, eventually ceasing to stretch and contract to allow the jumper to be freed from the cord. The jumper may be freed after reaching the lowest extremity of the cord (e.g., just above water) or after being raised to the launching point at the conclusion of the jump (e.g., from a building or canyon rim).

The sport's name is linked to the word *bungee*, which is an elasticized cord used especially as a fastening or shock-absorbing device.

Bungee jumping has its roots in vine jumping of the Pacific Ocean. Pentecost (Pentecôte) Island, named by the French explorer de Bougainville on the day of the Pentecost in 1768, is one of eighty-three islands of Vanuatu. The Pentecost Island village of Bunlap has a legacy of local myth and rites of courage. A local legend tells of a woman who dived from a banyan tree, with concealed vines tied to her legs, to escape unwelcome attentions of her pursuing husband, who leaped after her with no such restraining vines. Her escape and his death are commemorated annually, with men jumping from 30-meter-high towers. The jumps are associated with male puberty and are believed by the villagers to enhance the fertility of yam planting through a jumper's hands or hair touching the ground at the base of his leap. Such vine jumping, known as the "N'gol," "Nagol," or "Gkol" land-diving ritual, possibly dates from the 1500s and takes place from April to May.

The Pentecost Island rites were brought to the notice of European audiences through the photography of Charles Lagus, who visited Bunlap with the naturalist David Attenborough in the late 1950s. The Attenborough production was seen by members of the Oxford-based Dangerous Sports Club (DSC), a group of thrill-seeking amateurs led by David Kirke, who sought new and unconventional physical challenges.

On 1 April 1977, the DSC imitated the Pentecost vine divers by leaping from the 73-meter-high Clifton Suspension Bridge in Bristol, England. Employing nylon-braided, rubber shock cords, they leaped simultaneously, resplendent in formal dress. The club has undertaken eighty projects in forty countries with varying levels of compliance with local laws.

In the tradition of Sir Edmund Hillary, conqueror of Mount Everest in 1953, and Sandy Barwick, the first woman to complete a thousand-mile run in 1988, the development of bungee jumping is associated with another New Zealander, A. J. Hackett. Hackett, independent of the Dangerous Sports Club, had developed an interest in bungee jumping. His single-minded pursuit of this led to a range of commercial ventures.

Nowhere to Go but Down

Hackett and Henry Van Asch, a fellow New Zealand speed skier, had met at Wanaka in southern New Zealand. They were taken by the adrenaline charge of bungee jumping. They jumped 91 meters at Tignes, France, from a ski gondola. Hackett followed that jump with his epic leap from the Eiffel Tower in 1987. This jump drew global attention to the sport.

After a bungee-jumping experiment at Ohakune, North Island, New Zealand, in early 1988 by Hackett and Chris Allum of New Zealand, the former's interest was stimulated by the thrills and entrepreneurial possibilities of commercial bungee jumping. Hackett became a force in the spread of bungee jumping in New Zealand and beyond.

Acceptance of the sport was facilitated by recognition of bodies setting commercial and sport safety standards. In New Zealand the Bungee Code of Practice was published in

1989, and the New Zealand/Australia Bungee Jump Standard has become an industry marker. Other countries have followed suit. For example, England established the British Elastic Rope Sports Association Code of Practice.

In the United States brothers Peter and John Kockelman of California set up the pioneering Bungee Adventures commercial venture. John Kockelman leaped from the Golden Gate Bridge as a publicity stunt, then bungee jumped at Wards Ferry and sandbag jumped in the Sierra Foothills in northern California. In sandbag jumping the jumper carries a sandbag or other weight or another person during the descent and releases the weight at the bottom of the fall. This sudden weight loss causes the sudden upward propulsion of the jumper. If it is done without detailed planning, the jumper can hit the launching point on the upward thrust. After the 1980s the Kockelmans were innovative jumpers from hot air balloons and cranes.

The sport has spread internationally. For example, a 1993 road show in the United Kingdom brought attention to bungee jumping; the U.K. Bungee Club is a major operator in Europe; in 1993 the Auckland Harbor Bridge, New Zealand, added a purpose-built pod and new form of retrieval developed by Van Asch, Hackett's fellow adventurer; in 1994 sites were set up in the United States at Las Vegas and Kissimmee Bay, Florida.

The cinema world boosted the sport in 1995 with the seventeenth James Bond film, *Goldeneye*, starring Pierce Brosnan. Bond jumped from a 220-meter-high dam in Angelsk, Russia (in reality, Verzasca, Switzerland), dropping for almost seven seconds. Today bungee jumping from a platform in the middle of this dam is a commercial enterprise, with opportunities ranging from taking classic falls (swan and backward) of 220 meters to falling from a helicopter.

The legacy of A. J. Hackett is still seen in his native country. For example, in 1995 the Ledge jump site opened in Queenstown. The Ledge provides night bungee jumping with a free fall of 400 meters. Located at the top of the Queenstown gondola, the site offers striking vistas over Queenstown. The Ledge urban sky swing opened in 2000, also offering a panoramic view over Queenstown. In 1999 the Nevis High Wire, 134 meters high, was constructed with a purpose-built bungee gondola to give jumpers the experience of free fall for 8.5 seconds over the Nevis Valley. In 2004 the upgrade of the Kawarau Bridge Bungee Center was a major financial investment in the extreme sport's future. This experience offers falls forward, backward, in tandem, in spin, or in a somersault. The falls allow

---

"Bungy Zone Madness"

In the extracts below, writer Goody Niosi offers the advice she was given for her first bungee jump.

"First there's the ultimate swing," Cox-Jansen explains. "You sit on the platform on the bridge; the exciting part is when the platform gives way from under you and you swing through the canyon at about 140 kph; you keep swinging—it's a wild swing—and then you slowly stop swinging and get lowered into a boat. In the flying fox, you're harnessed in, you sit on the edge of the bridge and it's a wire—you're actually traveling along a wire at about 100 kph. Rap jumping is rappelling off the side of the bridge—down 140 feet."

Cox-Jansen asks which of the rides I'm trying. "What's the safest one?" I ask.

"They're all safe." I'm assured. "We had a safety inspector come up from the States," says Cox-Jansen. "He inspects every new ride in North America and he said it's the best ride he's ever done—and he's done them all."

Cox-Jansen recommends the ultimate swing. "It's the best one," Cox-Jansen says. "You're going to be terrified anyway—whether you do bungy jumping or the swing—so you may as well get the best ride."

Source: Goody, N. (n.d.). Bungee zone madness: Retrieved February 5, 2007, from http://www.vancouverisland.com/guestwriters/niosi_goody/bungyzonemadness.htm

---

a jumper to bob above water, touch the water, or be submerged momentarily. A pipeline bungee was set up by two past employees of the A. J. Hackett Bungee Company. The pipeline bungee platform is 102 meters above the Shotover River, with bungee jumper speeds reaching 150 kilometers per hour.

Stretching Out

In the late 1990s bungee jumping expanded to more international sites, such as Bali, Germany, and Acapulco. In northern Queensland, Australia, a jungle swing was set up in 2000. In 2005 the Go Fast Games in Colorado featured

A man rebounds back after being dunked in the river during his bungee jump in New Zealand. Source: istock/Ron Sumners.

bungee jumping from the world's highest suspension bridge, the 320-meter-high Royal Gorge Bridge.

Bungee jumping may be broadly classified in three categories. The first is that of standard or regular bungee vertical jumping with retrieval of the jumper to the point of departure or lowering of the jumper to the nearest point below the jumper's descent. The jumper may jump facing the platform or facing away from it. Second, the catapult, reverse bungee jump, and bungee rocket offer a propulsion experience, as does the twin tower thrill, which is a more specialized form of the catapult in which the cord is tied between two pillars. The third or "other" category includes such innovations as the g-max and the bungee run. Troy Griffin of New Zealand is credited with inventing the g-max, a reverse bungee jump in which a three-seater pod is thrust upward at up to six G forces. In the bungee run the runner runs from a base, fastened to an elastic cord, until the tension draws the runner back.

Far from the vine-clad trees of Vanuatu, bungee jumping is now practiced from buildings, cranes, natural landscape features, towers, airborne bases such as helicopters or hot air balloons, bridges, cable cars, and gondolas. New Zealand bungee-jumping operations tend to use unbraided

cords in which latex strands are not enclosed in sheaths. Users regard these cords as offering more elasticity and a greater fluidity of fall. Cords used by many operators in other countries customarily enclose latex strands in a strong sheath. Participants usually have the elastic cord tied to their lower legs or to a body harness. In the former arrangement the cord is usually tied over specially made ankle covers, which are tightened with straps. If a body harness is used, the cord is usually fastened to it on the chest.

The observance of safety considerations by reputable bungee-jumping operators has meant relatively few serious injuries or fatalities. After three deaths in France in 1987, the French government temporarily banned bungee jumping. An analysis of literature and limited research indicates that human error is the major factor in mishaps. Correct jumping position, proper fitting of the harness, skilled use of a static line, thorough preparation and testing, detailed planning of the site, and the employment of experienced operators are all important in ensuring safe jumping. Compliance with safety and bungee jumping codes is another factor to be looked for by prospective jumpers.

Limitations are usually placed on bungee jumpers. The weight range of jumpers is usually between 35 and 235 kilograms. Ten to twelve years is typically the minimum age, and an upper limit is often governed by the jumper's medical condition. Health conditions considered by reputable operators as being inappropriate for jumpers may include high blood pressure, pregnancy, bone disorders, or epilepsy or fainting disorders. Reputable operators may require medical certificates from older jumpers. Bungee jumpers may experience dizziness, headache, numbness in their limbs or pain in their neck or back, or blurred vision in their plunge. These symptoms should pass quickly.

The Pentecost Islanders, the Dangerous Sports Club, and commercial entrepreneurs such as A. J. Hackett helped establish a sport that attracts thrill seekers and adventure tourists across the globe today.

Robin C. McConnell

See also Vine Jumping

Further Reading

Harris, M. (1992, December). The ups and downs of bungee jumping. *British Medical Journal, 305,* 1520

Hite, P. R., Green, K.A., Levy, D.I., Jackimczyk, K. (1993, June). Injuries resulting from bungee-cord jumping. *Annals of Emergency Medicine, 22*(6), 1060–1063.

Kuryzman, J. (2005). Sports tourism categories. *Journal of Sport and Tourism, 10*(1), 15–20.

Martin, T., & Martin, J. (1994) The physics of bungee jumping. *Physics Education, 29*(4), 247–248.

Soden, G. (2005). *Defying gravity.* New York: Norton.

Young, C. C. (2002). Extreme sports injuries and medical coverage. *Current Sports Medicine Reports, 1,* 306–311.

Young, C. C., Raasch, W. G., & Boynton, M. D. (1988, May). After the fall: Symptoms in bungy jumping. *The Physician and Sportsmedicine, 26*(5).

Carmichael, Ricky

Ricky Carmichael (b. 1979), nicknamed "R.C." or "G.O.A.T." (Greatest of All Times), was born in Clearwater, Florida, and began racing motorcycles at the age of five. In twelve years as an amateur motocross racer he won sixty-seven championships.

Carmichael turned pro in 1996 and won every race in the 125-cubic centimeter Supercross Series and won the American Motorcyclist Association (AMA) Motocross Rookie of the Year Award. In 2000 he collected $100,000 for winning first place in game developer THQ's U.S. Open and won nine of twelve races in the 250-cubic centimeter AMA Motocross Series, breaking the twenty-two-year-old single-season record for most 250-cubic centimeter motocross wins in a season. Subsequently he took the crown from "King of Supercross" Jeremy McGrath in 2001 for the supercross and outdoor motocross titles.

In 2001 Carmichael moved from Team Kawasaki to Team Honda, where he was reputedly paid $2 million. In 2002 he was the first person to ride a perfect season in the 250-cubic centimeter national championship. Because of a knee injury he did not participate in the 2004 THQ AMA Supercross. In 2005 he moved to Team Makita Suzuki Racing and won the World Supercross GP Championship, the AMA Supercross Championship, the AMA Motocross Championship, and the U.S. Open of Supercross and led Team U.S.A. to victory at the Motocross des Nations and was thus named AMA Rider of the Year. By 2006 Carmichael had won four supercross titles and nine motocross championships. He is both a mentor and a role model to the other 2006 Team Makita Suzuki Racing riders, Broc Hepler and Ivan Tedesco.

In an interview Carmichael stated that "I think I'll always have a great reputation for winning a lot of races and championships, but unfortunately the nature of the sport is that you're only as good as your last race" (AMA Pro Racing 2005, 6). When asked how he stays motivated to race, he stated, "I set goals every year and I have little things that keep me motivated. When the year's up I try to find things that I need to improve on. I try to make myself a better rider and become more physically fit" (AMA Pro Racing 2005, 7).

In 2002 Carmichael married Ursula Holly. When asked when he and his wife might start a family, he said they want to wait until he had finished racing. "We want to raise our kids at home and not on the road. I love what I do and have a passion for it and want to be able to give 110 percent. I don't think it would be fair to my sponsors, myself or the kid . . . I love kids, but the timing isn't right and we're still young too" (AMA Pro Racing 2005, 8). When his contract with Suzuki expires in 2007, he will be twenty-eight years old and does not plan on being a full-time racer after reaching thirty years of age.

Carmichael says he would love to race NASCAR and after retiring from full-time racing would still compete in select races. He stated that "I'd like to do some GPs (Grand Prix), Daytona and a few supercross or motocross races. Being around the fans is a great feeling. I'll probably end up . . . doing some of the things that I sacrificed to get to where I am today" (AMA Pro Racing 2005, 8).

Jan Lewis

See also Motocross

Further Reading

AMA Pro Racing. (2001). *Career highlights*. Retrieved April 18, 2006, from http://www.amaproracing.com/archive/00sxms/RIDERS/RIDERBIO/RCARMIC.HTM

AMA Pro Racing. (2005). *Interview: Ricky Carmichael*. Retrieved June 28, 2006, from http://www.amamotocross.com/article.php?aid=5487&UID=Mb8H4scK6NG4KJIdM5fRIeUSGSNqOd.

AMA Pro Racing. (2006). *Career highlights 2001*. Retrieved June 28, 2006, from http://www.amaproracing.com/archive/00sxmx/RIDERS/RIDERBIO/RCARMIC.HTM

EXPN.com. (2006). *Chat wrap: Ricky Carmichael 2003*. Retrieved June 28, 2006, from http://expn.go.com/mtx/s/wrap_carmichael.html

Faught, K., & Bonnello, J. (2006). *Ricky Carmichael: Winning ways of a motocross champion*. Osceola, WI: Motorbooks Intl.

Makita. (2006). *Ricky Carmichael no. 4*. Retrieved June 28, 2006, from http://www.makita.com/racing_callthefinish/bio_photo.htm

Martin, M. (2004). *Ricky Carmichael: Motocross champion*. Mankato, MN: Edge Books.

Motocross.com. (2006). *Monster Energy signs the GOAT!! Ricky Carmichael is thirsty!* Retrieved June 28, 2006, from http://www.motocross.com/s/admin/pageserver/storyserver.asp?a=showpage&id=3372

Team Makita Suzuki. (2006). *Word from the team*. Retrieved June 28, 2006, from http://www.makita.com/racing/makitaSuzuki.htm

THQ Inc. (2006). MX2002 featuring Ricky Carmichael. Retrieved June 28, 2006, from http://www.thq.com/MX2002/CarCorner.html

Cave Diving

Cave diving is a type of technical diving in which specialized SCUBA (self-contained underwater breathing apparatus) equipment is used to enable the exploration of natural or artificial caves which are at least partially filled with water.

Cave Diving

Over the past forty years cave diving has evolved from being a relatively unknown and baffling extension of scuba diving to a highly recognized and respected sport. Although it remains an interest of a very small percentage of those involved in the diving world (estimates are less than 1 percent), participation has increased dramatically. Driven by the technological advances in diving equipment and techniques, cave diving now offers trained divers a fascinating environment to experience and explore. This extreme sport tests divers to the limit in endurance, psychology, ability, and training. It is highly specialized and requires specific equipment, procedures, and techniques for safe participation. Venturing untrained into a water-filled cave can only lead to disaster. Judgment is at the very heart of cave diving as human error is the main cause of accidents.

Extreme Sport

Cave diving has not relished its greatest claim to fame—being the world's most dangerous sport. It gained this repu-

tation in the late 1970s and 1980s when on average one in fifteen dives resulted in death. Cave diving conjures up all kinds of frightening images. This is best illustrated by the countless horror stories that have emerged from failed dives. This account puts this all into perspective: "When their bodies were recovered later, there was every evidence that their pre-death experience was panic-stricken, horrifying, and filled with thoughts of their own stupidity, their families, their dead buddies and their own lost life" (San Marcos Area Recovery Team 2004).

On a more positive note, the thrill, lure, and challenge of being where no one has ever been is enthralling. The beauty and geological features of this environment give an adrenaline rush so powerful that it is an exhilarating experience par excellence.

The knowledge, skills, attitude, and judgment needed to cave dive as safely as possible mean that very few people will actually participate in the sport. It is a challenge literally to the extreme, both to the body and the mind. Cave diving is perceived as one of the most dangerous sports in the world. This perception is debatable because the vast majority

---

Cave Diving Safety Warnings

Cave diving is incredibly risky. Unlike other diving, including free diving and scuba diving, cave diving does not provide the diver an easy escape to the surface. The following are from warning signs that have been placed at the entrances of several underwater caves.

Do You Need to Read This?
Are you planning a CAVE DIVE but you are...

- Neither formally trained nor certified in Cavern or Cave Diving?
- Trained in Cave Diving, but planing a dive beyond your level of training?
- Making one of your initial dives into a spring, cave, or blue hole?
- Not using at least two dependable underwater lights, a guideline on a reel, a submersible pressure gauge, and an additional second stage?

If your answer was "yes" to any of these questions, then you are typical of most cave-diving fatali-

ties. Since 1960, more than 431 divers fitting the above description—that is, untrained, inexperienced, and improperly equipped—have died in cave diving accidents in Florida, Mexico and the Caribbean.

STOP, Prevent Your Death! Go No Farther
- Fact: More than 300 divers, including open water scuba instructors, have died in caves just like this one.
- Fact: You need training to dive. You need cave training and cave equipment to cave dive.
- Fact: Without cave training and cave equipment, divers can die here.
- Fact: It can happen to you!

There's nothing in this cave worth dying for! Do not go beyond this point.

Source: Cave Diving Safety Notices: Cave Diving Section of the National Speleological Society (NSS-CDS). (n.d.). Retrieved December 20, 2006, from http://www.nsscds.org/pamphlt.htm

of divers who have lost their lives in caves have either not undergone specialized training or have had equipment inadequate for the environment. In fact it can be argued that cave diving is statistically much safer than recreational diving due to the necessary restrictions of advanced training, wealth of experience, specialized equipment, and soaring financial resources needed to fund the venture.

History and Background

It is widely accepted that Jacques-Yves Cousteau, (French naval officer and co-inventor of the first scuba equipment in 1943) was the world's first scuba diver and the world's first cave diver. However, there seems to be a disagreement here with early United Kingdom cave-diving history, which asserts that the first dive (in the Mendips Hills, Somerset) was made by Jack Sheppard on 4 October 1936 using a homemade dry suit, surface fed from a modified bicycle pump. In the U.K., the Cave Diving Group (CDG) formed in 1946 (informally existing from 1935) is the oldest surviving continuously exisiting diving club in the world. In America, Sheck Exley led the way by being the first to explore the many Florida underwater cave systems and indeed many other underwater cave systems throughout the world.

World War II provided a lot of surplus diving equipment, and the CDG made rapid progress exploring and mapping caves using this advanced equipment. Basic equipment at that time included a rubber diving suit (for insulation), an oxygen diving cylinder, a soda lime absorbent canister (to remove CO_2) and counterlung (part of a rebreather air system), lights, line-reel, compass, notebook (for the survey), and batteries. Divers used the "bottom-walking" method (perceived to be less dangerous than swimming). Oxygen use put a depth limit on the dive. In the 1960s new techniques using wetsuits (providing both insulation and buoyancy), twin open-circuit scuba air systems, helmet-mounted lights, and free-swimming with fins helped to extend diving time and therefore increase exploration and participation.

Cave-diving Basics

Open-water divers can always make independent, controlled emergency swimming ascents (CESAs). This is because they are usually less than 100 feet (recommended depth limit) from the surface and never more than 130 feet from air.

Any deeper or farther than this would make CESAS difficult. In addition (except for cavern, wreck, and ice diving), open-water divers are never under overhead obstructions that would prevent them from making an immediate direct ascent to the surface (www.cavediving.com).

It is important here to make the distinction between cavern diving and cave diving. In cavern diving exploration of the overhead environments always takes place while remaining within sight of the entrance. Table 1 highlights the key differences.

Cave Diving: Why Do It?

There are a number of motivations put forward for cave diving. Although itemizing them can be difficult, here is a list of the most important ones:

- Underground caves—their geology, clear water, and general environment—are often perceived to be magnificent.
- The conditions of cave diving are also unique. There are no wind or waves, no seasickness. Visibility (although often a problem) in many freshwater caves measures hundreds of meters. This is considerably clearer than any ocean water at even the best dive resorts.
- Excitement, the thrill, adrenalin surge, enthralling, riveting, and gripping are all descriptions that cave divers apply to the cave-diving experience.
- Unique insights are gained and a pioneering spirit often results. No one has been there before. Cave diving provides an opportunity to enter a unique environment and gives a window of how life evolved on earth.
- Cave divers share inquisitiveness for technical problem solving.
- Elite sport? Not everyone can cave dive. Only a small percentage of people have the knowledge, skills, experience, attitude, and judgment necessary.
- You learn self-reliance and practice self-mastery. Powers of judgment are vital. Cave divers need to be confident and calm enough to master even the most basic bodily reactions. A cave diver can achieve a sense of increased authority, bringing an improved ability to cope in the workplace as a result of the experience of mastering such alien environments (Ball n.d.).

 Cave Diving

Table 1 Differences between Cavern Diving and Cave Diving	
Cavern diving	*Cave diving*
Cavern divers generally go no farther than 130 feet from the surface.	Divers often go thousands of yards from entrance.
Cavern divers keep the entrance clearly in sight at all times.	Entrance is not visible, requiring the utmost in self-sufficiency and self reliance.
Divers remain within the controlled emergency swimming ascent zone (CESA).	Divers go beyond the CESA zone, i.e., into overhead environments.
Cavern diving is a form of recreational diving.	Cave diving involves "technical" diving, which requires extensive training, experience, and specialized equipment.
Certifications in cavern diving can be obtained from open-water training agencies such as National Association of Underwater Instructors (NAUI), Professional Association of Diving Instructors (PADI), Scuba Diving International (SDI), and Scuba Schools International (SSI).	Cave diving certifications are available only through cave diving organizations: National Speleological Society Cave Diving Section (NSS-CDS), National Association for Cave Diving (NACD), and technical diving organizations, such as Global Underwater Explorers (GUE), International Association of Nitrox and Technical Divers (IANTD), NAUI, and Technical Diving International (TDI).
Cavern divers use similar equipment as that used in open-water diving—a few modifications are made.	Cave divers use highly specialized equipment to reduce risks to an acceptable level; e.g., gas-delivery systems
Cavern diving is an activity that a large number of experienced recreational divers can learn and enjoy.	Divers must possess near-instructor-quality skills and be committed to diving in a highly disciplined and methodical manner. A very small percentage of divers have the sufficient inherent skills.

Source: Adapted from www.metu.edu.tr/home/wwwsat/madag/yayinlar/cavern&cavediving.doc

Training Requirements

Many accidents resulted (and continue to do so) from the following conditions:

- *Inadequate training:* The vast majority of cave-diving fatalities were untrained in cavern-diving or cave-diving procedures and were making one of their first cave dives.
- *Lack of experience:* Many lacked knowledge of the environment they were entering and were relatively new to cave diving.
- *Improper equipment:* Fatalities occurred when divers used recreational (as opposed to technical) diving equipment.

- *Lack of caution:* An inexperienced and overly inquisitve diver's "quick peak" all too often led to trouble.

Therefore a number of factors need to be considered in order to provide adequate training:

- Recognize and prepare to deal with the hazards unique to cave diving.
- Making a free ascent to the surface is impossible. This seems obvious but the need to fully think through equipment capacity and safety margins is vital.
- Normal open water swimming techniques can easily stir up silt, which can result in low or zero

visibility. Cave divers learn the more controlled, advanced, fin texhniques for swimming in such an environment (as opposed to flapping).

- Understand that the rules for air reserves are completely inadequate in water-filled caves.
- Remember that it will usually take at least as much air to exit the cave as it took to enter.
- Divers must swim back out of the cave the same way they went in—any problems encountered could be disastrous.

Cave diving is technical diving and special training is necessary. Cave diving safely involves many skills and activities that can only be learned in cave-diving training. Here are a few examples:

- *Guideline and reel use:* Its use is very different from open diving and a main cause of difficulty.
- *Specialized buoyancy control:* This is an integral part of the training process. Body position and propulsion techniques: Caves can silt up very quickly and special techniques need to be learned to minimize the disruption caused.
- *Equipment modification:* Special guidelines and mixtures need to be followed. Dive planning: The

breathing, gas-management sequence, depth, duration, distance, and direction all need accurate measurement.

There are few formal prerequisites for cave-diver training, other than Advanced Diver certification. The fact remains that students who successfully complete training typically have the following traits in common:

- *Training and experience:* At least to the Rescue Diver level; Nitrox Diver certification.
- *Ability:* To master specific skills, e.g., body position, helicopter turn, hover motionlessly, and achieve a perfectly horizontal hover.
- *Fitness:* Cave diving is physically demanding and being fit reduces the risk of decompression illness. Diet/body mass knowledge, low body mass index, and regular aerobic exercise are all relevant contributing factors.

The Future

Cave diving has had a checkered history. In the 1970s and 1980s misinformation and untrained divers led to cave diving being openly frowned upon. Discussions also centered

A diver entering an underwater cave. Source: istock/Stephen Giordano.

on whether it should be banned. Today, it is viewed as an acceptable area of sporting interest. The following aspects are important in any future scenario:

- Training organizations have done remarkably well in the education and training for the modern day acceptance of cave diving. This is likely to continue and lead to increased participation.
- There is a growing interest in cave diving as participation in scuba diving grows and horizons continually expand.
- Improvements in equipment (e.g., larger gas cylinders, clothing, and computers) aid longer, more comfortable, and undoubtedly safer diving.
- Technology will continue to improve providing safer diving conditions.
- The sport continues to claim lives every year. In Florida, where cave diving remains controversial, legislation has been considered to outlaw the sport because of the extreme risk involved. Cave diving does not easily forgive mistakes; there is little margin for error. As the National Speleological Society–Cave Diving Section puts it on their website (www.nsscds.com), "Anyone could enter a cave . . . but only the trained cave diver knows how to exit."

Tom Robinson

Further Reading
Ball, A. (n.d.) Cave diving: Your ticket to real. Retrieved January 30, 2007, from http://www.myprimetime.com/play/travel/content/cavedive/index.shtml
Burgess R. F. (1999). *The cave divers*. Essex, UK: Aqua Press.
Cave Diving. (2007). Retrieved January 30, 2007, from http://en.wikipedia.org/wiki/Cave_diving
Cave Diving Group of Great Britain. (2005). Retrieved January 30, 2007, from http://www.cavedivinggroup.org.uk
Cavediving.org. (2006). Retrieved January 30, 2007, from http://cavediving.org
Exley, S. (1986) *Basic cave diving: A blueprint for survival*. Huntsville, AL: National Speleological Society.
Farr, M. (1991). *The darkness beckons*. Trenton, NJ: Cave Books.
National Association for Cave Diving. (n.d.). http://www.safecavediving.com
National Speleological Society–Cave Diving Section. (2007). Retrieved January 30, 2007, from http://www.nsscds.com
North Florida Cave and Technical Diving. (2006). Retrieved January 30, 2007, from http://www.cavediving.com
Prosser, J., & Grey, H. V. (Eds.). *Cave diving manual*. Huntsville, AL: National Speleological Society.
San Marcos Area Recovery Team. (2004). Cave diving. Retrieved January 30, 2007, from http://www.smartdivers.com/cavediving.html

Caving

Cavers, sometimes referred to as "wild cavers," are people who explore, in small groups and in relatively short duration, remote and uncharted caves. Such caves are most often formed in limestone; however, caves can form in gypsum, granite, sandstone, loess, and marble. Ice caves, which form under glaciers, and lava caves, also called "tubes," are significant in some geographical areas. Wild cavers usually complete their trips in eight to ten hours. These cavers may be distinguished from "expeditionary" cavers, whose explorations last for days, weeks, or months, as well as from "tourist" cavers, whose experiences are limited to commercial caves.

Spelunking is the term that noncavers use to refer to the practice of cave exploration, but few cavers use the term. In fact, one popular bumper sticker among cavers in the United States proclaims: "Cavers Rescue Spelunkers." Although important regional and cultural differences exist in how cavers relate to and deal with the noncaving public, caving is practiced in most every location on the globe. This universality is partially evidenced by the fact that the Internet hosts websites devoted to caving in forty-one countries.

Although anthropological records indicate a long history of cave dwelling and cave exploration, less is known about contemporary cavers. Most cave research can be categorized in three ways: geological studies of cave formation, mapping techniques, or conservation; nonanalytical historical accounts of cave discoveries and cave commercialization; and autobiographies or biographies of cave discoverers. Surveys conducted by caving organizations, however, suggest that people from a wide range of economic and educational levels participate in caving. However, caving does not seem to be very diverse in terms of race or gender. Most wild cavers are white males, even though caving does not require the types of skills and assets that traditionally favor males: Physical power is rarely needed, and being large in stature can actually be a detriment in a cave. The skill requirements vary from cave to cave, but in general cavers must possess muscular endurance and physical flexibility. In addition, cavers must have an unflinching ability to function in small spaces and be able to maneuver across or around deep dropoffs and to withstand a dark and often cold environment for hours.

Low Tech

When compared with many other extreme sports, caving is practically antitechnological in nature. The most important recent technological innovation in caving was the replacement of carbide lamps with battery-operated headlights and flashlights. Some "old-timers" still cave with carbide lamps, although because of the damage that carbide waste can inflict on the cave environment, most cavers frown on their use. Caving equipment generally consists of a helmet with a mounted light, (at least) two other independent sources of light, heavy clothing, boots, and a pack to carry water and high-energy food. Single-rope technique gear is required for vertical caving, and if one is available, a cave map is utilized. Without a map, cavers rely on a compass and (preferably) years of caving experience to avoid becoming lost in the dark underworld.

Cavers are among the most environmentally conscious of all outdoor enthusiasts, often sanctioning or exiling members who violate caving conservation ethics or whose "gung-ho" caving techniques place other cavers at risk for injury. Despite noncavers' perceptions that cavers are risk-taking loners, wild caving is rarely (and unadvisedly) a solo practice. Because of the physical risks in this environment, caving requires complete commitment to individual safety and to the well-being of all members on a caving trip. If a person is injured while caving, she or he becomes a liability to everyone else on the trip, who must then either assume responsibility for getting the person out or attempt to bring outsiders into the cave. Because of its complexity, cave rescue can involve up to one hundred personnel. Such rescues often reaffirm stereotypical assumptions that cavers are reckless thrill seekers.

Misperceptions exist not only about people who engage in caving, but also about the underground world that cavers explore. The term *caving* conjures images of people maneuvering through dark holes in the ground, digging, squeezing, and crawling through cold and muddy spaces. Although tight passages exist, there is much more to the environment. The caves of the Appalachian region of the United States, for example, can contain vertical pitches, waterfalls, lakes, rivers, domes, arches, and sand dunes, none of which looks quite like its counterparts on the surface. The longest known cave system in the world is found in this region: Mammoth Cave, in Kentucky, has 585 kilometers of explored passageways, long enough to stretch from New York City nearly to the District of Columbia. There are domed rooms in some caves large enough to fly a light aircraft through, and a freefall pit in one cave in Georgia is deep enough to accommodate the Washington Monument. Caves in the eastern United States and in the United Kingdom tend to be "wet" caves, with humidity approaching 100 percent. Caves in the Yorkshire area of England can flood dangerously quickly if there is heavy rainfall on the surface. However, caves in the southwestern United States, Mexico, and South America tend to be dry. In all parts of the world, the temperature inside a cave generally reflects the mean annual temperature on the surface.

Caving is arduous, both psychologically and physically. Exploring underground environments can be dangerous, and nearly every caving organization in the world has a section devoted to issues of safety. Some organizations even publish summaries of accident and death reports and provide them to organization members. Although some accidents are a result of the stresses placed on cavers and caving equipment, others are clearly a result of participants' inexperience with managing the esoteric caving environment. Even veteran rock climbers have been fatally injured while exploring caves. Unlike rock climbing or mountain climbing, caving cannot always be planned in advance. Many times cavers do not have maps of the places they explore and do not know what obstacles will arise until they are faced with them. Furthermore, because most caves have only one entrance, every obstacle must be managed twice—going in and coming out. However, it is not risk taking itself that bonds members of the wild caving subculture. Rather, it is the experience of being in places that have remained isolated and relatively untouched for centuries from which cavers derive pleasure. It is the knowledge, shared among cavers, that they are set apart from those who would not risk venturing into the deep, dark, secret world underground. And it's the dream of discovering some unknown place that creates caving's lure and its lore.

Caving is one of the few extreme sports that is unobservable to the nonparticipant. One does not need, for example, to actually climb rocks, surf, or in-line skate to watch others engage in these activities and to participate—albeit vicariously. One cannot, in contrast, watch somebody engaged in wild caving: There are no bleachers in caves for spectators, and even the most sophisticated video equipment cannot come close to capturing the essence of a caving experience. Furthermore, cavers in the United States are characteristically among the most tight-lipped of all outdoor enthusiasts and are recognized even among the international caving community as being secretive.

Low Profile

Secrecy was first advocated in the 1950s by members of a caving club in Stanford who argued it was in the best interests of caves to limit the number of people who explored them. Today the National Speleological Society, whose membership numbers more than twelve thousand, still maintains a low profile because of concerns over wild cave conservation. There are thousands of wild caves in the United States, most of which are located on privately owned land. Missouri, for example, has 3,000, and Virginia has 2,500 caves. Although caves are found in every state, cave grottoes (caving clubs) rarely share information regarding cave locations, entrances, or surveys. One grotto in Ohio has published a

Floyd Collins

1888–1925 (death estimated)

Floyd Collins (1888–1925) was a professional cave hunter who died in February 1925 after being trapped for sixteen days in Sand Cave—now called "Floyd Collins Crystal Caverns"—in Cave City, Kentucky. Attempts to free Collins led to one of the first media events of the twentieth century, capturing front page headlines in the *New York Times* from 2–17 February 1925, and attracting some 10,000 visitors per day to the rescue site. William Burke "Skeets" Miller, reporter from the *Louisville Courier-Journal* who covered and became a key actor in the rescue efforts, was awarded the Pulitzer Prize for journalism for his daily dispatches from Sand Cave.

Collins lived in what cavers in the United States refer to as "cave country"—the area that encompasses the Flint-Mammoth Cave System. Mammoth Cave, now recognized as the longest cave in the world, is located in this system. However, in 1925, explorers had not realized the fact that many seemingly independent caves were connected to Mammoth's passages. During this time, there were a number of cave hunters in the region whose dream it was to discover and commercialize a cave, thus providing for themselves or the landowners a source of income. The competition between caves for tourist dollars led to "cave wars" and many cave hunters used any means necessary in their attempts to widen cave entrances. Collins had already discovered one large commercial cave and was exploring Sand Cave, located about two miles from Mammoth Cave, for its revenue-earning potential. To save time, he used dynamite to enlarge the cave's opening. Local legend has it that one weekend he told his stepmother that he dreamed of being trapped in Sand Cave and that he was rescued by angels.

On 30 January 1925, while on his way out of a small passage in Sand Cave, a 27-pound rock dislodged from the roof and pinned his left foot, rendering him unable to move and trapping him about 100 feet from the entrance and 50–60 feet from the surface. He was found the next day by a local boy who was unable to reach him and who returned to the outside prompting the rescue attempt. Collins was lodged in a form-fitting passage; he lay at a 40-degree upward slope, with a cold stream passing over him. William Burke "Skeets" Miller, a slightly-built man who stood five feet, five inches tall, was able to reach Collins but could not free him. Even though cracks began appearing in the cave wall, indicating a collapse in the passage, Miller made seven trips to Collins' placement. After the fifth day, a new cave-in did occur and rescuers could no long provide Collins with food. Rather than dying from hypothermia, starvation, or shock Collins survived for two weeks while the media event unfolded above him. On 16 February, eighteen days after he was trapped, rescuers reached Collins by digging a new shaft, only to find the caver had died some two days prior.

The story of Collins' entrapment and death has risen to mythic significance among contemporary cavers in the Appalachian Region of the United States. Decades after this tragedy, Collins' saga has inspired an award-winning musical, a film, and a number of Internet sites.

Kimberly S. Schimmel

Further Reading

Murray, R. & Brucker, R. (1979). *Trapped: The story of the struggle to rescue Floyd Collins from a Kentucky cave.* New York: G. P. Putnam & Sons.

A man crawling through mud, 450 feet underground, on a caving weekend in Northern California. Source: istock/Joshua Lurie-Terrell.

newsletter since 1945 and occupies a position of high status in the U.S. caving community; however, few people outside of the caving community even know of its existence. In the United States an old caving adage holds that "no publicity is good publicity." One of the consequences of secrecy policies is that cave explorers' feats are rarely recognized beyond word-of-mouth communication between members of the caving subculture.

In a practice referred to as "recycling," some cave explorers keep cave discoveries completely secret, thus allowing others to experience the thrill of discovery at a later date. The ethic of cave conservation and commitment to the values of wild caving is often deemed to be more important than individual accomplishment.

In contrast, caving practices in other parts of the world are not nearly so low profile. For example, the caving culture in the United Kingdom and most of mainland Europe is quite open, and cave locations are well publicized. Though cave discoveries are usually kept secret until they have been surveyed, maps often get published in one of the many caving guides. Then entry to caves usually requires nothing more than the landowner's permission and a good-will fee of fifty pence to a pound. In addition, caving is promoted

as recreational activity, and clubs are found on most college campuses, which offer instruction in caving techniques and sponsor caving trips. The most popular sites for caving in the United Kingdom are the vertical caves of the Dales and the extensive horizontal caving systems of South Wales, although challenging caves can also be found in Derbyshire and Mendip. The British Cave Research Association and the National Caving Association provide information on local caving clubs in England and Scotland. The Speleological Union of Ireland is the main caving organization for both the Republic and Northern Ireland.

Kimberly S. Schimmel

See also Gender

Further Reading

Alderson, L. (1982, April–May). Caving: The passions and the pitfalls. *National Wildlife*.

Hose, L. D. (1994). Secrecy: An alternative and successful model for cave exploration. *NSS Bulletin, 54*, 17–24.

National Speleological Society. (2007). Retrieved January 30, 2007, from http://www.caves.org

Rea, T. (1992). *Caving basics*. Huntsville, AL: National Speleological Society.

Taylor, M. R. (1996). *Cave passages*. New York: Vintage Books.
Traister, R. J. (1983). *Cave exploring*. Blue Ridge Summit, PA: TAB Books.

Climbing

Although climbing is not an Olympic sport and not likely to become one in the foreseeable future, it enjoys great popularity worldwide. Climbing is definitely more than moving from point A to point B. In particular, climbing in its extreme form is a calculated vertical game that leads to many questions and many surprises. It encompasses sub-disciplines ranging from Alpine climbing to rock climbing to ice climbing. Of these three subdisciplines, the majority of participants rock climb.

The history of Alpine climbing can be traced to the ascent of Mont Blanc (a mountain peak 4,807 meters high on the border of France, Italy, and Switzerland) in 1786 by Michel Gabriel Paccard and Jacques Balmat, but ascribing a date to the origins of rock climbing in its pure form is more difficult. Nonetheless, Gustaf Nedt was one pioneer of rock climbing. In 1885 he climbed the formidable western tower of Towerkop located above the town of Ladysmith in South Africa. This feat was not repeated for another sixty-four years.

Rock climbing offers a variety of possibilities. In its simplest form it entails climbing over boulders or little rocks. However, it also can entail climbing big-wall routes, which demand physical strength, precise technique, and, above all, a positive mental approach.

One of the world's most traditional climbing areas is the Yosemite Valley in California, which features many of the biggest and most beautiful climbing routes. Since the 1960s the valley has played an important role in the culture of climbing. The legendary Camp IV was founded there by society dropouts who delighted in climbing routes by day and having metaphysical discussions by night. According to the North American Grading System, Class I requires 1–2 hours, Class II half a day, Class III most of a day, and Class IV a very long day. The University of Berkeley, which was a center of the hippie movement in the 1960s, became prominent as a place for educating the children of the climbing culture in Camp IV. The climbers in Yosemite Valley achieved great feats on the rocks or on the walls. By the end of the 1960s Jim Bridwill and Mark Klemens had climbed harder routes called Grade 8. In the mid-1970s Ray Jardine, Ron Kauk, and John Bachar introduced Grade 9. Pictures of their extraordinary climbing performances were watched worldwide and inspired many climbers on other continents. People who had the time and money traveled to the Yosemite Valley to enjoy the community atmosphere and to learn from climbing experts. They took climbing knowledge back to their home countries, where it gave rise to a climbing movement. Although today Camp IV has lost some of its pioneering spirit, Yosemite Valley continues to be a key destination for those seeking challenging climbing. The ascent of the wall called "the Nose" on El Capitan in Yosemite Valley is a valued adventure for experienced climbers. Warren Harding was the first to climb this wall more than fifty years ago. In the 1980s Lynn Hill made her name by climbing it. Between 1986 and 1992 she was one of the top female climbers in the world and won more than thirty international titles.

Rock Climbing

Rock climbing encompasses a wide range of styles, among which free climbing, soloing, and big-wall climbing are the most spectacular. The term *free climbing* often leads to confusion. Free climbing is not climbing without a rope. Free climbers use ropes and protection gear but only for safety reasons. The function of the ropes is to arrest a fall but not to be a direct aid in climbing the mountain or in making height. When a rope is used for direct aid the variety is not known as "free climbing" but rather as "aided climbing." Free climbing had its origins in Saxon Switzerland, Germany, at the beginning of the twentieth century. Beginning in 1910 rigorous climbing rules were established, but climbing aids are forbidden. Germans Oscar Schuster, Rudolf Fehrmann, and Fritz Wiessner were pioneers of free climbing. In the 1930s Wiessner immigrated to the United States and introduced the rules of free climbing to the climbers of the New World. In the 1960s the rules imported by Wiessner were embraced by the climbers of Camp IV. The grading system of free climbing is a complex one and often differs from country to country. In general one can say that the smaller the hand/foot holds, the more difficult the climb and the higher the grade.

Soloing and free soloing are other varieties of rock climbing. The nature of these two varieties are often confused or misunderstood. "Soloing" does not necessarily mean climbing without a rope. "Soloing" refers to athletes climbing without a partner. Because ropes are used for protection, one can call this variety "rope soloing" as well. If one climbs without a partner and a rope, the climbing is called "free soloing." On the one hand, this is the most pure, challenging, and rewarding variety because the climber's ascent is not supported by ropes and other technical equipment. On the other hand, free soloing is the preserve of strong-minded and first-class climbers. Climbing a high rock wall without protection means that even the slightest miscalculation or briefest lapse of concentration could lead to severe injuries or even loss of life. Rope soloing is less risky. Of course, a lot of climbers favor this variety even though it is time consuming because one has to organize the equipment, set up self-delay systems, and remove them.

Because free soloing can be regarded as extreme climbing this term can also be used for big-wall climbing. Tony Lourens gives the following definition of this extreme variety of rock climbing in his book *Complete Climbing Manual* (2005, 124):

> Any steep, unbroken wall of 500m (1640ft) or more that demands lots of artificial (or aid) climbing, and requires two or more days of swinging in the vertical world, can be regarded as a big wall. However, it is rare that a big wall will not involve a few short sections of free climbing. Indeed, some of the benchmark big wall aid climbs of the 1950s and 1960s have not gone entirely free (some climbed in less than a day), but they are still regarded as big wall routes.

By this definition big-wall climbing is a mixture of free and aided climbing demanding experience, physical fitness, and a sense of adventure. Because this extreme variety of climbing often involves climbers staying on the wall for a day or more they must carry a lot of equipment, food, water, and warm clothing. The material is stored in a bag that is lifted after a rope length has been climbed. To facilitate the climbers' overnight stay, sleeping bases known as "portaledges" have been developed. These stable portable ledges can be anchored to steep cliffs with special hooks to provide a place to sleep.

Indoor Climbing

Climbing in the outdoors often requires travel to remote destinations. Such climbing is not only expensive, but also time consuming and often incompatible with the life of climbers. Furthermore, outdoor climbing is dependent upon the weather: Climbers are often forced to abort or even cancel their climb. A solution to the problem of traveling long distances has been the construction of artificial climbing walls, which can often be found in cities. Most of these walls are made of a multiplex board with holes at regular intervals. The holes contain a specially constructed T-nut, which allows modular hand holds to be screwed onto the walls.

The artificial climbing wall was developed in the United Kingdom. In the late 1960s some climbers stuck bits of rock onto a wall. Based on this beginning, the first commercial wall was built in Sheffield, which is close to the Peak District, England's traditional center for climbing. However, artificial outdoor walls offer no protection from wind and bad weather. Indoor walls do and have grown in number over the last two decades as a way to simulate the experience of outdoor climbing. With the exception of big-wall climbing, the most popular climbing varieties, including rope soloing and free soloing, can be performed indoors. Some indoor climbers are first class—even though some of them have never climbed outside the secure walls of the gym. These climbers are often ironically called "princes of plastic."

Indoor artificial climbing halls have given rise to competitive climbing. Artificial walls allow for the design of different routes and a precise route for every competition. Every year hundreds of such competitions take place around the world. In 1988 a world series was organized. The first world championship was hosted in Frankfurt, Germany, in 1991 and is held every second year. The annual World Youth Championships were established in 1992, with the first event held in Basel, Switzerland. The popularity of this event is an indication of the attraction climbing has for the younger generation.

In the World Cup Series, the world championship competitors are assessed by the difficulty of their climb. Each competitor has to climb a route set by officials. To ensure fair play, competitors are not allowed to watch how other competitors climb the route. Only one climber is on the wall; the others must wait in isolated chambers. In the difficult competition challenging routes of 49 to 60 feet in height are climbed. Each competitor is assessed by the maximum height that he/she has reached. The climbers who reached the highest point in any particular round make their way to the next round. In this way it is climbed until the routes become so difficult that only one competitor is left.

Speed competitions are also popular. In these competi-

Bloody Nose and Cold Fingers

This is an excerpt from an interview with Ines Papert, ice bouldering champion. Few athletes can claim to have dominated a sport as convincingly as Ines. Papert is the winner of the Ice Bouldering World Cup in 2001 and 2003, World Difficulty Champion in 2002, 2003 and 2004, and World Bouldering Champion in 2005.

Q: Ines, how did your passion for ice climbing come about?

A: My first ever experience on ice was on Alpamayo in 1998. It was quite hard to climb that steep 60° ice to the top, and I didn't feel strong enough to climb ice. That was the reason why I started: I wanted to try climbing frozen waterfalls, but I have to say that the first times I went were very painful—I ended up with a bloody nose, cold fingers . . . It was so painful I preferred to continue ski mountaineering in the sun.

Perhaps the reason for this unsuccessful start was that my friends took me to routes that were way to[o] hard. Then in 2000 they even took me to Saas Fee, my first ever competition. And I placed second. I then took 8 months off from my job as a physiotherapist and I started again, this time on easier routes and I simply had fun! I was really impressed by Will Gadd and Kim Kiszmazia from Canada when they climbed X-Files in Cogne. In those months I learned a lot about ice and how to climb it, and things progressed from there.

Q: What qualities must an ice climber possess?

A: [A climber] has to be tough and feel at ease in cold temperatures. That's the reason why we have to eat a lot: to gather our energy and to keep warm. Thin sport climbers [. . .] probably find this sport hard. And of course you really have to like the element ice, to feel it inside you. You shouldn't ever fight it, just go with its flow. Ice climbing makes much more fun when you're fast. Of course you only get fast when you climb lots. That's when it really starts to become fun.

Q: What are the most important things in ice climbing (technique, strength, knowledge of the terrain . . .)

A: All of [the] things you've mentioned are important. And the ability to trust the ice itself and remain strong psychologically, to keep your head even in difficult situations.

Source: Interview with Ines Papert, winner in Valle di Daone in 2005. (2005). Retrieved February 1, 2007, from http://www.daoneicemaster.it/page.lasso?l=2&cl=5&lvl1=44&lvl2=607&sez=1

tions the athletes must climb against each other on identical walls with identical routes. Although not part of the World Cup Series these competitions are often spectacular to watch because only the winner in a race of two will advance to the next round. To add to the excitement, the winner of a race hits a buzzer at the top of the route and then leaps off to make a spectacular fall that is arrested after 5–6 meters.

However, indoor climbing halls are not used only for competitive or speed climbing. For example, they are often used for employee team-building sessions or for incentives offered by big companies for their most successful employees. Children also enjoy climbing halls. Young climbers tend to have a lot of energy, and many are quick to embrace climbing. In fact, the climbing hall is becoming a regular venue for children's birthday parties.

The Thrill of the Hill

Perhaps the following quotation in Tony Lourens's *Complete Climbing Manual* (2005) best expresses the appeal of climbing:

> Many a time I have sat on the summit after a difficult climb, ravenous, my nerves worn out, my strength exhausted, but blissfully happy. It is that feeling that drives us climbers ever and again up into the high mountains tracts, remote from all life; which impels us to undertake the most fearful exertions, which drives us far beyond the narrow confines of the world.

Climbing can be a form of escapism from daily life. In particular the consumption of mass communication and the interactive handling of information can lead to an estrangement from reality. Stimulus satiation by modern media can push people into a passive receptivity that leads to a loss of first-hand experiences. Climbing is a way of alleviating that.

The primary motivation of most climbers is the opportunity to explore their personal limits, to gain a sense of their own capabilities. To do this they push themselves to the edge of their physical and mental limits. The ability to assess one's physical and mental limits is the most important precondition for free soloing. The majority of free solo and big-wall climbers are by no means lunatics longing for the ultimate thrill. Of course, they push their mental and physical abilities to the limit, but they are aware that the slightest error can have a disastrous result. Therefore, even the most extreme climbers plan their adventures carefully.

A man climbing on ice on a glacier in Austria. Source: istock/Stefan Hosemann.

They often know the route by heart and plan the ascent meticulously. Before entering the wall free soloists and big-wall climbers know what is ahead of them; they have an intricate understanding of where the most difficult sections are located, how they should attempt to climb them, and what the alternative routes are, just in case they are unable to master the most difficult sections. In other words, the climbers have to visualize the route and the moves necessary to conquer it in the safest way. Climbing at the edge of one's mental and physical limits can lead to the so-called flow experience in which the climber is caught up in the impressions of the moment. Despite taking many precautions, that climber lives on the edge of life. The risk of injury and even death is ever present for the free solo or big-wall climber. However, according to Lourens, fewer solo climbers are killed than climbers in the high mountains of the Himalayas and other extreme areas.

Climbing also offers a way for athletes to express individuality. They can leave their own traces on a wall, find their own route in the ascent of a rock or a wall. They can choose which route is the best for their own physical and mental abilities. They can display their achievement particularly with the first ascent of a rock or a wall. As the first climber of a route, an athlete has the right to name the route and to determine the grading of the route. By this right he or she signals athletic achievement to other climbers and contributes to the history of rock climbing. The German Kurt Albert was a pioneer in establishing the individuality of climbs. He invented red point climbing when in 1975 he began to mark with a red point routes that he had climbed without the direct help of material and ascents on which he used only natural foot and finger holds on the rock.

Rock climbing as an outdoor sport also offers climbers a multitude of possibilities to experience and value nature. Why does nature play such an important role among climbers? It is not simply because nature is the object of the sport itself. Nature is also the partner of the climber, and the climber's will and task are to accept both the purity and strength of nature. Advocates of outdoor climbing often say they feel in the outdoors the therapeutic impact of nature on their lives, which are dominated by the hectic pace of business. In the course of climbing an athlete is exposed to nature in its purest form. One has to deal with weather conditions, which often change several times a day, and the variations of light, which change by the seasons. Rock climbing in the outdoors provides climbers with insights that often arouse a desire to preserve nature.

Nature has much to offer climbers. However, to preserve all that nature offers, climbers must respect it. As the popularity of climbing increases, so, too, does the risk of damaging the environment, and many climbers advocate a coexistence. For example, Railay Beach in Thailand has become an international destination for climbers. Unfortunately, this formerly remote peninsula has suffered increasing environmental problems as a result of its popularity. The Thai people gladly accept the economic benefits of attracting climbers from all over the world. However, to make the playground for climbers more comfortable, every season more bungalows have been built and more trees have been cut down.

The exploitation of nature for tourism and sport, including climbing, has increased the necessity to designate areas as national parks and wilderness reserves. Because many climbing areas are located within these parks, access for climbers is often impossible. Where it is still possible, climbers often have to pay high entrance fees. Although most climbers accept nature as their partner, they are often the victims of restrictions caused by people who feel little obligation to preserve nature.

During the last few decades climbing has become an international movement. Climbers have spread their symbols and their passion to almost every continent, including, for example, the granite walls of California's Yosemite Valley, the mountains of the Himalayas, and the climbing areas in Thailand, France, and Patagonia. The many books on climbing feature illustrated articles, and reports on the sport have contributed much to the development of climbing as a global movement. In fact, many extreme climbers travel around the world looking for new adventures. A positive side effect of the internationality of climbing is that it helps to support transnational understanding. Of course, climbers are visitors when they climb in a foreign country, but the climbing experience provides them with the opportunity to come into contact with people who share their interests. These interests often help to build bridges to help understand the customs and different approaches of climbers from other nations.

Stephan Wassong

Further Reading
Gifford, T. (2005). *The joy of climbing: Terry Gifford's classic climbs.* Caithness, UK: Whittles Publishing.
Long, J. (2004). *How to climb* (4th ed.). Guilford, CT: Falcon.
Lourens, T. (2005). *Complete climbing manual.* London: New Holland.

Coleman, Bessie

From humble beginnings Bessie Coleman (1892–1926) became one of the most influential women in aviation history. One of thirteen children, Coleman was born into a poor family in the Jim Crow South. When her father, part Cherokee and part African American, proposed moving to the "Indian Territory" in Oklahoma in the hopes of a better future, Coleman's mother refused. Along with her sisters, Coleman remained with her mother in their hometown of Waxahachie, Texas. Intellectually bright and inquisitive, Coleman sought to satisfy her desire for a formal education interrupted by the necessity to work for a wage by borrowing books from a traveling library. In 1910 she enrolled at the Colored Agricultural and Normal University (now Langston University) but finished only one semester because she did not have the money to continue.

Driven by a desire to "amount to something" in the world, Coleman left Texas in 1915 to join two of her brothers in Chicago. After completing a course at a beauty school, she became a manicurist in the White Sox Barber Shop, which was owned by the trainer of the Chicago baseball team. Through this job Coleman came to know some of the wealthiest and most influential black leaders in Chicago, one of whom was Robert Abbott, editor and publisher of the *Chicago Defender.*

As Coleman contemplated her future, she was taken with stories of World War I aviation heroes in local newspapers. One of her brothers pointed out that French women flew during the war effort. Intrigued with the challenge of becoming a pilot, Coleman sought to enroll in flying schools in the United States, all of which turned her away. Frustrated by the rejections, Coleman eventually settled on pursuing her dream in France, with Robert Abbott and others serving as benefactors.

Upon arriving in France, Coleman completed a course of study in seven months at the École des Freres Caudron at Le Crotoy, where she learned to fly in a Nieuport Type 82 biplane, an 8-meter plane known to frequently fail in the air. In 1921, after passing a qualifying exam, Coleman was awarded her international pilot's license from the Federation Aeronautique Internationale.

Coleman would be greeted as a celebrity upon her return to the States, but she still faced the prospect of making a living as a flyer at a time when airline transportation had not yet become a part of U.S. life. Left with the alternative of becoming a barnstormer, Coleman created a persona around the strengths she had available—her skill as a pilot, her flair for the theatrical, and her cultivated personal style. Reigning over the skies as "Queen Bessie," Coleman began her career at an air show sponsored by the *Chicago Defender* to honor veterans of the all-black 269th American Expeditionary Force of World War I in September 1922.

With the goal of opening a flying school for African Americans, Coleman traveled the country performing for audiences. However, she would be denied the opportunity to achieve her goal when she died in an air accident while preparing for a performance. Thousands mourned her loss, and others during the passage of almost a century would honor her. Black aviators formed Bessie Coleman Aero Clubs to perpetuate her memory. A road at O'Hare Airport in Chicago bears her name, and the U.S. Postal Service in 1995 issued a stamp commemorating "her singular accomplishment in becoming the world's first African American pilot and, by definition, an American legend."

Ellen J. Staurowsky

See also Gender

Further Reading

Brooks-Pazmany, K. (1991). *United States women in aviation, 1919–1929.* Washington, DC: Smithsonian Institution Press.

Freydberg, E. H. (1994). *Bessie Coleman: The brownskin lady bird.* New York: Garland Publishing.

Hart, P. (1992). *Flying free: America's first black aviators.* Minneapolis, MN: Lerner Publications.

Rich, D. L. (1993). *Queen Bess: Daredevil aviator.* Washington, DC: Smithsonian Institution Press.

Universal legacy. (n.d.) Retrieved October 30, 2006, from http://www. bessiecoleman.com

Commercialization

Extreme sports are a multimillion-dollar industry that attracts significant market and media interest. Such interest brings the accusation that proponents of these sports have "sold out," rendering their once-alternative sports mainstream. These two facts dominate debates about extreme sports in the academic literature as well as the popular culture more broadly. As Humphreys notes, "debates over selling-out pervade—and consume—this new leisure movement" (Humphreys 2003, 417).

Sports have been transformed into a product through which individuals and organizations stand to reap enormous financial rewards from their involvement as athletes, broadcasters, marketers, and the like. Although as far back as 590 BCE Greek athletes were rewarded financially for a victory in the Olympic Games, in no previous era have sports been so irretrievably linked to commerce. As Slack points out, "sport is big business and big businesses are heavily involved in sport" (Slack 1995). Indeed, sports teams are traded on the stock market, players and athletes are hugely marketable commodities and celebrities, and the sponsorship and broadcasting rights of major sports events are a multimillion-dollar (and frequently multinational) business.

The commercialization of extreme sports has a particular character to it. Although sharing many of the properties of the commercialization of mainstream spectator sports more broadly—such as market and media appropriation—global consumer culture nonetheless penetrates and dominates extreme sports in alternatively sympathetic and antagonistic ways. On the one hand, those activities that are subsumed under the rubric of "extreme sports" are highly attractive to those in the business of marketing and advertising because of, in part, the particular discourses of identity and "hero making" that these sports trade in. On the other hand, however, these same commercial forces fuel a counterdebate that extreme sports have "sold out": buckled under an ever-expanding world of consumer capitalism at the expense of the authentic, "alternative" cultural identity that proponents of extreme sports initially embraced in opposition to these mainstream global forces. For others, this argument is somewhat circular. That is, the centrality of specialized equipment and clothing has meant that consumer culture has always been a key part of most extreme sports. Indeed, it is precisely through dress and/or the possession of particular forms of equipment that the authenticity of an extreme sports identity is constructed for some proponents of these sports.

Before elaborating on the particular nature of commercialization in extreme sports, a brief definition and overview of the commercialization of sports more broadly are perhaps needed.

Products and Profits

In general terms commercialization is simply the process of transforming something into a product, service, or activity that may be used for profit. That is, commercialization is es-

A row of ticket sales counters at a large sports stadium, where more and more extreme sports event are now held. Source: istock.

sentially an economic transaction that, increasingly, brings with it media and market interest. In terms of sports, this media and market interest means that many sporting events (the Olympic Games and the World Cup most notably) have become "spectacularized" and "globalized" on a scale without parallel and that consumer goods and ephemera have become central to the entire experience of that sport or event. The supermarket shelves of Australia, for example, in 2006 were stocked with bottles of Coca-Cola that had been repackaged in gold to resemble the winner's trophy in the football World Cup, and clothing, equipment, magazines, and PlayStation games, to name but a few, are among the extensive and ever-expanding array of commodities that are now part of the contemporary sports landscape. To quote the French intellectual Guy Debord: "[sports have become] the spectacle; this is the moment when the commodity has attained the total occupation of social life" (Debord 1972, 42).

Throughout history sports have been used to generate profit. The Tour de France, for example, was first staged in 1903 as a money-spinner for *L'Auto*, a new newspaper in France. The famous *maillot jaune* or yellow jersey worn by the overall winner of this epic bicycle race was named, not after any great heroic feat or person, but rather after the color of the pages of the newspaper that first sponsored the race. Over the years such associations of sports with media

and with profit have become increasingly commonplace, to the point that at no other historical moment have commercial or economic factors totally dominated the landscape of sports. Never before have "corporate interests had so much control over the meaning, organization and *purpose* of sport" (Coakley 2003, 364, emphasis added).

Commercialization has rendered problematic the increasing intervention of the media and the market into the *purpose* of sports. Indeed, the subtext of commercialization is that in transforming something into a product, service, or activity that may be used for profit, that product, service, or activity has been exploited or spoiled in some way. In other words, the purpose of the sport, once played for noble or pure reasons, is, according to some critics, now just about turning a profit.

Generally speaking, those sports that are commercialized share a number of key characteristics:

1. They are typically followed and watched by individuals and groups who possess or control the economic resources or capital of that society. Indeed, Coakley argues "it is only when sports promote the interests of powerful and wealthy people that they are likely to be commercialized" (Coakley 1998, 328).
2. They are typically played in countries where the material rewards of sports (large salaries, sponsorship

deals, etc.) are highly valued. One has only to witness the exorbitant salaries paid to many sports stars (e.g., British soccer star David Beckham) to recognize that those countries that value the material rewards of sports are also those countries with a sizeable celebrity culture.

3. They are typically dependent on spectator appeal, which in turn is dependent on people having considerable leisure time and disposable income to devote to sports spectatorship. The contexts where this is more likely to occur tend to be wealthy, Western, urban, postindustrial societies where people are not occupied with the day-to-day business of simply feeding and clothing themselves and their families.

4. They are typically sports that attract much media attention (largely because of the dramatic action and "riskiness" of many of the sports themselves). Once more, the broader political economy dictates that Western countries will be those where this is more likely to occur.

5. They are typically sports with a high degree of dependency on equipment, technology, and paraphernalia. Again, particular social and economic conditions are needed for this situation to occur.

Let's now look at these characteristics and conditions in terms of the commercialization of extreme sports.

Qualities and Consequences

As noted, the commercialization of extreme sports raises a number of issues for academics, the broader community, and proponents of the sports alike. Three main aspects of the commercialization debate are the commercial power of extreme sports, the particular qualities or characteristics of extreme sports that lend themselves to commercialization, and the consequences of commercialization for proponents of extreme sports.

Extreme sports are without doubt a lucrative business. To cite a few examples, skateboarding has been estimated to be a $2.3-million-a-year industry, the global surfing industry in 2002 was reported to be worth around $5.7 billion, while the 2002 Gravity Games generated upward of $25 million for the local economy of Cleveland, Ohio, the host city for the games that year. The key to such commercial success

is the dovetailing of aspects of consumer capitalism more broadly with the sports themselves. That is, elements such as rock music, commodities, and consumer goods have been incorporated into the iconography of the sports.

Here two issues are of concern when thinking about commercialization. First, these sports attract considerable commercial interest in terms of sponsorship for the athletes and events, which some people see as little more than a shrewd marketing ploy, and second, they provide an inexhaustible amount of commodities, products, and ephemera for proponents of these sports (or simply "wannabes") to purchase, which raises a number of issues for identity and authenticity.

To take each in turn, the sponsorship of extreme sports is a serious growth industry. In 1993 sponsorship revenue exceeded $23 million, but by 1998 sponsors had realized revenue of more than $135 million from the extreme sports genre. Not surprisingly, several major corporate sponsors in the United States such as Mountain Dew and Taco Bell have formed relationships with sports broadcasters, including ESPN, which hosts the Extreme Games, and NBC, which hosts the Gorge Games and the Gravity Games. In 1999 corporate sponsors paid up to $3 million each for the top-tier packages for the Gravity Games, while ESPN generated approximately $22 million from endorsement packages the same year. In many ways such televised events are as much a battle between brands as they are between competitors. Indeed, many popular items and commodities are now advertised as having some kind of reference to extreme sports. Whether it is young people kite surfing while drinking Coca-Cola or mountain biking while drinking Mountain Dew, the media and the market economy have certainly found their product niche in extreme sports.

Of course, this intersection of marketing and sports is not without its critics. As the former Canadian alpine ski coach Curry Chapman points out, somewhat pithily, "it is not just an athlete going down the mountain anymore, but it's also a bank, a drug store, and a car parts chain as well" (Kidd 1988, 23).

What makes extreme sports so attractive to commercial sponsors and advertisers is the market segment that comprises the key audience for events such as the Gravity Games or the Extreme Games. A generation of consumers known as "Generation X" is the key market for such events. Coined by Douglas Coupland (1991), the phrase "Generation Y" refers to a particular cohort of people, typically born between 1979 and 1994. The defining characteristic of this cohort is that members are media savvy, commercially aware, and have no financial commitments; they can spend their disposable income arbitrarily. McCarthy suggests that, in the United States alone, extreme sports currently boast more than 58 million consumers between the ages of ten and twenty-four, a generation "who wield US$250 billion in buying power" (McCarthy 2001, 22).

Indeed, proponents of extreme sports tend to be young and affluent, with considerable disposable income to spend on the accoutrements of popular culture. Certainly, the dependence of extreme sports on specialized equipment and clothing means that an ever-expanding array of consumer goods is available for this market to purchase. Some critics regard this association with global goods as representing the demise of a particular cultural identity that early proponents of extreme sports embraced in opposition to such global consumer culture. McCarthy, for example, argues that members of Generation Y tend to regard extreme sports more as a lifestyle and culture than as a physical activity. "These types of [extreme] sports have gone from being an activity of fringe groups to an ingrained part of a generation that influences its fashion, music and entertainment" (McCarthy 2001, 22).

Going Mainstream?

Following on from this, the second issue raised by the commercialization of extreme sports is that they provide an inexhaustible amount of commodities, products, and ephemera for proponents of these sports (or simply "wannabes") to purchase. That is, the clothing once worn by aficionados of extreme sports is also adopted as part of a broader "street culture." Indeed, the centrality of specialized equipment and associated paraphernalia to extreme sports makes the growth of a sizeable commercial industry that promotes a tantalizing range of state-of-the-art sporting exotica in no way surprising. As Palmer notes, "gloves, sunglasses, helmets, T-shirts, sandshoes, protective padding, bikes, karabiners and surf wax are all on sale for the discerning extreme buyer" (Palmer 2004, 56).

The issue of "wannabes" appropriating the clothing and products of extreme sports is perhaps the most contentious in the whole commercialization debate. No longer simply markers of identity that are particular to the sporting subcultures that participate in extreme sports, the nonspecialized media have recognized the rise in popularity of these sports and employ many of the insider themes to sell their products and paraphernalia. Previously "on the edge" behavior—a characteristic of many extreme sports—now features in a whole range of media to sell a whole range of mainstream commodities such as sunglasses, soft drinks, watches, alcoholic beverages, and clothing that has no relationship to the sports themselves. As Gliddon notes in relation to the commercial co-option of surfing: "surfing has appeal far beyond the surfers who provide the marketing cool. There's a surf shop in Singapore, but the roughest water is the condensation on the windows. A boutique surf store competes with Chanel and Prada for the consumer waves of down town New York" (Arthur 2003, 162).

Even so-called alternative youth cannot escape the media and market appropriation of their sports. Writing more than a decade ago about subcultural resistance in skateboarding, Beal notes that there are "individuals who bought the commercially produced paraphernalia and plastered all their belongings with corporate logos" (Beal 1995, 255).

Risky Business

So what is it about extreme sports that lends them to such commercialization? First, some attention needs to be paid to one of the central qualities of extreme sports. Extreme sports are risky sports. By their very nature, they are dangerous sports that provide their practitioners with a substantial chance of injury or even death. Such risk and unpredictability set up a particular narrative theme that is immensely attractive to sponsors and marketers, and these sports principally trade in the construction of a particular kind of extreme sports hero.

Many corporate sponsors are attracted to extreme sports because of the inherent "riskiness" of the sports. Frequently billed as "high thrill," many extreme sports lend themselves to the construction of a particular discourse of extremity that is then embellished in television commercials, on billboards, and in magazine advertising. This discourse of extremity routinely promotes its sports as being exceptional, cool, and not for the faint hearted.

Such messages are repeatedly amplified through the specialized and general sports media. Trading on the notion that extreme athletes are among a sporting elite, advertisements for the Hydra Fuel brand of sports drink, for example, claim "we didn't make them for the masses. We didn't make them for the average jock. We didn't make them for

"Bite into Xcitement!"

This passage details how Heinz was able to use the X Games to restructure and improve the company's marketing strategy when sales dropped for one of their snack foods.

For years, Heinz Bagel Bites had directed its marketing message to moms, a tack that helped catapult the little-known regional brand into the No. 2 slot in the frozen snack category . . . But even as consumers continued to opt for quick, on-the-go snacks over traditional meals—a trend borne out as the category sizzled with double-digit growth last year—Bagel Bites chilled to a 3 percent drop, causing marketers at the Pittsburgh-based packaged foods giant to rethink their strategy.

Rather than introducing new extensions, the company chose instead to strengthen the core positioning of its current offerings, mini-bagels with a variety of toppings including cheese, pepperoni and sausage. "We saw an opportunity to differentiate ourselves by targeting the end-user: tweens," Yoder said.

And that was the initial spark for "Bite into Xcitement!," a $3 million promotion built around sponsorship of ESPN's X Games, incorporating a sweepstakes, product giveaways and the visibility of pitchman, iconic skateboarding champion Tony Hawk. The promo kicked off in January, ran through the Winter X Games in early February and culminated with a sweeps . . . offering eight lucky winners (plus three pals each) an all-expense-paid trip to the summer X Games last month in San Francisco.

In order to take the "cool, unique" message of Bagel Bites directly to young consumers, Yoder said, "we knew we had to focus on brand-building activity instead of trade-driven deals. This was about creating a lasting brand image in their minds."

Research showed that among tweens' favorite activities, the Winter X Games was the most popular, second only to the Olympics. Marketers then zeroed in on snowboarding, which is currently the No. 1 sport among male teens and tweens: it's also the sport that gave birth to the X Games.

Source: Reyes, S. (2000, September 18). Bite me: Heinz Bagel Bites X Games promotion. Retrieved January 31, 2007, from http://findarticles.com/p/articles/mi_moBDW/is_36_41/ai_65485175

---

athletes who settle for second best," while those for Exceed sports nutrition products feature the slogan "Don't tell me I can't," suggesting that these are products for people for whom nothing is impossible.

The following commercial for Mountain Dew soft drink, which aired during the inaugural ESPN Extreme Games in 1995, sends a similar message:

Announcer: "Extreme mountain biking . . . forty-five miles an hour."

Biker 1: "Did it."

Announcer: ". . . 65 miles an hour."

Biker 2: "Done it."

Announcer: ". . . blindfolded."

Biker 3: "Been there."

Announcer: ". . . a 4,000-foot vertical drop."

Biker 4: "Tried that."

Announcer: ". . . All while slamming a Dew."

All bikers: "Whoa."

Announcer: "Nothing's more intense than slamming Mountain Dew. Oh, yeah—while watching the Extreme Games on ESPN."

All bikers: "Decent."

As such examples show, the media presentation of many extreme sports plays with the notion that they offer more than sports as sports are customarily imagined; extreme sports take their adherents faster, higher, and farther than all others. These are exceptional, cool sports that not just anyone can play; and it is from the considerable media resources that accompany the sponsorship, promotion, and selling of extreme sports that the extreme athlete emerges as a "fearless figure, supremely brave and ever adventurous as he or she negotiates a series of hair raising episodes" (Palmer 2004, 57). As Koerner observes:

> With their unwavering cool in the face of extraordinary circumstances, [they] resemble the romantic heroes of spaghetti westerns or Indiana Jones style adventures and thus pique the imaginations of those secretly wishing to put the Man With No Name swagger in their step—if not full time, at least for a few brief moments on Saturday or Sunday. (Koerner 1997, 59)

Social and Economic Conditions

To return to the key characteristics that enable sports to be commercialized, we can see how many extreme sports are a natural fit for market and media forces. As outlined earlier, those sports that are commercialized—turned into a product for financial gain or profit—are those that are followed and watched by the individuals and groups who possess or control economic resources. In the case of extreme sports, the spending power of Generation Y makes this market segment an economic force to be reckoned with.

Those sports that are commercialized are also frequently played in countries where the material rewards and the celebrity culture of sport are highly valued. That the skateboarding star Tony Hawk can be voted the "coolest big-time athlete" in a 2002 poll in the United States is testament to this dimension of the commercialization of extreme sports.

Those sports that are commercialized are also ones that are typically dependent on spectator appeal, which in turn is dependent on people having considerable leisure time and disposable income to devote to sports spectatorship. Once again, the demographic profile of Generation Y enables this particular condition for the commercialization of extreme sports.

Sports that are commercialized are typically those that attract much media attention (largely because of the dramatic action and riskiness of many of the sports themselves). The ever-present possibility of danger and even death means that the possibility for heroic and dramatic performances is never far from the action in extreme sports, which sets up a number of narrative themes that sponsors and marketers can use to sell their products.

Sports that are commercialized are typically those that

have a high degree of dependency on equipment, technology, and paraphernalia. This has been one of the consistent, defining features of extreme sports over the years.

Cashing In, Selling Out?

Two key consequences have emerged from the commercialization of extreme sports. The first is that, in being transformed from a physical pursuit to a commercial pursuit, extreme sports have been exploited and tainted. In extreme sports the notion of commercialization is often a shorthand for selling out, for forfeiting the purity of the sports for commercial gain. The commercial co-option of extreme sports is a central debate in the broader research literature on extreme sports.

The second consequence to emerge from the commercialization of extreme sports is that the incorporation of an iconography of risk-taking behavior into a whole range of popular cultural products creates the impression that *anyone* can take part in these activities. The use of "extreme images" to sell mainstream cultural products (such as bungee jumping to advertise deodorant) has been critically addressed by Palmer in her examination of the selling of risk in adventure tourism. Researchers Beal and Thompson have also explored and critiqued the ways in which risk taking has gone mainstream in relation to skateboarding.

Such is the irony of the commercialization of extreme sports that it actually makes the extraordinary quite ordinary. On the one hand, much of the commercial interest in the sports trades in the narratives of the extraordinary athlete undertaking hair-raising exploits. On the other hand, however, the fact that inexperienced actors (rather than athletes) can leap from a plane, tow-in surf, or street luge creates the impression that no extraordinary expertise is in fact needed to engage in extreme sports; they are now part and parcel of mainstream popular culture.

Questions Remain

If extreme sports are, as Rinehart suggests, meant to be activities that "either ideologically or practically provide alternatives to mainstream sports and to mainstream values" (Rinehart 2000, 506), then the centrality of commercialization, so much a part of modern sports more broadly, leaves two key questions unanswered: (1) Do extreme sports offer a counter to the commercially exploitative world of mainstream sports, or do they simply reproduce such commercialization? and (2) Do extreme sports offer an alternative culture to dominant sporting practices, or do they simply reproduce the dominant sporting practices of class inequities, media domination, and market influence? Such questions will remain central to the commercialization debate.

Catherine Palmer

See also Meaning of Extreme, The

Further Reading

Andrews, D., & Jackson, S. (2001). *Sports stars: The cultural politics of sporting celebrities.* London: Routledge.

Arthur, D. (2003). Corporate sponsorship of sport: Its impact on surfing and surf culture. In J. Skinner, K. Gilbert, & A. Edwards (Eds.), *Some like it hot: The beach as a cultural dimension* (pp. 160–171). Oxford, UK: Meyer & Meyer Sport.

Beal, B. (1995). Disqualifying the official: An exploration of social resistance through the subculture of skate boarding. *Sociology of Sport Journal, 12,* 252–267.

Beal, B., & Wilson, C. (2004). Chicks dig scars. In B. Wheaton (Ed.), *Understanding lifestyle sports: Consumption, identity and difference* (pp. 31–54). London: Routledge.

Bennett, G., Henson, R., & Zhang, J. (2002). Action sports sponsorship recognition. *Sports Marketing Quarterly, 11*(30), 185–196.

Bourdieu, P. (1993). How can one be a sports fan? In S. During (Ed.), *The cultural studies reader* (pp. 427–440). London: Routledge.

Cashmore, E. (2002). *Beckham.* London: Polity.

Cleland, K. (2001). Action sports form fabric of generation: Marines to Mountain Dew quick to join games in search of teens. *Advertising Age, 72*(16), 22–23.

Coakley, J. (1998). *Sports in society: Issues and controversies* (6th ed.). New York: McGraw-Hill.

Coakley, J. (2003). *Sports in society: Issues and controversies* (7th ed.). New York: McGraw-Hill.

Coupland, D. (1991). *Generation X: Tales for an accelerated culture.* New York: St. Martin's Press.

Debord, G. (1972). *Society of the spectacle.* Detroit, MI: Black and Red Books.

Featherstone, M. (1991). *Consumer culture and postmodernism.* London: Sage.

Harris, H. A. (1964). *Greek athletes and athletics.* London: Hutchinson.

Harvey, J., & Cantelon, H. (Eds.). (1988). *Not just a game.* Ottawa, Canada: University of Ottawa Press.

Henio, R. (2000). What's so punk about snowboarding? *Journal of Sport and Social Issues, 24*(2), 176–191.

Hochman, P. (1999). Street lugers, stunt bikers, and Colgate-Palmolive live! Spokesmen with nose rings. *Fortune, 140,* 60.

Humphreys, D. (2003). Selling out snowboarding: The alternative response to commercial co-option. In R. Rinehart & S. Syder (Eds.), *To the extreme: Alternative sports, inside and out* (pp. 407–428). Albany: State University of New York Press.

Kidd, B. (1988). The philosophy of excellence: Olympic performances, class power and the Canadian state. In P. J. Galasso (Ed.), *Philosophy of sport and physical activity: Issues and concepts* (pp. 17–29). Toronto: Canadian Scholars' Press.

Koerner, B. L. (1997). Extreeeme. *U.S. News & World Report, 122*(25), 51–60.

McCarthy, M. (2001, August 14). ESPN's promotion of X Games goes to extremes. *USA Today,* (B03).

Midol, N. (1993). Cultural dissents and technical innovations in the "whiz" sports. *International Review for the Sociology of Sport, 28*(1), 23–32.

Midol, N., & Broyer, G. (1995). Towards an anthropological analysis of new sport culture: The case of whiz sports in France. *Sociology of Sport Journal, 12,* 204–212.

Palmer, C. (2004). Death, danger and the selling of risk in adventure sports. In B. Wheaton (Ed.), *Understanding lifestyle sports: Consumption, identity and difference* (pp. 55–69). London: Routledge.

Rinehart, R. (2000). Emerging arriving sport: Alternatives to formal sport. In J. Coakley & E. Dunning (Eds.), *Handbook of sports studies* (pp. 110–123). London: Sage.

Rinehart, R., & Syder, S. (Eds.). (2003). *To the extreme: Alternative sports, inside and out.* Albany: State University of New York Press.

Slack, T. (1998) Studying the commercialization of sport: The need for critical analysis. *Sociology of Sport Online.* Retrieved July 8, 2006, from http://physed.otago.ac.nz/sosol/v1i1/v1i1a6.htm

SPAUSA (Skatepark Association of the United States of America). (2001). Are you contributing to the delinquency of a minor? Retrieved July 29, 2006, from http://www.spausa.org/introduction.html

Wheaton, B. (Ed.). (2004). *Understanding lifestyle sports: Consumption, identity and difference.* London: Routledge.

Crandal, Louise

Louise Crandal (b. 1971) is a two-time world champion paraglider, trainer of birds of prey, and journalist. As a child in Denmark she rode horses, as did her grandmother, who was a jockey; thus, Crandal shared a family interest in racing and challenging the forces of nature. Crandal discovered paragliding in Switzerland in 1992 (Denmark lacks the mountains necessary for paragliding). With her brother Mads Crandal and a few friends she took up paragliding and developed the sport in Denmark during the 1990s.

Paragliding is a sport developed from the parachute. Modern paraglider wings are made of high-performance non-porous fabrics and are often used in mountain regions where flying is based around thermal currents. Paragliders, who usually carry parachutes, risk injury, especially when crashing from lower altitudes where there is not enough time for a parachute to be deployed.

As paragliding became more organized Crandal participated in her first competition in 1995 in Italy. Women have been a minority in paragliding as a sport and in competition.

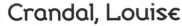
However, the number of women has increased, as is the case in many extreme sports, and women and men usually compete at the same levels during tournaments. The distance of the competition was 90 kilometers, but Crandal's longest distance to date was 28 kilometers. After three hours in the air she had reached 45 kilometers. Thinking back, she said: "That day I learned that you are able to challenge yourself to achieve much more than you actually think you are able to do." (Bach 2002)

In 1998 Crandal won her first competition, beating all the men paragliders in the Argentinean championship. In 2001 she won her first title as world champion of women and later that year set a world record in distance for women by flying 215 kilometers in Brazil. The Danish elite sports organization, Team Denmark, supported Crandal in international competitions during 2000–2003.

Crandal's first serious crash occurred when she hit a pine tree. And indeed the sport has taken the lives of friends in the international paragliding community. However, in her first book, published in 2003, she elaborates on the dangers of flying but also on the joy, excitement, and physical challenges that keep her in the air. She writes about traveling with the paragliding community, seeing the world from above:

> While flying we are not limited by only two dimensions, we are able to use the space above and we are moving around where the forces of nature are sovereign. We are able to fly over mountains that it otherwise will take days to climb. We are able to see places we never would be able to see—we are able to feel like we are birds. (Crandal 2003)

In 2003 Crandal came in third at the world championship for women. In 2005 she won the title again and decided to stop competing.

During her years of flying over landscapes of all continents Crandal developed an interest in birds and especially birds of prey. This interest led her to begin training birds of prey such as hawks in a new sport called "parahawking." Crandal is the first person to train a bird to land on her hand while paragliding. She has trained a steppe eagle, named "Coorsak," to fly along with her as she paraglides. A TV documentary, *Flying with Eagles*, showing Crandal and Coorsak in the air was filmed in Denmark and Italy.

Alice Riis Bach

See also Gender

Further Reading

Bach, A. R. (2002). *Kvinder på banen—sport, køn og medier* [Women at center court—Sport, gender and media]. Copenhagen, Denmark: Forlaget Rosinante.

Crandal.dk. (2006, July 20). Forside og nyheder [Frontpage and news] Retrieved August 15, 2006, from www.crandal.dk

Crandal, L. (2003). *At flyve med fugle* [Flying along with the birds]. Copenhagen, Denmark: Aschehaug.

Gin Gliders. (n.d.). News. Retrieved August 15, 2006, from http://www.gingliders.com/news/00000113.php

ParaVision. (n.d.). View our work samples. Retrieved August 15, 2006, from http://www.paravision.dk

da Silva, Fabiola

Fabiola da Silva (b. 1979) is a pioneer both in the realm of aggressive inline skating as well as in the larger realm of women's sports. She is the most decorated female athlete in extreme sports, as the winner of eight world championships, as well as the most decorated inline skater either female or male. She competes successfully in all three events of inline skating—vert, park, and street. Her dominance in the sport prompted the Aggressive Skaters Association Pro Tour to institute what is known as the "Fabiola Rule." The Fabiola Rule allows female athletes to prequalify and compete against men in inline vert competitions. Not only has she competed against men, but also she has proven a tough competitor, finishing as high as second place.

Born in Sao Paolo, Brazil, the skater who likes to be referred to as "Fab" was given her first pair of roller skates at age fourteen by her father. Only a year later Fab was introduced to inline skates when her mother saved to purchase them for her. Shortly thereafter Fab was signed by Rollerblade, the company that produces the only type of inline skates she has ever used, and by the age of sixteen she was traveling to the United States to join the Pro Tour circuit. Her first pro competition was the 1996 Summer X Games, where she began her dynasty by taking first place in the women's vert competition. Not only did she take home the gold medal, but also she made history by becoming the first inline skater to land a backflip in competition. *Sports Illustrated* described this performance as one of the most memorable in the history of the sport.

Her streak of first place finishes in vert competitions between 1996 and 2001 was interrupted only once, in 1999, when she took second. She also took gold in park in 2002 and 2003.

The Fabiola Rule allowed Fab to continue competing in vert despite the event being dropped for women by the Aggressive Skaters Association (Morfit, 2002). She worked her way up the ranks in male competition, taking second place at the 2004 Latin X Games and sixth at the 2004 Summer X Games. Da Silva's focus, commitment, and desire have made her an inspiration not only to the extreme sports athletes who follow her career but also to women everywhere.

Fabiola has crossed over from athlete to actress: She is set to star in the movie *Slammin'*, currently in production by Warner Brothers. The story brings her own life to mind because it follows a Brazilian girl who is struggling to rise in the world of competitive inline skating against men. Because of Fabiola's dominance in the sport and her pioneering attitude, many people believe she will become the heir to Tony Hawk, who is regarded by many as the father of modern skateboarding. Fab, however, skates out of love and wants to prove that girls and women can be and do anything. "I hope some little girl out there watches me and knows that you can be anything, even a pro in-line skater, if you are a girl" (Dial 2003, 11C).

Jaclyn Miller and Ellen J. Staurowsky

See also Gender; Inline Skating; Meaning of Extreme, The

Further Reading

Dial, J. (2003, May 26). Da Silva enjoys winning medals, respect: Brazilian makes a name for herself competing against men. *San Antonio Express News*, p. 11C.

Kaplan, B. (1999, May). Fabiola da Silva. *Sports Illustrated for Kids, 11*(5), 58.

MacPherson, B. (2005, August 1). A decade of x-cellence. *Sports Illustrated*, A12.

Morfit, C. (2002, September). Fabiola da Silva—Profile. *Sports Illustrated for Women, 4*(5), 128.

Rutsch, D. (2005, August 30). Heirs to the air: Extreme sports stars aim high to emulate Tony Hawk. *Sacramento Bee*, p. E1.

Dakides, Tara

Tara Dakides (b. 1975) is a three-time world champion snowboarder, five-time X Games gold medalist, and professional snowboarder. Growing up in southern California's Laguna Hills, Dakides played sports, including gymnastics, skateboarding, and soccer. She began snowboarding in her early teenage years and found solace from a messy home life in the terrain park. In her own words, "I was never a good student, and I always got in trouble. I was definitely a rebellious kid." At fifteen she left home, and by sixteen she had found her way to Mammoth, California, were she lived the snowboarding lifestyle and pursued a snowboarding career by riding in local competitions, promoting herself at industry trade shows, and producing sponsor-me videos. Riding rails and jumps in the early 1990s, Dakides was called "a pioneer of the women's jib [snowboarding on jumps and rails] movement." Sponsors took notice, and in 1994 she turned professional.

Nicknamed the "Terrorizer," Dakides fundamentally changed women's snowboarding at the Big Air finals at the 1998 Vans Triple Crown competition at Breckenridge, Colorado, with her revolutionary back-flip, a trick no woman had previously attempted in competition. She has played a significant role in altering popular perceptions that female riders are less capable than their male counterparts. According to snowboarding journalist Jardine Hammond, Dakides has "taken not only the standard for women in sport, but the standard of riders of either gender to the next level" (Hammond 2000). Almost every article acknowledges her role in narrowing the gap between genders. One fan explains: "Your riding destroys all preconceived notions and inspires a playing field devoid of gender separation." During the late 1990s and early 2000s Dakides dominated many of the contemporary disciplines, including big air, slope style, and rails. Her victories include five Winter X Games gold medals and three World Snowboarding Championships. Dakides's "aggressive, hard, and fast" styles have gained the respect of her peers, who voted her Best Female Freestyle Rider in 1999, 2000, and 2001, Best Overall Female Rider in 2000 and 2001, and Best Female Rail Rider in 2001 at the *Transworld Snowboarding* Rider's Poll Awards. Dakides was also *Snowboarder Magazine*'s Female Snowboarder of the Year in 2000, 2001, and 2002.

Dakides demonstrates a fearless attitude to snowboarding. In her own words, "If it scares me then I just want to do it more, I don't like being scared and I don't like thinking that I'm not going to do something because I'm scared of it" (Watson 2001). She "rides with the same level of confidence and courage as a guy does," says Jake Burton. "Although there have been other women along the way who have done that, it's never been in this sort of technical, freestyle way with rails and big airs. The way she charges is freakin' impressive" (Reed 2005, 158). Furthermore, Dakides provided inspiration to many female boarders. According to one core female snowboarder, "I was never really inspired by girls until Tara Dakides in 1998. I really looked up to Tara, not only did she rip, but she was also a gorgeous girl. I think it's important to be able to step it up on the hill and still have a bit of femininity too." As a role model Dakides has proved to males and females alike that gender is not a limiting factor in snowboarding.

Dakides has also developed a marketable image. According to EXPN.com, Dakides combines a courageous and powerful riding style with a "rad SoCal style, gnarly fashion sense, *lovely looks*, and sense of humour" to become "one of snowboarding's most prominent divas." Shirtless quartets of admiring males with "T-A-R-A" spelled across their chests greet her at finish lines. Online chats often leave Dakides fending off marriage proposals, along with more salacious offerings. A fearless attitude combined with a marketable image contributed to making Dakides "arguably the most popular snowboarder at the Winter X Games" (Seelenbradt 2001).

With her sporting success Dakides has gained eminence in the culture, with major corporate sponsors, including Mountain Dew and Campbell's Soup, and a range of product sponsors, including Jeenyus Snowboards, Billabong, Von Zipper, Vans, and Pro Tec Helmets, all using her signature on their designs. Dakides has also achieved broader celebrity status, being featured in *Rolling Stone*, *Sports Illustrated*, and *Maxim*. After appearing on the cover of *FHM* (in nothing but body paint), readers voted Dakides one of the "Top 100 Sexiest Women in the World." She also was featured on the cover of *Sports Illustrated for Women* and was named "the Coolest Sports Woman in 2001." She has judged the Miss Teen America pageant and appeared on the David Letterman show. The latter, however, did not go as planned.

Having recently won a silver medal in the X Games slope-style event and being featured on the cover of *FHM*, Dakides was invited to become the first female to complete a live stunt on *The Late Show with David Letterman* in February 2004. The producers built a massive wooden ramp outside the studio in the middle of New York's 53rd Street and then covered it in snow. It was supposed to launch Dakides over a 6-meter gap. However, various factors, including lack of building materials, warm weather that melted the snow, and the pressure of a big-time production, diminished Dakides's chances of successfully completing the backside 360-degree maneuver she had planned. Falling on asphalt from an estimated height of 7.6 meters, Dakides was knocked unconscious and split her head in front of a stunned crowd and live national audience. Letterman cancelled two shows scheduled later that night because of the "horrific, miserable tragedy." Every major U.S. newspaper covered the event, which also led local news programs across the country. Dakides later returned to the Letterman show, sans snowboard, and appeared on *Last Call*, *The Early Show*, *Deborah Norville Tonight*, and the *Howard Stern Show*. A benefit from the incident, according to Dakides, is that "a lot more people know my name now," but she also observes the inherent dangers for the athlete within this new highly mediatized context: "They build these big obstacles to watch us do gnarlier and gnarlier tricks, and I'm risking my entire season and all my other goals . . . laying in bed for a month is not fun" (Roenigk 2004).

Certainly Dakides has suffered her share of injuries, including a fractured back, dislocated elbows, torn ligaments in each knee, a broken fibula, as well as numerous concussions. Despite numerous surgeries and rehabilitation programs, she continues to compete. She also satisfies her hunger for adventure with a serving of other extreme sports. She surfs and skateboards; she races motocross; she drives a variety of race cars, including shifter cars and formula race cars; and in 2003 she raced in the Baja 1000, traveling 320 kilometers across the Mexican desert in a custom Baja race car.

Holly Thorpe

See also Gender; Snowboarding

Further Reading

Floros, S. (2004, June). Close up: Tara Dakides. *SG: The Girls Surf, Snow, Skate, Lifestyle Magazine,* 7(4), 34–38.

Reed, R. (2005). *The way of the snowboarder.* New York: Harry N. Abrams.

Taradakides.com. (n.d.). Retrieved June 27, 2006, from http://www.tara dakides.com

Roenigk, A. (2004, February 17). Tara Dakides talks, part one. Retrieved February 1, 2007, from http://expn.go.com/expn/story?pageName=040211_tara_dakides

Watson, C. L. (2001, February 4). Sweet repeat. Retrieved February 1, 2007, from http://expn.go.com/xgames/wxg/2001/s/women_bigair.html

Yant, N. (2001, March 1). Features 14.7: Tara Dakides interview. *Transworld Snowboarding.* Retrieved June 26, 2006, from http://www.transworldsnowboarding.com/snow/magazine/article/0,14304,243261,00.html

altitudes, especially opening his parachute at the last moment. After winning two French national titles and a silver medal at the 1986 World Freefall Parachuting Championships, de Gayardon increasingly devoted his efforts to BASE (building, antenna, span, Earth) jumping.

In 1992 he joined the No Limit Sector Team. He secured several big sponsors, including Sector, and received much publicity. In 1995 in Moscow he jumped from a height of 12,700 meters without an oxygen set and established a world record. In 1996 he won the first World Skysurfing Championships, a contest that he promoted. In the 1990s de Gayardon worked on a project that earned him the nickname "Icarus." He developed a flying suit that allowed him to glide; in so doing he contributed to realizing the eternal human dream of flying unassisted. The suit incorporated a number of scientific advancements, including the ability to resist air and move the wearer horizontally. During one test de Gayardon jumped from 4,000 meters, glided more than 5,000 meters, and returned to the plane that launched him. De Gayardon became so accomplished at this feat that it became his trademark. However, in 1998 he crashed to the ground and was killed while testing a new wingsuit in Hawaii. Neither his main parachute nor his reserve opened.

Gherardo Bonini

Further Reading

Leonardo.it. (n.d.). Patrick de Gayardon: Icaro: la scienza e l'audacia. Retrieved June 7, 2006, from http://biografie.leonardo.it/biografia.htm?BioID=1271&biografia=Patrick+De+Gayardon.htm

Passe, P., and Smith W. (2003). *Eyes in the sky.* Bethune, France: ParaMag.

de Gayardon, Patrick

In Europe the name of Patrick de Gayardon (1960–1998) is synonymous with extreme sports. Some people even compare him with Icarus, the mythological hero who built wings to escape from prison but who fell into the sea and died.

Patrick de Gayardon de Fenayl was born in Oulins, near Paris. He studied in Lyon at the abbey of Marie's Fathers before graduating in law. Throughout his youth de Gayardon showed an aptitude for a wide range of sports, including windsurfing, lawn tennis, golf, and Alpine skiing. His first love, however, was parachuting. He mastered the technical aspects of the sport and most of the techniques that he would apply to freefalls—skydiving—from higher

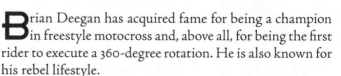

Deegan, Brian

Brian Deegan has acquired fame for being a champion in freestyle motocross and, above all, for being the first rider to execute a 360-degree rotation. He is also known for his rebel lifestyle.

Born in Omaha, Nebraska, on 9 May 1975, Deegan rode his first motorbike at age eight; just two years later he competed in his first junior races. He also competed in the ranks of the National Motocross Association, winning local and national events. In 1992 he turned professional and rapidly became a star both in indoor and outdoor competitions. In 1997 he won his first Supercross event (the main outdoor motocross event managed by the Amateur Motocross Association). After winning a round of the outdoor series in 1999, Deegan celebrated by removing his hands from the bars and assuming a number of high-risk positions. Although his actions excited the fans, the Amateur Motocross Association fined him $1,000. Notwithstanding this fine, he continued to repeat his postrace tricks and entered the world of freestyle motocross, where he flourished. In 1999 Deegan won the world championships and earned a silver medal in the Gravity Games, a multisport event based in Providence, Rhode Island, dedicated to extreme sports. These were the first steps in a career in which he has earned large prize monies and sponsorships. With his friend Larry Linkogle, Deegan formed Metal Mulisha, a group composed initially by the two riders, but later extended to all fans, with its own clothing, slogans, and gadgets. Fans rushed to purchase Metal Mulisha gear and further swelled Deegan's financial worth.

By 2006 Deegan had won ten medals at ESPN's X Games and two at the Gravity Games. He has appeared on the cover of many magazines, including *Penthouse*, *Tattoo*, and *ESPN The Magazine*, and acted as stuntman in various films, including *Spiderman* and *Fantastic 4*. In 2004 he received an ESPN award for best male action sport athlete, having been the first motocross rider to achieve a 360-degree rotation (despite breaking his femur and both wrists). In May 2004 at the Winter Extreme Games Deegan tried another 360-degree rotation, this time on a snow surface, but failed and again re-

ceived severe injures. After recovering Deegan restarted his career with the aim of finally achieving the 360-degree rotation. However, in May 2005 he had another serious accident and had a kidney removed. Nonetheless, Deegan plans to continue his career in the freestyle motocross circuit.

Gherardo Bonini

Further Reading

Schaefer, A. (2004). *Extreme freestyle motocross moves*. Mankato, MN: Capstone Press.
Schwarz, T. (2003). *Dirt bikes, motocross freestyle*. Mankato, MN: Capstone Press.

Dogtown and Z-Boys

The film *Dogtown and Z-Boys* (2001) was directed by Stacy Peralta, a Dogtown resident, skateboard champion, and eventual skateboard industry mogul, and cowritten by Peralta and surf and skate culture writer Craig Stecyk. The film traces the development of a uniquely urban skateboarding subculture in Venice, California, during the middle to late 1970s. The film's subtitle, *The Birth of Extreme*, expresses both the sense of extreme culture and extreme performance.

A professional skateboarder in action. Source: istock.

Stacy Peralta on Dogtown and Z-Boys

Skateboarding icon Stacy Peralta and Switch Magazine's *Emerson Brown discuss Peralta's award-winning skateboarding documentary* Dogtown and Z-Boys.

Emerson Brown: You've said that you want young skaters to see [*Dogtown and Z-Boys*]. Do you think skateboarding culture has instilled within itself an appreciation for its past? Or do you think it's more like pop music and everybody is continually looking for the next big thing?

Stacy Peralta: I think it's both. I think the kids are certainly looking for the next big thing. But, what has surprised me is a couple of things that happened that made me realize that people both old and young took the film seriously. Number one, there were a couple of kids on my block that, after having seen the film, went out and made their own wooden boards. I couldn't believe it. They started doing birds on the ground and slides. That made me realize, wow, these kids really connected. They really got it. And to make your own skateboard is a very personal thing for a kid to do because it puts him in touch with what that board's about.

EB: It's almost like shaping your own surfboard.

Stacy Peralta: Exactly. I thought that was really, really special. The other thing is a lot of adults that formally used to skateboard that now have kids are starting to skateboard again because they're starting to realize there's a part of their life that's missing. The local skateboard shop recently told me that all these 45-year-

old guys are coming in the shop going "I want to buy a skateboard." And they're just doing it to roll around and feel that feeling of movement again. The thing is there's never been a historical skateboard film before. So, this was the first one and it was just a matter of letting it out there.

EB: Regarding history and skateboarding. In this film, style is everything. You've inferred in some things you've said that style isn't as important in skateboarding today. I wondered what you meant by that.

Stacy Peralta: We live in the age of extremism. Today, going big is all that matters. Because of the danger of the tricks these guys are doing, they don't really have time to look particularly graceful or aesthetically pleasing when they're doing it because they have one foot over the back truck and the other foot over the front truck. And it's all about going as high or as far or as big as you can. In our day, it wasn't about going big. It was about really looking good and having your soul exposed while you were skateboarding because the way you skated was clearly a manifestation of who you were. It was just a difference. It's not to say one's better than the other, but at some point the two are going to hybridize together, and it's going to make something altogether new.

Source: Brown, E. (2004, February 14). Stacy Peralta on *Dogtown and Z-Boys*. Retrieved February 1, 2007, from http://www.switchmagazine.com/skateboard_storys/dogtown_zboys.html

---

The film explains the term *Dogtown* as a derivative of the "dog days" of summer, those long, hot days when the surf would be ruined by onshore winds and young people hanging around the neighborhood would skateboard outside the Zephyr surf shop (hence "Z-Boys") on Main Street in Santa Monica and on the road down to the beach parking lot across Main Street at the end of Bicknell Drive. The term *Dogtown* also refers to a beachside strip of Santa Monica and Venice Beach extending the length of Main Street from the Santa Monica Pier south to around the Venice Pier. Although a largely wealthy and regentrified area from the

mid-1990s onward, in the 1970s the area was known as a beachside slum, the seaside ruins of what was once a series of entertainment piers culminating in a several-block simulation of Venice by the Sea, complete with artificial canals and the Pacific Ocean Park amusement pier.

Although the film focuses on skateboarding, it also shows how the sport's redevelopment in the mid-1970s through the advent of urethane skateboard wheels was inspired by and emulative of the extreme transformation of surfing through the shortboard revolution, which allowed new and radical maneuvers on the waves previously impos-

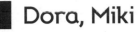
sible on the longboards of the previous decade. The film traces the development of the Zephyr skateboard team from the Zephyr surf team, which ruled a surf spot in the ruins of the Pacific Ocean Park pier called the "T," inadvertently formed by a collapsed and partially submerged roller coaster. Its metal beams jutted perpendicularly and presented a dangerous obstacle. The film includes footage (compiled from Super 8 and 16-millimeter film taken during the 1970s) of surfers riding dangerously close to the wreckage and even riding through the center of the T. The film then documents the rise of the Zephyr team through the skateboarding revival to the team's dissolution at the beginning of the 1980s.

The film is effective in its use of stock archival images, still photographs, and Super 8 film taken by Craig Stecyk and Glen E. Friedman, who also coauthored the book *Fuck You Heroes*, which features Friedman's photography of the Dogtown surf/skate and punk rock scene. The film creates extensive montages that compare surf and skateboard styles and confront Abbot Kinney's early twentieth-century creation of Venice as a "West Coast Coney Island" and "California Riviera" with its post–World War II degeneration into what came to be known as "Dogtown."

Although the film stresses that the influence of contemporary shortboard surfing transformed skateboarding beyond its original emulation of classic longboarding style, it also points out how the performances of the Z-Boys pushed skateboarding beyond the limitations of surfing through the development of pool skating. The film focuses especially on the significance of aerial maneuvers in which a skateboarder rides up the side of a pool, past the top of the wall and into the air, and then comes back down into the pool, landing safely and skating back up the other side. Not until the early 1990s would surfers inspired by skateboarding be able to perform similar aerials above the waves, thus allowing skateboarding to return the favor of influence. The popularity of *Dogtown and Z-Boys* led to a feature film, *Lords of Dogtown* (2005), based on the characters.

Kevin Fisher

See also Meaning of Extreme, The; Skateboarding; Surfing

Further Reading

Brooke, M. (1999). *Concrete wave: The history of skateboarding*. Lynchburg, VA: Warwick House.

Hardwicke, C. (2005). *Behind the scene: Lords of Dogtown*. Lynchburg, VA: Warwick House.

Stecyk, C. (2002). *Dogtown: The legend of the Z-Boys*. Los Angeles: Burning Flags Press.

Stecyk, C., & Friedman, G. (1994). *Fuck you heroes*. Los Angeles: Burning Flags Press.

Dora, Miki

Miki Dora (1934–2002) was a figure known for his extreme behavior as part of the 1950s and 1960s Malibu surf culture that centered on the legendary right-hand point break just north of Los Angeles on Pacific Coast Highway. Miklos Sandor Dora III was born in Budapest, Hungary, on 11 August 1934 and immigrated to the United States as a child with his mother. Following his parents divorce, the young Dora was introduced to surfing by his stepfather, and by famous early California surfer, Gard Chapin. Dora built a huge reputation for himself at Malibu throughout the 1950s, riding the long, hot-dog waves of First Point with style and aggressiveness. Miki attended Hollywood High but was absent whenever the surf was up at Malibu.

Dora the "Stylemaster"

Miki distinguished himself by his calculated casualness on the wave that set the standard of surfing style and earned him the nickname, "Da Cat." His moniker also had a double meaning; he had another pastime as a "cat burglar," with a penchant for petty thefts, scams, and other nonviolent crimes. Dora's outward behavior was also highly iconoclastic, alternately dressing the part of the young aristocrat in tennis outfits and wearing Nazi trench coats to the beach, as well as painting swastikas on his surfboard—perhaps the most antisocial statement one could make in 1950s America. The term *surf Nazis* may well have originated in reference to Dora. On the other hand, Dora's style was effete, many described his mannerisms as effeminate, and rumors swarmed that he was homosexual. In a recent *Vanity Fair* article an ex-girlfriend described him as "a eunuch," ineffectual and disinterested in sex.

Dora–Surfing Movie Star

Miki played an ambivalent role in the popularization of surfing within the burgeoning youth culture of the early 1960s.

He was a featured character in the novel *Gidget* and its film adaptation, both of which first brought the surfing subculture of Malibu to wider audiences. Because of his surfing abilities and classic movie-star looks, Dora was able to profit from Hollywood's mass marketing of surf culture, landing work as a stunt double in films such as *Muscle Beach Party* (1964), *Bikini Beach* (1964), *How to Stuff a Wild Bikini* (1965), *Beach Blanket Bingo* (1965), and *Ski Party* (1965).

In *Ride the Wild Surf* (1964), Dora, though not typically known as a big-wave surfer, was paid to take several horrendous wipeouts in huge surf at Waimea Bay, one of the most feared big-wave spots on the North Shore of Oahu.

Dora was ambivalent about his new media profile, and while he worked to exploit the system, he also did everything he could to undermine the image it was promoting. Dora was articulate and known for his pithy if cryptic prognostications about surfing, culture, and politics. He spoke his mind about these issues in now-famous interviews in *Surfing Guide* and *Surfer Magazine* in 1963–1964. When asked in the *Surfer* interview if he was ruthless in the water, Dora replied: "It's a lie. I'm vicious. We're all pushing and shoving, jockeying for position, and if I get the wave first—if I'm in the best position—then I feel I deserve it." In the *Surfing Guide* interview earlier that year, he related the following story: "So anyhow, I'm coming across the Point on this thing and I was completely locked in. I couldn't pull out ... I couldn't do anything. And here's this jerkus swimming toward his board on the beach, with his tiny head sticking out of the water ... Well, I came across and my skeg went into his back like a tomahawk" (Cleary, 1963).

Although widely renowned as the best small-wave surfer in the world during the mid to late 1960s, Dora was notoriously hostile to the emerging surf-contest format and what he saw as the soulless transformation of surfing from art form into sport. Dora made several jabs at the emerging institution of professional surfing. In one contest he rode a 12-foot tandem board in the final event; in another he threw his first-place trophy in the sand from the winner's podium in front of fans, judges, media, and fellow surfers; and in the 1967 Malibu Invitational Dora pulled down his board shorts on a wave and "mooned" the gathered crowd as he rode all the way down the point.

Dora in Exile

Miki Dora vanished mysteriously from Malibu around 1971, after which the words *Dora Lives* appeared in large graffiti on the wall at Malibu that demarcated "the pit"—the hangout spot of the early Malibu crew still favored by longboarders today. Over the next three decades, Dora toured the world surfing while on the run from U.S. authorities pursuing him for charges of credit card fraud. He spent most of the 1970s in the Gisborne region of New Zealand but was eventually extradited back to the United States where he spent a short time in prison. Dora made France his base for most of the 1990s from which he embarked on surf trips to Africa and around Europe. Sightings and correspondences with Dora appeared sporadically within the surfing media, and he made a rare appearance in the documentary, *Surfers: The Movie* (1990), while traveling and surfing in Mexico.

In 2001 rumor began to spread in the surfing community that Dora was seriously ill, and he returned to the United States where he died on 3 January 2002 at his father's home in Montecito, California, from inoperable pancreatic cancer. A short interview with Dora conducted three weeks before his death appeared in a memorial issue of *The Surfer's Journal*. An article written by Dora, "The Aquatic Ape," also appeared posthumously in *The Surfer's Journal* later that year. In it Dora stipulated an alternative form of surfing contest, which was enacted in 2005 and recorded in the 2006 film, *Chasing Dora*. The "Dora Lives" graffiti has been painted over by the city of Malibu several times, but it perennially reappears, and it was reconsecrated by the spray can work of world longboard champion Joel Tudor in the 2004 film, *Sprout*. Recent and forthcoming projects about Dora include an anthology, *Dora Lives*. The cinematic rights to Miki Dora's life story have recently been acquired by Leonardo DiCaprio, who reportedly plans to star as "Da Cat."

Kevin Fisher

Further Reading

Cleary, B. (1963). Miki Dora: The angry young man of surfing. *Surf Guide Magazine, 1*(7).

Cleary, B. (1964). Malibu: Characters and waves. *Surf Guide Magazine. 2*(10).

Dora, M. (1965). Mickey Dora speaks out. *Surfer Magazine, 6*(5).

Dora, M. (2003). The aquatic ape. *The Surfer's Journal, 12*(1).

Kampion, D. (1997). *Stoked: A history of surf culture.* Los Angeles: General Publishing.

Kohner, F., & Kohner-Zuckerman, K. (1962). *Gidget.* New York: Berkeley Publishing Group.

Pezman, S. (2002). The Cat's ninth life. *The Surfer's Journal, 11*(2), 86–91.

Stecyk, C.R., & Kampion, D. (2005). *Dora lives: The authorized story of Miki Dora.* Los Angeles: T. Alder Books.

Weller, S. (2006, August). Malibu's lost boys. *Vanity Fair,* 120–133.

Eisenberg, Arlo

Arlo David Eisenberg (b. 1973) is a pioneer in aggressive inline skating. He was born in Dallas, Texas, to Arthur and Vicki Eisenberg, both originally from Kansas City, Missouri. His sister, Josie Brook Eisenberg, is married to inline skater Chris Smith.

Eisenberg has a passion for art, and his parents recognized that passion while he was attending Hamilton Park Elementary at the age of nine. He went to W. E. Greiner Middle School and polished his artistic talents at the Arts Magnet, part of the Booker T. Washington High School for the Performing and Visual Arts. During high school Eisenberg noticed some Rollerblades and discovered that they could be used in a sport that involves aspects of ice skating and skateboarding, thus the evolution of aggressive inline skating.

Eisenberg attended the University of Texas for three semesters, but his love for roller skating dominated his passion for art. He began his skating career on the National Inline Skating Series (NISS), the first tour for skaters. He won the first NISS championship for street competition in 1994. He then entered the Aggressive Skaters Association (ASA) tour, winning the championship in 1995, 1996, and 1998. He also won the second X Games in inline street skating in 1996.

Eisenberg began promoting aggressive inline skating in 1993 by starting Senate, an accessory company that made such items as wheels, grind plates, bearings, socks, combs, T-shirts, and jeans. He wrote editorial content for *Daily Bread*, the first magazine for skaters, of which he was editor at one time. Eisenberg also was involved in *Hoax 2*, a video that was influential in developing inline skating.

In 1997 he opened Eisenbergs Skatepark in Dallas, one of the first complexes catering to inline skaters, skateboarders, and bikers. His family operates the park. He helped design the first skates for aggressive inline skaters, the Majestic 12. He hosts the annual Texas Showdown at the Hoedown, a competition free of judges that showcases skaters from all over the globe, held at Eisenbergs Skatepark.

Eisenberg also provides graphic design services to skate brands such as Xsjado, Salomon, and USD. He creates all the designs for Franco Shade, a clothing company, and broadcasts for the LG Action Sports Championships Series. He has a daughter, LuLu Ann Eisenberg, from his previous marriage to Lisa Keller. He resides in Santa Ana, California.

Jose Angel Pablo Alaniz

See also Inline Skating

Further Reading

Arlo. (n.d.). Myspace.com. Retrieved May 16, 2006, from http://searchresults.myspace.com/index.cfm?fuseaction=advancedFind.results&websearch=1&spotId=2

Arlo Eisenberg of the United States. (n.d.). Skatelog.com. Retrieved May 24, 2006, from http://skatelog.com/skaters/arlo-eisenberg

Eisenbergs. (n.d.). Myspace.com. Retrieved May 17, 2006, from http://myspace.com/eisenbergs

Hensell, L. (1997, May 2). Arlo's family starts extreme skate park in Plano. *Dallas Business Journal*. Retrieved May 18, 2006, from http://www.bizjournals.com/dallas/stories/1997/05/05/story4.html

Who is the digital messiah? (n.d.). Retrieved May 16, 2006, from http://www.thedigitalmessiah.com/about.html

Extreme Ironing

One day in 1997 Phil Shaw returned home from working in a Leicester, England, knitwear factory and felt like doing anything but his ironing. To make the best of a less-than-desirable situation, Shaw combined his love of rock climbing with his need to iron his clothes. He carried his ironing board, an extension cord, and his wrinkled clothes into his back garden and created the newest sport for thrill seekers—extreme ironing.

Shaw (nicknamed "Steam") and his roommate Paul Cartwright (nicknamed "Spray") began perfecting techniques for the new sport and soon recruited friends and others. They formed the Extreme Ironing Bureau to promote development of the sport.

Two years later Shaw and a fellow ironer, nicknamed "Short Fuse," launched a worldwide tour, promoting the sport in the United States, Fiji, New Zealand, Australia, and southern Africa. While in New Zealand, they met a group of Germans whose members were excited by the new sport and whose pants needed ironing. This meeting led to formation of Extreme Ironing International and the German Extreme Ironing Section (GEIS).

A Man of the Cloth

Shaw defines extreme ironing as "a sport involving ironing clothes outdoors in dangerous or unusual locations" (Shaw 2003). Participants, called "ironists," iron in locations ranging from the remote to the inhospitable and from dangerous to unusual. They may combine ironing with another sport, including rock climbing, canoeing, scuba diving, and surfing.

Underwater Press

In extreme ironing, the focus isn't always on getting the wrinkles out. Sometimes it's the journey the athletes take, especially when ironing underwater (as evidenced by the extract below from extremeironing.com).

Another week, another world record. The world depth record for ironing under water has yet again been broken—or more accurately reclaimed—by Louise Trewavas, aka Dive Girl. The London Eye is 135m high. The new world record for extreme ironing, set by Louise Trewavas (Dive Girl) is a depth of 137m (452 feet).

According to Dive Girl's press release, she: "took an ironing board and iron to 137m in the Blue Hole, at the Red Sea resort of Dahab, to reclaim her extreme ironing world record. The event took place on 17 August [2006] and was captured on underwater video by dive buddy Steve Brown. Dive computers carried by both divers recorded the depth of the dive, and the divers had to spend over three hours in the water carrying out decompression stops in order to avoid the bends."

It looks pretty straight to us and we're happy to re-award the status of world record holder to Louise. Here at the EIB, we're not surprised she's taken the steps to reclaim her crown—just a little surprised it was so quick.

The extreme ironing underwater record was first set by the 39-year-old Londoner in 2003 with an impressive display of linen-pressing at 100m. Last month, however, Teignmouth-based diver John Rudolph challenged for the title by ironing a T-shirt on a 129m dive.

Not to be out-laundered, Louise Trewavas sank to new depths to reclaim her title. "Records are there to be broken, but the boys will have to do better than that if they want to beat me. Bring it on," Louise says.

Source: Dive girl goes to new depths to re-claim record. (2006). Retrieved September 1, 2006, from http://www. extremeironing.com/modules.php?op=modload&name= News&file=article&sid=145&mode=thread&order= 0&thold=0

Thus, ironists are able to spend the weekend participating in an extreme sport and return to work on Monday with a well-pressed shirt or blouse.

Although ironists focus on the extreme nature of the sport, the Extreme Ironing Bureau encourages novices to train in safer environments to acquaint themselves with the heat of the irons. Shaw notes that rock climbing is difficult enough and that the addition of the weight of the ironing board and the heat of the iron dramatically increases the level of difficulty.

How the iron is powered is one of the biggest mysteries to nonironists. In competition power sources are made available to contestants, with each iron hot enough to iron one shirt. Therefore, part of the challenge is to complete the ironing before losing heat. Although battery-powered irons are under consideration, they have not yet entered mainstream extreme ironing. Other power sources include generators, long extension cords, and primus stoves to heat the iron's plate. Just as important as the iron is the ironing board, and although improvised boards have been used routinely, Shaw notes that there is no substitute for the thrill of getting a full-size board into a unique setting.

A New Wrinkle

Although extreme ironing originated from rock climbing, as the sport grew in popularity, other styles evolved. In forest style ironing, for example, one irons in the forest—on the ground, in trees, in rainforests, or in the bush. Such locales offer the ironist privacy and are recommended for newcomers to the sport. Water style ironing, originating in Germany in 1997, is considered to be a level higher than forest style. Although ironing in the water at first seems contradictory and counterproductive, Shaw notes that ironing typically involves water sprayed from the iron. Water style ironing, he says, simply takes that process to the next logical step. Underwater style takes that process still further. This style typically requires scuba diving equipment and a wet suit to protect the ironist from the cold water. Urban style ironing involves ironing on the street in front of large crowds. Although this style is characterized by the Extreme Ironing Bureau as moderate, it requires the ironist to use skateboarding and rollerblading techniques. Freestyle ironing also has a moderate difficulty rating. In this style "anything goes." It combines freedom of movement, imagination, and artistic expression with the thrill of an extreme sport. Freestyle ironing has been performed while engaged in synchronized swimming, bouncing on a trampoline, skating on ice, and creating a human pyramid, with the ironing board and ironist on top. Rocky style commonly involves climbing mountains or cliffs and ironing clothes at the peak. It has been called the "king of extreme ironing" and has been voted the most popular. Shaw notes that extreme ironing purists claim this style is the only true form of the sport, requiring both high skill levels and strong nerves. Rocky style ironing gained popularity when a group of ironists based in London scaled the French Alps to iron tea towels. More than any other style, this one requires at least one partner, both for the technique of climbing and for safety. The final style is underground, in which ironists take their ironing into caves. This is one of the newest styles and is slowing gaining in popularity.

Some Like It Hot

Extreme ironing has spread around the world from England. In 1999 the British Extreme Ironing Team launched its Join the Extreme Ironing Club Tour to encourage other countries to start their own teams. This tour was successful, with ironists appearing first in Germany in 2000 and then in twenty other countries, including Australia, Austria, Canada, Chile, Croatia, Iceland, Japan, Madagascar, New Zealand, South Africa, Taiwan, and the United States. The German Extreme Ironing Section (founded in 2000) put its research and development team to work and introduced ironists to *eso* ironing, a combination of ironing and meditation. The Austrian Extreme Ironing Team One was founded in 2002.

As the home of the sport, Great Britain naturally has a strong extreme ironing following. Well versed in many, if not all, of the ironing styles, British ironists take the sport seriously. Their bitter rivals, the German team, run by the GEIS, are the largest group of ironists outside of Great Britain. GEIS hosted the first Extreme Ironing World Championships in Munich in 2002. GEIS also developed a nonpowered sport iron, used effectively in water style ironing and more recently in *eso* ironing.

Founder Shaw has noticed differences in extreme ironing in different countries, most notably in the abilities of ironists. For example, Australian ironists, in keeping with their local terrain, are more likely to master ironing styles involving water. Ironists in Australia are so adept at water style (and underwater style) that they hosted the first extreme ironing competition outside of Europe. Similarly, ironists in New Zealand also excel at water style. Icelandic

ironists are skilled climbers who prefer rocky style, in keeping with their country's mountains, glaciers, volcanoes, and waterfalls. Similarly, Austrians prefer rocky style as well, which reflects their love of altitude and sports involving climbing.

Pressed Fest

The first Extreme Ironing World Championships included twelve teams from ten countries. This competition required ironists to compete in all five styles and to iron a variety of fabrics. Competitors were judged on their athletic skills as well as their ironing skills. It was only fitting that Great Britain, the home of extreme ironing, won the gold medal.

In competitions contestants move from station to station, using a different ironing style at each. They carry their full-size ironing board with them from task to task, and preheated irons are available at each station. Each style has its own team of international judges to assess each ironist on the speed of his or her transition from station to station, the style and level of difficulty of each move, and the quality of the ironing.

In addition to the larger competitions, smaller competitions are becoming more prevalent, including the Australian Extreme Underwater Ironing Competition. Similarly, the Rowenta Tour was established by the Extreme Ironing Bureau in 2004 to bring the sport to the United States and included events at Mount Rushmore in South Dakota, New York City, Boston, and Devils Tower, Wyoming.

For people who want the thrill of competition but have a limited travel budget, the sport has photography competitions. The Extreme Ironing Bureau sponsors a competition in which ironists submit photographs of extreme ironing for judging.

Ironist Joe "Ironinside" Sterling notes that although it is best for ironists to have a photo to prove they were there and did the ironing, the point of the sport is to have fun, not to prove themselves. The competitions are just the icing on the cake.

Full Steam Ahead

Extreme ironists have asked the International Olympic Committee to include the sports in the Olympic Games, although they have had little success so far. With the 2012 Olympic Games to be held in England, they have renewed their efforts, hoping to at least showcase the sport at the Games.

The words of Phil Shaw (2003) sum up the sport: "Extreme ironing is the latest danger sport that combines the thrills of an extreme outdoor activity with the satisfaction of a well pressed shirt."

Beth Pamela Skott

Further Reading

Pearson, H. (2006). In their element. *Eastern Airways Magazine*. Retrieved August 9, 2006, from http://www.easternairways.com/files/e-mag.pdf

Shaw, P. (2003). *Extreme ironing*. London: New Holland Publishers.

Extreme Media

Specialist magazines and films have long played a major role in the diffusion of values and attitudes among members of subcultures, including those of sports. More recently videos, DVDs, and websites have joined these niche media in assisting the communication among members of subcultures, including those of extreme sports. Four examples of these niche media are *Big Brother* skateboarding magazine, *Blunt* snowboarding magazine, *Jackass* videos, and *Whiskey* videos. These niche magazines and videos target a particular cohort of extreme sports enthusiast: the young male. In so doing, they help produce and reproduce the fratriarchal cultures at the core of skateboarding, snowboarding, and other extreme sports.

A fratriarchy is a group of young men whose members compete for prestige through demonstrations of physical prowess, courage, and gameness. A fratriarchy is the "rule of the brother-hoods." Remy notes that a fratriarchy (1) "is a mode of male domination which is concerned with a quite different set of values from those of patriarchy"; (2) "is based simply on the self-interest of the association of men itself"; (3) "reflects the demand of a group of lads to have the 'freedom' to do as they please, to have a good time"; and (4) "implies primarily the domination of the *age set* .. of young men who have not taken on family responsibilities" (Remy as cited in Loy 1995, 265). Across the social world young men engage in action situations in which they display, test, and subject their behavior to social evaluation. Not surprisingly, this fratriarchal behavior is apparent in skateboarding and snowboarding; in 2005 the average age of skateboarders was

fourteen, and approximately 75 percent of these participants were male. The same year more than 75 percent of snowboarders were under the age of twenty-four, and between 60 and 70 percent were male. Thus, young men in their late teens and early twenties inevitably constitute a dominant force at the core of these extreme sports cultures. Indeed, *Big Brother* and *Blunt* magazines and *Jackass* and *Whiskey* videos epitomize the boarding fratriarchy.

Big Brother

Founded in 1992 by ex-professional skateboarder Steve Rocco, *Big Brother* magazine represented the "less-than-parent-friendly side of skateboarding" (Skim the Fat n.d., para. 1). As well as features, interviews, and photographs of progressive skateboarders, it included female nudity, profanities, stunts, and pranks. Despite, or perhaps because of, its R-18 rating, core skateboarders considered the magazine the "bible" (Purpus 2002, para. 7). *Big Brother* also produced a series of skateboarding videos (*Shit*, 1996; *Number Two*, 1998; *Boob*, 1999; *Crap*, 2001). Like the magazine, these videos constituted roughly one-third skateboarding and two-thirds pranks. *Crap*, for example, featured skateboarding footage and strippers, diapers, beer, cattle prods, fighting, and colorful language. In 1997 Larry Flynt Publications (publisher of more than thirty pornography magazines) purchased *Big Brother* magazine. Ironically, in an attempt to sell more magazines, the editors of *Big Brother* reduced the level of nudity.

However, in 2000 a Larry Flynt Publications employee accidentally confused the subscriber lists of *Big Brother* and *Taboo* (a hardcore pornography magazine). As a result, the predominately teenage male readership of *Big Brother* received a copy of the magazine touting "America's most twisted porn," and *Taboo* readers were issued the latest skateboarding magazine. *The Tonight Show with Jay Leno* parodied the mix-up and so alerted conservatives, particularly the parents of *Big Brother* subscribers, who were vociferous in their condemnation. Although the incident did little to damage the popularity of the magazine among core skateboarders, Larry Flynt Publications abandoned it in 2004.

Blunt

Inspired by "the hard-line editorials and risky content" of *Big Brother* (Blehm 2003, 27), snowboarders Ken Block and

A throng of photographers at a surfing competition. Source: Brook Thorpe.

Damon Way established *Blunt* snowboarding magazine in 1993. *Blunt* quickly gained cultural credibility among core snowboarders, who considered it authentic. Professional snowboarder Todd Richards described the *Blunt* formula as "alcohol, party, party, party, oh, and snowboarding," adding that "it was really popular among snowboarders and really unpopular among ski resorts, parents, and snowboarding companies because of its blatant disregard for authority. As well as covering the most progressive snowboarders, *Blunt* turned down advertising from big companies like Burton and Morrow" (Richards 2003, 162).

In 1998 *Blunt* folded under political and economic pressure. "Distributors and advertisers wanted mainstream readers, while mainstream readers' parents wanted a more subdued, politically correct publication," explained one industry insider (Blehm 2003, 33). Although it is difficult to know the extent of parents' control over the reading habits and tastes of their teenage sons, this example does highlight the politics involved in producing knowledge in extreme sport cultures. Despite *Blunt*'s appeal to core snowboarders, the magazine (much like its skateboarding equivalent, *Big Brother*) challenged the snowboarding industry. And with reduced advertising it withered. The juvenile pranks, softcore pornography, and disregard for authority promoted in *Big Brother* and *Blunt* magazines became hallmarks of the *Jackass* and *Whiskey* videos.

Jackass

The *Jackass* phenomenon began in the late 1990s with a group of male skateboarders in their late teens, including Johnny Knoxville and Bam Margera. They produced low-grade homemade videos featuring their friends performing dangerous acts (e.g., riding blindfolded), performing annoying stunts on unsuspecting members of the public (e.g., Knoxville hides in shrubbery at an exclusive golf course and sounds an air horn at golfers in midswing), and inflicting pain on themselves (e.g., Steve-O's "butterfly" involved his stapling his scrotum to his thighs) and their peers (e.g., firing crossbows at one another). Many members of the *Jackass* crew (e.g., Jeff Tremaine, Dave Carnie, Rick Kosick, Chris Pontius, Johnny Knoxville, and Dave England) worked for, or contributed to, *Big Brother* magazine. Indeed, the *Big Brother* videos provided a platform for professional skateboarder Johnny Knoxville to showcase his bizarre stunts and acts of self-mutilation. For example, in *Number Two* Knoxville was shot with a Taser, sprayed with Mace, and then shot while wearing a bulletproof vest. The destructive

behavior and indifference to their bodies exhibited by members of the *Jackass* crew found an enthusiastic audience in the skateboarding population.

In 2000 *Jackass* became a regular feature on MTV. Airing up to ten times per week, *Jackass* was the highest-rated show of the network, but its success attracted controversy. Although *Jackass* programs frequently featured warnings and disclaimers, critics blamed it for a number of deaths and injuries involving young males imitating the stunts. In 2000 Senator Joseph Lieberman (and other politicians) campaigned to have the program banned. In response MTV rescheduled *Jackass* after 10 P.M. and cancelled several spin-off projects, including a book and soundtrack. MTV continued to censor and edit *Jackass* content, which irked the show's cast and crew. Voicing his disapproval, Knoxville stated, "the most objectionable things will be taken out" and "all the funny things will be gone" (News Shorts 2001, para. 4). Frustrated by the constraints placed on them by MTV, members of the *Jackass* crew left the network at the end of the third season in 2002.

Later that year, however, the cast reunited to produce *Jackass: The Movie*, which earned more than $22 million in its opening weekend. The movie format allowed the *Jackass* crew to circumvent the censors. However, not all moviegoers appreciated the raw sense of humor. As one irritated reviewer wrote:

> Not long after the debut of the wacky stunt show so appropriately named "Jackass" on *MTV* young people all over the country could be found attempting to reproduce the nitwitted, cartoon-like stunts that star Johnny Knoxville and his team of human monkeys subject themselves to: jumping in front of moving cars, taking shopping cart rides down steep public streets, setting themselves on fire, etc. After the debut of "Jackass: The Movie," don't be surprised if you hear of some-less-than-bright Jackass-wannabe blowing his own genitals off. That's just one of the "stunts" that the Jackasses undertake in the film, though the penis technically stays attached. If you're into guys sticking odd things up their butts and in their mouths, hurling themselves into walls and off buildings, eating the uneatable, challenging alligators, hanging out in raw sewage, insulting the entire country of Japan, and then doing a lot of really sick stuff, then "Jackass: The Movie" is the film for you. (Cogshell 2002, para. 1)

Nonetheless, another reviewer saw the appeal:

Extreme Sports Participants

A recent international online survey of the media preferences of 1,100 extreme sports participants, conducted by researchers at Auburn University Montgomery, found:

Type of Media or Event	% of Participants Who Indicated Frequent Use
Online Forums/ Bulletin Boards	71%
Radio	52
Magazines	47
Newspapers	40
TV	40
Ipod/mp3	27
Concerts	21
Music Festivals	16
Myspace/Facebook	13
Satellite Radio	12

The respondents, from forty-eight U.S. states and forty other countries, were 86 percent male and 14 percent female. The median age group was 25–34 years old.

Source: Survey conducted by Carolyn Sara (Casey) Findley, M.B.A., Auburn University Montgomery. Supervised by Donald Raymond Self, D.B.A., Auburn University Montgomery.

The stunts like Wee-man, the midget, kicking himself in the head, and sounding off air horns during golf games make us 18- to 30-year-olds laugh until our cheeks are sore. "Jackass: The Movie" is what every bored teenager thinks of doing but can't because of laws, penalties, parents or lack of money. I mean, what person hasn't thought of renting a car and returning it totally destroyed? Knoxville acted out our destructive dreams in the movie when he returned his rental car after a stint in a demolition derby. (Townsend 2002, para. 11)

The juvenile masculinity exhibited in *Jackass* has found widespread acclaim among young men (and some women) across the Western world. Indeed, *Jackass* fans embraced the release in 2006 of a second full-length motion picture, *Jackass: Number Two*, with the film grossing US$29 million during its opening weekend alone.

Whiskey

The *Whiskey* videos produced by Canadian snowboarders Sean Kearns and Sean Johnson in the mid- to late 1990s epitomized the irreverence and hedonism at the core of the snowboarding culture. The low-budget *Whiskey* videos were the first to document these aspects of the boarding lifestyle and predated the *Jackass* phenomenon by at least three years. They featured young male snowboarders, many of whom were also keen skateboarders, consuming excessive amounts of alcohol, vomiting, performing violent acts against themselves and others (e.g., smashing empty beer bottles over their own heads or over their friends' heads, often repeatedly), and engaging in destructive behavior (e.g., smashing windows). Women appeared only as adjuncts of soft pornography. "In those days, *Whiskey* was the dope shit," recalls Kearns, "fuckin' smash, break and crash—that was it" (as cited in LeFebvre 2005, para. 9). In the first *Whiskey* video a conversation between snowboarder Kris Markovich (who is in the act of vomiting violently) and the unknown camera operator reveals the criteria for inclusion in these videos:

Kris: "Someone told me the only way to get into the *Whiskey* videos was to throw up."

Camera operator: "It's either that or you smash a bottle over your head. You choose the easier way."

Kris: "I'll do the bottle later." (*Whiskey: The Movie* 1994)

The men in the *Whiskey* and *Jackass* videos show a complete disregard for the safety and health of themselves and their friends. Despite the increasing professionalism in snowboarding and skateboarding since the production of these early videos, many of the stunts promoted in these videos retain force within the contemporary boarding cultures. For example, much like the stars of the *Whiskey* and *Jackass* videos, many young male (and some female) skaters and snowboarders accept injury and risk taking as part of the core boarding experience.

In recent years skateboarding and snowboarding have undergone rapid institutionalization and commercialization. Although contemporary skateboarding and snowboarding magazines and videos continue to represent the profane and hedonistic lifestyles of core participants, in this new context they tend to be more conservative than *Big Brother*, *Blunt*, *Jackass*, or *Whiskey*. Certainly these extreme forms of niche media found an audience among young male skateboarders and snowboarders in the 1990s, but the content offended many cultural outsiders (as well as some insiders). *Big Brother*, *Blunt*, *Jackass*, and *Whiskey* faced intense public scrutiny and censorship, and only *Jackass* survived.

Holly Thorpe

See also Meaning of Extreme, The; Media and Extreme Sport

Further Reading

Attwood, F. (2005). Tits and ass, porn and fighting: Male heterosexuality in magazines for men. *International Journal of Cultural Studies*, 8(1), 83–100.

Benwell, B. (Ed.). (2003). *Masculinity and men's lifestyle magazines*. Oxford, UK: Blackwell.

Benwell, B. (2004). Ironic discourse: Evasive masculinity in men's lifestyle magazines. *Men and Masculinities*, 7(1), 3–21.

Blehm, E. (2003). *Agents of change: The story of DC shoes and its athletes*. New York: Reagan Books.

Cogshell, T. (2002). *Jackass*: The movie. Retrieved April 9, 2006, from http://www.boxoff.com/scripts/fiw.dll?GetReview?&where=ID& terms=6997

Kearns, S. and Johnson, S. (1994) *Whiskey: The movie*. TSP Productions.

LeFebvre, E. (2005, August 29). Shut the f—k up (an interview with Sean Kearns). *Transworld Snowboarding*. Retrieved April 1, 2006, from http://www.transworldsnowboarding.com/snow/features/article/ 0,13009,1099403,00.html

Loy, J. W. (1995). The dark side of Agon: Fratriarchies, performative masculinities, sport involvement, and the phenomenon of gang rape. In K. H. Better & A. Rutten (Eds.), *International sociology of sport contemporary issues: Festschrift in honor of Gunther Luschen* (pp. 263–282). Stuttgart, Germany: Naglschmid.

News shorts. (2001, August 16). Retrieved October 30, 2006, from http://www.medialifemagazine.com/news2001/aug01/aug13/4_thurs/news7thursday.html

Purpus, M. (2002). Skate town, part 3. Retrieved October 30, 2006, from http://easyreader.hermosawave.net/news2002/sotrypage.asp

Richards, T. (2003). *P3: Parks, pipes and powder*. New York: Harper Collins.

Skim the fat: Your guide to skateboarding videos. (n.d.). Retrieved from http://www.skimthefat.com/provideos/showvideo

Townsend, C. (2002, November 1). It's ok to laugh at *Jackass*. Retrieved April 9, 2006, from http://www.santacruzsentinel.com/archive/2002/November/01/style/stories/02style.htm

Wheaton, B. (2003). Lifestyle sport magazines and the discourses of sporting masculinity. In B. Benwell (Ed.), *Masculinity and men's lifestyle magazines* (pp. 193–221). Oxford, UK: Blackwell.

Ferreras Rodriguez, Francisco

Francisco "Pipin" Ferreras Rodriguez (b. 1962) is one of free diving's best known and most controversial figures. Millions of fans in Europe, Latin America, and Japan know the Cuban-born champion by the single name, Pipin. Swimming since infancy, he began competing in Europe and soon set a constant-ballast record of 58 meters before emigrating from Cuba to the United States in 1993.

After setting a world record for no-limits free diving in 1996 by riding a weighted sled 116 meters beneath the sea and rocketing back to the surface under an inflated lift bag, Pipin reportedly turned his attention to business ventures that included a dive shop and a Miami, Florida, nightclub. Both of those efforts failed. He continued diving, performing spectacles such as "two-breath" dives, using a single breath from a scuba tank to extend the depth of an otherwise standard no-limits dive. He also pursued a vigorous campaign to promote both the sport of free diving and his own public image, leading the United States representative to the Confédération Mondiale des Activitiés Subaquatiques (CMAS) to dismiss him as "a freak show." As the international body that coordinates underwater sports, CMAS stopped sanctioning no-limits free diving over safety concerns in 1970. Pipin himself broke away from the Association Internationale pour le Développement de l'Apnée (AIDA) that had emerged to support free diving, including no-limits diving, helping to found the International Association of Free Divers (IAFD) instead.

Pipin met French marine biology student Audrey Mestre (1975–2002) in 1996. The two were wed shortly thereafter, and Audrey quickly became a champion free diver herself. On 12 October 2002, her attempted IAFD world-record no-limits dive of 148 meters turned fatal. She reached the target depth, but the three-minute dive extended to over eight minutes before she was pulled from the water unconscious by her husband. IAFD subsequently recognized one of her practice dives, to 147 meters, as the new world record.

This was not the first accident involving Pipin. In 1996 two of his safety divers reportedly died while supporting his training dives. Pipin suffered an apparent case of decompression sickness while training for a 1997 "two-breath" dive. In that incident he followed a "two-breath" descent to 105 meters with a scuba dive to 52 meters to retrieve the sled used during his first dive.

Pipin became determined to complete the record dive that had claimed his wife, doing so on the first anniversary of her death. The story of their romance and diving careers is recounted in Pipin's book, *The Dive: A Story of Love and Obsession.*

Jeffery A. Charlston

Further Reading

Ferreras, F. (2004). *The dive: A story of love and obsession.* New York: Regan.

Pelizzarri, U., & Tovaglieri, S. (2004). *Manual of freediving: Underwater on a single breath.* Naples, Italy: Idelson Gnocchi.

Mick Foley

Mick Foley (b. 1965), the "Hardcore Legend," is a professional wrestler and author, and his name is almost synonymous with extreme forms of pro wrestling. His ability, and willingness, to take risks and withstand punishment in the "fake" world of pro wrestling have made a lasting impression on the business.

Mick Foley was born on 7 June 1965, and raised on Long Island, New York. He began wrestling in his own backyard in the early 1980s, where he acted out matches with his friends. A frequently replayed home movie from this time shows Foley diving off his roof onto a mattress below. As cultural studies scholar Sut Jhally states in the 2002 documentary, *Wrestling with Manhood: Boys, Bullying, and Battering,* Foley became an icon within backyard wrestling circles. So-called backyard wrestling federations formed across the U.S., as well as England, starting in the 1990s. The federations gave thousands of young (mostly) men a chance to emulate often dangerous moves of trained professional wrestlers. Most are very small and informal, with matches held, literally, in participants' backyards (or their parents'). Most matches are characterized to some extent by at least some of the characteristics of extreme wrestling, including the use of ladders, barbed wire, and fire, among other props. In one of his books, Foley warned backyard wrestlers against taking extreme risks and suggested that they get proper in-ring training.

Foley began wrestling professionally in 1985 and worked on the independent wrestling circuit for several years. He quickly became known for his propensity to take painful "bumps" and work through pain. For example, while working a match in Munich for World Championship

Wrestling in March of 1994, Foley became entangled in the ring ropes, his right ear was torn off, and he still finished the match. In August of 1995, he traveled to Japan, where he won the prestigious IWA Japan King of the Death match tournament. The final match, against friend and mentor Terry Funk, was an exploding barbed wire match that left both wrestlers badly bloodied and burned. Though choreographed, exploding barbed wire matches are highly dangerous matches in which explosive C4 charges are fixed to barbed wire-wrapped boards. At a designated point in the match, a wrestler falls or is thrown into the wire, which triggers the usually low-level explosion. After returning to Eastern Championship Wrestling (ECW) in 1995, Foley began an "anti-hardcore" gimmick, which was partly a response to some fans desire to see increasing levels of blood and injuries in matches.

Foley's next major step toward mainstream celebrity came in 1996, when he entered the WWE as "Mankind," a character who wore a leather mask during his matches. Foley was given the WWE championship belt three times, and in 1998 Vince McMahon awarded Foley the first ever "Hardcore" title belt. Foley's presence is often credited as helping to usher in the WWE "Attitude" era, which was partly characterized by an increased emphasis on more extreme matches. Foley's most enduring image in the WWE, however, came in the "Hell in a Cell" cage match in 1998, where he took two heavily replayed bumps, one from the top of a 16-foot cage and another through the roof of the cage onto the mat below. One book notes that this match "reinvented the standard by which high-risk wrestling was judged" (Assael and Mooneyham 2004, 201).

In 1999 Foley published his first autobiography at a time when he was still wrestling in WWE, and he was the first major wrestling figure to release an autobiographical, non-kayfabe (i.e., written largely out of character) book without a ghostwriter. He also gained mainstream attention in the well-reviewed Barry Blaustein documentary film, *Beyond the Mat*. Foley has also been politically outspoken, having attended the Democratic National Convention in 2004, and he received praised from the U.S. military for his visits to troops. As of June 2006, Foley is semiretired, and he has wrestled sparingly since his first official retirement in 2000. However, he has occasionally reentered the ring for hardcore matches. Most recently, Foley participated in a tag match against sixty-one-year-old Terry Funk, in which they both became entangled in barbed wire.

Ted Butryn

Further Reading

Assael S., & Mooneyham, M. (2004). *Sex, lies, and headlocks: The real story of Vince McMahon and World Wrestling Entertainment*. New York: Three Rivers Press.

Foley, M. (1999). *Have a nice day!: A tale of blood and sweatsocks*. New York: Regan Books.

Foley, M. (2001). *Foley is good: And the real world is faker than wrestling*. New York: Regan Books.

Jhally, S. (2002). *Wrestling with manhood: Boys, bullying, and battering* [Film]. Northhampton, MA: Media Education Foundation.

Kulkus, E. (2004, July 28). How to get the youth vote: Beauties and the beasts. *Post-Standard*, p. A9.

Loverro, T. (2005, August 3). Wrestler a legend among hurt troops. *Washington Times*, p. A01.

Pope, K., & Whebbe Jr., R. (2003). *The encyclopedia of professional wrestling* (2nd ed.). Iola, WI: Krause Publications.

Foucan, Sébastien

One of *parkour*'s most vocal leaders is Sébastien Foucan (b. 1975), a thirty-one-year-old Frenchman who began the sport with his childhood friend, David Belle. *Parkour* is the sport of using existing urban structures to create a sort of obstacle course. This intense athlete encourages others to enjoy the thrill of *parkour*, but he also applies his own philosophy to the sport, giving it deeper meaning. Additionally, he works to increase awareness of *parkour* throughout the world through his appearances on television and in movies. His dedication to his craft has become a way of life for him and his followers.

Foucan developed the sport of *parkour* with Belle in the Paris suburb of Lisse. *Parkour*'s big break came with two documentaries on the British Channel 4. *Jump London* and *Jump Britain* featured *parkour*'s founders practicing their new sport at popular sites around the British Isles. This publicity for the sport and for Foucan led to further opportunities. The *parkour* group he started with Belle, Yamakasi, was picked to be the center of a film, *Yamakasi—Les samouraï des temps modernes*. After the film, the two split for ideological differences. Belle felt that the film criminalized *parkour*, and he opposed the commercialization of the sport, while Foucan liked the film and how it portrayed *parkour*.

Foucan was heavily influenced by Asian philosophies and forms of movement, such as Tai Chi, and takes *parkour* very seriously, even creating his own personal philosophy

to back the sport and enhance its meaning. On his Web site, http://*parkour*.com, Foucan calls *parkour* an "evolution of the mind." His goal is to have people think about their actions, looking past simple actions to realize how moving from point to point physically can help one overcome obstacles in personal life as well. For Foucan, *parkour* is a lifestyle, one that helps create balance in life and combat negative energies.

As Foucan grew and evolved within *parkour*, so did his practice of the sport. Many consider what he does, free running, to be a branch of *parkour*. In a post on foucan.com, he states that "free-running is following your own way, and this is my way." As an offshoot of the original *parkour*, free running is more comprehensive, including using more of Foucan's philosophy to help determine its movements.

Today, Foucan regards himself as a worldwide ambassador of his style of free running. He uses many means of publicity, including stunts such as the one he performed at Millennium Stadium in Wales. He jumped across a 39-foot gap in the retractable roof, 295 feet above the ground, actually having to repeat the feat when the cameraman failed to properly catch it on film. Foucan trained the new James Bond, Daniel Craig, in the ways of *parkour* for his starring role in *Casino Royale*, in which the sport plays a large part. Foucan also has a featured role in the film. Most recently, Foucan joined Madonna's Confessions tour as an on-stage performer along with several other *traceurs*, and the sport's followers are known.

As Foucan continues to promote his sport, he keeps in mind its dangerous nature. His website has many warnings and he personally reminds fans of the training and precautions necessary to safely practice free running. What started as a game with a friend has grown into an empire for Sébastien Foucan. His public appearances, commercial website, and athletic talent all ensure that he will be a front-runner within the *parkour* world for many years to come.

Dana M. Weigel

Further Reading

Freerunning World. Retrieved April 10, 2006, from http://www.foucan.forumactif.com

Madge spider dance. (2006, April 9). *Sunday Mirror*. p. 3.

Powers, K. No strings attached. (2006, April 23). *Los Angeles Times*. p. 22.

Seb's into the groove. (2006, April 23). *Wales on Sunday*. p. 17.

Smith, L. C. (October, 2003). Le *parkour*. Rolling Stone, 95.

France

The mountains of France cover 102,000 square kilometers, accounting for one-fifth of the nation's area. Of this mountainous area, 1,200 square kilometers (1.18 percent) are equipped for winter sports. France has 357 ski resorts on six mountain ranges: the Alps, Pyrenees, Massif Central, Jura, Les Vosges, and Corsica, constituting one of the great skiing areas of the world. Every year eight million people, 20 percent of them foreigners, practice winter sports in France. This number is one-fourth of the European market, surpassing the number of skiers in Austria, Switzerland, and Italy. The selection of ski slopes and ski lifts, the quality of the snow, and the potential for off-trail skiing on virgin snow are among the main attractions of French ski resorts.

For the past few years the stations have joined efforts to increase access skiable grounds by adding features such as ski lifts, as one example, to offer the consumer a better and more sophisticated skiing experience. For example, the North Alps in Savoie (composed of the valleys of St. Bon,

A snowboarder catching air over the Alps. Source: istock.

Avalanche Statistics

It is notoriously difficult to collect comprehensive worldwide statistics about avalanches. The Cyber Snow and Avalanche Centre, however, keeps a running tally of avalanche accidents and fatalities each year.

A quick analysis of its incident pages shows around 200 deaths from avalanches each year, although this probably represents only a proportion of the true figure; compared to the number of road deaths worldwide, avalanches are not a major killer.

The fact is that you are far more likely to die traveling to or from a ski resort than in an avalanche. But that is little comfort for the thousands of people whose lives have been ruined by losing a loved one in this tragic way.

Ski and Ride Safely
The ferocity of the 1998/99 European winter can clearly be seen in the jump to 95 fatalities from 20–30 deaths in previous seasons.

Source: Cyber Snow and Avalanche Centre. Retrieved February 1, 2007 from http://www.ifyouski.com/avalanche/nivologie/

Avalanche Fatalities by Geography and Year

Continent	1996/97	1997/98	1998/99	1999/00	2000/01
North America	33	48	49	35	21
Europe	31	20	95	54	30
Asia	109	45	42	11	3
Latin America	2	3	—	7	—
Australia/New Zealand	3	—	—	2	—
Russia & ex–CIS	4	57	8	19	—
Middle East (Turkey, Iran, etc.)	6	47	4	20	12
Total	188	220	198	148	66

Allues, and Bellevilles) have five resorts of international standard making it today's biggest skiing domain in the world.

Some resorts are known for extreme (off-piste) skiing. The most famous are Chamonix and La Grave, which are located, respectively, at the foot of Mont Blanc (4,810 meters) and La Meije (3,982 meters). During the past fifteen years the practices of ski touring and snowboarding (with ascents with sealskins or snowshoes) have also developed as an alternative to skiing at resorts. However, the use of helicopters for this kind of skiing is still forbidden in France.

The first ski resort constructed in France was Megève, built in 1920. At the time people practiced only cross-country skiing. A major revolution occurred a few years later with the invention of the ski lift, inaugurated in 1933 at Rochebrune in Megève.

Since then many ski resorts and ski lifts have been built. Construction peaked during the 1960s. During the 1970s the mountains' urbanization policy was contested by those worried about the number of buildings that were being added to the mountain landscape, and the sports practiced in the ski resorts were diversified, in particular with the addition of snowboarding. These transformations had their origins in the evolution of French society in general and in the evolution of sporting practices in particular. They also were influenced by the U.S. counterculture ideology of the 1960s.

Skiing is still the first winter sport in France, but snowboarding now claims one-fourth of the market.

Véronique Reynier and Kévin Vermeir

See also Skiing; Snowboarding

Further Reading

Arnaud, D. (1975). *La neige empoisonnée* [The poisoned snow]. Paris: Moreau.

Bosso, A., & Lazier, I. (1994). *La grande histoire du ski* [The big story of skiing]. Grenoble, France: Musée Dauphinois.

Cognat, B. (1973). *La montagne colonisée* [The colonized mountain]. Paris: Les Editions du Cerf.

Reynier, V., Vermeir, K., & Soulé, B. (2004). Sports d'hiver. Les nouvelles glisses se banalisent [Winter sports: New practices become mainstream]. *Revue Espaces, 214,* 12–14.

Ski France. (2006). Retrieved August 15, 2006, from http://www.ski france.fr/index.cfm?fuseaction=sf.mag&langue=fr&IDA=14

Free Diving

Free diving, also known as skin diving, is the act of submerging beneath the water's surface sustained only by the air in one's lungs. Any swimmer who plunges beneath the surface for a closer look at the aquatic world transitions into free diving. As such it is an ancient activity, long practiced to hunt for food or otherwise pursue underwater goals without the complicated life-support systems found in scuba diving. Groups such as Japan's pearl divers or Mediterranean sponge divers perfected the basic techniques of free diving long before it developed into a popular recreational activity or extreme sport.

Recreation

Like scuba diving, free diving emerged as a popular form of recreation following World War II. The availability of fins, specialized goggles, and other equipment made free diving more accessible and enjoyable. Underwater hunting in particular benefited from the new technology. In the 1950s and 1960s, thousands of new enthusiasts around the world took up spear fishing or shellfish collection as forms of recreation, rather than as a means of subsistence or commercial activity. As a result the population of many species declined precipitously in popular hunting areas, a process accelerated by the introduction of scuba diving equipment to underwater hunting. Hunting with either form of diving has become increasingly regulated since the 1970s, and both diving communities have become active in environmental issues.

Unlike scuba divers, free divers are not subject to decompression sickness or nitrogen narcosis since they do not use external life support equipment. Free diving does not require any equipment, but it does benefit from some simple tools. Fins for improved motion and a diving mask, swimming goggles that enclose the nose so that the pressure in their internal air space can be equalized with external water pressure, make the activity far more enjoyable. A snorkel permits normal breathing while the face is submerged, and many people unknowingly join the ranks of free divers when they transition from swimming with a snorkel to fully entering the aquatic environment. Finally, many free divers find a wetsuit very useful indeed. In addition to protection from the sun and other environmental hazards, a wetsuit provides welcome warmth during long excursions or in colder waters.

Hazards

As an extension of swimming, the basic dangers of free diving are well known to anyone fond of the water. Hazards such as sunburn and jellyfish stings are by no means unique to free diving. Shallow water blackout is another matter entirely.

As a diver submerges, her body is subject to increasing pressure. This phenomenon is felt in the air spaces of the ears and diving mask, if one is used, and requires equalization of their internal pressure with the pressure of surrounding water. The lungs are also affected, as water pressure increases by one atmosphere for every 10 meters of descent. At 10 meters the volume of the lungs has been reduced to half their surface volume. Air contained within the lungs compresses to twice the surface pressure as a result, and the space that the lungs formerly filled in the chest cavity is filled with bodily fluids. On extended deep dives the increased pressure of the air in the lungs allows the diver to metabolize more of the oxygen that they contain than would be possible at the surface. If the diver allows this process to continue for too long, the remaining oxygen may not be sufficient to sustain consciousness as pressure decreases on ascent. Shallow water blackout follows.

For that and other safety reasons, free divers are well advised to never dive alone. A diver should always be

A free diver spear fishing for tuna off the northern-most part of the Philippines. Source: istock/Rex Crystal.

accompanied and supervised, particularly when experimenting with new skills or extending personal limits. At the recreational level free diving is a seemingly benign activity. But once a free diver leaves the surface, her life is dependent on the limited supply of air in her lungs and safe return to the surface.

Competition

Free diving can be extended into one of several competitive sports. Spear fishing contests are the most traditional, but the full range of underwater competition is greater than the uninitiated usually recognize. It includes the obscure sports of underwater hockey and apnea, competitions that push the human body up to, and occasionally beyond, its limitations in an alien and inherently deadly environment. A number of organizations have emerged to govern the potentially dangerous sport of apnea, the extreme form of free diving.

The Confédération Mondiale des Activités Subaquatiques (World Confederation of Underwater Activities) is the oldest and best known international organization governing underwater sports, including apnea. But the orga-

nization stopped sanctioning no-limits free diving in 1970 as a small group began pushing their dives to increasingly dangerous levels below beyond 100 meters. The Association Internationale pour le Developpement de l'Apnee (International Association for the Development of Apnea) developed to fill the gap, with member organizations in some forty countries by 2000. A rival organization, the International Association of Free Divers, emerged in the late 1990s despite the extremely small number of competitive free divers, indicating the continuing tensions within the community.

No-limits diving, ambiguously depicted by Luc Besson in his 1988 movie, *The Big Blue*, remains a controversial and extremely demanding sport. The diver rides a weighted sled down a line at great velocity in an attempt to reach the greatest possible depth and is carried back to the surface by an inflated lift bag. In this deepest form of apnea, a diver may experience over eighteen times surface pressure, with all of the accompanying physiological affects. The depths involved leave little room for error. Accompanying safety divers on scuba equipment have very few rescue options at such depths, and they are well below the generally accepted safe depth limits for scuba diving themselves. This can have tragic consequences for all concerned, as exempli-

fied by the 1996 deaths of two safety divers while free diver Francisco "Pipin" Ferreras Rodriguez trained for record-setting dives.

Other forms of apnea are more conservative. In variable ballast diving the athlete also descends on a sled, but must return to the surface under his own power by either kicking or pulling himself up the guideline. Constant ballast is regarded by many divers as the purest form of competitive free diving. In that event a diver is completely unassisted, descending and ascending only by kicking, using a guideline only for visual reference. Any weight carried down must also be carried up. Free immersion follows similar rules, but in this event the diver ascends and descends by pulling herself along the guideline.

Two forms of apnea are conducted in swimming pools. In dynamic apnea the competitor swims horizontally not more than 1 meter beneath the surface. The event is further subdivided, as participants swim unaided or with the use of fins. Finally, in static apnea the contestant floats face down in a swimming pool. The goal in both of these forms is to maximize the time spent underwater without breathing.

All forms of apnea match the individual's will power against the physical limitations of the human body in a dangerous and potentially fatal environment. In the 1999 world championships off Sardinia, the elite athletes reportedly suffered fifteen blackouts and one heart attack. Despite the potential dangers, apnea continues to grow in popularity. Champion free divers like Tanya Streeter have played an important role in popularizing the sport through their activities on behalf of environmental causes and marine education.

Underwater Hockey

Another form of free diving competition enjoys growing popularity in swimming clubs and on college campuses around the world. The sport of underwater hockey pits single-gender or mixed-gender teams of ten against each other in an effort to move a small metal disk across the bottom of a 2-meter-deep pool. Players use 30-centimeter bats resembling small hockey sticks to drive the disk into the opposing team's goal. All play is conducted underwater while free diving.

Developed by Great Britain's Royal Navy in the 1950s, the sport was originally as a way to improve the skills of

The Zen of Free Diving

Besides taking an incredible amount of endurance, stamina, energy, and lung capacity, free diving is also a mental challenge. But, in Palm Beach, Florida, there is a growing movement to focus on that mental, pure, aspect of free diving.

You float on the surface, breathing deep and slowly, watching the bottom 40 feet below you ... In tune with your body, you begin to slow your hear rate down ... 100 ... 90 ... 80 ... 70 ... 65 ... 55 beats per minute ...

With a last completely full breath, you jackknife, your feet rise up out of the water and their weight above its surface begins to thrust your body downward.

You take big, almost stiff–legged kicks, very slow frequency, but with large amplitude. You almost try to sleep your way down to the bottom, staying as relaxed as possible, exerting the minimum amount possible.

Twenty seconds later you are moving along the bottom about 50 feet deep, effortless and free, watching the antics of damselfish, triggers and the constant schools of mangrove snappers among the bright hues of sponges, gorgonians, and complex coral colonies.

You hit the surface exhaling hard through the snorkel, and the fresh taste of air has never felt so good. Your body feels somewhat heavy all over, from lactate developed throughout your body as it was forced to power you with anaerobic metabolism. You now pay back the oxygen debt, converting the blood lactate to a form of blood sugar (pyruvate), and your muscles begin to "sing" with new energy and they feel great. It's a perfect workout. Your focus and concentration improves with each dive, and the euphoria of the activity keeps you compelled towards several hours of more freedives until exhaustion suggests you retire until your next opportunity on another day.

Source: The zen of freediving. Retrieved February 1, 2007, from http://www.sfdj.com/sand/freedive.html

navy divers. Seemingly simple, it draws upon the skills of dynamic apnea, hand-eye coordination, and teamwork in a fast-paced athletic contest allowing for three-dimensional maneuvers. By its very nature underwater hockey is not a sport that is easily enjoyed by spectators, despite its resemblance to the popular sport of ice hockey. But it does feature biannual world championships and contests at the national, regional, and local levels in many countries.

Community

The social bonds formed by sharing exploration of the underwater world are part of the attraction of free diving. At the recreational level free divers form both their own community and share a sense of identity with scuba divers in a larger diving community. Resorts catering to scuba, free diving, and snorkeling may be found worldwide, and most scuba instructors can also provide basic instruction in free diving as an aspect of snorkeling. More advanced instruction in free diving and competitive apnea is available from a limited number of sources.

Competitors in apnea form an exclusive elite. Apnea competitions are heavily publicized in some nations, and the sport's fans significantly outnumber the number of participants. The sport is still very small in terms of absolute numbers, with contenders numbering in the thousands worldwide. The Internet has emerged as a significant force within the apnea community, where a number of dedicated websites and discussion forums provide information and a sense of community for the sport's widely dispersed enthusiasts.

Underwater hockey enjoys less publicity than apnea, but it boasts a larger total number of competitors. A participant sport by nature, its enthusiasts are also connected by Internet communications and informal networks. Underwater hockey draws on the skills of swimmers and free divers, and on better-known team sports such as ice hockey, water polo, and basketball. For that reason players tend to have a variety of other sporting interests, producing an unusually eclectic community bound by enjoyment of a most unusual sport.

Jeffery A. Charlston

Further Reading

Bookspan, J. (1995). *Diving physiology in plain English*. Kensington, MD: Undersea and Hyperbaric Medical Association.

Mass, T., & Sipperly, D. (1998). *Freedive!* Ventura, CA: Bluewater Freedivers.

Pelizzarri, U., & Tovaglieri, S. (2004). *Manual of freediving: Underwater on a single breath*. Naples, Italy: Idelson Gnocchi.

Gender

Extreme sports have a relatively short history. Many of them came into existence during the 1960s and 1970s at a critical juncture when increasing female participation challenged sports as an exclusive male bastion. Unlike in modern sports, females participated widely in the early forms of many extreme sports. Although fewer in number than men, women often participated alongside men, and thus it might be argued that extreme sports were not burdened by the years of entrenched sexism that plagues most other sports. Certainly some evidence suggests growing levels of participation and opportunities for women in extreme sports brought about by liberal endeavours supporting the development of strong, individual women who are unafraid to challenge their male counterparts. Yet, like most other modern sports, extreme sports are a social institution created by men for men.

Women and Risk

Extreme sports cultures have a strong emphasis on male physicality. Participants earn prestige and respect from their peers through displays of physical prowess, including finely honed combinations of skill, muscular strength, aggression, toughness, and, above all, courage. Among the general population such attributes are desirable or "natural" male traits. Everyday discourses and humor illuminate this perspective, as a joke in *Transworld Snowboarding* magazine, highlighting the commonly assumed differences between male and female participants, reveals:

> Question: What's the difference between snow-men and snow-women?
>
> Answer: Snow balls.

Extreme sports media regularly reinforce the popular belief that male participants are superior because they "have balls" and take more risks. The following narrative regarding Canadian free-ride mountain biker Darren Berrecloth is a good example:

> On a steep 30-degree descent . . . his front wheel came loose . . . his fork and his head dug into the rocks, knocking him unconscious and grinding his face into a mass of bleeding, rototilled skin. He

emerged from the hospital with ten stitches under his bottom lip, eight across the bridge of his nose, and puss and blood soaking through the bandages. Most people would have taken such a fall as a sign to stay away from mountain biking, but not "Bear Claw." The combination of pain and pleasure ignited a passion for the sport. (Brandt 2005, 110)

Engaging in risky behavior and sustaining injury prove dedication and toughness and are a masculinizing experience. Extreme sports magazines regularly feature photos of male participants proudly displaying gashes, black eyes, bruises, stitches, swelling, and broken bones, thus reinforcing the notion that these sports require manly courage. *Transworld Snowboarding* magazine emphasizes the health risks associated with aggressive boarding: "ever slam so hard that you get that weird metallic flavor in your mouth?" The article goes on to advise readers: "it's cerebral fluid released on impact" (Broken Off 2002, 168). Whereas some women happily engage risk, the glorification of physical injury in extreme sports cultures undoubtedly deters many more. As sports sociologist Helen Lenskyj argues, "the clearest way that . . . sport is consolidated as male territory is through the exclusion of women from sport on the basis that it is too risky" (Young, White, and McTeer 1994, 178).

Biological reductionism features strongly as an implicit defense of male superiority throughout extreme sports cultures. For example, surfer Buzzy Trent declared: "Girls are weaker than men and have a lesser chance of survival in giant wipeouts . . . Girls are better off and look more feminine riding average size waves" (Booth 2002, 3). According to one male snowboarder interviewed, named Tom: "Guys are always going to be better. Chicks are only just doing 900s [degrees of rotation on a jump or in the half-pipe]. Guys have been doing 900s for ages. They aren't strong enough. Girls are girls . . . they are always weaker, the average girl is scared to even put on a snowboard and go down the hill" (Tom, personal communication, August 2004).

Many of the attitudes surrounding female participation in extreme sports are informed by broader social expectations of what young women should and should not do. In particular, mainstream culture pressures women to protect their bodies and avoid dangerous situations that might cause injury. The following example is revealing. Having reached the summit of Switzerland's Mount Eiger in 1988, Alison Hargreaves stirred controversy when the public learned that she was five months pregnant. British journalist Nigella Lawson described her as personifying "me-first mountaineering" (Palmer 2002, 332); Hargreaves's climb represented a neurosis that "showed a reality-denying self-centeredness." "I was pregnant, not sick," Hargreaves countered. In 1995 she became the second person, male or female, to climb Mount Everest solo without using oxygen. However, in 1998 Hargreaves died descending her second successful summit of Mount Everest, and the media positioned her as an "errant, unthinking mother" rather than as an accomplished climber. She had "effectively abandoned her children by taking such extraordinary risks." The discourse of extremity is, as Catherine Palmer observes, "unquestionably highly gendered" (Palmer 2002, 332).

According to sports sociologist Lois Bryson, "women collude with male hegemony and largely accept the biological explanations offered for their 'inferior' performances, even when there is no validity for such explanations" (Bryson 1990, 175). Even though many female extreme sports enthusiasts display particular combinations of force and skill much more effectively than many male participants, the persistence of "normal" differences in physical ability remains one of the main ways in which the superiority of men becomes "naturalized." The key issue here is that these ideologies serve as symbolic proof of men's superiority and right to rule and work to justify women's exclusion from events and media outlets.

A Jump and a Leap of Faith

Many female extreme sports participants describe experiencing risk and dealing with fear differently from their male counterparts. Despite setting a Guinness world record for the longest jump on a motorcycle by a woman (48 meters), New Zealand freestyle motocross rider Mary Perkins believes "girls have a lot more fear than guys." After breaking her leg, Perkins admitted that regaining her confidence on her bike and getting over her "female fears" were "a real mental task" (cited in Simpson 2006, para. 10). When asked about the topic of fear, Olympic snowboarder Pamela Bell said she has "always admired how boys could have less fear. Girls have so much more self-preservation" (personal communication, September 2005). The authors of one study of skateboarding found that the fear of falling and getting hurt prevents more girls from taking up the sport. Interestingly, some women in extreme sports see the value in a more "feminine" approach to risk. Three-time world champion kitesurfer and instructor Cindy Mosey, for example, observes that her female students listen more and exercise

more caution than men. She suggests that this is perhaps one reason they tend to succeed.

Female extreme sports athletes often discuss the importance of acknowledging their fears and listening to their intuition; few males do the equivalent. Top U.S. climber Beth Rodden proclaims: "I'm not in it for the adrenaline. I'm not going out just to live on the edge. I get scared every time I go up, but you learn how to harness that" (Siber 2005, 32). Kristen Lignell, a U.S. mountaineer, observes gender differences in approaches to mountaineering and prefers climbing with women because their:

> egos don't get in the way as much as with men. Guys are more likely to get bummed because they think someone else might beat them to the top. That's such a guy thing. That's what usually gets men in trouble. As long as you don't have summit fever, you'll do better. No summit is worth injury or death. If we have to quit, we have to quit. I think that's why women make good mountaineers. They're patient. (Olsen 2001, 99)

Rock climber Lynn Hill also acknowledges the danger of the "male ego" and warns that "a climb is not an ego trip. If you let your ego get in the way of what you're trying to do, you're done before you start. Egotism is a very self defeating emotion" (Olsen 2001, 64). Although Hill has often been labeled an "extreme athlete," she refutes the label: "Extreme to me means doing something that is dangerous and risky. And that was never my motivation as a climber. It has nothing to do with how dangerous it is. [Successful climbing] involves listening to your inner voice, using your intuition" (Olsen 2001, 59) Clearly this "feminine" approach to risk taking worked for Hill, who in 1993 became the first person, male or female, to free climb the Nose at El Capitan (Yosemite Valley, California), "the most famous big wall climb in the world." This feat was not repeated until 2005, when husband and wife Tommy Caldwell and Beth Rodden "team freed" the route. Some extreme sports, such as climbing, clearly lend themselves to a more "feminine" approach.

Young women in the contemporary Western world are said to be more confident and resilient than ever before; they have "the world at their feet." At the same time research, journalism, and popular debates suggest increasing risk behaviors among young women. Tina-Marie Morrison, journalist for *The Dominion*, for example, describes the teen generation as alienated, cynical, experimental and increasingly savvy. In her words they "lose their virginity young, start smoking and taking drugs and are binge-drinking at 15." Moreover, a recent study of the risk-taking behaviors of young Australian women confirmed that 70 percent of women aged eighteen to twenty-three engage in "binge drinking," and twice the number of teenage girls use or experiment with drugs compared with their male counterparts. Simply put, contemporary young women are more readily engaging in risk-taking behaviors. This also seems true in the context of sports. More young women are participating in "risky" sports where the threat of injury is real. In fact, a recent study showed that 40 percent of all sports injuries in the United States were incurred by women. Furthermore, women accounted for 37 percent of all emergency rescue sports injuries. In some extreme sports the risk of injury is, in fact, higher for women than for men. For example, female skiers incur three times as many knee (tibial plateau) fractures as their male counterparts, and female mountain bike racers are 1.94 times more likely than men to experience injury and 4.17 times more likely to sustain a fracture. Despite the high risk of injury for some extreme sports, many young women are flocking to these sports and embracing a go-for-it attitude.

Like their male counterparts, some female extreme sports participants are embracing short-range views on participation. For example, professional female snowboarder Annie Boulanger explains that she plans to continue snowboarding "until Advil [painkillers] in the morning doesn't do it anymore." Moreover, many female extreme sports participants are embodying the cultural values of courage, taking risks, and experiencing their share of injuries. Top U.S. skateboarder Vanessa Torres is determined to "show people that I'm as good as the best guy out there. I want to throw myself down everything...big rails, huge gaps, everything. Even though you may not pull it off your first try, you gotta be like, 'yeah, I know I can do this'" (www.sexysportschicks.com/vanessatorres).

For many female participants, serious injury is simply part of the experience; some even wear their scars like "badges of honor." Describing her battered and scarred hands, New Zealand world champion kayaker Nikki Kelly proudly explains that her good friend and fellow kayaker John Grace said, "I got these scars 'cause I'm no fluffy bitch" (Daley 2005, 78). Male peers and media commentators alike praise female participants for displays of physical prowess, skill, aggression, and courage. For example, after she completed the first female descent of the challenging Grand Teton (Wyoming), *Powder* magazine included U.S. skier Kristen Ulmer as the first women in its "Big Balls Skier Hall

A woman rock climbing in the Blue Mountains, Australia. Source: istock/Scott Hailstone.

of Fame." Access to, and equality in, the male-dominated institution of extreme sports requires women to imitate men; they must prove themselves according to masculine-based standards of dedication, skill, and courage.

Women in Extreme Sports Cultures

Some extreme sports appeal to women more than others. Women constitute an estimated 51 percent of all inline skaters, 46 percent of Alpine skiers, 40 percent of mountain and rock climbers, 40 percent of windsurfers, 34 percent of snowboarders, 33 percent of surfers, 30 percent of mountain bikers, and 26 percent of skateboarders. In contrast, they constitute only 15 percent of skydivers, and the numbers of women participating in sports such as motocross, BMX, and drag racing are negligible. Certainly extreme sports have their own distinctive histories, environments, geographies, identities, development patterns, equipment, and physical requirements and thus gender relations. Some extreme sports are clearly more male dominated than others. However, an important commonality is the prevalence of young men at the core of most extreme sports cultures. Hence, the following discussion examines the youthful masculinity in extreme sports and the positions of women within these cultures.

A "fratriarchy" is a group of young men whose members compete for prestige through demonstrations of physical prowess, courage, and gameness. Fratriarchy is the "rule of the brother(hood)s." Sociologist John Remy notes that fratriarchy (1) "is a mode of male domination which is concerned with a quite different set of values from those of patriarchy"; (2) "is based simply on the self-interest of the association of men itself"; (3) "reflects the demand of a group of lads to have the 'freedom' to do as they please, to have a good time"; and (4) "implies primarily the domination of the *age set* ... of young men who have not taken on family responsibilities"

(Remy, 1990). Across the social world young men engage in action situations in which they display, test, and subject their behavior to social evaluation. This fratriarchial behavior is also apparent in many extreme sports, particularly at the core of the cultures. A high proportion of extreme sports enthusiasts are young and male; the average age of male skateboarders, snowboarders, artificial wall climbers, and in-line skaters is 14, 19, 19.9, and 20.5 years, respectively. Thus, young men in their late teens and early twenties constitute a dominant force in most extreme sports cultures. As one female windsurfer observes: "It's a laddishness you get, like a boy's club, sort of thing. It's a macho thing...they have to be tough, hard, masculine, successful, attractive, [and] to be able 'to pull' [demonstrate heterosexual prowess]" (cited in Wheaton 2000, 440).

The importance of male bonding as an exclusionary practice, or of the desire of men to differentiate themselves from women, should not be underestimated. The presence of women as objects of ridicule, humiliation, and abuse helps strengthen fraternal bonds and reinforce male domination. Although blatant abuse in extreme sports is rare, media representations frequently ridicule and humiliate women by promoting them as sex objects. For example, an advertisement for Treble Cone ski resort (Wanaka, New Zealand) in the July/August 2003 edition of *New Zealand*

Young Women in Extreme Sports

Extreme sports have always been dominated by men, as many sports have. While women are breaking into the arena, equality is still a ways off, as this excerpt from an article in Wire Tap *magazine explores.*

Like most arenas, the extreme sports world has its share of objectification. Some female athletes say they are judged based on how they look and whom they know versus their athletic ability. Then there's the media and advertising that surrounds these sports, which is, as you might guess, not the most respectful of women in general.

Even Sasha, who is only 14, says she often feels uncomfortable about the way skate magazines and the images on skate decks themselves portray women. And, she says, she chooses her sponsors accordingly.

"There are certain companies I wouldn't ride for be-

cause of their [portrayal] of women," she says. Sasha says that companies like World Industries, 151, and Blind are "always using women as sex objects."

Some women's clothing companies hire models to wear the clothes in ads, instead of the female athletes themselves—something that would never fly when it comes to selling men's sporting apparel.

So it's no wonder young girls have a hard time finding female athletes as role models—when they pick up a skate or BMX magazine the only women they see are half-dressed and standing on the sidelines, or in group fashion spreads surrounding male athletes.

Source: Dirksen, E. (2002, November 5). Young women in extreme sport. *Wire Tap*. Retrieved February 1, 2007, from http://www.wiretapmag.org/stories/14477

Snowboarder magazine features a male snowboarder glancing back at a near-naked female tied to his bed as he leaves to go snowboarding. The accompanying text reads: "Sorry, babe. Extremely big powder day." A radical case of female humiliation resulted in a court case in which two French boarders, Julian Joud (a former snowboard champion) and Jeremy Boissonnet, were found guilty of splicing pornographic footage into a snowboarding video. According to a press release, Joud admitted it was "a really bad idea to film the sex" that took place between his friend and the unwitting woman. "I did it as a laugh, but it was a bad joke." The court found the men guilty of invading the woman's privacy and making pornography available to minors; they were fined five thousand euros, to be paid to the woman in the video, and given suspended prison sentences of eight months. Similarly, in his discussion of skydiving culture, Jason Laurendeau found that male jumpers routinely excuse misogynist songs and other subcultural texts (e.g., videos bordering on soft-core pornography) as "having a little bit of harmless fun" (Laurendeau 2004, 414). Sports sociologist Robert Rinehart also observes advertisements in skateboarding and inline skating magazines as overtly sexualizing women such that they "might be deemed X-rated." He describes such advertisements as "reflect[ing] an outlaw image, or a bad-boy kind of clubbishness" (Rinehart 2005, 243). Certainly, ridiculing and humiliating women encourage male bonding and encourage the exclusion of women from the extreme sports brotherhood.

Yet, some women refuse to be excluded and negotiate spaces for themselves within the extreme sports fratriarchy. However, little room exists within these fraternal structures for women to represent themselves as women. That to excel in extreme sports requires inherently male qualities is accepted as "common sense." Thus, to be accepted into the extreme sports fratriarchy, a woman must behave in a "masculine" manner. She must demonstrate the same attributes that young men are thought to possess. For example, a top New Zealand snowboarder who rides, lives, works, and travels with a group of "guy friends," is treated "like one of the boys" because she "ride[s] as hard as them." She admits in an interview that to gain the respect of her male peers and inclusion into this group she has to "hit the same features as them, and don't be a wimp. Sometimes I have to tell myself to stop being a pussy and just do it; I have to be able to take the crashes and falls." She explains that she negotiated her way into this "boys club" by "learning to snowboard fast, keeping up with the boys, and not being bothered by boy talk." By demonstrating physical prowess and commitment, suppressing her femininity, and ignoring sexist banter, she has *earned* a place among her male peers. However, she also said she is conscious that other women are excluded from this group: "They treat me like one of the boys, but I've seen them treat their girlfriends much worse, like not inviting them to a kicker session [building a jump in the backcountry and then practicing maneuvers]."

For many women, to be treated like "one of the boys" and accepted into all-male groups constitute an achievement, indicating that the women have behaved in a "male" way and have thus removed the negative connotations associated with being female. Whether on the mountain, in the skate park, or in the waves, when a female displays superior athleticism it is common to hear that "she rides [climbs, skates, surfs, etc.] like a guy." Sociologist Mary Jo Kane terms this language a "re-gendering" mechanism and argues that it achieves two important goals. First, regendering helps reinforce the connection between maleness and superior athleticism while undermining female physicality and athleticism. Second, and more insidiously, the token compliments in such language create the impression that there is both acceptance of, and enthusiastic support for, female athleticism. However, rather than supporting the young girl or woman who exhibits such competence, the comment "she rides like a guy" naturalizes the superiority of males in extreme sports. For the most part those who utter such remarks do not set out consciously to devalue women. However, one consequence is the preservation of the "natural" gender order and the demarcation of sexed bodies. Simply put, whereas males in extreme sports work to prove they are "men," core female participants must work to prove they are not "women." In her search for subcultural identity as a core participant, the female extreme sports enthusiast faces a difficult task of negotiating the traditional codes of femininity—difficulties not faced by boys or men. As the following quote from professional snowboarder Tina Basich's (2003) autobiography illustrates, some women find it difficult to combine their physical skills and snowboarding identity, and maintain their femininity:

> As a girl, and the only girl on the team, I felt like I had to at least do everything the guys were doing to stay in the game. Not only did I have to get big air jumping cliffs and ride fast and hang with the guys, but be cool, pretty and feminine. For example, I liked riding with my ponytail flying behind me so there was no question of femininity. I was so proud to be a snowboarder girl. But the balance between

being a great rider and a girl was schizophrenic, and there were only a handful of girls out there who were supposedly doing that dance right. (70)

"Hanging" and Hungry

Even for those women who do negotiate their way into the homosocial extreme sports fratriarchy, male participants continue to subtly reinforce their difference. One of New Zealand's top female snowboarding judges said in a 2005 interview she enjoys "hanging out with the boys" because "they are all out ruckus fun, and they ride harder, are easier to get on with, and there's way more of them." However, whereas her male friends treat her "like 'one of the boys' 98 per cent of the time," they treat her "like a girl two per cent of the time": when they are hungry for food and sex. Although conscious of their attitudes and antics, she opts to ignore them, perhaps in fear of being excluded from this group. However, in so doing she offers a powerful reminder that whether women are included or excluded, extreme sports are ultimately defined by male standards. Young male participants successfully defend the "maleness" of extreme sports by reinforcing difference and distancing themselves from behavior associated with femininity. Extreme sports fratriarchies adopt a variety of covert and overt strategies to exclude and marginalize women. Whereas some women recognize these strategies and act in ways to undercut them, others accept marginalization and demonstrate compliance.

Within extreme sports cultures female participants do not constitute a homogeneous category; women experience extreme sports in diverse ways. For some women participation is a gratifying experience and a key site for the creation and negotiation of cultural identity. Among committed female participants, the extreme sports culture is an important site at which they forge their identity in an environment in which female participants negotiate status and construct feminine identities as active sports participants. A core New Zealand snowboarder believes that snowboarding "gives you a sense of confidence—that is priceless." "I now know," she adds, "that I can do things that other people think are impossible, in fact, the more people think they aren't possible, the more I want to do it" (personal communication 2005). Similarly, a female windsurfer proclaims:

You feel stronger and more positive about yourself. If I am hooked in on a windy day, I feel strong and positive about what I am achieving. I come

out and feel, "yeah, like I am taking charge of the situation." Windsurfing does challenge ideas about femininity—it is quite masculine, you are taking a masculine pose. (Wheaton and Tomlinson 1998, 260)

Many scholars and practitioners also believe that outdoor recreation helps women resist traditional gender roles and leads to discovering a new sense of self. They argue that conformity to traditional female roles is not required in the natural environment. When top New Zealand snowboarder Hayley Holt was asked why she quit competitive ballroom dancing and chose to focus on a snowboarding career, she replied, "I didn't have to pretend to be a lady anymore" (Catsburg 2005, 110). In short, participation in extreme sports provides some women with a welcome escape from traditional gender roles.

Many core female extreme sports participants position themselves in opposition to the culturally valued discourse of "emphasized femininity." Sociologist R. W. Connell (1987) employed the term "emphasized femininity" to refer to femininity that is based on women's "compliance" with their subordination to men and accommodating the interests and desires of men (183). Professional snowboarder Tina Basich captures the tension that coexists between extreme sports and emphasized femininity. She describes her group of female snowboarding friends as "the misfits of the misfits—the anti-cheerleaders. We didn't fit in [at high school]. Snowboarding was a savior to us" (Basich 2003, xi). Many female skateboarders also disassociate themselves from emphasized femininity, which one participant defined as "skinny, thin, pretty, and makeup [wearing]" girls who "live their life for a guy" (Kelly, Pomerantiz and Currie, 2005). Another female skateboarder declares herself and her skateboarding friends "totally opposite" to girls who spend all their time trying "to be sexy" (Kelly, Pomerantiz and Currie 2005). Top U.S. surfer Amy Cobb describes herself as "a gnarly surfer girl" and warns "all those stupid chicks with their painted nails" to "watch out" (Strauss 2001). Extreme sports provide some women with an "alternative" identity and thus have the potential to empower core female participants via both their physical and cultural experiences.

In contrast to core female participants, "fashion seekers," "poseurs," "pro hos" (extreme sports' equivalent of groupies), and so-called girlfriends are often less committed. One male instructor defines this group as women who "use their snowboards purely as a fashion statement." Ideological differences have caused divisions between committed and rec-

reational participants and those whose participation is based on fashion, social status, and heterosexual pursuits. The presence of "poseurs" and "pro hos" threatens the identities of core female participants and precipitates the occasional struggle between these two groups. For example, Madeline, a Canadian female skateboarder, complains, "girls that have skateboards and go to skate-parks just to look at guys, kind of bug me" (Kelly, Pomerantiz and Currie 2005) A comment posted on an Internet snowboard forum by "Jenni" indicates similar hostility in the snowboarding culture: "girls who do things like stare at boys and sit in the pipe and on the sidelines of the park are just f**king poseurs. They need to get a life and go have a sleepover in their thongs" ("Girls and Snowboarding" 2003).

The athleticism of core female participants is now highly visible on the mountains, in the water, and in the media, and some evidence suggests that boys and men are adjusting, and in some cases radically altering, their perceptions of women's abilities. Recently, when Andreya Wharry, a British kitesurfer, shattered the world record for the longest continuous kitesurf passage (212 kilometers) in eight hours and six minutes, Henry Ashworth, founder of the Extreme Academy, proclaimed, "Dreya has really proved that in the world of extreme sport it has nothing to do with whether you are a man or a woman. In breaking this record Dreya has shown sheer guts and determination and is an inspiration to us all" ("Dreya's Kite Surf Challenge" 2005).

Indeed, some male participants who acknowledge the physical capabilities of their female counterparts enjoy extreme sports experiences with women. In short, gender hierarchies in some extreme sports cultures are being affected by new configurations of women's identity and practice—especially among younger women—that are increasingly acknowledged by younger men.

Commercialization and Women

In the twenty-first century the number of women in extreme sports is escalating. For example, in 2003 snowboarding, kayaking, and paintball were the three fastest-growing sports for U.S. women, respectively; skateboarding was the sixth fastest. Furthermore, the number of women who surf everyday grew 280 percent between 1999 and 2003. The increasingly visible role of female extreme sports athletes in the broader society has contributed to the popularity of these sports among women. The inclusion of females in globally televised events, including the X Games and Olympics (skiing, mountain biking, kayaking, snowboarding), blockbuster movies focusing on female surfers (e.g., *Blue Crush* 2002) and inline skaters (e.g., *Brink* 1998), and the representation of female extreme sports athletes in the mass media (e.g., *Seventeen, Glamour, Sports Illustrated for Women*) have all added to the visibility and legitimization of women in extreme sports.

Yet, some female extreme sports athletes are more visible in popular culture than others. For example, female snowboarders have been included in the X Games since their inception in 1997, whereas female skateboarders and freestyle skiers were excluded until 2002 and 2005, respectively; women continue to be barred from all motorbike and snowmobile events. Thus, whereas the number of female participants has exploded in some extreme sports, others remain the exclusive domain of males. Nevertheless, the marketability of female extreme sports athletes cannot be ignored. For example, although motor sports are perhaps the most male-dominated extreme sports, driver Danica Patrick is arguably one of the most visible competitors in the Indy Racing League. In fact, she has been credited with single-handedly increasing the television ratings of the 2005 Indianapolis 500 by 40 percent.

Companies have recently recognized the huge potential of the female niche market. Extreme sports–specific companies that entered the industry to cater for male participants are broadening their product lines to tap into the female market and are producing female-specific equipment (e.g., skateboards, surfboards, wetsuits, snowboards, kayaks, wakeboards, mountain bikes, skis, boots, etc.), clothing (e.g., board shorts), and accessories (e.g., goggles, helmets). Some large companies, seeking to further capitalize on the growing female market, have established separate female divisions. Examples include Quiksilver (Roxy Surf and Snow), Globe (Gallaz), and Volcom (Volcom Girls). These companies often use language that connotes "girl power" sentiments of autonomy, rights, independence, and power. For example, a range of Volcom Girls jeans features buttons that declare the wearer "liberated by Volcom." Yet, the marketing approaches of many of these companies tend to mirror those of mainstream companies; they privilege fashion over participation. Whereas many women appreciate the opportunity to purchase clothing and equipment designed specifically for their technical, physical, and/or cultural sporting needs, others are less than optimistic. New Zealand snowboarder, skateboarder, and mountain biker Pamela, in a 2005 interview, complained: "Too many of these companies still rely on male perspectives of what women want. I don't want butterflies, flowers and birds on my snowboard . . . and everything doesn't have to be pink." Female skateboarders express similar sentiments. The women's skate-clothing market is "shocking," says professional skateboarder Elissa Steamer: "I see girls out there skating in these tight pants. People want to see what tricks you're doing, not your ass. The clothes they make for girls are like club clothes or something. They make you look like you skate like a girl" ("Girl on Board" 2004).

As these comments show, production and marketing techniques that tout girl power messages, employ lesser-quality construction and traditionally feminine designs, and put cultural and physical limits on what constitutes a female extreme sports participant do not satisfy all female consumers. Responding to these concerns, some women have established female-specific companies, including Cold as Ice (snowboarding outerwear and accessories), Betty Rides (snowboarding outerwear), Nikita (snow, skate, and surf street clothing), Surf Diva (clothing), Rookie Skateboards, and Chorus (snow, surf, and skate boards), to focus solely on the cultural and physical needs of women in extreme sports.

Many of the new generation of top female extreme sports athletes have immersed themselves in the process of commercialization and have achieved superstar status within the culture, attracting corporate sponsors, including Red Bull, Nike, Mountain Dew, Powerbar, Campbell's Soup, and Boost Mobile. Some earn seven-figure salaries. Many of these women are aware of their commodity value and have no qualms about marketing their sexuality to boost their public profile and image and reaping the financial benefits. One journalist described the commercial appeal of snowboarder Tara Dakides's alternative femininity as "a knockout combo of skill, swagger and sex appeal," adding "it helps that she's beautiful: deep green eyes and toothpaste-ad grin, a hyper-athletic body, biceps bulging and abs rippling . . . pierced nostril and belly button, and an intriguing tattoo . . ." (Elliot 2001). Increasingly female snowboarders (e.g., Tara Dakides, Gretchen Bleiler, and Victoria Jealouse), surfers (e.g., Amy Cobb, Wendy Botha, Malia Jones, Lana Papke, Anastasia Ashley, Kira Sheppard, and Kelly Dahlberg), mountain bikers (e.g., Tara Llanes), NASCAR drivers (e.g., Danica Patrick), skiers (e.g., Kristen Ulmer), rock and ice climbers (e.g., Steph Davis), and BASE (building, antenna, span, Earth) jumpers (e.g., Lottie Aton) are posing in male magazines such as *FHM*, *Maxim*, *Sports Illustrated*, and *Playboy*. When they pose in ways that promote their heterosexual femininity, the female extreme sports body itself becomes something of a fetishized commodity, one that can be attractively packaged, marketed, and sold.

Second-wave feminists typically take offense at such overtly sexualized displays, arguing that as the product of a backlash against women they diminish women's power, trivialize their strength, and put them in their sexual place. However, third-wave feminists believe that bodies coded as athletic can redeem female sexuality and make it visible as an assertion of female presence. Canadian snowboarder, skier, and mountain biker Jamie, for one, reads these images as evidence of these women's "confidence in their lifestyle and their looks" (personal correspondence, 2005). Certainly the athletes do not see themselves as exploited or manipulated; as part of a third-wave feminist generation, they are aware of their economic worth and not afraid to state their demands. For example, professional snowboarder Gretchen Bleiler reminds potential sponsors that she expects them to "whip out your checkbooks" and "show me the money." If feminism in the 1970s was built on ideals of authenticity and solidarity, girl power in the twenty-first century appears to be built on dreams of celebrity and self-advancement. In this context, it may seem that the idea of doing something for the greater good has become an anachronism.

Yet, some women are cleverly exploiting the new opportunities available within this highly commercial context, and the female niche market more specifically, to improve women's situation in extreme sports. For example, women have established female-specific magazines (e.g., *SG*, *Curl*) and websites (e.g., www.xgirlsport.com, www.powderroom.net, www.mtbchick.com, www.dirtgirls.com, www.girlsskatebetter.com, www.wakechicks.com). These forums provide space for women to display their skills, gain and share cultural knowledge, and voice their opinions. Some women are also producing female-only videos with the goal of inspiring the next generation of participants (e.g., *AKA: Girl Skater* [skateboarding], *The Chick Flick* [wakeboarding], *Our Turn* [surfing, skateboarding, snowboarding], *As If* [snowboarding], *Dropstitch* [snowboarding]). Women have also been proactive in organizing women-only competitions and clinics (e.g., All Girls Skate Jam, Girls Day Out [wakeboarding], Queen of the Mountain [snowboarding]) and camps (e.g., Op Girls Learn to Ride [surfing, skateboarding, snowboarding, wakeboarding, motocross, mountain biking, and BMX]). Women-only camps claim to give women of all ages the chance to learn in a supportive, no-pressure, and noncompetitive atmosphere.

In summary, female extreme sports athletes are not simply victims of commercialization but rather are active agents who are capitalizing on the opportunities available within the female niche market to reshape the images and meanings circulated by global consumer culture. Thus, it seems inevitable that gender relations in extreme sports will continue to change for many years to come.

Holly Thorpe

See also Extreme Media; Meaning of Extreme, The; Media and Extreme Sport; Psychology of Risk; Sociology of Risk

Further Reading

Basich, T. (2003). *Pretty good for a girl: The autobiography of a snowboarding pioneer.* New York: HarperCollins.

Beal, B. (1996). Alternative masculinity and its effects on gender relations in the subculture of skateboarding. *Journal of Sport Behavior, 19*(3), 204–220.

Booth, D. (2002). From bikinis to boardshorts: Wahines and the paradoxes of the surfing culture. *Journal of Sport History, 28*(1), 3–22.

Booth, D. (2003). Expression sessions: Surfing, style and prestige. In R. Rinehart & S. Sydnor (Eds.), *To the extreme: Alternative sports, inside and out* (pp. 315–333). Albany: State University of New York Press.

Brandt, R. (2005). Darren Berrecloth. In *Faces outside: The 20 greatest athletes now.* Santa Fe, NM: Mariah Media.

Broken off: Five wicked wipe-outs. (2002, December). *Transworld Snowboarding,* 168–178.

Bryson, L. (1990). Challenges to male hegemony in sport. In M. Messner & D. Sabo (Eds.), *Sport, men and the gender order: Critical feminist perspectives* (pp. 173–184). Champaign, IL: Human Kinetics.

Catsburg, M. (2005). Sibling rivalry? *Manual: New Zealand Skate and Snow Culture, 18;* 110–116.

Connell, R. (1987). *Gender and power: Society, the person and sexual politics.* Cambridge, UK: Polity Press.

Dreya's kite surf challenge. (2005). BBC Extreme Features. Retrieved February 3, 2007, from http://www.bbc.co.uk/cornwall/content/articles/2005/07/25/extreme_sports_kitesurf_record_feature.shtml

Elliott, Josh. (2001, January 21). The it girl. *Sports Illustrated.* Retrieved February 3, 2007, from http://sportsillustrated.cnn.com/features/siadventure/11/it_girl

Girl on board. (2004, November 12). Retrieved February 3, 2007, from http://www.twsbiz.com/twbiz/women/article/0,21214,781904,00.html

Girls and snowboarding (2003, March 28). *Boardpass.com.* Retrieved January 19, 2004, from http://www.boardpass.com/search/snownews/replies.asp?IDCODE=829&MainCode=703

Kane, M-J. (1995). Resistance/transformation of the oppositional binary: Exposing sport as a continuum. *Journal of Sport and Social Issues, 19*(2), 191–215.

Kelly, D., Pomerantz, S., & Currie, D. (2005). Skater girlhood and emphasized femininity: "You can't land an ollie properly in heels." *Gender and Education, 17*(3), 229–248.

Knee injuries to skiers on rise. (2001, July 1). American Orthopedic Society for Sports Medicine. Retrieved June 26, 2006, from http://www.sportsmed.org/about/document.asp?did=54

Kronisch, R., Pfeiffer, R., Chow, T., & Hummel, C. (2002). Gender differences in acute mountain bike racing injuries. *Clinical Journal of Sport Medicine, 12*(3), 158–164.

Laurendeau, J. (2004). The "crack choir" and the "cock chorus": The intersection of gender and sexuality in skydiving texts. *Sociology of Sport Journal, 21*(4), 397–417.

Lenskyj, H. (1986). *Out of bounds: Women, sport and sexuality.* Toronto, Canada: Women's Press.

Olsen, M. (2001). *Women who risk: Profiles of women in extreme sports.* (pp 59–99). New York: Hatherleigh Press.

Palmer, C. (2002). "Shit happens": The selling of risk in extreme sport. *Australian Journal of Anthropology, 13*(3), 323–336.

Remy, J. (1990). Patriarchy and fratriarchy as forms of androcracy. In J. Hearn & D. Morgan (Eds.), *Men, masculinities and social theory* (pp. 43–54). Boston: Unwin Hyman.

Richards, T. (2003). *P3: Parks, pipes and powder.* New York: Harper Collins.

Rinehart, R. (2005). "Babes" and boards: Opportunities in new millennium sport? *Journal of Sport and Social Issues, 29*(3), 232–255.

Simpson, S. (April 19, 2006). Freestyle motorcross: Mary Perkins. Retrieved October 21, 2006, from http://www.nzgirl.co.nz/articles/6215

Thorpe, H. (2005). Jibbing the gender order: Females in the snowboarding culture. *Sport in Society, 8*(1), 75–99.

Thorpe, H. (2006). Beyond "decorative sociology": Contextualizing female surf, skate and snowboarding. *Sociology of Sport Journal, 23*(3),

Vanessa Torres. (2006). Retrieved February 20, 2007, from http://www.sexysportschicks.com/vanessatorres/

Wheaton, B. (2000). "New lads?" Masculinities and the "new sport" participant. *Men and Masculinities, 2*(4), 434–456.

Wheaton, B. (2004). Introduction: Mapping the lifestyle sport-scape. In B. Wheaton (Ed.), *Understanding lifestyle sports: Consumption, identity and difference* (pp. 1–28). London: Routledge.

Wheaton, B., & Tomlinson, A. (1998). The changing gender order in sport? The case of windsurfing subcultures. *Journal of Sport and Social Issues, 22*(3), 252–274.

Young K., White, P., & McTeer, W. (1994). Body talk: Male athletes reflect on sport injury and pain. *Sociology of Sport Journal, 11*(2), 175–194.

Gladiator Competitions

The first gladiator competitions were ceremonial and took place in Rome around 264 BCE. They were part of a noble funerary rite called a *"munus,"* meaning "a funeral gift for the dead" (aristocratic descendants felt they needed to honor ancestors), in which six slaves fought to the death. From these religious, ceremonial origins, gladiator competitions evolved into public spectacles staged by politicians and emperors. These new competitions were called *"munera."*

Emperors made each *munera* more impressive than the last. From the genesis of the competitions that starred six gladiators, the number was raised to seventy-four at a three-day event in 174 BCE. In 65 BCE the emperor Julius Caesar used 640 gladiators. In 107 CE the emperor Trajan held the largest contest with ten thousand gladiators.

The Colosseum

Gladiator competitions were conducted in the Colosseum. Its inauguration was held in 80 CE and included one hundred days of games in which nine thousand animals and two thousand gladiators lost their lives.

The Colosseum had an underground area that contained a maze of corridors, ramps, wild animal pens, and rooms for prisoners. From this underground area, unbeknownst to gladiators, wild animals and/or additional gladiators were raised via elevators into the arena and through wooden trap doors.

Gladiators

Gladiators (named after the Roman word *gladius*, which meant a 68-centimeter-long sword) were typically criminals, prisoners of war, and slaves (captured fugitives). Some gladiators were free men volunteering for the celebrity status (skilled gladiators had the same status as today's rock stars and athletes), excitement, and women (gladiators were the object of female adoration).

All gladiators bound themselves to the proprietor of a gladiatorial troupe by pledging, "I will endure to be burned, to be bound, to be beaten, and to be killed by the sword." By the end of the republic half of the gladiators were volunteers taking on the status of a slave for an agreed-upon period of time.

Gladiators fought two or three times a year, with the opportunity to be released after three years of service. Gladiators also had the opportunity to become wealthy. They were paid approximately one thousand gold pieces each time they fought. The prize money could be used to purchase the wooden sword *(rudius)* that symbolized their freedom. Freed gladiators could continue to fight for money but often became gladiatorial trainers or bodyguards for the wealthy.

Gladiator Categories

There were fourteen gladiator categories, distinguished by the type of armor worn, weapons used, and the style of fighting utilized. After a gladiator chose a category he usually stayed in that category throughout his career. The games themselves consisted of at least two categories of gladiators pitted against one another in the arena. The seven most popular gladiator categories were the following.

Thracian

The *thracian* used the weapons and equipment characteristic of his people. In time this category designated a type of gladiator using particular armor and fighting equipment that included (1) a wide-brimmed crested helmet with full visor (or open face) and plume called a "*galea*," (2) high greaves (shin guards) called "*ocrea*" that extended past the knees, (3) a right arm protector known as a "*manica*" (made of heavy linen quilting, leather bands or curved and overlapping segments of iron or bronze), (4) a small rectangular shield called a "*parma*," and (5) a short, curved sword called a "*sica*." The *thracian* did not wear chest armor.

Retiarius

The *retiarius* attempted to snare and entangle his opponent in the net that he would cast like a fisherman and then stab his opponent with the three-pronged trident spear he carried. *Retiarius* was the only type of gladiator whose head and face were uncovered. He wore practically no defensive armor (i.e., no helmet or shield) and thus was more mobile than most gladiators but more vulnerable to serious wounds. His weapons and equipment included (1) a large flared metal shoulder guard known as "*galerus*," (2) a large net known as an "*iaculum*" that had weights attached to the edges to assist in making the net flare out when thrown. The net also had a tether cord attached so the *retiarius* could draw it back if it failed to snare his adversary, (3) a trident also known as a "*fascina*," (4) a small dagger, and (5) a *manica* fastened to a leather backing held on by straps protecting his left arm. The *retiarius* was a special gladiator because his gear was not inspired by the military. In essence, he was a fisherman, as his net and trident imply.

Secutor

The *secutor* chased his opponent around the arena to exhaust him for the kill. He was the standard opponent of the *retiarius*. He fought virtually naked. Artillery and devices included (1) a legionary-style curved oblong shield known as the "*scutum*," (2) a greave on one leg, (3) a *manica* to protect his right arm, and (4) a *gladius*. The *secutor* wore an egg-

The Coliseum in Rome, Italy. Source: istock/Luke Daniek.

shaped, smooth-surfaced helmet (designed without any projection so it would not become ensnared in the net thrown by the *retiarius*) with small round eye-holes. The purpose of the small eye-holes was to prevent the narrow prongs of the *retiarius's* trident from penetrating the eyes. The helmet had no brim but included a low, thin crest. This style of helmet made the *secutor* look like a fish, thus making the *retiarius* his appropriate opponent.

Bestiarius

The *bestiarius* handled and fought animals. The *bestiarii* were the lowest-ranking gladiators and the least popular. There were three classes of *bestiarii*: The first was condemned individuals (enemies, prisoners, slaves, criminals) known as "*noxii*" (guilty) who were sentenced to death as they were tossed to the beasts naked and without weapons to defend themselves. Even if they succeeded in killing one beast, fresh

animals were continually let loose on them, until all the *bestiarii* were dead. The most popular *bestiarii* of this class were the Christians. The second class was young men who fought against beasts to become expert in managing their arms or "*bravados*" who exposed themselves to this treacherous combat to show their bravery, valor, and skill. They were not given armor but only cloth or leather garments to wear. They were equipped with whips or spears to defend themselves. The third class was trained hunters called "*venator*."

Hoplomachus

The *hoplomachus* wore a full set of armor, based on Greek infantrymen (hoplites). He (1) wielded a small round shield, (2) wore a *manica*, (3) dressed in a loin cloth with a belt called a "*subligaculum*," (4) wore greaves, and (5) wore a helmet with a stylized griffin on the crest. The *hoplomachi* were paired with *murmillos* or *thracians*.

Gladiators and Philosophy

Gladiators played a major role in the ancient world, and were often used by philosophers to explore characteristics and ideals. Below is an excerpt from Seneca's essays on morality (4 BCE).

On Anger

"Passion," some one says, "is useful, provided that it be moderate." No, only by its nature can it be useful. If, however, it will not submit to authority and reason, the only result of its moderation will be that the less there is of it, the less harm it will do. Consequently moderate passion is nothing else than a moderate evil. "But against the enemy," it is said, "anger is necessary." Nowhere is it less so; for there the attack ought not to be disorderly, but regulated and under control. What else is it, in fact, but their anger—its own worst foe—that reduces to impotency the barbarians, who are so much stronger of body than we, and so much better able to endure hardship? So, too, in the case of gladiators skill is their protection, anger their undoing. Of what use, further, is anger, when the same end may be accomplished by reason? Think you the hunter has anger toward wild beasts? Yet when they come, he takes them, and when they flee, he follows, and reason does it all without anger.

Source: Seneca, L. A. (1928) *Moral essays.* John W. Basore (trans). Retrieved February 9, 2007 from http://www.stoics.com/seneca_essays_book_1.html

Eques and the *Provocator*

The *eques* and the *provocator* were two gladiator categories that fought only opponents of the same category. The apparel of the *eques* included (1) a wide-brimmed, round helmet with visor and two feathers, (2) a tunic to midthigh (in comparison with the naked torso of most gladiators), (3) a spear, (4) a *gladius*, and (5) a *manica*. These gladiators were called "horsemen" because they began their fight (or entered the arena) on horseback. They did, however, finish their battle on foot. In contrast, the *provocatores* (1) wore a helmet without crest, (2) carried a curved, rectangular shield, and (3) brandished a sword with a straight blade. The *provocator* was the only gladiator who wore effective upper-body protection: a rectangular breastplate. The *provocator* therefore lacked what was a badge of honor for other heavily armed gladiators: a naked torso.

A Typical Day of Combat in the Colosseum

Gladiators entered the Colosseum in chariots or marched in an elaborate and colorful parade known as the *"pompa."* They were accompanied by jugglers, acrobats, and other performers led by the sponsor of the games, known as the *"editor"* (usually the emperor or a high-ranking magistrate known as the *"munerarius"*). They all marched in time with the music provided by musicians, who also performed during the actual fighting, producing the same effect as the background musical score of a movie.

Following the *pompa*, the performers exited the Colosseum. The gladiators progressed in full public view to the front of the emperor to draw lots. The lots decided who would fight whom. All gladiators then left the arena and came back according to the program.

The morning's events commenced with a mock fight that combined clowns and dwarfs in a satire resembling gladiator battles or reenactments of clashes from mythology. Other times it included gladiators engaged in a mock rehearsed fight with blunt weapons. When the people had seen enough, they bellowed to the trumpeters, who signaled for the fierce fighting to begin. Gladiators who lost courage were forced back with whips and hot irons. Sometimes a cowardly gladiator would ask for clemency by holding one finger up to the official in charge. The fate of that gladiator then fell upon the citizens of Rome.

It is not clear how the vote of life or death for the defeated opponent was decided, although it did involve the thumb. Contrary to popular belief, the crowd did not use the signal "thumbs down" or "thumbs up" to call for the killing or sparing the life of a gladiator. There is no visual evidence for this. Those signals were made up by moviemakers and flawed translations of Greek and Latin text. Scholars, historians, and researchers agree on this. However, they disagree on the meaning of the "written" evidence (words and pictures).

One theory proposes that persons wanting the gladiator killed waved their thumbs in any direction, demonstrating *pollicem vertere* (to turn the thumb) or turned the thumb sideways across or toward the chest. The persons who wanted the gladiator spared kept their thumbs pressed against their hands, demonstrating *pollicem premere* (to press the thumb).

A second theory advocates that "to press thumb" sentenced a gladiator to death. The confusion between the two interpretations comes from various mosaics that illustrate the crowd members, who, in conjunction with shouting "*pollicem premere*" (to press the thumb), seem to press their thumbs toward their own chests. If one sides with the first theory, this gesture is to show mercy, thus sparing the gladiator. If one sides with the second theory, the pressing of the thumb toward the chest symbolizes a sword through the heart, hence gesturing for the gladiator's death. Therefore, the second theory interprets "to turn the thumb" to mean "thumbs up," allowing the gladiator to be saved.

However, both theories were deemed by Augustus as an expression of empathetic mercy. He was the first emperor to forbid any turn of thumbs and decided that all gladiators must fight to the death.

Late Morning

Late morning events involved animal combats and the "hunting" and slaying of wild animals, including lions, panthers, leopards, bulls, rhinoceros, wild boars, and elephants by *bestiarii*. This competition was known as "*venatio*" (hunt).

As noted earlier, the *bestiarii* were thrust into the arena without armor or weapons to defend themselves against the wild beasts. They were referred to as "*damnatio ad bestias.*" The *bestiarii* and the animals took part in theatrical reenactments of mythological fables. One of the favorite betrayals was the myth of Dirce, who was killed by being tied to a bull. The *bestiarii* were also presented to the wild animals, either tied to a stake in the middle of the Colosseum or tied to a stake and wheeled out on a little cart.

Regardless of the method by which *bestiarii* were to die, they understood they were going to be maimed, killed, and eaten by a ferocious beast. Many *bestiarii* decided they did not want to die in that manner and took matters into their own hands. For instance, a disinclined *bestiarius* circumvented partaking in a *venatio* by thrusting his head through the spokes of the wheel of the cart in which he was being carried to the games, breaking his neck when the cart moved. There was also a story of a German prisoner of war who while in the lavatory stuffed a stick with a sponge down his throat. With his breathing passage obstructed, he choked to death.

In addition to the *bestiarii* hunting, and being hunted by, wild animals, the *venatio* involved animals pitted against each other. It was not uncommon for a bull to be tethered to a ring in the ground to force it to fight against elephants with riders. Much like the condemned *bestiarii*, many of the animals were reluctant to fight and had to be provoked.

Noon (Lunch) Time

Noon time was dedicated to executions of felons who had performed terrible crimes: murder, arson, and treason. Criminals were brutally killed by being burned, crucified, put to death by sword, or forced to fight and execute one another with no previous training (unlike the professional gladiators).

Participants and spectators alike knew death was a foregone conclusion because the champion had to fight other criminal opponents until he himself was killed. In this way the condemned executed one another. What happened to the ultimate winner is not known. Scholars speculate he was pardoned or at least allowed to live to fight another day.

Afternoon Games

The afternoon games were known as "*munus gladiatorium*" and were the high point of the day. These were the matches between gladiators with different types of armor and fighting styles. The contests pitted members of the same gladiatorial familia against each other, so if a duel ended in death often a man's own comrade had to deliver the fatal blow.

Gladiators fought in pairs: one gladiator against another. However, the emperor could request other combinations such as a *catervarii*, in which several gladiators fought in a melee as a group.

Contrary to the accepted belief, matches did not begin with the gladiators saying, "Those who are about to die salute you." The only evidence for this phrase is found in the description of the *naumachia* (a mock sea battle between prisoners of war and convicts) staged by Claudius in which the men said, "*Ave, imperator; morituri te salutant*" (Suetonius, *Claudius* 21.6). Because the purpose of the *naumachia* was to have the criminals slaughter each other, it is not surprising they are cynical about their survival. The *naumachia* was not a typical gladiatorial combat (because it was held one time on a lake) and therefore should not be used as evidence for typical practice.

Gladiatorial contests were not always exemplified by impulsive, fickle, and violent brutality and vindictiveness.

Ideally, the judgment of life or death was based on a code of justice. The audience anticipated a proficient presentation of skill and proficiency and rewarded life to those losing gladiators who fought well.

Consequently, a wounded gladiator wishing to concede defeat would hold up the index finger of the left hand. At this point the referee would hold the right hand of the victor, with both the victor and wounded awaiting the recommendation of the crowd.

The crowd indicated whether it wished the defeated gladiator to be killed or spared. Members of the crowd also indicated the gladiator's fate by calling out "*mitte*" (release him) while waving the hem of their garment or handkerchief or yelling "*lugula*" (cut his throat) if they wanted death.

The final decision to give the defeated gladiator a reprieve (*missio*) came from the emperor (or sponsor). The emperor wanted to please the crowd and therefore passed judgment based on the crowd's wishes. Another factor in determining whether to provide a *missio* was whether the gladiator was good or popular. Gladiators were too valuable to their owners and promoters because time, expense, and effort had been expended in their training.

If the gladiator was to be killed, he was expected to accept the final blow in a ritualized fashion, without crying out or flinching. With one knee on the ground, the defeated opponent would ceremoniously grasp the thigh of the victor. The victor, while holding the helmet or head of his defeated opponent, would slay him by plunging his sword into his neck. In addition, historians have found evidence that the wound may have been made so it appeared that the gladiator had been slain when in fact he was alive. The defeated gladiator would be hauled offstage and assassinated compassionately and in private by a backstage slayer who would kill the gladiator with a hammer strike to the forehead.

If the fallen warrior fought bravely, the bout was declared a draw, and both gladiators were allowed to leave to fight another day. An amazing competition among two gladiators named "Priscus" and "Verus" was recorded in which both fought so valiantly that when they signified surrender simultaneously, Titus (encouraged by shouts of "*missio*") awarded victory to both and gave them wooden swords.

If the gladiators were permitted to live, all necessary medical treatment (which was of the highest quality available) was granted to them. However, if the emperor (and/or the spectators) felt that the gladiators were not giving it their all (or if a gladiator turned and ran), they were punished by whipping or branding with hot irons.

Another outcome was one gladiator killing an opponent outright. In some instances the fallen combatant pretended to be dead. Few were successful at this ruse because costumed attendants dressed as Charon, the ferryman of Hades, ran out to make sure the fallen combatant was really dead by applying hot irons to the body. Pretenders promptly had their throats cut. If the gladiator died at the hands of Charon or was truly dead to begin with, a slave was called to drag the body with a hook through a gate called the "Porta Libitinensis" (Libitina was a death goddess). At other times a man dressed as Mercury (transporter of the dead) came out with Charon to strike the carcass with a hammer as it was whisked away.

The winner(s) would receive from the emperor a palm branch (which was a symbol of victory) and money. A laurel crown was awarded for an outstanding performance. The victor ran the perimeter of the Colosseum, waving the palm above his head. The ultimate accolade bestowed to a gladiator was permanent release. As a symbol of this accolade, the emperor presented the gladiator a *rudius*, suggesting he no longer had to fight with actual weaponry jeopardizing his life.

Termination of the Games

In 404 CE an incident put an end to the gladiator competitions. Telemachus, a Christian monk, jumped into the Colosseum arena to disengage two gladiators. The crowd went wild. Members scrambled over the walls into the arena, where they tore the monk limb from limb. In reaction to this scene, the emperor Honorius banned all gladiator competitions. The seven hundred-year age of the gladiator had been ended by the dogma of Christianity.

Joanne Margaret Hynes-Hunter

See also Agon Motif; Initiation/Hazing; Injury; Ultimate Fighting

Further Reading

Auguet, R. (1972). *Cruelty and civilization: The Roman games.* New York: Allen and Unwin.

Bartin, C. (1993). *The sorrows of the ancient Romans: The gladiator and the monster.* Princeton, NJ: Princeton University Press.

Bomgardner, D. L. (2000). *The story of the Roman amphitheater.* New York: Routledge.

Cagniart, P. (2000). The philosopher and the gladiator. *Classical World, 93*(6), 607–618.

Coleman, K. M. (1990). Fatal charades: Roman executions staged as mythological enactments. *Journal of Roman Studies, 80,* 44–73.

Futrell, A. (1997). *Blood in the arena: The spectacle of Roman power*. Austin: University of Texas Press.

Grant, M. (1967). *Gladiators*. New York: Barnes & Noble.

Harris, H. A. (1972). *Sport in Greece and Rome: Aspects of Greek and Roman life*. Ithaca, NY: Cornell University Press.

Hopkins, K. (1983). *Death and renewal*. Cambridge, UK: Cambridge University Press.

Humphrey, J. H. (1988). Roman games. In M. Grant & Rachel Kitzinger (Eds.), *Civilization of the ancient Mediterranean: Vol. 2. Greece and Rome* (pp. 153–165). New York: Charles Scribner's Sons.

Köhne, E., & Ewigleben, C. (2000). *The power of spectacle in ancient Rome: Gladiators and Caesars*. Berkeley and Los Angeles: University of California Press.

Kyle, D. (1998). *Spectacles of death in ancient Rome*. London: Routledge.

Pearson, J. (1973). *Arena: The story of the Colosseum*. New York: McGraw-Hill.

Plass, P. (1995). *Arena sport and political suicide*. Madison: University of Wisconsin Press.

Potter, D. S., & Mattingly, J. D. (1999). *Life, death, and entertainment in the Roman empire*. Ann Arbor: University of Michigan Press.

Wiedemann, T. (1995). *Emperors & gladiators*. London: Routledge.

Wistrand, M. (1992). *Entertainment and violence in ancient Rome: The attitudes of Roman writers of the first century A.D.* Göteborg, Sweden: Acta Universitatis Gothoburgensis Universitatis.

Haakonsen, Terje

Terje Haakonsen (b. 1974), five-time world champion snowboarder, grew up in the Telemark region of southern Norway in the village of Romot. He learned to cross-country ski at age three and to Alpine ski at age five. However, not until the winter of 1987 did he try snowboarding. Within three years Haakonsen had mastered the sport, signed a sponsorship deal with Burton Snowboards, and begun competing at the highest level. He made his debut in international snowboarding at the 1990 U.S. Open, as professional snowboarder Todd Richards recalls: "There was a little fifteen-year-old kid from Norway named Terje Haakonsen who dropped in [to the halfpipe] and blew the crowd away with big airs that seemed even bigger because of his size. Everybody who watched him ride that day suspected they might be watching the next Craig Kelly" (Richards and Blehm 2003, 100).

Haakonsen went on to become a five-time world champion, three-time U.S. Open champion, and five-time European champion. In the halfpipe he performed the most difficult maneuvers with huge amplitude and a sense of ease; he even developed a new aerial snowboarding maneuver called the "Haakonflip." He further solidified his mythic status in 1998 when, at the Mount Baker banked slalom event, he rode through the challenging course fakie (backward) and still finished fourth in the qualifying round. The following day he won the event.

Not only did Haakonsen win nearly every major halfpipe competition at least once during the 1990s, but also he played an integral role in redeveloping big mountain riding. Haakonsen was among the first snowboarders to mix freestyle snowboarding (jumps, aerials, spin maneuvers) with big mountain riding. "In TB4 [snowboarding video], he does a big front-side 180 off a cliff—a solid forty-foot cliff—and lands it. That's typical Terje. He's just the master," says snowboard cinematographer Mike Hatchett (Reed 2005, 138). During this period Haakonsen was also refining his skills on a surfboard. In his own words, "surfing has made me look at the terrain a little differently. The way I do power turns in the critical point in the mountains is similar to surfing. I think surfing has helped my snowboarding" (Brisick 2004, 132). Certainly, his combination of freestyle, free-riding, and surfing styles helped redefine big mountain riding.

During the mid- to late 1990s Haakonsen shifted his focus from competition to filming and continued to expand his legend with "unbelievable performances" in videos such as *RoadKill*, *The Garden*, and the *Totally Board* series. He then redefined the meaning of "going big" in *Subjekt Haakonsen* (1996) and *The Haakonsen Faktor* (2000). According to snowboarding journalist Jeff Galbraith, these videos reinforced Haakonsen's "feline propensity for landing on his feet from any height and any position" (Galbraith and Marcopoulos 2004, 65). For this reason he is nicknamed "The Cat."

When snowboarding was accepted into the 1998 Winter Olympic Games, Haakonsen was the world's best halfpipe rider. However, he fervently opposed snowboarding's inclusion in the Games. He argued that the International Olympic Committee (IOC) was a group of Mafialike officials and that competing in the event was tantamount to joining the army. He criticized the IOC's lack of understanding of snowboarding culture or consideration of snowboarders' needs. "The fact is that the big wigs ride in limousines and stay in fancy hotels while the athletes live in barracks in the woods," he argued (Humphreys 2003, 421). Not surprisingly, he refused to participate. In so doing, he questioned the validity of a gold medal. "Every snowboarder who came to the Olympics basically knew he was battling it out for second," said fellow professional boarder Peter Line (Reed 2005, 135). In 1999 Haakonsen backed up his convictions by co-founding the Arctic Challenge, an annual snowboarding event that is held in a traditional Norse village and prioritizes athletes over all else. He listened to riders' needs and tailored the competition accordingly. The event is one of the most respected in the sport.

The master of amplitude and style in the halfpipe and quarterpipe, Haakonsen is also one of the fastest riders in the world. In 2004 he set a record by winning his sixth Mount Baker banked slalom. Cultural commentator Rob Reed describes him as "a master of all trades, from World Cup halfpipes to death-defying Alaskan lines. He's got the vision to push innovation and the physical and technical ability to pull it off" (Reed 2005, 135). Jake Burton, owner of the world's largest snowboarding company and Haakonsen's primary sponsor for more than a quarter of a century, proclaims Haakonsen as "the kind of kid who is afraid of nothing" (Reed 2005, 135).

"He goes the biggest, wins the most, rides the fastest, and just does everything the best," says Reed (Reed 2005, 126). Although Haakonsen rarely competes anymore, he occasionally appears in snowboarding films and recently starred in the snowboarding movie *First Descent* (2005). In the words of journalist Jeff Galbraith, Haakonsen has "de-

fined snowboarding's attitude, style and soul like none other" (Galbraith and Marcopoulos 2004, 65).

Holly Thorpe

Further Reading

Brisick, J. (2004). *Have board will travel: The definitive history of surf, skate, and snow.* New York: Harper Entertainment.

Curly, K., & Harrison, K. (Director/Producers). (2005). *First descent: The story of the snowboarding revolution* [Motion picture]. United States: Universal Pictures.

Galbraith, J., & Marcopoulos, A. (2004). Terje Haakonsen. *Frequency: The Snowboarder's Journal,* 62–83.

Humphreys, D. (2003). Selling out snowboarding: The alternative response to commercial co-optation. In R. Rinehart and S. Sydnor (Eds.) *To the extreme: Alternative sports, inside and out* (pp. 407–428). Albany: State University of New York Press.

Reed, R. (2005). *The way of the snowboarder.* New York: Harry N. Abrams.

Richards, T., & Blehm, E. (2003). *P3: Pipes, parks, and powder.* New York: HarperCollins.

Hackett, A. J.

Born in 1958 on the North Shore of Auckland, New Zealand, A. J. Hackett was educated in that city. In his youth he showed an interest in machines and movement. He became an apprentice carpenter and developed interests in snowboarding and skiing.

Hackett's life changed when he viewed his first bungee jump, outside the Melanesian island of Pentecost, in 1977. In 1986 Hackett made his first bungee jump, with Chris Sigglekow, from the Greenhithe Bridge on the North Shore of Auckland.

Hackett and Henry Van Asch, another New Zealand with strong adventure sport interests, were energized by the possibilities of antigravity thrills. This led to their jumping at Tignes, in France, and the ensuing 1987 bungee jump by Hackett from the Eiffel Tower. This headline-grabbing leap generated publicity across nations and spurred Hackett on to consider other jumping possibilities.

Hackett returned to New Zealand where he made the first jump from a building, the Auckland Stock Exchange Tower, in 1988. He set up the first part-time commercial bungee jumping operation, open for certain weekends in that year at Ohakune, jumping with another New Zealander, Chris Allum, and set up a year-round jump site in Queenstown, in the lower region of the South Island of New Zealand. His commercial ventures provided a focus on Queenstown as an "adventure capital" when his commercial bungee jumping operation opened at the Kawarau Bridge. In July 1989 Hackett opened what was then then highest bungee jump in the Southern Hemisphere, the Nevis Highwire, in the Queenstown region, at a height of 134 meters.

Hackett became a critical figure in the global expansion of bungee jumping, through his own commercial enterprise and his publicizing of the extreme sport. The decade of the 1990s saw Hackett expand his bungee interests, including the introduction of commercial sites in overseas countries, such as France (Normandy) and Australia (Cairns), innovative leaps (from a helicopter), and the development of new cords that allowed greater accuracy in jumping (used in the Auckland Sky Tower leap in the central business district of New Zealand's largest city). More recently, he has expanded his business linkages to include one with Pulse GP to provide input into the Grand Prix company's event marketing.

The A. J. Hackett bungee jump at Kawarau Bridge, Queenstown, "the world's first bungee jumping leap" is still an active lure for thrill seekers. For the enquiring adventure tourist the A. J. Hackett site has the innovative "Secrets of Bungee Jumping" tour that provides "behind the scenes" insights into bungee viewing and an understandings of equipment and knowledge of bungee history.

Hackett was recognized by the New Zealand government, being given significant tourism awards in 1991 and 1992. Separated with three children, Hackett currently lives in the French Alps, where he can engage in his love of mountains and the activities they offer.

Robin C. McConnell

Further Reading

Wilmouth, P. (2006, August 6). The fall guy. *The Sunday Age Extra.* p. 15

Hamilton, Laird

Professional surfer, stuntman, model, waterman, and big-wave rider, Laird Hamilton (b. 1964), along with Buzzy Kerbox and Darrick Doerner, pioneered tow-in surfing in the early 1990s. In 2000 Hamilton rode what many consider to be the most treacherous wave ever, a 6-meter-high slab of water of unfathomable mass and power that collapsed onto a shallow razor-sharp reef at Teahupoo, Tahiti. The ride won

Hamilton the Action Sport Feat of the Year Award at the ESPN Action Sports and Music Awards in 2001.

Born in San Francisco, Laird—the name is Scottish for "lord"—arrived on the North Shore of Oahu, Hawaii, with his mother, JoAnn Zerfas, in 1967 shortly after the breakdown of her marriage. Playing in the shore break at Pupukea, Laird became entangled with legendary surfer Billy Hamilton. Back on the beach Laird looked Hamilton in the eye and, according to Billy, said, "I want you to be my daddy. So you have to meet my mommy. Come meet her" (Jenkins 1997, 87). Laird Hamilton confirms the story: "I chose Bill. He was Superman to me. Superman's my father, and I'm gonna do everything just like him" (Jenkins 1997, 93). Billy and JoAnn married shortly after, and Laird took the "Hamilton" surname.

From an early age Laird Hamilton's notion of fun was taking risks. At five he attached one end of a rope to a slab of building tile that he buried and the other end to his waist. He then threw himself into the raging shore break at Pipeline, where the lateral current was running around 20 knots. At age eight he leaped 18 meters from the famous Waimea dive rock; at age thirteen he surfed Hanalei at 3.6 meters; his first bungee jump was 213 meters from a bridge in Sacramento; and he rode his first street luge head-first—his face traveling at 96 kilometers per hour mere inches from the concrete track.

In 1992 Buzzy Kerbox persuaded Hamilton to try tow-in surfing behind the former's inflatable motorized boat. Initially the pair experimented at Backyards, near Sunset Beach (North Shore, Oahu). At the suggestion of Pipeline surfer Jerry Lopez, they transferred the experiment the following year to the north coast of Maui and the big-wave location of Peahi (known more popularly as "Jaws"). There the waves break at 6 meters perhaps a half-dozen times a year and occasionally twice that size. In the Peahi laboratory Hamilton and a coterie of friends, known as the "strapped crew," developed tow-in surfing; they replaced inflatable boats with jet skis, designed and manufactured specialized boards with straps for the feet, and practiced their teamwork and safety drills. In this extreme environment Hamilton took command of the activity and within a few years established a reputation as the world's tow-in expert and big-wave rider.

Hamilton developed an early dislike of organized surfing competitions, a dislike he attributes to watching his stepfather being "burned" in controversial events and to what he considers to be a system that manipulates young people. "How do you judge art?" he scoffs. Thus, Hamilton shies away from big-wave competitions such as the Tow-In World Cup, the K2 Big-Wave Challenge, and the Billabong XXL

Global Big Wave Awards. Hamilton does not boast about his achievements: "You'll never hear from me, 'I rode the biggest wave'" (Duane 2004, 2). Such boasting, he argues, merely establishes a "benchmark that people want to step over" and ultimately undermines one's credibility. Hamilton insists that success is much more than a single performance on one big wave; rather it is "about your body of work." Yet, Hamilton clearly understands that in the quest for social prestige he must be seen and that he cannot totally remove himself from his peers. In the late 1980s and early 1990s, for example, Hamilton spent several seasons at Pipeline establishing his credentials: "At that point in my life, I needed to find out if I could surf at that level. I needed to surf Pipe just like everyone else did. And I had local guys giving me shit. So I had to go through the lineup, each guy, and have a confrontation. Fortunately for me—and them—I didn't have to go to brawls. A lot of people understood how serious I was" (Jenkins 1997, 103).

Today Hamilton's views about competition and publicity seem more grounded in marketing strategy than principle. As Daniel Duane comments, "by staying above the fray, surfing only for himself, he has become a lone, untouchable Neptune, reigning over a swelling pantheon of competing demigods" (Duane 2004, 2). Indeed, Hamilton artfully employs the media to enhance his profile and status. Among his media appearances Hamilton has been a correspondent for the syndicated cable series *The Extremists*, host of Fox Sports Network's *Planet Extreme Championships*, surfing stunt double for Pierce Brosnan in the James Bond film *Die Another Day*, a performer in the Artisan Entertainment surf documentary *Step into Liquid* and the Sony Pictures big-wave documentary *Riding Giants*. More recently he started his own company, BamMan Productions, which will allow him to serve as the star, producer, and owner of every second of Laird water-action footage.

Hamilton's detractors criticize his ego and maniacal attitude. Yet, tellingly, they speak publicly only on condition of anonymity. On the other hand, Hamilton's supporters shower him with praise. "Laird," says big-wave rider Brian Keaulana, "is like every single element known to man. Raw power that the ocean has. Strong foundations of mother earth. He can be as calm as the sea, as strong and swift as the wind" (Jenkins 1997, 120).

Douglas Booth

Further Reading

Duane, D. (2004, December). Laird Hamilton: Big-wave surfer. *Outside Magazine*. Retrieved July 20, 2006, from http://outside.away.com/outside/features/200412/laird-hamilton_1.html

Jenkins, B. (1997). Laird Hamilton: 20th century man. *The Australian Surfer's Journal*, 1(1), 84–121.

Kachmer, J. (Producer), & Monaghan, T. (Director). (2001). *Laird* [Motion picture]. United States: Image Entertainment.

Kachmer, J. (Producer), & Peralta, S. (Director). (2004). *Riding giants* [Motion picture]. United States: Sony Pictures.

Laird. (n.d.). Retrieved July 20, 2006, from www.lairdhamilton.com/

Warshaw, M. (2004). *The encyclopedia of surfing*. London: Viking.

Hang Gliding

A man gliding over a mountain terrain.
Soruce: istock/Andrzej Burak.

Hang gliding is a sport in which people soar using a hang glider—a wing made of an aluminum or carbon fiber frame and a synthetic sail and a triangular-shaped structure below the wing that allows a pilot to carry and maneuver the glider. The pilot wears a harness that is hooked to the glider and takes off on foot on a slope or is towed aloft by a vehicle on flatlands. Hang gliding allows a pilot to admire fantastic views in the company of soaring birds with only the rush of the wind to break the silence.

Hang gliding pilots find rising air currents and use them to climb, stay aloft, and fly over the landscape. With the right weather pattern hang gliders can travel long distances—the world record (regularly broken) stands at 703 kilometers (437 miles), flown by Mike Barber in 2002 in Texas. Pilots can reach altitudes of more than 6,000 meters (countries set their own legal altitude limits).

History

Hang gliding is a relatively new sport that began during the early 1970s, but its development had a long evolution. Legends, including that of Icarus in Greek mythology, show that people dreamed to fly even during ancient times. The Italian Renaissance artist and inventor, Leonardo da Vinci, studied flight, as did many inventors during the nineteenth century: Otto Lilienthal of Germany, Sir George Cayley of England, and John Montgomery of the United States built successful motorless flying machines. The development of powered flight by Wilbur and Orville Wright of the United States during the early 1900s started with nonpowered soaring flights from the dunes of North Carolina. The pursuit of powered flight put soaring on the sidelines, and it resurfaced in Germany only after World War I. In the United States during the 1960s National Aeronautics and Space Administration (NASA) engineer Francis Rogallo and his wife, Gertrude, developed a triangular wing designed as a reentry device for spacecraft. By the early 1970s the design was adapted to launching on foot and spread throughout the United States and Europe. The sport of hang gliding was born.

Instructors use two main methods to teach hang gliding: training hill sessions and tandem flying. Most schools use a combination of both. The development of safe towing practices using a winch or an ultralight (a light recreational aircraft typically for one person and powered by a small gasoline engine) has promoted tandem flying, which is less physically demanding and appeals more to women. Tandem flying is done on a larger hang glider that is designed for two persons: a pilot (or instructor) and a passenger (or student). This arrangement allows a student to learn skills with hands-on experience under the supervision of an instructor.

Women in Hang Gliding

Women historically have been a minority in hang gliding (5–10 percent of participants). However, the development of smaller and lighter gliders and the evolution of teaching techniques during recent years have promoted the participation of women. With new technology and materials the equipment is better adapted to lighter-weight pilots. Some participants believe that hang gliding is popular among women because it is aesthetically appealing and requires finesse in control. The glider is controlled by weight shift, which requires upper body motions but not excessive strength.

Kari Castle of the United States holds the hang gliding world distance record for women. In 2001 she flew 350 kilometers (217.5 miles) from Zapata, Texas. Judy Leden of England holds the *Guinness World Records* altitude record (for men and women): On 25 October 1994, she took off at 11,856 meters (38,898 feet) from a balloon over Wadi Rum, Jordan, and flew back to Earth.

Competition at the Top

With the exception of the Women's World Meet held every other year, men and women compete together in hang gliding competitions. Hang gliding has three forms of competition: aerobatics, speed gliding, and cross-country. Aerobatics (or freestyle) is a routine of aesthetically pleas-

Hang Gliding Improvements Over Time

Since its inception, hang gliding has been considered an unsafe and extreme sport. Early hang gliders tended to develop technologies and learn their sport through "trial and error," and thus fatalities and serious injuries were not uncommon among these pioneers. One of the earliest fatalities occurred on 9 August 1896, when a gust of wind fractured the wing of the German "Glider King" Otto Lilienthal's glider and he fell from a height of 17m (56 ft), breaking his spine. He died the next day, saying, "Opfer müssen gebracht werden!" ("Sacrifices must be made!"). While modern hang gliders are fairly sturdy in comparison to the technologies used by Lilienthal, they remain lightweight crafts that can be easily damaged, either through misuse or by continued operation in unsafe wind and weather conditions. The inherent danger of gliding at the mercy of unpredictable thermal and wind currents, often in proximity to dangerous terrain, has resulted in numerous fatal accidents and many serious injuries over the years, even to experienced pilots, and the resultant adverse publicity has affected the popularity of hang gliding.

Glider safety is, as in all other forms of aviation, a matter of training (through certified instructors) and self-discipline. Many contemporary gliders are engaging in intensive training regimens and taking saftey precautions. As a backup, pilots carry a parachute with them in the harness. In case of serious problems the parachute is deployed (thrown by hand) and carries both pilot and glider down to earth. Pilots also wear helmets and generally carry other safety items such as hook knives (for cutting their parachute bridle after impact or cutting their harness lines and straps in case of a tree or water landing), light ropes (for lowering from trees to haul up tools or climbing ropes), radios (for calling for help), and first aid equipment. Despite some preventative strategies being put in place, there is still a "culture of extremism" among many passionate hang gliders, such that "they're not particularly interested in regulations or having any operating restrictions placed on them" (Rex Kenny, New Zealand civil aviation authority sports and recreation manager, cited in Jamieson, 2006, para. 9). Ross Grey, hang glider and New Zealand hang gliding and paragliding association chief executive, also describes hang gliding as "a very free sport and a very individual sport. You're in your own aircraft doing your own thing" which "makes managing the sport a little like herding cats" (cited in Jamieson, 2006, para. 6). Indeed, the image of hang gliding as an extreme sport continues to pervade the broader culture.

Holly Thorpe

Source: Jamieson, D. (2006, March 18). Queenstown has become the hub of New Zealand's commercial hang-gliding industry, but with the boom have come some bust-ups. *The Press*. Retrieved December 15, 2006, from http://www.nzhgpa.org.nz/phpBB/viewtopic.php?p=753&sid=e128451daa615a151e42eebccecfe8a0

ing maneuvers judged on precision, technique, and elegance. Speed gliding, the newest form, is a short race close to the ground between pylons.

Cross-country, the most common form of competition, is a long race along a course that is determined by turnpoints (reference points such as the takeoff and landing spot) and a goal. Cross-country competitions typically last one to two weeks. A different task is set for competitors every day. Each task may be on a course that is from 80 to 240 kilometers in length and may last from two to six hours. The course may be a straight line to the goal, a series of doglegs, an out-and-return course, or a triangular course. Competitors prove that they have flown the task along the course by taking aerial photographs of the turnpoints or by recording their flight path with a GPS (Global Positioning System). To complete the course competitors must find rising air currents along their way and plan their flight so that they achieve the fastest time. Accomplishing this requires knowledge of weather conditions on the large scale and small scale and honed soaring skills. (The terms soaring and gliding are often used interchangeably; however, soaring refers particularly to using air currents to stay aloft.)

The two main types of soaring are ridge soaring and thermal soaring. Ridge soaring takes place when wind strikes a slope and is deflected upward. A pilot can ride this upward wind and stay up above the ridge. Thermal soaring uses rising columns of warm air known as "thermals." Thermals develop over dry, darker, or rocky terrain that absorbs and then radiates heat from the sun. A pilot uses a thermal by circling and climbing in it. To aid in soaring pilots use altimeters (to measure altitude) and variometers (to measure the rate of climb or descent).

The Future

Hang gliding, like any other type of aviation, is constantly evolving as new technologies and materials cause the gliders to change form. Through the years gliders have become safer and more efficient, their rates of descent becoming slower and their speeds faster. These changes improve performance while soaring and traveling distances.

Claire Vassort

Further Reading

Cheney, P. (1997). *Hang gliding for beginner pilots.* Colorado Springs, CO: United States Hang Gliding Association.

Leden, J. (1996). *Flying with condors.* Spring Mills, PA: Sport Aviation Publications.

Pagen, D. (1991). *Understanding the sky.* Spring Mills, PA: Sport Aviation Publications.

Pagen, D. (1993). *Performance flying.* Spring Mills, PA: Sport Aviation Publications.

Pagen, D. (1995). *Hang gliding training manual.* Spring Mills, PA: Sport Aviation Publications.

Palmieri, J., & Palmieri, M. (1997). *Sky adventures, fantasies of free flight: True stories by pilots.* Roanoke, VA: Sky Dog Publications.

Palmieri, J., & Palmieri, M. (1998). *Sky adventures, stories of our heritage.* Roanoke, VA: Sky Dog Publications.

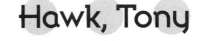

Hawk, Tony

Tony Hawk (b. 1968) is widely regarded as skateboarding's first global superstar. A "vert" skater (vert skaters are so named because they skate in half-pipes that provide both a horizontal and vertical dimension to their performances), Hawk was the first person to complete the "720" (two midair spins) and the "900" (two-and-a-half midair spins). He is also attributed with inventing over eighty tricks, including the stalefish, kickflip McTwist, and 360 shove-it nose ground.

Hawk received significant support from his father who not only drove him to skateparks, but who also was instrumental in establishing the California Amateur Skateboard League and later the National Skateboard Association; these two organizations gave the emergent sport increased legitimacy.

A professional skateboarder since his teenage years, Hawk won 73 of the 103 professional contests that he entered and placed second in an additional 19 events. Since his retirement from competitive skateboarding in 1999, Hawk has remained the most well-known athlete in the sport by virtue of numerous successful business initiatives. He established Birdhouse Projects in the early 1990s to oversee his commercial endorsements. As a celebrity endorser, his familiarity and appeal is among the highest in the industry. He has appeared in television commercials for nonskateboarding brands such as Schick, Levi's, Coca-Cola, and Pepsi, as well as numerous appearances in films and on television. In 1999, Activision, an American computer and video game company, released Tony Hawk's Pro Skater. Updated on a near-annual basis, this video game is among the biggest sellers ever with retail sales in excess of $1 billion. Hawk Clothing, an apparel line, was sold to Quiksilver in 2000. Hawk turned his entrepreneurial skills toward event management in 2002 with the launch of Boom Boom HuckJam. Conducted in large sports arenas, this event choreographs elite-level skateboarding, BMX riding, and motocross riding with pyrotechnics, light shows, and contemporary music. At the same time he also created Tony Hawk's Gigantic Skatepark Tour for the ESPN television network. It's ratings are second only to those of the X Games. Through the Tony Hawk Foundation, Hawk channels some of his fortune toward the creation of public skateboard parks and other related initiatives.

Perhaps more than any other skater, Hawk was responsible for skateboarding's transformation from an informal recreational activity in suburban Los Angeles into a legitimate global sporting phenomenon. In 2006 the U.S.-based *Sporting News* described Hawk as an "action sports entrepreneur" and ranked him number 72 on its list of the 100 most powerful people in sports. Two features underpin Hawk's fame, fortune, and influence: his exceptional skateboarding skills and the ability to preserve his counterculture credibility while maximizing his commercial revenues.

Geoff Dickson

Further Reading

Hawk, T. (2001). *HAWK: Occupation, skateboarder.* New York: Harper Collins.

Layden, T. (2002). What is this 34-year-old man doing on a skateboard? Making millions. *Sports Illustrated, 96*(24), 82–96.

Peterson, T. (2005). *Tony Hawk: Skateboarder and businessman.* New York: Ferguson Publishing Company.

The Sporting News: Power 100. Retrieved August 10, 2006 from http://www.sportingnews.com/exclusives/20060103/692920-p.html

Hazing

See Initiation/Hazing

Hillary, Sir Edmund and Tenzing Norgay

Edmund Hillary (b. 1919), a New Zealand mountaineer and explorer, and Tenzing Norgay (1914–1986), a Sherpa mountaineer from the Himalayas, made the first ascent of Mount Everest on 29 May 1953. Both men rose from humble origins to reach the summit of the world's highest mountain (8,850 meters).

Hillary was born in Auckland, New Zealand, and dropped out of college to join the family beekeeping business. Ed Hillary became an accomplished snow-and-ice climber on holiday trips to the mountains of New Zealand. After climbing in the Himalayas, he joined British expeditions to Everest in 1951 and Cho Oyu the next year. Tenzing was born in Tsa-chu, a village in Tibet near Chomolungma (as Everest is known locally), and he grew up farming and herding in Solu Khumbu, Nepal. He went to Darjeeling, India, to become a porter on Everest expeditions in the 1930s. After World War II he joined many mountaineering expeditions, and in 1952 he came to within about 250 meters of the summit of Everest with Raymond Lambert, a Swiss climber.

The 1953 British Everest expedition was the culmination of the many attempts to summit since the 1920s. Col. John Hunt's party was well organized and benefited from the Swiss experience and improved equipment and knowledge of high altitudes. Hunt chose Hillary and Tenzing for the summit since they proved to be the strongest pair of climbers. Just below the summit they reached the crux of the climb, now called the Hillary Step, and wriggled up a dangerous and exposed crack between rock and an ice cornice overhanging the 3,048-meter Kangshung Face. On the summit Hillary photographed Tenzing holding his ice axe with the flags of Britain, Nepal, India, and the United Nations. On their return from the mountain, the climbers were showered with awards around the world.

After Everest, Hillary's drive and competitiveness were evident in Antarctica and the Himalayas. On a Commonwealth expedition across Antarctica with motor-sledges (1956–1958), Hillary was supposed to support another group but launched his own push to the pole resulting in a "race" that Hillary won easily. In the Himalayas, Hillary led attempts on Makalu that combined climbing, scientific tests, and a search for the Yeti. He also traveled by jet boat up the Ganges from the ocean to its headwaters in the Himalayas.

When a Sherpa told Hillary that "our children have eyes but they cannot see" (Hillary 1999), he built a village school to provide education. After the early 1960s, Hillary built many other schools and hospitals, helped restore a Buddhist monastery after a fire, and promoted reforestation in Nepal through the Himalayan Trust. Hillary served as New Zealand's ambassador in India in the 1980s and was able to attend Tenzing's funeral in 1986.

Tenzing served as director of the Himalayan Mountaineering Institute in Darjeeling from 1954 to 1976 and trained generations of Sherpas and Indian mountaineers. After retirement he traveled occasionally as a guide for tourists and goodwill ambassador and was known for his wide smile and humble dignity.

In recent years Hillary has become an outspoken critic of the guided ascents, piles of trash, and climbing ethics on Everest. Fixed ropes on the Hillary Step may have reduced the extreme risks encountered in the first ascent. Even though these ropes remain, despite Hillary's protests, the risks faced by Hillary and Tenzing have not been eliminated.

Peter H. Hansen

Further Reading
Douglas, E. (2003). *Tenzing: Hero of Everest*. Washington, DC: National Geographic.
Hansen, P. (2000). Confetti of empire: The Conquest of Everest in Nepal, India, Britain and New Zealand. *Comparative Studies in Society and History 42*(2), 307–332.
Hillary, E. (1999). *View from the summit*. London: Doubleday.

# Hoffman, Mat

The influence of Mat Hoffman (b. 1972) on all aspects of BMX (bicycle motocross) riding—from participation to the production, marketing, administration, and media representation of BMX events—has been considerable.

Born in Oklahoma City, Oklahoma, the "Condor," as Hoffman is nicknamed, began to influence BMX when he turned pro at the age of fifteen. He immediately redefined the discipline of vert riding. The inventor of more than one hundred tricks, Hoffman was the first person to perform a 900-degree and a backflip in a vert competition. Even after coming out of retirement in 2002 at the age of thirty, he demonstrated that he could still take the sport to new levels when he landed the first no-handed 900-degree, a trick no other rider had accomplished in competition up to that point.

Hoffman is the athlete who, arguably, has most successfully capitalized on the cultural attention and profitability of extreme sports from the mid-1990s to the present. When only in his early twenties, Hoffman established his own BMX bicycle manufacturing company—Hoffman Bikes. Later he created a BMX event promotion company, Hoffman Sports Association, to work with cable TV network ESPN to put on the X Games and international bike stunt competitions. More recently he developed the website hsacentral. com, which boasts of being "the most comprehensive and complete coverage of bicycle stunt events/competitions on the web" (www.hsacentral.com). In addition, Hoffman has played a role in building BMX stunt riding into a professional sport by creating the Bicycle Stunt (BS) and Crazy Freakin' Bikers (CFB) series so that riders from around the globe could compete to qualify for the annual Summer X Games. In 2005 he was elected president of the International BMX Freestyle Federation (the international governing body of bicycle stunt riding).

Hoffman was quick to promote BMX riding via the creation of ancillary youth-oriented products not previously associated with BMX riding cultures. For example, Hoffman worked with Activision to develop the video game Mat Hoffman's Pro BMX, as well as with toy companies to create Flix Trix finger bikes and even a Mat Hoffman action figure as a means of introducing BMX riding to new generations of youth in ways that do not involve riding. Further, Hoffman produced, directed, and hosted a number of television series on BMX riding and action sports for ESPN (*Kids in the Way*, *HBTV*, and *Mat's World*) to popularize BMX riding. In 2002 Hoffman wrote his autobiography, *The Ride of My Life*.

Hoffman also has exemplified many of the core values of extreme sports, such as treating sport as a lifestyle, emphasizing participant control over sport, resisting conformity, and maintaining an entrepreneurial spirit. Hoffman also embodies the extreme nature of extreme sports. An avowed masochist who does not shy away from pain, Hoffman once endured knee surgery to replace a torn ligament without anesthesia or other painkillers.

Kyle Kusz

See also BMX

Further Reading
Hoffman Sports Association. (2007). Retrieved February 3, 2007, from http://www.hsacentral.com
Mat Hoffman. (2002). Retrieved February 3, 2007, from http://expn. go.com/athletes/bios/HOFFMAN_MAT.html
Mat Hoffman. (2006). http://www.mathoffman.com

Ice Yachting

As ice yachters skim across a frozen lake, river, or bay on a boat propelled by the wind, danger, like the ice, is a cold, hard fact. At high speed, if an ice yacht's metal runner blade becomes caught in an ice crack, the yacht can splinter into hundreds of shards of wood and metal. Even when the ice is glassy smooth and thick, unseen dangers like ferry slips—ramps that extend into the water for the docking of ferries or barges—or collisions lurk for the unsuspecting ice yachter.

Origins

The first known record of an ice yacht is a second-century Scandinavian woodcut that depicts a boat skimming over bumpy ice as it is being pulled by a reindeer while four passengers watch the path ahead. By the 1600s Dutch master painter Hendrick Avercamp's artwork showed sails attached to large boats with runners underneath, possibly of the same type of metal that the Dutch used on their wood-based ice skates, which had been adapted to boats.

North American Beginnings

Canadians experimented with ice yachting on Toronto Bay in the 1820s. The sport soon spread south. By 1866 Poughkeepsie, located on the Hudson River in New York State, had become the center of ice yachting in the United States. By 1871 Poughkeepsie had its first ice yachting fatal accident, arguably making ice yachting one of the first extreme sports.

The early ice yacht designs in Poughkeepsie likely were inspired by a mixture of sailing cultures, including that of the Dutch. Poughkeepsie's first fleet of ice yachts was owned by wealthy people who lived along "millionaires row" on the Hudson River. However, their new technological thrill machines were generally sailed by hired professionals. The largest yacht, nearly 21 meters long, was the *Icicle*, owned by an uncle of future president Theodore Roosevelt. The *Icicle* was huge by today's standards and was extremely heavy, able to carry seven to nine passengers. These ruddered stern-steerers were not easily controlled; bow-steerers later proved to be safer and more efficient. Reports of crashes and perilous journeys filled the newspapers.

For example, in January 1866 Poughkeepsie's fleet of three boats, the *Minnehaha*, *Snow Flake*, and *Haze*, raced 144 kilometers on the Hudson from Poughkeepsie to Albany in two "leisurely" days.

At the start of the race, after the sails were set, the three vessels were put head to the wind—sails flapping vigorously in a heavy wind and a 45-mile-long continuous sheet of smooth, glassy Hudson River black ice lay before them." There was no need for a "look-out" man to shout "humps to the larboard" or "humps to the starboard."

After stops in Rhinebeck and Tivoli, the racers were greeted by the Athens Ice-Boat Association. After 64 kilometers in one day, the racers crossed the river to the town of Hudson and stayed the night at the White House Hotel; with sails taken down, the boats remained on the river until the next morning, when the final stage of the race to Albany began. The three boats traveled another 64 kilometers in about two hours. They had almost reached Albany when the *Snow Flake* hit loose ice and broke through, but was rescued. A little farther on the steering apparatus of the *Haze* malfunctioned, and more time was lost; finally all the boats were greeted in Albany, the *Minnehaha* arriving first. Enchanted by their new toys of a new technology, Poughkeepsians enjoyed racing their ice yachts against the trains that ran alongside the Hudson River. With a wind "on the beam" ice yachts always beat the trains, reaching 96–112 kilometers per hour; "a mile a minute" was a regularly quoted speed. By outracing trains, ice yachts became the fastest vehicles of that time.

Having outraced trains, ice yachters next set out to outrace the faster ice yacht. They tried new designs, new materials, experimented with sail size. More clubs were founded: besides Poughkeepsie, Newburgh, Athens, North Shrewsbury, and Albany founded clubs. By 1880 the North Shrewsbury River Ice Yacht Club, located near New York City, had its own fleet of boats, and the racing rivalry with Poughkeepsie grew more intense.

The two clubs still get together socially, but the meetings are no longer so intense. Modern ice yachts are smaller, designs more stable, procedures safer. In 2003, on the frozen Navesink River in Red Bank, New Jersey, the two clubs met to sail the big stern-steerers with canvas sails in a reenactment race. North Shrewsbury retained the Van Nostrand Challenge Cup, which it first won in 1889 when the Hudson River clubs had tried to regain their 1860s status.

Good ice was not always available in those early days, but when it was, ice yachters flocked to the river. So did many open-river skaters, who made the same journey north

Ice yachting on a lake n
Bavaria. Source: istock/
Georg Winkens.

to Albany. Whereas river skaters relished the thrill of jumping over water spots or cracked ice, ice yachters went too fast to see approaching dangers.

When ice yachts raced upriver to Albany, rarely did they make it back without incident. Sometimes a boat's metal runner blades became caught in an ice crack, causing following boats to crash into the stalled boat. In 1871 young Jacob Best was pierced just above the heart by the lancelike bowsprit of a colliding boat. He cried, "Oh, dear!" once, a newspaper reported, "gasped twice, and was a corpse." Other deaths would follow. Other deaths would follow, but Best's death was the first fatal incident teaching sailors about dangers never before experienced.

Culture of Speed

By 1824 a culture of speed had already gripped Hudson River communities as steamboats began to race one another. In 1824 the steamboat *Aetna* burst one of her three iron boilers in New York Harbor, killing about thirteen people. In 1845 the *Swallow* ran aground on a small island while racing, taking twelve lives. In 1852 the most famous steamboat racing tragedy occurred along the steamboat corridor from Albany to New York City. Eighty-two people died on the

steamboat *Henry Clay* in a fire caused by bursting boilers. On that day when the *Henry Clay* raced the *Armenia*, the competition was so intense that crewmen threw fine furniture and woodwork into the boilers for fuel. Other accidents followed until the *Henry Clay* tragedy helped create a turning point when steamers finally began to learn that reckless speed kills. However, ice yachting had years to go before it implemented safety codes and reduced the risks. By 2006 recklessness was almost unknown among ice yachters.

During the 1870s, as the U.S. frontier continued to expand, a long-distance culture developed alongside the speed culture: Ice yachters, long-distance runners (pedestrians), and open-river ice skaters attempted to travel the longest distance in the shortest time; for example, 965 kilometers in six days was a standard goal for ice skaters and pedestrians, a few losing their life along the way to heat exhaustion and dehydration or drowning.

Today ice yachters are interested in safety and the thrill of the fast ride, not the dangerous ride or the world speed record. Racing, however, remains important. Clubs with competitive members race in regattas with their bow-steerers, such as the popular DN models, which were invented in 1933 in Detroit, Michigan. Championships are held on the regional, North American, European, and world levels.

When Poughkeepsie was the center of U.S. ice yachting

Dangers of Ice Boating

Ice yachting, or ice boating, involves traveling across expanses of ice, wind-propelled and sometimes only inches from cracks, holes, and other dangers that could plunge you into life-threatening conditions. Safety under these conditions is paramount.

Facts on Safety

60 percent of ice rescue victims are would-be rescuers.

New, clear ice is generally the strongest.

Lake ice is stronger than ice found on creeks, rivers, or anything with a current.

Snow and water erode ice and add weight.

When ice pulls away from the shore, it is also eroding from above and below.

Hypothermia

Water causes heat loss 25 times faster than air.

Water under 70° is considered cold.

Levels of Hypothermia

Mild: shivering, slurred speech

Moderate: disorientation, drowsiness

Severe: bodily functions stop, hallucinations

Terminal: unconsciousness, death

When the water temperature is 32.5° F or below your survival time is 15–45 minutes.

Source: Whitehorse, D. & The Four Lakes Ice Yacht Club. *Safety.* Retrieved Feb. 1, 2007 from http://www.iceboat.org/safety.htm

---

enjoy their social atmosphere as it is and do not want to be identified with the lifestyle of those extreme sports that stand in sharp contrast to conservative, middle-class sporting values. As one Hudson River Ice-Yachting commodore said in 2006: "We are weekend sailors—at the end of the day we go home and live very normal lives and may not see each other for another year. There is no money in our sport—no yacht syndicates, no endorsements, no prizes, no guest spots on the late night television shows, no groupies" (Commodore John Sperr e-mail, June 6, 2006).

However, because ice yacht speeds can surpass 225 kilometers per hour, the sport can be considered extreme. When ice yachters feel that they're holding their own in a strong wind, they push the edge and "hike" the boat up onto metal runner blades and ride "on the edge," knowing that the risk of wiping out is real. Most ice yacht deaths are caused by drowning; broken bones, bruises, and concussions are minimized by crash helmets and better safety regulations. Nonetheless, after a death in a collision on Lake Sunapee in New Hampshire in 2006, some clubs are rethinking their safety standards.

Fear of Extinction

The total number of ice yachters in the world is fewer than five thousand. That number is not expected to increase. Thus, dedicated ice yachters fear gradual extinction. Organizers want better opportunities for good ice as prospects fade in an age of threatening glacial melt, and more ways to entice young people to seek thrills.

As the Earth's ice melts, so does the promise of that annual thrill of skimming over good ice in the Northern Hemisphere. However, as long as good ice continues to return each winter, the serious ice yachters also will return. Whether leisurely social or marginally extreme, they'll be sailing on the edge.

Paul J. DeLoca

See also Meaning of Extreme, The

during the last half of the nineteenth century, ice yachting was a sport for the upper class, but no longer. Ice yachting has become affordable to the general public.

"Extreme"? Not So Fast Now

Some of the older clubs, such as the Hudson River Ice-Yachting Association, fearful of losing a tradition, have distanced themselves from the "extreme sport" label. They

Further Reading

Andresen, J. (1974). *Sailing on ice.* New York: A. S. Barnes.

Chadwick, H. (1879). *Handbook of winter sports; embracing skating, (on the ice and on rollers), rink-ball, curling, ice-boating, and American football.* New York: Beadle and Adams.

Gardner, F. (1938). *Wings on ice.* New York: Yachting Pub. Corp.

Levy, N. (1978). *Iceboating: Your guide to the fundamentals and fine points of buying, sailing, racing, and maintaining your craft.* New York: McKay.

New Jersey Bureau of Recreation. (1966). *Ice boating in New Jersey: A general guide for ice boating, sailing, racing and safety on ice.* Trenton, NJ: Author.
Roberts, L. (1980). *Think ice!: The DN ice boating book.* Decatur, IL: International DN Ice Yacht Racing Association.
Smith, S. (1962). *Ice boating.* Princeton, NJ: Van Nostrand.
Stone, H. L. (1913). *Ice boating: The latest opinions of the foremost authorities in America.* New York: Outing Publishing.
Summers, J. (1992). The coldest sport in the world: Ice boating in Toronto Harbour, 1824–1941. *Material History Review, 35,* 35–46.
Whitehorse, D. (2004). All for the glory of Madison. *Historic Madison: A Journal of the Four Lakes Region, 19,* 4–17.
Whitehorse, D. (2006). History of the Four Lakes Ice Yacht Club. Retrieved December 4, 2006, from www.iceboat.org/history.htm

Iditarod

Dogsled racing, or "mushing," is both a way of life and a sporting competition for participants, most of whom come from cold, snowy climates in North America and Europe. The Iditarod Trail sled dog race, commonly referred to as the "Iditarod" or "The Last Great Race on Earth," is probably the best-known dogsled race in the world. On the first Saturday in March, mushers from across the world enter the Iditarod, starting in Anchorage, Alaska, and finishing about 1,100 miles later in Nome. The Iditarod is one of several sled dog races, which vary by location (for example, the Yukon Quest, a 1,000-mile race run each year between Whitehorse, Yukon, and Fairbanks, Alaska), by distance (for example, the Open North American Sled Dog Race Championship for sprint racing, held annually in Fairbanks since 1936), or by distance covered per day (for example, the multiday stage races occurring in North America and Europe that involve a defined distance per day, which are similar to the Tour de France in cycling).

Races such as the Iditarod Trail require extreme physical and mental endurance. Mushers handle heavy sleds and teams of up to twelve dogs for days on end, often on just a few hours sleep. They race through blizzards causing white-out conditions, and sub-zero weather and gale-force winds, which can cause the wind-chill to reach −100° F (−75° C). "I think I've had every single cold related injury," says DeeDee Jonrowe, one of the most successful women in the sport, "I haven't had any amputations, but I have had severe frostbite on my fingers, cheeks and nose" (Olsen 2001, 85). When caught in a snowstorm during a training expedition, Jonrowe was forced to wait three days in a tent without matches, food or water. She experienced severe hypothermia, and was "shivering so hard" that her "diaphragm would seize up" (Olsen 2001, 85). Despite such risks, Jonrowe, like many passionate mushers, continues to train year-round for the Iditarod event

A sled dog team on the move.
Source: istock/Iztok Noc.

because, in her own words, it is "a real adventure . . . that puts me out there on the edge" (Olsen 2001, 76).

History

Dogs, typically huskies and malamutes, have been used traditionally in northern parts of North America to help pull humans and their equipment over the rugged landscape. Competitive racing with dog teams commonly occurred in Native villages, and in 1908, a 408-mile all-Alaska sweepstakes race was begun in Nome, Alaska. But it was a 1925 diphtheria outbreak in Nome, which required a serum delivery from a town 647 miles away (Nenana) by dog teams facing blizzard conditions, which caught the media's attention. It is this serum run that is commemorated by the modern Iditarod.

It was Dorothy G. Page (c. 1920–1989), the secretary of the Aurora Dog Mushers Association, chair of the Wasilla-Knik Centennial Committee, and mother of the Iditarod, who promoted the idea of holding a sled-dog race in 1967 on the Iditarod Trail as part of the one-hundreth anniver-

sary of Alaska's purchase from Russia. This historic seven-hundred-mile trail had originally been used by dog teams to transport supplies, mail, and gold to the inland mining town of Iditarod. Page wanted to celebrate the history of the trail and the important place of sled dogs in Alaskan history. She worked with Joe Redington Sr. (1917–1999), a skillful musher from Oklahoma, often called the father of the Iditarod, to create a fifty-mile race along this trail. Redington, who had been using dog teams since he moved to Alaska in 1948, was concerned that dog teams were disappearing from native villages due to the increasing popularity of snow machines. After this race was successfully held a second time in 1969, Page suggested that the distance be increased to five hundred miles, finishing at the ghost town of Iditarod. Redington and others extended this idea into a thousand-mile race, past Iditarod to better-known Nome. This would also allow the race to commemorate the 1925 diphtheria serum run.

The first Iditarod was run in 1973. Redington guaranteed a $50,000 purse, an enormous amount for a dogsled race at that time. He ended up cosigning a loan for $30,000 of that amount with his home as collateral. Fundraising ef-

---

The Iditarod

The Iditarod dog sled race is held every year in Alaska and is considered one of the greatest winter extreme races someone can attempt. Since its first official run in 1973, the Iditarod has seen all sorts of competitors, winter conditions, and challenges that set it apart from nearly any other race.

The Last Great Race on Earth

You can't compare it to any other competitive event in the world! A race over 1150 miles of the roughest, most beautiful terrain Mother Nature has to offer. She throws jagged mountain ranges, frozen river, dense forest, desolate tundra and miles of windswept coast at the mushers and their dog teams. Add to that temperatures far below zero, winds that can cause a complete loss of visibility, the hazards of overflow, long hours of darkness and treacherous climbs and side hills, and you have the Iditarod. A race extraordinaire. A race only possible in Alaska.

From Anchorage, in south central Alaska, to Nome on the western Bering Sea coast, each team of twelve to sixteen dogs and their musher cover[s] over 1,150 miles in ten to seventeen days.

It has been called the "Last Great Race on Earth" and it has won worldwide acclaim and interest. German, Spanish, British, Japanese and American film crews have covered the event. Journalists from outdoor magazines, adventure magazines, newspapers and wire services flock to Anchorage and Nome to record the excitement. It's not just a dog sled race, it's a race in which unique men and woman compete. Mushers enter from all walks of life. Fishermen, lawyers, doctors, miners, artists, natives, Canadians, Swiss, French and others; men and women each with their own story, each with their own reasons for going the distance. It's a race organized and run primarily by volunteers, thousands of volunteers, men and women, students and village residents.

Source: http://www.iditarod.com/2-0.html

forts kept him from competing in this first race, which was won twenty days later by Dick Wilmarth. Thirty-four teams started on a trail no one had used for forty-eight years. Spectators as well as mushers wondered if anyone could finish it, but twenty-two teams completed it. The last-place musher, John Shultz, took thirty-two days and was awarded the first Red Lantern, the prize always given to the last musher to complete the race. Redington entered the next nineteen races; he completed his last race at the age of 80 in 1997.

The race consists of two routes: the southern route, which is run in odd years, and the northern route, which is run in even years. The actual race distance varies with each route and the conditions that prevail that year, but it is approximately 1,100 miles. Race times have come down dramatically since the beginning of the Iditarod; the first 10-day Iditarod was completed by Martin Buser in 1992. The 2004 Iditarod was won by Mitch Seavey in a time of 9 days, 12 hours, and 20 minutes.

The race begins in downtown Anchorage at 10 a.m. on the first Saturday in March. The mushers first race twenty miles to Eagle River as part of a fundraiser called the Idita-Rider. Fans bid to ride in a musher's sled, and this money is used to pay as much as $1,049 to mushers who finish from thirty-first place to last place. The teams are then trucked twenty-nine miles to Wasilla, where the race begins in earnest the next day. Teams leave at two-minute intervals, and the time difference is adjusted during the mandatory twenty-four-hour stop. Racers also have to take two eight-hour mandatory stops.

Numerous en route awards are provided in addition to the purses. For example, a seven-course gourmet meal is prepared for the first musher reaching the Yukon River, who also gets $3,500 in $1 bills. Another award, which includes a trophy and $2,500 in gold nuggets, goes to the first musher to arrive in Unalakleet, on the coast. The Iditarod Hall of Fame was created in 1997 by the *Anchorage Daily News* to honor those who have contributed to this race, such as mushers, veterinarians, and trailbreakers.

Volunteers are an integral part of this event. For example, volunteer veterinarians from across North America come to monitor the dogs before and after the race and at each checkpoint. They also do random drug testing on the dogs. Other volunteers, including individuals from villages along the route, complete tasks needed to ensure the race runs successfully, such as breaking trails with snow machines and helping to move trail supplies to drop spots.

The Iditarod is one sporting event where women compete on a par with men. The first two women to run the Iditarod both completed the race in 1974. Libby Riddles became the first female champion in 1985. Susan Butcher is the most successful female champion, having won the Iditarod four times between 1986 and 1990. She ran the race seventeen times, and was the first woman to place in the money when she came in nineteenth in the 1978 race.

Significance

The Iditarod, and sled-dog racing in general, are among the most important sporting activities in Alaska. The Iditarod is Alaska's official sled-dog race, and at the turn of the millennium, several of Alaska's top-ten athletes of the century were dog mushers. Mushers, the media, and spectators from around the world contribute to the local economy. Volunteers—such as members of small communities along the trail, pilots who drop off supplies for the mushers and fly out injured dogs, and veterinarians who take time from their practices across North America to assist in this race—reinforce its importance through their ongoing involvement. Commonly portrayed as one of the last great sporting adventures, it is an important cultural event in the lives of Northerners and an exciting sporting competition for spectators.

Most importantly, it provides participants with a way of life that brings them meaning. The Iditarod may occur over a few weeks each March, but the dedicated athletes who compete—the mushers and their dogs—live this preferred way of life throughout the year.

Victoria Paraschak

Further Reading

Beeman, S. (2003). The Iditarod. *Alaska Geographic, 28*(4).

Brown, T. (1998). *Iditarod country: Exploring the route of the last great race.* Fairbanks, AK: Epicenter Press.

Dolan, E. (1993). *Susan Butcher and the Iditarod trail.* New York: Walker Publishing.

Freedman, L. (1993). *George Attla: The legend of the sled-dog trail.* Harrisburg, PA: Stackpole Books.

Freedman, L. (1999). *Father of the Iditarod: The Joe Redington story.* Fairbanks, AK: Epicenter Press.

Freedman, L., & Jonrowe, D. (1995). *Iditarod dreams: A year in the life of Alaskan sled dog racer DeeDee Jonrowe.* Fairbanks, AK: Epicenter Press.

Hood, M. (1996). *A fan's guide to the Iditarod.* Colorado: Alpine Blue Ribbon Books.

Mattson, S. (Ed.). (2001). *Iditarod fact book: A complete guide to the last great race.* Fairbanks, AK: Epicenter Press.

O'Donoghue, B. P. (1999). *Honest dogs: A story of triumph and regret from the world's toughest sled dog race.* Fairbanks, AK: Epicenter Press.

Olsen, M. (2001). Dream big and dare to fail: A profile of DeeDee Jonrowe. In M. Olsen, *Women who Risk: Profiles of Women in Extreme Sports* (pp. 70–92). New York, Hatherleigh Press.

Wendt, R. (1996). *Alaska dog mushing guide: Facts, legends, & oddities.* Wasilla, AK: Goldstream Publications.

Initiation/Hazing

For most men and to some extent women in Western countries, avoiding initiation is virtually impossible. Hazing ceremonies have been described in junior and senior high school, the military, private schools, paramilitary organizations, fraternities and sororities, as well as sport.

Many of the initiation practices are configured to introduce new members into the power-based, hierarchical structure of the team and to the "masculine model" that the initiation ceremony reinforces. Although there are female examples that do mimic the hostility and masculinity of traditional hazing ceremonies, there are also examples of female welcoming ceremonies which do not go to the same extremes. The continuation of potentially harmful, traditional initiations is contingent on a matrix of factors including the use of alcohol, secrecy, attire, hierarchy, confinement, gender, tradition, heterosexism, homoeroticism, misogyny, power, masculinity, cohesion, symbolism, ritual and the cycle of status from initiated to initiator. The extreme nature of athletes to haze strenuously has led to injury, both physical and psychological, and in some cases has led to death. Sport is typically recognized as a culture that promotes character building and positive values, yet researchers continue to highlight some of the faces of sport which in fact, do just the opposite.

Historical Overview

Behavior that would meet today's definition of hazing has been documented among male educational and military groups for centuries. The term *hazing*, however, was not commonly used until the Civil War period when it emerged as a descriptor of initiation jokes played on newcomers to the ranks of the military. After the Civil War, hazing was used to describe practices of initiating new students to the university and maintaining order within the established hierarchy between classes of students (i.e., upperclassmen versus freshmen). Such activities typically included expectations of personal servitude and other displays of subordination to students in the upper ranks. Occasionally, however, hazing involved what was termed *disorderly conduct* and sometimes escalated into physical brawls causing serious injuries and even fatalities.

Modern hazing practices continue to reflect the masculine historical roots of military units and universities. However, documentation of hazing in high schools and in organized athletics, as well as in professional groups like police academies and firefighting units, has grown considerably. Over the last century, and especially the last three decades, awareness and concern about the dangers of hazing have increased, marked, for example, by their inclusion in many school and university codes of student conduct. Since the 1970s there has been at least one student fatality involving hazing each year. Such tragedies often led to increased public scrutiny and sometimes resulted in the passage of statutory legislation rendering hazing a criminal act. In the United States forty-four states have enacted antihazing laws that vary widely in scope and consequence but are typically restricted to behavior occurring in educational arenas. Although some individual Canadian universities such as McMaster, Western, Windsor, and Toronto universities have specific student athlete codes of conduct policy outlining hazing infractions, the CIS (Canadian Intrauniversity Sport) and some Canadian institutions do not have specific hazing laws, tending instead to defer to the criminal code, or in the case of university infractions, utilizing the umbrella student code of conduct on an individual case basis.

Hazing in School

Disturbingly, in an Alfred University study (1999), 42 percent of the surveyed students reported that they were hazed in high school. Hazing rituals at the high school level might seem to set up and perpetuate the notion in students and athletes that hazing is something very natural, that it is part of joining any group. This mentality surely breeds a cycle. When hazing begins for an individual in high school, or even when the individual is a child, it may be more readily accepted when the individual continues into college and university years. The individual is not necessarily blind in this acceptance, but still, the acceptance may lead the individual to unconsciously believe that hazing is part of joining any team or group, in the belief that it is an important part of bonding. But this kind of belief can be dangerous, given that violent, demeaning, or sexualized behavior may be an integral part of the so-called bonding tradition.

Hank Nuwer's 1990 study is an excellent resource for readers to heighten their awareness of some of the behaviors that are required through hazing. For example: In 1924 two girls from Brooklyn, New York, had Greek letters branded into their foreheads with nitrate of silver. Sadly, the school principal's only response was to say that the sorority that the girls were trying to join had no affiliation with the high school. In another instance, in 1989 a Loris High School initiate of the National Future Farmers of America had to crawl under an electrified cattle fence while wet and naked, while in yet another case, at the same school, initiates were forced to stick bananas up their noses until their noses bled.

If 42 percent of varsity athletes surveyed reported being hazed in some fashion at the high school level, then the examples presented must be less exceptional than they first appear. This percentage represents a significant number, and its implication begs further attention.

After World War II, there was an increase in the number of college fraternities on campus and with it, a sharp increase in hazing. At Texas A & M, for example, a dean of students noted that by 1947, as a result of the rise of hazing, 48 percent of dormitory students dropped out after the first semester.

A tragic event occurred 23 September 2000, when a seventeen-year-old athlete for the rugby team at the University of New Brunswick almost died because of alcohol poisoning at a "rookie party." The team was promptly suspended between 26 September and 2 October 2000 as a result of the incident. And yet, in another case in the same year, in the same province, on 14 October, the Mount St. Allison women's volleyball team was charged in connection with an initiation party that saw rookies "suck beer from condoms, peeing in stolen garbage buckets and nose-writing in cat food casserole" (MacIntyre 2001, 4).

It should be mentioned that in the United States there have also been documented incidents involving violence, including branding. Many African-American fraternities have been known, for example, to brand their pledges with the Greek letter associated with the respective fraternity. In one such case at Ball State University in Missouri in 1987, a student went on record and described the experience of being branded in the following way: "Three seconds more—I wouldn't have gotten it ... I was losing my nerve ... The pain isn't intense. You just smell your skin burning and you hear it crackling. To some, that might be enough

to drive them crazy. You can't move because they'll make a mistake. Once you move it's hard to correct the mistake" (Nuwer 1990, 210).

It should be noted, too, that many of these incidents occur during orientation week or "Frosh Week," during which first-year students are initiated. During one opening week at the University of Saskatchewan campus, one man was found dead at the bottom of an elevator shaft, and there was little doubt as to what contributed to his death because, when he was found, his body was covered in whipped cream and fire extinguisher fluid (Nuwer 1990, 250). Unfortunately, being covered with food and liquids does not appear to be uncommon in hazing rituals."

Modern Sport Hazing

In 1998 two universities in Ontario were forced to address the issue of initiations on their varsity teams. The University of Western Ontario's football team was sanctioned for a hazing-related incident. The terms of the sanctions included the voluntary withdrawal of head coach, Larry Haylor, for a period of two games; the ineligibility of all upper-year players for athletic awards for the 1998–1999 season; and, the requirement that all football players take part in seminars designed to educate about initiation activities. The football team was placed on a two-year's probation during which any further infractions could lead to further sanctions and/or suspensions (*London Free Press* 1998).

McMaster University sanctioned two varsity teams, men's rugby and men's volleyball, for initiation activities that violated both the athletics and student codes of conduct. Both teams were penalized with a one-game suspension from Ontario University Athletics (OUA) competition, resulting in the forfeit of the two points for that competition in their overall league standing, a punishment that affects the entire league by skewing the standings. The teams were also required to perform community service and to design welcoming activities that would provide an alternative to hazing for their incoming high school student athletes (*Hamilton Spectator* 1998a, 1998b, 1998c).

More recently, the University of Vermont (Lively 2000) took action to cancel the remainder of their men's hockey season after Corey Latulippe, a first-year goalie with the team, filed a civil lawsuit against the university. Latulippe was seeking justice for emotional damage and financial loss that he experienced after being hazed against his will by his former teammates.

A man "shotgunning" a beer, an activity not uncommon in hazing and initiation rituals. Source: istock/Tyler Stalman.

These cases are representative of hazing in the 1990s. While there might be a counter argument that athletes are more enlightened and that hazing is no longer commonplace, the following accounts do not support this premise.

In the fall of 2005, the sports world was again shaken when McGill University in Montreal, Canada, revealed serious hazing activities within their football team, canceling the remainder of their season (Naylor 2005). Almost simultaneously, the Windsor Spitfires OHL (Ontario Hockey League) team experienced internal turmoil as a result of a player's resistance to an alleged hazing, challenging the traditions of the team's activities. The fallout from this latter case included the firing of the coach and the trading of the two key combatants in this situation, both highly skilled players. And in February of 2006, Simon Fraser University

suspended its men's and women's swim and dive teams in response to hazing.

The most comprehensive study to date regarding initiation and hazing in U.S. university sport was released 30 August 1999 by Alfred University. The study was sponsored by the National Collegiate Athletic Association (NCAA), and the report consisted of data collected from surveys of NCAA athletes, coaches, and athletic directors across the United States.

A summary of their findings based on a survey sample size of 2,027 is as follows: Over 325,000 athletes at more than 1,000 NCAA universities participated in intercollegiate sports during 1998–1999. Of those athletes involved, more than 250,000 experienced some form of hazing to join a college athletic team. These projections are from a weighted sample of respondents by gender and division of athletics.

Of the group who experienced hazing, one in five was subjected to unacceptable and potentially illegal hazing, including kidnapping, beatings, being tied up, or being abandoned. Some of these individuals were forced to commit crimes, destroy property, make prank phone calls, or harass others. Half were required to participate in drinking contests or alcohol-related games. Women were more likely to be involved in alcohol-related initiations than other forms of hazing, while two-thirds were subjected to humiliating hazing, such as being yelled at, sworn at, forced to wear embarrassing clothing, or forced to deprive themselves of sleep, food, or personal hygiene. Of note is the fact that only one in five participated exclusively in positive initiations, such as camping trips or ropes courses.

According to this study, athletes who were deemed to be most at risk for any kind of hazing for university sports were men: nonfraternity members, either swimmers, divers, soccer players, or lacrosse players. Football players were perceived to be most at risk for dangerous and potentially harmful hazing.

The campuses where hazings were most likely to occur were primarily in eastern or southern states with no antihazing laws. Eastern and western campuses had the most alcohol-related hazing, while southern and midwestern campuses had the greatest incidence of dangerous and potentially illegal hazing. Nonfraternity members were most at risk of being hazed from athletics, though a fraternity system on campus is a significant predictor of hazing.

Coaches reported that they were aware of the positive initiations, but unaware of the prevalence of hazing and alcohol use. Only 10 percent of coaches and administra-

tors reported that they knew of hazing on their campuses or of the use of alcohol during the initiation ceremony. In fact a number of these individuals denied the need to discuss the issue of hazing and its prevention. However, there was agreement on strategies to prevent hazing by athletes, coaches, and administrators who did acknowledge the problem. These included sending a clear antihazing message in policy, education, and enforcement and an expectation of responsibility, integrity, and civility on the part of the athletes, team captains, coaches, and administrators, as well as offering team-building initiation rites facilitated by trained coaches and adults

Recent research, national news accounts of hazing, and anecdotal evidence point toward gender differences in hazing activities. In general a common conclusion drawn is that hazing among men is more likely to be violent in nature and hazing among women is more likely to be psychological/emotional in nature, although this demographic is in a state of flux illustrated by recent high-profile hazing cases involving girls and women.

Such perspectives align with and also reinforce predominant understandings of differences between the genders. The results of the Alfred/NCAA study revealed differences between types of hazing experienced by male and female athletes. Notably, women were less likely than men to be subjected to unacceptable acts including destroying or stealing property, beatings, being tied up or taped, confined to small places, paddled, kidnapped, or transported and abandoned. This finding supports the assertion that sex/gender differences in hazing experiences do exist.

Sport Subculture and Identity

A part of the large body of work on sport subcultures involves an examination of socialization into subcultures. Such socialization often involves establishing an identity as a member of a particular subculture and having that identity confirmed by established members. One of the ways in which team sport athletes have frequently had their identities confirmed is by successfully negotiating the rigors of "Rookie Night" hazing ceremonies. Athletes who choose to take part in the initiation ceremony do so of their own volition, or so it would seem. However, the necessity of making that choice is in direct correlation with their desire to belong to a new group.

Donnelly and Young (1988, 223–225) define *subcultures* as "small social structures within the larger dominant culture."

In this domain the group communes with shared values, clothing, attitudes, language, practices, and ceremonies; it is these shared attributes that separate the subculture from culture. When discussing subcultures, it is possible to categorize, for example, being a member of a rugby subculture, as different from the greater culture in which its members develop and share common goals, equipment, language, use of the body, values, beliefs, and rituals. Within that subculture, however, there can exist further slight or gross divisions between teams.

Membership within the team community extends beyond physical ability and athletic prowess. An athlete's acceptance within this culture can be facilitated or hindered by social factors stemming from his or her willingness to demonstrate loyalty and commitment to teammates as well as the team. The greater the resistance to the desires of the team, the more difficult the transition will be into the community.

Team Cohesion (Bonding)

Many members within team sport cultures share the belief that hazing equates with cohesion, which in turn fosters success. As Donnelly and Young (1988) contend, acceptance is contingent on various conditions, many of which are in place to create a sense of cohesion. *Group cohesion* is described as "the dynamic process which is reflected in the tendency for a group to stick together and remain united in the pursuit of goals and objectives" (Carron 1982, 124). The basis of group cohesion stems from the idea that a group of individuals working together is far more effective than the same individuals working independently, and it has also been established that members of cohesive teams enjoy a certain attraction to one another. While the literature on cohesion does not deal specifically with the role of initiation into the team unit itself as a means of developing group cohesion, Widmeyer and Martens (1993) determined that cohesiveness is actively promoted by coaches through such practices as establishing athletic dormitories, common clothing that identifies the players as members of the team, social activities, communal goal setting and ritualistic activities, which would clearly include initiation ceremonies. Cohesion is actively pursued by both players and coaches and often is cited as an excuse for the continuation of initiation and hazing ceremonies.

During the initiation ceremony all of the participants come together for a common purpose. Some players hold onto the belief that it is the initiation ceremony that gels the team and allows cohesion to occur. Cohesion, real or perceived, is one of the motivating factors for the continuation of the initiation ceremony.

Conformity

There is a dynamic aspect to groups: peer pressure, mob antics, a need to appease the "vets," or to conform and cause the least amount of ripples possible. This is the coercive pull of a hegemonic system, which allows the participant a sense of autonomy and choice yet limits the routes he or she can take. The pull toward the intoxicating environment, one rich with power-laden overtones, and which is accessible to the neophyte who needs only endure the initiation is, for some, easy to justify.

The alluring draw toward the team culture can entice individuals to, at times, compromise their integrity and free will and to enter into situations that under normal circumstances would seem corrupt and unethical. Participation in the initiation ceremony is then justified and sold to the participants as a necessary transition for the good of the team, to forge strong bonds, to keep the tradition alive, to succeed. This is internalized and reproduced within the subculture.

People engaged in hazing usually accept its proposed effects. A new group member who refuses to accept hazing is usually considered a deviant or ostracized and humiliated, forced to the periphery in a bid by the group to reestablish its dominance and the importance of the rituals that are at the core of its belief and practical system. The ability to go through with an initiation can stem from a need to be accepted. While it is recognized that people need to be valued by their peers, it must be noted that although most social groups have some type of entry ritual, not all groups do. Hazing allows for this acceptance and it is difficult for those outside of the community not familiar with the culture of hazing to understand this (Nuwer 1999). Yet it provides a contradictory response from administrators and coaches, who, as former athletes and "insiders" in the sport culture, both publicly condemn and privately condone hazing practices, effectively allowing practices to flourish.

Hierarchy and Power

Various techniques are used to reinforce the power structure imbedded within the team. The hierarchical needs of the power-holders are established and reproduced throughout the initiation, educating the neophytes as to both their position within the system and their means by which to attain it. This domination is exerted over the rookies through violence, forced menial labor, hierarchal seating and locker assignments, and initiations. During the hazing ceremony the novitiates are inducted into the cyclical nature of the system that bestows the rookies with the eventual means of becoming the initiaton.

The hierarchy is established by the veteran players as a means of control over the first-year players. They exert this control through the expectation that the players will fulfill their prescribed "Rookie Duties." Although the tasks may vary from team to team, the basis of this system is to construct a tiered system that can only be negotiated through compliance and the unquestioning fulfillment of the ascribed responsibilities. The creation of this type of hierarchical structure is a crucial element of the initiation ceremony, not only in terms of a rite of passage, but also as a means to convey to the neophytes their position within the structure of the team and the processes they must endure to achieve eventual power.

The threat of the incoming rookie contingent is dealt with through the initiation ceremony. The veteran players use the ceremony, often in violent ways, to establish a system of dominance, which favors senior players and demands the subservience of the neophyte. This represents a marked divergence from cultural initiations in which the initiation is to mark entry into the culture, not to establish a system of dominance and submission.

Role of Alcohol

Various components of initiation ceremonies serve to produce and reproduce a veteran–rookie relationship based on power. The initiation functions to instill within the rookie a sense of subservience, while at the same time revealing the means by which to attain power (e.g., by asserting dominance over newer members). The ceremony explicitly defines the role of the novitiate in the community, often with the aid of alcohol. Alcohol serves a dual purpose. Not only is it used to relax the inhibitions of the initiates, it is also the tool through which the veterans exert their power. Alcohol taken in sufficient quantities results in uncharacteristic behavior, impaired thinking, and decreased awareness of one's surroundings. During initiations veterans encourage, coerce, or force rookies to consume alcohol in quantities that, in most

cases, result in unruly behavior, vomiting, and/or unconsciousness (events that precede or indicate alcohol poisoning). Occasionally, the alcohol poisoning of initiates is severe enough to require emergency medical attention. Under the influence of alcohol, initiates can be more easily coerced by the veterans into performing humiliating or dangerous acts since their own decision-making abilities are depressed. By limiting the ability of initiates to make rational choices of their own, and at the same time impairing their physical wellness, the veterans can assert their physical, social, and behavioral dominance over the rookies.

For some first-year players, who may be as young as seventeen, this ceremony can be their introduction to alcohol. The veterans, who claim authority over the rookies and the activities of initiation events, position themselves as "experts" in alcohol consumption, drinking games, and initiations, establishing the rookies in a subservient position. The rule of the "experts" encourages the initiates to uncritically accept the alcohol, games, and other rites as mandatory and safe. Stories are rampant of passing out, blacking out, throwing up, unruly behavior, two-day hangovers, playing games designed to get them drunk faster, and never having been "so pissed" in their lives. The use of alcohol during the initiation is a means to an end; under its influence alcohol can relax rookies' social inhibitions and sense of personal responsibility, establishing the veteran as the authority in those areas. A relationship of power, the veteran holding power over the rookie, is therefore established.

Cycle of Initiation

The cyclical nature of the initiation is defined by those who endured the initiation as an initiate and then assumed the role of initiator. This is a frequently cited reason for the perpetuation of the ceremonies. This cycle is one that feeds on the need to "outdo," or at least to match, the previous year's activities. It embeds in the psyche of those who have been initiated the desire to exert their power over the rookie contingent in subsequent seasons. The language describing the ceremonies is for the most part harsh and suggestive of an event, which is not altogether pleasant or welcoming. Yet the need for most participants to become initiators allows the cycle to persist. A product of the initiation ceremony is the folklore and grandiose tales that are generated through the feats of rookie participants. These stories are revisited by team members in order to protract the myths and legends of team dedication and cohesion passed on to the rookie

Long-term Affects of Hazing

Hazing and initiation rituals can have an immediate, embarrassing result, but as reporting of these incidents increases, the long-term damage is becoming more evident.

Affects of Hazing Last Long After Pledging Process

Sam Zwecker '04 at Cornell University, stood tired and barefoot on shards of broken glass with the rest of his fraternity pledge class. For seven hours, Zwecker and his pledge mates had been pelted by eggs and forced to do push-ups by the brothers at his chosen fraternity, activities designed to initiate aspiring members into the organization. The exercise may sound extreme, but it was just another night of hazing for a pledge class in 2001.

"That was one of the nights when you go home and you wonder, 'What the hell am I doing?'" Zwecker said. "The frat brothers tried to justify it by saying that it would build unity for us, but it was kind of just a stupid, gross experience."

Zwecker's story is posted in detail at hazing.cornell.edu, a University-operated website designed to foster community awareness about the incidence of hazing on campus. Hazing incidents like those experienced by Zwecker would ultimately inspire Susan Murphy, vice president for student and services, to appoint a Task Force on Hazing in 2001. That group would eventually recommend the launch of the University's hazing website four years later.

Noah Grynberg

Source: Grynmberg, N. (Jan. 26, 2007). Effects of Hazing Last Long After Pledging Process. *The Cornell Daily Sun*. Retrieved Feb. 1 2007 from http://www.cornellsun.com/node/20926

contingent in hopes of keeping the bond alive. This form of hype is an attempt to convey to rookie candidates the dedication, desire, and sense of sacrifice that members demonstrate to the team. The revisiting of these tales generates both an interest within the audience to belong and a means of passing on the traditional folklore of the team.

The possible role that the coach assumes concerning the cycle of initiation falls into two categories: nonparticipation and participation. The coaches who are nonparticipants are either adamant in their demands that no initiation take place, or they feign ignorance of any knowledge of what the team is planning until after the event, at which time they choose to acknowledge the initiation with mock disapproval or silent acceptance. The coaches who participate are either full participants or they take part in a minor capacity. The direct involvement of the coach is paramount to the successful paradigm shift that will change the very fabric of the group. Without strong leadership initiation practices will simply find an existence out of the reach of the administration.

Model for Change

In a bid to change the problematic, dangerous elements surrounding the culture of hazing and initiations, it is crucial to discuss the status quo and the need for replacing the old traditions with the newer sport concept of orientation in the form of adventure-based programming. Why are athletes eager to comply with the demands of the hazing ritual in a bid for membership? What is actually happening across most campuses? Successful implementation and change is dependent on sensitivity to the power imbalance in relationships between new and veteran players and coaches. The power imbalance comes from the status of new players as "rookies" and is linked to the ability of veteran players to establish team norms and withhold membership and acceptance. Many of the alternatives—such as adventure-based education and outdoor education—are viable only if new players are extended the same privileges and rights as their older peers. Coaches and student leaders recognize that the need of new players to feel they belong may have a tremendous impact on their willingness to participate in initiation and hazing activities.

Teams that persist in carrying out inappropriate initiation rituals must face appropriate sanctions, which may include reduction or removal of funding and restrictions on, or denial of, access to competitive privileges, resources, and facilities. The teams must be educated prior to the commencement of their season as to what are unacceptable practices and to the possible sanctions for indulging in them. Although there have been limited sanctions handed out for infractions, for example, by McMaster University, the University of Western Ontario, McGill University, and the University of Vermont, there are some questions as to whether sanctions are enough to eliminate the hazing practices of certain teams. The University of Toronto and McMaster University have been very proactive in attempting to stop hazing in response to a few public cases of hazing both in their residences and on varsity teams. Their examples can be viewed as models toward changing the culture of hazing of which a longitudinal study would serve to illuminate potential successes.

Some University athletic policies, like the example of the University of Western Ontario, also prohibit activities of a sexually exploitative nature at orientation events. It is extremely difficult to distinguish between willingness to participate in sexually oriented activities. Orientation events which are sexually oriented do not represent welcoming experience for all students. "Some former participants have experienced post-traumatic stress disorder, similar to those experienced by soldiers, as a result of such experiences" (Winslow 1999, 26). It is crucial to create and offer activities that are attractive and exciting, and that come to be seen as "real" alternatives to traditional hazing practices. It is equally important to include the veteran athletes in the planning process so that the membership is able to derive a sense of ownership over the welcoming ceremony in a bid to establish a new tradition that emanates from them as opposed to the administration.

There are guidelines about hazing in some student handbooks, but often these are ignored as according to the research, 60 percent of American high school students and 80 percent of college athletes, particularly those involved in sport, said they had experienced hazing, half of them before the age of thirteen; only 20 percent found the practice positive.

There is still pressure to mark a new player's entry onto the team. Although research that examines hazing in a sporting context is limited, there is a growing body of literature that describes some of the experiences and phenomena of athletes in the traditional methods of initiating. There is no literature that discusses institutions that have implemented alternative policies and are actively seeking alternative methods for teams to orient themselves to counter some of the damaging and questionable practices currently practiced by some sport teams. Some of the alternatives have been adventure-based orientations such as canoeing, high and low rope courses, cooperative games, and climbing wall activities.

It is important that teams adopt a strategy of education, open communication, strong leadership supportive of the inclusive ideal, a concise understanding of a clearly defined policy, and sanctions and activities which promote a welcoming environment while shedding their traditional pasts. At the varsity level, athletic departments should be including budgetary commitments to actively promote and establish alternative opportunities for teams. To effectively change the culture of hazing, those participating must be educated as to the damaging and harmful potential that exists in these ceremonies. However, there must be a ritualized rite of passage to fill the void in the wake of the elimination of traditional hazing practices. Adventure-based and outdoor education can fill that void.

Historically, much of the affects of such extreme humiliation and abusive practices would have been left to the individual to internalize or would be seen as an internal matter for the team or group to resolve. As the discourse around such practices becomes more pronounced, the legal and social ramifications of such actions increase, perpetrators are being held accountable, and there is a contestation of what is "play" and what is cruelty. This mirrors what happens as social norms evolve in many areas; racist and sexist jokes have become less acceptable to a wide range of people.

Jay Johnson

Further Reading

Bryshun, J. (1997). Hazing in sport: An exploratory study of veteran/rookie relations. Unpublished master's thesis, University of Calgary, Calgary, Canada.

Burstyn, V. (1999). *The rites of men: Manhood, politics, and the culture of sport.* Toronto, Ontario, Canada: University of Toronto Press.

Campo S., Poulos G., & Sipple, J. W. (2005). Prevalence and profiling: Hazing among college students and points of intervention. *American Journal of Health Behavior, 29*(2), 137–149.

Carron, A. V. (1982). Cohesiveness in sport groups: Interpretations and considerations. *Journal of Sport Psychology, 4,* 123–138.

Crow, R., & Rosner, S. (2002). Institutional and organizational liability for hazing in intercollegiate and professional team sports. *St. John's Law Review, 76*(1), 87–114.

Donnelly, P., & Young, K. (1988). The construction and confirmation of identity in sport subcultures. *Sociology of Sport Journal, 5,* 223–240.

Eliade, M. (1975). *Rites and symbols of initiations and the mysteries of birth and rebirth.* New York: Harper and Row.

Fitchett, A. (1995). Motivation, cohesion and success in male and female soccer teams. Unpublished master's thesis, Queen's University, Kingston, Canada.

Garfinkel, H. (1999). Conditions of successful degradation ceremonies. *American Journal of Sociology 3*(4), 139–154.

Hamilton Spectator. (1998a, October 16). HAZING: The education must continue.

Hamilton Spectator. (1998b, October 19). Mac's on-side with hazing crackdown.

Hamilton Spectator. (1998c, November 2). Hazing punishment at Mac is justified.

Holman, M. (1997, November). *Hazing in sport.* Paper presented at the North American Society for the Sociology of Sport, Toronto, Canada.

Hoover, N. (1999). *National survey: Initiation rites and athletics for NCAA sports teams.* Retrieved May 15, 2003 from: http://www.alfred.edu/news/html/hazing_study_99.html

Johnson, J., & Donnelly, P. (2004). In their own words: Athletic administrators, coaches and athletes at two universities discuss hazing policy initiatives. In J. Johnson & M. Holman (Eds.), *Making the team: Inside the world of sport initiations and hazing.* Toronto, Ontario, Canada: Canadian Scholars Press.

Linhares de Albuquerque, C. L., & Paes-Machado, E. (2004). The hazing machine: The shaping of Brazilian military police recruits. *Policing and Society 14*(2), 175–192.

Lively, K. (2000, February 4). U. Vermont cancels men's hockey season. *The Chronicle of Higher Education,* Athletics: A. 56.

London Free Press, (1998, October 26). Western pulls a sneak play on initiation antics.

Mac hazing costly. (1998, October 15). *The Toronto Sun,* p. 17.

Malszecki, G. (2004). No mercy shown, nor asked: Toughness, test or torture?: Hazing in military combat units and its collateral damage. In J. Johnson & M. Holman (Eds.), *Making the team: Inside the world of sport initiations and hazing.* Toronto, Ontario, Canada: Canadian Scholars Press.

Moss, M. (2001). *Manliness and militarism: Educating young boys in Ontario for war.* Toronto, Ontario: Oxford University Press.

Naylor, D. (2005, September 21). Hazing allegation under investigation. *The Globe and Mail.*

Nuwer, H. (1999). *Wrongs of passage.* Bloomington, IN: Indiana University Press.

Robinson, L. (1998). *Crossing the line: Violence and sexual assault in Canada's national sport.* Toronto, Canada: McClelland & Stewart.

Sabo, D., & Panepinto, J. (1990). Football ritual and the social production of masculinity. In M. Messner & D. Sabo (Eds.), *Sport, men and the gender order.* Champaign, IL: Human Kinetics.

White, P., & Young, K. (1999). Is sports injury gendered? In P. White & K. Young (Eds.), *Sport and gender in Canada* (pp. 69–84). Don Mills, Ontario, Canada: Oxford University Press.

Widmeyer, W. N., & Martens, R. (1993). When cohesion predicts performance outcomes in sport. *The Research Quarterly, 49*(3), 372–380.

Winslow, D. (1999). Rites of passage and group bonding in the Canadian airborne. *Armed Forces and Society, 25*(3), 429–457.

Young, K. (1993). Violence, risk, and liability in male sports culture. *Sociology of Sport Journal, 10*(4), 373–396.

Injury

Extreme sports, by definition, contain elements of risk. The spaces in which such sports take place often cannot be controlled because they include the ocean or mountains or places where wind, precipitation, and temperature contribute to a volatile environment. In such unpredictable spaces, the risk of injury, and even death, is higher than in many other sporting contexts. In addition, to be regarded as an authentic participant in an extreme sport usually requires a high level of technical skill and a particular attitude, which often includes thrill seeking for personal gratification. As a result, although most extreme sports are individual and noncontact activities and thus may appear "safe," the fact that they take place in challenging physical environments by participants seeking an "adrenaline rush" means that such sports carry an intrinsic risk of injury.

Injury may be broadly defined as damage to which the body is unable to immediately adapt and which may have varied potential consequences. These consequences include preventing athletes from continuing to participate in the sport, impairing their quality of life, and reducing their life expectancy. Ultimately, injuries may even be life threatening. Sports-related injuries may be categorized under two main types: acute or chronic. Acute injuries most commonly take the form of fractures and are usually the result of a specific traumatic event, such as falling off a skateboard or skis. Forearm fractures are the most common injury among young people participating in skateboarding, often because of the failure to wear wristguards and armguards. Chronic injuries include sprains and contusions and generally develop slowly through overuse. For example, climbers who continually practice the same move often damage their fingers and can develop tendonitis in their shoulders. Meanwhile, the damage to surfers' auditory canals through extended time in cold water has become known in common parlance as "surfer's ear." In addition, chronic injuries may be caused by training with a previous injury.

Researchers cannot easily determine the exact number of injuries incurred through participation in extreme sports because the nature of the sports means that many participants are amateur and do not belong to clubs, which means that injuries sustained may not be recorded. However, the increasing popularity of such sports means that, inevitably, the number of related injuries also appears to be increasing. For example, in the United States inline skating is thought to be the nation's fastest-growing sport, with approximately 29 million skaters. Each year approximately sixty-five thousand children receive medical treatment for inline skating injuries, the most common of which are bone fractures and injuries to the head or face. Surveys of extreme sports injuries indicate that snowboarding carries the highest risk of injury, followed by surfing, mountain biking, skateboarding, and BMX (bicycle motocross) riding.

Causes of Injury

Injuries may be caused by factors that are internal to the athlete as well as by external factors. Risk factors that are internal to the athlete's body are easier to control. For example, athletes who do not undertake an appropriate training program or warm up thoroughly before participating may find that their body is insufficiently strong and flexible or that their muscles fail to contract and relax properly, and so they risk injury. The Chiropractors Association of Australia, witnessing a growth in snowboarding injuries, advocates a minimum of seven minutes to warm up and warm down to avoid damage to the musculoskeletal system risked through skiing and snowboarding. In extreme sports these risks are worsened by the fact that these sports are not in mainstream physical education curricula, nor do many have an established club base, and so participants are often self-taught, having received no training in such activities at school or in sports clubs.

However, many injuries in extreme sports are caused by factors external to the athlete's body, such as a challenging physical environment, collisions, and the use of poor equipment or insufficient safety equipment. The BMX rider Dave Mirra told of how he injured his spleen after falling because he wore inappropriate clothing: His shirt got caught in his bike while performing a trick at a state fair. In motocross Carey Hart collided with a tractor working on the track, causing six breaks to his femurs, a broken shin, and a broken wrist. BASE (building, antenna, span, Earth) jumpers are often seriously injured or killed if their parachute fails to open or if they collide with a wall or antenna. And in bull riding a thrown rider can break bones and even be killed if the bull then lands on top of him or her.

Many of those injured in extreme sports were not wearing protective clothing such as helmets, elbow pads, or wristguards, which might have prevented their injury. In extreme water sports, failure to wear protective clothing places the participant at risk of jellyfish stings or other bites, skin abrasions, and sunburn.

However, sometimes the equipment is responsible for injuries. Many advances in equipment enable participants to travel at higher speeds and perform more adventurous tricks but often without a concomitant improvement in safety. For example, the design of surfboard fins includes sharp edges and a specific tip profile to improve performance, but these features simultaneously increase the risk of injury if the surfer is struck by the board. Most injuries are caused by direct contact with the surfer's own board as a result of increased use of short boards, which are leashed to the surfer and so recoil when the surfer falls off the board. The most common injuries are lacerations, sprains, and less frequently loss of sight. An additional development in surfing has been the emergence of tow-in surfing, whereby surfers are towed out to surf bigger waves, usually on the back of a jet ski, so increasing the risk of injury and fatalities. The most common causes of injuries in windsurfing are also related to the equipment, with athletes experiencing contusions and lower back pain related to the boom and mast, while ankle injuries often result from the use of foot straps.

In speed skiing, wakeboarding, and street luging, the use of specialized skis and modified boards, often combined with aerodynamic clothes, enables participants to reach speeds equivalent to traveling in a car but without the protection of the metal surround. In skiing, participants may reach 257 kilometers per hour, and in street luging they may race down a hill (sometimes in traffic) at 128 kilometers per hour. Wakeboarders, towed behind a boat, frequently experience injuries to their knees as a result of the rotational force from the board and also impact injuries from hitting the water face-on at high speed. In a similar sport, water skiers may reach speeds of 80 kilometers per hour, and injuries are most common as a result of entanglement with the towrope (including amputation of fingers wrapped up in the rope), collision with the boat, and injuries to the vagina and rectum. Free divers are able to plunge to greater depths because of equipment improvements, often to 120 meters with a single breath and without breathing equipment, but this advancement has led to blackouts and death because the brain is starved of oxygen.

In addition, the equipment that has been developed to enable athletes with physical disabilities to be more mobile is also being further adapted to facilitate involvement in extreme sports. Extreme wheelchair sports feature wheelchair stunts, similar to BMX tricks, and trail and street riding. In addition, sports such as skiing have been adapted to sit-ski and bi-ski to enable skiing in a seated position. Such developments enable faster and more dangerous levels of participation. In addition, any subsequent injury carries new significance when the athlete already has frequent pain and functional impairment because of physical disability.

An all too familiar sign at a hospital. Source: istock/Paul Hart.

Common Extreme Sports Injuries

There are some injuries that, over time, become attributed with certain sports such as concussions in rugby, torn shoulder muscles in baseball, or knee injuries in football. Extreme sports carry their own risks, and many of the same injuries. Below are some descriptions of more common "extreme injuries."

When a skateboarder is practicing tricks on a 15-foot ramp (commonly called a half-pipe), or a mountain biker is flying down a rock-strewn single track trail, and he makes a mistake and falls—well, it's going to hurt a little. Okay, maybe a lot.

Matt Donovan, a pro downhill mountain bike racer from Massachusetts, said that when he first got serious about racing, his season was "very injury-laden. I had two concussions, a separated shoulder, a broken hand, multiple cuts, and lacerations. And I cracked a rib."

Yes, extreme sports can often lead to extreme in-juries. The most common injuries in alternative sports are broken bones, strains, sprains, serious bruising, and facial cuts. But studies show that nearly 75 percent of all people who get injured participating in extreme sports incurred their injuries because they didn't wear any protective gear.

Of the estimated 65,000 children receiving medical treatment for inline skating injuries each year, almost half have fractured a bone and 7,000 have injured the head or face.

Skaters most often injure their wrists and elbows.

Wrist guards and elbow pads afford the same amount of protection to inline skaters as helmets do for cyclists—85 percent.

Source: Kids and extreme sports. (n.d.). Retrieved February 2, 2007, from http://life.familyeducation.com/sports/29462.html

"Just Do It"? Why Do It?

Given the potential for injury incurred through participation in extreme sports, one might ask why people take such risks. It is possible that people with particular personality types may be more likely to engage in such risky behavior. People with an extrovert personality often seek excitement, stimulation, and thrills through risk taking and are also likely to have a high pain threshold. These traits mean that such people are more likely to both become injured and to continue to participate while in pain. They may also be bored by rehabilitation, particularly if it requires rest, and so may not complete any program of therapy. Psychologist Frank Farley refers to people with such traits as having a "Type T" personality. He notes that many such people engage in dangerous sports. At the extreme people with psychopathic personalities may have a desire to harm themselves or others, and even a death wish, and so engage in high-risk behavior to prove superiority. However, some people also suffer what is known as "akrasia," which includes difficulty in making logical decisions, for example, an inability to correctly perceive danger and the potential for injury. For such people involve-

ment in extreme sports is a less rational decision than it is for those with a Type T personality. Clearly the reason why people become involved in extreme sports is more complex than just an issue of personality type.

Another explanation for such behavior may be related to changes in societies that leave people seeking excitement. Since the Middle Ages most Western societies have witnessed increased state control over people's behavior, along with broader social pressures on people to exercise self-restraint, especially in physical violence. Such social processes are reflected in sports, including the ban on many blood sports and the imposition of tighter controls to limit violence and injury in many other sports. For example, the rules of many mainstream sports require participants to wear protective clothing, and athletes are penalized by "red cards" or "sin bins" for rule infringement and behavior that may cause injury to an opponent. As a result of such processes, many people seek alternative outlets to satisfy their desire for excitement, which is no longer readily available within the constraints of many organized sport forms. Risking their body in extreme sports may be one consequence of these civilizing processes. As the tagline reads on one extreme sports website (www.extremesportscafe.com): "Remember, we don't measure life by how many breaths we take, but by how many moments take our breath away." Thus, in sports such as climbing, many athletes have resisted technological developments that have made the sport more routine and rational through the deliberate placing of bolts on routes for climbers to follow. Instead, traditional climbers embrace the inherent injury risk in following the natural rock and so deliberately increase the uncertainty and danger. Similarly, in skateboarding the ramp and vert styles of skating are more controlled, with requirements that participants wear safety equipment. As a result, the street style of skating maintains a higher status because it is unsupervised and values physical (and sometimes illegal) risk taking, with participants resisting the wearing of padding, thus increasing the likelihood of injury.

Some extreme sports also involve a deliberate infliction of injury on an opponent. This fact is illustrated most obviously in ultimate fighting, which is a mixed martial arts sport. The sport originated in the United States in the 1990s and in its earliest manifestation promoted itself as a "no rules" sport. Competitors would fight until there was a victor, with no weight categories and few limits on the techniques that could be used. Perceptions of violence and injury risk led to calls to ban the sport. U.S. Senator John McCain described it as a form of "human cockfighting." As a result, in line with developments in other sports, ultimate fighting has also become more "civilized," with rules introduced to penalize some of the more dangerous actions and even a name change to "mixed martial arts." However, even in the more regulated sport, victory is often achieved by forcing a submission with holds that cut off the oxygen supply or risk limb breakage, and a "no holds barred" competition survives in the Ultimate Fighting Championships. Although exact rates of injury are not known, the most common injuries include broken bones, torn knees, and shoulder and ankle sprains. In addition, fatality rates are estimated to be twice those of athletes in boxing, most commonly as a result of subdural hematoma, in which a strike to the head causes tearing of the veins around the brain, leading to a blood clot. Despite the contentious nature of the sport, ultimate fighting is still celebrated with its own television show on Spike TV in the United States, and there is an ultimate fighting competition hall of fame, with many fighters having some celebrity status, perhaps most notably Ken Shamrock, who describes himself as the "world's most dangerous man" and has the catchphrase "I'm gonna beat you into the living death."

Celebrating Extreme Injuries

As mentioned, many of the most successful extreme sports athletes are media celebrities, not least in ESPN's X Games, which is broadcast globally in more than twenty languages. When athletes become injured, such injuries also become part of the mediated sports spectacle—so much so that injury in extreme sports may be normalized and even celebrated. Some specialist magazines have titles reinforcing the culture of extremity, such as the climbing magazine *On the Edge* and skiing's *Ballistic*. Many even have columns dedicated to admiring injuries. For example, the skateboarding magazine *Thrasher* has "Hall of Merit," and *Skateboarder* has "Skate Anatomy," while Internet sites such as www.kidzworld.com have an online vote for "grossest extreme injury." Extreme sports presented in the media also often use production techniques such as slow-motion replay of injurious events and freeze-frames focusing on the injured athlete, and journalists will often confer heroic status on the athlete willing to play hurt, all of which serves to belie the agony experienced by the injured athlete.

Such media coverage of extreme sports injuries has implications for athletes and spectators. The athletes learn that being portrayed as a risk taker and participating while injured are beneficial to their athletic status. In addition, such coverage indicates to spectators what is required for achievement at the highest level of performance in extreme sports. Young people will try to emulate the skills of elite extreme sports athletes, risking pain and injury in the process. However, injury is often celebrated among sports performers as an indication of commitment and accomplishment, such as when participants in ultimate Frisbee compete for the "worst injury" prize at many tournaments.

Selling Extreme Injuries

The celebration of risk taking in extreme sports has also provided the basis for a leisure market: adventure tourism. Adventure travel companies sell extreme holidays to novice athletes seeking the thrill of extreme activities such as bungee jumping, mountaineering, or canyoning. In buying the extreme, these people risk injury, and in some cases death, because their desire for the thrill of the activity often exceeds their ability to safely participate. For example, in bungee jumping participants, who are often holidaying backpackers without any training, may suffer injuries from rope burns, visual impairment as a result of a damaged retina, quadriplegia, and even death.

Sports such as mountaineering or canyoning, which require high levels of training and skill, have been made available through these companies to amateur tourists who pay a financial (and sometimes a health) price. Among the most infamous incidents on such adventure holidays was the Interlaken tragedy in 1999, when twenty-one people died canyoning in white water in the Swiss Saxtenbach Gorge. A flash flood filled the narrow gorge with water, sweeping to their deaths those negotiating the rapids with nothing more than a wetsuit and buoyancy aid. More generally, injuries to such tourists are estimated to be equivalent to the annual number of traffic injuries. Most common are falls in mountaineering, horseback riding, skiing, and cycling.

Gendering Extreme Injuries

The majority of sports-related injuries occur among young males. This fact is most likely because this group has the highest number of participants. Also, whereas females are often raised to take care of their bodies, males learn that taking risks and enduring the pain of participation while injured are a sign of masculinity. For example, BASE jumpers accept that being injured is not a case of "if," but rather "when," with predictions of a 5 percent chance of death and a 95 percent chance of serious injury. Notably, the majority of BASE jumpers are male. In skateboarding the physical display of injury is seen as an attractive quality in males, as demonstrated in the slogan on a T-shirt worn by one male skater: "Chicks Dig Scars" (Beal and Wilson 2004, 38), suggesting that women are attracted to risk-taking males.

However, many extreme sports are less gender differentiated than mainstream activities, and where there are high rates of female participation, the risk of injury is comparable with that of their male counterparts. Therefore, although extreme sports enable women to challenge the gender inequities that have surrounded the development of most mainstream sports, this challenge is countered by the apparent trend of these women being exposed to, and frequently adopting, masculine norms of sacrificing their body for their sport. For example, in rock climbing the risk and tolerance of injury have often been viewed as a positive indication of masculinity. As more women become involved in climbing, they also have to take risks to demonstrate commitment and character in a male-dominated domain and in so doing experience climbing-related injuries.

Adventure racing is an example of an extreme sport whose rules of competition require mixed-sex teams. These teams complete a designated course that may include mountain biking, horseback riding, paddling, climbing, and/or trekking, sometimes over several days. Women often become injured in adventure racing because they have to push harder or take greater risks with their bodies in order to be taken seriously as an athlete on a team containing males. As a result, although the increased involvement of women in previously male-exclusive environments offers the potential to challenge violent and injurious behavior, women feel that they are treading on male territory, accept the masculine norms in these activities, and end up risking their own health.

Future Possibilities

The world of extreme sports appears to be dominated by people who seek risk and are prepared to compromise their bodily well-being in practicing such sports. Sports such as rock climbing, mountaineering, BMX, and snowboarding carry an intrinsic risk of injury, and for participants this is central to the pleasure in the sport. As a result, many athletes who have been injured while participating in extreme sports find it difficult to terminate their engagement with such sports. Psychologists sometimes refer to this phenomenon as "reversal theory": People seek situations that have the potential for high arousal and excitement but find a way to construct these situations as safe despite the injurious consequences. Sometimes this process occurs because these athletes are dependent on the high arousal experience and may even be addicted to the experience of excitement. Although for many athletes this process is appropriated into their lifestyle (and, in fact, extreme sports are often referred to as "lifestyle" sports), there is now the further danger that inexperienced and sometimes ill-informed people are risking their bodies and sometimes their lives while buying into adventure tourism.

One possible consequence for extreme sports, as they increasingly move into the mainstream, is the development of specialized insurance packages for those engaged in activities that may require particular help, ranging from people wishing to take their cars off road to people seeking evacuation from a hazardous space after an injurious accident. Insurance premiums for extreme sports athletes are high, given the nature of these activities and the likelihood of injury, which means that some professional athletes have considered unionizing to gain group insurance packages.

The use of legal support is also reflected in increased litigation to police and punish those people deemed responsible for sports-related injuries. Legal intervention in such cases is complicated by the belief that athletes are voluntarily engaging in extreme sports, including adventure tourism, knowing the potential for harm to their body. This belief is based on the English common law notion of *volenti non fit injuria* (the voluntary assumption of risk). However, legal action in sports-related injury cases appears to be increasing. Companies now specialize in sports injury litigation, dealing with claims that include becoming injured under supervision and suffering trauma related to witnessing a sports-related death such as might occur on adventure holidays. No doubt litigation will have an impact on the future of extreme sports, not least through the consequences of even higher insurance costs for participants and those organizing extreme sports competitions and tourism.

Elizabeth C. J. Pike

See also Gender; Meaning of Extreme, The; Media and Extreme Sport; Physiology of Risk; Psychology of Risk; Sociology of Risk; X Games

Further Reading

Beal, B., & Wilson, C. (2004). "Chicks dig scars": Commercialisation and the transformations of skateboarders' identities. In B. Wheaton (Ed.), *Understanding lifestyle sports: Consumption, identity and difference* (pp. 31–54). London: Routledge.

Bird, S., Black, N., & Newton, P. (1997). *Sports injuries: Causes, diagnosis, treatment and prevention.* Cheltenham, UK: Stanley Thornes.

Coakley, J. (2007). *Sports in society: Issues and controversies.* London: McGraw-Hill.

Crossman, J. (2001). *Coping with sports injuries: Psychological strategies for rehabilitation.* Oxford, UK: Oxford University Press.

Donnelly, P. (2004). Sport and risk culture. In K. Young (Ed.), *Sporting bodies, damaged selves: Sociological studies of sports-related injuries* (pp. 29–58). Oxford, UK: Elsevier Science Press.

Dunning, E. (2002). Figurational contributions to the sociological study of sport. In J. Maguire & K. Young (Eds.), *Theory, sport and society* (pp. 211–238). Oxford, UK: Elsevier.

Goksøyr, M. (2006). Pains and strains on the ice: Some thoughts on the physical and mental struggles of polar adventurers. In S. Loland, B. Skirstad, & I. Waddington (Eds.), *Pain and injury in sport* (pp. 76–88). London: Routledge.

Grayson, E. (1999). *Ethics, injuries and the law in sports medicine.* Oxford, UK: Oxford University Press.

Hutson, M. (2001). *Sports injuries: Recognition and management.* Oxford, UK: Oxford University Press.

Miller, J. (2005, June). Extreme water sports. *SportsMed,* 1–5.

Nicholl, J., Colman, P., & Williams, B. (1993). *Injuries in sport and exercise.* London: Sports Council.

Palmer, C. (2004). Death, danger and the selling of risk in adventure sports. In B. Wheaton (Ed.), *Understanding lifestyle sports: Consumption, identity and difference* (pp. 55–69). London: Routledge.

Pargman, D. (1999). *Psychological bases of sport injuries.* Morgantown, WV: Fitness Information Technology.

Parry, J. (2006). The intentional infliction of pain in sport: Ethical perspectives. In S. Loland, B. Skirstad, & I. Waddington (Eds.), *Pain and injury in sport* (pp. 144–162). London: Routledge.

Pike, E., & Maguire, J. (2003). Injury in women's sport: Classifying key elements of "risk encounters." *Sociology of Sport Journal, 20*(3), 232–251.

Robinson, V. (2004). Taking risks: Identity, masculinities and rock climbing. In B. Wheaton (Ed.), *Understanding lifestyle sports: Consumption, identity and difference* (pp. 113–130). London: Routledge.

Roderick, M. (2006). The sociology of pain and injury in sport: Main perspectives and problems. In S. Loland, B. Skirstad, & I. Waddington (Eds.), *Pain and injury in sport* (pp. 17–33). London: Routledge.

Thornton, A. (2004). "Anyone can play this game": Ultimate Frisbee, identity and difference. In B. Wheaton (Ed.), *Understanding lifestyle sports: Consumption, identity and difference* (pp. 175–196). London: Routledge.

Tulloch, J., & Lupton, D. (2003). *Risk and everyday life.* London: Sage.

Young, K. (2004). Sports-related pain and injury: Sociological notes. In K. Young (Ed.), *Sporting bodies, damaged selves: Sociological studies of sports-related injuries* (pp. 1–28). Oxford, UK: Elsevier Science Press.

Inline Skating/ Rollerblading

Thrill seekers have been skating on wheels for more than two hundred years. From the origin of the four-wheeled (quad) skate in the 1700s to today's inline skate, skating's combination of speed, independence, and glide is difficult to duplicate in other sports and has helped inline skating to become one of the most popular sports of the past twenty years. Today's inline skaters are typically well educated, financially stable, and contributing members of the community. Participants are divided equally between males and females. Many new participants have taken up the sport for recreation and fitness reasons. Other participants look for competitive and extreme opportunities through speed skating events, aggressive skating competitions, inline hockey leagues, and skating marathons.

Inline skating can reach an extreme level as the risk associated with the sport increases. Adding speed, elevation, creativity, and aggressiveness to one's skating gradually increases the risk of injury and even death. For example, an inline skater can reach speeds of 80 kilometers per hour, depending on the slope of the terrain and the skater's ability to accelerate. Additionally, inline skaters are not known to be overly cautious, and many elect to not wear any type of protective gear, such as helmet and padding. Some reports suggest that only half of all inline skaters wear any protective gear at all, even though they skate on hard surfaces. The result has frequently been injury, such as broken bones. In fact, more than 40 percent of inline skating accidents result in fractures. In addition, inline "skitching," the act of hanging on to the bumper or side of a moving motorized vehicle while skating, has resulted in serious injuries and even fatalities.

Types of Inline Skates

Inline skates usually consist of four or five wheels arranged in a single line on the bottom of the shoe or boot. A stopping mechanism, usually a heel stop rather than a toe stop, is also included. Inline skating is often performed on the same surfaces as skateboarding: on the road, sidewalk, and public furnishings such as fences and steps and on special tracks and areas, including skate parks and halfpipes. An appropriate type of skate exists for each need. The general difference between types of skates is the core features, such as the wheels, the frame/outsole structures, and the bearings. Recreational skates consist of a plastic boot, four wheels, and a brake and are designed for beginning skaters who occasionally skate for a short amount of time and for short distances. Fitness skates have larger wheels and are designed for skaters who skate at longer distances in order to receive fitness benefits from their workout.

Specialty skates are designed for aggressive, speed, or roller hockey skating. Aggressive skates, usually worn by participants in competitive skating events, are usually made of thick plastic with small wheels for quick movement and have grind plates to protect the skates during tricks. Freestyle skates have three wheels and a kick stop for tricks. Racing skates have five wheels and usually no brake.

Evolution of the Inline Skate

Inline skating has a history that is intertwined with that of the quad skate. Joseph Merlin, a Belgian inventor and ice skater, introduced the quad skate in London in 1760. The first inline skate was patented by Robert John Tyers of London on 22 April 1823. Tyers referred to his invention as a "Rolito." It consisted of five wheels in a row attached to the bottom of a shoe. In 1863 James Leonard Plimpton invented an improved quad roller skate that could maneuver in a smooth curve and allowed for the ability to skate backward. This enhanced quad skate consisted of two wheels under the ball of the foot and two wheels under the heel of the foot. The four wheels were made of boxwood and worked on rubber springs. This improvement is considered to be the ancestor of the modern four-wheeled roller skate. Limited by the technology of the late nineteenth century, inline skates could not be designed to function as well as conventional roller skates.

By 1930 roller skates had found a permanent place in society, becoming a fixture of community recreation and sociality. Wooden-wheeled skates were the norm and satisfied skaters of the time. Twenty-nine years (1959) passed before someone mass produced a metal-wheeled skate, which would prove to be much more durable and resistant to regular skating than the wooden-wheeled skate. The next significant development in skating technology came in 1973, when the skate was further improved by the introduction of polyurethane wheels. These wheels provided a skater with a smoother, faster, more responsive ride on a variety of surfaces. For much of the 1980s and into the 1990s inline skates were mostly manufactured with a hard plastic boot, similar to ski boots. By the mid-1990s "soft boot" designs were introduced by sporting goods manufacturers and promoted by fitness skaters. By the early twenty-first century the use of hard-shell skates was primarily limited to the aggressive skating discipline. Additional technologies, such as ventilated shells, advanced braking systems, and temperature-regulated materials, have contributed to the types of inline skates available.

On a Roll

In the late 1970s Scott Olson and Brennan Olson of Minneapolis, Minnesota, were looking for off-season ice hockey training options. They discovered an outdated inline skate while rummaging through a sporting goods store. They redesigned the skate by using modern materials for wheels and attaching them to ice hockey boots. The brothers soon were manufacturing their first inline skates in their parents' basement. Ice hockey players embraced the skates and were soon turning heads as they glided down Minnesota roads in the summer. Nordic and Alpine skiers also adopted these new inline skates to their summer training regimens.

**A skater practices at
a public skating park.
Source: istock/Chris Johnson.**

The Olson brothers launched Rollerblade, Inc. in 1983 and marketed their new skates. These first mass-produced Rollerblades, although progressive, did have a few design flaws. They were difficult to put on and adjust, prone to collect dirt and moisture in the ball bearings, easily damaged, and had poor braking systems. The Olson brothers, possibly lacking the necessary capital to enhance their product, sold Rollerblade, Inc. The new owners apparently had the funds to invest in product design. Design improvements included the use of Fiberglas in the boot frame, better-protected wheels, and stronger brakes placed in the rear. Through strategic marketing the Rollerblade brand of skates became so synonymous with "inline skates" and skating that many people came to incorrectly call any form of skating "Rollerblading." Rollerblade brand skates became so popular that other companies began to manufacture comparable skates. This increase in popularity elevated the inline skate to a more prominent market position than that of traditional quad skates.

Maturation of Inline Skating

The growth of inline skating in the United States was explosive from the mid-1980s to the mid-1990s. Skating center owners capitalized by renting inline skates and promoting the safety benefits of skating indoors. During this decade of growth, skating centers began to expand into family entertainment centers by offering a wider variety of entertainment choices, with inline skating and roller skating serving as the business foundation. By the mid-1990s inline skating and inline hockey had become two of the most popular sports in the United States.

As inline skating reached the masses and as the

marketplace became saturated with inline skates, interest in the new sport waned. National sporting goods participation data suggest that inline skating participation peaked in the mid-1990s at 30 million skaters. During the second half of the 1990s sales began to drop as the sport's trendy status began to fade. Data suggest that participation decreased from 19.2 million in 2000 to 13.1 million in 2005. Inline skates were left on store shelves while kick scooters experienced a renewed interest among children and a skateboard revival occurred among adolescents.

Competitive Speed Skating

The "need for speed" of some inline skating enthusiasts is not satisfied by recreational inline skating. Their need to skate as fast and as far as possible can be met only by participating in speed skating competitions. Speed skating is fast-paced, competitive, and somewhat dangerous. Although not considered a contact sport, speed skating requires skaters to use their skills to maneuver cleanly through a pack of skating competitors and into a winning position. Speed skating develops health, strength, and discipline while instilling the importance of teamwork, persistence, goal setting, and sportsmanship. Pushing, blocking, forcing another racer out of position, and using arms, legs, or hands in any way to gain an advantage are viewed as unsportsmanlike and result in disqualification from an event. Because of the speeds reached by participants, helmets are required to be worn during competition.

A 100-meter oval track is the standard for individual and relay events in indoor speed skating competitions. Age groups determine distances and divisions. Points earned by participants in the final races of each distance are used to determine winners. In relay events members of teams—single gender or mixed—combine their skills against those of other relay teams. National competitions are held for quad skates and for inline skates.

Outdoor competition is the international standard for speed skating. The two main categories of competition are road racing and track racing. A road course usually is an irregular closed loop with no bank on either side or a length of closed road. Endurance is a key to success because such courses require constant power with little or no opportu-

Skitching

With the rise in popularity of skateboarding, inline skating, and other roller sports, came the concept of using a motorized vehicle and "hitching a ride" on a car or truck to get around. This is considered incredibly dangerous, but has been popularized in movies and television.

Even though the actor Michael J. Fox made it look easy and cool as the character Marty McFly on a skateboard in the 1985 movie "Back to the Future," skitching is an extreme extension of roller sports that is dangerous and potentially deadly. Skitching was also made popular in the 1993 video game "Skitchin'" where skitchers raced against each other. Skitching has also been incorporated in many of the Tony Hawk series of skateboarding video games.

Inline skitching is when an inline skater holds on to the rear bumper of a moving motor vehicle and hitches a "free ride." Skitching is also called "ski-hitching" or "skate-hitching" depending on what the skitcher is doing at the time. Skitching with shoes or boots is common under certain weather conditions, such as when the roads get slick in icy or snowy conditions. It is common in urban areas with roller skates, a bicycle, or a skateboard. For many, skitching provides a quick, exhilarating experience on wheels. However, this "free ride" can turn into a "death ride" for the thrill seeker.

Once the driver of the skitched vehicle becomes aware of the skitcher, a typical response is to swerve and try to shake the skitcher, or accelerate faster than the skitcher can handle. This often causes the skitcher to lose their grip of the vehicle, leading to loss of skating balance and control.

Serious injury, and even death, has occurred under these extreme skating circumstances. In September 2001, Canadian Daniel Peterson died of injuries sustained while skitching on inline skates, hanging onto a friend's truck near Toronto, Canada.

Jon Oliver

nity to coast. Track races are held on a closed oval course, usually measuring 200 meters and featuring banked sides. Outdoor speed skating is almost exclusively performed on inline skates. Inline skates made their debut at the 1992 World Speed Championships, and quads have since disappeared from these events.

Skating Marathons

Like the foot-race marathon, skating marathons are 26.2 miles (42.1 kilometers) in length. Skating marathons provide the excitement of a race among thousands of skaters with, many times, a complementary weekend of fun activities associated with the race. Although the popularity of the skating marathon has not yet equaled the popularity of the foot-race marathon, interest is increasing, fueled by corporate-sponsored events on the national and international levels. In fact, skating marathons have been sponsored around the world, including in Europe, Asia, and North America.

Aggressive Skating

Aggressive skating arguably involves more risk, creativity, and courage than recreational inline skating, speed skating, or skating marathons. Aggressive skaters push the boundaries of the sport through the use of unique equipment and settings, such as halfpipes, bowls, and rails. They display their creativity by performing "coping-high tricks," "head-high airs," and "lip tricks"—jumps, flips, tricks and rotations performed high above their ramps. Such skaters often perform their acrobatic moves without the aid of safety cushions, nets, or mats.

Aggressive skating has struck a chord with Generation X, whose members often display an appetite for thrills and risk. The development of a global professional competition circuit has also pushed the sport into the public's eye. Aggressive skating has become a key component of extreme events and television programs, such as the Entertainment and Sports Programming Network (ESPN) Extreme Games, that also feature skateboarding, freestyle BMX, free skiing, music, and freestyle motocross. As of 2006 numerous professional competitions were scheduled to be broadcast nationally in the United States—evidence that aggressive skating is positioning itself as a mainstream international sport.

Inline Hockey

Inline hockey is a variation of roller hockey with characteristics similar to those of ice hockey. The game is played by two teams, each consisting of four skaters and one goalie, on a dry rink divided into two halves by a center line, with one net at each end of the rink. The playing time is two twenty-minute periods. Inline hockey is less extreme than ice hockey because it is usually played as a nonchecking sport. However, players tend to have more time on the puck, and the game is often more free flowing.

USA Hockey Inline is the rule-making association for inline hockey. Whereas competitive-level inline hockey is strictly bound by USA Hockey Inline rules, recreational hockey leagues may modify certain rules to suit local requirements (size of rink, length of periods and penalties) and resources. In the United States inline hockey is organized by the Amateur Athletic Union in partnership with USA Roller Sports and USA Hockey Inline.

Warming Up to Inline Skating

Inline skating has established strong roots in warm areas such as California, Texas, and Florida, where sunny skies, warm temperatures, and low humidity offer perfect conditions. In fact, retailers, skating instructors, and media and sales representatives were surveyed on the places that have the best skating paths, ease of access to lessons, skate rentals, and safety skate patrols. Four of the top ten sites were located in California, Texas, and Florida.

The Los Angeles area has embraced a variety of extreme sports, including aggressive inline skating. The weather is good, as is the multitude of inline skating parks, paths, and other facilities along the Pacific Coast.

Big Wheels

Inline skating and ice skating are connected in many ways. Some of the most famous ice skaters in the world have a background in roller sports such as inline skating. In fact, eleven former inline speed skaters competed in the 2006 winter Olympics in Turin, Italy, some winning medals in their contests. For instance, Chad Hedrick, who won bronze, silver, and gold, started his career in inline speed skating, winning fifty world championships. Joey Cheek and Apolo Anton Ohno each won at least two medals. And at the 1998 winter Olympics Tara Lipinski, a former figure roller skater, won gold in figure skating.

Governing Bodies

International and national organizations govern inline skating. The International Ice Hockey Federation (IIHF) is a federation of national hockey associations that governs ice hockey and inline hockey for both men and women. The IIHF sponsors the international Inline Hockey World Championships.

The Federation Internationale de Roller Skating (FIRS) and the United States Olympic Committee (USOC) recognize USA Roller Sports (USARS) as the national governing body for competitive roller sports in the United States. USARS successfully lobbied FIRS to permit inline skates in international competition beginning in 1992. USARS also was the promotional force behind inline speed skating being reviewed by the International Olympic Committee (IOC) to be included in the 2012 Olympic Games. Although the bid fell short, USARS is renewing educational and promotional efforts in hopes that inline skating will be included in the 2016 summer Olympics.

USA Hockey Inline is assisting USA Roller Sports in promoting inline skating in the United States. The mission of USA Hockey Inline is to promote inline hockey at all levels, including college, club, high school, middle school, and youth. The organization promotes public awareness and participation, sponsors competitions, and assists USARS in lobbying to get inline hockey included in future Olympics.

On the collegiate level the National Collegiate Roller Hockey Association (NCRHA) is the governing body for inline hockey. With approximately 200 teams and 2,500 players nationwide, interest in inline hockey as a collegiate club sport is increasing.

What's Next?

With the emergence of aggressive skating as a key component of a global professional competition circuit, the growth of inline hockey at the grassroots level, the increasing popularity of skating marathons, and the growing support to add inline skating to the summer Olympics, the future of inline skating is promising. Although injuries will continue to be sustained by adventurous—and sometimes careless—inline skaters, the excitement of the sport will continue to push inline skaters to the edge and possibly beyond.

Jon Oliver

See also Commercialization; Meaning of Extreme, The; Skateboarding; X Games

Further Reading

Aggressive Skaters Association. (n.d.). About ASA events. Retrieved September 15, 2006, from http://www.lgactionsports.com/about_asa.html

American Academy of Pediatrics: Committee on Injury and Poison Prevention and Committee on Sports Medicine and Fitness. (1998). In-line skating injuries in children and adolescents. *Pediatrics, 101*(4), 720–722.,

Bellis, M. (2002). The invention of the wheel: An overview of the evolution of dry land skating. Retrieved September 14, 2006, from http://inventors.about.com/library/weekly/aa050997.htm

Bellis, M. (2006). History of rollerblades. Retrieved September 14, 2006, from http://inventors.about.com/od/rstartinventions/a/Roller_Blades.htm

Business Week Online. (2005, June 29). A new slant on inline skates. Retrieved September 15, 2006, from http://www.businessweekonline

Centers for Disease Control and Prevention. (1995). In-line skating injuries: Epidemiology and recommendations for prevention. Retrieved September 15, 2006, from http://aepo-xdv-www.epo.cdc.gov/wonder/prevguid/p0000450/P0000450.asp

Centers for Disease Control and Prevention. (n.d.). Inline skating activity card. Retrieved September 16, 2006, from http://www.bam.gov/sub_physicalactivity/activitycards_inlineskating.html

Clark, G. (1998, July). Inline skating: Coming to a community near you. *Parks & Recreation (Ashburn, VA.), 33*(7), 58–67.

Dendy, C. (1999, September). On a roll: Inline skating appeals to every segment of the population. *Parks & Recreation (Ashburn, VA.), 34*(9), 152–159.

ESPN Internet Ventures. (2005). Retrieved September 16, 2006, from http://expn.go.com/expn/index

FreeSkateLesson.Com. (n.d.). Benefits of inline skating. Retrieved September 18, 2006, from http://www.freeskatelesson.com/benefits.htm

Glidewell, S. (2003). *Inline skating: Extreme sports.* London: David West Children's Books.

Graham, G. (2006). Building the PIHA: Brian Yingling and Justin Silvia are helping the Professional Inline Hockey Association grow. Retrieved September 18, 2006, from http://www.inlinehockeycentral.com/article.php?article_id=51070

Inline Hockey Central. (n.d.). Retrieved September 18, 2006, from http://www.inlinehockeycentral.com/index.php

Inline Skating Resource Center. (n.d.). Health benefits of inline skating. Retrieved September 7, 2006, from http://www.iisa.org/resources/health.htm

Inline Skating Resource Center. (n.d.). Rollerblade's top 10 U.S. skating locations. Retrieved September 18, 2006, from http://www.iisa.org/places/top10.htm

Inline Skating Resource Center. (n.d.). Skate marathons. Retrieved September 7, 2006, from http://www.iisa.org/travel/marathons.htm

Inline skating tips. (2006). Retrieved September 7, 2006, from http://inlineskating.about.com/od/allskatingtips/

International Ice Hockey Federation. (n.d.). Purposes and objectives. Retrieved September 18, 2006, from http://www.iihf.com/iihf/organisation/purpose.htm

Loy, B., & Della Giustina, D. (2003). Skating on wheels: Safety concerns lie in the shadow of popularity. *Journal of Physical Education, Recreation, and Dance, 74*(2), 21–23.

Miller, L. (1998). *Get rolling: The beginner's guide to in-line skating.* New York: McGraw-Hill.

National Association Skate Museum. (n.d.). Roller skating history of the United States. Retrieved September 13, 2006, from http://www.skateland.com/rshis.html

National Collegiate Roller Hockey Association. (n.d.). About the NCRHA. Retrieved September 18, 2006, from http://www.ncrha.org/page.php?page=about

National Safety Council. (n.d.). Inline skating. Retrieved September 13, 2006, from http://www.nsc.org/library/facts/inline.htm

National Sporting Goods Association. (2006). 2005 participation—Alphabetically. Retrieved September 13, 2006, from http://www.nsga.org/public/pages/index.cfm?pageid=149

Nottinghman, S., & Fedel, F. (1997). *Fitness in-line skating.* Champaign, IL: Human Kinetics.

Oneil, M. (1998). *In-line skating facts.* Minnetonka, MN: Rollerblade, Inc.

Powell, M., & Svensson, J. (1993). *Inline skating: The skills for fun and fitness on wheels.* Champaign, IL: Human Kinetics.

Rappelfeld, J. (1992). *The complete blader.* New York: St. Martin's Press.

Rollerblade, Inc. (2006). How it all began. Retrieved September 13, 2006, from http://www.rollerblade.com/about_us/background.php?id=2

Roller Skating Association International. (n.d.). Evolution of roller skating. Retrieved September 7, 2006, from http://rsa.affiniscape.com/displaycommon.cfm?an=1&subarticlenbr=2

Ruibal, S. (2005, April 4). L.A.–X: City of angels is heaven for big air and big media. *USA TODAY,* p. 14C.

Trap, J., Barr, M., & Carlson, C. (1980). Roller skating from start to finish. London: Penguin.

USA Roller Sports. (2006). Speed skating. Retrieved September 7, 2006, from http://www.usarollersports.org/vnews/display.v/SEC/SPEED%20SKATING

Jaws

"Jaws" is the name of a wave break situated off the North Shore of the Hawaiian island of Maui. The 6–21-meter waves traveling at around 48 kilometers an hour at Jaws are produced only by specific wind and swell conditions. The local ocean topography, specifically a large underwater ridge around 0.8 kilometers offshore, causes waves to jack up (grow in height) and refract.

These conditions make Jaws one of the most intense wave breaks in Hawaii, and it has become one of the most famous worldwide. It was popularized originally by tow-in surfers such as Dave Kalama and Laird Hamilton. They developed tow-in surfing as a means of riding inaccessible and big waves like those at Jaws, which move too fast to be paddled into and are difficult to access via traditional paddle from shore surfing.

A driver on a watercraft such as a Jet Ski (originally an inflatable boat) tows a partner riding a specially designed short surfboard with straps out behind the break. As the driver overtakes the wave from behind, the rider lets go of the tow rope and rides the wave, often for up to a minute.

Jaws became popularized by tow-in surfers such as Hamilton, Mike Waltze, Derrick Doerner, and Pete Cabrinha, most of whom were professional windsurfers living in Maui who had learned about Jaws through windsurfing. Kalama, one of the members of the original group who started tow-in surfing Jaws around 1992, had first windsurfed there four years earlier in 1988. As Waltze claims, "It's funny that tow-in surfing came from a bunch of windsurfers because our ultimate goal with windsurfing was to get on a wave and just pitch the sail. You wish your board could just turn into a little surf board. Now that's exactly what it's become" (Waltze as cited in Lyon and Lyon 1997, 182).

Today Jaws is popular with the elite of the wind-surfing and kite-surfing communities, and among the Jaws regulars are many who have surfed, wind surfed, and kite surfed the waves.

Debates over whether tow-in surfing is "real" surfing have raged in the surfing media—for purists it is not "authentic" or "real" surfing. Nevertheless, big wave surfing—whether on a surfboard, strap board, windsurfer, or a kite—is considered the highest-status form of these sports, and demonstrating prowess in big waves is a significant part of masculine identity performance and subcultural status. As Booth has argued, "Big-wave riders are surfing's warrior caste: riding giant waves bestows the greatest prestige" (Booth 2004, 104). "Big wave sailing is what I wait for; it's the peak of the season. You only get the conditions five or

Surfing Into Jaws

Off the coast of Maui, Hawaii, is a unique convergence of waves, barrier reefs and wind that come to create the Jaws wave break. It is a water athlete's dream.

A few times each year, storm swells originating as far away as Alaska's Aleutian Islands make their way to the Maui surf spot locals call Jaws. There, a barrier reef, just over a half mile off shore, sculpts the swells into 40- to 70-foot walls of water.

The waves' speed—roughly 30 miles per hour—and the rocky cove where it breaks make traditional, paddle-from-shore surfing impossible.

Drivers on personal watercraft tow their partners on short boards specially designed with straps, out to Jaws. As the driver overtakes a wave from behind, the surfer releases the towrope and rides down the front. Total surf time is nearly a minute—an eon compared to the typical 5- to 30-second rides of smaller waves.

Nicole Davis

When you let go of the rope and you drop in, you go in a warrior mode—you flex your muscles, you grit your teeth, you're ready for anything. I'm so focused I can't hear the wave when I'm riding it. It can be spiritual to be next to that much raw power. A wave is essentially energy passing through the ocean until it breaks and disperses. To be that close to that much energy can be humbling.

Dave Kalama

Source: National Geographic Adventure (July 2002) *Big Wave Surfer*, retrieved Feb. 1, 2007 from http://www.nationalgeographic.com/adventure/0207/q_n_a.html

six times a year. . . . It's the motivation that keeps you ready" (Naish as cited in Lyon and Lyon 1997, 180).

Jaws breaks only infrequently—perhaps twelve times a year, and only a handful of days produce good wave-riding conditions. The surfing lifestyle has been described as a culture of commitment. This is particularly true for the big wave surfers, who must set up their whole life to be ready when the swell arrives. Most are professionals, funded by sponsorship and endorsements. However, they do it for the adrenaline rush, the experience. As Mark Angulo, another of the pioneering big wave surfers, puts it (Lyon and Lyon 1997, 26): "We didn't do this for the press or money. We just did it because it was there. It was a challenge and no one else was doing it. Money and press came but it was all after the fact. We do it for the love of it and we do it for each other, to keep each other alive and to help each other realise our dreams."

Belinda Wheaton

See also Big Wave Contests; Hamilton, Laird; Kite Surfing; Surfing; Windsurfing

Further Reading

Booth, D. (2004). Surfing: From one (cultural) extreme to another. In B. Wheaton (Ed.), *Understanding lifestyle sports: Consumption, identity and difference* (pp. 94–109). London: Routledge.

Davis, N. (2002, July.). Surfing into jaws: Q & A. *National Geographic Adventure Magazine.* Retrieved October 2, 2006, from www.nationalgeographic.com/adventure/0207/q_n_a.html

Fearing, K., & Dalrymple, R. (2006). Wave refraction at Jaws, Maui. Newark: University of Delaware Press.

Lyon, C., & Lyon, L. (1997). *Jaws Maui.* Hong Kong: Peter Canon.

Wheaton, B. (2003). Windsurfing: A subculture of commitment. In R. Rinehart & S. Sydor (Eds.), *To the extreme: Alternative sports, inside and out* (pp. 75–101). Albany: State University of New York Press.

 **Jet Skiing**

Jet skiing is performed on a small, self-propelled vehicle that is ridden on water, usually by one person. The jet ski, also known as a "personal watercraft," is classified as a Class A inboard boat by the U.S. Coast Guard; operators must follow all rules of boating, such as wearing life jackets. Jet skiing is considered an extreme sport because there are many dangers associated with it. Along with the high speeds the watercraft travel at, jet skiers typically ride, and compete, in turbulent waters that can make for a dangerous experience for those who do not follow the necessary precautions.

Clayton Jacobsen II invented the jet ski in the 1960s to operate on lakes in Arizona. According to Luke Thompson,

Cruiseship Saves Jet Ski

Stranded in the middle of the ocean, a jet skier was fortunate to cross paths with a cruise ship, and fortunate the cruise ship took notice.

I took the July 17 sailing of Explorer of the Seas. We were scheduled to have a short stop in Nassau on Saturday, July 23, from 1 to 7 PM. About 7:30 AM the captain stopped the ship & turned it around. The rescue boat was launched. They picked up a jet skier who had been lost from Nassau since Wednesday evening. The man, about 27 years old, married with two children, had been out on his jet ski with friends on Wednesday evening. He lost power and somehow his friends left him. He was reported missing. He was on his jet ski in the water for three nights. The Coast Guard told cruise ships in the vicinity to be on the lookout for him. He was spotted from the bridge of Explorer. Can you imagine being alone in shark infested waters clinging to a jet ski for three nights? The man was taken to the ship's infirmary where it was reported that he was lucid, happy, and healthy and only a bit dehydrated. They credited his demeanor of the relaxed Bahamian attitude to saving his life. He just stayed on his jet ski & waited for rescue.

Flipper

Source: *Cruise ship rescue*, retrieved Feb. 1, 2007 from http://www.tripso.com/forum/archive/index.php/t-1348.html

Types of Personal Watercraft

Two types of personal watercraft exist. Although the two are similar, one major difference makes them easily distinguishable: A rider stands on one type (the jet ski); a rider sits on the other type (the waverunner). In competition most riders prefer the jet ski. Waverunners, capable of carrying up to four people, are used for recreation.

Some personal watercraft are designed to tow waterskiers, some are designed to handle more aggressive action. Some allow the rider to get wet; some are designed to prevent the rider from getting wet. Jet skis are also frequently used to tow surfers out to distant wave breaks, or in to shore when waters become too dangerous. Also, if surfers fall off their boards, a jet ski is a quick way to get to the board and surfer, minimizing the chance of injury.

Similarities between Jet Skis

All jet skis are powered by jet propulsion, which is not only effective, but also safe for the rider. Jet propulsion produces the same effect as propellers but without the blades that could cause injury if a rider fell off a blade-propelled ski. To power his jet ski, Jacobsen used a device called an "impeller," which is essentially a propeller that has been fitted into a tunnel. Water is pushed through the impeller by the engine. During this process the water is pressurized in the tunnel, and after the pressure has built to a certain level, the water is forced out of the tunnel through a nozzle at the back end of the jet ski. The pressurized water that is forced out of the back end propels the jet ski forward.

Competition

The design of stand-up jet skis makes them easy to race; they are lightweight and easy to maneuver. One of the largest jet-skiing events is the International Jet Sports Boating Association (IJSBA) Watercross Nationals. This worldwide event often lasts about a month starting in September and features day-long competitions called "watercrosses."

Each watercross features different divisions of races. The three typical divisions are ski, waverunner, and runabout. The ski division is only for jet skis. The waverunner division is for smaller waverunners that require only one rider, and the runabout division is for larger waverunners that require more than one rider.

author of *Jet Ski*, Jacobsen's first jet ski was "a cross between a motorcycle, a speedboat, and a jet aircraft" (Thompson 2001, 8). It was steered by handlebars, like a motorcycle; it traveled rapidly on water, like a speedboat; and it used a special type of jet propulsion, which made it safer for the rider.

Jacobsen sold the concept to the Bombardier company, which then attempted to market the product. However, most people wanted a boat that the whole family could use rather than a boat for the individual. When Bombardier was unable to sell the jet ski, Kawasaki bought it and began to sell it in the early 1970s as people became more interested in boats that could be used as a form of individual entertainment.

The IJSBA uses six types of courses: closed course, slalom, freestyle, drag race, endurance/offshore, and indoor. In the closed course, riders race around a course in multiple laps. This course tests both speed and ability. In the slalom riders race through a course marked by zigzagged buoys. Riders must weave in and out of the buoys, reaching the end after 86 meters. In the freestyle course riders must perform tricks during a two-minute period. Riders are judged by the difficulty of the tricks and by the creativity in which they perform them. The drag race, unlike the freestyle, is all about speed. The goal is to reach the end of a specified distance (usually an eighth of a mile) with the fastest speed and finish first. The endurance race spans a long period of time. Indoor races are held either indoors or on rivers.

A rider can perform numerous tricks during a freestyle event. Six popular tricks are the tail stand, the barrel roll, the hurricane, the turning sub, the fountain, and barefooting. The tail stand is easy for beginners to learn. It requires the rider to pull the nose of the jet ski into the air and hold it as long as possible. In the barrel roll the rider rolls the jet ski over into the water. In the hurricane the rider spins the jet ski around in tight circles while keeping one foot off the jet ski. The turning sub is more difficult and requires a great deal of either weight or strength. In this trick the rider pushes the jet ski completely underwater, nose first, then turns it while underwater so that when the jet ski emerges it is pointing in a different direction than it was when it

submerged. In the fountain trick the rider moves his or her weight to the front of the jet ski so that the end of the jet ski rises out of the water, shooting water from the impeller into the air. Barefooting requires the rider to lift both feet off the jet ski while riding.

In 2000 the IJSBA held a total of eight rounds for its national tournament. The rounds were held in many states, with the finals taking place in Chicago. Most of the races were held close to shore, allowing spectators to watch.

Talented racers of the IJSBA include Nicolas Rius and Dustin Farthing, who competed for Team Yamaha in the 2000 nationals. Rius has been racing since 1989, and his list of wins is impressive. Born in France, he moved to the United States to become a better jet skier by racing better riders. He has won fourteen consecutive competitions in European, world, and national championships.

Danger and Safety

The average jet ski reaches speeds of 72 kilometers per hour. Competition jet skis reach speeds of 112 kilometers per hour. That's fast enough to injure a rider who is not riding safely. One way to avoid injury is to learn the proper way to fall off a jet ski. When falling one should push himself or herself from the handlebars and then roll into the water.

Several devices and laws were designed to increase the

A jet ski racer rounding a buoy. Source: istock/ Graham Heywood.

safety of jet skiers. For example, the lanyard is a cord that is connected to the rider's wrist and to the on/off switch of the jet ski. If the rider falls off, the lanyard is pulled out, and the engine is shut off. This device prevents the jet ski from moving without a rider in control of it. Jet skiers are also required by law to wear a life jacket. There are three types of life jackets, also called "personal flotation devices" (PFDs). A Type 1 PFD is by far the best. It ensures that an unconscious person remains face up in the water, minimizing risk of drowning. Type 2 PFDs ensure that most people remain face up, but they are not as good as Type 1 PFDs. Type 3 PFDs are the most common type because they are more comfortable and allow the wearer to be more mobile, but they do not have the strength to ensure that an unconscious person remains face up in the water.

Four other recommended—but not required—items of safety equipment are the wetsuit, gloves, eye protection, and footwear. Wetsuits keep the rider warm, allowing him or her to ride in colder climates for longer periods of time. Gloves prevent the rider from developing blisters. Eye protection keeps water and sand out of the rider's eyes, and footwear prevents the rider from stepping on sharp rocks. Many experts recommend that a small fire extinguisher be kept on a jet ski in case of a fire.

Because the U.S. Coast Guard classifies a jet ski as a Class A inboard boat, the rider must be in control of the vehicle at all times, even if he or she falls off. If the rider falls off, and the jet ski injures someone, the rider is held responsible. According to the Personal Watercraft Industry Association (PWIA), a person must be at least sixteen years of age and have a valid driver's license to rent a jet ski. The PWIA recommends that no one under the age of fourteen operate a jet ski. By law, the jet ski must be registered and have an identification number (which is assigned when the jet ski is registered). The personal flotation device that is worn should fit properly and be approved by the Coast Guard. Alcohol or drug use while operating a jet ski is illegal, the same as with driving a car. These substances can have a serious effect on the rider, increasing their chances of being in an accident. Often times, there are speed limits which the riders must obey. Along with speed limits, there are other warning signs for riders, including "no wake zones." A wake is the wave that is formed as the jet ski moves forward. Finally, a jet-ski rider must be aware that bigger boats always have the right-of-way and that the jet ski, being one of the smallest boats on the water, must yield to bigger boats.

Riders should keep a safe distance between themselves and other boats. If a rider is being passed by someone else, the rider should be sure that the passer is completely by before performing any maneuvers or tricks or before turning. It is recommended that riders keep to the right when approaching a boat head on. Avoiding boat channels as much as possible will allow a jet skier to avoid many situations with larger boats. In areas with numerous other boats, riders should travel more slowly. There are some areas that are designated for swimming, and these areas should be avoided due to the fact that a swimmer could be injured. Dams and waterfalls make riding dangerous for the jet skier, and should be avoided. Jet skis are only designed to handle so much weight, so placing an excess amount could be damaging to the boats. Some other precautions include avoiding stormy weather and avoiding restricted areas.

Riders should keep hands, feet, hair, or other objects away from the impeller intake and not ride a jet ski in less than 60 centimeters of water to avoid sand being sucked into the impeller system.

The Future

The popularity of jet skiing is growing as technology makes the vehicles more efficient, allowing riders to perform more tricks at faster speeds in relative safety.

Melissa Mead

Further Reading

American Watercraft Association. (n.d.). Retrieved October 7, 2006, from http://www.watercraft association.com

Children's Hospital of Pittsburgh. (n.d.). Jet skiing. Retrieved October 7, 2006, from http://www.chp.edu/besafe/adults/02jetski.php

Italia, B. (1991). *Jet skiing.* Minneapolis, MN: Abdo and Daughters.

Jetski.com. (n.d.). Retrieved October 7, 2006, from http://www.jetski.com

Nicolas Rius Racing. (n.d.). Retrieved October 7, 2006, from http://www.nicolasrius.com

Personal Watercraft Industry Association. (n.d.). Retrieved October 7, 2006, from http://www.pwia.org

Thompson, L. (2001). *Built for speed: Jet ski.* New York: Rosen Book Works.

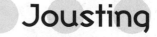

Jousting

The word *joust* derives from the Latin word *juxtare*, which means "to meet together." Jousting tournaments were believed to be first organized by Henry the Fowler (876–936 CE) of Germany, but jousting did not gain popu-

larity in Germany until somewhat later. Jousting appeared in written records in the middle of the eleventh century CE with the reference to an organized jousting event in the year 1066. The reference mentions Godfrey de Preuilly, a Norman knight responsible for the first "official" rules of the sport. According to contemporary chronicles, he was killed while jousting.

Even though the sport was organized by a German, it was the people from France who first embraced it. Once jousting gained popularity in France, it spread throughout Germany, then to England, and into southern Europe. It was at the peak of its popularity during the fourteenth to sixteenth centuries. The major tournaments between the tenth and twelfth centuries were held in Germany.

What Is Jousting?

In jousting, two knights, each holding a sharp lance (a pole weapon based on the spear), charge at each other from opposite directions on horses. In addition to the lance, historically each knight was equipped with (1) a one-handed sword (a long weapon consisting of a hilt and a two-edged blade for striking, cutting, and thrusting) and (2) a rondel (a side-arm dagger worn at the waist).

On the playing field the two knights were separated by a low wooden fence to prevent accidental collisions. The fence was introduced around 1420 as a safety measure to reduce injury to horses. Each knight charged along one side of the fence, seeing little more through the eye holes of his helmet than the head and shoulders of his opponent.

The object of the joust was not to try to kill the opponent but rather to score points by breaking the lance of the opponent or by knocking the opponent off his horse, which was difficult because the back of the saddle was about 30 centimeters tall. The point of aim was either the four nails of the shield, the chest, or throat armor. Later developments included a crest mounted atop the helmet that became an allowable target.

This form of jousting was also known as "tilting." The word is derived from the Scandinavian-based Middle English word *tilten*, meaning "to cause to fall." In a tilt a combatant armed with a lance attempted to "tilt" his opponent from the saddle. The knight's bridle arm was on the tilt side, and thus the blunted lance struck at an angle on the armor. This form of contest was also known as *"joust a plaisir"* or *"au plaisance"* (for pleasure). A winner was declared on the basis of the best of three rounds or on points scored.

A knight won a round (1) if he broke his lance at the minimum length on a strike to the opposing knight's chest or helmet (a break caused by hitting the other's saddle did not win a round), (2) if he was the last knight standing if both knights were knocked off their mounts at the same time and engaged in ground sword combat, or (3) if the knight dismounted his opponent. In some tournaments winning three rounds entitled the victor to the loser's horse. However, if a knight struck his opponent's horse, he was disqualified.

Points were scored thusly: (1) One point was awarded for a strike to the torso or a clean hit to the center of the shield shattering the lance, (2) two points were awarded for breaking a lance at the opponent's helmet, and (3) three points were awarded for knocking the opponent off his horse. However, in point jousting, if a combatant struck either rider or horse he was disqualified. In either form (round or point) the joust could last for days because all knights would compete in it.

Even though this form of jousting was for pleasure and the object was not to kill the opponent, mishaps did occur. For example, King Henry II of France died from the stroke of Gabriel de Montgomeri, who failed to cast his lance up in time. Many knights were killed because the visor of the protective helmet accidentally opened during a run; thus, the opponent's lance or debris from a breaking lance hit the unprotected face of the knight. Thus, jousting became known as one of the first "extreme" and violent sports in the world.

In their earliest form jousting contests were held as exercises between knights and nobles simulating battles for training during times of peace. These public contests were attended by royalty. They developed as a result of two factors: (1) a natural inclination toward weapons and feats of skill and military valor and (2) a need for regular military training. Such contests, starting peacefully, often turned into bloody battles between jealous champions.

In the Beginning

Jealous champions and knights seeking revenge, as well as men of noble birth and those of the privileged class, arranged jousting contests on some pretext. These became no-holds-barred events, fought with real weapons in the preferred style of the day and were therefore brutal and fatal.

These events were small battles in which hostile tactics were applied. They lasted several hours or days and spanned a wide topographical area, occasionally spilling into nearby settlements. This form of jousting was called "*au outrance*," "melee," or "tourney proper." It was performed "to the death" using solid oak lances with sharpened tips. A significant strike was needed to shatter the lances. Sharpened weaponry and heavy field armor were called "*armes a outrance*" (arms of war).

The rules were straightforward and rudimentary. A safe zone was established where the wounded and captured were taken to remove them from combat. Teams with flags on their backs gathered on their side of the field, facing their opponents. All participants, upon hearing the command to charge, crashed onto the countryside and proceeded to knock the flags off or to unhorse their opponents by any method at hand. When the charges had ground to a halt, the two sides began to pound one another. The melee would become a swirling mass of horses and riders, the participants slashing at one another in an attempt to win the advantage for their side until a winner was determined.

Jousting events were also held on water. Each knight held a lance and tried to knock his opponent off his boat while other participants rowed forward.

The *au outrance* "to the death" melee was popular because honor and fortune were gained through participation in this style of jousting. Instead of claiming mere points, the winning team either (1) held the losers for ransom, accepting their horses and armor as payment with a value equivalent to $300,000 today (many knights made their fortune in these events, and many lost theirs as well) or (2) seized the armor and weapons of a fallen adversary.

During battle knights employed kippers (who were usually vassals of the knights), whose job was to collect the armor and weapons of a fallen adversary. Kippers did not participate in the fighting. The word comes from various sources such as the Icelandic word *kippa*, which means "to pull, snatch," and the Danish word *kippen*, which means "to seize."

If a fallen adversary was not completely subdued and not ready to give up his armor and arms, a kipper would bang on him with blunt, nonlethal instruments, such as heavy sticks or clubs, in order to knock him unconscious so that his armor and weapons could be removed without further protest.

During the later Middle Ages kippers were frowned upon as tournaments began to resemble real warfare less and the chivalric code became more popular, encouraging less warlike and more honorable tournament conduct.

Knights traveled from land to land, offering and accepting challenges from other knights in hopes of increas-

ing their fame and fortune by virtue of their skill at this dangerous sport.

Armor Used

In the beginning protective armor included chain mail (small metal rings linked together in a pattern to form a mesh), a heavy one-piece helmet called a "great helm," and a shield. The "great helm" was replaced in the 1400s with full suits of plate armor (made from large metal plates, worn on the chest and sometimes the entire body). However, the plate armor was hot and weighed 22 kilograms or more. Gloves were molded without joints; thus, the jouster could not move his fingers. The horses wore armor, too.

Formalizing the Sport into Tournaments

The sport was taken "off the streets" around the eleventh century as the initial melee rendezvous became more popular with spectators. This move brought the meetings into an arena, where a new melee (the word has not changed in a millennium), with shattered lances, clanging swords, and flailing arms and legs, went on for days. At this point the jousting melee arena meetings were given the name "tournaments."

A knight might win fame and fortune while participating in such battles. However, the disadvantages are obvious: facing the prospect of death or dysentery, sleeping on the cold, stony ground, and baking in one's armor harness under a blazing sun. However, while participating in jousting tournaments, a knight could enjoy all the excitement, danger, and glory of war with less of the dirt, flies, disease, and discomfort. After the joust he could soak his bruised, bloody limbs in a warm bath, eat a good dinner, and retire, appropriately accompanied, to a soft bed.

Because of the nature of this brutal sport, its history of killed and wounded in the chronicle books is extensive. For example, the first of the Montagu earls of Salisbury died of wounds incurred at a Windsor jousting. Geoffrey de Magneville, count of Essex, was killed in 1216, and the count of Holland in 1234. In 1240, at the tournament of Nuys, near Cologne, sixty knights and squires perished, trampled or crushed to death by their horses. William Longéspee in 1256 was so bruised that he never recovered his strength. According to the chronicler of an English

A participant in a modern jousting tournament. Source: istock/Stuart Brill.

tournament in 1256, many of the noble contestants "never afterward recovered their health." Perhaps the most deplorable incident of all occurred at Windsor, where the earl of Salisbury's grandson, Sir William Montagu, was killed by his own father at a tournament in 1382. At least one king, Henry II of France, died in 1559 while jousting. A splinter from a broken lance entered the eye slot on his helmet and lodged in his brain.

However, knights and nobles were not the only casualties of this lethal sport. Peasant spectators also became victims when a knight's horse went out of control (and they did so frequently).

Banning Tournaments

Tournaments became so savage that popes and English kings banned jousting. Popes preached against them, and the Church of England eventually forbade the Christian burial of those killed in tournaments. "Those who fall in tourneys will go to hell," scolded one monk. The church excommunicated English subjects who persisting in jousting. The church disapproved of tournaments because they distracted knights from the Crusades. The state disapproved of tournaments because of the unwarranted loss of life. Kings regarded them with unease because such a large gathering of military forces could threaten politically unstable regions.

However, the church and state were powerless to stop tournaments entirely because the enthusiasm of knights was too great. Church and state were forced to extend a grudging tolerance to the sport.

Statute of Arms for Tournaments

In 1292 the church, the earls and barons, and the knighthood of England banded together to structure these bloody conflicts into more civilized tournaments. These new tournaments were conducted according to a basic code of rules known as the "Statute of Arms for Tournaments."

This statute curtailed the bloodshed at tournaments. All knights were automatically considered gentlemen, much like a congressional edict in the United States makes all commissioned armed forces personnel "officers and gentlemen." Knights were required to abide by the ideals of chivalry and fair play, thus reducing the church's disgust considerably.

Under the statute knights were not to use pointed swords, pointed daggers, clubs, or maces. Swords were dulled, and an alternative form of lance, the "lance of peace," was developed. This lance was similar in most respects to its deadlier predecessor except that its tip was blunted with a *coronal* (little crown) to prevent it from penetrating armor. Some authorities also believe that the lance was deliberately weakened.

With the advent of the Statute of Arms for Tournaments and the increasing number of women spectators, the dangers of jousting were greatly reduced. By the fifteenth century the jousting tournament was transformed into a pageant of horsemanship, gallantry, and sporting prowess. For example, the sword blades used during the Jousts of Peace at Windsor Park were made of whalebone and parchment, the chest "armor" made of boiled leather, and the shields of light timber. If a knight was knocked off his horse, fights continued with blunted swords or with stylized wooden maces. Such armaments were called "*armes a plaisance*" (arms of courtesy). However, jousting remained a rough sport, and severe injuries were still common.

Training

Medieval manuscripts show that training for the joust first required a knight to ride a wooden horse on wheels pulled by several men. The trainee had to hit a rectangular board. The board had a slit through which the trainer could observe the trainee. When a knight was training with a real horse, a target (simulating an opponent) called a "*quintain*" would rotate when hit. The *quintain* had either a shield or a square wooden board target mounted on a horizontal revolving pole that had either an iron ball or a sandbag on the other end. If the trainee hit the board head-on and in the center, the *quintain* spun around, and the weight would miss him. If his lance struck off center and/or the trainee was not fast enough, the weight swung around with enough velocity to strike the trainee on the head or back and unseated him.

The second form of training was known as "riding the rings" or "running at the ring." The object was to ride at a fast

---

Jousting

An article from The Lynchburg News and Advance *about a family whose life revolves around modern day jousting.*

Riding unarmored on a horse going 35 mph, Jesse Eubank lifted himself from the saddle and aimed his 12-pound lance at a series of rings the size of a LifeSaver candy.

He had eight seconds to hook three of them.

Jesse snagged one of the rings and missed another. A third bounced off his lance. He stopped, then turned to head back across the 80-yard track on his family's farm while his father, John Eubank set up the rings again . . .

At twenty, Jesse has jousted for almost half his life. He's the fourth generation of his family to participate in the Amherst County Jousting Association, which has met regularly for more than six decades . . .

The jousting isn't the kind most people know from movies. There's no armor, though John Eubank said that some riders choose to wear headgear.

He said that instead of going up against one another, jousters try to hook rings of different sizes, which was a training exercise used in medieval times.

Though this type of jousting may not sound as dangerous as the kind with armor and swords, there's still plenty of risk. . . .

Once, his father said, Jesse fell off his horse and was knocked out.

After being diagnosed with a concussion, he came back to his competition and won for his class. On another occasion, Jesse lost two of his fingertips when they became tangled in a horse's rope.

Participants in the jousts don't expect to make a living at it. The purse for a jousting competition is sometimes as low as a trophy and $35 in cash.

"You do it for the love of the game," John Eubank said. "If you win, I doubt you'll be able to pay for your gas."

Source: Smith, Z. (2006, May 8). A battle of coordination. *The Lynchburg News and Advance.* Retrieved on July 19, 2006, from http://www.newsadvance.com/servlet/Satellite?c= MGArticle&cid=1137835926789&pagename=LNA/MGArticle/ LNA_BasicArticle

canter or gallop, to spear a small ring that was (1) suspended on a cord, (2) tossed into the air, (3) attached along a fence rail or (4) held by persons on the ground, and to carry it off on the tip of the knight's lance.

By teaching themselves to strike relatively small targets in such a fashion, knights developed considerable accuracy with their lances.

Tent pegging was a form of training in which a knight riding at a gallop used a lance to pierce and carry away a small ground target or a series of ground targets. Tent pegging games included lemon sticking (the rider tried to stab or slice a lemon suspended from a cord or sitting on a platform) and Parthian (mounted) archery.

Training included (1) targets of different sizes, (2) targets of different compositions (3) varying numbers of consecutive targets placed on a course, (4) sword, lance, or bow of different dimensions and weights, (5) the minimum time in which a course must be covered, and (6) the way a target must be struck, cut, or carried.

The term *tent pegging* derives from the practice of knights mounting a surprise predawn raid on an enemy camp and using the game's skills to uproot tent pegs, thus collapsing the tents on their sleeping occupants.

Jousting's Decline

Many factors account for jousting's decline. The development of more modern methods of warfare such as the longbow and the crossbow (missile weapons that could defeat the heaviest personal armor from a distance) and the invention of gunpowder and cannons made armored duels such as jousting seem quaint and somewhat old-fashioned. Gunpowder was introduced to Europe from the Orient in the 1500s. Guns made warfare by horse-mounted lancers obsolete overnight. Also, after the death of King Henry II in 1559, direct-combat competitions declined, and ring-threading events gained popularity. After the Crusades literature that had exalted chivalry and the superiority of the horseman in warfare began to react against such extravagances.

Knighthood became merely an award or title of social distinction given to persons who served king or country, which it remains to this day. However, jousting based on tilting can still be viewed at Renaissance fairs. Many persons also enjoy modern-day variants, including bike jousting, jet ski jousting, and, most recently, downhill ski jousting. Many hardcore Renaissance performers find these sports appalling, but they are gaining popularity among younger people.

Joanne Margaret Hynes-Hunter

See also Meaning of Extreme, The; Violence

Further Reading

Barber, R., & Barker, J. (1989). *Tournaments, jousts, chivalry and pageants in the Middle Ages.* Suffolk, UK: Boydell Press.

Clephan, R. C. (1995). *The medieval tournament.* New York: Dover Publications.

Coss, P. (1993). *The knight in medieval England 1000–1400.* Stroud, UK: Alan Sutton.

Entertainment Magazine Online. (n.d.). The story of jousting. Retrieved August 21, 2006, from http://emol.org/azrenfest/azrenjoust.html

Flesh in Armor. (n.d.). History of jousting. Retrieved August 21, 2006, from http://home.comcast.net/~flesh_in_armor/history.htm

Gies, F. (1984). *The knight in history.* New York: Harper & Row.

Gravett, C. (1988). *Knights at tournament.* Sterling Heights, MI: Osprey.

Hopkins, A. (1990). *Knights.* New York: Artabras.

National Jousting Association. (n.d.). History of jousting. Retrieved August 21, 2006, from http://www.nationaljousting.com/history/history.htm

Renaissance-Faire.com. (n.d.). History of jousting. Retrieved August 21, 2006, from http://renaissance-faire.com/Renfaires/Entertainment/jousting.htm

Turnbull, S. (1985). *The book of the medieval knight.* London: Guild Publishing.

 # Julio, Jon

Jon Julio (b.1977) is a legend in the extreme sport of inline skating. He has helped elevate inline skating to the aggressive sport it has become not only through his skating technique, but also by using his business acumen. His achievements and involvement in the sport have earned him nicknames such as "The Head" or "The President."

Jonathan Julio was born in Milpitas, California, to Victor and Flor Julio. Jon's father, originally from Manila, Philippines, met his mother when he was in the U.S. Navy. Jon is the younger of two children. He has an older brother, Victor. The peripatetic Julio family moved to Japan when Julio was two years old and lived there for three years. Then they returned to California for five years, finally relocating to Hawaii when Jon was ten years old.

Jon got involved in karate in Hawaii and spent a lot of time around the ocean; those experiences were vital in developing his skating style when, back in California, he started inline skating when he was fifteen. His skating style was also influenced by some activities he and his friends were involved in, such as playing hockey, DJ-ing, and B-boying (break dancing). He skated along with inline skaters Ted Simpson and Jess Dyrenforth, who created Fifty/50, a skate company, which Jon skated for.

Jon sent videos of himself to skate companies. Roces, one of the larger corporations he contacted,, eventually took notice and sponsored him, allowing Jon to become a professional inline skater. As a pro skater Jon achieved superstar status when he won the National In-Line Skating Series (NISS) championship in 1996. As a result he was soon featured in many skate videos, magazines, and ads.

Jon Julio is also known in the world of inline skating as a skating entrepreneur. Jon cofounded England clothing in 1996 with Jess Dyrenforth and Brook Howard-Smith. Other businesses owned/previously owned by Jon included Runner's Project (backpacks), Dyna (wheels), Valo (skates, clothing), and Headcaselife (videos). He also has investments in other companies, such as Synergy (bearings), USD (skates, clothing), United (wheels), and Sifika (shoes).

Jon has also produced various skating products that made him more popular in the sport of inline skating. He has some skates named after him, like the Valo JJ1, USD Jon Julio, and USD Julio Psirus 3 UFS, and skate accessories, such as the 50/50 UFS Jon Julio (frames), Julio Pro Dyna wheels, 50/50 Julio Grindplate, and Julio Liner (USD). In 2002 Jon launched *Rolling*, a video game, that has fifteen pro skaters, including himself, skating in fourteen parks.

Jon is a strong advocate of street skating and promotes street competitions through his I Match Your Trick Association (IMYTA) established in 2002. Apart from his business ventures, Julio skates in the Aggressive Skaters Association (ASA), Mobile SkatePark Series (MSS), and with his Valo team.

Jose Angel Pablo Alaniz

Further Reading

Era, C. (1999). *Jon Julio: Profile*. Retrieved June 1, 2006, from http://www.asaskate.com/members/session/01/julio.html

EXPN.com. (2006). *Jon Julio*. Retrieved June 1, 2006, from http://www.expn.go.com/athletes/bios/JULIO_JON.html

Fry, K. (Ed.). (2006). *Jon Julio fan site: Legendary inline street skater*. Retrieved June 1, 2006, from http://skatelog.com/skaters/jon-julio/

Mitchell, C. (2005). *Rollerblading revolutionary*. Retrieved June 1, 2006, from http://www.expn.go.com/inl/s/inl_c_julio_012900.html

Profile: Jon Julio. (2006). Retrieved June 1, 2006, from http://valo-brand.com/version%202/pages/new_team_julio.htm

Stir Jon Julio interview.(2006). Retrieved June 1, 2006, from http://video.google.com/videoplay?docid=8189430972760359298&q=Jon+Julio

Wilson, M. (2004). *Why IMYTA is*. Retrieved June 1, 2006, from http://www.imyta.com/html/history.htm

Kelly, Craig

Craig Kelly (1966–2003), four-time World Champion snowboarder, legendary big mountain rider, and back-country guide. Craig Kelly grew up in the North West American town of Mount Vernon, not far from Mount Baker Ski Area. He tried snowboarding for the first time in 1981, and was among the first snowboarders allowed on Mount Baker the following year. During the 1980s the teen-age Kelly was part of a tight-knit group of snowboarding friends including Jeff Fulton, Carter Turk, and Eric Janko, commonly known within the culture as the Mount Baker Hard Core Crew. The infamously harsh weather and var-ied terrain of Mount Baker helped nurture this group into all-round free-riders. During the winter of 1983 Tom Sims, early pioneer and owner of Sims Snowboards, on his first trip to Mount Baker, discovered Kelly. "When I saw Craig ride," Sims remembers, "I knew he was special." Sims quickly signed Kelly to his snowboarding team. In 1985, eighteen-year-old Kelly took fourth in the inaugural Mount Baker Banked Slalom event, and in 1987 won his first half-pipe World Championship. Kelly proceeded to win three more World Championship titles and three U.S. Open titles, along with the Baker Banked Slalom in 1988, 1991, and 1993. According to cultural commentator Rob Reed (2005):

> [Kelly] etched for himself a new level of stature in the sport: the best-snowboarder the world had ever known. His freestyle technique—the Kelly stance and his tweaked-out method airs, in particular—transcended that of the individual and quickly be-came *the way* to ride, the archetype for freestyle riding in general.

During this period, Burton Snowboards, Kelly's new sponsor, produced the first signature board, the "Craig Kelly Air." Some commentators rank this as the most famous snowboard ever built. Certainly, many teenagers during the time coveted it as *the* board.

At the peak of his career Kelly retired from competitive snowboarding to become the sport's "original soul rider." In his own words:

> Snowboarding is something that I think should be done on your own terms. Society is full of rules, and I use the time I spend in the mountains as an opportunity to free myself of all constraints. Dur-

ing the past winter I decided that competing on the World Tour restricted the freedom that I found with snowboarding in the first place, so I decided to try a year with very little competing. Now that I have recaptured the feeling that made snowboard-ing special to me, I am not about to give it up. This is not retirement. I am simply revolving my snow-boarding around free-riding rather than competing. It sure feels right. (O'Connor 2000)

He told Jeff Galbraith, founding editor of *Frequency* magazine, that he sought not "the most dangerous line but the one that feels the best—the grooviest." His signature style embodied this "groovy-ness" and was very graceful; it "flowed with the terrain like equal forces at odds and in per-fect harmony," says Rob Reed. For Kelly, snowboarding in the backcountry transcended both the physical and mental realms. In his own words:

> When I go into the backcountry, I sort of feel this elation at being out there and the purity and the freedom that comes with the experience. It sort of lends itself to believing that there is another dimen-sion to everything we do. All of a sudden you have this feeling of clarity. (O'Connor 2000)

According to Tom Sims, Kelly was "a Zen snowboarder" who "sacrificed material wealth to seek oneness with his rid-ing and the backcountry." Certainly, Craig Kelly was the quintessential soul-boarder.

Rather than being cocky, loud and irresponsible (like many professional snowboarders during this period), Kelly was humble, non-aggressive, and non-materialistic. He of-fered a new generation an alternative to the dominant snow-boarding identity. Snowboarding legend Terje Haakonsen recalls:

> Craig was my inspiration. When I finally met him [in 1989] he turned out to be the best possible role model. Not just because of his snowboarding but also for his lifestyle and love of the mountains. I don't know anybody that loved mountain riding as much as he did. Nor do I know anybody who had the style and grace coming down the mountain. (O'Connor 2000)

On January 21, 2003, Craig Kelly, "the greatest snow-boarder ever," was tragically killed by an avalanche while working with Selkirk Mountain Experience (SME), a backcountry ski-touring business based in Revelstoke, British Columbia (Canada). "To the world of snowboarding, losing Craig Kelly was like the passing of a Pope or the untimely death of Princess Diana, resonating with immeasurable grief," says cultural commentator Rob Reed. "I can't think of a bigger loss to the sport and to all of us personally," said Jake Burton, "Craig was the epitome of core."

Holly Thorpe

Further Reading

Blehm, E. (September 26, 2003). Craig Kelly—The Gatekeeper. *Transworld Snowboarding*, retrieved from http://www.transworldsnowboarding.com/snow/magazine/article/0,14304,490411,00.html

Howe, S. (1998). *(SICK) A Cultural History of Snowboarding*. New York: St Martin's Press.

O'Connor, M. (2000). Interview with Craig Kelly. *MountainZone.com*, retrieved from http://classic.mountainzone.com/snowboarding/2000/interviews/kelly/

Reed, R. (2005). *The Way of the Snowboarder*. New York: Harry N. Abrams.

Khris, Taïg

Taïg Khris (b. 1975) is a world-renowned inline skating superstar, who has won a medal in almost every inline skating competition in which he has participated throughout his pro career. Apart from his skating and his business interests, Taïg is a multitalented pianist, dancer, actor, tennis player, and, of course, magician. "The Magician" is his nickname in the extreme sport of inline skating.

Taïg Khris was born in Algeria to parents of Greek and French descent and is a citizen of Greece and France. He has spent the majority of his life in Paris, where he learned to roller-skate with his brother at the age of six. School for Taïg was difficult, but roller-skating was not as difficult, as he and his brother began building their own ramps and doing various jumps and tricks.

Khris skated on quad skates for the first time on a half-pipe when he was fifteen. It was at this age also that he met some well-known European skaters, including Raphael Sandoz, Rene Hulgreen, and Toto, at a German competition. In 1996, when inline skates became available globally, the extreme sport of inline skating was introduced worldwide, changing the world of thousands of skaters, including Khris. He participated in the Aggressive Skaters Association (ASA) Amateur Tour that same year and became so good on inline skates that the Rollerblade company offered to sponsor him for the ASA Pro Tour the following year, thus making Khris a professional inline skater.

Khris did well as a pro his first year, winning 22 out of 33 contests, and medaling in the other competitions, coming in second 8 times, and third 3 times. His rookie pro record in 1997 was so incredible that the ASA named Khris its rookie of the year. His success continued on the next five years as he won 49 out of 70 events, placing second 7 times, third 11 times, and failing to medal in only three contests.

The Magician is known in the world of inline skating for his patented double flat spin and for being the first inline skater to complete a double back flip in competition, a stunt that only a few skaters can land. Other tricks that Khris performs in competition include the alley-oop, the switch fakie 900, and the 720-degree flip.

Besides Rollerblade, Khris is also sponsored by Club Med, Yoo-Hoo, Haribo, 2Advanced Studios, and BodyPack. Khris also promotes inline skating in other ways. He operates a skate shop in Paris called Ilios and owns a ramp company. He teaches beginning skaters the basics of inline skating at the Taïg Khris Ramp School at Club Med's Sandpiper resort in West Palm Beach, Florida. He also teaches classes and leads roller hikes in Vincennes, France. In 2002 he helped develop Aggressive Inline, a Playstation 2 video game in which he is featured. He resides part-time in Greece, Paris, Monaco, and Redondo Beach, California.

Jose Angel Pablo Alaniz

Further Reading

BBC interview. (n.d.). Retrieved May 28, 2006, from http://www.bbc.co.uk/scotland/sportscotland/airtight/inline/interviews/taig_khris.shtml

Mahaney, I. (2005). *Taïg Khris: In-line skating champion*. New York: Rosen Publishing Group.

Rosenberg, A. (2005). *Taïg Khris: In-line skating superstar*. New York: Rosen Publishing Group.

Taïg Khris. (2003). Retrieved May 27, 2006, from http://expn.go.com/athletes/bios/KHRIS_TAIG.html

Kite Surfing

Kite surfing, also known as "kiteboarding" or "flysurfing," draws from skateboarding, snowboarding, wakeboarding, surfing, wind surfing, and paragliding to form a sport that can be practiced on still water or among ocean swells

and breaking waves. The kite surfer stands with feet attached to a kiteboard. A kite attached by two to five lines to a kite control device is then used to harness wind energy and propel the kite surfer across the water and through the air. Kite surfing provides a physical, psychological, and even spiritual experience among the natural elements of water, wind, and air.

Origins

Kites originated in China between 500 and 400 BCE. The use of kites to move people across water dates back to the twelfth century, when Indonesian and Polynesian fishermen built kite-powered canoes for fishing and transportation. In 1826 British inventor George Pocock received the first patent for a fully controllable four-line kite system that he used to power boats as well as carts on land. In 1948 Italian American Francis Rogallo developed the "flex-wing" kite. All modern hang-gliding and delta-shaped kite designs originate from the flex-wing, including Englishman Peter Powell's two-line delta kites, which were the first kites sold commercially to propel boats and buggies.

The first patent for the sport of kite surfing was issued in the Netherlands in 1977 to Gijsbertus Adrianus Panhuise of the Netherlands. Considered the originator of the sport, Panhuise described kite surfing as "a 'water sport' using a 'floating board' of a 'surf board type' where a pilot standing upon it is pulled by a 'wind catching device' of a 'parachute type' tied to his harness on a 'trapeze type belt'" (kitesurf. nl 2006).

Kite design progressed well in the following decade. In 1978 Dave Culp of the United States pioneered the first kite with an inflated leading edge. In 1987 the French brothers Dominique and Bruno Legaignoux received a patent for their "self-relaunching marine wing," called the "wipika." At this time Cory Roeseler of the United States also began experimenting with the "kiteski," which enabled him to sail upwind for the first time. Roeseler continued to refine his kiteski and in 1994 was granted a patent.

Kite surfing was now ready for the world, and in 1996 images of high-profile big wave rider Laird Hamilton and windsurfer Manu Bertin completing soaring jumps and board-style maneuvers in the waters off Hawaii appeared in surfing and wind-surfing magazines across the globe. In 1998 kite-surfing pioneer Stefano Rosso of Brazil formed the Kitesurfing Group. The multinational group is credited with shaping the sport of kite surfing. Contributors

include such pioneers as Bruno Legaignoux, Raphael Salles, and Laurent Ness of France; Michel Montmigny and Chris Glazier of Canada; Cory Roeseler, Dave Culp, Ken Winner, Don Montague, and Robby Naish of the United States; Ian Young and Tim Mellor of Australia; and Hung Vu of Vietnam.

From just a few kite surfers in 1998 the sport has grown to 150,000 to 200,000 worldwide in 2006. Concentrations of kite surfers have formed in Europe, Africa, Canada, North and South America, the Caribbean, Hawaii, Australia, and Asia. Each area has prime locations, such as Noordwijk Beach (Netherlands), Tarifa (Spain), Walvis Bay (Namibia), Western Cape (South Africa), Iles de la Madeleine (Canada), Cape Hatteras, Hood River, and Maui (United States), La Ventana (Mexico), Tranque Puclaro (Chile), Combuco (Brazil), Silver Sands (Barbados), Cabarete (Dominican Republic), Perth and Port Douglas (Australia), Chumpon (Thailand), and Boracay Island (Philippines). Each location offers prevailing wind and surface conditions that may be best suited to one or more of the common styles of kite surfing:

- Cruise style—free-riding fun in a variety of wind and surface conditions
- Freestyle—technical jumps and skills such as spins, inverted tricks, surface tricks, one-foot and board-off tricks, grabs, where the kite surfer holds their kite board with one or two hands during a trick, and kite loops, usually on flat water, and may include human-made ramps, rails, and other structures
- Jumping—focuses on height, airtime, and distance of jumps
- Speed—flat-out speed runs over a particular distance or marked course
- Wake style—low-angled power carving, usually on flat water
- Wave style—carving and aerial maneuvers performed on breaking waves

Extreme Kite Surfing

Kite surfing in any style can provide an exhilarating ride. Speeds of 40 to 50 kilometers per hour and airtime during jumps of five to ten seconds are not uncommon for experienced kite surfers in the right conditions. The world speed record is 77.40 kilometers per hour, set by South African Olaf Marting on 12 October 2005 over a 500-meter course at

Walvis Bay, Namibia. On the same day over the same course Aurelia Herpin of France set the women's world speed record at 65.19 kilometers per hour. The record for airtime is considered to be held by Erik Eck, who survived ascending to approximately 50 meters and staying airborne for thirty-nine seconds during an accidental "kitemare" at Mokuleia Beach Park, Hawaii, in 2006.

A kitemare (an amalgam of "kite" and "nightmare") is a dangerous kite-surfing accident. With the speed, height, and airtime that kite surfers can achieve, a kitemare highlights why kite surfing is an extreme sport—risk of injury and even death. Kite surfing is practiced in an uncontrollable and largely unpredictable environment. The elements of wind, water, waves, and air continually change in speed, direction, and force. At any time a gust of wind can carry a kite surfer off into the air and hurl him or her violently back into the water or a fixed object such as the ground, trees, buildings, or power lines. Wave-style kite surfing adds the risk of breaking waves pounding a kite surfer and holding him or her underwater. In addition, equipment such as the kiteboard with foot straps, bindings, sharp edges, and fins; the kite control device; long kite lines; and even the kite itself can cause injury to an out-of-control pilot.

Although research into kite-surfing injuries is limited, one recent study of 235 kite surfers found a self-reported injury rate of 7 per 1,000 hours of practice over a six-month period. The most frequent injuries involved the foot and ankle (28 percent), skull (14 percent), chest (13 percent), and knee (13 percent). Fifty-six percent of all injuries were linked to the inability to detach the kite from the harness when kite control was lost; kite surfers using a quick-release system reported fewer injuries than those not using such a release system. At least seventeen kite-surfing fatalities have been recorded since 2000.

Kite surfers, particularly inexperienced kite surfers, may also inadvertently become a hazard to others nearby. Hence, participants are required to obey local water-safety regulations, and kite surfing may be restricted or even banned in areas with high public use for other water-based activities. In addition experts recommend that surfers use standard safety equipment such as helmets, impact vests, bar floats, and quick-release harness systems and tune in to local weather forecasts.

Psychologically kite surfing may also be defined as an extreme experience. The uncertainty and potential for harm that come with activities practiced in natural settings provide an opportunity for intense cognitive and affective or emotional absorption. Fear and adrenaline are ever present, and persons who participate in such sports tend to score higher than the general population on psychometric measurements of "sensation seeking" (the desire to seek risky, complex, or novel experiences) and "type-T" or "type thrill" personality (the tendency to engage in high-thrill, high-stimulation, high arousal-producing behavior). In addition, personal expression and aesthetics form the basis for kite-surfing performance, and the spontaneity involved as the kite surfer strives for energy, harmony, and freedom among the natural elements is conducive to being in *flow*—the psychological process of peak experience.

Collective Culture

Just as kite surfing combines elements from a number of land- and water-based board sports, kite-surfing culture began as a collective of board-sport customs and attitudes. At the core are the free-form thinking, creativity, and innovation of elder board sports such as surfing, wind surfing, and skateboarding. Voicing beliefs and ideals that diverge from conservative, mainstream standards is readily accepted among people immersed in the dynamic, youth-oriented world of kite surfing. Indeed, the challenges that kite-surfing culture presents to mainstream social and cultural conventions further serves to define this rapidly evolving pursuit as an extreme sport.

The culture is lifestyle based and distinct from cultures of mainstream sports such as cricket, football, or basketball, where challenging tradition and modifying convention are rare. In kite surfing individual expression and aesthetics prevail. Experimentation is encouraged and change embraced as new possibilities for kite-surfing performance emerge. Advances in the technical complexity of freestyle tricks as well as refinements in equipment during the last five years are clear testament. In fact, even the manufacture of handmade kiteboards is considered an art form. Beginning simply with a vision, kiteboard shapers spend hours crafting their range of directional and bidirectional designs with skill and affection.

Kite-surfing culture can pervade all dimensions of a participant's existence, and the committed kite surfer can become compelled to base his or her entire life around the sport. Personal, social, educational, and vocational decisions, along with geographical choices of residence and vacation time, often stem from a desire for maximum opportunity for kite surfing. Whereas the classic "beach style" look is apparent among coastal kite surfers, expectations about fashions or appearance among the global kite-surfing community appear

A man kite boarding on the ocean. Source: istock/Arturo Limon.

absent. The same goes for preferences in music, entertainment, and broader hobbies or interests. In addition, just as kite surfers may allow their surfing roots to influence many other dimensions of their life, they may also allow anything from outside kite surfing that looks or feels good to influence their kite-surfing experience. Aesthetic modifications to standard equipment are a prime example, and it is not uncommon to see kite surfers wearing wetsuits covered in flame designs or riding kiteboards airbrushed with original artwork.

Kite-surfing language is evolving, too. Naturally, some terms refer to tricks—back-side tricks, front-side tricks, grabs, and spins—that originated in established board sports that influenced kite surfing, such as skateboarding and snowboarding. However, kite surfers are creating their own jargon to describe surface tricks, kite loops, handle pass tricks, and other tricks unique to their sport. Kite-surfing experiences present opportunity to create new dialogue with phrases such as "tea bagging" (used to describe dropping the kite in and out of the water intermittently because of light, gusty wind or poor flying skills), "send it" (used to describe moving the kite up aggressively through the power zone), or "I'd hate to be that good" (used to describe a kite surfer who is performing well, a genuine compliment).

Kite-surfing culture is displayed globally through sport-specific websites, DVD productions, and print media in major kite-surfing regions. The sport also regularly appears in mainstream media productions. The commercial industry is expanding, and in tandem with advances in performance, the culture of kite surfing is establishing its own customs, symbols, and marketplace.

Governance and Competition

Kite surfing has become a well-organized recreational and competitive sport. Local and national associations regulate practices and competition in the core kite-surfing regions of Europe, Africa, North and South America, Asia, Australia, and the Pacific. Formed in 2001, the International Kiteboarding Organisation (IKO) promotes safe kite-surfing practices and develops standards for kite-surfing coach accreditation, provides accident and liability insurance for kite surfers, and nurtures key organizational, professional, and industry relationships for the benefit of the sport. The IKO network includes more than 110 affiliated centers across 29 countries with 15 examiners and more than 1,600 accredited instructors.

Two world championship circuits and many extreme games and exhibition events are available for competitive kite surfers. The Kiteboard Pro World Tour (KPWT) began in 1999 with world cup freestyle events and in 2003 introduced wave masters events. Since 1999 the KPWT has

Common Terms in Kite Surfing

Like any sport, the jargon and lingo that accompanies kite surfing is unique. Here is a brief glossary of those terms.

- **Buoyancy aid:** Flotation jacket designed to keep you afloat. Not to be confused with a life jacket which, technically, will keep your head above water if unconscious.
- **Canopy:** The material that links the struts and the leading edge. The canopy is the most visable part of the kite.
- **Chicken loop:** The loop below the control bar where you hook into with your harness hook.
- **Impact jacket:** A jacket with slight amount of flotation, but is designed to absorb some of the impact after a wipeout.
- **Kite knife:** A hook shaped knife where the gap between the plastic and the knife is only big enough for the lines to fit through. Allows you to cut yourself free in case of a dangerous tangle.
- **Larks head:** The self tightening knot used to attach the lines to the kite.
- **Leash:** the strong line that attaches you to either your kite or your board.
- **Pig tails:** The bits of rope that come off the wing tips of the kite. This is where the lines attach to from the bar.
- **Quiver:** a name used to describe all your kites. For example, "my quiver consists of a 9m and a 12m."

Source: British Kite Surfing Association, *Terminology* retrieved Feb. 1, 2007 from http://www.britishkitesurfing association.co.uk/content/view/78/101/

men's wave masters world champion is Jose Luengo of Spain. In 2006 more than fifty professional riders will compete in a series of international events to decide the next KPWT freestyle and wave masters world champions.

The Professional Kite Riders Association (PKRA) formed in 2002 to create cohesion, professionalism, and direction for professional kite riders. In keeping with kite-surfing culture, the PKRA was created "by the riders, for the riders," and a democratic process based on this credo is followed throughout PKRA guideline development (such as for event rules and judging criteria) and decision making (such as for event dates and locations).

Athletes ranging from elder kite-surfing pioneers to the young generation of radical freestyle riders compete on the PKRA World Tour each year. The women's PKRA world champion is Kristin Boese of Germany, and in the men's division the champion is eighteen-year-old Aaron Hadlow of Great Britain. In 2006 hundreds of athletes from more than twenty-eight countries will compete in eight PKRA World Tour events in Europe, the Canary Islands, Canada, South America, and the Caribbean. Each event will include a freestyle competition along with exhibition rounds (such as speed trials or best trick) suited to prevailing wind and surface conditions, with technical difficulty, height, smoothness, power, style, variety, and innovation forming the basis of judging criteria.

The PKRA also sanctions the Kite Speed World Championships, which are decided each year across four events in high-wind regions of Namibia, France, and the Canary Islands. Speed trials are run over a standard 500-meter course, and results from each event count toward the overall kite speed world championship. The women's kite speed world champion and kite speed world record holder is Aurelia Herpin of France, and the men's kite speed world champion is Christophe Prin-Guenon, also of France.

As in the world tour circuits of elder board sports such as surfing and skateboarding, extreme performance and the cultural core of kite surfing are epitomized by the sport's elite competitors. Each event serves as a breeding ground for new tricks, and the sport's growth is largely because competitive kite surfers challenge one another at the highest level.

held thirty-seven events in twelve countries. The women's KPWT world champion in both junior and open divisions of freestyle and wave masters is twelve-year-old Gisela Pulido Borrell of Spain. The men's open KPWT world champion in freestyle is Thomas Cocquelet of France, and the

The Sky's the Limit

Freestyle kite surfers started by performing high jumps and then progressed to taking the board off the feet during jumps, performing handle pass tricks, and then going for

more wakeboard-style low center-of-gravity power moves. Top kite surfers believe that in the future riders will develop tricks with more speed, power, height, airtime, and technical difficulty. Tricks will be higher and will combine several technical skills at once, such as board off feet, kite loops, twists, grabs, and handle passes as well as skills yet to be developed.

Several forms of kite surfing have also emerged from the traditional form, for example, kite boating on water, kite snowboarding, kite skiing,, kite snow blading, and kite skating on snow and ice, kite skateboarding, and kite buggying on land. Clearly, only the sky is the limit for this rapidly evolving, modern extreme sport.

Richard Bennett

See also Hamilton, Laird; Meaning of Extreme, The; Skateboarding; Snowboarding; Surfing; Wakeboarding; Windsurfing

Further Reading

Bennett, R. J. (2004). *The surfer's mind: The complete, practical guide to surf psychology.* Sydney, Australia: The Surfer's Mind.

Cooper, A. (1998). *Playing in the zone: Exploring the spiritual dimensions of sports.* Boston: Shambhala.

Csikszentmihalyi, M. (1990). *Flow: The psychology of optimal experience.* New York: Harper and Row.

Currer, I. (2002). *Kite surfing: The complete guide.* Cumbria, UK: Lakes Paragliding.

Elias, N., & Dunning, E. (1986). *Quest for excitement: Sport and leisure in the civilizing process.* Oxford, UK: Blackwell.

Farley, F. (1991). The type-T personality. In L. Lipsitt & L. Mitnick (Eds.), *Selfregulatory behaviour and risk taking* (pp. 371–382). New York: Wiley & Sons.

Holyfield, L. (1999). Manufacturing adventure. *Journal of Contemporary Ethnography, 28(1),* 3–32.

Hunt, J. (1995). Divers' accounts of normal risk. *Symbolic Interaction, 18(4),* 439–462.

Hunt, J. (1996). Diving the wreck: Risk and injury in sport scuba diving. *Psychoanalytic Quarterly, 65,* 591–622.

Jackson, S. A., & Csikszentmihalyi, M. (1999). *Flow in sports: The keys to optimal experiences and performances.* Champaign, IL: Human Kinetics.

Murphy, S., & White, R. A. (1995). *In the zone: Transcendent experience in sports.* New York: Penguin.

Nickel, C., Zernial, O., Musahl, V., Hansen, U., Zantop, T., & Peterson, W. (2004). A prospective study of kitesurfing injuries. *The American Journal of Sports Medicine, 32,* 921–927.

Robinson, D. W. (1992). The risk-sport process: An alternative approach for humanistic physical education. *Quest, 44,* 88–104.

Schrader, M. P., & Wann, D. L. (1999). High-risk recreation: The relationship between participant characteristics and degree of involvement. *Journal of Sport Behaviour, 22(3),* 426–431.

Schultheis, R. (1996). *Bone games: Extreme sports, shamanism, zen, and the search for transcendence.* New York: Breakaway Books.

Shoham, A., Rose, G. M., & Kahle, L. R. (2000). Practitioners of risky sports: A quantitative examination. *Journal of Business Research, 47,* 237–251.

Slanger, E., & Rudestam, K. E. (1997). Motivation and disinhibition in high risk sports: Sensation seeking and self-efficacy. *Journal of Research in Personality, 31,* 355–374.

Wheaton, B. (2004). Understanding lifestyle sport: Consumption, identity and difference. Abingdon, UK: Routledge.

Zuckerman, M. (1971). Dimensions of sensation seeking. *Journal of Consulting and Clinical Psychology, 36(1),* 45–52.

Zuckerman, M. (1984). Sensation seeking: A comparative approach to a human trait. *The Behaviour and Brain Sciences, 7,* 413–471.

Knievel, Evel

Evel Knievel (Robert Craig Knievel, b. 1938) was born in the copper-mining town of Butte, Montana. At the age of eight he was a spectator at Joey Chitwood's Auto Daredevil Show and recalls that experience as sparking his lifelong passion for stunts and motorcycles.

However, Knievel's career focused on much more than daredevil histrionics. Following army service in which he pole vaulted and ran the 220-yard (201-meter) sprint he operated a hunting guide service in Montana. He was so appalled to discover that excess elk were being killed in Yellowstone National Park that he hitchhiked to Washington, D.C., and petitioned for congressional intervention.

From 1962 to 1965 Knievel did some motorcycle racing, sold policies for the Combined Insurance Company of America, and operated a Honda motorcycle dealership in Washington State. In 1965 he launched a troupe called "Evel Knievel's Motorcycle Daredevils." The following year he went solo and, like a one-man band, packaged his brand of entertainment that spotlighted himself as publicist and performer. His spills and tumbles rather than his courage or skill or theatrics captured the public's imagination. For example, despite clearing a jump of 46 meters across the fountains at Caesar's Palace in Las Vegas in January 1968 the headlines spotlighted a thirty-day hospital stay in which he gradually recovered from his "landing" injuries.

The pinnacle of Knievel's career was his famous (or infamous, depending on personal viewpoint) attempt to blast himself over the Snake River Canyon in Idaho in 1974 on his specially built rocket-powered "Sky-Cycle." Steve Rushin, writing a retrospective profile on Knievel in 1999, gives a vivid picture of a performer who had become the master of hype, hoopla, and hysteria. Rushin recalls Knievel thusly:

There was the star-spangled, bell-bottomed, white-leather jumpsuits. The pterodactyl-wing collars. The belt buckle with the raised monogram (like a license plate, only larger). The gold-and-ebony inlaid walking stick. The pinky ring. The diamond cuff links. The sideburns like shag-carpet swatches. In hindsight he was a charisma kleptomaniac, his magnetism lifted largely from Elvis. (Rushin 1999)

Knievel is also well captured on the cover of *Sports Illustrated* (2 September 1974). The nine-page narrative on Knievel by Robert F. Jones is a biography in miniature and essential reading for coming to terms with a man whose credo was fame through excess. Knievel is quoted as saying, "I think it's better to risk my life and be a has-been than to never have been at all!"

The Snake River stunt, masterminded by boxing promoter Bob Arum, took place on 8 September 1974, in front of fifteen thousand rowdy fans and more than one million closed-circuit viewers with David Frost, Normal Mailer, and Bobby Riggs as color commentators. Knievel shot up the 32-meter ramp, accelerating his Sky-Cycle toward 482 kilometers per hour. However, a safety parachute deployed early, and Rushin writes of Evel dribbling Earthward by parachute and landing unscathed, an "Icarus in mutton-chops." Although Knievel claimed that he grossed $6 million from his extravaganza, in reality his gross may have been only $250,000.

Although he retired in 1976 a decade later he made astronomical amounts of money with a popular line of Evel Knievel toys. His memorabilia is held by the Museum of American History, Smithsonian Institution, Washington, D.C. A 1996 article in *Sports Illustrated* by Richard Hoffer reviews a life that has had a series of low points marked by drinking, spending, and gambling. Nevertheless, Hoffer highlights a showman who was the quintessential promotional genius. Nobody has marketed and exploited extreme sports in the manner of Evel Knievel. To this day, the last weekend of July is a celebration of Butte's most famous son—the Evel Knievel Summer Festival.

Scott A. G. M. Crawford

Further Reading

Hoffer, R. (1996). Where Evel lurks. *Sports Illustrated, 85*(15), 78.

Jones, R. F. (1974). Make or break. *Sports Illustrated, 41*(10), 52–62.

Rushin, S. (1999). Seeing all the good in Evel. *Sports Illustrated, 92*(21), 116.

Sager, M. (1999). What I've learned—Evel Knievel. *Esquire, 132*(1), 98.

Schwarz, F. D. (1999). The time machine. *American Heritage, 50*(5), 93.

Leadership and Extreme Sport

Leadership in sports has received increased academic and practitioner attention during the final decades of the twentieth century and the beginning of the twenty-first century. The attention, however, has been on leadership in "conventional" or traditional sports and rarely on leadership in extreme sports. The latter has demands of safety and risk management that are beyond those faced by most leaders in traditional sports. Initially considered almost solely in terms of coaching, sports leadership has also been examined in terms of team cohesion, captaincy, management structures, and operations of sports bodies. The worlds of education, business, and commerce have drawn from their perceptions of leadership in sports, placing a focus on workplace teams and coaching. This focus has often been on what coaches do, rather than on a firsthand knowledge of what actually occurs in the sports coaching context.

Researchers have studied sports leadership in team sports, individual sports, and roles within sports organizations. Studies of the former have usually focused on athletes' perceptions of coaches and/or their traits and actions revealed when carrying out their coaching roles. The number of sports leadership researchers who have carried out investigations in the field is small. Even smaller is the number of sports leadership researchers who have tested their research findings through on-site guidance of, and interaction with, coaches, captains, or administrators within sports organizations.

In the worlds of academia and sports organizational practice, sports *management* has received greater attention than sports *leadership*. Coaching books tend to present conventional leadership theory and to treat leadership as management with little innovation or practical application of sports leadership research. One of the world's most successful coaches, Ric Charlesworth of Australia, has provided an insight into leadership of the dual Olympic gold-winning women's field hockey team. A researcher and writer who has brought sports leadership to the attention of academics and sports practitioners is Packianathan Chelladurai of Ohio State University. Chelladurai's research led to his formulation of a sports leadership scale and a range of publications that stimulated academic interest in the subject. Key researchers include Albert Carron, with a body of literature on team dynamics and cohesion, and John Salmela of Canada, who has explored perceptions of coaches held by athletes in different sports settings. Robin McConnell of New Zealand conducted a participant observation study of elite sports team leadership during four years that presented multifaceted insights into the coach and captain as elite team leaders. Findings from this study have been incorporated into the leadership of club, regional, national, and international coaches and captains. Despite such literature and an expanding domain of sports leadership research and programs of sports leader development that offer opportunities for replication studies, little has been written or researched in the domain of leadership in extreme sports.

Components of Sports Leadership

Sports leadership may be defined as "an influence relationship, in a sport context, through which the leader and followers share a common vision and pursue agreed goals to which they are individually committed" (McConnell 2005, 2).

Vision is the "picture" or envisaged future state of an organization or individual. It is the critical element of sports leadership, being the basis of goal-setting, and should be clear, uplifting, challenging, and attainable. The leader and followers agree on it without ambiguity or undue compromise. Mobley notes, "By focusing on a vision, the leader operates on the emotional and spiritual resources of the organisation, on its values, commitment and aspirations. The manager, by contrast, operates on the physical resources of the organisation, on its capital, human skills, raw materials and technology" (Mobley 1986). With a clear understanding of the vision, the leader and followers set goals that relate directly to the realization of that vision and are clear, measurable, and agreed upon by the participants involved. These goals lead to the setting up of structures, operations, and processes that lead to their realization.

Conventional definitions of leadership note the importance of vision and goals that are acceptable to, or agreed upon, by leaders and followers. In sports, however, the commitment of *individuals* to the vision and goals is also an essential consideration. This commitment is an integral element of team cohesion as, for example, in a football team's individuals being committed to the game plan that best meets the team's goals. It is also important in individual sports, in which an athlete needs to commit to goal achievement rather than simply have a competition goal that is acceptable or agreed upon.

In the realities of both conventional and extreme sports, leadership and management are often linked, requiring the enactment of leadership *and* management by the one person or group of persons. In part this is because of the small size of many sports organizations, whether they are comprised of an administrative structure or competitive unit. The management elements are optimized when they are based on clear and agreed leadership vision and goals.

The definition of sports leadership noted earlier is concomitant with leadership in extreme sports, but its actualization requires a range of leadership applications in the extreme sports context not readily found in conventional sports. These applications usually center on the risks, safety, and wider participation parameters of extreme sports.

Extreme Sports Leadership Groups

Leadership roles in extreme sports may be broadly considered in four groupings that are not mutually exclusive and that, arguably, vary more than in conventional sports. These roles draw upon skills and situational responses seldom asked of conventional sports leaders.

The first grouping of extreme sports leaders is that of national or regional administrators of a particular sport.

Such sports (e.g., kayaking and skydiving) usually have national structures, national rules, a central organization with overall responsibility for each sport, and administrative levels from the voluntary, amateur, or club level through to the national and professional levels. Leadership in this context has similarities with leadership in conventional sports in terms of governing the sport, operating a national structure, and supporting the sport from club to elite levels. In contrast to the leaders of conventional sports, the leaders of extreme sports bodies have cognizance of special factors associated with risk, relations with local and national authorities, and the operation and marketing of extreme challenges. Official or governmental standards and regulations are integral to the administration of many extreme sports. Goals arising from the leaders' vision are thus often tempered in the processes leading to goal attainment, with realities of safety regulations, environmental concerns, risk management, common law, vehicle or equipment operation, and local government requirements. This fact also applies to leaders of independent extreme sports clubs, adventure sites, and extreme sports bodies, who face leadership and management considerations beyond those of their conventional sports counterparts.

The second grouping of extreme sports leaders is that of event managers. These leaders have a vision that must temper commercial interests with risk management and

Leadership is important in extreme sports that require teamwork, such as climbing. Source: iastock/René Mansi.

realities of situation and environment beyond those in traditional sports. Consider the organizers or event managers of a multisport coast-to-coast competition whose participants may kayak in turbulent waters, run through wilderness territory, and mountain bike in dangerous areas. The leaders in this grouping face leadership considerations similar to those faced by national sport-specific administrators but apply considerations of safety, environmental concerns, legal requirements, risk management, and local government regulations to a specific area and specific extreme sport. This site-specific knowledge is critical because the event manager, as leader, must have the ability to frame a vision for the event that is uplifting and realizable in the local setting yet be framed with an understanding of the event's setting and risk factors explicit and implicit in that setting. The framing of goals, to achieve the vision, must strike a balance between safety and risk. The processes enabling the goals to be attained require strong local knowledge, appropriate athlete entry skills, thorough preparation, legal compliance, clear briefing of participants, and close monitoring of the event.

Coaches, managers, and team leaders comprise the third extreme sports leadership grouping. The demands on their leadership transcend the demands on the leadership of their counterparts in conventional sports. Members of this grouping face critical challenges in their team's planning and participation. From team selection to successful completion of the competitive event, these team leaders face decisions on safety, campcraft, medical emergencies, risk management, interpersonal support, and environmental challenges that characterize many extreme sports. For example, in free climbing can athletes handle a particular life-challenging task? In whitewater rafting can a course be taken through particular rapids if the river has risen? Extreme sports coaches and team leaders must know their athletes and their personal and skill capabilities because these may be crucial in life-or-death situations—situations not faced by coaches in conventional sports. Knowledge of the environment and weather is more vital to extreme sports leaders, as are the actions to be taken in emergency situations. Decision making, then, becomes a critical skill, with overtones of mortality, for the extreme sports team leader.

The final grouping of extreme sports leaders is that of extreme sports athletes who engage in self-leadership in order to be successful. Warren Bennis, a writer and researcher of leadership, notes that leadership of one's self is essential. Self-led athletes in extreme sports have demands on their self-leadership similar to the demands on leaders in the third grouping of extreme sports leaders. Self-leadership

may be defined as "self-setting a vision and goals that lead to performance enhancing and self-fulfilling actions, independent of a formal coach or mentor" (McConnell 2005, 7). Sports participants in individual sports who can formulate a clear vision and set resultant goals to which they commit themselves are better placed to succeed than those with unclear, ambiguous, or shifting goals. Whether self-coached or coached by another person, the athlete in extreme sports faces self-leadership challenges greater than those faced by the athlete in conventional sports. The street luge or skysurfing competitor, for example, has considerations of safety, equipment, and environment that are critical to the competitor's well-being and goal attainment beyond those required of competitors in conventional sports.

Leadership Skills and Situational Responses

Leaders in an extreme sport push beyond usual boundaries of conventional sports leaders in addressing challenges of their sport when they develop their vision, goals, and processes. McConnell (2005) noted five broad categories of such skills and situational responses that are essential to extreme sports leadership and that are either not necessarily required by leaders in conventional sports or not required to the same extent.

■ Leaders translate their visionary aspirations into reality through goals and processes, but in extreme sports the realities of risk lie outside those of most conventional sports. Risk management is critical in extreme sports. A risk management strategy would note the context of the sport, identify the risks, plan to reduce or eliminate the risks, ensure that the risks are managed as well as possible in the sports context, and then monitor the effectiveness of this process. National organization leaders should ensure that such a policy is formulated for their sport, even if generic. At the competitive level the leader ensures that the policy is understood in the competitive environment, agreed upon by the team (if engaged in a team sport), and implemented with team commitment. In conventional sports on-site officials, such as referees or umpires, are present with the athletes throughout an encounter, supervising competition free of undue risk to participants, whereas in extreme sports this safeguard is not continually present, and greater responsibility is vested in the on-site leader.

(a) The leader's risk management includes goals and processes that ensure that management processes are on hand for emergency situations, particularly medical emergencies. Leaders in conventional sports face moments of concern for their athletes in medical emergencies, but these emergencies are the responsibility of on-site officials and medical personnel. For example, a support crew for an endurance event, when an emergency occurs in difficult and remote terrain or when a race vehicle crashes, relies on the on-site leader's behavior and judgments in the immediacy of an emergency before the crew arrives. The leader in extreme sports, who may not have emergency services immediately on hand, has responsibilities for ensuring that an available support crew is qualified, trained for sport-specific injuries and emergencies, is well-briefed, and can operate with judgment and efficiency in a rapid response.

(b) Risk factors related to campcraft and equipment fall within extreme sports leadership and managerial roles, for example, considerations of location, safety, shelter, warmth, meals, disposal of waste matter, selection of equipment, and repair of equipment.

(c) Technical skills are, arguably, more important for extreme sports leaders than for their counterparts in conventional sports on safety grounds alone. These skills require realistic understandings of the land, water, or air environment and of the technical skills required to prevail in that particular environment. Challenges of location in some extreme sports require leaders to ensure that technical skills include compass and map reading, route planning, weather analysis, flight planning, and precompetition analysis of the event setting. The experienced paragliding or parapenting instructor, tandem parachutist, cave diver, and balloonist, for example, need such skills.

■ Competition in extreme sports places a premium on environmental challenges beyond those customarily apparent in conventional sports. An emphasis is placed on competing against the elements *and* one's self and, in some sports, an opponent. Such leaders must know the competitive setting, which may change for each competitive event, unlike conventional sports arenas, courts, and fields, which are more inclined to be standardized. The regional or national leaders of an extreme sport frame a vision and goals that are sufficiently generic to fit all participatory circumstances, but the event manager, team leader, or athlete must address specific environmental challenges. Given the need for risk management, the team leader usually traverses the competition course to check possible dangers firsthand, carefully selects and plans camping sites (if relevant), and ensures that the environment will be respected. Checking the course also includes considering the course's demands on particular technical skills.

■ Organizational culture—the way things are done in the organization—is basically similar in extreme and conventional sports. However, in extreme sports the interdependence of team members is reliant on absolute trust, a shared and total commitment, more than in conventional sports because these team culture elements will affect competition success and may affect safety and even survival. To ensure full consideration of factors that are important in the safe and successful completion of a course or event, the extreme sports leader must be skilled in the avoidance of groupthink. This phenomenon—the compliance of all team members with a certain expressed view—may not unduly affect a conventional sports team's results, especially given a core of strong achievers, but it can lead to a critical view on safety or technique not being expressed and considered in an extreme sports setting.

■ Ethics in conventional and extreme sports have a similar focus on the need to respect rules, comply with organizers' and arbiters' decisions, and compete or participate fairly. The world of extreme sports leadership has the added challenge of environmental stewardship. The football or basketball coach does not have this challenge, but the coaches, participants, and leaders in bungee jumping, mountain biking, or heli-skiing face considerations of environmental damage, compliance with local regulations and laws on land use, the image of their sport, and access to places of sports activity. The observance of ethics is integral to campcraft also.

The True Champion

Robert Quercetani writes of his meeting with Czechoslovakian Olympic runner Emil Zátopek.

I am among those lucky track fans who saw Emil Zátopek in his Week of Weeks at the Helsinki Olympics in 1952. Twenty-six years later I had a chat with him during the European Championships in Prague. I found him as kind and humorous as ever, even though he had gone through troubled times for siding with those who turned out to be the (temporary) losers during the Prague Spring of 1968.

I invited him to give me his retrospective views on his track career. What he said was a monument to his proverbial modesty. In sharp contrast to the type of champion from yesteryear who likes to take refuge in the ivory tower of "his good old days," he candidly told me: "I think I had a fair amount of luck. Track thrived at a low-level temperature in those days. Most countries still had to heal the wounds of World War II and the turnover of talents was relatively slow. Finland's great runners from pre-war days had disappeared. Recalling the 1952 Olympic marathon (his first ever!) he said: "In a way, that was probably my easiest victory. It was not the 'new' distance that frightened me but rather the possibility of a fast pace throughout—but nobody chose to resort to that."

Robert Quercetani

■ Personal skills are similar for leaders in both conventional and extreme sports. Communication skills in extreme sports may affect survival, use forms of emergency contact, require understandings of certain technologies, and employ nonverbal signals. Kouzes and Posner (2001) note credibility as the heart of leadership, being essential for followers and a key to generating respect. Other personal strengths include charisma and empathy, the ability to give a vision excitement and relevance, the ability to resolve conflict, the ability to foster team commitment and unity, single-mindedness, humor, respect for individuals, and interpersonal skills.

Extreme Sports Leadership Training

Training extreme sports leaders is often haphazard and places a premium on experience, although a range of institutions has developed training programs in wilderness leadership and outdoor education leadership. Examples are Outward Bound, California Extreme Sports Camps, and the National Outdoor Leadership School (NOLS) in Wyoming. Koesler found that feedback and the mentoring influence were especially important for their impact on the wilderness leader's self-efficacy. The use of extreme and adventure sports settings for the development of leaders is seen in different countries. Examples are Outward Bound and the recent leader and self-development experiences of A. J. Hackett, the primary developer of commercial bungee jumping, who is based in France.

Looking Ahead

Leadership in extreme sports is, essentially, similar to that in conventional sports, with a vision, goals, and resultant processes having the commitment of those people directly affected. However, extreme sports leadership has wider parameters and a greater range of safety and risk considerations that engender critical planning, leadership actions, and decision making.

Robin Charles McConnell

See also Meaning of Extreme, The; Psychology of Risk; Sociology of Risk

Further Reading

Bennis, W., Spreitzer, G. M., & Cummings, T. G. (Eds.). (2001). *The future of leadership*. San Francisco: Jossey-Bass.

Carron, A., & Hausenblaus, H. A. (1998). *Group dynamics in sport* (2nd ed.). Morgantown, WV: Fitness Information Technology.

Charlesworth, R. (2001). *The coach: Managing for success*. Sydney, Australia: Macmillan.

Chelladurai, P. (1980). Leadership in sports organizations. *Canadian Journal of Applied Sports Sciences*, 15(4), 226–231.

Chelladurai, P., & Saleh, S. D. (1978). Preferred leadership in sports. *Canadian Journal of Applied Sports Sciences*, 13 3(2), 85–92.

Koesler, R., & Propst, D. (1994, August). *Factors influencing leadership development in wilderness education: Final report.* Ann Arbor, MI: University of Michigan.

Kouzes, J. M., & Posner, B. Z. (2001). Bringing leadership lessons from the past into the future. In W. Bennis, G. M. Spreitzer, & T. G. Cummings (Eds.), *The future of leadership* (pp. 81–90). San Francisco: Jossey-Bass.

McConnell, R. C. (2005). *The leadership challenge in adventure and extreme sports.* Jordanstown, UK: University of Ulster Press.

McConnell, R. C., & McConnell, C. D. (1996). Leadership. In D. Levinson & K. Christensen (Eds.), *Encyclopedia of world sport* (Vol. 2, pp. 573–576). Santa Barbara, CA: ABC-CLIO.

Martin, J. L. (2005, August 8). Leadership is an extreme sport: Richard Hames at Future Summit. *Australian Financial Review.*

Mobley, T. A. (1986). Thoughts on management and leadership. *Journal of Parks and Recreation Management*, 4(1).

Rost, J. C. (1991). *Leadership for the twenty-first century.* New York: Praeger.

Stark, P. (2001). *Last breath: Cautionary tales from the limits of human endurance.* New York: Ballantine Books.

Tomlinson, J. (2002). *Ultimate encyclopedia of extreme sports.* London: Carlton Books.

Long Distance Racing and Pedestrianism

Long distance running has been a prime activity of humans since time immemorial, associated with hunting, fighting, or delivering messages. The earliest example of running for sport occurred in the Panhellenic contests of antiquity (Olympic, Pythian, Isthmian, and Nemean Games), in which the *dolichos* was the longest of the running events.

Long distance running can well be included under the label "extreme" as it symbolizes man's challenge in terms of endurance-to-speed. Challenging distance is tantamount to challenging fatigue. Notwithstanding the progress made in training methods with the support of science applied to sport, endurance to suffering remains an unavoidable factor (the more so, of course, if we consider longer events such as the marathon and ultradistances).

At Olympia racing was first included in the program in 720 BCE, and the race was won by Akanthos of Sparta. The race was 20 stades (3,845.4 meters) in length. According to one tale, after winning the *dolichos* during the morning

hours at the Olympic Games in 328 BCE, Ageas of Argos set off again and arrived at Argos in the late evening to announce his victory to fellow citizens. He thus ran approximately 110 kilometers in one day. There were no doubt outstanding distance runners in other remote civilizations, too. For example, the Tarahumara Indians of Mexico were famous for their endurance feats. In most tribes "learning to run" was considered one of the prime necessities of life.

Pedestrianism

The dawn of long distance racing in modern times is usually identified with pedestrianism, a form of professional athletics practiced in the British Isles between the seventeenth and nineteenth centuries. It was a mixed type of activity described as "go as you please," in which competitors were free to alternate between running and walking. Most famous in the United States was Lewis Bennett (c. 1830–1895), a Native American of the Seneca tribe. Known as "Deerfoot" for his smooth running style, he ran in the traditional costume of his tribe, "with a slight red apron around his waist and a band around his head, with one eagle feather." He made the news on both sides of the Atlantic, and his most significant achievement was a one-hour record of 18,589 meters, made in London in 1863—an achievement that remained unsurpassed for forty-one years among amateurs. This mark was set in a race of more than 19 kilometers, at the end of which "Deerfoot" "lost" by 1 meter to William Lang of England, who had a 91-meter head start.

Also famous at that time was John "Jack" White (1838–1910), a tiny British runner from Gateshead who in 1863 broke the half-hour barrier in the 6 miles (9.6 kilometers) with 29 minutes 50 seconds (29:50.0), then went on to reach 10 miles (16 kilometers) in 52:14.0, beating Lang and "Deerfoot," among others. Even more remarkable was that White ran on a narrow 260-yard (237-meter) cinder track and at a steadily decreasing pace—first mile (1.6 kilometers) in 4:40, last mile in 5:10.

Throughout the nineteenth century professionals invariably outshone their amateur counterparts. As well as good economic incentives, the pros also competed under looser rules. Amateur athletics, born in the best British schools and colleges, operated under strict rules and received the backing of influential patrons; in the end such factors were to turn the tide in its favor with the creation of national federations governing the sport. Quite prominent near the end of the nineteenth century was the frail-looking, willowy

Walter George of England (1858–1943). In 1884, his best year, he achieved the following times, all of which were amateur bests: 1 mile (1.6 kilometers) in 4:18, 2 miles (3.2 kilometers) in 9:17, 3 miles (4.8 kilometers) in 14:39.0, 6 miles (9.6 kilometers) in 30:21, 10 miles (16 kilometers) in 51:20.0, 11.5 miles (18,555 meters) in 60:0. His races with Lon Myers, an American who reigned over a wide spectrum of distances (100 yards to 1 mile) in his own country, were among the competitive highlights of athletics in the nineteenth century, but, of course, they rather belong to the domain of middle distance running.

The earliest attempts at more than 5,000 and 10,000 meters date from the last decade of the nineteenth century and were invariably made by continental Europeans. Yet, the fastest 10,000-meter mark of that century should be credited to Walter George: 31:40.0, taken at 6.25 miles in 1884 en route to a 12-mile (19.3-kilometer) tape.

Marathon

The inaugural Olympics of the modern era, held in Athens in 1896, featured only one long distance race, called the "marathon," about 40 kilometers in length. The race was a tribute to ancient Greek traditions; Marathon is a village in Attica northeast of Athens, where the Athenians defeated the Persians in 490 BCE. As legend has it, a Greek messenger, Pheidippides, ran all the way from the Plain of Marathon to Athens to carry news of the victory to the citizens of the capital. On arrival he fell dead. Michel Bréal, a French linguist and historian as well as a friend of Olympic organizer Pierre de Coubertin, advocated the inclusion of an endurance test named after Marathon in the program of the modern Olympic Games. The inaugural event was won by a Greek—the previously unheralded Spiridon Louis (1873–1940), a shepherd from Maroussi whose victory transformed him into a national icon almost overnight. He came home after 2:58.50. The event sent a loud echo in athletics circles around the world, and marathon races became popular, particularly in the United States and France. The Boston marathon was run for the first time in 1897, along a course just under 40 kilometers in length. Still in vogue today, it ranks as the oldest of non-Olympic marathons.

The first distance runner likely to be considered a "modern" in more than one way was Alfred Shrubb of Great Britain (1878–1964). Although he never appeared in the Olympics, he rewrote the record book with times such as 9:09 (2 miles/3.2 kilometers), 14:17 (3 miles/4.8 kilometers),

Close-up of a road runner's feet pounding a paved road. Source: istock.

29:59 (6 miles/9.6 kilometers), 31:02 (6.2 miles/10 kilometers), 50:40 (10 miles/16 kilometers), and 60:0 (11.6 miles/18.7 kilometers). The last four were run at Glasgow on 5 November 1904. He later revealed that in the thirty days preceding that race he covered 286 kilometers in training. Each session consisted of a single long race at a pace varying from "fairly slow" to "goodish."

One of the most enduring marathon memories occurred at the conclusion of the Olympic event in 1908 in London. Italy's Dorando Pietri (1885–1942) entered the White City Stadium first but, being exhausted, fell several times. Doctors and officials rushed to assist him and thereby helped him to finish. He came to the end of his odyssey after 2:54.46 but was subsequently disqualified. Victory went to John Hayes of the United States (2:55.18). Worldwide popular interest in long events increased considerably. Pietri, Hayes, and others turned pro and starred during the "marathon craze" that subsequently swept the United States.

The London race of 1908 was also famous for another reason: Its length (26 miles 385 yards/42.1 kilometers) was curiously adopted as official for all marathon races of international significance. As a result, the event so often referred to as "the classic Greek distance" actually originated from an English convenience—the distance from Windsor Castle, where the race started, to White City Stadium.

Finnish Era

Finland played a prominent role in the advancement of distance running in the early decades of the twentieth century. The man who put Finland on the map of athletics was Hannes Kolehmainen (1889–1966), who won a 5,000/10,000-meter double at the 1912 Olympics in Stockholm and came back eight years later, after World War I, to win the marathon at Antwerp. In his wake there arose a phalanx of worthy successors who made Finland the leading distance running nation for many years. Foremost among them was Paavo Nurmi (1897–1973), who won twelve medals in the Olympics (nine gold, three silver) and set twenty-nine world records at distances ranging from 1,500 to 20,000 meters. His best times at Olympic distances were 3:52.6 (1,500 meters), 14:28.2 (5,000 meters), and 30:06.2 (10,000 meters), all in 1924. He covered 19,210 meters in one hour (1928). In his book *Olympiavoittajen Testamenttii* (Testament of an Olympic Champion) he said that his physical fitness was the result of many years of hard work as a teenager. Most of his training consisted of long races at a steady pace. Only in his later years did he pay adequate attention to "speed work." Even though he enjoyed great popularity—in 1925 he made a triumphant tour of the United States—he always remained faithful to his parsimonious habits in speech and behavior.

Finnish runners continued to dominate the track throughout the 1930s. Leading Finnish runners included Lauri Lehtinen, Gunnar Höckert, and Ilmari Salminen, who improved on Nurmi's records. In the marathon new runners included Juan Carlos Zabala of Argentina and Kee-Chung Sohn, a Korean-born Japanese, who won that event at Los Angeles (1932) and Berlin (1936), respectively.

Although the Olympic Games of 1940 and 1944 were cancelled during World War II, in 1942 the Swede Gunder Hägg (1918–2004), a tall, strong farm boy from Jämtland, became the first man to break the fourteen-minute barrier in the 5,000 meters (13:58.2). Two years later Viljo Heino of Finland also made history with a sensational 29:35.4 time over 10,000 meters.

"Ironman" Zátopek

The first great distance runner of the postwar years was Emil "Ironman" Zátopek of Czechoslovakia (1922–2000), who had a great impact on his contemporaries. He was four times an Olympic champion (10,000 meters in 1948, 5,000 and 10,000 meters and the marathon in 1952 for a unique triple), and between 1949 and 1955 he set eighteen world records at distances ranging from 5,000 to 30,000 meters. His best times included 13:57.2 (5,000 meters), 28:54.2 (10,000 meters), and 60:0 (20,052 meters). He thrived on "interval training," running over a fixed distance many times and slowing down to a dog trot during intervals. A Ukrainian from the Soviet Union, Vladimir Kuts (1927–1975), further lowered the world records for the 5,000 meters and 10,000 meters to 13:35.0 (1957) and 28:30.4 (1956), respectively. Kuts destroyed the morale of his rivals by going out early at a fast pace. He even scored a double at the Melbourne Olympics in 1956 but did not equal Zátopek in longevity.

Champions are preferably rated on the strength of their competitive record on big occasions rather than on their achievements against the clock in "cold" races. However, if one exception is to be made, that would be Ron Clarke (b. 1937). Between 1963 and 1968 Clarke amassed eighteen world records. His best times were 13:16.6 (5,000 meters), 27:39.4 (10,000 meters), and 60:0 (20,232 meters). He "failed" at the Olympics, winning a mere bronze in Tokyo in 1964, and like many runners was severely disadvantaged by the atmosphere of Mexico City (2,300 meters above sea level) in the 1968 Games. Africans, usually more accustomed to such conditions, won all six medals at stake in the 5,000 and 10,000 meters. In 1960 there had been a foreshadowing of the incoming "African wave" when an unheralded runner from Ethiopia, Abebe Bikila (1933–1973), won the Olympic marathon in Rome. He did it again four years later in Tokyo, with the fastest time on record (2:12.11) up to then. Finland had a comeback of sorts in the 1970s thanks to Lasse Viren (b. 1949), a "lone wolf" from the forest region of Myrskylä, who achieved the 5,000/10,000-meter double in two consecutive editions of the Olympics, 1972 and 1976.

Advent of Africa

What came after that was mostly, if not entirely, an African epic. Runners from that continent have ruled long distance racing in recent years. Miruts Yifter (b. 1944), an aging distance runner from Ethiopia, won both track events at the 1980 Olympics in Moscow. Even greater was the impact of Said Aouita of Morocco, whose range covered all distances between 800 and 10,000 meters. The two stars of recent years have come from Ethiopia, Haile Gebrselassie (b. 1973) and Kenenisa Bekele (b. 1982). The former broke the world records for 5,000 and 10,000 meters time and again, his best times being 12:39.36 and 26:22.75, both in 1998. The latter took over in an impressive fashion with 12:37.35 (2004) and 26:17.53 (2005). Bekele can also point to an imposing record in cross-country competitions. The one-hour world record belongs to Auturo Barrios (b. 1963) of Mexico, who later became a U.S. citizen: 21,101 meters at La Flèche, France, in 1991.

Honors have been more evenly split in the marathon, but here again Africa has had the last word so far with Paul Tergat of Kenya, who, after a great but partly checkered career on the track, lowered the world record for the marathon to 2:04.55 in the Berlin classic of 2003. And he needed just that to stay ahead of runner-up Sammy Korir of Kenya, who finished a bare second behind. The success of distance runners from Africa can be attributed to several factors. First, they have natural talent—qualities inherited either at birth or acquired through living habits in the years of childhood—fostered through years of running uphill and downhill since childhood. Second, they are generally accustomed to a different rhythm of life and tend to be more relaxed than their European counterparts. Third, they often have an ambition to use sports as a vehicle toward a better life. Many leading African runners have trained in U.S. colleges and/or European clubs. And younger runners now benefit from training centers recently created on their own continent by the International Association of Athletics Federations (IAAF). European runners are no longer prominent in distance running. Europe's last noteworthy success occurred at the 1992 Olympics in Barcelona, when Dieter Baumann of Germany outsprinted his African rivals in the closing stage of the 5,000 meters. The current European records for the classic distances (12:49.71 and 26:52.30) are held by Mohammed Mourhit of Belgium, a Moroccan at birth. Current U.S. records are held by Meb Keflezighi (10,000 meters) and Khalid Khannouchi (marathon), who hail from Eritrea and Morocco, respectively.

Women

In modern times the earliest references to athletic activity by women date from the middle of the seventeenth century, mostly in connection with English fairs and wakes. For incipient forms of the sport as we know it today one had to wait until the 1890s, when women's meets were held in several English-speaking countries on both sides of the Atlantic. For a long time even illustrious men seemed to have reservations about the participation of women in sports. Not surprisingly, the real boost to an international competition came from a group of sports-loving women headed by Alice Milliat of France. The group was responsible for

Endurance Runner on the Newry Road

The solitary figure spurns
siren heat to ghost
In headlights

In white flight energy
Her compulsive tempo
Spinning syllables

Paced in sinewed time,
taut with fragile space
and spirit burned

passing through. My
Mother would aver it is
More genteel for such a girl

To lay down her burden
Mile and burn not a zealous
Candle of rue to the

Inner-ness that drives
The pale body running
On consummate threads

Of flesh and spirit addiction
To discard the ravel reach of
Her pacemaker moon.

Robin McConnell

organizing the first multinational meet, the Women's World Games, held at Stade Pershing, Paris, in 1922. The longest running event on the program was a 1,000-meter race. Six years later, when women were admitted to the Olympics for the first time, the longest race was 800 meters. However, only in the late 1960s did women begin to partake in long distance running en masse.

Van Aaken's Theory

Dr. Ernst Van Aaken of Germany, a coach and physician, championed the cause of women's distance running. He argued that women have the ideal physical and mental prerequisites to excel in the sport. He believed that women would come closer to men's standards over long distances than in the sprints. Even so, one had to wait until the 1980s to see the inclusion of the longer races in the Olympic women's program. Joan Benoit (b. 1957) of the United States won the inaugural women's marathon in 1984 with a brilliant 2:24.52. Benoit beat Grete Waitz (b. 1953) of Norway and Rosa Mota (b. 1958) of Portugal in that race, but over time Waitz and Mota would have an even greater influence on the evolution of the event. Waitz scored nine victories in the New York marathon.

Another Norwegian, Ingrid Kristiansen (b. 1956), broke such barriers as fifteen minutes for the 5,000 meters (14:58.89 in 1984) and thirty-one minutes for the 10,000 meters (30:59.42 in 1985). At the longer distance she later improved to 30:13.74. However, the real revolution occurred in 1993 when Chinese women, trained by coach Ma Junren, entered the stage. Foremost among them was Wang Junxia (b. 1973), who ran 3,000 meters in 8:06.11 and 10,000 meters in 29:31.78. No one has matched this performance.

Female distance runners from Africa have challenged the Chinese. At the 2005 World Championships Tirunesh Dibaba (b. 1985) of Ethiopia won both 5,000 and 10,000 meters, and her teammates assured a complete medal sweep for that country. Early in 2006 another Ethiopian, Meseret Deafr (b. 1983), lowered the world's 5,000 record to 14:24.53. The one-hour world record belongs to Tegla Loroupe (b. 1971) of Kenya: 18,340 meters at Borgholzhausen, Germany, in 1998.

And There Came Radcliffe

After learning the art of long distance running on the track, Paula Radcliffe (b. 1973), a student of European languages from Britain, has emerged as a new marathon champion. In 2003 she won the London marathon in 2:15.25, a time bettered by only one man in the 1960 Olympic marathon. Much of the success in women's long distance running can be attributed to a blend of interval training, endurance training, and the shift from high quantity to high quality.

Roberto L. Quercetani

Further reading

Alfred Schrubb: World champion runner. (n.d.). Retrieved February 11, 2007, from www.alfieshrubb.ca

Hamilton, B. (2000), East African running dominance: What is behind it. *British Journal of Sports Medicine, 34,* 391–394.

www.paularadcliffe.com

Meaning of Extreme, The

"Extreme" is a popular adjective used to describe a range of individualistic, adventure-type pursuits and sports with obvious elements of risk. Although the list of pursuits and sports described as "extreme" is long, some of the better known ones include adventure racing, BASE (building, antenna, span, Earth) jumping, bungee jumping, canyoning, free climbing, in-line skating, kite surfing, mountain boarding, *parkour* (an activity in which athletes try to pass obstacles in the fastest and most direct manner), skysurfing, speed biking, street luge, tough man competitions, and wakeboarding. Although these activities are easily differentiated from well-established sports such as athletics, baseball, baseball, basketball, cricket, football, and hockey, in other cases the line between the two blurs. Skiing and snowboarding, for example, are two fast, dangerous mountain activities and codified sports, yet in the popular imagination the latter connotes extreme. Lest readers equate "extreme" with recently invented physical activities, history is a less than reliable point of differentiation.

Some extreme pursuits, such as bungee jumping, surfing, mountaineering, ultimate fighting, and skyflying have long histories; others, such as buildering (climbing over urban features), extreme ironing (in which participants iron shirts at remote locations), and skyjumping with unrelated objects (e.g., water heaters, wagons, golf carts), reflect the long-recognized human penchant for transgression, stepping outside social convention and playing with norms. Other extreme pursuits, like many established sports, have their origins in work; tree climbing, for example, is popular among arborists.

Defining Extreme Sports

Extreme sports, as noted, do not constitute an objective class of physical activity. Some exist as codified sports with a formal competitive, contest-based structure characterized by agreed-upon rules, set criteria for determining winners, and zero-sum outcomes (e.g., street luge). Others are unstructured with highly playful and expressive dimensions (e.g., adventure climbing, bungee jumping, whitewater rafting). Many others include elements of both (e.g., in-line skating, snowboarding, surfing, wakeboarding). Still others, such

as buildering and BASE jumping are illegal. In order to analyze extreme pursuits—here for simplicity's sake labeled "sports"—we identify a range of characteristics that enables a comparison with established sports. The process of comparison reveals considerable similarities between the two forms of physical activity and less differences than might initially be thought.

Similarities in Extreme Sports and Established Sports

In addition to committing significant amounts of time and money to their activities, disciples of extreme sports and established sports share a willingness to take risks, a social ideology of fun, and a tendency toward codifying and institutionalizing their interests.

▶ **Risk** In physical activity "risk" refers to exposure to injury; in physical competitions and games risk also includes exposure to (symbolic) defeat, loss of face, and esteem. Exposure to injury is a universal trait of all physical activity, regardless of how innocuous (e.g., showering, descending stairs, crossing roads). Before undertaking a physical activity, whether as part of day-to-day life, work, or leisure, most people will consider, either consciously or subconsciously, the level of risk. Continuation with the activity thus involves a calculation that connects means and ends and/or causes and effects. Such calculations invariably lead individuals to introduce mechanisms of control whereby they adopt strategies to reduce the probability of injury (e.g., slipping in the shower—holding on to a rail; drowning in big surf—wearing a life vest). In game situations some individuals and teams may also adopt negative strategies to reduce the chances of losing (e.g., retaining possession of the ball without attempting to score and thus potentially turning the ball over to stronger opponents). In both these senses then risk becomes an analytical concept for either making the unpredictable predictable or calculating unpredictable consequences.

However, no universal standard of objective risk exists in established sports or extreme sports; participants define their own level of risk, and an activity that one individual defines as risk free, another may consider high risk. Moreover, individuals constantly reappraise their calculations of risk; what appears high risk at one moment might seem perfectly safe the next—and vice versa. Joe Tomlinson illustrates the complexity of risk calculations in the case of BASE jumping

A partial dictionary definition of "risk," one of the key elements of extreme sports. Source: istock.

when he lists "the most important skill any BASE jumper can possess" as "the ability to differentiate between a jump that can be made, and one that can but shouldn't" (Tomlinson 2004, 15). Further complicating these calculations, psychologists observe that in game situations individuals attempt to balance the level of difficulty and degree of risk and that they will adjust their behavior in order to maintain the balance and satisfy a threshold of risk.

Notwithstanding the willingness of participants to accept some risk, minimization of the risk threshold has been a hallmark of the codification of modern sports and ongoing changes to rules in different codes. Among the better known early examples of rules intended to reduce injury are the rule mandating the wearing of "fair size" gloves in boxing under the 1867 Marquess of Queensberry rules, the Rugby Football Union's 1871 prohibition against "hacking" (kicking an opponent to the ground), and the embryonic National Collegiate Athletic Association's adoption of the forward pass in American football (intended to open the game and eliminate brutal mass plays such as the "flying wedge," held responsible for the deaths of eighteen players in 1905). More recent examples of risk reduction in modern sports include safety equipment (e.g., mouthguards in Australian football, helmets in cricket, minimum-length skis in downhill skiing, expansion bolts—for attaching carabiners [rings with one spring-hinged side used as a connector and to hold a freely

running rope]—in sport climbing, full-face shields in ice hockey, footguards in field hockey, frangible [breakable] fences in equestrian events) and rule changes (e.g., the ban against "spearing" [using the top of the helmet when tackling an opponent] in American football, and the prohibition against checking from behind in ice hockey).

In many cases new equipment and new rules have significantly reduced the risk of injury. Full-face shields have eliminated eye injuries in ice hockey, and the ban against spearing decreased fatalities by 74 percent and serious head injuries by 84 percent in American football. Yet, safety equipment is not necessarily a panacea, as Ken Sheard argues in the case of boxing. Gloves worn by boxers have certainly eliminated "the gore, the broken bones, and bunged-up eyes of the bare-knuckle era, but in their place is a more brutal and insidious legacy that is difficult to measure or predict: brain-damage" (Sheard 2004, 25). With their hands protected, Sheard observes, modern boxers tend to hit their opponents harder, more often, and from angles that produce the "rotational forces...which cause the brain to swirl inside the skull" (Sheard 2004, 27) and lead to brain damage. In addition, the introduction of safety equipment or safety-inspired rules may disrupt an individual's perceptions of the balance between difficulty and risk, and in order to restore that tension he or she may compensate for lower levels of risk in one area by adopting more risky behavior in others.

The mania for risk in extreme sports—captured by the "If it can't kill you, it ain't extreme" annual tow-in surfing event—suggests that devotees accept higher levels of danger than participants in established sports. Statistical evidence seems to provide confirmation. In climbing and air sports the estimated death rate is about 800 per 100 million person-days, compared with 70 for water sports, 30 for horse riding, 16 for rugby, and 5 for boxing. Yet, on closer inspection, high risk per se does not stand out as a characteristic of extreme sports. Many activities labeled "extreme" are actually very safe. Sports journalist Rick Arnett might cast bungee jumping as "suicide on-a-string" (Arnett 2006), but statistics show it is no more dangerous than riding a roller coaster. Such comparisons lead Michael Bane, author of *Over the Edge*, to approach extreme from an alternative perspective: thrill as a state of physiological arousal.

A form of response to novel stimulus (e.g., perception of danger, sense of vertigo, acute stress), physical thrills trigger specific physiological actions that are collectively and popularly known as an "adrenaline rush." On perceiving a stimulus, the brain relays signals through the central nervous system. This process initiates the release of the hormones epinephrine and norepinephrine into the blood, which in turn causes stimulatory reactions throughout the body, including increases in the heart rate and breathing, and the redirecting of blood into potentially active muscles. The accumulation of epinephrine and norepinephrine may cause a form of overloading that precipitates a number of spontaneous or intuitive behaviors popularly described as "fight or flight." Some physiologists believe that in other cases these stimulatory reactions may enable individuals to maintain control in chaotic situations and avoid fear-induced paralysis. Describing a version of the control response, professional snowboarder Andrew Crawford admits to being "scared to death every time I get on my snowboard" but, he maintains, it is a "feeling that pushes you and makes you try your hardest" (Sherowski 2006, 192). Some researchers also hypothesize that these physiological mechanisms may produce an addiction to thrill-seeking behavior; the body also releases dopamine in response to arousal, and this hormone is involved with the sensation of pleasure. Anecdotal evidence supports this hypothesis. "You float like a bird out there," raves paraglider Mike Carr: "you can go as high as 18,000 feet and go for 200 miles. That's magic" (Greenfeld 1999). Similarly, one devotee of snow kiting likens the activity to "a pure drug."

Anthropologists and sociologists, on the other hand, analyze risk within the context of physically based, hierarchical cultures that celebrate and glorify risk. In these (typically macho) cultures, risks constitute challenges, and meeting these challenges earn members—predominantly young men—rewards (e.g., peer recognition and prestige). Far from highlighting their calculations of, and strategies to manage, risk, members of these cultures publicly endorse and embrace risk. A common bedfellow here is the media, which, in appropriating a rhetoric of progress and development through physical activity, happily regale readers with stories of young men risking all to prove their skills and their mettle. Thus, we read, for example, about snowboarder Scotty Wittlake, who, in his quest to land the perfect jump, has broken teeth, ribs, ankles, and nose, collapsed a lung, cracked a femur, crushed cheekbones, and lost sight in one eye—all without the slightest complaint.

Regardless of the analytical framework, no evidence indicates that disciples of extreme have completely abandoned concerns for safety. On the contrary, many participants in extreme sports deny accusations that they are risk takers; many insist that they are as conscious of safety as participants in established sports. Felix Baumgartner spent months preparing for his 7.5-second BASE jump into the Mamet cave (Croatia). Preparations included making practice jumps from a hot air balloon, taking laser measurements of the interior of the cave, and illuminating the floor of the cave with flares. In his study of high-risk competitors, including skydivers, racing car drivers, fencers, and aerobatic pilots, Bruce Ogilvie concluded that they are success oriented and rarely reckless risk takers. Their risk taking, he said, is cool and calculated. Similarly, Joe Tomlinson dismisses notions of extreme disciples as "fanatics seeking a buzz" without regard for consequences. He argues that they all "perform within their limits" (Tomlinson 2004, 6). On the other hand, Stephen Lyng observes that many participants in extreme sports believe that they possess innate survival capacities. "I wasn't thinking at all," says one skydiver recounting an incident of parachute malfunction: "I just did what I had to do." Interestingly, Lyng identifies a tautology in this notion of survival capacity among test pilots; they believe that innate ability is their insurance against fatal accidents and that those who die simply did not possess the basic survival capacities in the first place.

Most accounts of extreme sports emphasize the importance of safety equipment and support partners/teams. Tow-in surfers venturing into massive surf carry pure-grade oxygen and choose their partners carefully. Canyoners wear helmets, wetsuits, life jackets, and climbing harnesses. Adventure climbers limit the distance between running belays to prevent lead climbers from long and potentially deadly falls. Following high numbers of fatalities in their new pursuit in the 1960s, skydivers replaced round, military-surplus canopies with safer, rectangular ram-air parachutes (that act more like inflatable gliders) and began using automatic opening devices to deploy reserve canopies in the event of the main canopy failing. Of course, as the statistics cited imply, the nature of the environment means that the consequences of failure tend to be more severe in extreme sports than established sports. In 1999 Jan Davis, an experienced BASE jumper with three thousand jumps, died jumping from a cliff at Yosemite National Park; she had arranged the jump to prove that parachuting from cliffs, a pursuit banned by the United States Park Service, is safe.

On the other hand, for all the apparent moves to make established sports safer, some participants still willingly risk fractures, dislocations, wounds, bruises, strains, burns, willfully violent opponents, spinal injuries, concussions, and even death. "Willy," a participant in research into men's experiences of fear, pain, and pleasure in rugby, recalls feeling "good" playing the game at school during lunchtimes "because we took the hits, scratches, grazes, and stuff." Even today as a young adult, Willy affords the highest esteem to those who embrace pain. In his eyes New Zealand representative Norm Hewitt, who once continued playing with a broken arm, is "the man!" "That's what you have to do in rugby, suck it in," Willy says. In short, the risks in established sports are often as great as in extreme sports (e.g., downhill skiing versus extreme skiing, boxing versus extreme fighting); some individuals in established sports will appear as addicted to risk as devotees of extreme sports, while other disciples of extreme sports will show high aversion to risk. Regardless of their disposition (and more research into the physiology and psychology of individual risk takers is required), most devotees will perform careful calculations of the risk factors associated with their actions.

▶ **Fun** Participants and spectators often use the term *fun* to describe their involvement in established sports and extreme sports. "Snowboarders are dead serious about having fun," says devotee and equipment manufacturer Jake Burton, adding that "we have always had a helluva lot of fun busting our asses to create a sport and [the] successful [Burton] company" (Burton 2003, 401–406). Similarly, when asked why he keeps returning to the slopes, professional snowboarder Terje Haakonsen replied, "it's just a joy, the joy of ... playing" (Galbraith and Marcopoulos 2004, 62–83). Whereas the Dutch scholar Johan Huizinga maintains that "the *fun* of playing resists all analysis, all logical interpretation" (Huiz-

inga 1955, 3), John Loy and Jay Coakley (2006) observe in the literature several theoretical concepts related to fun, including Georg Simmel's "sociability," Erving Goffman's "euphoric interaction," Norbert Elias and Eric Dunning's "quest for excitement," and Brian Sutton Smith's "emotional dialectics." These characteristics exist across the gamut of established sports and extreme sports.

Defined by Georg Simmel as the "play form" of human interaction, sociability is a characteristic of established sports and extreme sports as participants willingly confront artificial obstacles such as opposing teams or treacherous natural environments, cooperate with and support teammates and partners, and cast aside social distinctions (e.g., income, occupation, education, race) for the duration of the activity in which they act, and treat each other, as social equals. Bonding, for example, is as important in competition adventure racing and skysurfing as in basketball and football. Compelled by the rules to finish the race together, adventure racers are, in Martha Bell's words, "under intense pressure to make safe judgements, for speed, time, and their stamina" and to "communicate and 'journey' well" (Bell 2003, 229).

Erving Goffman analyzed fun (pleasurable sociability) as the euphoric interaction found in gaming environments. He attributed euphoria to three conditions: uncertain outcomes, displays of sanctioned behavior, and tensions. Whether based on luck, the idiosyncrasies and nuances of competition, or unforeseen obstacles, uncertain outcomes characterize established sports and extreme sports; likewise, both forms also sanction displays of athletic excellence and physical prowess. Although many extreme sports are solitary endeavors or take place in environments unsuited to mass spectatorship, one of the paradoxes of these activities in the context of sanctioned displays is that devotees go to inordinate lengths to ensure their visibility among peers. When BMX (bicycle motocross) rider Mat Hoffman achieved the "highest air" on record (15.4 meters) in March 2001, he invited a camera crew from *ABC Wide World of Sports* to the site and organized a team of professional photographers to record the attempt at different angles from an elaborate scaffolding system. Regardless of the activity, visibility is a prerequisite of cultural legitimacy and status. Lastly, all gaming situations involve stakes—whether they be status or physical risks—that precipitate tension- (and possibly thrill-) producing forms of excitement.

The quest for excitement figures prominently in the research of Norbert Elias and Eric Dunning. They hold that sport "stir[s] the emotions" and "evoke[s] tension" (Loy and Coakley 2006) in a playful and pleasurable manner. Although many of the emotions and tensions in sports mimic those in everyday life (e.g., challenge, pleasure, triumph, despair, loss, rivalry, torment), they do not carry the same levels of risk because sports are, ultimately, set aside from life as only a game. As discussed earlier, devotees of extreme sports also manage the level of risk in their quest for mimetic excitement.

Brian Sutton Smith concurs with Huizinga that fun is the primary purpose of play, and he agrees with Elias and Dunning that playful fun offers mimetic excitement. However, he also analyzes fun as a dialectical relationship between excess and constraint in societies that impose constraints on forms of play that involve excessive emotions and noise and riotous behaviors. The history of established sports and extreme sports reveals numerous examples of local authorities acting against players, devotees, and spectators whose behaviors they deem as threatening the social order. Examples include bans against football and cricket played on Sundays in the early nineteenth century and those against surfing and snowboarding at different beaches and mountain resorts in the late twentieth century. Interestingly, many scholars, including Loy and Coakley, conceptualize institutionalization as an amalgam of social and political processes designed to harness, control, and regulate the expressive dimensions of play.

▶ **Institutionalization** Loy and Coakley locate physical activity on a continuum of expressivity–instrumentality; *expressivity* refers to the principles of play, pleasure, and participation in unstructured games and activities, and *instrumentality* articulates the principles of performance, profit, and prestige found in professional and representational (especially national team) sports. Extreme sports, too, reside on this continuum. Institutionalization is a reasonably good measure of instrumentality, and in order to illustrate comparable levels of institutionalization across established sports and extreme sports, we apply four questions recommended by Loy and Coakley to both:

- What is the social structure of the activity?
- How does mainstream thought regard the activity?
- Who participates in the activity?
- How widely has the activity diffused across society?

At the center of the social structure of established sports sits the process of rationalization, a process integral to the systematic improvement of performance, profit, and prestige. Extreme sports have embraced instrumental rationalization, as is evident in the formalization of rules, specialization of skills, quantification of outcomes, bureaucratization of administration, the appearance of professional events, circuits, and athletes, and the broadcasting of those same events by the mass media. In our examination of the rationalization of extreme sports two examples must suffice: the formalization of rules and the quantification of outcomes.

Ultimate fighting, a form of brawling in which opponents battle in a cage using their fists, feet, and legs, offers a good example of rationalization. After facing bans in most states across North America, organizers prohibited head butting and introduced weight divisions, a scoring system, and rigorous medical testing. These new rules and codes immediately earned the sport official sanction in twenty states. Simultaneously, ultimate fighting secured a television contract with Spike TV (part of MTV Networks, a subsidiary of Viacom), a cable network that initially referred to itself as "the first network for men" but that recently underwent a rebranding exercise that incorporated the line "Get More Action."

"The phenomenon of collecting and documenting 'firsts,' 'landmark performances,' or 'records' in all facets of extreme sports," note Robert Rinehart and Synthia Sydnor, replicates that which "occurred in mainstream sports such as baseball and basketball in the past century" (Rinehart and Sydnor 2003, 1–17). The annals of extreme sports—typically dedicated magazines and websites—judiciously record the fastest speeds (e.g., speed skiing—Jeff Hamilton, 241 kilometers per hour; speed biking—Christian Taillefer, 212 kilometers per hour), latest maneuvers (e.g., skateboarding, 900-degree spin—Tony Hawk; vert BMX, no-handed 900-degree spin—Mat Hoffman; snowmobiling, backflip—Jim Rippey; motocross, backflip—Mike Metzger; barefoot water skiing, inverted jumping style—Mike Seipel), the deepest dives (e.g., fixed-weight category, Eric Charrier, 73 meters; absolute category, Francisco Ferraras, 168 meters), and the simply unique (e.g., BASE jumper Felix Baumgartner's low jump from the statue of Christ in Rio de Janeiro, his high jump from the eighty-eight-story Petronas Towers in Kuala Lumpur, and his fourteen-minute sky flight across the English Channel). Record keeping, we should note, facilitates competition among participants as they set out to become the first to achieve a task or maneuver or to better a previous record (distance, time).

Although devotees of extreme sports insist that they oppose formal administrative structures, which they equate with intrusion, unwarranted attempts to control and dictate, and ultimately corruption, in numerous instances, such as ultimate fighting, they have rationalized their activities as a strategic move to counter adverse publicity, circumvent controls and/or bans, and minimize external interference. Of course, all physical activities require a critical mass of participants to achieve recognition and legitimacy, and that mass in turn necessitates a level of coordination and administration. Invariably, both legitimacy and administration involve relationships with official institutions such as government agencies, and, as Peter Donnelly reminds us, even "apparently innocent links with government" through, for example, securing minor funding for administration and education, mean "accountability and a certain amount of implicit control" (Donnelly 2003, 301).

At first glance the structures that frame extreme sports appear less stable and more susceptible to change than those that frame established sports. Robert Rinehart observes that changes to the rules in established sports almost invariably spark debates; he attributes such a reaction to an apprehension associated with disrupting "the nostalgia that reaffirms people's connections with the sport" (Rinehart 2000, 509). By contrast, he argues, change is more inherent in extreme sports, and nostalgia appears shortlived. At the very least, extreme sports seem to mutate rapidly as devotees add new twists to established activities or combine existing sports in ways that sometimes spawn bizarre variations. Land yachting and ice yachting, for example, apply the principles of ocean sailing to different surfaces, BASE jumping is a form of skydiving from fixed objects, and snow kiting, an offshoot of kite surfing, involves snowboarding or skiing with a kite. Although new technologies (e.g., carbon fiber wings for skyflying, specialized chassis, grind plates, and wheels for inline skating, three- and four-wheeled mountainboards for riding mountain slopes) and entrepreneurial activity among participants seeking new commercial opportunities account for many of the developments in extreme sports, established sports, too, have long histories of fracturing (e.g., rugby union and rugby league), mutating (e.g., football— American football, Association football [soccer], Australian football, Gaelic football, rugby football), and compounding (e.g., decathlon, triathlon). Struggles over the right to define what is legitimate and acceptable (e.g., with respect to body actions and styles, training and technology) and over who is included and who is excluded (e.g., gender and race as well as sporting codes in multievent pageants) are as intense in established sports as in extreme sports. Moreover, although the history of sports reveals innumerable instances of divergent groups organizing in opposition to established institutions, by definition the survivors invariably become official institutions and defenders of the status quo.

Mainstream opinion is critical to the legitimization of extreme sports. Just as the rhetoric and discourse of personal development, social development, health and wellness, community spirit, national prestige, escapism, entertainment, and corporate profit helped legitimize violent sports such as rugby and boxing in the nineteenth century, so, too, they legitimize contemporary extreme sports. The fitness industry, for example, now touts snowboarding, the one-time activity of "13–18-year-olds with raging hormones," as a "total body workout." It works your "abs, arms, and just about every other muscle group," proclaims one U.S. journalist. Even those who confront near-death experiences couch them in a rhetoric of psychological well-being. After losing his board in big surf at Pipeline (Oahu, Hawaii), Corb Donohue began swimming to the beach; twenty exhausting minutes later he found himself in a surge carrying him across a shallow reef and into a rip toward an outcrop of flesh-tearing and bone-crunching rocks. Although nauseous and fearful, Donohue knew he had to focus and swim across the surge into less dangerous surf that would deliver him to the beach. Fifteen minutes later he crawled onto the sand, "exhausted but... more alive and exhilarated: 'something happened to me out there. It was a bottom line encounter with fear and self-doubt. I confronted them... and in so doing, they vanished. It was one of the highest, most rewarding experiences of my life" (Grissim 1982, 48). When a BASE jump from a cliff in South Africa went wrong, Jeb Corliss broke multiple ribs and his back in three places. He also endured an hour-long wait in freezing water, with crabs eating his flesh, while awaiting rescue. "It's what's known as a life experience," said Corliss, adding that, "not all life experiences are fun, but I wouldn't change it for the world" (Duhigg 2004).

As well as propagating notions of a global village and peaceful brotherhoods and sisterhoods, devotees of extreme sports insist that their activities challenge the elitism fostered by established sports. They claim that their activities are more democratic and that members encourage broader social participation. In part, these claims rest on alternative objectives for participation such as "personal expression and gratification," "the thrill of vertigo," and level of "adrenaline rush," which, as Belinda Wheaton (2004) explains, exist independently of the traditional forms of identity promoted by established sports, such as race, ethnicity, nationality, and gender. Rather, these alternative objectives of participation broaden the base for forming identity by incorporating new notions of technical skill, commitment, courage, style, and authenticity. Nonetheless, anecdotal evidence and published research suggest that the young, white, middle-class men who dominate most extreme sports do not readily welcome those outside their demographic profile. Wary of the reactions of younger skateboarders, forty-five-year-old devotee Bret Connolly describes "sneaking around" skate parks and visiting them in "early mornings." Becky Beal and Charlene Wilson (2004) report that although "skaters will claim that their activity is open to all," the reality is that "the informal male networks tend to restrict and control female participation." Like the media that cover established sports, the specialized media that cover extreme sports tend to stereotype and demean female participants; remarks such as "awww, did you hurt your bottom?" and "your hair got messed up on that one!" are regularly made by commentators on extreme sports television. Fierce debates among devotees around cultural authenticity also belie claims of social equity in extreme sports. "Self-identified core members," says Michele Donnelly, strategically deploy "discourses of authenticity" to "aggrandize and legitimize themselves" and to "identify and marginalize other participants" (Donnelly 2006, 220) as unworthy. Lastly, accusations that the institutional structures of established sports are discriminatory increasingly ring hollow in the face of their efforts to integrate and open their ranks to all social classes, genders, sexualities, and people of color as well as their support for special populations (e.g., paralympians, gay athletes, special olympians).

Extreme sports have diffused around the world at a phenomenal rate and far faster than established sports. However, in this process extreme sports have benefited from a historically unique conjuncture of mass communications, corporate sponsors, entertainment industries, political aspirations of cities, and a burgeoning affluent and young demographic. At the center of this diffusion sits the cable television network ESPN (Entertainment and Sports Programming Network, which is owned by ABC, which in turn is owned by the Walt Disney Group), the creator and broadcaster of the Extreme Games (later the X Games). With corporate sponsorship from Advil, Mountain Dew, Taco Bell, Chevy Trucks, AT&T, Nike, and Miller Lite Ice, ESPN broadcast the first Summer X Games in mid-1995. Staged at Newport (Providence), Middletown (Rhode Island), and Mount Snow (Vermont), the inaugural games featured twenty-seven events in nine categories: bungee jumping, eco-challenge, inline skating, skateboarding, skysurfing, sport climbing, street luge, biking, and water sports. Twelve months later X Games II attracted around 200,000 spectators, and early in 1997 ESPN staged the first Winter X Games at Snow Summit Mountain Resort (California).

An Adventurous First Step

In one of author Dana Weigel's first extreme adventures, she takes the uncharacteristic leap of faith, paragliding off a cliff in France.

I've never been a particularly adventurous person. I'm terrified of breaking a bone, and have a mild case of vertigo. I've never even been skiing but there was something about paragliding that pulled me in. I was studying in south eastern France for a semester and went to see the Coupe Icare, a huge paragliding and hangliding festival in the tiny village of Sainte Hilaire du Touvet. The sight of people flying peacefully above the valley made me want to join them.

I found a place in the village that offered *parapente en biplace,* a tandem paragliding flight. That sounded good, someone else does all the work and I just enjoy the view. I arrived, signed in, was handed a harness and headed for the cliff. Praying that the harness was sturdy and my guide knew what he was doing, I ran off the edge of the cliff and into the air. This did not sound like something sane people would do and it was certainly the most terrifying thing I have ever chosen to do.

When my guide found a good air pocket and we were slightly more stable, I gathered the courage to open my eyes. The terror of being hundreds of feet from solid ground gave way to awe. What an amazing view. The fall foliage along the cliffside and the valley below was stunning, snow on Mont Blanc glimmered in the distance. Forty-five minutes later we landed at the bottom of the valley and my only regret was that it hadn't lasted longer.

Dana M. Weigel

As well as drawing thirty-eight thousand spectators, the initial Winter X Games were televised in 198 countries and territories in twenty-one languages. Although venues limit the number of spectators (usually around 250,000 people over the duration of the summer version and 40,000 at the winter event), the X Games have witnessed exponential growth in terms of participants and television audiences in the decade since the first games. Today competitors in the X Games qualify via regional games staged across North America, Latin America, Asia, and Europe. A television audience of 63 million people watched X Games VIII in 2002 on ESPN, ESPN2, and ABC Sports. In 2003 ESPN began live broadcasts of its X Games. Among the target demographic of boys and men aged thirteen to thirty-four, the Summer and Winter X Games are a staple of the global sporting culture. Like the corporate sponsors of established sports, those that sponsor the X Games view their associations with extreme sports as a means to convey an insider mentality. (Corporations typically communicate this mentality through advertising and sponsorship of specific events and awards.) Although corporate sponsors of extreme sports highlight risk taking and individualism, in contrast to sponsors of established sports who emphasize teamwork and cooperation, both continue to underscore traditional notions of masculinity.

On the political front, cities are showing an increasing interest in hosting the multiextreme sports events, including the summer and winter versions of the X Games. The competition for hosting these events is equal to that between cities looking to host world cups in individual sports such as athletics, cricket, and rugby. In 2005 ESPN signed a contract to keep the X Games in Los Angeles until 2009, and the following year it signed a contract with the Aspen Skiing Company to retain the Winter X Games in Colorado until 2010.

Differences in Extreme Sports and Established Sports

Despite the breadth and depth of similarities between extreme sports and established sports, extreme sports are most certainly more significant than some scholars give credit; Allen Guttmann, for example, likens extreme sports to an "animal found only in the imaginary zoo of sociological speculation" (Guttmann 2004, 323). Indeed, four key differences stand out: participation, relationships with environment, values, and presentation.

▶ **Participation** The biggest difference between established sports and extreme sports lies in the unit and objectives of participation. The most popular established sports are team events, whereas individuals and occasionally pairs are the principal units of participation in extreme sports. (Team-based extreme competitions are rare, notwithstanding their appeal to ESPN and other media companies that encourage their promotion.) Moreover, extreme sports put much greater emphasis on participation than established sports, the popularity of which derives more from spectating. Of course, one must be wary of overstating the case: Many consumers of extreme sports are *poseurs* who express their "devotion" by simply purchasing the accoutrements of the activity or playing video game versions.

The primary objectives of participation in extreme sports also differ significantly from those in established sports. Rather than conceptualizing their participation in simple terms of victory or defeat, disciples of extreme sports tend to frame their involvement in terms of meeting personal challenges, testing themselves, and competing against themselves. Describing the rationale of *parkour*, Sébastien Foucan, the sport's cofounder, refers to participants striving to "overtake themselves." Likewise, *traceur* (the term used for a participant of *parkour*) Rhys James describes *parkour* as a philosophy that combines body and soul: "it's about being motivated to better yourself, not just in a physical way, but to develop your mind as well. It helps you make choices in your life" (Creagh 2006). Thus, unlike in gymnastics, says journalist and social commentator Josie Appleton, where athletes must perform limited moves on standard equipment in set time, free runners perform jumps and aerial acrobatics across the urban landscape in their own way. In other words, extreme sports redefine winning in terms of conquering one's fears rather than outscoring an opponent. Victory in adventure races, says the director of one event, "is more than winning—it is success in completing an exceptional task, an extraordinary experience." This difference is also reflected in the fact that there is less overt aggression in extreme sports, few of which involve body contact.

However, it must be stressed that participation in extreme sports, like that in established sports, takes diverse forms. Some disciples seek escape, privacy, health, and healing; some practice their pursuits as regimens of asceticism and decry the promotion of their activity into the mainstream. Other participants consciously link themselves to corporations as commodities in search of iconic status. Some devotees are obsessed; such is their commitment to the activity that it organizes their whole lives. Others are casuals or samplers who "graze" on several activities without fully committing to, or living, one.

The objectives of extreme sports also overlap with, and extend into, special relationships with the environment. These relationships are quite different from those experienced in established sports, where the body acts on artificial, formally constituted spaces (e.g., courts, arenas, fields, ovals, tracks, pistes) in formally recognized times (e.g., start, finish). By contrast, extreme sports tend to blur the boundaries between the body and the environment.

▶ **Environment** Many extreme sports take place in the sky, mountains, oceans, lakes, rivers, and canyons and involve close interaction with the Earth's natural forces: "The air is like a second home to me," says BASE jumper and skyflier Felix Baumgartner (Cave Jump 2005, 15).When these forces swirl in violent vortexes of energy, survival can depend on an intimate knowledge of the elements and their various relationships. Gravity, Joe Tomlinson reminds us, is "the force that pulls climbers off rock faces, skiers down slopes and off cliffs, hang gliders toward the ground, and water downstream" (Tomlinson 2004, 7). Although some devotees conceptualize their involvement in extreme sports in terms of conquering the environment (e.g., a mountain, a set of rapids, a wave), more often they attach spiritual and religious personas to the Earth's forces and stress harmonious relationships with "mother nature." Surfing pioneer Tom Blake says that "nature is synonymous with God: for a brief period of the ride, [the surfer shares] God-given energy.... One might say surfriding is prayer of a high order, that the sea is a beautiful church, the wave a silent sermon" (Blake 2000, 11). This harmony also often extends into equipment. Nick Ford and David Brown, for example, refer to the surfer's board as a "kind of hybrid extension of the body," and Ian Borden describes the skateboard as "a prosthetic device, an extension of the body as a kind of fifth limb, absorbed into and diffused inside the body-terrain encounter" (Borden 2001, 100).

Ulrich Beck's reference to the merging of nature and culture—"today if we talk about nature we talk about culture, and if we talk about culture we talk about nature" (Beck 1999, 145)—undoubtedly captures something of the relationship that disciples of extreme sports hold with the environment and the way they position technology in that relationship. The extent and complexity of this relationship become even clearer when comparing different attitudes toward the environment and technology in closely related extreme sports and established sports such as free (adventure) climbing and sport climbing. Free climbers typically frown upon sports climbers, whom they variously charge with detracting from the wilderness experience, damaging rock faces and features by attaching permanent protection devices (e.g., expansion bolts, pitons) and devaluing the achievements of the first persons who climbed a particular route (Donnelly 2003). Such distinctions arguably highlight fundamentally different values in the two forms of activity.

Devotees of extreme sports also reconceptualize urban landforms and terrain. Skateboarders, for example, quickly recognize asphalt and concrete drains and backyard swimming pools as urban waves; curbs, stairs, and railings become sites for artistic acrobatics. After taking up *parkour*, college student Billy Hughes looked at the built environment through fresh eyes: Architects think that they are constructing monuments, the *traceur* says, but really "they're building obstacles. They're building our playground." Not surprisingly, such reconceptualizations bring disciplines of extreme sports into conflict with urban and municipal authorities for whom pedestrian plazas, public seating, handrails, statues, fences, and staircases serve only one function—that approved by the official commissioning committee. By contrast, the skateboarder, for example, in the words of Craig Stecyk—architect of the 1970s skateboarding scene in Dogtown (Los Angeles) and co-writer and production designer for *Dogtown and Z-Boys*—"makes everyday use of the useless artifacts of the technological burden. The skating urban anarchist employs [structures] in a thousand ways that the original architects could never dream of" (Beato 1999). In this clash of cultures it is hardly surprisingly that Stecyk should paint skateboarders as "anarchists" and "urban guerrillas."

▶ **Values** Much of the analysis of extreme sports focuses on their social values. Comparing extreme sports with established sports, Robert Rinehart defines the former as "activities that either ideologically or practically provide alternatives to mainstream sports and to mainstream values" (Rinehart 2000, 506). We "have a completely different culture from the norms of the world's society. We dress differently, we have our own language, use our own slang, and live by our own rules," says one skateboarder (Beal 1995, 256). Indeed, many participants cultivate "outlaw" images and convey general states of irreverence. Danny Kass embodies the outlaw image of extreme participants; at a trade show in Las Vegas in 2001 the snowboarder who would go on to win two Olympic silver medals in the halfpipe, stole a ski bike and urinated behind a display booth.

Similarly, BMX freestyler Mat Hoffman's obvious delight at transgressing sponsored events captures the irreverent culture of extreme sports. When "companies set up a televised event, build a course and put barricades around," bikers like to "use the ramp to jump the barricade and ride it into the parking lot. And the suits will say, 'what are you guys trippin'? Are you insane?'" Hoffman retorts, "that's what we do all day—extend the boundaries of our sport and our playground" (Hochman 1999). Indeed, such irreverence illustrates the fundamentally different sets of values found in established sports and extreme sports. Robert Rinehart notes that whereas professional athletes in established sports "see their sport primarily as their work," those in extreme sports "insist their sport is part of their lifestyle, thus still fun" (Rinehart 2003, 32). Belinda Wheaton also stresses the lifestyle dimensions of extreme sports. She comments that extreme sports are typically associated with youth who want to explore the boundaries of physical performance and culture such as fashion and music; thus they appropriate the appellations "alternative" and "lifestyle." Modern lifestyles, she continues, are about "choice, differentiation, self expression, creativity, fitness, health and the body" (Wheaton 2004, 4–5). Most importantly, extreme sports often facilitate identities that contrast sharply with traditional notions of identity based on work, gender, ethnicity, religion, and age.

▶ **Presentation** Lastly, Rinehart and Sydnor refer to the way that extreme sports are presented electronically, which, they argue, is quite different from presentations of established sports. Broadcast forms of established sports continue to privilege "centered wide-angle panning with a large part of the field in sight of the television audience. Additionally, the whole contest is often broadcast" (Rinehart and Sydnor 2003, 6–7). In contradistinction, coverage of extreme sports emphasizes "discontinuous shots, short (time duration) events, quick off-centered collage-type shots, blurred frames, super slow-motion cinematography, jolts of musical accompaniment, voyeuristic body shots, neon and holographic colors, and shocking up-close scenarios of sport-induced injury, illness, or 'crashes'" (Rinehart and Sydnor 2003, 7). Extreme sports videos exemplify the new modes of presentation. For example, Catherine Palmer likens the technical styles and modes of production in the rock-climbing video *Coming at Ya Hyper* (1998) to "a rock music video." In her words, "fast cuts, images coming in and out of focus and constant movement between locations, the footage of these lithe men and women dicing with death is unquestionably dramatic. Accompanied by a pumping soundtrack, *Coming at Ya Hyper* is a relentless introduction to the ways in which a very particular discourse of extremity is promoted and packed for its own audience" (Palmer 2002, 324–5).

The preceding analysis has emphasized some of the differences between extreme sports and established sports, especially in the areas of participation, relationship to environment, ideology, and presentation. Yet, as a comparison of similarities between the two forms of physical activity reveals, it would be easy to overstate the level of differences, especially with respect to risk. Although in popular thought the terms *high risk* and *extreme sports* are synonymous, many participants in established sports also embrace risk. At this point then it is pertinent to inquire into the source of popular perceptions of extreme sports. In order to address this issue we turn to the historical context of extreme sports.

Contextualizing Extreme Sports

Although reliable contemporary statistics are rare, evidence shows that interest in established team sports is waning, whereas interest in extreme sports is gaining in popularity. Participation in baseball in the United States declined by 28 percent to 10.9 million players between 1987 and 2000, and involvement in softball and volleyball plunged by 37 percent and 36 percent, respectively, in the same period. Falling levels of participation extend into compacting revenues for broadcasters of established sports: Television contracts for football, baseball, and basketball now lose the major networks billions of dollars. By contrast, the appeal of, and revenues generated by, extreme sports keeps growing. More than 50 million people watched some of the Summer X Games on television in 2003, and 37 million watched part of the Winter X Games the same year. The X Games were instrumental in launching ESPN2 and helped spawn dozens of licensing deals, including an IMAX movie, X Games skateparks, X Games DVDs, and toys.

How do scholars explain the surging popularity of extreme sports at the expense of established sports? In order to answer this question we turn to cultural developments in late modernity. Although some extreme sports such as bungee jumping, surfing, mountaineering, and ultimate fighting have deep historical roots (the ancient Greeks, for example, practiced a form of ultimate fighting known as the *pankration*), most came to prominence in the last quarter of the twentieth century, a period that some social theorists refer to as "late modernity." The philosophy (ideas and values) and zeitgeist (mood) of late modernity provide a useful context for understanding the rise of extreme sports, their cultural significance, and escalating popularity. However, the concept of late modernity also presupposes the existence of an earlier phase, modernity. This phase, too, offers a context for examining the origins of modern sports (subsequently established sports) and their later apparent waning, as reflected in the statistics cited earlier.

Modernity, Social Control, and Risk

The transformation from traditional to modern society (from premodernity to modernity) fueled immense social uncertainty and disruption. However, as well as ushering in unheralded material prosperity, modernity, as framed by Enlightenment thought (relating to a philosophic movement of the eighteenth century marked by a rejection of traditional social, religious, and political ideas and an emphasis on rationalism), also promised progress and certainty. Modernity would reduce threats to individual well-being posed by the new (capitalist) social relationships of exploitation, marginalization, and alienation in the burgeoning industrial cities. Moreover, the industrial and scientific technology of modernity held out the promise of overcoming natural threats such as floods, droughts, fires, and earthquakes.

Central to the removal of risk in modernity is the nation-state, an all-encompassing bureaucratic structure dedicated to protecting citizens from a host of threats: foreign invasion (e.g., permanent military and intelligence-gathering forces), terrorism (e.g., security police), economic collapse (e.g., central banks), workplace incapacitation (e.g., health and safety legislation), and natural disasters (e.g., infrastructures—drains, dikes, reservoirs, dams—and qualified professional experts—firefighters, building inspectors). During the first half of the twentieth century the nation-state extended the provision of services (e.g., health care, education) and insurance schemes (e.g., pensions, unemployment benefits) to further increase the security and well-being of its citizens.

The modern state is also an instrument of social control, a structure that disciplines and normalizes citizens. Conformity and universality underpin every function of the modern welfare state from education (e.g., setting standard primary and secondary school curricula) to citizenship (e.g., requiring oaths of allegiance) and even to road rules (e.g., setting speed limits). In these tasks the modern state received assistance from an early form of capitalism known as "Fordism," after Henry Ford's system of production for

motor vehicles. Although Fordism expanded the range of goods available to consumers, it was nonetheless an inflexible system geared toward production for mass markets, a system in which producers, not consumers, dictated uniform styles. In short, Fordism contributed to standardization and conformity in social life by limiting consumers' choices to basic forms.

Sports, too, played a part in the promises of, and social controls associated with, modernity. Organized sports arose in the nineteenth century amid the contingencies and uncertainties of modern urban life and provided new identities in chaotic, disorienting, and heterogeneous cities. As well as offering coherence and stability to the lives of disparate individuals and groups, sports nurtured a sense of certainty in social life. For example, "certainty" in a sporting sense refers to the repetitiveness of seasonal and weekly sporting cycles (e.g., football in winter, training on Tuesdays and Thursdays, playing on Saturdays) and enduring identities attached to sporting communities such as towns, suburbs, cities, regions, and nations. A host of "petty rituals" (e.g., dressing in team colors on match day, eating fish and chips before, and pies during, the game, cavorting in the streets after victory) makes the sporting world appear even more familiar and comfortable. In short, modern sports promised regularity, camaraderie, intimacy, warmth, emotional support, community identity, and belonging.

Modern sports also helped order and control local populations. For example, factory owners sponsored team sports as a strategy to bond workers and tie them to the company; middle-class cultural brokers in churches, schools, and voluntary agencies founded sports clubs to rationalize the use of time and to promote individual and collective discipline and community identity. The culture of modern sports championed and elevated commitment, fair play, character, teamwork, interdependence, and trust as ideal social values.

Welfare states (including the former socialist versions of eastern Europe) also seized on sports as an ideological rallying call, as a means to indoctrinate young citizens, and as a policy instrument to produce healthy citizens. As part of their strategies of control and risk minimization, states invested in sporting infrastructures (e.g., pools, tracks, stadia) and conferred with sports authorities to legislate against violent and dangerous practices and channel socially questionable behaviors into constructive forms. For example, in 1905 U.S. President Theodore Roosevelt called a conference of football authorities to address questions relating to rough and foul play in the game.

Fully fledged welfare states tackled risk with new gusto in the mid-twentieth century. Every aspect of life, including physical activities, became subjected to risk analysis, regulation, and litigation. As Michael Bane observed, states "defined product liability so strictly that they would close playgrounds rather than risk someone's falling out of a swing" (Bane 1996, 91). Indeed, school districts across the United States, including some in Washington, Florida, and Oregon, prohibit children running in the playground as a safety precaution, and many skateboard parks in North America collapsed in the 1970s under the burden of insurance liability. These are sad expressions of what Chris Rojek describes as a "social order macerating the human body, numbing the mind and murdering the soul" (Rojek 1995, 82). According to Rojek, modern forms of leisure "offer only timid freedoms and weak choices." He argues that "the capacity for arousal and pleasure associated with the passions is denied because the passions are themselves reined in by the requirements of respectable society. The result is the production of pleasure-seeking individuals who are incapable of finding pleasure and the reproduction of a society which values the accumulation of pleasure as one of the highest social goals but which also legally and morally inhibits goal achievement" (Rojek 1995, 82).

However, a plethora of contradictions and paradoxes challenges the modern welfare state's policies of risk management. Key driving forces of the conformity, normalization, and standardization inherent in the modern welfare state are the numerically and politically dominant middle classes. However, they also subscribe to an alternative set of values, which Mike Brake lists as expressivity, dissociation, subjectivity, individualism, anticompetitiveness, and antimaterialism. In one way or another these values invite people, in the words of Ulrich Beck, to "constitute themselves as individuals, to plan, understand, design themselves as individuals" (Beck 1999, 9). Beck discusses individualism within the context of a structural concept he calls "individualization." Although Beck links individualization to the welfare state (i.e., "most of the rights and entitlements of the welfare state are designed for individuals rather than for families"), individualization also manifests in the "me-first society," which is based on the dissolution of community and group solidarity, the decline of values, the culture of narcissism, and an entitlement-orientated hedonism. As Beck puts it, "in the old system of values, the self remained subordinated to patterns of the collective, today it is the opposite" (Beck 1999, 10–11).

Critically, the middle classes, especially youth, are attracted to activities that, in the words of Chris Rojek, "they perceive as being richer and more colorful than the mundane order of ordinary life." "It is as if," he continues, "the freedom, self-determination and choice offered by modernity are rejected in favor of the possibility of a transcending experience" (Rojek 1995, 100). "Our society is so surgically sterile," (Greenfeld 1999) laments Jonathan Senk; in search of his soul and his limitations he turned to adventure racing. Thus, whereas the state's focus on risk emphasized "what should not be done," the ideology of individualism and the structure of individualization guided the middle classes to focus on "what can we do." (By contrast, Stephen Lyng argues that devotees of extreme sports on lower-income rungs tend to "gravitate toward high risk occupations such as police work, fire fighting, or combat soldiering" [Lyng 1990, 876].) In these senses then, Josie Appleton believes that extreme sports serve as "an antidote to our safety-first, shrink-wrapped world" and as opportunities for individuals "to carve their own path and find out where their limits lie" (Appleton 2005).

Late Modernity and the Reemergence of Risk

Questions about the unrealistic promises of certainty and the state's attempts to eliminate risk from social life abound in late modernity. Whereas professionals working in and with the welfare, health, and higher education sectors are vociferous in expressing their doubts, others connected to the realm of physical leisure draw attention to the blandness and conformity of modernity. "Team sports are dying and the activities taking their place are all about individualism, making up your own rules as you go along and taking everything to the limit," says Joe Tomlinson. "After all, what's life worth without a little bit of danger?" he asks (Tomlinson 2004). None of this should surprise, given that voluntary physical activity is such a central site of agency or what psychologists call "self-actualization," the feeling that one has direct authorship of one's actions and is totally free from all forms of coercion.

A host of new terms, including *whiz sports*, *alternative sports*, *lifestyle sports*, *action sports*, *panic sports*, *postmodern sports*, *postindustrial sports*, and *new sports*, articulates the philosophy of physical activity in late modernity. Notwithstanding problems of definition and the lack of precision in these terms, they all convey a number of interrelated anti-modern sentiments: fierce individualism, civil disobedience, the quest for human potential, taking control of one's own life, and intimate engagements with the environment. Vince Nye expresses this sentiment while riding his skateboard across corporate plazas in the dead of night: "stolen apples taste sweeter," he says, reminding us of the thrill of the forbidden. Meanwhile, canyoners rappel, hike, and climb into river gorges to engage cold and furious water, submerged logs, and slippery and jagged rocks. These activities illustrate what Ulrich Beck calls "manufactured uncertainties," another phrase capturing the reaction against the blandness and conformity of modernity.

Such are the profile and popularity of some extreme sports that, combined with the aesthetic appeal and obvious courage of the leading practitioners, the state has had to reappraise its position, at least in some instances, notably under pressure from economic imperatives and from commercial interests. For example, some states have passed legislation prohibiting cities from being sued for accidents at city-owned skate parks. Despite bans against BASE jumping in all 370 national parks across the United States, the New River Gorge National River in West Virginia allows devotees to leap 870 meters from New River Bridge on the third Saturday of each October. When the park service took over the bridge it bowed to pressure from the local chamber of commerce, which enjoyed the money brought into the area by BASE jumpers and tourists.

Of course, support for and opposition to extreme sports are not clear alternatives. As Christopher Lasch reminds us, the middle classes invariably want it both ways, advocating more state involvement when they want someone else to take responsibility and more individual rights when they perceive their freedoms under attack. Echoes of these tensions and contradictory positions appeared in the *New York Times* in 1999 after a sudden downpour swept nineteen canyoners to their deaths near Interlaken (Switzerland). According to an editorial in the newspaper, "the flood that overtook them was a predictable event—led by paid guides. Trouble arises not when you decide to risk your life in one extreme sport or another but when you do not know that that is what you are doing—when in other words, you let someone else risk your life for you. The danger is not extreme sport or nature itself. The danger is our anesthetized, Disneyfied view of nature as a place where the conventions of urban life still apply, where the burden of self-preservation, at its most basic level, can be handed

off to the authorities, to a guide or counselor or instructor" (Risking Nature 1999, A14).

The Commercialism of Extreme

Although the complex relationships between middle-class citizens and the state in late modernity provide a context for understanding the rise of extreme sports, no explanation would be complete without consideration of corporate forces. Extreme skier Rob Deloria attributes the first use of the term *extreme* to the apparel company North Face, which began using the term in the 1970s. Since then it has become ubiquitous; as Robert Rinehart and Synthia Sydnor observe, contemporary marketers and advertisers employ *extreme* or *X* to "convey radical, extraordinary, unusual properties to nearly any product" (Rinehart and Sydnor 2003,2). *Extreme* is a prefix for "soft drinks, health food, celebrity behavior, fashion and makeup, sexual technique, athletic shoes, cars, music, and of course, sport" (Rinehart and Sydnor 2003, 3). Simultaneously, extreme sports such as mountaineering, canyoning, bouldering, freestyle motocross, tow-in surfing, snowboarding, and street luge appear in feature movies, music film clips, and television commercials for soft drinks, sandshoes, and sunglasses.

Extreme is the password for corporations and advertisers to access young men in the 13-to-34-year-old demographic. Whereas the median age of the baseball demographic is the mid-40s, the X Games and Gravity Games (a joint venture between NBC Sports Ventures and EMAP Petersen, a special interest publisher) are primarily watched by 12- to 17-year-olds. Brad Adgate, from Horizon Media, calls extreme a "demographic sweet spot" combining physical activity and entertainment. When Toyota signed up as an exclusive automotive sponsor of the Gravity Games, Don Cecconi, the company's merchandise and marketing director, described the sponsorship as an opportunity to capture the attention of an audience that had traditionally bypassed Toyota: "We have new products coming out that will be targeted to the youth market. The Gravity Games look to be a great avenue to communicate with the youthful buyer" (Pare 1999). Indeed, such alignments have proved beneficial in select cases. Marketing professor Douglas Holt attributes the economic success of PepsiCo's Mountain Dew to its "Do the Dew" advertising campaigns in the 1990s. The advertisements "featured daredevil stunts juxtaposed with the ironic, unimpressed commentary of four teenage boys: 'Done that. Did that. Been there. Tried that'" (Holt 1989).

According to Holt, the advertisements increased sales by 40 million cases, and since 1993 Mountain Dew has "led the carbonated soft drinks category in share growth," "now ranks third in retail sales behind Coke and Pepsi" (Holt 1989), and is a $4.7 billion business.

Commercializing extreme is a complex exercise. Notwithstanding the corporate world's successful appropriation of extreme images, the extreme movement is ultimately an organic entity that cannot be reproduced or manufactured according to a formula. The folding of XFL, an extreme version of American football that sought to build on the success of both National Football League (NFL) football and World Wrestling Federation (WWF) wrestling, after just one season is a case in point. XFL was the brainchild of Vince McMahon, who built a wrestling empire and hoped to translate that success to a spring football league. He found a partner in NBC, which had lost NFL rights to CBS and was in the market for Saturday night sports programming. However, XFL failed to captivate those audiences who, in late modernity, demand novelty and excitement and who quickly grow tired and bored with repetition. Hence corporate interests rely on participants themselves to drive interest by inventing new tricks and thrills. And those who produce the most daring and spectacular shows are typically the "hardcore," who, by definition, take up their pursuits to escape scrutiny, supervision, and commodification. The hardcore are often the least willing to cooperate with corporate interests. Labeling him a "corporate" is "one of the worst things you could ever call me. It means I let some company tell me what to do and how to act. It means I'm a sell out," (Hochman 1999) declares freestyle motocross rider Brian Deegan.

Needless to say, in late modernity the contradictions are palpable. Announcing the launch of the "If it can't kill you, it ain't extreme" tow-in surfing event, Garrett McNamara declared, "we're not going out there looking for sponsorship, prize money and media mayhem." Instead, "we're putting the money up our selves. There's a handful of us who surf extreme waves simply because we love to. We want to get out from under any rigid contest rules and restrictions and open it up to extreme surfing—pure and simple" (Towsurfer. com 2003). Among the sponsors of the event, prominently displayed on the website, are Ford, United Airlines, and Fox Sports.

Another problem for corporate interests is that many extreme sports are simply unsuited to television, the source of the big audiences that draw the large sponsorships. Caving, for example, is inaccessible to television, an issue compounded by the fact that secrecy is a hallmark of the subculture; one caver adage declares "no publicity is good publicity." "The trouble with watching any kind of climbing," notes David Dorian, whose words identify a more universal problem, "is that once you've been exposed to the novel environment a couple of times and the initial surge of sympathetic fear and vertigo wears off, there's little about the activity that is obviously impressive. It's slow moving, competitors never face one another on the course, [and] worse, the good performers are usually less exciting than the bad ones" (Dorian 2003, 283).

The successful Summer and Winter X Games demonstrate that the corporate and extreme worlds can work together. However, the relationship derives more from mutual need than mutual respect: ESPN needs extreme athletes to produce the events that draw audiences and sponsors; as noted earlier, hardcore extreme participants rely on exposure in the media for cultural legitimacy and status among their peers. And relationships between the two groups are fragile. Although the participants understand that the X Games are simply a platform to secure lucrative commercial sponsorships, complaints nonetheless abound about the paltry prize money. In 2004 the total prize money for all 250 athletes at the Winter X Games was $576,000—the cost of one reserve quarterback in the NFL. Against this background some participants have made moves to form a union, which, paradoxically, is the very form of institution that they seek to escape.

All Things Considered

Although extreme sports appear to resonate with the philosophy and zeitgeist of late modernity, close analysis reveals a surprisingly vague and ambiguous notion. In many respects "extreme" is simply a label adopted by corporate media and marketers to portray a certain style of physical endeavor rather than an objective field of activities recognized by participants. Robert Rinehart and Synthia Sydnor comment that the Disney Corporation, ESPN, ESPN2, ABC, MTV, the Discovery Channel, and large corporations such as Pepsi, Coke, and Nike have "essentially appropriated and determined much of the electronic imaging of extreme sports to the world" (Rinehart and Sydnor 2003, 4). Indeed, products with the "extreme" label attached—television programs, graffiti art, design, drinks, and clothing—are frequently bigger business than the pursuits themselves. It is doubtful whether many of the estimated 20 million people who watch the Extreme Sports Channel in Europe actually venture anywhere near the terrains of extreme sports. *Traceurs* probably number in the hundreds, skyflyers probably less than a dozen. In short, corporate interests have successfully transformed living on the edge into an aspirational consumer product: wearing North Face gear, drinking Mountain Dew, talking on an X Games mobile phone are about appearance and the passive consumption of risk.

Yet, if extreme sports lack coherence when applied to participation in physical activity, in the context of late modernity they do at least reveal something about the philosophy and zeitgeist of the times. Perhaps the best way of summing up that philosophy and zeitgeist is as a reaction to modernity and, in the case of physical activity, the shallow freedoms and conformity of modern sports. However, even here one must be wary of overstating the differences. Ultimately modern sports and extreme sports are tests (mostly, but by no means exclusively) of men's character. One hundred years ago the ideal man demonstrated his physical skill on a wicket under a scorching sun. The cricketer won the respect of his peers by standing firm before the fast bowler, a man with menace in his heart who brandished a ball of hard cork bound in string and leather; he received universal admiration for his graceful strokes with a narrow wooden bat used to play a ball delivered at breakneck speed. Today the ideal man displays his physical skill on a 6-meter wall of collapsing water. The surfboard rider wins the respect of peers by turning his ultra-thin polyurethane and fiberglass board under the guillotine-like lip of a wave that spits over his head before violently collapsing on a reef of sharpened coral; he is feted for his poise and balance as he gracefully sprints deep inside the bowels of mother nature. Regardless of the era both men live at the frontier of mind and body, both play with risk, and both know all too well the physical and social consequences of failure.

Douglas Booth and Holly Thorpe

See also Commercialization; Gender; Injury; Media and Extreme Sport; Physiology of Risk; Psychology of Risk; Sociology of Risk; X-Games

Further Reading

Adelman, M. (1989). *A sporting time: New York City and the rise of modern athletics, 1820–70.* Urbana: University of Illinois Press.

Andrews, M. (2001). Examining the XFL: The good, the bad, and the ugly. Retrieved April 30, 2006, from http://www.allsports.com/cgi-bin/showstory.cgi?story_id=15414

Appleton, J. (2005). What's so extreme about extreme sports? Retrieved August 30, 2006, from http://www.spiked-online.com

Arnett, R. (2006). Tiger's antics in New Zealand should be questioned. *Sports Illustrated.* Retrieved April 25, 2006, from http://sportsillustrated.cnn.com/2006/writers/rick_arnett/04/25/tiger/index.html

Bane, M. (1996). *Over the edge: A regular guy's odyssey in extreme sports.* New York: Macmillan.

Beal, B. (1995). Disqualifying the official: An exploration of social resistance through the subculture of skateboarding, *Sociology of Sport Journal, 12,* 252–267.

Beal, B., & Wilson, C. (2004). Chicks dig scars: Commercialisation and the transformations of skateboarders' identities. In B. Wheaton (Ed.), *Understanding lifestyle sports: Consumption, identity and difference* (pp. 31–54). London: Routledge.

Beato, G. (1999). The lords of Dogtown. *Spin Magazine.* Retrieved July 11, 2006, from http://www.angelfire.com/ca/alva3/spin.html

Beck, U. (1992). *Risk society.* London: Sage Publications.

Beck, U. (1999). *World risk society.* Oxford, UK: Polity.

Bell, M. (2003). Another kind of life: Adventure racing and epic expeditions. In R. E. Rinehart & S. Sydnor (Eds.), *To the extreme: Alternative sports, inside and out* (pp. 219–253). Albany: State University of New York Press.

Benson, B. (2005). *Epidemiology of ice hockey injuries and mechanisms of injury.* Paper presented at the First World Congress on Sports Injury Prevention, Oslo, Norway. Retrieved July 11, 2006, from http://www.ostrc.no/Congress2005

Blake, T. (2000). Voice of the wave. *The Australian Surfer's Journal, 3*(1), 11.

Blehm, E. (2003). *Agents of change: The story of DC shoes and its athletes.* New York: Reagan Books.

Booth, D. (2003). Expression sessions: Surfing, style, and prestige. In R. E. Rinehart & S. Sydnor (Eds.), *To the extreme: Alternative sports, inside and out* (pp. 315–333). Albany: State University of New York Press.

Borden, I. (2001). *Skateboarding, space and the city: Architecture and the body.* London: Berg.

Borsay, P. (2006). *A history of leisure.* Houndmills, UK: Palgrave Macmillan.

Brake, M. (1980). *The sociology of youth culture and youth subcultures: Sex and drugs and rock 'n' roll.* London: Routledge & Kegan Paul.

Burke, M. (2004, February 2). X-treme economics. *Forbes Magazine,* 42–44.

Burton, J. (2003). Snowboarding: The essence is fun. In R. E. Rinehart & S. Sydnor (Eds.), *To the extreme: Alternative sports, inside and out* (pp. 401–406). Albany: State University of New York Press.

Cantu, R. (2005). *Catastrophic spine injuries in American football—Effect of athletic education and rule changes.* Paper presented at the First World Congress on Sports Injury Prevention, Oslo, Norway. Retrieved July 11, 2006, from http://www.ostrc.no/Congress2005

Cauchon, D. (2006, March 27). Amateur fighting rounds up crowds and controversy. *USA Today.* Retrieved July 11, 2006, from http://www.usatoday.com.news/nation/2006-03-27-toughman-popularity_x.html

Cave jump. (2005, December–January). *New Zealand Adventure,* 13–15.

Creagh, S. (2006, April 1). Look! Up in the sky! It's…No, it's parkour man. *Sydney Morning Herald.* Retrieved July 11, 2006, from http://www.smh.com.au/articles/nation/2006/03/31/1143441337754.html

Donnelly, M. (2006). Studying extreme sports: Beyond the core participants. *Journal of Sport & Social Issues, 30*(2), 219–224.

Donnelly, P. (2003). The great divide: Sport climbing vs. adventure climbing. In R. E. Rinehart & S. Sydnor (Eds.), *To the extreme: Alternative sports, inside and out* (pp. 291–304). Albany: State University of New York Press.

Dorian, D. (2003). Xtreem. In R. E. Rinehart & S. Sydnor (Eds.), *To the extreme: Alternative sports, inside and out* (pp. 281–289). Albany: State University of New York Press.

Duhigg, C. (2004). Risk is sport for those who leap at chance to, well, leap. Retrieved July 11, 2006, from http://www.theeagle.com/brazossunday/122604thrills.php

Espneventmedia.com. (2006). Life of X: A brief history of the X Games. Retrieved July 11, 2006, from http://www.espneventmedia.com/xabout.php

Ford, N., & Brown, D. (2006). *Surfing and social theory: Experience, embodiment and narrative of the dream glide.* London: Routledge.

Fries, P. (2006, January 23). Freefall to death. *The Australian.*

Galbraith, J., & Marcopoulos, A. (2004). Terje Haakonsen. *Frequency: The Snowboarder's Journal, 3*(3), 62–83.

Giddens, A. (1991). *The consequences of modernity.* Palo Alto, CA: Stanford University Press.

Greenfeld, K. (1999, September 6). Life on the edge. *Time.*

Grissim, J. (1982). *Pure stoke.* New York: Harper Colophon.

Guttmann, A. (2004). *Sports: The first five millennia.* Amherst: University of Massachusetts Press.

Harkin, B. (2001). XFL: Gone but is it too late! Retrieved May 14, 2006, from http://www.allsports.com/cgi-bin/showstory.cgi?story_id=15885

Harvey, D. (1995). *The condition of postmodernity.* Oxford, UK: Blackwell.

Hochman, P. (1999, November 22). Street lugers, stunt bikers, and—Colgate Palmolive. *Fortune.*

Holt, R. (1989). *Sport and the British: A modern history.* Oxford, UK: Clarendon Press.

Huizinga, J. (1955). *Homo ludens: A study of the play element in culture.* Boston: Beacon Press.

Humphreys, D. (2003). Selling out snowboarding: The alternative response to commercial co-optation. In R. E. Rinehart & S. Sydnor (Eds.), *To the extreme: Alternative sports, inside and out* (pp. 407–428). Albany: State University of New York Press.

Kitemare.com. (n.d.). Snow kiting. Retrieved July 11, 2006, from http://www.kitemare.com.snow_kiting.html

Kumar, K. (1986). *Prophecy and progress: The sociology of industrial and post-industrial society.* Harmondsworth, UK: Penguin.

Kusz, K. (2001). I want to be the minority: The politics of youthful white masculinities in sport and popular culture in 1990s America. *Journal of Sport and Social Issues, 25*(4), 390–416.

KXAN.com. (2006, February 13). Snowboarding growing in popularity. Retrieved July 11, 2006, from http://www.kxan.com/Global/story.asp?s=4497975

Lagace, M. (2002). Building brandtopias—How top brands tap in to society. *Working Knowledge Newsletter.* Retrieved June 24, 2006, from http://hbswk.hbs.edu/item.jhtml?id=2985&t=marketing

Lasch, C. (1979). *The culture of narcissism.* New York: W. W. Norton.

Lash, S. (1990). *The sociology of postmodernism.* London: Routledge.

Le Breton, D. (2000). Playing symbolically with death in extreme sports. *Body & Society, 6*(1), 1–11.

Levinson, D., & Christensen, K. (1996). *Encyclopedia of world sport.* Santa Barbara, CA: ABC-Clio.

Lieber, J., & Ruibal, S. (2002, February 12). Extreme success continues: USA sweeps men's snowboarding halfpipe. *USA Today,* p. D1.

Loy, J., & Coakley, J. (2006). Sport. In G. Ritzer (Ed.), *Blackwell encyclopedia of sociology.* Oxford, UK: Blackwell.

Lyng, S. (1990). Edgework: A social psychological analysis of voluntary risk taking. *American Journal of Sociology, 95*(4), 851–886.

McCrory, P. (2005). *Preventing head and cervical spine injuries.* Paper presented at the First World Congress on Sports Injury Prevention, Oslo, Norway. Retrieved July 10, 2006, from http://www.ostrc.no/Congress2005

McIntosh, A. (2005). *Do helmets prevent head injury in sport?* Paper presented at the First World Congress on Sports Injury Prevention, Oslo, Norway. Retrieved July 10, 2006, from http://www.ostrc.no/Congress2005

Meadows-Ingram, B. (2002, June). Roll out. *Vibe,* 123–126.

Meeuwisse, W. (2005). *Key components of collection and classification of sports injuries.* Paper presented at the First World Congress on Sports Injury Prevention, Oslo, Norway. Retrieved July 10, 2006, from http://www.ostrc.no/Congress2005

Midol, N., & Broyer, G. (1995). Toward an anthropological analysis of new sport cultures: The case of whiz sports in France. *Sociology of Sport Journal, 12,* 204–212.

National parks: Thrilled to death. (1999, November 13). *The Economist.*

Ogilvie, B. (1974). Stimulus addiction: The sweet psychic jolt of danger. *Psychology Today, 8*(5), 88–94.

Palmer, C. (2002). Shit happens—The selling of risk in extreme sports. *The Australian Journal of Anthropology, 13*(3), 323–336.

Pare, M. (1999, June 28). Here comes the Gravity Games: Look out below. *Providence Business News.*

Pedersen, P., & Kelly, M. (2000). ESPN X Games: Commercialized extreme sports for the masses. Retrieved July 10, 2006, from http://sptmgt.tamu.edu/espnx.htm

Poliakoff, M. (1987). *Combat sports in the ancient world.* New Haven, CT: Yale University Press.

Pringle, R., & Markula, P. (2005). No pain is sane after all: A Foucauldian analysis of masculinities and men's rugby experiences of fear, pain, and pleasure. *Sociology of Sport Journal, 22,* 472–497.

Raymond, J. (2002, June 1). Going to extremes—Marketing and extreme sports. *American Demographics.*

Rinehart, R. (2000). Arriving sport: Alternatives to formal sports. In J. Coakley & E. Dunning (Eds.), *Handbook of sports studies* (pp. 504–519). London: Sage.

Rinehart, R. (2003). Dropping into sight: Commodification and co-optation of in-line skating. In R. E. Rinehart & S. Sydnor (Eds.), *To the extreme: Alternative sports, inside and out* (pp. 27–51). New York: State University of New York Press.

Rinehart, R., & Sydnor, S. (2003). Proem. In R. E. Rinehart & S. Sydnor (Eds.), *To the extreme: Alternative sports, inside and out* (pp. 1–17). New York: State University of New York Press.

Risking nature. (1999, August 3). *New York Times,* p. A14.

Roberts, P. (1994). Risk. *Psychology Today, 27*(6), 50–53, 83–84.

Rojek, C. (1985). *Capitalism and leisure theory.* London: Tavistock.

Rojek, C. (1995). *Decentring leisure: Rethinking leisure theory.* London: Sage.

Ruibal, S. (2001, August 17–19). X games roll from the edge to the burbs. *USA Today,* p. A6.

Sheard, K. (2004). Boxing in the Western civilizing process. In E. Dunning, D. Malcolm, & I. Waddington (Eds.), *Sport histories: Figurational studies of the development of modern sports* (pp. 15–30). London: Routledge.

Sherowski, J. (2006, February). Three days with Andrew Crawford. *Transworld Snowboarding*, 188–192.

Smith, A. (2002). Australian tree-climbing championships. *The Sports Factor*. Retrieved July 10, 2006, from http://www.abc.net.au/rn/sports factor/stories/2002/678516.htm#

Stark, J. (2006). Time flies as dads with pads roll back the years. Retrieved July 11, 2006, from http://www.theage.com.au/articles/2006/04/01/1143441377688.html

Thorpe, H. (2004). Embodied boarders: Snowboarding, status and style. *Waikato Journal of Education, 10,* 181–201.

Tomlinson, J. (2004). *Extreme sports: In search of the ultimate thrill.* London: Carlton Books.

Towsurfer.com. (2003). Extreme surfing world champion Garrett McNamara announces new contest. Retrieved July 15, 2006, from http://www.towsurfer.com/ViewContent.asp?ContentID=67

Wasley, P. (2006, May 5). Parkour aficionados jump, roll, and dart across campuses. *Chronicle of Higher Education*, p. A8.

Watson, T. (1996). Injuries in sport. Retrieved July 11, 2006, from http://www.ul.ie/~childsp/Elements/Issue3/watson.html

Wheaton, B. (2004). Introduction: Mapping the lifestyle sport-scape. In B. Wheaton (Ed.), *Understanding lifestyle sports: Consumption, identity and difference* (pp. 1–28). London: Routledge.

Wikipedia. (2006). Mat Hoffman. Retrieved July 12, 2006, from http://en.wikipedia.org/wiki/Mat_Hoffman

Wren, C. (1999, July 29). Floods not only danger in canyoning craze. *Denver Post.*

XFL ceases operations after one season. (2001). Retrieved July 11, 2006, from http://www.allsports.com/cgi-bin/showstory.cgi?story_id=15773

Media and Extreme Sport

Risking death or serious injury in pursuit of a sports-induced adrenaline rush is probably nearly as old as civilization itself. Murals from ancient Crete showing young men and women vaulting over the horns of wild bulls represent one of the earliest examples of media coverage of so-called extreme sports. The ancient Roman gladiators who called out, "We who are about to die salute you," knew that if they survived their ordeal, they could become favorites of the crowd and have word of their deeds spread throughout the empire. In more recent times bullfighters who slaughtered their animal opponents with panache became stars.

In the nineteenth century the increasing need to sell newspapers in a competitive market led newspapers to publicize extreme travel accounts, such as the *New York Herald*'s 1869 publicity stunt that sent Henry Morton Stanley (1841–1904) to Africa to find Scottish missionary and explorer David Livingstone (1813–1873). This sort of adventure travel was translated into the popular culture in the French writer Jules Verne's *Around the World in 80 Days* (1872), and the nexus between extreme activities and their absorption into the popular culture continues unabated in contemporary times.

In the early twenty-first century athletes have used the insatiable public appetite for sports programming and abundant opportunities for self-promotion to perform their feats of derring-do for sometimes global audiences, and the exploits of these iconoclasts have increasingly become the stuff of advertisers and the dreams of promoters. Marketers, seeking a way to sell their products to the lucrative youth market, with the aid of media outlets, such as the Entertainment and Sports Programming Network (ESPN), have created a massive extreme sports industry.

Newspapers continue to publicize extreme sporting feats, making celebrities of the athletes involved, and these accounts have been joined by films, specialty magazines, video games, and websites. Whenever an athlete attempts the dangerous or unusual, a reporter is sure to be following along to record the action. Both men and women risk drowning by swimming the English Channel, U.S. aviator Charles Lindbergh made his celebrated solo crossing of the Atlantic amidst a blaze of publicity, and when asked why so many wanted to climb Mount Everest, George Leigh Mallory (1886–1924) became immortal by answering, "Because it's there."

The Austrian neurologist Sigmund Freud, in *Civilization and Its Discontents* (1930), described the troubles that accompany the ever-increasing strictures that society places upon the freedom of the individual, and these strictures are plainly on display on the bike path, where young children are equipped with nearly as much body armor as the knights of old. Modern society has attempted to make life as safe as possible, and these strictures chafe at some, causing them to flaunt the rules in pursuit of authentic experience.

The rebel image projected by extreme athletes has proven to be irresistible to marketers bent on selling to the youth audience. In the United States and other industrialized nations, where life has become too tame for a significant segment of the population, the image of the rebel, sanitized by corporate marketing departments, allows millions of young people to rebel while wearing the same tennis shoes and practicing the same "extreme" sports that have become the basis for cool.

Self-promotion: The Dangerous Sports Club

One of the first groups to capitalize on this hunger for the unusual in sports was the Dangerous Sports Club (DSC), a group of graduates and students from England's Oxford University. They not only became innovators in creating death-defying sports, but also helped set a pattern of self-promotion, making sure that the cameras were rolling and the media tipped off before they risked their lives. Their sports and their quest for publicity would lead to a surge in the popularity of extreme sports.

The idea for the club began in 1977 when David Kirke and Ed Hulton met Chris Baker, an early hang gliding enthusiast. In those days hang gliding was a much more dangerous sport, with gliders that were difficult to steer and could fall apart in midflight. Over drinks after Kirke and Hulton's initial flights, the three decided to form the DSC, which officially began in 1978, to serve as a vehicle for pushing the envelope of conventional sports and to create ever more daring sports to make up for their humdrum existences. The club drew from friends and acquaintances whom these pioneers had met during their years at Oxford University or whom they would meet through their self-proclaimed insanity.

Martin Lyster, who later joined the club and who wrote a book about it, stated the philosophy of the members when he wrote: "One of the Freedoms we enjoy is the freedom to take personal risks, deciding for ourselves where to draw the line; while society as a whole tends to pull the other way, constantly seeking to make us all safer. So, in writing a song of praise to the joys of dangerous sports, I realize that I may give offence to those who see bicycle helmets, decaffeination, and traffic calming as symbols of progress" (Lyster 1997, 7). This attitude neatly sums up the collective ethos of the extreme sports movement at large. Whether they actually risk life and limb, those practicing such sports could, at the very least, see themselves as being rebels in the mold of the Dangerous Sports Club.

Nearly from the start Kirke saw the possibilities for making money from publicizing the antics of the club and began to seek opportunities to capture video images of the members' efforts. In 1979 the first commercial venture involved taking a film crew to Africa to film hang gliding from the slopes of Mount Kilimanjaro. The expedition and the film met with various disasters, such as broken gliders, pilots who suffered altitude sickness, and helicopter delays. *The History of the Dangerous Sports Club*, with additional footage of other club adventures, was not released until 1981 as a short film. Despite the complications in bringing the film to the public, it became the eighth-largest grossing film of 1982 in Britain.

The stunt that truly put the DSC into the public eye on a global basis was the invention of the Western version of the sport of bungee jumping. This sport had originated on Pentecost Island in Vanuatu, part of the Micronesia island chain in the South Pacific. The natives of the island tied grass ropes to their feet and jumped off towers, trusting in the ropes to slow them enough to prevent death. After watching a 1950s BBC film by David Attenborough, which featured demonstrations of this manhood ritual, Chris Baker, one of the charter members of the club, conceived the idea of using elasticized bungee cords, which the club used to lash down their hang gliders when traveling, instead of grass ropes and decided to test his theory that the jumper would spring back safely rather than strike the ground in a somewhat controlled crash.

When plans for a trip to New Guinea to test the theory fell through, Baker decided instead to try his jump from the Clifton Suspension Bridge near his home in Bristol, England. Ironically, Baker arrived late for the jump, scheduled for April Fool's Day in 1979, and missed the inauguration of the new sport when his friends took advantage of the retreat of police officers sent to prevent the jump and jumped without him. David Kirke, Alan Weston, Simon Keeling, and Tim Hunt therefore were the first to test Baker's theory that the elasticity of the bungee cords would make the sport survivable (Baker, in the best traditions of the club, declined to test his hypothesis before jumping).

The media, of course, had been tipped off to the event, and photos of the jumpers fired the public imagination. Club members dressed in top hats and tails, which lent an eccentric air to the event, and their eventual arrest and conviction for breach of the peace garnered additional publicity for the club and the sport. The media coverage also allowed Kirke to publicize the club's creed, saying that, "People may think we are mad. We think they are insane to endure such humdrum lives" (Lyster 1997, 35).

The threat of police interference or arrest added spice to the exploits of the club, and the next big jump, off the

Golden Gate Bridge in San Francisco, California, in October 1979, garnered wide publicity in the U.S. and worldwide media. Baker again failed to make the jump when his cord tangled in the bridge structure, and again those who were not able to escape were arrested, this time for trespassing, which kept their adventures in the media.

This spectacle led producers of the U.S. television program *That's Incredible* to offer the club a spot on their show and $20,000 to perform their stunt from the Royal Gorge Bridge in Colorado, which, at more than 300 meters, was then the highest suspension bridge in the world. This time there were no arrests, but the exposure of a highly rated television show spread the allure of the new death-defying sport, as did an article in *Playboy* magazine written by Geoff Tabin, one of the jumpers.

Bungee jumping is now a familiar pastime at a multitude of venues and has been tamed enough for grandparents to enjoy. As sports such as hang gliding and bungee jumping became sanitized for a mass audience, their allure faded for the members of the DSC, and they sought even more extreme experiences. While some bungee jumpers still attempt to push the envelope, which sometimes results in death or serious injury, the DSC moved on to bolder frontiers. One of its latest attempts to tempt death or serious injury was the trebuchet, a medieval catapult designed to propel rocks at castle walls. It also can propel a person 21 meters high, at 80 kilometers per hour, toward a net target. The club abandoned the human catapult when one participant was killed in 2002.

Alternative Media

The DSC epitomizes the extreme sports movement, which searches for ever more spectacular adrenaline rushes while using its adventures as a means of self-promotion. The increasing ease with which individuals can create films that can be disseminated to the public has caused an explosion of extreme sports spotlighted in the media. In 1978 parachutist and cinematographer Carl Boenish (1941–1984) filmed his jump off El Capitan, a 914-meter-tall rock formation in California's Yosemite Valley. He was not the first to jump from El Capitan, but he was the first to film the experience. His footage was included in a *National Geographic* special and thus began BASE (building, antenna, span, Earth) jumping. BASE jumpers launch themselves for a thrill that they describe as superior to that of jumping from an airplane because the nearness of objects, either natural or human-made, adds a sensation of speed that is missing in the free space of the freefall.

After Boenish's film appeared in the *National Geographic* special, other parachutists began to emulate his feat, expanding the repertoire of objects leaped from until they had covered all the BASEs. The early BASE jumpers from El Capitan spread word of the thrill they experienced, and the National Park Service briefly allowed jumpers to buy permits but soon halted the practice. Before dying in a jump from the Troll Wall in Norway, Boenish worked diligently to promote the sport he helped to popularize, making additional films, publishing *BASE Magazine*, and creating a numbering system to recognize those who had completed jumps from all four types of objects.

Tony Hawk is an example of an extreme athlete who has created a media empire of his own. After becoming a world champion skateboarder performing tricks such as the 900, which entails spinning around in the air two and a half times, through 900 degrees, and landing on the board, Hawk translated his skill on the halfpipe (a cement structure that resembles a pipe sawed in half) into international stardom beyond the skateboarding world in film and television appearances and commercials. Hawk is also an example of the current trend in extreme sports: the star who made his reputation in an extreme sport and has been sought out by corporate America to promote the products that it wishes to label as "extreme" in order to gain a larger share of the youth market.

This trend has had a pulling effect in the popular culture as media outlets such as Music Television (MTV) and ESPN have sought to create television programs that exploit the popularity of extreme sports. Whereas adventurers such as the DSC and Carl Boenish created sports before or at the same time the media discovered them, the new trend is to create sports for television.

The X Games

One such media effort is the X Games, which began in 1995 when ESPN created a venue for extreme sports competition. The original Extreme Games, whose name was shortened to solidify its connection to the so-called Generation X, which followed the Baby Boom generation, included aggressive in-line skating, bicycle stunt riding, skateboarding, skysurfing, snowboarding, sport climbing, street luge racing, wakeboarding, and skating. Although at first ridiculed, the X Games have proven to be a winner for ESPN, and now some of the events are also carried on the American Broadcasting Corporation (ABC), which, along with ESPN, is owned by the Disney Corporation. The X Games led to the popularization of sports such as snowboarding, street luge, skysurfing, and trick skateboarding and created a climate that applied the adjective *extreme* to advertise nearly any product or activity.

Other programs such as MTV's *Jackass*, which featured crazy stunts that usually ended in injuries, and the National Broadcasting Corporation's (NBC) *Fear Factor*, which asked contestants to brave extreme situations, have likewise tried to tap this market. *Jackass* was blamed for prompting copycat attempts to perform stunts, such as jumping over a moving car, that resulted in some deaths. Other attempts to cash in on the "extreme" label have not fared so well. The shortlived XFL, which sought to create a hybrid between professional football and wrestling, did not gain much interest.

Extreme sports have found a considerable niche at the box office, and adventure films such as *The Adventures of the Dangerous Sports Club* and *National Geographic* specials on bungee jumping and BASE jumping have helped popularize those sports. The critically acclaimed *Dogtown and Z Boys* (2001) did much to repopularize both the sport and culture of skateboarding. The conflict between skiers and snowboarders has also been a part of several teen movies. The extreme sports industry, whose ethos has rippled through the popular culture, has also resulted in, among other changes, even venerable action characters such as Tarzan (1999) and James Bond going to extremes: Tarzan skateboarded in 1999, and Bond snowboarded in *Die Another Day* in 2002. The Bond franchise, at least, was reacting to the popularity of *Triple X* (2002), which featured Vin Diesel as a prototypical extreme sports star-turned-secret agent.

The Future

Despite a few setbacks, the melding of extreme sports and the media has been successful. The Extreme Sports Channel, owned by a British company and based in the Netherlands, now offers nonstop coverage of such sports, and the need for programming to fill the schedule will no doubt lead to even more extremities. Extreme ironing, for example, is a sport that features people in inaccessible locations ironing their laundry. Whatever the event, the urge to escape the strictures of a society bent on safety and the pull of marketers seeking the lucrative twelve-to-thirty-four-year-old

demographic have created a powerful force that is likely to persist.

Russ Crawford

See also Commercialization; Injuries; Meaning of Extreme, The

Further Reading

Adrenaline addicts invent more kinds of extreme sports to grate on their own nerves. (2006, March 5). *Pravda*, Retrieved on July 24, 2006, from http://english.pravda.ru/society/stories/03-05-2006/79781-extreme-0

Appleton, J. (2005, August 30). What's so extreme about extreme sports? Retrieved July 12, 2006, from www.spiked-online.com/Prntable/0000000CAD26.htm

Barboza, D. (1996, June 27). Mountain Dew's promotion angers children's advocates. *New York Times*, D7.

Club Tony Hawk. (n.d.). Tony Hawk bio. Retrieved July 12, 2006, from http://www.tonyhawk.com/bio.html

Dafjones.com. (n.d.). The Dangerous Sports Club. Retrieved July 12, 2006, from http://www.btinternet.com/~dafyddk/dsc.htm

Di Giovanni, N. (n.d.). BASE jumping history. Retrieved July 12, 2006, from http://www.basicresearch.com/base_history.htm

For thrills, lovers and others leap. (1999, June 31). *New York Times*, A13.

Kannapell, A. (1998, October 11). Taking sports to the limit. *New York Times*, NJ1.

Lyster, M. (1997). *The strange adventures of the Dangerous Sports Club*. London: Do-Not Press.

Mirra, Dave

Dave Mirra (b. 1974) has won many BMX (bicycle motocross) competitions, appeared on television shows, and starred in his own movie and video game. Born in a small town outside of Syracuse, New York, Mirra was BMX riding with his brother and his friends at the age of four. He competed in his first flatland competition at the age of thirteen. In fact, in the same year he earned his first sponsorship from General Bikes. Just a year later Mirra began riding ramps and by 1991 had evolved mainly into a vert rider in competitions. In 1992 he turned pro at the age of eighteen.

However, Mirra's BMX professional career almost did not make it off the ground. In 1994 Mirra was struck by a drunk driver traveling at 56 kilometers per hour. Mirra suffered a skull fracture and a serious injury to his shoulder. Doctors were not sure he would survive, let alone ride again. It took Mirra nearly a year and a half to regain his nerve to ride again aggressively. Yet, he recovered just in time to earn

a silver medal in vert in ESPN's inaugural Extreme Games (later named the "X Games") in 1995.

Mirra has won more medals—including more gold medals—than any other X Games athlete. In 1997 alone he won X Games gold in the street, vert, and vert doubles competitions. Just a year earlier he was the overall Bicycle Stunt Series champion in street. Mirra is credited with inventing a number of tricks, most notably the framestand peg-pick, barspin tailwhip, and backside weasel. He is also the first rider to execute a double backflip in competition. In 2000 Mirra was named "Freestyler of the Year" by *BMX Magazine* and won the ESPN Action Sports and Music Award for BMX Rider of the Year.

Like his contemporaries, skateboarder Tony Hawk and fellow BMX rider Mat Hoffman, Mirra is one of the few extreme sports athletes who has transcended their sport and carved out a place for himself in the U.S. mainstream. He has appeared a number of times on television shows such as MTV's *Punk'd*, *Cribs*, and *The Real World*, *Road Rules Challenge* (which he hosted). Mirra has also appeared on NBC's *Las Vegas* and been a guest on CBS's *The Late Show with David Letterman*. He has also teamed up with PlayStation to create his own video game, *Dave Mirra Freestyle BMX*, which debuted in 2000 and is now into its second version. His biography, *Mirra Images*, has also helped to make him one of the most recognizable extreme sports athletes in the United States. With fellow BMX professional Ryan Nyquist and a number of other lesser known riders, Mirra has made Greenville, North Carolina, a key locale in the BMX riding landscape of the United States.

Kyle Kusz

Further Reading

Mirra, D. (n.d.). Retrieved February 11, 2007, from http://expn.go.com/athletes/bios/MIRRA_DAVE.html

Mirra, D. (2003). *Mirra images: The story of my life.* New York: Regan Books.

Motocross

In the 1980s riders in motocross (a closed-course motorcycle race over natural or simulated rough terrain) began performing acrobatic exhibitions. During the next decade these exhibitions developed into the autonomous and codified sport of freestyle motocross. Riding light, two-stroke 125- or 250-cubic-centimeter motocross bikes, riders execute risky and spectacular tricks in which they launch themselves into the air from ramps. The sport grew rapidly, and in 2006 the international governing body of motorcycle racing and motocross, the Fédération Internationale de Motocyclisme (FIM), joined the main governing body for freestyle, the International Freestyle Motocross Federation (IFMXF), to organize the World Cup circuit.

Development

In the mid-1980s a group of motocross riders began taking both hands off the handlebars in midair. This risky trick became known as a "no-hander." After initial opposition the American Motocross Association (AMA) accepted the trick, which riders said is a reaction against the boring routines of the standard circuit. No-handers quickly became standard routines at AMA-sanctioned outdoor supercross events (open air, natural tracks) and indoor arenacross events (open air or limited and closed halls for arranged tracks, often with artificial obstacles). No-handers also spawned other innovative maneuvers that were displayed at the conclusion of races and performances. The maneuvers appealed to television and spectators, and amateur and professional videos began documenting professional riders practicing for these maneuvers.

The television film *Crusty Demons of Dirt* (1993) played a critical role in the diffusion of freestyle motocross and helped the sport to gain popularity. Since then many freestyle motocross riders have produced videos to promote their sport and themselves. Further impetus for growth came from the All Clear Channel, which provided financing and airtime and filmed excited crowds watching riders change the direction of their bikes and leave their seats. Corporate sponsors quickly followed suit. In 1997 the network Four Leaf Entertainment organized the first U.S. freestyle motocross event. In the next year the network assisted in creation of the International Freestyle Motocross Association (IFMA). Although a U.S.-based organization, IFMA welcomed non-U.S. riders as members. Also in 1998 IFMA organized the first Free Air Festival Freestyle Motocross contest with a purse of $175,000. In 1999 freestyle motocross appeared on the programs of both the Xtreme Games and the Gravity Games.

In freestyle motocross, judges, most of whom are former riders, trainers, or journalists, award points, from 0 to 100, across five categories: amplitude, transitions, degree of difficulty, originality, and overall impressions. Most jumps range between 18 and 27 meters. In 2000 the Vans Triple Crown contest offered $175,000 in prize money for three events. Freestyle motocross developed in Europe a little later. The Night of Jumps, organized in Germany in 2001, was a landmark event for the new sport in Europe. As the name suggests, the Night of Jumps was conducted under artificial light. Although particularly appealing to young people, the event attracted a cross-section of ages. Most European riders joined the IFMXF, which in 2006 received recognition by the FIM. Also in 2001 the World Freestyle Association (WFA), sponsored by networks, organized a world championship. In 2002 at the Xtreme Games Heidi Henry of the United States performed a series of spectacular maneuvers to mark the official entrance of women into the discipline. In 2004 the IFMXF organized the first world championships.

Kenny Bartram of the United States was the first rider to win both the IFMA and WFA world titles. He also won the Vans Triple Crown to complete an unprecedented set of achievements.

Although IFMXF, IFMA and WFA are competing organizations, the FIM welcomes riders from the other organizations, providing they register and comply with FIM rules. FIM rules prohibit wooden ramps and rocks on the track, set the height of ramps between 2.5 and 3.2 meters, and stipulate a minimum distance of 10 meters between the ramp and the landing area. Only riders with an IFMXF license may take part in the FIM/IFMXF world championship; for every stage of this championship the first nineteen riders earn points: 12 for the winner, 10 for the runner-up, 8 for third place, 7 for fourth, 6 for fifth, 5 for sixth, 4 for seventh and eighth, 3 for ninth and tenth, 2 for eleventh and twelfth, and 1 point for the remaining seven placed riders. In 2004 the Swiss rider Mathieu Rebeaud became the first FIM/IFMXF world champion.

Hard-core Freestyle

At first glance the rapid evolution of freestyle motocross suggests a dichotomy of attitudes between European and U.S. riders and their respective associations. The Europeans seemed to liken freestyle motocross to freestyle

A motorcycle rider in midair. Source: istock/ Christopher O Driscoll.

skiing, a dangerous but nonetheless rule-governed sport. However, U.S. riders and the IFMA also promote races outside arenas and at venues such as canyons, snow tracks, and dried lakes. These venues appear outside the domains set out by FIM. Thus, despite its codification, freestyle is an extreme sport. The skills of daredevil riders continue to grow, as do the risks, although, paradoxically, as the time riders spend in the air increases so, too, does the time available to regain full control of their machines and to manage treacherous landings. The ranges and the sizes of objects challenged by freestyle motocross riders continue to expand, with riders performing in the snow, on hills, over bars normally set for high jumping or pole vaulting, and over obstacles such as planes or trucks. Synchronized performances, with several riders executing jumps and landings one after the other, add to the excitement. These exhibitions seem more extreme than the more regulated European-style competitions.

Bike Preparation

The preparation and customization of bikes are fundamental aspects of freestyle motocross. In general, riders prefer a 250-cubic-centimeter, two-stroke engine that combines consistent horsepower and adequate maneuverability. However, some riders prefer a special kind of Yamaha, still the main supplier of bikes on both the freestyle circuit and the general motocross circuit. This four-stroke model provides more reliability on some slippery surfaces. Standard modifications include the addition of grips to the seat, lowered front wheels, adjustments to the pipes and portals on the engine, and stiffened suspensions.

Tricks of the Trade

Leading freestyle motocross riders have a repertoire of more than thirty tricks. In the "nac-nac," first performed by Jeremy McGrath in 1993, the rider whips the bike sideways while removing one leg and extending it back behind the seat and, at the same time, turning his or her trunk to face the public.

Gordon Ward invented the heel clicker, but Mike Metzger popularized it. In this trick the rider puts his legs over the handlebars, flexes his legs over the elbows, and clicks them at the level of his number plate. Many experts consider this trick a good one for beginners.

The cliffhanger is a particularly spectacular trick. After leaving the ramp the rider adopts a standing position, and the rider's hands leave the handlebars. After the hands have left the handlebars, the rider's feet leave the pedals and contact the handlebars, so the feet and lower legs form a right angle, on the handlebars. With the feet still on the handlebars, the arms stretch back, bringing back also the trunk. Finally the rider resumes the original position, the arms completing the circling and retaking the handlebars, and the feet and legs help the rider to resume a sitting position.

The bar hop is popular among IFMA stars. The rider places his legs over the handlebars and then straightens them. In order to return to the normal sitting position he has to repeat the move in reverse, which demands strength and athleticism to avoid hitting the handlebars.

The Hart attack, named after Carey Hart, is one of most spectacular tricks and invariably draws great response from crowds. After the jump the rider glides backward from the sitting position in order to free her legs. One of her hands also leaves the handlebar to grasp the seat. The rider then pushes her legs upward into a vertical position before returning to the seat.

In the kiss of death trick the rider completely leaves his seat and adopts a vertical position with both hands on the handlebars. In the descending phase he approaches the metal cover of the front wheel, simulating a kiss with the helmet, then reassumes the sitting position just before landing.

Backflips and double backflips—single and double somersaults, respectively—and 360-degree rotations are particularly dangerous tricks. Insurance companies in the United States refuse to insure riders who attempt them. Metzger executed the first backflip, and Brian Deegan the first 360-degree.

Freestyle motocross probably will continue to expand, with riders performing in more paid exhibitions. Certainly they will continue to invent more spectacular tricks.

Gherardo Bonini

Flags of Motocross

Between high speeds, and loud noises, no one can really expect to be heard during a motocross tournament. To avoid problems, motocross organizations have adopted a system of flags and other rules to govern the sport.

Excerpts from the Motocross Racing Association official rulebook

Flags

1. GREEN—start of the race.
2. WHITE—one lap to go to finish of the race.
3. YELLOW—when a yellow flag is displayed, all racers will exercise caution and CANNOT PASS until they have passed the incident which caused the flag to be displayed. Failure to do so WILL result in disqualification from the day's event.
4. BLACK—disqualification of an individual racer. Report to the Referee at once.
5. LIGHT BLUE—move over at once, another racer is trying to pass.
6. WHITE WITH RED CROSS—ambulance flag indicates that ambulance personnel is needed on the track.
7. BLACK & WHITE CHECKERED FLAG—finished, end of race.
8. RED—stopping of a race for an emergency situation.

Any racer whose machine is disabled before he reaches the finish line may, by his own unaided muscular energy, push or carry his machine (in the direction of the track) across the finish line to receive the checkered flag, and under such conditions will be considered as having completed the event, provided he has completed 50% of the laps completed by the winner of the event.

Source: Motocross Racing Association. *The Motocross Racing Association Rulebook.* Retrieved Feb. 1, 2007 from http://www.racemra.com/06_files/the%20_MRA_rule_book.pdf

Further Reading

Fédération Internationale de Motocyclisme. (2006). International free-style motocross appendix and freestyle motocross world championship regulations. Retrieved June 7, 2006, from http://www.fim.ch/fr/rules/Sportifs/cms/2006/MX%20FREESTYLE_031.pdf

International Freestyle Motocross Association. (n.d.). Retrieved June 7, 2006, from http://fmx.cc.com

Milan, G. (2000). *Freestyle motocross: Jump tricks from the pros*. Osceola, FL: MBI Publishing.

Milan, G. (2002). *Freestyle motocross 2: Air sickness: More jump tricks from the pros*. Osceola, FL: MBI Publishing.

Motorvehicle Sports

The specter of injury and even death always goes along for a ride when motor-racing competitors race their cars at breakneck speeds. The sport originated in Europe, with Germany's Karl Benz and Gottlieb Daimler being credited with inventing the car, a petrol-fired prototype in 1885, while France invented motor racing by staging the first race. The date of this first race is disputed, with some historians asserting that a race between Paris and Rouen in 1894 was the first, whereas other historians claim that race was merely a reliability trial in preparation for the first race in 1895 from Paris to Bordeaux and back. These two races were staged on public roads, with later races being held throughout Europe. The French government banned road racing before relenting to pressure from the automobile industry, although racing was finally banned outright after deaths of competitors and spectators during the 1903 Paris-to-Madrid race.

After the tragedy of 1903, motor racing moved to rural roads, racing on a closed circuit rather than from city to city. Although road racing remained popular in most of Europe, purpose-built racing circuits emerged after construction of the Monza track near Milan in 1922, allowing "road racing" to be held on closed circuits designed like road courses, as well as the opportunity to charge spectators for attendance. In Britain and the United States road racing had never been permitted, with both countries restricting racing to large banked oval circuits, the most notable being built at Indianapolis in 1909. Whereas Britain gradually adopted the European-style purpose-built circuits, the United States continued to favor banked ovals, providing a venue to race the larger passenger cars (with larger engines) that were being produced in the United States and attracting a large paying audience. These two circuit designs have by and large permeated the U.S. and European styles of racing.

Many people participate in a range of motor-racing formats. The most basic format, cart racing, offers speed and danger for its competitors and is often the entry level for drivers before they progress to different cars and competitions. The most popular form of motor racing in the United States is the National Association for Stock Car Auto Racing (NASCAR), a stock car racing series with origins in the transportation of moonshine in the South from the 1930s to the 1950s. The United States also has two open-wheeler series, the Indy Racing League (IRL) and Champ Cars (CART), with the IRL staging arguably the United States' most prestigious race, the Indy 500. Because NASCAR and the IRL are primarily oval-based racing (CART is circuit-based), they offer global viewing audiences the spectacle of cars racing at 320 kilometers per hour inches away from both concrete walls and other competitors. The potential for a crash is obvious, and it is rare to watch a NASCAR race without seeing a multiple-car collision.

Outside of the United States, Rally offers another variation that attracts a large global audience. Predominantly staged in Europe, Rally carries substantial risks for drivers, who participate in timed runs over a variety of surfaces that include tarmac, gravel, rocks, and even snow in Sweden as part of the World Rally Championship (WRC). Danger is ever present, either for the spectators, who often line the roads only meters away from the cars, or for the competitors, who are likely to collide with trees, rocks, ditches, or spectators or even drive over cliff edges if they lose control of their cars or leave the road.

Two other elite motor-racing variations are worth noting. The first is drag racing, which features two rocket-powered cars accelerating from a standing start over a quarter-mile. With volatile fuel and a quest for speed, crashes in drag racing are dangerous, with cars often launching into the air or exploding into a fireball of debris. Drag races are held at various places around the world, although, without a unified competition, the National Hot Rod Association (NHRA) of the United States arguably sponsors the elite drag-racing competition. Additionally, Saloon or Touring Car racing series are staged around the world. These series are raced in a variety of classes (e.g., Le Mans Endurance, Porsche Carrera Cup, British Touring Car Championship, and the V8 Supercars competition in Australasia), so determining the top class is difficult. In the United States NASCAR is the premier stock-car series, followed by a range of second-tier races. In Europe either the World Touring Car Championship or the DTM series, often raced by ex—Formula One drivers (e.g., Heinz-Harald Frentzen, Mika Hakkinen, and Jean Alesi in 2006), is regarded as the elite series. All of these series have high speeds, close-formation racing, and the presence of barriers and walls as dangerous elements.

Formula One: The Pinnacle of Motor Sport

Formula One racing is the pinnacle of single-seater, open-wheel racing, if not the pinnacle of *all* forms of motor sport. As Noble and Hughes assert,

> Formula One stands at the technological pinnacle of all motorsport. It's also the richest, most intense, most difficult, most political, and most international racing championship in the world. Most of the world's best drivers are either there or aspire to be there. (Noble and Hughes 2004, 20)

The term *Formula One* is derived from the "formula" of rules and regulations for competing in terms of the size, weight, and power of the cars. The "one" signifies Formula One's designation as the pinnacle of the sport and marks a distinction from the lower divisions, such as Formula Three, Formula 3000, and Formula Ford, each with its own restrictions and regulations. Reaching speeds in excess of 320 kilometers per hour, Formula One racing is an extreme sport. As Noble and Hughes note, "Racing a 200 mph missile loaded with fuel is never going to be an intrinsically safe activity. For many, this inherent danger is part of the sport's appeal" (Noble and Hughes 2004, 24). Perversely, to some extent the danger may also account for Formula One's global audience. As Shirley suggests, Formula One drivers are "speed kings who find it impossible to escape from their own mortality in a sport where death is always on the agenda. It is an extreme existence, but the danger of death or serious injury makes for great entertainment" (Shirley 2000, xiv).

With improved safety measures, Formula One racing has not suffered a driver fatality since 1994. Rather, with the speed and technological efficiency of these hybrid rocket-cars, driver bravado and danger come to the fore. Interestingly, open-wheel cars of the IRL and CART in the United States actually reach higher speeds than Formula One cars. The U.S. cars are generically produced, are less regulated, and race on oval tracks that require minimal braking or turning to facilitate consistent high speeds. For example, IRL cars exceed 350 kilometers per hour on some oval circuits. In contrast, Formula One is more constrained, being a technology-based sport in which each team builds its own car in accordance with strict regulations (e.g., in 2006 engines had to be V8s with no turbos or superchargers). In addition, Formula One

A Grand Prix in Sepang, Malaysia. Source: istock/ Ahmad Faizal Yahya.

Jacques Villeneuve

Formula One risk-taker

Described as a "daredevil" (Donaldson, 2001) or "macho racer" (Benson, 2000), the 1997 World Champion Jacques Villeneuve stood out in contemporary Formula One due to his fearless approach to racing. Despite numerous big crashes throughout his career (1996–2006), Villeneuve employed a spectacular "hard-charging" driving style (Hughes, 2004) which often extended beyond the "edge" of track space available to maximize his momentum. Villeneuve's bravado was most visible with the annual challenge he used to set himself, attempting to take the notorious Eau Rogue section at Spa, Belgium, "flat" (not lift off the accelerator). Eau Rogue is an uphill, left-right-left configuration, with gradient shifts, concealed exits and exerts up to 4.6 lateral g-forces on the driver (Peagam, 2005). Unsuccessful in 1998, Villeneuve crashed into the barriers at 185mph, exclaiming, "That was a big one . . . easily the biggest in my Formula One career and one of the biggest I have ever had . . . It was the best crash of my F1 career" (Villeneuve in Shirley 2000, p. 131). Villeneuve repeated the feat in 1999, this now taking the mantle of his "best crash," although he noted, "The 1999 accident was not fun, and I saw stars . . . but it makes you feel strong" (Villeneuve in Donaldson 2001, p. 60). Post-2001, new electronic systems on the cars made it possible for every driver to take Eau Rogue "flat," forcing Villeneuve to adapt his driving style and relinquish elements of his risk-taking until his retirement in 2006.

Damion Sturm

Further Reading

Benson, A. (2000, n.d.). Villeneuve—The only man Schumacher fears. Inside the mind of Formula 1's last macho racer. Reproduced on *geocities*. Retrieved January 11, 2001, from http://www.geocities.com/jvlover_group/article1.html

Donaldson, G. (2001, April). The daredevil inside Jacques Villeneuve. *Formula 1 Magazine, 1*, 2, pp. 54–61.

Hughes, M. (2004). *The unofficial Formula One encyclopedia* (Rev. ed.). London: Anness.

Peagam, O. (2005, September). Whoah Rogue! *F1 Racing, Australian Edition*, pp. 78–81.

Shirley, P. (2000). *Deadly obsessions. Life and death in Formula One.* London: HarperCollins.

does not race on ovals but rather on circuits that have numerous turns and heavy braking points. Nevertheless, a Formula One car is lighter, more agile, more powerful, and quicker over a single lap than its U.S. counterpart.

A Formula One race is called a "grand prix" and although the first grand prix was held at Le Mans, France, in 1906, it was not a Formula One race. Irregularly held races continued throughout Europe during the early twentieth century before the first official Formula One World Championship race was staged at Silverstone, England, in 1950. During these formative years the competitors (known as "privateers" or "enthusiasts") raced in their national colors (e.g., British racing green or Italian red) and manufactured their own cars. The complexion of the sport changed drastically in the late 1960s with the advent of car sponsorship by tobacco companies and others as well as the increased involvement of car manufacturers. Costs rose as teams pursued technical and performance advantages, and increasingly these escalating production costs required sponsor and manufacturer backing, literally driving many privateers out of the sport. Throughout much of its early history Formula One was also staged haphazardly as, even in the 1970s, each race was independent and required negotiation between teams and circuit owners to determine fees and entrants.

Commercialization/Globalization

Since the early 1980s Formula One has been transformed into a global series of sixteen to nineteen races at various localities around the world. It draws an estimated 50 billion television viewers annually. In the early 1980s Bernie Ecclestone, as president of the Formula One Constructors Association (FOCA), began streamlining the sport. He sensed the commercial possibilities of the sport and, in particular, the influential role that televised coverage could play. As Hotten says, "Ecclestone's masterstroke was to promise circuit owners a full grid of teams; teams had to commit themselves to a full season of racing. This pleased the crowds, it pleased the sponsors, and it pleased the television stations" (Hotten 1999, 29). Ecclestone was responsible for negotiating worldwide television rights, and by the end of the 1980s he had established a television product that was strong on production values and highly sought by an array of global networks. In particular, through technologies such as on-board cameras mounted on the cars, televised Formula One attracts a large viewing audience by enhancing the sense of realism and the spectacle for viewers.

With its technological emphasis and its status as the pinnacle of motor sports, Formula One has a strong commercial and corporate orientation. The cost of running a team and the reliance on sponsorship from both car manufacturers and multinational companies make Formula One as much a business as a sport. As team principal Sir Frank Williams said, "Between the hours of two o'clock and four o'clock most Sunday afternoons at Grand Prix races, it is a sport . . . The rest of the time it is a business" (Turner 2004, 102). The budgets of Formula One teams are staggering, with *F1 Racing* magazine estimating that the sport as a whole (inclusive of testing, salaries, engine budgets, etc.) costs $2.1–2.5 billion annually for all the teams involved. Between 2003 and 2005 Ferrari was consistently the biggest spender of all the teams, with an operating budget of more than $400 million per season, while Toyota, McLaren, Williams, and British American Racing (BAR) spent $350 million or more annually. Sponsors contribute vast sums to these operating budgets, and, in return, the cars, team members, and drivers are adorned with sponsor logos. Tobacco companies were the predominant sponsors of Formula One teams from the late 1960s until 31 July 2005, when new antitobacco legislation went into effect in Europe. This legislation prohibited tobacco branding and forced most tobacco firms to leave Formula One. Only Philip Morris (Marlboro) remained after 2006.

Sponsors are also influential in the sport by either stating their preferences in driver selection or by paying for a race seat for a particular driver (pending final approval from the team). As Turner asserts, "Don't be fooled into thinking Formula One showcases the twenty best drivers in the world—it doesn't. It offers a stage to those lucky enough to carry the logos of ambitious multinational corporations" (Turner 2004, 201). Problematically, because of the cost of running a Formula One team, some drivers bring cash or sponsorship with them to buy a race seat with a smaller team. An example of a "pay driver" with more money than driving talent was Argentinean Gaston Mazzacane, who was "hired" by the Prost team in 2001 because of his estimated $41 million of sponsorship. As Peagam explains,

"It all comes down to sponsorship and cash. PanAmerican Sports Network (PSN) hold the rights to F1 in Argentina. They have around $41 million to spend in F1. They also sponsor Mazzacane" (Peagam 2001, 103). Prost needed the money but dumped Mazzacane after a handful of disappointing races and appeased sponsors by replacing him with another South American, Brazilian Luciano Burti.

Formula One is also a gendered sport, with almost all the drivers and team owners and most of the crews and media personnel being male. Only five females have competed in Formula One, the last in 1992. With men as the risk takers or team leaders, the few women who work in Formula One are often cast in a supporting role. Primarily they function as adornments for the men and their cars, the young and beautiful "grid girls" or "pit babes" sprawled over the cars dressed in tight, revealing Lycra suits, miniskirts, or bikinis adorned with sponsors' logos. Such displays may be the foundation of Formula One's "glamorous" image, although the expense, prestige, luxury, exotic locations, and jet-set lifestyles also contribute to the image. The fast cars also contribute. As Noble and Hughes observe,

> A Formula One car . . . is a very different beast to anything else you see on the road. It is the ultimate prototype machine, featuring design ideas, technology, and materials that many people associate more with a modern day fighter jet than with an automobile . . . their design has been centred on the quest for speed rather than comfort, and they are almost literally rockets on wheels. (Noble and Hughes 2004, 13)

Unfortunately, with its technological sophistication and expense, Formula One is also an elite sport; the Formula One driving experience is limited to its drivers. Thus, the closest the masses can get to the Formula One driving experience is visual reproduction: either watching the on-board camera or playing one of the Formula One video games.

Speed versus Safety

During its early decades Formula One was even more dangerous, with risk and bravado far outweighing concerns with safety. Formula One racing was at its extreme during the 1950s and 1960s because cars had limited safety features, and drivers wore little protective gear. Drivers also had to contend with spectators, trees, fences, and concrete walls if they ran off the track. Indeed, during the 1960s twelve drivers and sixteen spectators were killed, and drivers were reluctant to wear even seat belts for fear of being trapped in a burning car. Three-time world champion Jackie Stewart became a crusader for improved safety in the sport in 1966 after he was trapped in his overturned car at the Spa-Francorchamps circuit in Belgium. As potentially explosive petrol poured over his body, his fellow drivers rescued him, but he waited another twenty minutes for trackside assistance to arrive. By the late 1960s Stewart's campaign had brought about improved safety for cars and drivers, such as drivers wearing fireproof overalls, and teams seal fuel tanks with rubber cells to reduce ruptures and potential fires. Stewart also brought about radical changes in circuit safety, such as the removal of trees and other dangerous trackside objects, the installation of Armco barriers (metal barriers that absorb the force of cars on impact, allowing them to slow and skim along the barrier), and improvements in marshal training and medical facilities. Despite these improvements, Formula One remained dangerous. Seventeen drivers died, and more than one hundred were seriously injured between 1963 and 1997. Even with continual changes to car design, circuit layouts, and safety features, there was statistically still more than one driver fatality a season during the 1970s.

Between the 1980s and 2000 Formula One underwent marked improvements in safety and a significant reduction in driver fatalities. The last two driver fatalities occurred in 1994 at Imola, Italy. Prior to that, the last fatality was Gilles Villeneuve in Belgium in 1982. These improvements can be attributed to British neurosurgeon Sid Watkins, who, from the late 1970s until his retirement in 2005, brought about far-reaching improvements in driver safety. Watkins realized that expert medical attention needs to be readily available to prevent driver fatalities, and he ensured that all races have teams of medical experts located around the circuit as well as medical cars and a medical helicopter on standby. Watkins also made on-site medical centers mandatory at every circuit. In 1998 he said that, with the staff, equipment, and basic operating theaters available, "the facilities at many of these circuits are now superior to some hospitals you find in the outside world!" (Henry 1998, 105).

The race at Imola in 1994 was a dark stain on the sport. Ominously, in Friday practice Rubens Barrichello was fortunate to survive a 257-kilometer-per-hour crash that sent his car airborne. The next day Roland Ratzenberger was killed during practice, and three-time world champion Aryton Senna, revered as one of the sport's greatest drivers, lost his life during the race after hitting a concrete wall at 300 kilometers per hour. After four more drivers suffered major injuries during the 1994 season, drastic changes were made to the sport. In particular, Formula One improved driver safety. Traditional high-speed circuits such as Imola, Monza, and Hockenheim were revamped to reduce speeds by installing chicanes—corners or other track changes added to a previously straight section of course—or even removing fast sections, such as breaking up the long straights at Hockenheim. Improvements have been made to the composition of materials used for cars, and stringent structural tests have been introduced. The speeds of the cars have also been restricted by the introduction of grooved tires since 1998 (which appears to be a dubious safety measure because it actually reduces grip), as well as by regulation changes to aerodynamics and engine specifications. Driver safety equipment is continually undergoing refinement, notably with the introduction in 2003 of the HANS (head and neck support) device, which is attached to the helmet to limit head and neck movements in a crash.

Although no driver fatalities occurred between 1995 and 2006, some horrific injuries occurred. Two-time world champion Mika Hakkinen fractured his skull after a 240-kilometer-per-hour crash while qualifying in Australia in 1995. Doctors performed a trackside tracheotomy after Hakkinen stopped breathing. In 1997 Oliver Panis broke both legs in a crash in Canada, an injury shared by seven-time world champion Michael Schumacher when his brakes failed during the 1999 British Grand Prix. Two accidents in 2001 were close to fatal, with the 1997 world champion Jacques Villeneuve lucky to escape with only minor cuts and bruises after his car became airborne and disintegrated as it skimmed along fencing before crashing at the Australian Grand Prix. And in Belgium television viewers saw Luciano Burti leave the circuit at full throttle, failing to reduce his speed as he plowed into the tire barriers at 300 kilometers per hour. Burti was extracted from the tire wall and was fortunate to not suffer any long-term injuries, although he never raced in Formula One again. However, two trackside marshals were killed during the 2001 season. One was struck by Villeneuve's errant flying tire in Australia, and flying debris from multiple-car crash at Monza killed another during the Italian Grand Prix.

Despite all the safety improvements, the speed and power of these cars make Formula One an extreme sport for all involved. Because Formula One cars have great acceleration and cornering ability, they will continue to become airborne, as happened to Pedro Diniz in 1999, Luciano Burti in 2001, Ralf Schumacher in 2002, Christian Klien in 2005, and Nick Heidfeld in 2006. Additionally, rain does not usually prevent Formula One races. Treacherous track conditions have resulted in numerous crashes, most notably an eighteen-car pileup in Belgium in 1998 and six identical crashes at turn three during the 2003 Brazilian Grand Prix. With high-speed circuits such as Monza and Silverstone, temporary street circuits in Melbourne and Montreal, and the narrow streets of Monaco, the Formula One World Championship provides challenges for its competitors. With drivers pushing the envelope of speed and engaging in close-quarter racing in hybrid rocket-cars on narrow courses, Formula One remains an extreme sport.

Damion Sturm

See also Gender; Meaning of Extreme, The

Further Reading

F fever grips UK. (2002, March). *Formula 1 Magazine, 2,* 1, 18.
Henry, A. (1998). *Formula 1: Creating the spectacle.* Sussex, UK: Hazleton.
Henry, A. (2003). Counting the cost. *F1 Racing, Australian Edition,* 62–70, 72.
Henry, A. (2004, April). Counting the cost. *F1 Racing, Australian Edition,* 64–70.
Henry, A. (2005, April). Counting the cost. *F1 Racing, Australian Edition,* 46–53.
Hotten, R. (1999). *Formula One: The business of winning: The people, money and profits that power the world's richest sport.* London: Orion Business Books.
Hughes, M. (2004). *The unofficial Formula One encyclopedia* (Rev. ed.). London: Anness.
Noble, J., & Hughes, M. (2004). *Formula One racing for dummies: An insider's guide to Formula One.* Chichester, UK: John Wiley & Sons.
Peagam, O. (2001, May). Can you hear me at the back? *F1 Racing, Australian Edition,* 100–103.
Rendall, I. (2000). *The power game: The history of Formula 1 and the world championship.* London: Cassell & Co.
Shackleford, B. A. (1999). Masculinity, hierarchy, and the auto racing fraternity: The pit stop as a celebration of social roles. *Men and Masculinities, 2*(2), 180–196.
Shirley, P. (2000). *Deadly obsessions: Life and death in Formula One.* London: HarperCollins
Turner, B. (2004). *The pits: The real world of Formula One.* London: Atlantic.
Vergeer, K. (2004). *Formula One fanatic.* London: Bloomsbury.

Mountain Bike Racing

Despite the worldwide popularity of the mountain bike as a means of recreation and transportation, the sport of mountain bike racing and the media portrayal of Generation X and Generation Y "adrenaline junkies" hurtling downhill at speeds in excess of 90 kilometers per hour have helped to ensure that this sporting practice is perceived of as "extreme" in the popular imagination.

The development of mountain bike racing relied significantly on the technological development of the mountain bike itself. In fact mountain bike racing is one of the few sports that encourages technological innovation and does not overly restrict the implementation of new equipment or designs. This "innovate or die" ethos—as captured in a popular ad campaign by *Specialized Bicycles,* one of the first widely successful mountain bike companies—seems to attract a mixed assortment of designers, engineers, and athletes who willingly put their bodies on the line to test the latest products in the hopes of shaving precious seconds off racing times.

While riding bicycles off-road is hardly a new practice, the pioneering spirit of harnessing technology in order to conquer increasingly more extreme terrain, leading to modern international mountain bike racing, is a relatively recent phenomenon.

Early Days

Ignaz and Frank W. Schwinn introduced the forerunner of the mountain bike—the Schwinn Excelsior, a balloon tire bike—in the mid-1930s. The popularity of the Schwinn Excelsior waned, but surfers and college students rediscovered the bikes several decades later. The larger tires, upright riding position, heavy-duty construction, relative availability, and low cost made these so-called "ballooners" or "clunkers" a natural for commuting to and from the beach and campus. By the 1970s a small group of cycling enthusiasts began to transform the one-speed clunker of the 1930s into the fastest growing sport bike of the 1990s. It difficult to say with certainly who fitted the first single-speed balloon-tire bike with gears and hand brakes, yet most accounts lead to northern California.

The precursor of the modern mountain bike and the first mountain bike races were probably introduced in the early 1970s in Cupertino, California. The Morrow Dirt Riders, a group of about ten people, would meet regularly to ride down the fire roads around Cupertino on modified coaster-brake bikes. At the 1974 California State Cyclocross championships, a group of the Morrow riders entered the event on their specially modified 26-inch-wheeled dirt bikes to the curiosity of the rest of the participants who were on more traditional road bikes. The bikes would leave an impression on several of the racers and soon-to-be pioneers of the burgeoning sport, including Joe Breeze, Charlie Kelly, and Gary Fisher, since none of them had seen such bikes fitted with gears.

At around the same time a small group of road bike racers from the Velo Club Tamalpas—a bicycle racing club in Marin County—were introduced to "clunking" by Marc Vendetti, who had ridden with a group of fat-tire riders called the Larkespur Canyon Gang. The "gang" was riding fat-tire, single-speed bikes with coaster brakes in the mountains of Marin and even had an informal race from the top of a mountain back down to Larkspur Canyon with the winner claiming first prize: reportedly an envelope of marijuana! Inevitably, riders began experimenting with different parts while cannibalizing old bicycles and even motorcycles to construct bikes that would go up as well as down the mountain. The addition of gears and powerful brakes first introduced by Gary Fisher in 1974 sparked a flurry of innovations that would see major corporate involvement and the development of an organized sport in less than ten years.

Racing and Innovating

Despite evidence suggesting that a group of French riders, the Velo Cross Club Parisien, developed a sport in 1951 that was similar to present-day mountain bike racing, the strong belief that mountain bike racing began as a uniquely American pastime, due to its mythic California roots, endures, despite the country's lack of success in international competition since at least the mid-1990s.

The first organized mountain bike race was held on Pine Mountain just north of San Francisco in 1976. It was named the "Repack" Downhill race and got its name from the fact that after each four-and-a-half-minute run down the mountain, the wheel hub bearings would have to be repacked since the friction of the ride would vaporize the old grease. These and subsequent races were pivotal in the development of the modern mountain bike. The harsh conditions of the early races coupled with antiquated equipment would often necessitate custom fabrication to deal with the rugged conditions, thereby allowing riders to conquer increasingly extreme terrain at greater velocities. By 1980 MountainBikes, a company founded by Gary Fisher and Charlie Kelly in northern California, had sold 150 bikes in the United States, about half of all the mountain bikes sold in the country at the time. In just three years the number of mountain bikes in the United States would skyrocket to 200,000, due in large part to a growing Japanese influence that would change the mountain bike industry forever. Cheap production costs in Taiwan and specially built components designed by Japanese companies like Shimano and Suntour cemented the

A racer descending a trail at top speed. Source: istock/Brad Ralph.

Rules of Mountain Bike Racing

As extreme sports become more and more popular in mainstream culture, rules have been adapted and created to avoid unnecessary risk. Below are the National Off-Road Bicycle Association rules.

- I will yield the right of way to other non-motorized recreationists. I realize that people judge cyclists by my actions.
- I will slow down and use caution when approaching or overtaking another and will make my presence known well in advance.
- I will maintain control of my speed at all times and will approach turns in anticipation of someone around the bend.
- I will stay on designated trails to avoid trampling native vegetation and minimize potential erosion to trails by not using muddy trails or shortcutting switchbacks.
- I will not disturb wildlife or livestock.

- I will not litter, I will pack out what I pack in and I will pack out more than my share whenever possible.
- I will respect public and private property, including trail use signs and no trespassing signs and will leave gates as I have found them.
- I will always be self-sufficient, and my destination and travel speed will be determined by my ability, my equipment, the terrain and the present and potential weather conditions.
- I will not travel solo when biking in remote areas. I will leave word of my destination and when I plan to return.
- I will observe the practice of minimum impact bicycling by "taking only pictures and leaving only waffle prints."
- I will always wear a helmet whenever I ride.

Source: Mountain Bike Policies. Retrieved Feb. 1, 2007 from http://www.steamboat.com/summer-int.aspx?CategoryId=653

corporate partnership between the northern California racer/builders and the mainstream bike industry.

Pushing the Limits

Since its inception, the mountain bike has been influenced by the racing set. As such, it is not surprising that many of those attracted to the sport were interested in pushing the boundaries of speed and gravity. Riding down mountain trails at high speed remains one of the fundamental and unique aspects of mountain bike riding and racing. Racers demanding more responsive equipment have led to a host of developments from high-tech frame materials to motorcycle-like shock absorbers and disc brakes on the front and rear of the bicycle. The thrilling sight of racers avoiding obstacles, catching "big-air" while sailing over jumps, and "stacking" (or crashing) hard when a miscalculation snaps equipment, or worse, bones, is indeed enduring. It is this extreme aspect, no doubt, that captured the attention of riders, spectators, and promoters alike. The leaders of the sport were quick to include racing events that showcased the acrobatic skills

of riders as they battled head to head on ski-slalom type courses. This television-friendly competition made for exciting viewing and led to an influx of sponsor dollars.

The high-adrenaline nature of mountain biking has also lent itself well to the antiestablishment image of other extreme sports like skateboarding, snowboarding, bicycle motocross (BMX), and in-line skating. In fact television networks like ESPN2, which cater to young male viewers, literally created high-energy sporting events such as the X Games and Gravity Games in an attempt to capitalize on the energy and aggression inherent in mountain bike racing.

The Growth of Racing

In 1983 the National Off-Road Bicycling Association (NORBA) was formed to govern the increasing number of races that were being promoted in the United States. In the early days of organized mountain bike racing, Americans and Canadians dominated the mostly U.S.–based racing circuit. However, it would not take long before mountain bike racing would spread to Europe and beyond. Given the historical and cultural importance of European bicycle racing, and the sheer numbers of racers and ex-racers looking to extend their professional careers, the American's domination of the sport was short-lived. The introduction of the first world championship event held in Purgatory, Colorado, in 1990 in many ways marked a dramatic shift in the sport. The laid-back communal atmosphere that typified the early racing scene gave way to the high-pressure world of international sport. By 1996 the first-ever mountain bike racing medals would be awarded at the Atlanta Olympics, reflecting, in part, the stratospheric growth in popularity of the mountain bike itself, which had eclipsed the road bike in worldwide sales.

Mountain bike racing takes on many variations, but it is generally split into two separate categories: cross-country racing and downhill racing. Cross-county racing typically involves racing longer distances where endurance is a factor. Many cross-country courses have a significant amount of vertical assent followed by moderate-to-steep downhill sections. Single-track narrow, twisting trails that challenge riders technical skills are usually incorporated into a cross-county racecourse. Professional riders race about 35 miles in international cross-country competitions or about 60 miles in a newly created format called the marathon race. In the United States the short-track cross-country event is a mass-start race on a short dirt loop, not more than 1 or 2 miles long. These events are shorter in duration and involve more team strategy, moreover, they are fan and television friendly since one does not have to hike several miles into the woods to see their favorite racers as is usually necessary when watching cross-country racing.

Until recently, one unique aspect of cross-country racing required that the racers had to repair any mechanical malfunction themselves during an event; no outside assistance was permitted. This feature of racing had arguably pushed designers to produce equipment that was less prone to failure. With the introduction of new international rules by the Union Cycliste Internationale (UCI), the international governing body of bicycle racing, competitors in UCI–sanctioned events are allowed to receive aid in the event of a mechanical incident, to the dismay of many traditionalists.

Downhill racing is the simplest form of mountain bike racing. The racer who covers the course in the least amount of time is the winner. In downhill racing riders are given qualifying runs and seeded according to the times that they post. Similarly, dual-slalom racing involves a head-to-head competition on a man-made racecourse that has turns, jumps, and berms. It is adapted from ski racing; each rider takes a turn on each of the two runs, thereby negating the advantage of a faster run. The four-cross event pits four riders on the same course from starting gates to finish. There can only be one winner per heat, so the races can quickly eliminate riders, making the running of the day's events faster. For this reason as well as the television-friendly nature of this exciting event, four-cross replaced the dual-slalom in the UCI World Cup series in 2002.

Another popular form of mountain bike racing is the twenty-four-hour event. Teams of four or five racers and individuals in the solo category compete to see who can go the farthest in a twenty-four-hour period. The teams are responsible for maintaining their own equipment and must ride throughout the night with the aid of a helmet-mounted headlamp. This type of event is gaining popularity because the real accomplishment is to have participated and finished. For many this format of racing, while certainly extreme in one respect, connects competitors in the camaraderie of the precorporate, grassroots racing ethos of the late 1970s and early 1980s.

Back to the Future

Due, in part, to the growing bureaucracy and commercialization of international-level mountain bike racing, alternative racing forms that push the very limits of human performance have emerged. The events, including the Iditasport Extreme, a 300-mile mountain bike race across the frozen Alaskan tundra, and the La Ruta de Los Conquistadores, a three-day, 300-mile wilderness race in Costa Rica, as well as countless others, hint at a new direction for the sport. In addition to the growth of ultraendurance races, single-speed racing represents a clear backlash against the technology that has transformed the modern mountain bike. By using bikes that are fitted with only one gear, the growing group of single-speed racers can be seen riding in every discipline of mountain bike racing, from twenty-four-hour events, to cross country to downhill. Despite often utilizing high-tech frames and components, the single-speeders are paradoxically viewed as the "low-tech" extreme fringe of mountain bike racing—since their athletic accomplishments are attributed to mental and physical skills rather than the technology of the bicycles they ride.

Perhaps harkening back to its counterculture roots in northern California, mountain bike racing still attracts adrenaline junkies and tattooed and pierced young men and women. However owing, in part, to the popularization of the mountain bike, the sport now attracts equal numbers of highly disciplined elite athletes as well as families who enjoy spending their leisure time at race festivals hosted at favorite biking destinations worldwide.

Matthew A. Masucci

Further Reading

Berto, F. (1999). *The birth of dirt: Origins of mountain biking.* San Francisco: Van der Plas Publications.

Breeze, J. (1996, March). Who really invented the mountain bike? *Bicycling, 37,* 60–65.

Easom, S. (2003). Mountain biking madness. In R. Rinehart & S. Sydnor (Eds.), *To the extreme: Alternative sports, inside and out* (pp. 191–203). Albany: State University of New York Press.

Hughes, S., Case, H., Stuempfle, K., & Evans, D. (2003). Personality profiles of Iditasport Ultra-Marathon participants. *Journal of Applied Sport Psychology, 15*(3), 256–261.

Imhof, D. (Ed.). (1999). *Fat tire: A celebration of the mountain bike by Amici Design.* San Francisco: Chronicle Books.

Kelly, C., & Crane, N. (1988). *Richard's mountain bike book.* London: Richard's Bicycle Books Ltd.

Pridemore, J., & Hurd, J. (1995). *The American bicycle.* Osceola, WI: MBI Publishers.

Muldowney, Shirley

Imagine sitting behind the wheel of a finely tuned 2,500-horsepower nitromethane-burning top fuel dragster that accelerates from 0 to 100 miles per hour in less than a second, generates enough G forces to make you feel like an astronaut, and travels down a quarter strip of speedway at over 300 miles per hour? Shirley Muldowney (b. 1940), known as the "First Lady of Racing," not only imagined this but also lived it.

In a professional career that spanned thirty years, Muldowney won thirty-one national event races, three National Hot Rod Association (NHRA) titles, and an American Hot Rod Association (AHRA) championship. To put these accomplishments in perspective, "She was the first woman to race an NHRA top fuel dragster, the first woman to win the top fuel championship, and the first person of either sex to win it more than once" (Bechtel 2003, 28).

Muldowney's passion for racing developed in the 1950s while growing up in Schenectady, New York. At the age of fifteen, she was racing her 1951 blue Mercury hot rod on the streets and out of the sight of law enforcement. The racing fraternity was slow in offering her acceptance and energetic

in their efforts to discourage Muldowney from competing during her first few years as a driver. Muldowney's characteristic response to her detractors came in the form of her famous hot pink dragster and racing suit and her attitude. In a sport where drivers pride themselves on toughness and aggression, Muldowney more than held her own.

Despite the NHRA's initial reluctance to issue a license to a driver who would eventually be voted fifth among the top fifty greatest drivers in the history of the sport (Staff 2003, 46), she became a fixture on the circuit and a force to be reckoned with. During her career she progressed from Top Gas category to Funny Car to Top Fuel. In 1984, while racing at Sanair Speedway near Montreal, Muldowney hit a ditch at 250 miles per hour after one of her front tires failed. She sustained massive injuries, including a crushed pelvis, multiple fractures to her legs, and significant damage to her hands. When Muldowney returned to race again after six operations and eighteen months of rehabilitation, she redefined what constitutes a career-ending crash in drag racing. Where others would have retired, she went on to race for another sixteen years, registering the fastest time of her career just several months after her return.

Muldowney is one of the few drag racers to transcend the sport and achieve iconic status. She is the only drag racer to appear on the *Tonight Show* with legendary host, Johnny Carson. After her first NHRA title win, Muldowney was awarded an outstanding achievement award by the United States House of Representatives. And her rivalries with Big Daddy Don Garlits and former crew chief Connie Kalitta inspired the 1983 biographical movie *Heart Like a Wheel.*

Adding to the list of hall of fame honors bestowed on Muldowney, she was inducted into the International Motorsports Hall of Fame in 2004, becoming only the second woman to achieve that distinction. Muldowney continues to contribute to the sport to which she devoted her life. In 2005 she became the team and sponsor relations representative for driver Dave Grubnic and his team. She is also mentoring a new generation of women racers, working to support Hillary Will in her attempt to become just the sixteenth woman to compete in the NHRA Top Fuel category in a national event.

Ellen J. Staurowsky

Further Reading

Allen, K. (2000, May 25). Muldowney can't slow down: Racer remains as opinionated as ever as she nears 60. *USA Today,* 13C.

Andrews, N. (1984, June 8). Feminism fuels the drag: *Heart Like a Wheel. Financial Times (London),* Section I, The Arts, Cinema, p. 13.

Bechtel, M. (2003, November 3). The drag queen departs: A woman who whipped the good ol' boys retires—for her husband. *Sports Illustrated*, 99(17), 28.

Burgess, P. (2006, March 3). Five minutes with Hillary Will. *National Dragster*, 47(7), 28.

Lowe, J. (2005, July 7). Shirley Muldowney: Even in retirement the former drag racing champion can't keep herself out of the garage. *Sports Illustrated*, 146. Retrieved May 25, 206, from http://sportsillustrated.cnn.com/2005/magazine/where.muldowney0711/index.html

McDonald, N. (2003, November 22). A pioneering driver takes her last pass. *Toronto Star*, p. G02.

Muldowney, S., & Johnson, S. (2005). *Tales from the track*. Champaign, IL: Sports Publishing LLC.

Staff. (2003, December 12). Muldowney closes book on legendary career. *National Dragster*, 44(48), 46.

Staff. (2004, June 18). NHRA legend Muldowney inducted into International Motorsports Hall of Fame. *National Dragster*, 45 (21), 6.

Staff. (2005, February 11). Heeeere's Shirley. *National Dragster*, 46(4), 13.

Zeiger, D. (2006, February 25). Drag racing queens: Women have made more success in NHRA than in any other motorsports series. *The Tribune Business Series*, p. 1.

Mullen, Rodney

Rodney Mullen (b. 1966) is perhaps the world's most innovative and creative skateboarder. He was voted Skater of the Year in 2002 by *Transworld Skateboarding* magazine. Born into an athletic family in Gainsville, Florida, Mullen's early interest in sport was compromised by his being severely pigeon-toed. Mullen started skating at age ten, was sponsored by a local skateboard shop within a year, and at age thirteen won the first freestyle contest he entered. Soon after he turned professional when he joined the legendary Powell Peralta skateboard company and began a ten-year career as a professional freestyle skater, winning all but one event—in which he finished second.

Freestyle skating is done on flat ground with skaters stopping constantly to perform stationery tricks. Unlike street skating, there are no ramps, rails, or any other obstacles. Contests would usually incorporate two-minute runs choreographed to music.

By the early 1990s, freestyle skating's popularity was usurped by the emergence of street skating, and Mullen drew on his freestyle background to be in the vanguard of the street-skating revolution. Mullen developed many of the technical moves that revolutionized skateboarding including the Flatground Ollie, Casper 360 Flip, Caballerial impossible, and the Half-cab kickflip underflip. The ability to ollie on flatground—popping the board off of the ground and landing back on the board while moving—was the technique that laid the foundation for modern street skating.

In addition to his skating prowess, Mullen is also one of the skateboarding's foremost business leaders. In 1987 Mullen left Powell Peralta and skated for World Industries. At the same time Mullen invested in the company that would evolve into Kubic, the world's leading marketer of skate hardgoods that owned leading brands such as Darkstar, World Industries, Blind, and Tensor. In 2002 Australian-based Globe International purchased Kubic for $45.9 million. At the time of the purchase, it was estimated that Kubic accounted for an estimated 20 percent of world skate hardgoods sales, approximately twice as much as their nearest rival.

Mullen dominated freestyle skateboarding for over a decade and pioneered the development of street skating. These achievements combined with the success of his skateboarding businesses have made him one of the sport's most influential figures.

Geoff Dickson

Further Reading

Brooke, M. (1999). The concrete wave: The history of skateboarding. Toronto: Warwick Publishing.

Mullen, R., & Mortimer, S. (2004). The Mutt: How to skateboard and not kill yourself. New York: HarperCollins.

Noll, Greg

Greg Noll (b. 1937) is a legendary big wave rider who has worked as lifeguard, surfboard maker, surf-film cinematographer, professional surfer and fisherman. As a member of the U.S. lifeguard team who toured Australia in 1956, Noll introduced lightweight malibu surfboard technology to Australian surfers and in so doing helped precipitate the surfing craze "down under."

He was also a member of the first generation—which included José Angel, Peter Cole, Pat Curren, George Dowling, Ricky Grigg, and Buzzy Trent—to ride the now-famous big wave locations on the North Shore of Oahu, Hawaii. Noll quickly established his reputation as a big wave rider. However, his ride on a 7.6-meter (25–30 feet) wave at Makaha, Hawaii, on 4 December 1969—a feat immortalized by Ken Auster in his widely reproduced serigraph *Makaha 1969*—cemented Noll's status as a legend.

Noll grew up at Manhattan Beach, California, where he learned to surf in 1948 at age eleven. His first surfboard was solid redwood and weighed about 50 kilograms. He spent the entire first summer trying to catch a wave. While still a schoolboy, Noll began regularly visiting Hawaii. In 1954 he temporarily moved to the islands, where he lived in a Quonset hut at Makaha, spending most of his time surfing, diving, and fishing. Returning to the mainland, he left school and shaped surfboards while working part-time as a lifeguard. Initially operating out of a garage, Noll's business grew quickly, and he opened a small shop at Manhattan Beach. He later moved to a larger shop at Hermosa Beach before building a combined surfboard factory and shop at Hermosa in 1965. Intense competition forced the factory to close in 1971.

Noll has provided a graphic account of his experience at Makaha in 1969 when he paddled into, took off, rode, and then wiped out on the 7.6-meter wave. It is a testimony to his courage.

Finally a set came thundering down...I caught a glimpse of my wave. I turned and began paddling, hard. I felt a rush of adrenalin as the wave approached, lifted me and my board began to accelerate. Then I was on my feet, committed. You could have stacked two eighteen-wheel semis on top of each other against the face of that wave and still have had room left over to ride it....my board began to howl like a goddamn jet...I flew down the face, past the lip of the wave, and when I got to the bottom...I looked ahead and saw the sonofabitch starting to break in a section that stretched a block and a half in front of me. The wave threw out a sheet of water over my head and engulfed me. My board flew out from under me. I hit the water going so fast that it was like hitting concrete...tons of white water exploded over me. It pounded me under. It thrashed and rolled me beneath the surface until my lungs burned and there was so much pressure that I felt my eardrums were going to burst ...the white water finally began to dissipate and the turbulence released me. I made it to the surface, gulped for air and quickly looked outside. There was another monster heading my way. (Noll and Gabbard 1989, 7–8)

A sense of letdown overwhelmed Noll after his exploit, and shortly afterward he ceased going to Hawaii. The period coincided with the death of his stepfather, Ash, and mounting economic pressures and the abandonment of his surf factory. He sold the shop and returned briefly to working as a lifeguard. He then departed for Alaska, where he became a commercial fisherman for the next decade and a half.

I just wanted to find some place quiet where I could enjoy my family, play with the kids, swim in the ocean and do some hunting and fishing. All the other stuff [the factory and shop] was a means of playing the game, playing along to make money, to get ahead, to do whatever it is society tells you to do to succeed. I finally decided, piss on that. It wasn't worth the pretense. Time to get back to the adage, "if it feels good, do it." (Noll and Gabbard 1989, 175)

More recently Noll has returned to the surfing scene—shaping reproductions of original Hawaiian surfboards. He is a lauded elder of the surfing community, one of the early modern riders to venture into, and survive, the extreme.

Douglas Booth

Further Reading

Kampion, D. (1997). *Stoked: A history of surf culture.* Los Angeles: General Publishing.

Noll, G., & Gabbard, A. (1989). *Da Bull: Life over the edge.* Berkeley, CA: North Atlantic Books.

Nyquist, Ryan

As a twelve-year-old trying to keep up with his brother and friends, Ryan Nyquist (b. 1979) started riding a BMX (bicycle motocross) bike over dirt trails and on the street in 1991 in Los Gatos, California. Four years later Nyquist turned professional and began competing regularly on the BMX riding circuit. Nyquist is described on one BMX website as "one of the leaders of the new school" of riding.

Some of the tricks Nyquist is known for performing are the suicide no-hander, the 720-degree lookback, and the 360-degree flip over a spine. He prefers competing in dirt jumping, park (street), and vert contests to specializing in one of these disciplines. At the 1999 X Games Nyquist was the only rider to place in the top ten of the vert, park, and dirt jumping competitions.

Nyquist has won medals eight times in X Games competition. From 2001 to 2004 he won the Vans Triple Crown Dirt Competition eleven straight times. He is also the only BMX rider to win gold medals in both the dirt jumping and park events during the same X Games (2003). In fact, the 2003 season proved to be, by far, Nyquist's most successful as a professional as he won every contest he entered except one—the Gravity Games park event, where he settled for second place. In recognition of his 2003 season, he was awarded the 2004 ESPY Award for Best Action Sport Athlete.

Nyquist has been sponsored by a number of companies, such as Haro bikes, Oakley sunglasses, Butterfinger candy, T-Mobile cellular phones, and Napster software. Another of his sponsors, Adidas, created a signature series shoe with Nyquist's name on it.

However, unlike other BMX riders who quickly turn themselves into a brand so they can profit from their talents, Nyquist has chosen not to market himself as aggressively, choosing instead to focus his energies on his riding and remaining true to the reason he says he began riding BMX bikes in the first place—to enjoy the camaraderie of his friends. Nonetheless, a likeness of Nyquist does appear in the video game Dave Mirra Freestyle BMX of riding icon Dave Mirra. And like many BMX riders, Ryan is featured in a number of BMX videos, which circulate underground within communities of BMX riders across the globe. Most notably, Nyquist is featured in the film *Miracle Boy & Nyquist*, in which he appears with his friend Mirra.

Kyle Kusz

Further Reading

Ryan Nyquist. (n.d.). Retrieved February 11, 2007, from http://expn.go.com/athletes/bios/NYQUIST_RYAN.html

Ryan Nyquist Fan Site. (n.d.). Retrieved February 11, 2007, from http://www.skatelog.com/bmx/ryan-nyquist.htm

Split Team Riders: Ryan Nyquist. (n.d.). Retrieved February 11, 2007, from http://www.splitusa.com/riders/nyquist.html

Open Water Swimming

Swimming 80 kilometers and more in the open waters of lakes, rivers, and oceans, wearing only a light costume, cap, and goggles, tests endurance and physical and mental toughness. The best-known feats of open water swimming take place in particularly cold or treacherous bodies of water—sometimes both. Hallmark open water swims include Alcatraz Island (San Francisco Bay), Bering Strait (between Asia and North America), Cape Agulhas (most southern point of Africa), Cook Strait (between the North and South Islands of New Zealand), English Channel (between England and France), Foveaux Strait (between the South and Stewart Islands of New Zealand), Gibraltar Straits (between Spain and Morocco), Gulf of Aqaba (Middle East), the Kattegut (between Norway and Sweden), Manhattan Island (New York), the Oresund (between Denmark and Sweden), Robben Island (Cape Town, South Africa), and Strait of Magellan (between Tierra del Fuego and mainland South America).

In addition to environmental extremes (e.g., freezing temperatures, rough water, tides, currents, gale-force winds, hail, fog), open water swimmers can face a range of hazards, including creatures of various kinds (e.g., jellyfish, sea snakes, sharks, polar bears), ships and other motorized craft, floating and submerged debris, and sewage and other forms of toxic and disease-bearing pollution. The water temperature was 0°C when Lewis Pugh—who holds records for swimming at the northernmost and southernmost latitudes—swam one kilometer at Petermann Island off the Antarctic Peninsula at 65 degrees south in December 2005. Pugh called it his hardest swim in cold water; several months earlier he had swum one kilometer in 3°C water at 80 degrees north on the most northern point of Spitsbergen (Svalbard Archipelago) in the Arctic Ocean. "The difference between swimming in 0°C water in the Antarctic and 3°C in the Arctic," Pugh said, "was the difference between night and day. As soon as I dived in, I had a screaming pain all over my body. After three minutes, I'd lost all feeling in my hands and feet. And after six minutes I lost all feeling throughout my arms and legs" (Extreme 365, 2005).

Shelley Taylor-Smith completed her record-breaking swim around Manhattan Island in 1985 immediately after heavy rain, and the water was "crowded with litter and debris" and "all manner of human and animal waste" (Taylor-Smith 1996, 65). When she left the water, more than six hours later, her body was "stinging from collisions with debris." However, the situation got worse. Only after Taylor-Smith removed her bathers (swimming costume) hours later did she realize that her "neck was raw from all the banging against stray planks and suchlike. I looked like I'd been strangled. Worst of all, I found a noodle in my belly button! It grossed me out. All I could think of was, 'who ate this noodle?'" (Taylor-Smith 1996, 70). Unfortunately for Taylor-Smith the headline in one newspaper—"Queen of the Sewers"—proved prophetic: She was soon stricken with dysentery.

In addition to absorbing heavy repetitive strain, the shoulders of open water swimmers sometimes confront the forces of nature. Pulled from the English Channel suffering from dehydration and hypothermia after eight hours, Ned Denison likened the experience of the prevailing waves pounding his left shoulder to "hitting a heavy bag 16,000 times" (Denison 2006). Nor is nature the only obstacle. Des Renford abandoned one attempted crossing of the English Channel after his escort boat plowed into him and dislocated his shoulder.

Asked why they swim in open water, participants often refer to hydrophilia (love of water). Lynne Cox, who swam the English Channel at age fifteen in a record-shattering 9 hours, 36 minutes and who is the first person to swim the Bering Strait, "always loved the sound, feeling, smell, look and taste of water" (Dellinger 2003). "I think," she says, "it has to do with growing up on the East Coast. My parents, my brother, and my sisters and I were always swimming in either sweet open-water ponds or in the Atlantic Ocean" (Dellinger 2003). English adventure swimmer Roger Deakin describes the feeling of "absolute freedom" in natural water; he attributes this sensation to the "boldness that comes with the sheer liberation of nakedness as well as weightlessness" (Deakin 2000, 79). Indeed, the motto of the British Long Distance Swimming Association captures the notion of freedom in open water swimming: "no roof, no walls, no chlorine, no lane ropes, no lines on the bottom, no tumble turns! Just all the natural elements—sunshine, blue sky, clouds, wind, rain, sometimes all at the same time!" (Channel Swimming Association, n.d.). Nonetheless, nothing is innate about open water swimming. On the contrary, it is a sport with its own social history, one closely intertwined with the histories of the sea and the beach as sites of leisure as well as ideas about cold water, health, and the body.

History

Western culture has variously embraced, rebuffed, and rediscovered the idea of bathing in cold water. According to Alain Corbin, the ancient Greeks were the first Westerners to invent the sea as a site of recreation. Prior to them, the sea, "that watery monsters' den, was a damned world in whose darkness accursed creatures devoured one another" (Corbin 1994, 7). "The grey winter ocean, dismal and cold," was a prime source of untoward fears: "it fosters the haunting dread of being caught by sudden death and deprived of extreme unction, far from the home fires" and "of being delivered, body and soul, unburied, to these endless waves that know no rest" (Corbin 1994, 13). The Romans developed a passion for the beach. Seaside pursuits became the lifeblood of civilized pleasures, and, from the end of the republic until the middle of the second century, resorts thrived along the shores of Latium and Campania as both the masses and the upper classes fled each summer from overcrowded, sultry, and putrid Rome. Neither the sea nor the beach survived the collapse of the Roman Empire, and for a thousand years, write Lena Lenček and Gideon Bosker (1998), "a mantle of dread and prohibition" shrouded "the body, the beach and even pleasure."

Apocalyptic and ascetic Christian doctrines disavowed the hedonistic practices and hygienic codes of behavior that characterized the Greek and Roman leisure at the seaside. Notions of abyss in the Old Testament promulgated a "disquieting perspective of the sea," while Christian spirituality "denigrated the value of the body" and "looked askance" at institutions and practices that indulged pleasures of the flesh. "Except during strictly limited periods of permissiveness," (Lenček and Bosker 1998, 38) notably carnivals and a few scattered holidays, Christianity largely denied the needs of the body. Plagues that rampaged across Europe in the fourteenth century caused the "moral and hygienic prestige" of water to plummet still further. Medical theory, consistent with prevailing Christian theology, blamed pestilence on exposure to infected air and water that penetrated the pores and disrupted the equilibrium of the organs. Even in the sixteenth century, said George Ryley Scott, "bathing as a hygienic protocol was quite unthinkable. Cleanliness manifested in clothing not the body. Quite contrary to the classical paradigm, water was thought to enfeeble" (Scott 1939, 70).

Spurred on by medical practitioners "touting the miraculous healing properties of cold water," bathing slowly returned to fashion at the end of the sixteenth century, observe Lenček and Bosker (1998, 74). A century later Sir John Floyer, author of the *History of Cold Bathing* (1701–1702), "recommended the cold bath for nearly every malady in the medical dictionary" (Lenček and Bosker 1998, 38). Whereas previous medical theory deemed the "permeable body ill-equipped to defend" itself against immersion, Floyer discovered that the human physiology thrives in cold water:

> Cold baths cause a sense of chillness, and that, as well as the Terror and Surprise, very much contracts the Nervous membrane and tubes, in which the aerial spirits are contained, and they being kept tense and compressed, do most easily communicate, all external expressions to the Sensitive soul. Not only the external senses are more lively in cold water, but all our animal actions and reasoning's [*sic*] are then more vigorous by the external compressure of cold air. (Scott 1939, 70)

Scores of authorities, among them Dr. Joseph Browne, Dr. William Buchan, Sir Arthur Clarke, Dr. Richard Kentish, and John Wesley (the founder of Methodism), followed Floyer in singing the high praises of cold water bathing. In 1764 Dr. E. Baynard captured what, by then, had become a new orthodoxy in a poem entitled "Health":

> Of exercises, swimming's best,
> Strengthens the muscles and the chest,
> And all their fleshy parts confirms.
>
> Extends, and stretches legs and arms,
> And, with a nimble retro-spring,
> Contracts, and brings them back again.
>
> As 'tis the best, so 'tis the sum
> Of exercises all in one,
> And of all motions most compleat,
> Because 'tis vi'lent without heat.
> (Sinclair and Henry 1912, 18–19)

In their history of swimming, published in the early twentieth century, Archibald Sinclair and William Henry comment that "cold-water bathing has so often been strongly recommended by the medical profession that it requires no defense of ours" (Sinclair and Henry 1912, 153). According to these two founders of the Royal Life Saving Society, "there are many men who bathe all year round, even when their favorite water is ice-bound, and by habitual practice they have come to enjoy their morning dip so greatly and to reap such

A woman swimming in the open sea. Source: istock.

benefits from it that they would rather miss their breakfast than their bath" (Sinclair and Henry 1912, 153).

Against this background it is hardly surprising that cold-water bathers would seek physical tests of endurance, the most obvious being the 33-kilometer-wide channel between England and France. History records Mathew Webb as the first person to swim the English Channel, a feat he completed in 1875 on his second attempt. Webb learned to swim in the Severn River (Shropshire); in 1863 he saved his younger brother Thomas from drowning in that river. Webb served as an apprentice seaman for three years and became a national hero when, as a second mate, he jumped overboard in the middle of the Atlantic to save a fellow seaman. In 1874 he left the sea to become a professional endurance swimmer. Webb's channel crossing, between Dover and Calais, took 21 hours, 45 minutes; his seconds calculated that with currents and tides he swam 62 kilometers. (Webb died in 1883 while trying to swim the rapids of Niagara Falls.)

The first woman, and only the sixth person, to swim the English Channel was Gertrude Ederle, who had won gold and bronze medals in swimming events at the 1924 Olympic Games. Unlike previous swimmers she used the freestyle stroke. Ederle completed the crossing on her second attempt in 1926; she wore a revolutionary two-piece bathing suit and personally designed wraparound goggles kept watertight with molten candle wax. Her time of 14 hours, 31 minutes

smashed the record of 16 hours, 23 minutes set three years earlier by Sebastian Tirabocchi. Experts calculated that Ederle had swum 56 kilometers. Upon her return home to New York City more than two million people greeted the nineteen-year-old in a ticker-tape parade. Ederle's record stood until 1950, when Florence Chadwick completed the crossing in 13 hours, 20 minutes.

In response to a series of bogus claims to have swum the English Channel, a group of devotees formed the Channel Swimming Association (CSA) in 1927. The CSA authenticates claims of having swum the channel and verifies their times. According to CSA records, by the end of 2005, 665 people had made 982 successful crossings, including twenty-four double crossings and three triple crossings. The CSA's most prestigious awards are "King of the Channel" and "Queen of the Channel." Michael Read holds the former title with thirty-three crossings, and Alison Streeter holds the latter with forty-three crossings (including seven in one year, 1992).

The quest for titles has fired some noteworthy rivalries. The competition between Des Renford and Kevin Murphy for "King of the Channel" in the late 1970s was particularly intense and culminated in a challenge comprising three races. Murphy won the first, more than 16 kilometers, in Sydney Harbor. Renford took the honors in the second race across the English Channel. Neither swimmer completed the third race in the freezing waters of Loch Ness in Scotland. Although Murphy swam for two and one-half hours longer than Renford—who was pulled unconscious from the water after six and one-half hours and placed in intensive care—the two men agreed to an honorable draw.

As the references to Ederle, Chadwick, and Streeter indicate, women often perform better than men in open water swimming, much to the chagrin of some males. Between 1984 and 1995 Shelly Taylor-Smith defeated both men and women competitors in eight of the forty-five major events she entered (as well as being the first woman home on thirty-five occasions). Although Taylor-Smith says most men accepted her victories, she adds that "it wasn't all sweetness and light" (Taylor-Smith 1996, 112). Indeed, one jolted male swimmer told Taylor-Smith to "take a hike" and added a "far-from-complimentary forearm salute complete with clenched fist" (Taylor-Smith 1996, 124) after she beat him for a second time in consecutive races. The International Marathon Swimming Federation separated men and women in the official rankings a few months after this incident. The history of gender discrimination in sports lends weight to Taylor-Smith's speculation that the decision was "probably not entirely coincidental" (Taylor-Smith 1996, 124).

The geography of open water also makes the sport ripe for political statements. In this regard open water swimmer Lynne Cox has proved especially adroit. By swimming the Bering Strait from Little Diomede Island (Alaska) to Big Diomede Island (Soviet Union) in 1987, during the Cold War, Cox effectively opened a border that had been closed for forty-eight years. Four months later, during his meeting with President Reagan at the White House to sign the INF Missile Treaty, President Gorbachev proposed a toast in which he said:

> last summer it took one brave American by the name of Lynne Cox just two hours to swim from one of our countries to the other. We saw on television how sincere and friendly the meeting was between our people and the Americans when she stepped onto the Soviet shore. She proved by her courage how close to each other our peoples live. (Cox, 2004a)

In 1990 Cox swam the Beagle Channel between Argentina and Chile to promote cooperation between the two countries and later that year swam across the Spree River between the newly united German republics. Then in 1994 Cox swam through the Gulf of Aqaba from Egypt to Israel and from Israel to Jordan, tracing the progress of peace between the three countries. According to Cox,

> Egyptian, Israeli, and Jordanian officials supported the swim. The Jordanians opened the border between Israel and Jordan for the first time in 48 years

---

A Brisk Swim

What drives a swimmer to swim in the freezing water around the South Pole? Apparently world records have something to do with it.

British Swimmer Breaks Two World Records in Antarctica Swim

On the anniversary of Norwegian explorer Roald Amundsen reaching the South Pole, British swimmer Lewis Gordon Pugh has plunged into the icy waters off the Antarctic Peninsula to smash the world record for the most southern long distance swim ever undertaken. Wearing only Speedo trunks, goggles and a swimming cap, Lewis swam 1 kilometre (0.6 Miles) in 0°C (32°F) water.

Pugh, who has pioneered more swims around famous landmarks than any other swimmer in history (including a swim near the North Pole in August this year) is now the first person to have completed a long distance swim in both the Arctic and Antarctic. After the swim he admitted that the Antarctic waters were the most formidable. He said, "As soon as I dived in, I had a screaming pain all over my body. After three minutes, I'd lost all feeling in my hands and feet. And after six minutes I lost all feeling throughout my arms and legs. I am not sure how I kept on going for so long. I had to concentrate all the time and swim as fast as I could to keep the cold out."

Source: British swimmer breaks two world records in Antarctica swim. (n.d.). Retrieved February 1, 2007, from http://swimming. about.com/od/openwaterswims/a/pughantarticasw.htm

and let me swim to Jordan along with my American and Israeli crew. Afterward, Queen Noor had a wonderful reception for us in Aqaba, and I was invited to the treaty signing between Israel and Jordan a few days later. It was an incredible honor. (Dellinger, 2003)

Environmental activist Christopher Swain is another who has used open water swimming to make a political statement. He swam the entire 128 kilometers of the Charles River, from Hopkinton to Boston, to raise awareness about pollution in the waterway. One must avoid shopping carts, bicycles, and refrigerators at "pretty much every bridge" along the river, says Swain, "not to mention the glass, pesticides and raw sewage from storm drain runoffs" (Swimming with Sewage 2004).

Codification of Open Water Swimming

During the last decade open water swimming has developed into a popular sport with mass events in North and South America, Asia, Australasia, and Europe. Open water swimming enthusiasts in Australia, for example, staged sixty-eight events in New South Wales and eighteen in Victoria in the summer of 2005–2006. The sport particularly attracts aging baby boomers, to whom it offers the opportunity to extend their active and sporting lives. Fifty-three-year-old David Helsham talks about the "wonderful" activity that, unlike jogging, is easy on the joints; fifty-six-year-old Denise Elder took up open water swimming after retiring from netball when her hips started to hurt. The Cole Classic in Sydney, which began in 1983 and is one of the oldest open water swimming events in Australia, illustrates the rising popularity of the sport and its shifting demographic. Initially the 2-kilometer swim (staged at Bondi Beach before organizers shifted it to Manly Beach in 2005) attracted mainly elite swimmers and the iron men and iron women of surf life saving. In the late 1990s the numbers swelled, and of the 1,656 swimmers in the 2006 Cole Classic, 751 (just over 45 percent) were aged forty or older.

Anecdotal evidence suggests that open water swimming embraces something other than modernist pool swimming. As former Olympic gold medalist Shane Gould explains, "People don't like the mechanics of pool training, the structure of it. They want to be confronted by nature and challenged by it. There's the running on the sand, the elbowing out through the waves, around the buoys, the charge back in. It puts a little excitement into your life" (McDonald 2006). Such accounts add weight to David Le Breton's concept of extreme sports as symbolic play in late modernity. Le Breton argues that in contemporary society "reference points are both countless and contradictory" while "values are in crisis" and that "people are seeking, through a radical one-to-one contest, to test their strength of character, their courage and their personal resources" (Le Breton 2000, 1). Denise Elder agrees. "I was hesitant when I started" open water swimming, she recalls. "I was on the shore wetting myself but there was a guy next to me and he spoke about being scared too and there was a woman on my other side and it was her first ocean swim. So I thought 'we're all nervous, let's go'" (McDonald 2006). Le Breton believes that physicality is replacing the moral boundaries that have dissipated in late modernity and that "paradoxically, the more intense the suffering, the more the achievement has a reassuring personal significance, the more fulfilling the satisfaction of having resisted the temptation to give up" (Le Breton 2000, 1)

Yet, despite these late modern tendencies, it is not surprising, given its rapidly growing popularity, that swimming's governing bodies, including the Fédération Internationale de Natation (FINA), have appropriated open water swimming and codified it as a sport. Under FINA rules a long-distance swim is one up to 10 kilometers long, and a marathon swim is one more than 10 kilometers long. The FINA-sanctioned 2006 Marathon Swimming World Cup included five events in South America, seven in Europe and Africa, four in Asia, and three in North and Central America. Most events on the circuit are 10 kilometers, but they range up to 88 kilometers (Hernandarias-Parana, Argentina). Minimum prize money is $10,000, with a maximum of $40,000 (Lac St-Jean, Roberval, Canada). Following a recommendation by FINA the International Olympic Committee approved the addition of 10-kilometer open water swimming events for both men and women to the program for the Beijing Olympic Games in 2008.

Yet, although the codification of open water swimming and its inclusion in the Olympics will undoubtedly reduce some of the extreme physical elements traditionally associated with the sport, no doubt for many participants it will continue to symbolize a form of adventure in the wild.

Douglas Booth

Further Reading

Channel Swimming Association. (n.d.). Retrieved October 7, 2006, from http://www.channelswimmingassociation.com/

Cleveland, M. (2006). Gertrude Ederle. Dover Solo. Retrieved October 7, 2006, from http://www.doversolo.com/gertrudeederle.htm

Cole Classic Swim. (n.d.). Retrieved October 7, 2006, from http://www.coleclassic.com/

Corbin, A. (1994). *The lure of the sea.* Berkeley and Los Angeles: University of California Press.

Cox, L. (2004a). Interview. Harcourt Trade Publishers. Retrieved October 7, 2006, from http://www.harcourtbooks.com/authorinterviews/bookinterview_Cox.asp

Cox, L. (2004b). *Swimming to Antarctica.* New York: Knopf.

Deakin, R. (2000). *Waterlog: A swimmer's journey through Britain.* London: Vintage.

Dean, P. (1998). *Open water swimming.* Champaign, IL: Human Kinetics.

Dellinger, M. (2003). Swimming with the penguins. *The New Yorker Online.* Retrieved October 7, 2006, from http://www.newyorker.com/online/content/articles/030203on_onlineonly01

Denison, N. (2006). Ned Denison swims the English Channel. Retrieved October 7, 2006, from http://swimming.about.com/od/openwaterswims/a/channelswim_2.htm

Dover Museum. (2004). Swimming the English Channel. Retrieved October 7, 2006, from http://swimming.about.com/gi/dynamic/offsite.htm?site=http://www.dover.gov.uk/museum/resource/swim/swim1.asp

Extreme 365. (2005). Briton sets Antarctic record. Retrieved October 7, 2006, from http://www.extremesports365.com/news/story_75195.shtml

Fédération Internationale de Natation (FINA). (n.d.). Retrieved October 7, 2006, from http://www.fina.org/

Heaphy, L. (2001). Gertrude Ederle. In K. Christensen, A. Guttmann, & G. Pfister (Eds.), *International encyclopedia of women and sports* (pp. 358–360). New York: Macmillan Reference.

Le Breton, D. (2000). Playing symbolically with death in extreme sports. *Body & Society, 6*(1), 1–11.

Lenček, L., & Bosker, G. (1998). *The beach: The history of paradise on Earth.* New York: Viking.

Martin, D. (2000, February 2). Des Renford, 72, Channel swimmer is dead. *New York Times,* C30.

McDonald, M. (2006). Swim for your life. *The Australian.* Retrieved October 7, 2006, from http://www.theaustralian.news.com.au/printpage/0,5942,17721602,00.html

Ocean Swims. (n.d.). Retrieved October 7, 2006, from http://www.oceanswims.com

Scott, G. R. (1939). *The story of baths and bathing.* London: T. Werner Laurie.

Sinclair, A., & Henry, W. (1912). *Swimming.* London: Longmans Green.

Smith, A. (2000, December 8). Swimming: A feeling for water. Radio National, Australia. Retrieved October 7, 2006, from http://www.ausport.gov.au/fulltext/2000/sportsf/s221227.htm

Sprawson, C. (1993). *Haunts of the black masseur: The swimmer as hero.* London: Random House.

Swimming with sewage. (2004, Nov. 12). Retrieved October 7, 2006, from http://www.greaterboston.tv/features/gb_20041112_swimmer.html

Taylor-Smith, S. (1996). *Dangerous when wet: The Shelly Taylor-Smith story.* Sydney, Australia: Allen & Unwin.

Tomlinson, J. (2004). *Extreme sports.* London: Carlton Books.

USA Swimming. (2006). USA Swimming names open water national teams. Retrieved October 7, 2006, from http://www.usaswimming.org/USASWeb/ViewNewsArticle.aspx?TabId=0&Alias=Rainbow&Lang=en&ItemId=1124&mid=2713

Outrigger Canoe Racing

In outrigger canoe racing participants face the changeable conditions of the open sea and the constant risk of dehydration and fatigue. Marathon distances (more than 42 kilometers for crews of paddlers and more than 35 kilometers for solo paddlers) make such races the ultimate paddling challenge. Races include the Hawaiki Nui Va'a in Tahiti (three marathons raced over consecutive days between islands), the Super Aito solo canoe race in Tahiti (35 kilometers of rudderless racing between islands), and the Ouv'ea-to-Poindimie' race in New Caledonia (the longest one-day race, involving more than 140 kilometers of paddling across open ocean).

As knowledge and experience are growing in paddling communities, hundreds of competitors annually are completing races that might previously have been considered extreme. For example, the oldest Hawaiian race, the annual Bangkoh Moloka'i Hoe (66 kilometers), involves more than six hundred male paddlers and more than four hundred female paddlers. Nonetheless, ocean conditions and distance make this race an extreme challenge. Outrigger canoeing is not a mainstream sport; international media coverage and prize money are limited; no internationally sanctioned ranking system exists. Describing one paddler on day three of the Hawaiki Nui Va'a race, sports psychologist Jo Lukins commented:

> Just 30 minutes out from finishing the Tahaa–Bora Bora 60km stretch, he's super dehydrated and at boiling point and not far off shutting down. Back on the beach he is carried out and put in the medic tent where they recorded a body temperature of 41.7 degrees—3.5lt's of saline later he was near good enough to party. What did it take for him to continue to paddle? (Lukins 2000, 114)

Participants most often say they paddle for personal enjoyment. *Mana* (prestige, respect from others, and personal pride) and the opportunity to embody the voyaging spirit of canoe cultures past also motivate paddlers to undertake extreme races.

Voyaging and Canoe Culture

Historically outrigger canoes were common in many cultures around the world. Outrigger and sailing canoes were an integral part of the life of the ancestors of Southeast Asian, Melanesian, and Polynesian peoples. Sophisticated seafaring skills and navigation by the stars allowed people to migrate across the Pacific Ocean as far as Hawaii; Rapa Nui, Easter Island; and Aotearoa, New Zealand. In contemporary times people of many cultures participate in outrigger canoeing. However, the sport has found greatest expression in Polynesian peoples, particularly the Hawaiian, Tahitian, and Mäori peoples. In a sense marathon outrigger canoeing can be viewed as the contemporary manifestation of a voyaging heritage. Marathon open ocean races enable paddlers to reenact island-to-island journeys, facing personal risks and earning them the respect and admiration of their communities. According to *Kanu Culture* writer Steve West:

> Outrigger canoe racing has created a catalyst by which CANOE CULTURES of Oceania can focus the re-awakening of a cultural identity and pride. For them it is an activity of great significance. A fundamental part of an ancient culture commanding respect, custom, ritual and remembrance, serving to keep the legend of the outrigger canoe and its people alive.
>
> For those of us who find ourselves involved with outrigger canoe racing, whose cultural origins are not of a CANOE CULTURE, realize that this simple craft is considered the greatest vehicle in the history of humankind. Take time to understand more fully why this is, and your participation will take on new meaning. (West 1995, 3)

Outrigger canoe racing began as a serious sport in 1910 with competition between the Outrigger Canoe Club of Hawaii and the Hui Nalu Surfing Club. The first Hawaiian regatta was established in 1922, and formal rules and regulations were devised in 1940. Outrigger canoeing (*waʻa*) is the unofficial national sport in Hawaii, the official national sport of Tahiti, and is a fast growing sport in Aotearoa, New Zealand. Outrigger canoe clubs exist throughout Melane-

sia, Micronesia, and Polynesia, as well as in Australia, Hong Kong, Canada, California, Oregon, Washington State, New York, South Africa, Britain, France, Italy, Hungry, Austria, and Sweden. In addition to the most extreme marathon races, sprint (500 and 1,500 meters) and medium-distance (5–30 kilometers) races are held in rivers, lakes, lagoons, and open ocean. All races involve similar outrigger canoes.

Ancient Technology in the Twenty-first Century

The outrigger canoe utilizes ancient technology that survives today as testimony to the vision and sophistication of the canoe cultures. The outrigger canoe consists of a long hull (*kaʻle*) and a parallel float or pontoon (*ama*). Two or more spars (*iako*) are lashed by means of rope or rubber ties from thwarts (*wae waʻa*) on the hull gunnels and extend sideways to the float. The center of the hull of the canoe is designed to remain in the water, with the float providing stability on the left side. Flexibility in the construction and lashing of the spars allows the rig to withstand the torsion of waves and swells. With this rigging arrangement, the canoe has greater stability in swells and surf than a single-hulled canoe and can be paddled with single-blade paddles.

Traditionally canoe hulls were made from wood. Canoe builders used various materials to construct their hulls, including hollowed logs (dugout canoe), stitched wooden planks, or a combination of both. The wooden Hawaiian Koa canoe provided the template for the contemporary outrigger canoe, which is now typically made of Fiberglas. Six-person racing canoes measure approximately 13 meters in length. Two-person and solo canoes are also raced, and surfing canoes can seat four paddlers. Solo canoes vary in design and length, depending on the water conditions in which they are used. Canoes used in extreme events are designed and rigged carefully to both maximize speed and maintain stability in surf. Approaching a challenging reef pass, for example, not only the canoe, but also the paddler's confidence must withstand the challenge, as this excerpt reveals:

> Menacingly, a vertical wall rears its head... Hardcore racing leads to taking risks—the steerer constantly narrowing the angles, looking for that extra inch. It's at times like this you'll need to paddle your heart out—if fear overcomes you and you back off, consumed about the possibilities your mind

has created, you endanger yourself bringing those imaginings closer to reality. Paddle hard and survive, push through it and rise to the occasion! (West 2000, 177)

Confidence is crucial for paddlers facing extreme challenges.

Accepting the Challenges: Outrigger Canoe Paddlers

Facing the open ocean in a crew of six (or solo), outrigger canoe paddlers all share fitness, skill mastery, and a reasonable degree of personal confidence. Beyond these traits, though, paddlers who undertake extreme marathon races come from many cultures, are both male and female, and represent most adult age cohorts. Although paddlers most commonly participate in the sport for personal enjoyment, they also paddle to improve cardiovascular fitness and to release stress. The hours of training required simply to consider entering any marathon are many and must include preparation to paddle using explosive energy (when catching swells) and to paddle consistently over a long distance. Competitors usually cross-train, running, biking, or surfing, to complement their water training in the canoe. Strength training in gymnasiums is also common because most paddlers appreciate that enhancing their power-to-weight ratio is an effective way to improve performance. Being a repetitive action, paddling has the tendency to result in tendon injuries, muscle strains, or rotator cuff and lower spinal disc injuries. Paddlers also suffer from headaches, cramps, and dehydration in marathon races, making drinking water during racing crucial to survival.

A son helping his father launch his outrigger canoe to go fishing off the reef in Polynesia. Source: istock/Chris Burk.

Fortunately, deaths in extreme races occur rarely, in part because formal events provide medics and require support boats and in part because careful preparation and enthusiasm for life seem to go hand-in-hand with paddling. Paddling often becomes a lifestyle, with hours training on the water complemented by a desire to participate in cultural heritage. For this reason paddlers often speak indigenous languages, participate in cultural ceremonies, and learn about the design, crafting, rigging, and repair of canoes and paddles.

Have Paddle, Will Travel

Participation is key for outrigger paddlers; thus, owning a paddle, or a collection, is essential. Paddles were traditionally handcrafted of wood, but many types of wooden and composite paddles exist now. Paddles have a single blade offset from the shaft at an angle between three and fifteen degrees. The paddle shaft may be straight or curved or have a double curve. It ends in a T-shaped grip. A steerer's paddle, however, typically has a straight shaft with a dihedral shaping around the neck of the blade and a stronger construction. Blade size and paddle length vary, depending on the paddler's height, personal preference, and the paddling conditions. Paddle choice will also vary, depending on the type of paddling being undertaken. In a six-person canoe paddlers typically use similar paddle designs and sizes.

Paddling the Canoe Together

One of the distinctive aspects of outrigger canoeing is the need for crew members to paddle together. Each paddler is responsible for working with the others to move the canoe efficiently and quickly through the water. People use many paddling techniques, but efficiency over long distances is crucial to completing a marathon event and to avoiding injury. In general, "to pull rather than push the canoe through the water, reach forward as far as you can . . . at the beginning of the stroke and end the stroke just before your lower hand reaches your hip" (Ocean River Sports 2006). In a six-person canoe paddlers sit one behind the other and paddle on alternate sides of the hull. The crew members generally paddle in unison for sets of nine to fifteen strokes before changing sides. The stroke rate is typically sixty-five strokes per minute and increases up to seventy-five strokes per minute when running with swells.

Efficiency in paddling technique and synchronization is especially important over marathon distances. Each paddler also has some unique responsibilities to ensure that the canoe is stable and moves smoothly through the water. The first paddler, or stroke, will set the stroke rate and length for the crew to follow. Strokes need to remain focused, have good aerobic fitness, and be able to understand water conditions in order to vary the stroke rate as necessary. In races involving turns around markers, strokes must also help turn the front of the canoe. The second paddler must have excellent timing and good fitness because he or she must mirror the stroke. The third and fourth seats usually contain the heavier and more powerful paddlers. The third paddler calls "hut" or "hoe" to initiate the change from one side of the canoe to the other. The fourth paddler may be required to bail any water pooling in the canoe. The fifth paddler, also a power paddler, may help bail and should have some steering knowledge to assist the steerer if required. Additionally, the fifth paddler maintains careful watch over the float and canoe stability.

The steerer, often the captain of a six-person canoe, is responsible for navigation and carries the greatest responsibility for crew and canoe safety. Steerers may paddle with the crew, but their overall focus is to maintain the canoe's course. They slide their paddle alongside the hull, allowing the blade to function as a rudder or keel. An efficient steerer helps the canoe to run with swells, responds to currents and wind, and changes direction without unnecessarily reducing canoe speed. The steerer's level of ocean knowledge and skill mastery affect the performance of the crew as a whole. The steerer chooses the routes across the water to maximize the speed and efficiency of the canoe and considers the crew's capability and performance as the race unfolds. Paddling together as a crew requires commitment from all paddlers, trust in each other, and knowledge of the specific duties of each seat position.

Going Solo

Many paddlers believe that the most challenging outrigger paddling is solo. A solo paddler needs excellent navigation skills and aerobic fitness, combined with courage and determination to meet the challenges of the sea. Solo canoes can be fitted with or without a rudder; rudderless, an outrigger canoe requires skill and experience to paddle confidently in swells and surf. "The lack of a rudder makes very great demands on the paddler who must be fit, strong and perhaps have an even greater degree of ocean sense and knowledge in order to handle such craft in the open water" (West 1996, 22). Alone on the water, being faced with large ocean swells, burning sun, or gusting winds and having to make constant steering strokes to navigate the canoe toward a distant island, the solo paddler must meet every challenge with confidence simply in order to complete the race. Competence and trust in oneself instill competitive potential in such tests of endurance and skill.

Outrigger Canoe Marathons

An outrigger canoe marathon race requires years of skill development, months of training, fundraising and planning travel to remote Pacific islands, and fierce international competition. Thus, not only the long distances but also these contextual factors, alongside whatever the open ocean and weather offer during the race, make such races extreme. Some of the skills required of paddlers also relate to the particular way different marathons are completed. Iron races involve one crew of six paddlers (or one solo paddler), who races over the entire course. Relay races involve two or more crews (or solo paddlers), who paddle a stretch of the race and then exit, allowing fresh paddlers to continue.

However, changeover races introduce new skills and risks. Changeover races involve crews of nine to twelve paddlers who change in and out of the canoe throughout the race. Changeover races are challenging because the overall aim is to replace fatigued paddlers with fresh paddlers without losing canoe speed. Managed from a support boat traveling with the canoe, paddlers are dropped into the water ahead of the approaching canoe. On cue paddlers roll out of the canoe, and simultaneously fresh paddlers pull themselves from the water into their seats and take over paddling. "It requires many good qualities of strength, timing, swimming ability and a degree of nerve. Having a 40 foot canoe weighing over 1,500 lbs being aimed pretty much right at you, requires nerve. You only get one shot at it" (West 2005). Support boats travel with managers, food and water supplies, fresh paddlers for changeovers, and medics.

Many marathon races are held around the Pacific region. The most challenging include the Super Aito solo canoe race and the Hawaiki Nui Va'a race in Tahiti, the Ouv'ea-to-Poindimie' race in New Caledonia, the Moloka'i Hoe and Na Wahine o Ke Kai races in Hawaii, the Catalina Crossing race in California, the Cook Strait Crossing in Aotearoa, New Zealand, and the Hamilton Cup marathon

in Australia. Of these, arguably, the most extreme are the Super Aito solo race, the three-day Hawaiki Nui Va'a race, and the race from Ouv'ea to Poindimie.'

Super Aito

The Super Aito race has been held annually in Tahiti since 1993 and is arguably the toughest solo "iron" race. The race runs from Moorea Island to Point Venus on Tahiti and covers 35 kilometers, including a channel crossing. As one cultural commentator notes: "There is so much more to a race like this than paddler endurance and canoe speed, which seems fitting for a sport which is essentially a re-enactment and celebration of the skills and accomplishments of the ancestors of all the Polynesian people. Ocean steering and weather observation skills are as important as fitness and technology. I, for one, hope this does not change" (Kjeldsen 1997, 187). Paddlers from Tahiti must qualify in lead-up races to participate, and international paddlers may be invited to compete.

Hawaiki Nui Va'a

The Hawaiki Nui Va'a race held in October in Tahiti is a three-day event that covers 116 kilometers from Huahine to Raiatea on day one (45 kilometers), on to Tahaa on day two (27 kilometers), and to Bora Bora on the final day (57 kilometers). The race was established in 1992 as a changeover race and lures crews (typically of fourteen members) with prize money. Surprisingly, some of the best performances come from crews who choose to paddle all three days with the same six paddlers, essentially paddling three iron marathons races consecutively.

Ouv'ea-to-Poindimie' Race

The Ouv'ea-to-Poindimie' race held in New Caledonia is the longest one-day race, involving changeovers during 140 kilometers of paddling across open ocean from the northern island of Ouv'ea to Poindimie' on the east coast. The race is invitational only, making it a most prestigious event. The first race in 1998 was abandoned after only three hours as a result of huge seas and winds. In 1999 four crews completed the second attempt at the race. The race began at 4 A.M. in the dark with changeover crews of twelve paddlers and took

The Rituals of Canoe Building

Outrigger canoes are associated with Polynesia, which includes the Hawaiian islands. This account describes the supernatural forces and ritual required to produce a seaworthy canoe in traditional Hawaiian culture.

Canoe building (*'oihana wa'a*) was conducted by skilled craftsmen (*kahuna kalai wa'a*) who, in addition to eing expert in designing and shaping the vessels, possessed a knowledge of the religious ceremonies to be observed at various stages of the work. The religious ritual consisted of offerings and chanted prayers addressed to the tutelary deities of the craft. The gods of the craft, as listed by Kamakau, were Kupulupulu and five other forms of Ku. It is probable that the six names enumerated various attributes of the one god, Ku. In most of the other parts of Polynesia, Ku (or Tu) was the god of war, and the god of forests and canoe building was Kane (Tane). It is therefore evident that the Hawaiian ancestors confused the functions of the two gods and erroneously transferred the functions of Kane to Ku. However a god by any name would perform the functions attributed to it by its worshipers. Lea, as the wife of one of the forms of Ku, was the female deity of the craft. Her visible representative, or incarnation, was the *alapaea* woodpecker [probably the *elepaio*]. When a tree was felled for a canoe hull, Lea, represented by the bird, kindly gave expert advice as to the soundness of the tree. If, when the bird appeared, it walked the whole length of the trunk without pausing, the wood was sound. On the other hand, if the bird stopped and pecked at the bark, the tree had a hollow or flaw at the spot pecked and was thus condemned by the higher authority. A variant to this form of diagnosis was the interpretation of a dream by a priest to whom the prospective owner reported that he had located a suitable tree. The priest slept beside the shrine in the men's house (*mua*); and if a naked man or woman appeared in a dream, the tree was condemned as having some hidden flaw and the canoe seeker had to find another tree. If the priest dreamed that he saw a well-clad man or woman, the tree was approved as sound.

Source: Buck, Peter Henry, Sir. (1957). *Arts and crafts of Hawaii* (p. 254). Honolulu:, HI: Bishop Museum Press.

approximately twelve hours to complete. In 2002 five crews completed the race in mild seas but extreme heat. According to one participant, "This race is an epic adventure. It is in fact a truly great race to do, but the whole experience is made even more memorable through the unbelievable hospitality" of the local communities (Wilding 2002, 32). This race constitutes an extraordinary test of endurance, ocean navigation, and skill.

The Future

The traditions of outrigger canoe racing are firmly based in the Pacific, and with the growth of the sport throughout the region, outrigger canoeing will continue to challenge paddlers. New technologies allow for the improvement of canoes and paddles. Training programs enhanced by sports science and nutrition prepare paddlers to push themselves to the limits of human endurance. Longer races are likely to be undertaken with paddlers striving to win under the most challenging weather and sea conditions. However, the ancient technologies of canoe building and navigation and the cultural traditions of yesteryear are still relevant to paddlers today. Although competition may be the context of these extreme events, the fact that most paddlers participate for personal enjoyment indicates that outrigger paddlers will always engage in the traditions of canoe culture.

Karen Barbour

Further Reading

Feinberg, R. (1991, March). A long distance voyage in contemporary Polynesia. *The Journal of Polynesian Society, 100*(1), 25–44.

Guild, W. (1998). Solo technique. *Kanu Culture, 4,* 21–25.

Humphries, B., Abt, G. A., Stanton, R., & Sly, N. (2000). Kinanthropometric and physiological characteristics of outrigger canoe paddlers. *Journal of Sport Sciences, 18,* 395–399.

Kjeldsen, K. (1997). Super Aito, Tahiti. *Kanu Culture, 3,* 184–187.

Labman Hawaii. (2005, July). Outrigger canoe paddling performance standards. Retrieved July 4, 2006, from http://www.labman.org/canoe.html

Lewis, D. (1994). We, the navigators. *The ancient art of landfinding in the Pacific.* Sir Derek Oulton (Ed.) (2nd ed.). Honolulu: University of Hawaii Press.

Lukins, J. (2000). Pain management: Psychology in paddling. *Kanu Culture, 6,* 107–114.

Moloka'i Hoe. (2005, November). About. Retrieved July 3, 2006, from http://ohcra.com/molokaihoe/about.htm

Murch, B., & Verhagen, H. (2004, May–June). Bernie Murch and Heidie Verhagen prep for Molokai relay. *New Zealand Paddler Pasifika, 3,* 30–31.

Na Wahine O Ke Kai. (2005, September). History. Retrieved July 3, 2006, from http://www.nawahineokekai.com/

Ngaia, B. (2003, May). Cook Strait challenge 2003. Retrieved July 9, 2006, from http://nzwaka.wellington.net.nz/newsletter/newsletter.php?y=2003&doc=5

Ocean River Sports. (n.d.). The outrigger paddling stroke. Retrieved July 3, 2006, from http://www.performancepaddling.com/training_resources.php

Schultz, A. (2005). The Cook Strait crossing. Retrieved July 9, 2006, from http://crossing.wellington.net.nz/history/2002/index.php

Scott, S. (1998). Change overs. *Kanu Culture, 4,* 7–20.

Stanton, R. (1999, April). Strength training for outrigger canoe paddlers. *Strength and Conditioning Journal, 21(2),* 28–32.

Tahitiguide.com. (2005). Hawaiki Nui Va'a 2005. Retrieved July 5, 2006, from http://www.tahitiguide.com/@en-us/586/article.asp

Wallace, T. (2001). Moloka'i assault: Planning to fail, through failing to plan. *Kanu Culture, 7,* 8–13.

West, S. (1995). Introduction. *Kanu Culture, 1,* 3.

West, S. (1995). The outrigger canoe: Wa'a kaukahi. *Kanu Culture, 1,* 43–72.

West, S. (1996). Solo explosion. *Kanu Culture, 2,* 21–37.

West, S. (2000). Hawaiki Nui Va'a '99. *Kanu Culture, 6,* 68–85.

West, S. (2003). Hamilton Island. *Kanu Culture, 9,* 1–43.

West, S. (2005, January). Frequently asked questions: Kanu culture. Retrieved July 3, 2006, from http://www.kanuculture.com/faq.html

Wilding, G. (2002). Ouv'ea to Poindimie.' *Kanu Culture, 8,* 27–32.

Pankration

The Olympic Games began in Peloponnese, Greece, three thousand years ago. The first written mention of the competitions was in 776 BCE. The Games were held at Olympia every four years. In order to participate an athlete had to fulfill three criteria: be male, free, and Greek. Women, slaves, and foreigners were excluded from participation. In ancient Greece sport was an integral part of general education, and it was particularly encouraged because of its significance for physical and mental balance. The ancient Greek conception of balance, reflected in the philosopher Plato's writings, was that a sound mind can exist only in a sound body. The external beauty of the nude body was considered to reflect internal beauty. Greeks considered it to demonstrate the harmonious balance between body and mind. For this reason athletes always trained and competed in the nude.

The program of the Games consisted of only individual sports. The three combat sports were wrestling, boxing, and *pankration*. The term *pankration* comes from the Greek adjectives *pan* and *kratos* and means "all powers" or "all powerful." Equally, *pankratiatist* means "all powerful—he who conquers and keeps everything." The ancient author Plutarch wrote that the *pankration* was founded by the hero Theseus, who combined wrestling and boxing in order to defeat the Minotaur in the labyrinth in Knossos. This theory contrasts with Pausanias's view. According to the latter, the *pankration* was founded by Hercules, who was the first Olympic victor in this contest. (Tradition says Hercules was the first athlete to accomplish the greatest achievement at ancient Olympia: winning both the wrestling and the *pankration* contests in the same day.) However, other theories exist. According to the ancient Greek philosopher Aristotle, for instance, the founder of the *pankration* was the athlete Lefkaros of Akarnania. However, some authors regard other heroes or mortals as the founder of the contemporary *pankration*.

Regardless, the *pankration*, arguably one of the earliest extreme sports, was added to the Olympic Games in 648 BCE in the thirty-third Olympiad. It was the most popular and demanding of all events. The *pankration* was essentially a combination of wrestling and what we might call today "kickboxing." It included ground fighting and submission holds to standing fighting with all types of strikes. It was no-holds-barred fighting and was performed with bare hands, unlike the ancient boxing matches. The *pankration* aroused strong reactions from the audience. Because of its popularity, it was among the first sports to be taken over by professionals by the end of the fourth century BCE.

The *pankration* was a notoriously harsh competition, as is shown by the story of one of the great *pankratiatists*, Arrachion of Phigalia (or "Arrichion," according to some authors—only Pausanias among the ancient authors refers to him as "Arrachion"). According to Pausanias, Arrachion was being strangled by his opponent (a legal maneuver). As Arrachion was losing consciousness, he inflicted so much pain by twisting his foe's leg that his foe lifted his hand to signal defeat. As the judges declared Arrachion the winner, he lay dead before them.

According to the author Philostratos, the *pankration* was an excellent exercise in training warriors. He wrote that the *pankratiatists* practiced a dangerous brand of wrestling: "they have to endure black eyes . . . and learn holds by which one who has fallen can still win, and they must be skilful in various ways of strangulation. They bend ankles and twist arms and throw punches and jump on their opponents" (Woody 1936, 9). The *pankration* was taught as part of the Spartan warriors' regular training program. It was also basic to the Greek warriors who served under Alexander of Macedon during his invasion of India in 326 BCE. Later the *pankration* was taught as part of the gladiators' regular training program in the Roman Empire. According to Philostratos, the perfect *pankratiatists* were men who might be described as being the best wrestlers among the boxers and the best boxers among the wrestlers.

The Event

The *pankration* allowed kicks, punches, throws, knee attacks, elbow attacks, and head punches. The techniques included hook and uppercut punches, joint locks, and numerous submission chokeholds. A competitor was permitted to submit at the point of being strangled or having a bone broken. Victory was sought with no consideration of the danger to the health or life of one's opponent. Only biting and gouging an opponent's eyes, nose, or mouth with fingernails were banned (although the Spartans allowed these, too, in their local athletic festivals). However, some athletes often broke the rules and resorted to such measures in order to escape being seriously injured.

The athletes fought one-on-one. No weight divisions and no time limits existed. Contests were said to have lasted more than four hours on occasion. Both men's and boys' divisions existed. The fighting arena was 3 to 4 meters square.

Pankration Rankings

The following are the ten grade levels (taxis) recognized at the Spartan Academy. Student ranks are indicated by lowercase Greek letters; instructors by uppercase Greek letter symbols. Written and physical tests are administered for promotions from one level to the next up to senior instructor.

Mathitis (Student) Taxis

■ *Aharios* (learner): letter grade = *alpha, beta, gamma*

■ *Polemistes* (warrior/competing fighter): letter grade = *delta, epsilon*

Paidotrivis (Trainer) Taxis

■ *Voithos* (apprentice instructor): letter grade = *zeta*

■ *Thaskalos* (full instructor): letter grade = *eta*

■ *Theethaktor* (senior instructor): letter grade = *iota*

■ *Arhigos* (master instructor): letter grade = *kappa*

■ *Kerios* (grandmaster): letter grade = *lambda*

Source: The Spartan Academy of Modern Pankration, *Spartan Academy ranks*. Retrieved Feb. 1, 2007, from http://www.spartanacademy.com/ranks/index.htm

Referees were armed with stout rods to enforce the rules against biting and gouging. Contestants used no equipment. The two forms of the *pankration* were *ano* and *kato*. In the former opponents had to remain standing. If one opponent fell he had to stand up for the contest to resume. In the latter opponents started standing, and the contest continued after they fell to the ground to the point that one of them, because of pain or exhaustion, *"apagoreve"* (lifted his hand to signal defeat). The contest continued until one opponent either surrendered or suffered unconsciousness.

Most *pankration* matches were judged on the success of both striking and submission techniques. However, knockouts were also common. It was important for athletes to remain standing because falling to the ground put them in a vulnerable position. When an opponent fell, typically his opponent fell on top of him and immobilized him with his legs, thus leaving the opponent's hands free to apply a dangerous stranglehold. In the *pankration*, as opposed to boxing, competitors were also allowed to hold their opponent with one hand and to hit him with the other. The athlete who fell down could use his hands, legs, and back to protect himself. Kicking was an essential part of the *pankration*, especially powerful leg sweeps, which could take an opponent off his feet; kicks above the belt were used scarcely. According to the author Pindaros, Mellisos of Theves (one of the great *pankratiatists*) resembled a fox in ingenuity and cunning. He didn't have the stature of the great *pankratiatist* Orion, but he would lie down like a fox, extend his hands, pull his legs, and kick back with great power.

Legendary Champions

The feats of the ancient *pankratiatists* became legendary. Stories told of past champions who were considered invincible beings and had acquired godlike status. The names of Kleitomachos of Theves, Polydamas of Skotoussa, Sostratos of Sikiona, and Leondiskos of Messini are among the most recognizable. Sostratos would defeat his opponents by bending their fingers, thereby inflicting severe pain and forcing them to surrender. Leondiskos finished his career undefeated and had the remarkable ability to break his opponents' fingers. Another famous *pankratiatist* was Dioxippus. He was crowned Olympic champion by default in 336 BCE when no other *pankratiatist* dared to meet him on the field.

However, Polydamas of Skotoussa was probably the most legendary of all. He won the *pankration* in 408 BCE in the ninety-third Olympiad. Little is known about his Olympic victory and his physical appearance other than that his statue was notably tall. Tradition says he was more than 2.1 meters tall and had superhuman strength. Polydamas was said to have killed a lion with his bare hands and to have immobilized a moving chariot. The son of Artaxerxes I, Darius II Ochus, once asked him to fight three of his best soldiers in full armor. Polydamas, whose only weapon was a club, managed to kill them all. However, he died tragically. On a summer day Polydamas and some friends camped in a cave. Because of an earthquake, the walls of the cave began to fall. Tradition says Polydamas held up the roof of the cave with his hands in order to help his friends escape. Although his friends escaped, Polydamas was buried under the ruins of the cave.

As mentioned, according to tradition, the first athlete

to win both the wrestling and the *pankration* contests in the same day was Hercules. However, others after him, such as Aristomenis of Rhodes and Marion of Alexandria. also accomplished this remarkable achievement. In the 249th Olympiad the great *pankratiatist* Aurilios won in the *pankration* and wanted to compete in the wrestling contest. However, the judges didn't let him compete, saying Aurilios didn't have the required ethos. According to the judges, he was under the influence of the emperor Iliogavalos, who was mean and immoral. The judges didn't want to recognize Aurilios as the eighth athlete after Hercules to accomplish the achievement and sully the name of Hercules. To do so would have been against the philosophy of the Games. There is, however, also the view that the judges did not allow Aurilios to compete because they didn't want to sully the sacredness of the number seven. In ancient Greece the number seven was sacred to the god Apollo.

In a different event the *pankratiatist* Theagenis of Thasos failed to show up for the final match of the *pankration* contest. Despite having won the boxing contest and having participated in the *pankration* contest, he was too tired to fight against Dromeus of Theves in the final. The judges declared Dromeus the winner and punished Theagenis by forcing him to pay a money penalty. This kind of victory (in absentia) was against the conception of the sport, and Olympic law forbade it. The difference between boxing and the *pankration* on the one hand and wrestling on the other hand was that only in the latter did an athlete make the same effort both in the match and in the preparatory/warm-up/training matches. In the former two contests punches were forbidden in training matches. This was an injury-prevention strategy because the athletes fought with bare hands. Hence, only shadowboxing was allowed in the training boxing and training *pankration* matches. For this reason

Kickboxing, or Muay Thai, is a modern version of the ancient Greek extreme sport of *pankration*. Source: istock.

the judges could declare a wrestler the winner if his opponent failed to show up in the final. However, according to Olympic law, the judges weren't allowed to do the same in the *pankration* or boxing events. The case cited earlier was a rare exception to the rule.

Modern Pankration

When ancient Greek society dissolved and Greece eventually became part of the Roman Empire, the *pankration* found a new home in the Romans' athletic contests. The fighters were no longer expected to be unarmed. Rather, gladiators were armed with the deadly *caestus* (from the Latin *caedo*, meaning "strike"). *Caestus* were hard leather gloves that covered the hands, wrists, and forearms and into which metal studs, teeth, and spikes were inserted, a far cry from the boxing gloves of modern times, which are designed to lessen injury, not increase it. These gloves eventually diminished the skill and the aesthetic value that the ancient Greeks had come to see in their *pankratiatists*. The *pankration*, by that time, was broken down into several martial arts, and these spread into other countries. According to many commentators, this spread resulted in the development of martial arts such as Chinese kung fu and Okinawan karate. Most commentators link the fighting systems that have developed in both the Eastern and Western worlds to the ancient Greek *pankration*.

As boxing developed from the ancient Greek amateur boxing to pay-per-view professional boxing, *pankration* events developed into professional Ultimate Fighting cage matches. In the United States the Ultimate Fighting Championship (UFC), founded in 1993, promotes a no-holds-barred combination of martial arts and wrestling. In an attempt to resemble the *pankration* as much as possible, early UFC matches had no weight categories and no equipment for the competitors. The competitors wore no gloves, and only biting and gouging an opponent's eyes were banned. However, the brutality of the sport caused much concern, and the UFC had to make significant rule changes in order to legitimize the sport; weight classes were added, and competitors wore light gloves. Moreover, head butts and elbow strikes to the back of the head and spine were banned.

Several contemporary organizations hold *pankration*-inspired events. Two of the best-known events in the United States are Battlecade's Extreme Fighting and S.E.G.'s Ultimate Challenge events. Organizations in Japan, Brazil, and Russia also hold events inspired by the concept of the *pankration*. In Japan the Pride Fighting Championship and

K-1 are the top mixed-martial arts organizations. In addition, the United Full Contact Federation (UFCF) and the World Pankration Federation (WPF) are two major sanctioning bodies that use the term *pankration* and are dedicated to developing the sport throughout the world. The WPF conducts international competitions such as the World Pankration Championships, and it is attempting to have the *pankration* added to the modern Olympic Games. Such attempts, however, have been unsuccessful. People widely believed that Greece would reenter the *pankration* in the 2004 Olympic Games. However, in 1996 the International Olympic Committee (IOC) expressed doubts that the Greek government would be able to provide the needs of the 2004 Games. The IOC was convinced otherwise only with the provision that no new medal sports would be added, thus dashing hopes that the *pankration* would again be celebrated at the Olympics. Nonetheless, some enthusiasts remain optimistic that the *pankration* will eventually be included in the Olympic program. However, a more convincing case probably will be needed to sway those who oppose the brutality inherent in the *pankration*.

Dimitris Platchias

Further Reading

Auguet, R. (1972). *Cruelty and civilization. The Roman games.* London: Allen and Unwin.

Brophy, M & R. (1985). Deaths in the Pan-Hellenic games II: All combative sports. *The American Journal of Philology, 106*(2), 2, 171–198.

Gardiner, E. N. (1906). The pankration and wrestling,. *The Journal of Hellenic Studies, 26,* 4–22.

Gardiner, E. N. (1910). *Greek athletic sports and festivals.* London: Macmillan.

Gardiner, N. (1930). *Athletics of the ancient world.* Oxford, UK: Oxford University Press.

Glubok, S., & Tamarin, A. (1976). *Olympic games in ancient Greece.* New York: Harper and Row.

Pausanias. (1918–1935). *Description of Greece* (W. H. S. Jones, trans.), 5 vols. New York: G. P. Putnam's Sons.

Plutarch. (1878). *The morals.* Retrieved February 11, 2007, from http://oll.libertyfund.org/ToC/0062.php

Poliakoff, M. B. (1987). *Combat sports in the ancient world: Competition, violence and culture.* New Haven, CT: Yale University Press.

Woody T. (1936). Philostratos: Concerning gymnastics. *Journal of the American Physical Education Association, 7,* 3–26.

Paragliding

See Hang Gliding

Parkour

Parkour (also known as the "art of displacement" and "free-running") has been described as "a quasi acrobatic sport" and "urban-steeplechase aerobics" (Jones n.d., para. 1). The practice of *parkour* involves "traversing the urban environment and its obstacles in the quickest and most fluid way possible and normally involves a series of moves including jumping, vaulting, leaping and balancing" (Jones n.d., para. 3). *Parkour* draws on many influences, and while it may resemble certain other physical practices in appearance—such as gymnastics, dance or athletics—it is in fact far removed from any of these cousins. So much so, in fact, that defining *parkour* is extremely difficult: is it an extreme sport, an art, a philosophy, or a discipline?

Although many core practitioners would deny that *parkour* is an extreme sport, it is inherently risky. The practice of running, jumping, and leaping from a variety of urban structures (e.g., roof tops, staircases, raised surfaces, walls, etc.) and landing on concrete, of course, carries the potential for injury. Some of the most common injuries among practitioners include sprained ankles and repetitive strain injuries to the knees. However, excessive risk-taking runs in opposition to the philosophy of *parkour*. According to one participant, "one of the most striking differences between parkour and other so-called 'extreme' sports is that it is not concerned solely with the acquisition of physical skills, but also with the improvement of one's mental and spiritual well-being. Ensuring that physical progress is not at the expense of mental progress is one of the main aims of a good traceur (term used for a *parkour* practitioner)" (cited in Jones n.d., para. 22). The philosophy of *parkour* can be largely attributed to its French roots.

The French Connection

Since the beginning of humankind people have been running and leaping through the natural environment. Thus, pinpointing the exact moment of the birth of *parkour* is impossible. However, researchers acknowledge that *parkour*, as we understand the activity today, has French foundations. Researchers believe that David Belle combined a number of influences to create *parkour* in the 1980s. Growing up in the French suburban town of Lisses, Belle and his friends began to explore the urban-rural environment in new ways. David's father, Raymond Belle, was a key influence on their activi-

ties. In fact, the term *parkour* (actually coined by Hubert Kounde, a close friend of David Belle) is perhaps indirectly attributable to Raymond Belle, who introduced his son to the military training methods of Georges Hebert, a French physical educationalist and theorist.

Hebert was one of the earliest advocates of the *parcours*, an obstacle course for physical training. Inspired by the natural, physical conditioning of indigenous peoples from Africa, Hebert developed the "natural method," a form of training session that used the natural environment as an obstacle course. In explaining the natural method he wrote: "A (natural method) session is composed of exercises belonging to the ten fundamental groups: walking, running, jumping, quadrupedal movement, climbing, equilibrism (balancing), throwing, lifting, defending and swimming. A training session consists then, of exercise in an outdoor environment" (cited in Jones n.d., para. 8). While in the French military the senior Belle had trained using Hebert's method.

Drawing on the knowledge passed on by his father, David Belle and his companions played in the urban environment, testing their bodies and developing new techniques for jumping and landing efficiently. According to Sébastien Foucan, an early training partner and student of Belle, they didn't begin to experiment with "big jumps" until they reached their mid-teens. During this time, however, they began to develop a fundamental set of movements: vaults, jumps, climbs, and rolls. They taught themselves to be athletes, moving through their environment in a way never before seen in an urban setting. The "big jumps" have grabbed the attention of the world's media and mainstream consciousness, although all experienced practitioners are quick to play down the significance of the more spectacular aspects of *parkour*. They would argue that the goal is not to perform spectacular and risky maneuvers, but rather to employ techniques to traverse a space in a way that seems effortless. Indeed, the motion of a good *traceur* is often expressed as being "fluid like water." The comparison with water is "not only because of the idea of the grace and artistry of the movement but also through the thought that water can be associated with breaking down barriers and obstacles through its constant flowing force" (Jones n.d., para. 12). Some of the maneuvers developed by David Belle and his companions involve mimicking animal movements and carry names such as the Cat Leap, Monkey Vault, and Cat Balance. These maneuvers continue to be the foundation upon which contemporary *traceurs* around the world develop their own styles.

Although David Belle initiated and was integral to the development of *parkour*, he was by no means the only practitioner during the early years. Others, including Stephane Vigroux, Yahn Hnautra, David Malgogne, and Frederic Hnautra, also contributed. Stephane Vigroux, for example, was instrumental in the creation and development of the Saut de Chat movement (now known in English as the "King Kong Vault").

Parkour and the Philosophy of Movement

Not only is *parkour* a form of efficient, functional movement over any terrain, but it is also an expression and an exploration of the power and versatility of the human spirit. According to one cultural commentator, *parkour* is "a way of

A free runner back flips from high steps onto the sandy bank of the Thames River in London. Source: istock/Anthony Brown.

life and this philosophical side to the practice . . . is what distinguishes parkour from being just an extreme sport or a fun activity" (Jones n.d., para. 10). Sébastien Foucan promotes this mental aspect of the discipline as an "equal partner to the physical" (Jones n.d., para 10). For many practitioners, the mental and spiritual elements share a loose relationship with ancient Eastern philosophies and religion. According to one experienced *traceur*, "the most important element is the harmony between you and the obstacle" (Aoues cited in Jones, n.d., para. 13). Parallels have been drawn with Eastern philosophy in the form of the discipline and self-improvement that is central to *parkour* practice. As with all transformative practices, *parkour* is much more about mastering the self than about mastering a few high walls. Integral to the philosophy of *parkour* are the importance of adaptability in life; the ability to overcome any obstacle through perseverance and creativity; self-discipline; the concept of constant progression—always moving forward, both in life and in one's training; and strength, both inner and outer. Indeed, freedom of the body and mind is integral to the philosophy of *parkour*, such that the activity has been described as a way of "escaping from the clogging of modern suburbia" (Jones n.d., para. 13).

The Traceur and the Urban Environment

The architecture of the city provides the ultimate training ground for self-development. According to a *traceur* from San Francisco, respect for the environment is a key element of *parkour*: "Another aspect of parkour mentality is how you view and interact with your environment. Unlike sports like skateboarding, where skaters wax up curbs and structures and grind them, sometimes disrespecting and damaging the environment, traceurs adapt themselves to the space in an effort to 'flow' through it efficiently. It is often said that parkour is 'a way of life' and that is a very true statement. Even when not out free-running, traceurs will scan their environment, look for lines, evaluate space, and imagine themselves moving within it" (cited in Jones n.d., para. 16). Further explaining the relationship between the philosophy of *parkour* and urban settings and the built environment, another cultural commentator writes that "the art of moving from place to another with fluidity allows you to see your environment differently. The quest's goal is to become part of the environment in order to develop your mind and body" (Jones n.d., para. 25).

Showtime

Parkour is by nature a visually stunning activity, especially when displayed by experts such as Belle, Vigroux, and Foucan. As the reputation of the original practitioners spread, more people came to join them and to learn, and beyond these came those who saw the potential that *parkour* possesses as a money-making machine. Indeed, the media and many large companies have been attracted to the "high octane, fresh, and youthful edginess" of *parkour* (Jones n.d., para. 20). Commercials for the British Broadcasting Corporation (BBC), Nike, and Toyota featuring some of the French founders of the discipline caught the attention of interested parties around the world. The BBC commercial dubbed "Rush Hour," for example, starred David Belle as an innovative commuter who chooses to find an alternate route home via the roof tops of London to avoid the crush of people on the streets below.

Ultimately this swell in interest caused the first splits in the *parkour* community: between those who embraced the new opportunities for financial gain and those who spurned such opportunities. Luc Besson's 2001 film *Yamakasi: Les samouraïs des temps modernes*, (*Yamakasi: the Modern Samurai*) stars the group formed by Belle that called itself Yamakasi, a Lingala word meaning "strong man—strong spirit." This is considered a famous reference point in this cultural fragmentation. Luc Besson's film prompted a surge of interest in the activity; yet, along with that surge came *parkour's* first wave of injuries. Not only did many of the new participants suffer broken bones from falls, but also two deaths were, rightly or wrongly, attributed to copycat behavior. Describing the effect of the film, Paul Corkery, founder of Urban Freeflow, a group of London-based *traceurs*, explains: "You had kids going out thinking they could go out and jump off high objects. Very quickly they found out that to do so, you need to practice landings and how to roll and transfer the energy of the jump" (cited in George 2004, para. 14).

Furthermore, many of the new participants did not take time to learn the philosophy behind *parkour* and instead privileged the spectacular aspects of the activity. Sébastien Foucan describes the attitude of much of the post-film interest: "After *Yamakasi* it's another kind of people, it's just 'I jump I jump I jump, just like the movie, I'm on the roof, just like the movie'" (Interview with Foucan, retrieved from www.UrbanFreeFlow.com). Also observing the cultural fragmentation among contemporary *parkour* enthusiasts, Dan Jones writes: "there are definitely two pathways emerging: those that remain true to the original

---

Parkour Philosophy

Many people take the principles they learn through parkour and apply them to their lives, the art of navigating obstacles efficiently. By challenging themselves physically, it becomes easier to deal with everyday life situations. When an "obstacle" or difficult situation comes up in daily life, a *Traceur* (*parkour* practitioner) can see this as any other obstacle which they've learned to overcome quickly, efficiently, and without disruption to their intended path. According to *Parkour* pioneer David Belle, part of the overall *Parkour* philosophy is to be useful in a variety of situations. *Parkour* itself does not strive to be a "complete" discipline.

Mark Toorock

Source: American Parkour. (2006). Retrieved Feb. 1, 2007, from http://americanparkour.com/index.php?option=com_content&task=view&id=224&Itemid=237

---

philosophies of parkour, the way, and achieving the flow that is talked about in movement, and those that use the built environment as a human skatepark for entertainment and showmanship" (Jones n.d., para. 21). Having developed a somewhat skeptical view of the many newcomers to the discipline, the originators coined the term *traceur* to distinguish themselves from those drawn solely to the spectacle and adrenaline rush of *parkour*. *Traceur* means "bullet" and was chosen because of the emphasis that Belle and Foucan put on achieving direct, efficient, and fast movement over any terrain.

Parkour, then, is not easily categorized. Perhaps inevitably, however, as the community grew, attempts to define and classify became commonplace. By nature *parkour* is an art that encourages freedom of movement and individual expression; formalizing a structured system that contains it while allowing for the subjective approaches of its practitioners is difficult, if not impossible. Matters were further complicated by the fact that David Belle—acknowledged as the guru of *parkour*—chose at first not to release a clear definition for others to refer to, and so the debates raged and schisms between the different perspectives ensued. These debates tend to revolve around what does or does not constitute *parkour*: Does it include acrobatics (e.g., flips), or is this counter to the core philosophy of efficiency espoused by Belle? Is it purely a practical discipline, to be studied as if one were studying a fighting art, or can it be done simply for fun and the feeling of liberation that it brings? Such debates continue to rage at the core of the *parkour* culture.

Jump!

Although *parkour* had been displayed in the media, it had not been explained. In some parts of the world, people even wrongly referred to the discipline itself as "Yamakasi." Misunderstanding was rife. Not until 2003 was an accurate insight into the depths of the art released for public consumption when the United Kingdom's Channel 4 produced an award-winning documentary entitled *Jump London*, featuring Foucan and two colleagues showcasing their skills on the London cityscape. Foucan conveyed the philosophical aspects of *parkour* side-by-side with the physical brilliance, at last providing the wider public with a better understanding of the discipline. The response was telling. Groups of practitioners, also known as "clans" or "crews," sprang up throughout Europe, and the term *free-running* seeped into the mainstream vocabulary. In no small part because it had been the location for *Jump London*, London fast became a focal point for the nascent free-running community.

In 2004 another milestone was reached when the central members of Urban Freeflow united with Foucan and Jerome Ben-Aoues to star in the documentary sequel, *Jump Britain*. First aired in January 2005, this film was the dambreaker for *parkour*, cementing its position as a valid sport/ art for the modern age. Through the *Jump* series, *parkour* had literally leaped into the spotlight.

Moving Swiftly On

Since the 1980s *parkour* has eased itself stealthily from the shadows of Paris to the gritty streets of London and from there onto the world stage. *Parkour* has been featured in several movies, including the most recent James Bond film, and is being used in every form of media from television commercials to documentaries, billboard campaigns, fashion shoots, and live stage shows. Indeed, *parkour* has grown far beyond its roots in Lisses and is now a global practice with communities of free-runners and *traceurs* across the world. *Parkour* is beginning even to filter into the most mainstream of institutions: the educational system. *Parkour* is being

taught in some schools and county councils in the United Kingdom as part of the physical education curriculum. In sum, *parkour* is constantly being reborn as each new generation of practitioners picks it up and runs with it. And, as each person embraces *parkour*, so the discipline finds a new way of expressing itself. *Parkour* is here to stay: it isn't going anywhere. Or rather, it's going *everywhere*.

Dan Edwardes

Further Reading

Edwardes, D. (n.d.). Parkour *and the body*. Retrieved February 6, 2007, from http://www.urbanfreeflow.com/the_core_level/pages/archives/parkour_and_the_body.htm

Edwardes, D. (n.d.). Parkour *and the development of human potential*. Retrieved February 6, 2007, from http://www.urbanfreeflow.com/the_core_level/pages/archives/human_potential.htm

Edwardes, D. (n.d.). *The discipline of* parkour. Retrieved February 6, 2007, from http://www.urbanfreeflow.com/the_core_level/pages/archives/discipline.htm

Day, Andy. *An introduction to* parkour. (2003). Retrieved February 6, 2007, from http://www.kiell.com/parkour_research_paper.pdf

George, D. (2004, September 6). *Parkour*, a strange new urban sport, is like skateboarding but without the skateboards. Knight Ridder Newspapers. Retrieved February 5, 2007, from http://archive.dailyitem.com/archive/2004/0906/fea/stories/05fea.htm

Jones, D. (n.d.). Parkour: *A natural perspective*. Retrieved February 5, 2007, from http://www.urbanfreeflow.com/the_core_level/parkour_a_natural_perspective/parkour_a_natural_perspective.htm

Wolf, Tony. (n.d.).*George Hebert and the natural method of physical culture*. Retrieved February 6, 2007, from http://www.urbanfreeflow.com/the_core_level/pages/archives/methode_naturelle.htm

Physiology of Risk

Why are an increasing number of people drawn to sports that present them with a real risk of injury or death? Do we not have a biologically imprinted mandate to protect ourselves so that we may pass on our genetic information for generations to come? Clearly, given the recent increase in extreme sports such as hang gliding, rock climbing, big wave surfing, mountaineering, skydiving, and white water rafting, any such mandate is being ignored by the general population.

Is there a physiological reason for such sensation seeking, which has been labeled by some as an addiction? Marvin Zuckerman, a leading researcher in the field of risk taking, defines *sensation seeking* as a "need for varied, novel, complex,

A young man combines athletic ability with risk taking as he leaps across boulders. Source: istock/Galina Barskaya.

and intense sensations and experiences and the willingness to take physical, social, legal and financial risks for the sake of such experiences" (Zuckerman and Kuhlman 2000, 1000). Another explanation, according to Fletcher (2004), who spent eighteen months studying a group of white water rafters, is that at some level these extreme experiences enable the participant to transcend or escape the routine of everyday life. Indeed, this experience can be "inherently pleasurable and thus intrinsically motivating" (Fletcher 2004, 6). The risks associated with extreme sports are particularly conducive to the attainment of a transcendent state; however, at the same time they demand complete concentration to be focused on the task at hand. The fear inherent in risk taking can trigger the "fight-or-flight mechanism" of the sympathetic nervous system. This trigger results in the rapid release of certain substances (e.g., adrenaline) in anticipation of the need for instant action. This situation gives rise to the term *adrenalin rush* or *natural high.*

What is happening at a physiological level when athletes participate in extreme sports? We have all experienced that nervous feeling when we perceive a threat to our life or anticipate a stressful situation. This is typical of a range of physiological responses to the increased concentrations of

various biochemical messengers in our blood. For example, our heart rate increases, our rate and depth of breathing may change, and the distribution of our blood is altered to meet the needs of physical activity. Unsurprisingly, one study of novice male skydivers has shown that the potentially life-threatening event of leaping out of a plane results in a significant increase in the activity of the sympathetic nervous system. The results of this study supported earlier evidence that showed that urinary catecholamines and plasma noradrenaline levels rapidly increase in parachutists.

Three Chemicals

Three chemicals in the body help explain our responses to stressful or life-threatening events. The first chemical is adrenaline (also known as "epinephrine"). Adrenaline is a catecholamine that plays a central role in the physiological response to threatening or exciting conditions such as those experienced by extreme sports participants. When adrenaline is released into the bloodstream it increases heart rate, dilates the pupils, and increases blood supply to the muscles. It also elevates the blood sugar levels and initiates the breakdown of fat. These effects are often felt in anticipation of a stressful event, as well as during and after the stressful event.

A second important catecholamine is noradrenaline (also known as "norepinephrine"). Noradrenaline is a stress hormone and plays a role in activating the sympathetic nervous system to increase heart rate, release energy from fat, and increase muscle readiness. Noradrenaline affects the sections of the human brain where attention and impulsivity are controlled. Indeed, a lack of noradrenaline contributes to Attention Deficit Disorder (ADD). Medications for ADD, such as the psychostimulant Ritalin, help increase levels of noradrenaline and dopamine. The role of noradrenaline in enhancing attention and focus may provide a physiological mechanism to explain the "transcendence" described by extreme sports participants.

Dopamine is also a member of the catecholamine family and is a precursor to adrenaline and noradrenaline in the biosynthetic pathways for these hormones. Dopamine modulates the brain's movement control, and a shortage of dopamine has been implicated in causing Parkinson's disease, in which a person loses the ability to execute smooth, controlled movements. In humans drugs that reduce dopamine activity have been shown to induce an inability to experience pleasure (anhedonia). This inability has been reported to be more prevalent in a population of skydivers than in a population of rowers. Researchers Franken, Zijlstra, and Muris (2006) proposed that the frequent exposure to the "natural high" associated with skydiving is a result of a reduction in dopamine receptor density. Earlier work by Volkow and colleagues (2003) has shown a correlation between feelings of anhedonia and a reduction in dopamine receptor levels.

Another important physiological function of dopamine is its involvement in the brain's reward mechanism. Dopamine is commonly associated with providing feelings of enjoyment and as such can motivate us to participate in certain activities. Dopamine is released by naturally rewarding experiences such as food and sex and by the use of drugs such as cocaine and amphetamines. These drugs increase the bioavailability of dopamine and lead to excessive stimulation of the reward pathway, which in turn results in a feeling of intense pleasure and exhilaration. Interestingly, almost all known drugs of abuse in humans elevate the level of dopamine in the nucleus accumbens of the brain. Indeed, the euphoric effects of drugs of abuse are thought to be a direct result of the acute increase in accumbal dopamine. To quote J. Madelaine Nash (n.d.):

Genetically Extreme?

Medical research may have found some similarities between the adrenaline-junkie who goes out and tries extreme sports and those who are addicted to substances such as alcohol or drugs.

Hardwired for Thrills

Medical researchers believe some people are genetically destined to risk death in pursuit of fun and personal challenge. One scientist, Dr. Ernest Noble, believes extreme athletes may carry the gene also linked to alcoholism. Instead of reaching for the bottle, he says, these "dry alcoholics" climb an ice wall, ride a BMX bicycle off a jump or do something else to give their brains a boost. Noble has published research linking the D2 dopamine receptor gene to smoking, cocaine use and obesity, as well as alcoholism and risk-taking behaviour.

Dean Hamer is a prominent and controversial American geneticist who identified what some call "thrill" or "novelty-seeking" genes. He has since suggested a person's genetic makeup can predispose them to other behaviours as well. The notion that some people are predisposed to risky activities has been around for decades. In 1973, University of Illinois researcher Dr. Sol Roy Rosenthal told CBC Radio's *As It Happens* that humans have a natural drive for such sports because of an evolutionary holdover from the days when they had to hunt their own food. He argued that participating in "risk sports," such as horseback riding, swimming and sailing, is essential for physical and mental well-being.

Source: CBC News (25 February 1998) *Hardwired for thrills.* Retrieved Feb. 1, 2007, from http://archives.cbc.ca/400i.asp?IDCat =41&IDDos=1727&IDCli=11912&IDLan=1&NoCli=5&type=clip

At a purely chemical level, every experience humans find enjoyable—whether listening to music, embracing a lover, or savoring chocolate—amounts to little more than an explosion of dopamine in the nucleus accumbens as exhilarating and ephemeral as a firecracker.

This aspect of dopamine biochemistry may suggest a physiological pathway that could explain the "buzz" experienced during extreme sports as well as the "addiction" to such sports often talked about by onlookers. Indeed, Franken and colleagues (2006) found that skydivers demonstrated behaviors similar to those of heroine addicts. These authors suggested that the "natural high" experiences shared the same biological pathway as pharmacological addiction.

Seeking a Bigger Wave

Chronic elevation of dopamine will result in the downregulation of dopamine receptors available. This downregulation renders a person less able to respond to chemical signaling, and researchers hypothesize that this dulling of the responsiveness of the brain's reward pathways leads to desensitization to a set stimulus. Thus, there is an increased requirement for dopamine to maintain the same physiological response. This may explain why thrill seekers are constantly seeking a "bigger wave" or more precarious mountain peak just as drug addicts seek more frequent and higher doses of their drug of dependence.

Does this type of data suggest a physiological component that could explain the increase in popularity of high-risk sports? Obviously the growth of affluence in postindustrialized societies has provided more leisure time for workers and has contributed to this popularity. However, are extreme sports addictive? Information suggests that physiological mechanisms could indeed play a part in explaining the thrills associated with extreme sports.

So why are we not all "addicted" to skydiving or white water rafting? Are certain people biologically predisposed toward sensation seeking? The first association between a gene and a personality was made between the D4 dopamine receptor (D4DR) exon III and the trait of "novelty seeking." Zuckerman and Kuhlman (2000) reported that personality factors that influence risk taking had a "high degree of genetic influence," with genetic factors accounting for up to 70 percent of sensation-seeking behaviors. A further genetic

link between sensation seeking and biochemistry has been proposed by Zuckerman (2000, 1016). Monoamine oxidase (MAO) is an enzyme that is involved in the catabolism of dopamine. Zuckerman found that persons with conditions characterized by sensation seeking, disinhibition, and impulsivity had low levels of this enzyme and that low MAO levels are hereditary. Danish Professor Gunnar Breivik challenges the modernist view of humans as rational, safety-seeking creatures and points to our evolution as a reason for risk taking. Indeed, humans adapted to a life in the savannas of Africa that would have involved constant risks and challenges, and thus natural selection implies that risk taking is indeed "in our genes."

However, people searching for an "adrenaline rush" can easily find one in a task that has a high level of only perceived threat. For example, bungee jumping is safe, with very few accidents causing major injuries. Thus, sensation seekers can jump knowing that they are unlikely to incur harm but still can be extremely afraid and experience the associated biochemical "buzz." Furthermore, the commercialization of extreme sports has increased their popularity and their availability. People can now participate in extreme sports in most major cities of the world in one form or another.

Nicholas Gill and Martyn Beaven

Further Reading

Bardo, M. T., Donohew, R. L., & Harrington, N. G. (1996). Psychobiology of novelty seeking and drug seeking behaviour. *Behavioural Brain Research, 77*, 23–43.

Breivik, G. (1999). The quest for excitement and the safe society. *Philosophy of Safety, 2*(3), 1–10.

Celsi, R. L., Rose, R. L., & Leigh, T. W. (1993). An exploration of high-risk leisure consumption through skydiving. *Journal of Consumer Research, 20*, 1–23.

Chatterton, R. T., Vogelsong, K. M., Lu, Y., & Hudgens, G. A. (1997). Hormonal responses to psychological stress in men preparing for skydiving. *Journal of Clinical Endocrinology and Metabolism, 82*, 2503–2509.

Ebstein, R. P., Novick, O., Urmansky, R., Priel, B., Osher, Y., Blaine, D., Bennett, E. R., Nemanov, L., Katz, M., & Belmaker, R. H. (1996). Dopamine D4 receptor (D4DR) exon III polymorphism associated with the human personality trait novelty seeking. *Nature Genetics, 12*, 78–80.

Fletcher, R. (2004). Living on the edge: Affluent society and the rise of risk sports. Unpublished doctoral dissertation, University of California, Santa Barbara.

Franken, I. H. A., Zijlstra, C., & Muris, P. (2006). Are nonpharmacological induced rewards related to anhedonia? A study among skydivers. *Progress in Neuropharmacology & Biological Psychiatry, 30*, 297–300.

Hansen, J. R., Stoa, K. F., Schytte, B. A., & Ursin, H. (1978). Urinary levels of epinephrine and norepinephrine in parachutist trainees. In H. Ursin, E. Baade, & S. Levine (Eds.). *Psychobiology of stress: A study of coping men* (pp. 63–74). New York: Academic Press.

Nash, J. M. (n.d.). quoted in Hans Kosterlitz and the enkephalins. Retrieved July 13, 2006, from http://opioids.com/endogenous/index.html

Richter, S. D., Schurmeyer, T. H., Schledlowski, M., Hadicke, A., Tewes, U., Schmidt, R. E., & Wagner, T. O. F. (1996). Time kinetics of the endocrine response to acute psychological stress. *Journal of Clinical Endocrinology and Metabolism, 81,* 1956–1960.

Volkow, N. D., Fowler, J. S., & Wang, G. J. (2003). The addicted human brain: Insights from imaging studies. *The Journal of Clinical Investigation, 111,* 1444–1451.

Zuckerman, M. (1994). *Behavioural expressions and biosocial bases of sensation seeking.* New York: Cambridge University Press.

Zuckerman, M., & Kuhlman, D. M. (2000). Personality and risk-taking: Common biosocial factors. *Journal of Personality, 6*(8), 999–1029.

Playgrounds

In almost all countries the history of organized playgrounds can be traced to the mid-nineteenth century at the earliest. The most traditional playground was the sandpit, located in urban parks or in the backyards of crowded living areas. Whereas sandpits existed in Europe around the middle of the nineteenth century, the first sandpits in the United States did not appear until 1885 in Boston and were in fact "imported" from Germany by Maria Zakrezewska on behalf of the Massachusetts Emergency and Hygiene Association (MEHA):

The sandpit offered street children up to twelve years of age an opportunity to play safely away from the dangerous streets The sandpits were open three days a week and equipped with balls, shovels, buckets, and other sand tools. The Committee on Playgrounds, a subcommittee of the MEHA, was founded in 1887, and by 1896 more than thirty-five sandpits had been built in Boston under its patronage. However, the development of sandpits was not limited to Boston. They rapidly spread to other cities such as New York City, Chicago, Providence, and Philadelphia. In all of these cities the intent behind establishing sandpits was to keep children off the streets and out of mischief. Arguably, similar intentions are behind the development of contemporary extreme playgrounds such as skateboard parks and artificial climbing walls.

From Sandpits to Athletic Playgrounds

Although the development of sandpits was a success, a shortage of places for adolescents to play remained. Only children up to twelve years of age were allowed to play in sandpits. In addition, the sandpits tended to be too small for catch-and-run games or athletic activities preferred by older boys and girls. In order to solve this problem and to offer older children a place to play, the MEHA launched the Charlesbank Playground project. In 1889 the Charlesbank Playground was built at the Charles River close to the West End slum of Boston. This playground was subdivided into a men's and a women's division and included sandpits, athletic fields, and a gymnasium. It was open only during the summer, but it afforded adolescents the opportunity to spend their leisure time in a secure place. It marked the beginning of the playground movement in the United States. Playgrounds in many other cities were modeled after the Charlesbank Playground. Perhaps the best known was that at Hull House in Chicago. Hull House was founded by the settlement worker Jane Addams in 1889 and became internationally prominent as a well-organized settlement house. Although the Hull House playground, built in 1894, was limited in space, it did have enough room for athletic team games and track and field activities.

Until 1906 no national organization looked after playing fields and playgrounds. Although some local playground associations were formed, no umbrella organization was responsible for establishing a network across the country and for systematically publicizing the educational value of such facilities, especially in the big inner cities. That changed in 1906, when the Playground Association of America (PAA) was founded in Washington, D.C. The leaders of this organization were Henry S. Curtis, who was the leader of Playgrounds of the District of Columbia; Joseph Lee, who was president of the Massachusetts Civic Association; and Luther A. Gulick, who was prominent in the YMCA and president of the National Physical Education Association. Gulick became president of the PAA, and Curtis was secretary. In order to give the PAA the necessary high-profile political support, President Theodore Roosevelt became honorary president of the PAA. Roosevelt was an advocate of amateur sport and glorified the founding of the PAA as a patriotic project by which the educational values of play and sport could be spread among the masses. In particular Roosevelt referred to playgrounds in the inner cities and how they would offer children who lived there opportunities to engage in sport instead of hanging around in the streets unproductively. In the following years the PAA supported local playground associations in establishing city playgrounds. The PAA also published the monthly journal *The Playground* and organized conferences on the subject to help publicize the educational aims of the movement.

Before 1905 only eighty-seven playgrounds existed in twenty-one cities. Between 1906 and 1917, 3,940 playgrounds existed in more than 481 cities. However, leaders of the PAA, including Curtis, Lee, and Gulick, were not satisfied. They were concerned with lack of use because in some cities fewer than 10 percent of the adolescents visited playgrounds.

In 1911 the PAA was renamed "Playground and Recreation Association of America" (PRAA). In 1930 the PRAA became the National Recreation Association, the forerunner of today's National Recreation and Park Association (NRPA), which is the biggest organization in the United States to organize leisure sport activities for different target groups in parks and other settings.

Development of Adventure and Extreme Activity Playgrounds

The development of adventure playgrounds in their purest form began in Denmark during World War II. After 1945 development spread quickly throughout several European countries. In the United States the American Adventure Playground Association (AAPA) was founded in 1976. However, the traditional concept of the adventure playground has not gained a firm foothold in the United States.

The adventure playground is not an unmalleable environment. It has less fixed equipment than does a traditional playground. In addition, the fixed equipment, such as swings and slides, is constructed in a more complex way so that it can be used for alternative activities. For example, slides allow a variety of climbing maneuvers to reach the top, or they are located close to water or sand reservoirs, whose contents can be used by children to cover the surface of the slides. Loose tools, including tires, wood, paint, plants, and seed, are the most important equipment of adventure playgrounds, stimulating children to form their own play activities. In contrast to fixed structures in traditional

A young man at a survival-style playground at an amusement park. Source: istock/Antonius Johannes Slewe.

A New Look at the Jungle Gym

Playgrounds are not just for the students at recess, or the neighborhood park. As extreme sports have flourished, extreme playgrounds have found their place in society and offered adult athletes a way to satisfy their need for extreme sports.

What Would Tarzan & Jane Say About Ropes Challenge Courses?

Why would anyone want to play in an artificial zoo to recreate some sort of "Tarzan and Jane" experience?

There are two main reasons:

- Humans evolved from a climbing, tree-dwelling ancestry and have a vestigial proclivity for experiencing the potential psychosocial and physical rewards of being at height
- Due to massive urbanization and the removal of everyday life from direct engagement with nature, this vestigial urge to climb and explore is now being increasingly engaged through artificially constructed climbing experiences

It should be noted that the extent to which individuals are favorably disposed towards taking perceived physical risks at height varies greatly, both inherently and due to past experiences with taking physical and psychological risks at height.

It might also be noted that fear of height is one of only about a half a dozen core, inherent fears that humans seem to be born with (others include fear of drowning, fire, suffocation, etc.). By directly engaging with a core fear such as height in supportive conditions, a well-run ropes course program can be a significant and even transformative experience giving rise to a greater capacity for handling fear-type reactions in other settings.

Source: Neill, J. (2006). *What is a ropes challenge course?* Retrieved Feb. 1, 2007, from http://wilderdom.com/ropes/RopesWhatIs.html

---

playgrounds, moveable or loose materials can be arranged in multiple ways by children. The aim of this concept is to foster more creative play, which is thought to support social and cognitive development.

Particularly in the United States the traditional forms of adventure playgrounds have been changed into a form that stresses fixed material and equipment. However, in contrast to traditional playgrounds, the main facilities are not slides, swings, ladders, or fields for traditional team games. Such modified adventure playgrounds feature artificial climbing walls, ropes courses, ponds for rafting, and skateboard parks.

Without doubt the focus of these playgrounds is more on challenging physical activities. One can speak of extreme activity playgrounds as visitors are offered the possibility to climb difficult wall routes, perform stunts in skateboard half pipes, and master exercises in high ropes courses. Extreme playgrounds provide a space where youths (and some older devotees) can satisfy their quest for thrill and adventure, as well as providing an alternative to unsanctioned activities including skateboarding on crowded streets, illegal car races and even train surfing.

These questionable ways of spending leisure time are not only potentially very dangerous for the adolescents' health and even life but will also often lead to severe conflicts with the community or with the police. Extreme activity playgrounds can offer a sanctioned and safe outlet for the adolescents´ quest for excitement and non day-to-day experiences. One might even argue that the educational intent of the extreme activity playground is comparable with the intent of playgrounds in the late nineteenth and early twentieth centuries, namely, to keep children off the streets and out of mischief.

Stephan Wassong

Further Reading

Cavallo, D. (1981). *Muscles and morals: Organized playgrounds and urban reform, 1880–1920*. Philadelphia: University of Pennsylvania Press.

Cross, G. S. (Ed.). (2004). *Encyclopedia of recreation and leisure in America*. New York: Charles Scribner's Sons.

Frost, J. (1992). *Play and playscapes*. Clifton Park, NY: Thomson Delmar Learning.

Riess, S. (1989). *City games: The evolution of American urban society and the rise of sport*. Chicago: University of Illinois Press.

Professional Wrestling

Although not as popular as it was during the late 1990s when there were three nationally televised wrestling shows on the air in the United States, and when characters such as Sting, the Rock, and Stone Cold Steve Austin were referenced across numerous domains of popular culture, professional wrestling continues to be an immensely popular, profitable, and increasingly global business (Atkinson 2002; Hackett 2006). One aspect of pro wrestling that continues to draw both fan attention and critical ire is what has become known as "extreme" versions of what World Wrestling Entertainment (WWE) owner Vince McMahon calls "sports entertainment." The term *extreme wrestling* has many meanings, and what constitutes *extreme* is always socioculturally constructed. In contemporary wrestling, when wrestling matches, and in some cases entire promotions, are labeled extreme, they are characterized by: (1) depictions of more explicitly "violent" acts, (2) the use of some type of potentially dangerous implement or stipulation (i.e., barbed wire match; table, ladder, and chair matches; death match, etc.), and (3) the inclusion of risky behaviors and moves. In these ways extreme pro wrestling stands in opposition to mat-based matches that focus more on storytelling and ring logic than on violent spectacles and heavy blood content, and on technical skill more than brawling and high-flying aerials. Other terms related to the use of "extreme" as it relates to wrestling include *hardcore* wrestling and the more pejorative *garbage* wrestling.

Extreme wrestling, then, encompasses a range of match styles. Hardcore matches generally involve the use of what would otherwise be illegal tactics and a variety of implements, including tables, ladders, chairs, garbage cans, metal signs, canes, barbed wire boards, baseball bats, and virtually any other usable metal object. One interesting type of match, generally called a "fans bring the weapons" match, has yielded such random contributions as cheese graters, boat oars, and even spiny puffer fish. Sometimes, the weapons and implements are "gimmicked," which means that they have been altered in some way to reduce the amount of danger to the performers. For instance, rather than using steel garbage cans, many mainstream hardcore matches utilize cans made from much softer metal that dents easily while still providing a visual effect similar to that of harder metals. At the far end of the extreme form of wrestling contests are death matches, which are characterized by often-brutal violence (albeit within constraints that the two wrestlers agree to), massive amounts of blood, and the potential for permanent injury or death. For instance, the IWA Japan promotion held an annual "King of the Death Match" tournament that included exploding barbed wire boards and ring ropes made of barbed wire. U.S. wrestlers such as Terry Funk, Sabu, and Mick Foley all wrestled in death matches before being widely known as hardcore in the United States.

Adding "Color" to the Ring: Blood as Extreme

One salient element of extreme wrestling involves the practice of adding "color," or blood, to matches. Indeed, pro wrestling has employed numerous gimmick matches designed to add spectacle to bloody feuds for decades. For example, beginning in the early 1960s, wrestlers like the Sheik and Abdullah the Butcher had matches that were labeled as "bloodbaths." In fact, some of the current hardcore matches originated in the mid-twentieth century, including dog-collar matches, in which the two wrestlers are fitted with dog collars, connected with a steel chain. According to Kristian Pope and Ray Whebbe Jr. (2003), the first use of fire in matches was in Puerto Rico in the late 1980s by wrestling legend and promoter Carlos Colon. Arguably, the most common of the extreme matches throughout the latter twentieth century was the cage match, in which performers routinely "bladed" after being driven into the chain fence surrounding the ring. Despite its appearance bloodshed in the wrestling ring is almost always done by blading, or juicing, which involves the performer cutting himself (blading is seldom done by women wrestlers) on the forehead while hiding the act from the audience and television cameras.

Extreme Championship Wrestling

Mainstream attention to extreme elements of wrestling was bolstered by the emergence of Extreme Championship Wrestling (ECW) in 1994. Prior to 1994 what was then Eastern Championship Wrestling was a regional promotion in the northeastern United States that was affiliated with a larger umbrella organization, the National Wrestling Alliance (NWA). Following the rise of an "alternative" popular culture in the United States and the application (and commodification) of the "extreme" label to include everything

A Mexican masked professional wrestler at the start of a match. Source: istock/eva serrabassa.

from the X Games to deodorant, new ECW owner Paul Heyman repackaged the promotion as Extreme Championship Wrestling.

While the various written and video interviews with former ECW employees illustrates that the definition of extreme was broad, the antiauthoritarian approach of the company was meant to counter the two major promotions in the United States in the mid-1990s, World Wrestling Entertainment (WWE) and World Championship Wrestling (WCW). The lasting popular characterization of ECW, however, is the result of violently creative matches and the hardcore mentality of many of the wrestlers. Indeed, almost immediately after taking over the company, Heyman changed the type of wrestling in the promotion. While extreme matches and blood were not used much in WWE and were banned from television in the Ted Turner–owned WCW, violent storylines and big "bumps" (e.g., top-rope

moves, dives to the outside of the ring, etc.) became a central aspect of how pro wrestling was performed in ECW. By 1995 ECW included a number of characters who were known not only for their wrestling skills (or lack thereof), but also for their violent gimmicks and/or ability to take increasingly dangerous risks in matches. One of the most infamous and lasting ECW images—resulting from the "feud" between Raven and Sandman—involved Raven and his henchmen tying Sandman (wearing a barbed wire "crown") onto a wooden crucifix at ringside, a scene that left some of the otherwise hardened ECW fans offended.

Kendo sticks (essentially a long stick made of a batch of thin sticks bound together) had been used many times in wrestling, but Heyman drew from the 1994 Michael Fay incident in which a young American was caned for vandalism in Singapore. Soon after, the Kendo stick became Sandman's trademark weapon, and "Singapore cane match" became part of the ECW extreme brand. Some matches, such as the Axl and Ian Rotten brawls in which the "brothers" sliced each other with broken glass glued to their taped fists and forearms, did away with virtually any sense of traditional storytelling. In the ECW documentary, *Forever Hardcore* (Borash 2005), ECW alumnus Kid Kash even stated that "to me it was a little too much." As the author of a non-WWE published history of ECW states, "ECW got the rap of being the place where guys beat each other with chairs, broke tables, and had garbage-wrestling brawls." Interestingly, the company also broke new ground in other ways, including blurring the lines between the wrestlers and the fans, bringing in Lucha Libre stars from Mexico, and giving opportunities to little-known technical wrestlers like Chris Benoit and the late Eddy Guerrero.

Backlash Against Extreme Wrestling

Perhaps the most important event that prompted a strong backlash against extreme wrestling, and specifically ECW, was the "Mass Transit" incident in which a seventeen-year-old boy, accompanied by his father, misled Heyman about both his age and his level of training, and was severely bladed by the very hardcore performer, New Jack, in a match. Although all ECW parties were exonerated, a home videotape of the teen boy's head literally streaming blood was sent (no one knows for certain by whom) to the pay-per-view providers, and the ECW company lost its PPV market for several months.

As what became known as the "hardcore style" became more mainstream, there was also a backlash against the integration of scantily clad women in matches that would often result in these women being driven through tables or slammed on the mat much like their male counterparts. Ironically, even insiders expressed concern over the risky elements of ECW. Speaking of a time when New Jack sustained serious head injuries after plunging off a balcony, Terry Taylor, a former wrester and employee of both WCW and WWE, stated: "To me, two guys almost died. That's a big deal, and it's not a big deal to the fans because they're so MTV minded they're gonna say 'What's next?' unless you slow things down to let them understand the gravity of what they just saw" (Borash 2005).

The irony of the practice of extreme pro wrestling is that in a "fake" sport the acute and chronic injuries sustained by performers are anything but, and unlike "real" high-revenue sports such as soccer, football, and baseball, wrestlers do not have a union, nor do they have traditional forms of health benefits packages.

The Death and Rebirth of ECW

Although not public knowledge at the time, Vince McMahon's WWE had been financially supporting ECW in a number of ways throughout the late 1990s, in part, according to McMahon at least, to compensate Heyman for the loss of some of his wrestlers to WWE. By the time the WWE officially bought out and assumed control over the ECW brand in 2001, they had already adopted many of the hardcore elements of the matches and had essentially copied some of the angles used earlier by ECW, particularly after the "Hardcore Legend" Mick Foley left ECW for the WWE in 1996. In 1998 McMahon presented Foley with the first "Hardcore Title" belt, but it soon came to represent a watered-down version of the original grittiness of ECW. Ironically, the WWE version of extreme wrestling is arguably much safer for both the wrestlers and for the company's investment in the performers-as-laborers (you cannot draw fans when wrestlers are injured for long periods of time). However, many elements that seemed revolutionary in ECW now appear, to regular fans, as passé, most notably the use of metal signs and canes.

The rebirth of the ECW brand began with the surprisingly success of the WWE-produced DVD, *The Rise and Fall of ECW*, and the subsequent and also very successful ECW pay-per-view event presented on 12 June 2005. In June 2006 the WWE fully relaunched the ECW, essentially as one of its new brands, to accompany the established Raw and Smackdown brands. The weekly show, which began airing on 13 June on the Sci-Fi network in the United States, was again helmed by Paul Heyman, albeit with significant input from higher-ups in the WWE. Although

Selling the Show

Pro wrestling is an act, or so it is often said. But what does it take to keep up this act? The challenge and the risk and the athleticism is certainly real.

A wrestler unleashes four monstrous punches directly to his opponent's head. He then hurls him into the ropes, where he bounces off and runs headlong into a clothesline. The crowd hears the slap of flesh hitting flesh, and the opponent catapults into the air, slamming down onto the canvas with a solid thud.

If anyone really went through this, they'd probably end up with a concussion, a broken jaw and some cracked ribs at the very least. Pro wrestlers work very hard to make their moves look real, but inflict minimal damage. This is known as selling. If someone hits you with a pulled punch that barely touches you, but you time it correctly and leap backward as though you'd been smashed, then you've sold the move. Wrestlers really do hit each other, and it really does hurt. They just don't hit each other as hard as they make it appear.

While a match is going on, stage directions and signals are flying between the performers, the referee, ringside officials and ringside managers. Occasionally you can spot the wrestlers talking to each other, planning the next series of moves. When it's time for the match to end, the ref will tell one of the wrestlers to "bring it home."

Source: Grabianowski, E. Retrieved Jan. 20, 2007, from http://entertainment.howstuffworks.com/pro-wrestling3.htm

poorly received by "insider" fans, known as "smart marks," as well as wrestling publications such as the long-running *Wrestling Observer Newsletter*, the rebranded ECW was a ratings success for the network (2.8 rating). It remains to be seen if the McMahon-owned version of the company can meet the need for profitability while retaining the qualities that made ECW so influential in the 1990s.

The Future of Hardcore Wrestling

Some remnants of the ECW-style crowd behavior, most notably loud chants of "Holy shit! Holy shit!," are still standard fare whenever moves collectively deemed as extreme occur in various promotions. However, because the standards of what it takes to shock fans have been raised, simply crashing through a table or falling on tacks alone do not elicit as strong of a response when the event doesn't offer a rationale for the action. Thus, in this environment in order for the action to be perceived as extreme, wrestlers have to take risks that could very easily result in permanent disability or death. Further, even though serious injuries appear to be relatively rare, the proliferation of risky moves and big "bumps" potentially increases the number of wrestlers who have developed dependencies on pain medications.

The most noteworthy current bearer of the extreme wrestling label is the relatively small indie promotion, Combat Zone Wrestling (CZW). Though it also features performers who focus on high-flying spots and mat-based wrestling, CZW is most well known for its stiff working style and violent, bloody matches. For example, they hold a yearly Tournament of Death event in Delaware, featuring ultraviolent, bloody, and risky elements. In one CZW event, former wrestler Nick Mondo was actually "attacked" with a weedwacker. This type of wrestling, however, remains at the fringes of the popular consciousness. As sport sociologist Peter Donnelley (2004) has noted, the irony of risk activities, including sport, is that they exist in the current climate of post–September 11, 2001, a climate of hypercautiousness and, more generally, what author Barry Glassner (1999) calls the "culture of fear" that pervades the United States.

Ted Butryn

Further Reading

Atkinson, M. (2002). Fifty million viewers can't be wrong: Professional wrestling, sports-entertainment, and mimesis. *Sociology of Sport Journal, 19*, 47–66

Borash, J. (Director). (2005). *Forever hardcore: The documentary* [Film]. Sherman Oaks, CA: Big Vision Entertainment.

Donnelly, P. (2004). Sport and risk culture. In K. Young (Ed.), *Sporting bodies, damaged selves: Sociological studies of sports-related injury* (pp. 29–58). Boston: Elsevier Press.

Glassner, B. (1999). *The culture of fear: Why Americans are afraid of the wrong things.* New York: Basic Books.

Hackett, T. (2006). *Slaphappy: Pride, prejudice, and professional wrestling.* New York: HarperCollins.

Lister, J. (2005). *Turning the tables: The story of Extreme Championship Wrestling.* Liskeard, Cornwall, UK: Exposure Publishing.

Meltzer, D. (2005, June 20). *Wrestling Observer Newsletter.*

Pope, K., & Whebbe Jr., R. (2003). *The encyclopedia of professional wrestling* (2nd ed.). Iola, WI: Krause Publications.

Rahilly, L. (2005). Is Raw war?: Professional wrestling as popular S/M narrative. In N. Sammond (Ed.), *Steel chair to the head: The pleasure and pain of professional wrestling* (pp. 213–231). Durham, NC: Duke University Press.

Williams, S. E. (2006). *Hardcore history: The extremely unauthorized story of ECW.* Champaign, IL: Sports Publishing L.L.C.

Psychology of Risk

Risk is a common phenomenon in everyday life. The risk involved in any action can be defined as the probability of a negative outcome (harm or loss) occurring multiplied by the magnitude or seriousness of the consequences of that action. Risk has been analyzed from such diverse perspectives as financial activities, game theory, military strategy, politics, health behaviors, and sports.

Risk taking is a voluntary act that involves the intention of receiving a positive outcome. Risk tolerance is a measure of the level of risk that an individual is willing to assume to gain a particular positive outcome or to avoid a negative outcome. Some individuals may be willing to assume a risk that is proportionate to the potential for gain. Risk takers, or sensation seekers, are individuals who will accept a high level of risk in proportion to the anticipated return. Other people, referred to as "risk averse," will expect or be more willing to accept a significantly lower-than-optimum outcome if the possibility of loss is reduced, either relatively or absolutely. Risk takers, or sensation seekers, are commonly found in a variety of extreme sports because the inherent risk of extreme sports is attractive to them.

Antecedents of Risk Taking

Researchers have conducted a great deal of research on the causes of risk taking, also commonly referred to as "thrill seeking" or "sensation seeking." Researchers have suggested physiological and chemical, social and cultural, and psychological reasons for why people engage in risk taking.

In the biochemical field some researchers have found risk taking to be associated with deficient levels of monoamine oxidase (MAO)—an enzyme that regulates neurotransmitters (chemicals that send neurological messages between neurons)—and dopamine. Other researchers have pinpointed a specific gene, the D4DR gene, which is responsible for determining a person's propensity for risk taking. The long version of the gene is found in high thrill seekers. The short version of is found in risk-averse people. The long version of D4DR is more common in people whose ancestors migrated long distances to settle in another area. Researchers have discovered that genetics explain 60 percent of the variation in sensation seeking, which is a high degree of heritability. Finally, a strong link has been drawn between risk taking and high levels of testosterone. This link is illustrated by the fact that the majority of risk takers, particularly in extreme sports, are young and male. Evidence indicates that sensation-seeking behavior, as well as testosterone, begins to trail off with age.

Sociologists have found that extensive subcultures frequently develop around risk-taking activities. This is particularly the case with extreme sports participants. Each extreme sports subculture takes on its own identity, complete with its own language, rituals, symbols, and styles. Within the confines of its sport, such a subculture is conducive to risk taking and socially uninhibited behavior. Extreme sports subcultures attract risk takers because they promote a sense of belonging that is elusive to many risk takers who are surrounded by a risk-averse, normal population.

Researchers have not discovered a definitive, absolute cause of risk taking. The cause is most likely a combination of several theories. Psychology offers insights into the mental characteristics and processes that influence individuals to take risks. The mental characteristics are easier to test on a large scale than the biochemical and sociological characteristics and therefore are the most extensively developed.

Four Schools of Sports Psychological Thought

Four of the prevailing schools of psychological thought that researchers have used to study risk taking and extreme sports are the trait approach, the psychodynamic approach, the situational approach, and the interactional approach. The trait and interactional approaches are both frequently used in sports psychology. The trait approach is the most widely used. The interactional approach integrates the trait and situational approaches and adds additional insights. The situational and psychodynamic approaches have had less impact on the psychology of sports.

Trait Approach

The trait approach emphasizes the importance of personality characteristics, or traits, as the main influencers of behavior. This approach proposes that traits, which are primary building blocks of personality, remain relatively stable and consistent over time and a wide variety of situations. Followers of the trait approach believe that internal factors (traits) predispose an individual's behavior, without much consideration of environmental or situational factors.

Allport and Odbert identified some eighteen thousand words that attempt to describe personality, from which they developed a list of more than forty-five hundred traits that describe human behavior and are relatively stable and permanent. Models describing enthusiastic and impulsive individuals date back to the Vata personality in Ayurvedic medicine (3000 BCE). Hippocrates (4000 BCE) and Galen (150 CE) discussed the sanguine personality (optimistic and open to new experiences). The sanguine personality is an important part of the twentieth-century risk-taking research of Hans Eysenck.

Several well-known psychologists have employed the trait approach in ways that are useful for understanding the psychology of risk taking, especially that of extreme sports participants.

▶ **Frank Farley and the Type T Personality** Frank Farley is a pioneer in the psychology of risk taking and specifically thrill seeking. Farley developed the concept of a thrill-seeking personality type. People with this personality type are referred to as "Type Ts." The Type T personality consists of a series of continuums. First, if a person possesses a high level of thrill-seeking characteristics, then he or she is a "Big T." Conversely, if a person has a low degree of thrill-seeking characteristics, then he or she is a "little t." Most people fall somewhere in the middle of the continuum, with risk seekers and risk avoiders in the outer positions.

Next, Type Ts can express their personality in positive and negative ways. Extreme sports participation, firefighting, and entrepreneurship are examples of positive Type T behavior. Negative Type T behavior can take the form of excessive alcohol use, smoking, promiscuity, and criminal behavior. Type T individuals are not limited to either positive or negative thrill seeking. They sometimes engage in some positive and some negative activities. As a result, positive and negative thrill seeking may be represented as different subsets of the Type T personality.

Additionally, thrill seeking may take either or both of the forms of mental (cognitive) thrill seeking and physical (sensory) thrill seeking. Examples of mental thrill seeking are gambling and investment banking. Examples of physical thrill seeking are participating in extreme sports and riding roller coasters. A high level of either mental or physical thrill seeking in an individual Type T does not preclude a high level of the other type of thrill seeking. So, mental and physical thrill seeking are not mutually exclusive. Therefore, mental and physical thrill seeking also represent two separate continuums.

▶ **Farley's Type T Personality Continuums** Farley proposed that Type Ts comprise a distinct group of individuals. Farley and other researchers have found that Type Ts crave novelty, excitement, thrills, and risks. Individuals with Type T personalities are highly inclined toward extreme sports. They think creatively and abstractly and thrive in work environments that allow variety and provide mental or physical stimulation. Type Ts also prefer more variety in many aspects of their lives.

Farley's original insights have been expanded by several researchers who have developed instruments to measure the traits of thrill seeking and risk taking. Several of these researchers have developed subscales to measure individual components of thrill seeking or risk taking.

▶ **Marvin Zuckerman and Sensation Seeking** Arguably the most influential of these researchers is Marvin Zuckerman. Instead of "risk taking," he called the behavior "sensation seeking," and instead of "risk takers" or "Type Ts," he called those people with this type of personality "sensation seekers." Zuckerman characterized sensation seekers as people who have a need for a wide variety of new and involved sensations and experiences and are willing to take physical and social risks to achieve them. Zuckerman proposed that all individuals have an optimal level of arousal. Those who are high in sensation seeking have a higher optimal level of arousal than those who are low in sensation seeking.

Zuckerman found that sensation seeking tends to fade with age. Also, sensation seekers are more commonly male than female, although many women and older individuals are sensation seekers. Sensation seekers can be differentiated through their propensity to engage in risky health behaviors and extreme sports.

Zuckerman developed several scales. Zuckerman-Kuhlman's Personality Questionnaire (ZKPQ) has proven useful in identifying sensation seekers. The ZKPQ measures five qualities: sociability, neuroticism-anxiety, impulsive sensation seeking, aggression-hostility, and activity. Sociability (Sy) relates to a person's quantity of friends and the amount of time spent with them versus spending time alone. Neuroticism-anxiety (N-Anx) includes a variety of traits of emotionality, such as tension, fearfulness, and lack of self-confidence. Impulsive sensation seeking (ImpSS) combines lack of planning and foresight with the willingness to take risks for the sake of experience. Aggression-hostility (Agg-Host) comprises traits such as willingness to express verbal aggression and other rude or antisocial behavior. Activity (Act) describes the preference for staying busy and the distaste for inactivity.

High scores on impulsive sensation seeking, aggression-hostility, and sociability are the strongest indicators of risk taking, often taking the form of participation in extreme sports. Many sensation seekers have varying scores on neuroticism-anxiety, which provides a possible indication of whether an individual sensation seeker may lean toward risky health (high N-Anx) and/or (low N-Anx) risky sports activities. A high score on Activity may indicate an inclination to become involved in extreme sports.

Zuckerman's four-part sensation-seeking scale (SSS-V) is one of the most popular psychological scales currently used in research on risk taking. The SSS-V includes four factors: thrill and adventure seeking, experience seeking, disinhibition, and boredom susceptibility. A previous version of this scale also included impulsivity. Thrill and adventure seeking (TAS) is the desire to engage in extreme sports and/or other dangerous activities. Experience seeking (ES) is the desire to seek novel experiences through travel and unconventional friends and lifestyles. Disinhibition (Dis) is

A young woman engaged in a mind-body exercise as she balances on a stone cylinder. Source: istock.

a lack of inhibited social behavior involving promiscuity and substance use. Boredom susceptibility (BS) is distaste for repetitive, or routine, work and/or people. Sensation seekers score highly on all four subsets of the SSS-V.

Goma-i-Freixanet found a strong connection between the total SSS-V, as well as several of the subscales, and participation in extreme sports. Specifically, thrill and adventure seeking are strongly linked to scuba diving, skydiving, hang gliding, mountain and rock climbing, and whitewater kayaking. Experience seeking is linked to hang gliding, rock climbing, rodeo riding, and other sports. Disinhibition is linked to scuba diving, mountain climbing, hang gliding, and rodeo riding. Boredom susceptibility is linked to many of the extreme sports. The total score on the SSS-V scale was found to be strongly related to participation in scuba diving, skydiving, hang gliding, mountain and rock climbing, whitewater kayaking, extreme skiing, rodeo riding, and spelunking.

Type T personality and *sensation seeker* have become practically synonymous terms. Many researchers have built on Farley's and Zuckerman's findings. David Puretz has noted that sensation seekers or Type Ts are more inclined to do the following: "whitewater kayaking, having unprotected sex … perhaps with strangers, rock climbing, listening to complex music such as classical, jazz, or the most extreme forms of rock, binge drinking, hang gliding, driving fast, driving drunk, auto racing, sky-diving, eating hot, sour or crunchy food, gambling, using drugs, riding roller coasters, watching sex or horror films, traveling to exotic places, cliff jumping, and engaging in combat" (Puretz, 2003). Although Farley and Zuckerman may arguably be the most influential in the psychology of risk taking, other researchers' personality models are worth mentioning.

▶ **Hans Eysenck and the Big Three** Hans Eysenck developed the Eysenck Personality Questionnaire, which has since been revised, also known as the "Big Three structural model." The three subscales are psychoticism (P), extraversion (E), and neuroticism (N). Psychoticism is characterized by traits such as impulsivity, hostility, antisocial tendency, inappropriate emotional expression, recklessness, and disregard for common sense. Eysenck's psychoticism corresponds with Zuckerman's impulsive sensation seeking and aggression-hostility. Extraversion is characterized by traits such as outgoingness, talkativeness, assertiveness, and the tendency to enjoy social events. Eysenck's extraversion corresponds with Zuckerman's sociability and activity. Neuroticism is characterized by a lack of emotional stability, evident in conditions such as depression, anxiety, and obsessive-compulsive disorder. Eysenck's neuroticism is similar to Zuckerman's neuroticism.

Most of the research on Eysenck's Big Three personality dimensions and risk taking has been related to risky health behaviors. Researchers have found that high scores on all three of the dimensions indicate an inclination for health risk taking, such as cigarette smoking, alcohol abuse, sexual risk taking, and unsafe driving.

▶ **Paul Costa and Robert McCrae and the Big Five** Paul Costa and Robert McCrae developed the Neuroticism Extraversion Openness Personality Inventory (NEO-PI), also known as the "Big Five structural model" or the "Five Factor model." This model has become the standard in the psycho-logical literature. The five factors are neuroticism (N), extraversion (E), openness to experience (O), conscientiousness (C), and agreeableness (A). The definitions of Costa and McCrae's neuroticism and extraversion mirror those of Eysenck. In many texts "neuroticism" is referred to as "lack of emotional stability." Openness to experience is an appreciation for art, adventure, imaginative and creative ideas, and experience for the sake of experiencing. Conscientiousness is the tendency to be self-disciplined and conforming, to show self-restraint, and to behave dutifully. Conscientiousness also measures achievement and motivation. Agreeableness is characterized by compassion for, and cooperation with, others.

The Big Five model is a modification of the Big Three model. Eysenck, Costa, and McCrae agreed that extraversion and neuroticism are important aspects of personality. Although Costa and McCrae added dimensions, Eysenck claimed that his psychoticism subscale inversely measures the same constructs as Costa and McCrae's agreeableness and conscientiousness. Openness to experience is a new construct not covered under the Big Three.

In reference to both health-related and sports-related risk-taking behavior, Costa and McCrae's model provides clues to identifying risk takers or sensation seekers. Openness to experience and extraversion are positively related to risk-taking behavior. Agreeableness and conscientiousness are negatively related to risk-taking behavior. Levels of neuroticism often vary among risk takers. However, evidence suggests that those with high neuroticism may be more inclined to participate in risky health practices, whereas those with low neuroticism may be more inclined to participate in risky sports activities. Nonetheless, these statements are not absolute; plenty of risk takers are involved in both risky sports and risky health activities.

A significant amount of overlap exists between the models mentioned. All of them offer insight into risk-taking or sensation-seeking behavior. The relationships between the models should also be considered when testing individuals for risk-taking or sensation-seeking personality traits. The fact that some individual risk takers' personality traits may vary from these models should also be taken into consideration.

Psychodynamic Approach

The Austrian neurologist Sigmund Freud, along with his followers, developed and popularized the psychodynamic approach. It focuses on the unconscious determinants of be-

---

The Psychology of Risk

An excerpt from Betsy Cowles Partridge: Mountaineer, *a book detailing the travels of Partridge, one of the first women to climb extensively throughout the world.*

We crossed three wearisome ridges, like triplets each was so identical with the other except that it got a bit higher each time. From the top of the last we saw at leave five more and beyond, as unconcerned as may be, our mountain looking incredibly remote. Really, it looked further away than when we had started. We retreated like Napoleon from Moscow. When finally, in desperation, far below in the old labyrinth of cliffs and lakes, we decide to wade a last obstacle, we sank in mud up to our waists and probably would have disappeared completely and forever had we not clung by our ice axes to niches on the overhang above us. Paul declares it was the most dangerous moment of his life.

I just know that it was the dirtiest of mine.

Source: Robertson, J. (1998). *Betsy Cowles Partridge: mountaineer.* Niwot: University Press of Colorado.

havior and views a person as a whole entity instead of focusing on individual traits. Some psychoanalysts feel that risk-taking behavior is a sign of mental illness. They believe that no logical reason exists to take risks (particularly mountaineering) and that participation in extreme sports is most likely an expression of a "death wish" or a feeling of inferiority. However, little evidence supports these hypotheses. Many people who participate in extreme sports may argue that their self-esteem actually increases as a result of their sports. The psychodynamic approach has weaknesses that have led to its not being widely used in sports psychology. The most important weakness is that the psychodynamic approach is difficult to measure and test. Also, because it focuses on unconscious determinants of behavior, it does not consider environmental factors that may affect behavior. This approach is more widely used in Europe than in the United States.

Situational Approach

The situational approach is on the other end of the spectrum from the psychodynamic approach. It focuses on the relationship between behavior and environmental factors to the exclusion of internal factors. Proponents of the situational approach believe that all behavior is shaped by environmental influences. Whereas the environment may influence the behavior of some people in one way, other people may react differently to the same environmental stimulus. A sensation seeker's environment may influence the type of risk taking in which he or she engages. Studies have shown that the socioeconomic environment can have an impact because children with fewer economic resources often engage in more negative or delinquent forms of risk taking, whereas children who have ample economic resources can afford expensive sports equipment and lessons. Also, the geographic environment influences what sports a sensation seeker may practice. For example, a person who lives near a beach is more likely to surf, a person who lives near snow is more likely to snowboard, and a person who lives near mountains is more likely to rock climb. Another situational variable, peer acceptance and peer pressure, has proven to effectively frame promotional messages to sensation seekers.

Interactional Approach

The interactional approach is a combination of the trait and situational approaches. This approach recognizes that both an individual's personality traits and situational, or environmental, factors can influence behavior. Followers of the interactional approach believe that these two areas play an important role; however, the interaction between personality traits and situational factors has a synchronous influence on behavior. For example, sensation seekers who have access to the appropriate environments (i.e., oceans, mountains, airplanes) are even more likely to participate in extreme sports that necessitate those environments than are sensation seekers who do not have access to those environments. Also, those people who have a sensation-seeking personality and have access to the appropriate environments are far more likely to participate in extreme sports than are those without a sensation-seeking personality.

▶ **Values, Attitudes, and Lifestyles Survey (VALS)** Psychographics is an interactional approach that seeks to understand individual behavior by combining demographics with psychology. One of the most successful psychographic models—Values, Attitudes, and Lifestyles Survey (VALS) from SRI Consulting Business Intelligence—has been used to identify characteristics that match extreme sports enthusiasts. Two of the eight types in VALS—experiencers and innovators—have been related to participation in several extreme sports.

Experiencers, who are likely to be single (two-thirds) and young (about half under age twenty-five), comprise about one-eighth of the U.S. adult population. They are enthusiastic and impulsive and seek variety and excitement, including the risky. Behaviors or activities of experiencers are likely to include participation in mountain biking, snowboarding, skateboarding, surfing/windsurfing, in-line skating, and whitewater rafting.

Innovators are slightly older, with one-third under age thirty-five and a median age of forty-five. They represent about one-tenth of the U.S. population. Described as successful and active and having high self-esteem, these individuals continue to seek challenges and are open to change. Innovators are likely to backpack, ski, snowboard, in-line skate, windsurf, and rock climb.

Although VALS is not directly related to risk seeking, the details provided in reports from SRI provide a wealth of information about extreme sports participants—characteristic attitudes and behaviors, activities, purchases, and media.

▶ **Risk Homeostasis Theory** Geralde Wilde and John Adams have proposed the concept of risk homeostasis (a relatively stable state of equilibrium), which has also had a large impact on the psychology of risk taking. Risk Homeostasis Theory, originally identified by Sam Peltzman, helps explain why risk takers seek out risks. It should be noted, however, that rebuttals of this theory have come from within the insurance industry.

Risk Homeostasis Theory advances the idea that each person has his or her own target risk. Sensation seekers or risk takers have a higher acceptable level of target risk than do risk-averse people. When a situation presents more perceived risk than a person's target risk, he or she will make behavioral changes to bring the level of risk back to the target level. Conversely, if a situation presents less risk than a person's target risk, then he or she will become susceptible to boredom and find new ways to create risk in order to maintain the target risk. These changes produce a homeostatic effect because a person will constantly make changes to the situational level of risk to converge with his or her target risk.

Risk Homeostasis Theory is similar to ideas proposed by Zuckerman and Farley. Zuckerman's concept of optimal level of arousal is comparable with an acceptable level of target risk. In this case sensation seekers strive to maintain their optimal level of arousal through the introduction or removal of sensation. The optimal level of arousal also employs a homeostatic effect as a person continuously modifies his or her environment or situation. These concepts are virtually the same.

Early research on Risk Homeostasis Theory involved driving situations. Studies have shown that the introduction of safety requirements, such as mandatory seat-belt use, does not reduce the aggregate amount of deaths caused by driving accidents. The explanation is that seat belts reduce drivers' perceived level of risk. In response drivers introduce more risk to the situation in order to raise their perceived risk back to their acceptable level of target risk. For example, a driver may feel safer with a seat belt, so he or she may drive faster.

Risk Homeostasis Theory has also been applied to extreme sports. Vic Napier has pioneered the application of Risk Homeostasis Theory to fatalities in skydiving. He observed the effects of this theory in skydiving with the introduction of Cypres automatic activation devices (AAD). AADs are a fairly recent technology that automatically deploys the reserve parachute if a skydiver is still above a certain speed at a certain altitude. The speed and altitude can vary depending on whether the AAD is for a normal, student, or tandem parachute. Napier theorized that the introduction of AADs would reduce the number of deaths in the "no pull-low pull" category. However, because skydivers would have a lessened perceived risk, they would introduce new risk in order to maintain their level of perceived target risk. This development has coincided with an increasing number of deaths in other categories, such as open canopy fatalities, creating a homeostatic effect while keeping the aggregate number of deaths relatively stable. Napier collected data from the United States Parachute Association (USPA), Skydive.net, and SSK Industries (the manufacturer of the Cypres AAD). Indeed, he found that from 1989 through 1998 the introduction of Cypres AADs reduced the number of "no pull-low pull" fatalities, whereas the number of landing fatalities rose. He attributed this phenomenon to risk homeostasis.

In a report prepared for the U.S. Coast Guard, researchers also found evidence of Risk Homeostasis Theory in operation with the use of sponsons in kayaking. Sponsons are structures that can be attached to the sides of canoes and kayaks in order to add stability, increase flotation, and lessen the likelihood of capsizing and flooding. The findings concluded that, although the purpose of sponsons is to reduce the risk of kayaking, they often have an opposite effect: Sponsons gave paddlers a false sense of confidence, so that they took on situations that were beyond their skill levels. The findings concluded that additional safety devices, such as sponsons, are generally ineffective because users often increased their risk-taking behavior in response to lower perceived levels of risk.

Negative Risk Taking

Many thrill seekers may exhibit one or more negative health-related behaviors and traits. These include reckless driving, tobacco use, alcohol abuse, drug abuse, suicide, depression, and sexually transmitted diseases. Further, researchers have shown that adolescents who engage in one risky behavior are much more likely to engage in other risky behaviors. Childhood trauma and abuse may worsen these tendencies. Whether a sensation seeker follows a more positive direction, such as extreme sports, or a negative direction may be influenced by his or her childhood experiences and peer pressure. This is true especially because high sensation seekers are more affected by peer pressure than are low sensation seekers.

Future Implications

Researchers have extensively studied risk taking and specifically the expression of risk taking in the form of extreme sports. Many have arrived at hypotheses, but no one has produced a definitive and comprehensive rationale for risk taking. Researchers could survey many extreme sports participants as to why they do what they do, and the researchers would find thousands of differing reasons. This provides an opportunity for further research.

At some point researchers may discover that all risk-taking behavior is biochemical in nature. If so, this finding will not diminish the role of psychology in the study of risk-taking activities. Risk takers are an important segment of society with special wants, needs, and lifestyles. They may serve as opinion leaders in the adoption of new extreme sports and, possibly, new products and concepts. In analyzing the effectiveness of communicating with risk takers, researchers have found that messages delivered by electronic media to risk takers should pay more attention to ephemeral (cue-based content that requires minimal effort) and narrative processing, where the message is related in story form. This processing has proven more important than cognitive (analytically based reasoning) message processing. Messages that are novel, dramatic, intense, exciting, suspenseful, or fast provide higher attention and involvement.

Several research questions can help expand the knowledge base about risk takers. More information is needed about the relative impact of such cultural variables as family, mobility, and friends. More knowledge about the ephemeral processing elements would also be useful.

Risk takers tend to have behaviors and musical preferences that are different from those of risk-averse individuals, allowing them to be targeted as a different market segment. As tastes change in music and fashions, the preferences of sensation seekers will also change. These changes can be used to tailor messages that have a better chance of overcoming the boredom susceptibility problem.

Finally, more knowledge is needed about the substitution of alternate, positive activities for negative risk-taking activities. In addition to extreme sports, a wide range of aesthetic, intellectual, artistic, audio, and visual activities can stimulate risk takers.

Don Self and Carolyn Findley

See also Physiology of Risk; Sociology of Risk

Further Reading

Adams, J. (1995). *Risk*. London: UCL Press.

Baumgartner, H., & Steenkamp, J. (1994). An investigation into the construct validity of the arousal seeking tendency scale, version II. *Educational and Psychological Measurement*, 54(4), 993–1001.

Beal, B. (1995). Disqualifying the official: An exploration of social resistance through the subculture of skateboarding. *Sociology of Sport Journal*, 12, 252–267.

Celsi, R., Rose, R., & Leigh, T. (1993). An exploration of high-risk leisure consumption through skydiving. *Journal of Consumer Research*, 20, 1–23.

Costa, P. A., Jr., & McCrae, R. R. (1992). *Revised NEO personality inventory and NEO five-factor inventory, professional manual*. Odessa, FL: Psychological Assessment Resources.

Diehm, R., & Armatas, C. (2004). Surfing: An avenue for socially acceptable risk-taking, satisfying needs for sensation seeking and experience seeking. *Personality and Individual Differences*, 36(3), 663–677.

Farley, F. (1986). The big T in personality; thrill-seeking often produces the best achievers but it can also create the worst criminals. *Psychology Today*, 20, 44–48.

Goma-i-Freixanet, M. (2004). Sensation seeking and participation in physical risk sports. In R. M. Stelmack (Ed.), *On the psychobiology of personality: Essays in honor of Marvin Zuckerman* (pp. 185–202). Oxford, UK: Elsevier.

Howe, S. (1998). *(Sick): A cultural history of snowboarding*. New York: St. Martin's Press.

Humphreys, D. (1997). Shredheads go mainstream? Snowboarding and alternative youth. *International Review for the Sociology of Sport*, 32(2), 147–160.

Lauriola, M, Russo, P., Lucidi, F., Violani, C., & Levin, I. (2005). The role of personality in positively and negatively framed risky health decisions. *Personality and Individual Differences*, 38(1), 45–59.

Mehrabian, A., & Bekken, M. (1986). Temperament characteristics of individuals who participate in strenuous sports. *Research Quarterly for Exercise and Sport*, 57, 160–166.

O'Neill, B., & Williams, A. (1998). Risk homeostasis hypothesis; a rebuttal. *Injury Prevention*, 4, 92–93.

Peltzman, S. (1975). The effects of automobile safety regulation. *Journal of Political Economy*, 83(4), 677–725.

Puretz, D. E. (April 2003). The novelty seeking gene. *Buzzsaw Haircut*. Retrieved Jan. 19, 2007, from http://www.ithaca.edu/buzzsaw/0203 thrill.htm.

Roberts, P. (1994). Risk. *Psychology Today*, 24(6), 50.

Schwebel, D., Severson, J., Ball, K., & Rizzo, M. (2006). Individual difference factors in risky driving: The roles of anger/hostility, conscientiousness, and sensation-seeking. *Accident Analysis & Prevention*, 38(4), 801–810.

Sohn, E. (2004). Roller coaster thrills. Retrieved December 18, 2006, from http://www.sciencenewsforkids.org/articles/20040616/Feature1.asp

SRI Consulting Business Intelligence. (2003). *Understanding U.S. consumers*. Menlo Park, CA: Author.

Tenenbaum, D. (n.d.). T-types thrive on thrills. Retrieved December 18, 2006, from http://whyfiles.org/026fear/psych1.html

Trobst, K., Herbst, J., Master, H., & Costa, P. (2002). Personality pathways to unsafe sex: Personality, condom use, and HIV risk behaviors. *Journal of Research in Personality*, 36(2), 117–133.

Weinberg, R., & Gould, D. (2003). *Foundations of sport and exercise psychology* (3rd ed.). Champaign, IL: Human Kinetics.

Weiss, R. (1987). How dare we? Scientists seek the sources of risk-taking behavior. *Science News, 132,* 57.

Wheaton, B. (2000). "Just do it": Consumption, commitment, and identity in the windsurfing subculture. *Sociology of Sport Journal, 17,* 254–274.

Wilde, G. J. S. (1994). *Target risk, dealing with the danger of death, disease and damage in everyday decisions.* Toronto, Canada: PDE Publications.

Zuckerman, M. (1979). *Sensation seeking: Beyond the optimal level of arousal.* Hillsdale, NJ: Lawrence Erlbaum Associates.

Zuckerman, M. (1994). *Behavioral expression and biosocial bases of sensation seeking.* New York: Cambridge University Press.

Zuckerman, M. (2000). Are you a risk taker? *Psychology Today, 33*(6), 52.

Zuckerman, M., Kuhlman, D. M., Joireman, J., Teta, P., & Kraft, M. (1993). A comparison of three structural models for personality: The big three, the big five, and the alternative five. *Journal of Personality and Social Psychology, 65*(4), 757–768.

Queenstown

Queenstown, New Zealand, is located on the Queenstown Bay inlet of Lake Wakatipu in the Southern Lakes region of South Island. The town was originally known as "Tahuna" (shallows) by the indigenous Maori people and later called the "Camp" after gold miners in the 1860s gathered on W. G. Rees's sheep station. The present name may have come from a public gathering in 1863 when the government acquired the town and the government or citizens or both decided that the town was "fit for a queen." Another theory maintains that the town was evocative of Queenstown, Ireland, to many local miners.

An aerial view of Queenstown, and the lake.
Source: istock/Paulus Rusyanto.

Extreme Tourism

Queenstown is the extreme sports capital of the world, where the fearless go to frighten themselves.

The adventure business is the town's lifeblood. Tourists outnumber locals 100–1, and all of them want something unforgettable. When you talk about adventure tourism in New Zealand, this is where it all began. Queenstown was put on the map with the first commercial bungee jump on 12 November 1988. Since then 450,000 people have taken the plunge.

The secret to bungee's success is that even though it looks very dangerous, it is in fact pretty safe. What people pay US$85 for is the fear factor, according to bungee co-founder Henry Van Ash. "What is actually extreme is what people go through in their minds," he said. "From a marketing perspective, when we started out we had to convince people that we're very safe, and that it was a bit extreme."

New wave

Things have changed. In today's extreme sports game, innovation is the key. Making things taller and scarier than before brings visitors back for more, and makes headlines. The evolution of bungee is a good example. It was born as a fertility rite in the South Pacific, developed by the Oxford Dangerous Sports Club, and commercialized by the New Zealanders.

Source: Mahne, C. (April 19, 2004). New Zealand pushes tourism to the extreme. Retrieved Feb. 1, 2007 from http://news.bbc.co.uk/2/hi/business/3578973.stm

As the home of the world's commercial bungee jumping, jet-boating operations, and river-surfing ventures, Queenstown has acquired an international reputation for extreme sports and adventure tourism. The town is six hours southwest of Christchurch by car. It is accessible by international flight links and local flights from Dunedin, Christchurch, and Invercargill. The population in 2006 was 8,538.

Other local attractions include fishing, waterskiing, skydiving, canyoning, parapenting (soaring from a high point with a maneuverable parachute), hot air ballooning, mountain biking, climbing, canyon swinging, gondola riding, mountain walking, heliskiing, helirafting, and paragliding. Across the Wakatipu Basin the Remarkables mountain range looms over Queenstown with alpine terrain that provides challenges for adventure sports enthusiasts, including the Remarkable Ski Resort with an international standard superpipe and black terrain. Coronet Peak, opened as a ski field in 1947, offers snow sports for all levels, including night skiing with floodlit trails. Shotover Canyon claims the world's highest swing, where patrons can launch themselves off a 109-meter-high platform with a free fall of 60 meters before experiencing a 200-meter pendulum swing at 150 kilometers per hour. The Kawerau and Shotover Rivers offer jet boating and whitewater rafting with challenging rapids and tunnels. The former sport originated in New Zealand with the invention of jet-boat propulsion by Bill Hamilton. It offers speeds up to 85 kilometers per hour in water as shallow as 10 centimeters. Nearby Wanaka and Cardrona offer other outdoor and adventure sports.

The rise of adventure tourism and extreme sports around Queenstown has led retail businesses to cater to these sports with specialized shops for visitors, nightlife, casinos, restaurants, and accommodations ranging from backpacker hostels to international luxury hotels and resorts.

The Queenstown spring season (September through November) offers mountain biking; summer, (December through February) has a rodeo, a mountain run, and a half-marathon; autumn (March through May) has a marathon, the Motatapu Icebreaker, and Silverstone Race to the Sky; and winter (June through August) has snow and ice activities.

Robin Charles McConnell

See also Bungee Jumping; Hackett, A. J.

Further Reading

Extreme Air. (n.d.). Welcome to Extreme Air hang gliding and paragliding. Retrieved August 21, 2006, from www.extremeair.co.nz

Justqueenstown.co.nz. (n.d.). Queenstown, New Zealand: Directory and information. Retrieved August 21, 2006, from www.justqueenstown.co.nz

Queenstownnz.co.nz. (n.d). Queenstown, New Zealand, the Southern Hemisphere's premier 4 season alpine resort. Retrieved August 21, 2006, from www.queenstownnz.co.nz

Ryan, C., & Ruthe, J. (2003, January). Language and perceptions of an adventure location in New Zealand. *Tourist Culture & Communication, 4*(1) 29–40.

Southern Alpine Recreation. (n.d.). Snow reports. Retrieved August 21, 2006, from www.nzski.com

Rock Climbing

With the advent of commercial indoor climbing gyms during the late 1980s, rock climbing paradoxically gained popularity as an extreme sport at the same time it became the safest it has ever been. The 1993 movie *Cliffhanger* built on the image of rock climbing as a challenge against death and pitted Sylvester Stallone against a stranded group of would-be treasury thieves. The image of Stallone's body double climbing ropeless in the opening sequence, in contrast to the controlled environment of burgeoning climbing gyms, reflects the fundamental tension between safety and the thrill of risk that produced rock climbing as a modern extreme sport.

Historically, the key to a long rock climbing career was not to fall. As Chris McNamara states, once "climbers relied upon carpentry nails for protection, belay methods that *might* hold a fall, and shoulder stands to get past blank sections" (McNamara 2001a, 42). Key developments throughout the century and a half of technical rock climbing's history, including devices like piton, the removable chock, the spring-loaded camming device, and the permanent bolt, not only have made climbs safer, but also have opened up more difficult climbs. McNamara continues: "How many modern climbers would ever leave the group if rappels still required the Düffler method, with the rope wrapped under the groin and over the shoulder?" (McNamara 2001a, 42). Increased gear selection and reliability, however, has not done away with the risks of rock climbing. With new safety gear come both an increased need for knowledge and a desire on the part of some climbers to cast off the comfort of technological advances to choose a more dangerous path.

Although fatalities are not uncommon in rock climbing (1 per 320,000 climbs), most injuries are scrapes and fractures (5.63 per 1,000 climbs). Most accidents result from faulty use of safety gear, a concern reflected in climbing instruction manuals, which focus briefly on the physical skills of climbing, instead choosing to promote safe equipment practices. For many participants risk is an integral part of climbing; they choose a risky way of proceeding over a safer way, thus giving rock climbing a legitimate claim to the term *extreme*. The choice to accept risk comes from a culture in which "real climbing is seen to demand, from time to time, not just physical performance, not just *technical* qualities, but *moral* qualities, qualities of *character* as well" (Heywood 1994, 185). Thus, the style and ethics of climbing that a person follows, mandating the degree of difficulty, equipment used, and degree of risk, determine the level of legitimacy that person has within climbing communities. A style of climbing that allows safety and protection on a climb is often rejected in favor of a style that allows only passive, nonpermanent protection. The use of permanent bolts on some climbs has sparked heated debates in almost all climbing communities throughout the world.

Development

Rock climbing ethics, and the controversies surrounding it, arose from the development of climbing as a form of training for mountaineering during the late nineteenth century. Some of the earliest climbs in modern rock climbing were made in Germany, Italy, and England. Routes were established in Elbsandsteingebirge, near Dresden (Germany), as early as 1864; considerable developments in climbing were made in the Dolomites (Italy); and significant climbs were completed at Scafell crag in the Lake District (England) in 1898. The production of lighter ropes and cheaper equipment after World War II led to a rapid increase in the skills of rock climbers and the movement of these skills from Europe to North America. This movement facilitated a significant boom in climbing in Yosemite Valley, California, where 600–900-meter cliffs excited climbers' imaginations. In Yosemite many modern climbing techniques were developed, especially in the field of "aid" climbing. By using pitons inserted into cracks to hold their weight as they ascended, climbers could bypass previously unclimbable sections with confidence. Opposed to aid climbing, "free" climbing uses pitons and other forms of protection only to protect from a fall. Climbers in Yosemite and other parts of the world used a combination of free climbing and aid climbing to ascend cliffs, often spending several days on a cliff face without touching down.

Pushing the Limit

The evolution of climbing technology, offering more reliable safety systems, has allowed for increasingly difficult climbs to be made. Indeed, experts assume that climbers' skills will continue to improve, and the systems for rating the difficulty of a climb, which differ from country to country, are open-ended. During the 1970s these rating systems expanded through the sustained training on specific routes by U.S. climbers such as Ron Kauk, Ray Jardine, and Tony

Yaniro. Between 1984 and 1991 German climber Wolfgang Gullich established a new difficulty rating four times on climbs in Germany and Australia. Chris Sharma's Realization (France), Fred Roughing's Akira (France), Tommy Caldwell's Flex Luther (United States), and Yuji Hiriyama's Flat Mountain (Japan) are among the climbs that are considered the most difficult, with Sharma's climb receiving the most recognition.

The difficulty of a climbing route and the prestige gained from climbing that route are not based solely on the moves, but also on the length of the climb (distance and time) and the possibility of serious consequences from a fall. Climbing big walls, on cliffs of more than 300 meters, in Yosemite, the Dolomites, or in more remote locations such as Canada's Baffin Island or Pakistan's Trango Tower,

A man rock climbing in New Zealand.
Source: istock/Scott Hailstone.

has given many climbers prestige for the size, remoteness, and commitment of the route. Some of the big wall climbs that once took days to complete are now being completed without stopping. The most famous of these climbs is Lynn Hill's twenty-four-hour free-climbing ascent of Yosemite's Nose route in 1994, a feat repeated only by Tommy Caldwell in 2005. Hill's climb followed standard safety practices, but the prestige of faster ascents has made for "a hair raising approach, heavy on speed and light on protection" (McNamara 2001b, 95), including unroped solo climbing.

Cultural Conflicts

For many participants the roots of climbing are in contrast to a conformist way of life and "stand against the rationalizing tide engulfing so many other areas of social life" (Heywood 1994, 185). Talking about her early days of climbing in Yosemite, Lynn Hill called her climbs "a means of reaffirming our belief in the virtue of abandoning material comforts in favour of the kind of character building experiences that inevitably occur on these big wall journeys" (Hill 2003, 114). The Yosemite climbing community mirrors others throughout the world that follow what is known as "tradition," "trad," or "adventure climbing," in which climbers use only the features of the rock to put their protection in, leaving nothing behind at the end of the climb. Proponents suggest that this form of climbing resists the certainty and comfort of modern life. This resistance is often directly related to traditional climbers' acceptance of certain risks, when "the imposing of limits, such as the adventure climber's refusal to utilize a form of technology (the bolt) that would severely reduce the consequences of a fall, serves to keep alive the prospect of death" (Lewis 2000, 76).

During the 1980s the ethics of traditional climbing came into conflict with a style of climbing that valued the difficulty of a climb over the style of ascent. Sport climbing, which originated in France, uses bolts placed in the cliff (often on rappel, from the top down) to access lines that previously could not be safely climbed without bolts. These permanent bolts would offer more security on which to fall, thereby increasing the difficulty level of the climbs. Often described as a gymnastic form of climbing that concentrates on movement rather than the overall experience, sport climbing has opened climbing to a faster skill curve, allowing new climbers to try more difficult cliffs with relative comfort because bolts require less safety knowledge. Anticonformist climbers frown on such a degree of con-

Limits on Extreme Sports

The following rule "clarification" from the National Park Service was issued in response to rock climber Dean Potter's assent of the Delicate Arch rock formation in Utah's Arches National Park. The assent was not sanctioned by NPS, and there were claims that his use of ropes scarred the formation. The incident sparked an outcry in the climbing community, and ignited a debate between those in the climbing community who felt Potter broke one of the unwritten agreements between climbers and NPS, and those who defended the efforts of climbers like Potter who treated climbing as a way to commune with nature.

Effective May 9, 2006, under the authority of Title 36 Code of Federal Regulations (CFR), Part 1, Section 1.5(a)(1), all rock climbing or similar activities on any arch or natu-ral bridge named on the United States Geological Survey 7.5 minute topographical maps covering Arches National Park are prohibited.

In addition, slacklining in Arches National Park is pro-hibited. Slacklining is defined as walking on a rope or other line that is anchored between rock formations, trees, or any other natural features. Height of the rope above the ground is immaterial.

These closures are based upon a determination that such action is necessary for the maintenance of public health and safety, protection of environmental or scenic values, protection of natural resources and avoidance of conflict among visitor use activities.

Source: http://www.nps.gov/arch/parknews/news050606.htm

---

venience, perceiving it as the encroachment of modern life into their sport. Yet, as cultural commentator Jackie Keiwa argues, this encroachment may already exist for traditional climbers in the form of rigid adherence to traditional climbing rules.

Although sport climbing offers easy entry into the sport, the most important factor in the increasing appeal of climbing to the public was the development of artificial climbing walls. Throughout the 1960s and 1970s schools and clubs in England developed artificial climbing walls from brick, sometimes on the side of buildings. However, not until 1987 was the first full-service indoor climbing gym opened in Seattle, ushering in a new era of commercial rock climbing. Commercial climbing gyms allow younger climbers, more comfortable with the gymnastic moves needed on modern sport routes, to excel. Thus, teenaged climbers such as Katie Brown, Chris Sharma, and Charlotte Durif gained international recognition.

Competitions

With the development of climbing walls, competitions could be held with new routes each time. Although speed-climbing competitions had been held in the USSR since the 1940s, not until 1985 were the first difficulty competitions held. These first competitions, staged in Bardonecchia, Italy, were held on outdoor cliffs with an audience of ten thousand. In 1991 the Union Internationale des Associations d'Alpinism (UIAA), the governing body for climbing competitions, moved all official competitions to artificial walls to avoid environmental impact on cliffs. The UIAA developed a world cup circuit for difficult, bouldering, and ice climbing and demonstrated climbing at the 2006 Olympics in Turin, Italy, as a cultural event.

The rise of competitions brought to a head the tension between traditional climbers and the new sport climbers. French sport climbers, such as Francois Legrand and Catherine Destavilles, were celebrities in their country, receiving sponsorship endorsements and media coverage. In the United States, however, climbers had not wholeheartedly accepted sport climbing ethics, and most climbers were unknown outside climbing circles. In an effort to demonstrate the superiority of traditional climbers over "Eurostyle" or sport climbers, whose fashion choice at the time was predominately form-fitting spandex, U.S. climber Ron Kauk climbed an early competition in jeans, quipping that "John Wayne never wore lycra" (cited in Knapp 1997, 58). The competition was held shortly after veteran mountaineer Jeff Smoot critiqued U.S. climbers as a stagnant community surpassed in skill by Europeans. Kauk's comments, coming from the self-defined "hardman" brand of climbing, point to the national and gendered investments in different modes of climbing.

Soloing

Outdoor climbing always has an element of risk, and climbers who accept this risk at its highest level are "free soloists," or ropeless climbers. Not only does free soloing present the ultimate risk of climbing, but also it is a strong statement against the conformity of modernity, harkening back to days when the safety of a climb depended on one's ability to climb without falling. This experience, for Hans Florine, "is such a pleasant and unencumbered experience. All the bother of gear ropes, anchors, belaying, and rappelling are stripped away, all that is left is climbing" (Florine and Wright 2004, 69). Free soloists, a predominately male group, climb without ropes on entire climbs, where a fall would certainly be disastrous. Usually free soloists climb comfortably within their skill level, often on routes they have climbed many times before. Exceptions to this rule have included Peter Croft's 335-meter solo climb of Astroman in Yosemite and Alex Huber's solo climb of the difficult Kummunist in Austria. Not all climbers agree on the benefits of soloing, and online forums are filled with arguments about the appropriateness of climbing unroped. Jon Long said the pressures of solo climbing can "show us thoughts and feelings we have otherwise no access to" (Long 1999, 4), and climbers such as Huber and Dan Osmand and Jon Bacher highlight the focus gained from solo climbing. In an attempt to access those moments without the threat of death, climbers have turned to deep water soloing, in which routes are directly above a body of water deep enough to fall into.

All climbers make decisions about the risks that they wish to take. The differences arising from these decisions enable distinctions about types of climbers and the prestige accorded to each. These distinctions flow from the style of climbing but also illustrate an investment in regional, national, and, sometimes, gendered identities.

Bruce Erickson

Further Reading

Ament, P. (2002). *A history of free climbing in America: Wizards of rock.* Berkeley, CA: Wilderness.

Child, G. (1995). *Climbing: The complete reference to rock, ice and indoor climbing.* New York: Facts on File.

Florine, H., & Wright, B. (2004). *Speed climbing: How to climb faster and better.* Guilford, CT: Falcon.

Grimes, N. (2004). Big issues: Ethics and style. *Summit, 36,* 14–20.

Hankinson, A. (1972). *The first tigers: The early history of rock climbing in the Lake District.* London: J. M. Dent & Sons.

Heywood, I. (1994). Urgent dreams: Climbing, rationalization and ambivalence. *Leisure Studies, 13*(3), 179–194.

Hill, L. (2003). *Climbing free: My life in the vertical world.* New York: Norton.

Huber, A., Heinz, Z., & Nadya, S. (2003). *Yosemite: Fifty years of dynamic rock climbing.* London: Baton Wicks.

Kiewa, J. (2002). Control over self and space in rock climbing. *Journal of Leisure Research, 33*(4), 363–382.

Knapp, F. (1997). The whole natural art. *Rock and Ice, 81,* 50–60.

Lewis, N. (2000). The climbing body, nature and the experience of modernity. *Body & Society, 6*(3–4), 58–80.

Long, J. (1999). *The high lonesome: Epic solo climbing stories.* Guilford, CT: Falcon.

Long, J. (2003). *How to rock climb!* (4th ed.). Evergreen, CO: Chockstone.

McNamara, C. (2001a). Bold school. *Rock and Ice, 111,* 42–45.

McNamara, C. (2001b). Vertical velocity. *Climbing, 203,* 92–100.

Middendorf, J. (1999). The mechanical advantage: Tools for the wild vertical. In A. Steck, S. Roper, & D. Harris (Eds.), *Ascent: The climbing experience in word and image* (pp. 149–175). Golden, CO: American Alpine Club.

Paige, T., Fiore, D., & Houston, J. (1998). Injury in traditional and sport rock climbing. *Wilderness and Environmental Medicine, 9*(1), 2–7.

Rowell, G. (Ed.). (1974). *The vertical world of Yosemite: A collection of photographs and writings on rock climbing in Yosemite.* Berkeley, CA: Wilderness.

Williamson, J. (Ed.). (2005). *Accidents in North American mountaineering.* Golden, CO: American Alpine Club.

Rollerblading

See Inline Skating

Round-the-World Yacht Racing

Round-the-world yacht racing is the ultimate form of offshore racing, which must take place at least 50 nautical miles (92 kilometers) from mainland or island shores. Round-the-world yacht racing vessels, using sail power alone, travel a course that crosses the equator, both northbound and southbound, and the Atlantic, Indian, and Pacific Oceans.

The routes of round-the-world yacht racing can vary greatly, from harsh and remote oceans and dangerous maritime regions such as Cape Horn to canals such as the Panama Canal. The competitors themselves also vary from the professional to the amateur.

Round-the-world yacht racers sail into vulnerability, isolation, and extreme danger. To face the extremes of nature, particularly the ocean and the wind, is one of the oldest and most testing challenges for any man or woman. The greatest honor for any offshore yacht racer is to compete on the planet's greatest stage, the classic round-the-world course, which passes south of the three great capes—Cape of Good Hope (South Africa), Cape Leeuwin (Australia), and Cape Horn (South America). This course takes a sailor through the notorious Southern Ocean (South Polar Ocean), which is the only body of water that circumnavigates the globe uninterrupted by any landmass. The course exposes a sailor to every natural element in its enormity—hurricane-force winds and giant seas are common—and those who endure return to land with a new perception of calms, storms, heat, and cold. The course features every element and seascape that a mariner yearns to experience, for better and for worse.

Types of Crewed Races

Round-the-world races include the fully crewed—more than one sailor—professional Volvo Ocean Race (previously known as the "Whitbread Round the World Race"). The boats of the Volvo race are crewed by eleven sailors: ten crew members and the skipper. This race takes place every four years with stopovers at key ports around the world.

In fully crewed amateur races, such as the Clipper Round the World Race and the Global Challenge, amateur sailors race under the guidance of a professional skipper. These races also include stopover ports. The men and women who sign up for such a challenge come from all walks of life and are from eighteen to sixty-five years of age. Other than good physical health, few other requirements are made of amateur sailors. The steel yachts designed for these races are heavy, and they tend to bury themselves into waves and in doing so shift tons of water across their decks. With such power, injuries are commonplace; severe bruises, broken bones, concussions, or worse can afflict the crew. Although every safety precaution is taken to prevent injury, crew members are sailing in extreme conditions, and injuries are almost inevitable.

Only one nonstop round-the-world race has been held in multihulls—boats with two or three hulls as opposed to monohulls, which are boats with a single hull. This contest, held in 2000–2001, was called "the Race." Huge 33-meter catamarans (two hulls) known as "giant class multihulls"

raced flat-out around the world with a crew of thirteen, the leading boat finishing in just sixty-two days. In comparison, the winner of the Vendée Globe race in 2000–2001, onboard an 18-meter monohull, took ninety-three days.

"Short-Handed" Races

At the other extreme are the solo or double-handed (two-crew-member) round-the-world races, also known as "short-handed." The ultimate solo round-the-world race is the nonstop Vendée Globe, which is held every four years. This race was first held in 1968 (the year Neil Armstrong stepped on the moon) and was named the "Golden Globe." It was renamed the "Vendée Globe" in 1989. This race, in which triumph comes hand-in-hand with tragedy, has given sailing fans a rich history of drama.

In 1968 nine solo sailors staggered their departures over the course of five months in a race to be the first yachtsman to sail solo and nonstop around the world, paving the way for modern round-the-world sailors. This race was sponsored by a British newspaper, the *Sunday Times*, and the public was gripped by its story.

The fleet spent ten months at sea, and only one of the nine entrants finished. News from onboard the boats was relayed to the world via marine radio and the transfer of packages—containing mail, rolls of film, and copies of ship logs—to passing commercial vessels. While in a commanding position to win the race, Frenchman Bernard Moitessier decided on the home straight that his love was for the ocean, not the competition or the fame that would accompany his potential victory. Instead of racing north toward the finish, he altered course to the east and passed this message to a British Petroleum tanker off the coast of Cape Town, South Africa: "My intention is to continue this voyage, still nonstop, towards the Pacific islands, where there is plenty of sun and more peace that there is in Europe. Please do not think that I am trying to break a record. 'Record' is a very stupid word at sea. I am continuing because I am happy at sea, and perhaps I want to save my soul" (Werth, 1987).

While Moitessier was saving his soul, the rest of the world was reading news, relayed via radio communications, of the amazing rate of speed of another competitor in the race, Donald Crowhurst. The drama turned to dismay when Crowhurst's yacht *Teignmouth Electron* was found with no sign of life onboard. The ship's log revealed that Crowhurst had been living a lie, faking a passage around the bottom of the world when in fact he and his yacht never left the

Atlantic Ocean. His log also revealed that he was mentally unstable and that he had found living with such a lie unbearable. Some people believe that this pressure drove Crowhurst to take his own life.

The Golden Globe race was won by British yachtsman Robin Knox Johnston, who was later knighted for becoming the first person to sail nonstop around the world alone. Johnston is now the owner of the Clipper Race for amateur crews and the Velux 5 Oceans race, previously known as the "Around Alone," a solo race around the world with stopovers. Today the Vendée Globe race is the proving ground for sailing heroes, particularly within France, a nation of adventure sailing enthusiasts. Indeed, thousands of supporters turn up to witness the departure of the solo sailors as they debark on their journey around the world.

The newest round-the-world yacht race is the double-handed, nonstop Barcelona World Race, which will bring together sailors from the two sailing disciplines of solo and crewed in a two-up race. The transoceanic races are mere sprints in comparison with round-the-world races, but nonetheless these races are the proving ground for many sailors who eventually take on a full circumnavigation.

Records—Racing against the Clock

In a race other sailors are the opponent. However, when it comes to setting records, the clock is the greatest opponent. Records are set either while sailing solo or while sailing in a race, for example, the twenty-four-hour record. Records are recognized by the World Sailing Speed Record Council. Perhaps the two most sought-after records are the crewed, nonstop, round-the-world record and the solo, nonstop, round-the-world record.

The most coveted crewed trophy is the Jules Verne Trophy, which is awarded to the winners of a race that is sailed in large and fast catamarans. The start/finish line extends across the western entrance of the English Channel between France and the British Isles. The idea for the race was conceived in the early 1990s, inspired by the novel by Verne set in the 1870s and entitled *Around the World in 80 Days*. The novel raised the question of whether one could sail nonstop around the world in under eighty days.

Many sailors were excited by this challenge, and on 31 January 1993, Frenchman Bruno Peyron and his crew of four set off in a multihull yacht to prove that such a feat is possible. It was a risky adventure that was later documented by

U.S. crew member Cam Lewis in his book *Around the World in 79 Days*. The cover of Lewis's book reads: "In 1872 Jules Verne did it in his imagination. In 1993 five men set out to do it for real—or die trying." On 20 April 2003—79 days, 6 hours, 15 minutes, and 56 seconds after crossing the start line—Peyron and his crew answered the question. The Jules Verne Trophy was claimed with only 17 hours, 44 minutes, and 4 seconds to spare.

The Jules Verne Trophy remains the ultimate sailing speed trophy. To date only seven records have been set, yet one skipper has held that trophy three times in his career. The name of Bruno Peyron was the first engraved on the trophy, and he remains the record holder. In 2005 he set the current record of 50 days, 16 hours, 20 minutes, and 4 seconds at an average speed of 22.2 knots (40 kilometers per hour).

The need for speed on a round-the-world course has been the driving force behind the development of bigger and faster oceangoing multihulls. So far no fatalities have occurred on the Jules Verne Trophy course, but as designers and engineers push technological boundaries, danger also increases. With the continual quest for speed, the safety limits are continually pushed, and critical equipment failure is frequent. For example, the failure of a keel (the weighted appendage under the boat that keeps it upright) is common. Even with a good testing program, using any new material or design brings an element of uncertainty.

With fourteen crew members operating these giant vessels, the throttle can be kept tightly to the floor 100 percent of the time. For the solo round-the-world record, however, one person doing the work of fourteen crew members cannot sail the boat at 100 percent the entire time. The skipper must rely heavily on the autopilot to steer the boat when he or she is sleeping or performing a maneuver that takes him or her away from the helm. Furthermore, whereas members of crewed races are able to establish a watch system, in which part of the crew is on duty, and part of the crew is either on standby or off duty (i.e., sleeping or eating), for a solo sailor a twenty-four-hour day often consists of four hours of broken sleep obtained by twenty-minute catnaps, interrupted by the need to continue an active watch.

Recent solo round-the-world record attempts have also been undertaken in multihulls—to be precise, trimarans, which have three hulls. In effect, the central hull is where trimarans "live," and the two outer hulls are merely floats that balance the boat to carry the overtall mast. The fastest sailor to sail solo and nonstop around the world is Britain's Ellen MacArthur. In 2005 MacArthur set a record of 71 days, 14 hours, 18 minutes, and 33 seconds onboard a 22-meter tri-

Start of a sailing regatta. Sailing yachts are one type of boat used in long distance races. Source: istock/Alina Pavlova.

maran sailing the traditional route around the world (i.e., west to east). Another British woman, Dee Caffari, sailed her 23-meter monohull yacht around the world the "wrong way" (i.e., east to west) against the prevailing winds and currents. Caffari holds the current record of 178 days, 3 hours, 5 minutes, and 30 seconds. Considering that Caffari took 107 days longer than MacArthur, it is understandable why the east-west route is called the "wrong way."

History

Arguably, contemporary offshore yacht racing is a continuation of racing begun in the mid-1500s. During this period a frantic race to discover new continents was under way. Also, for those sailors delivering precious cargo to growing countries, arriving first enabled them to get the best price for their goods.

Four hundred years of maritime history preceded completion of the Panama Canal, which opened in 1914, when the first self-propelled, oceangoing vessel used the canal to sail from the Atlantic to the Pacific Ocean. Prior to this passage Cape Horn remained a ship's most convenient route between the Pacific and the Atlantic, but it was also the most treacherous. Many people undertaking this journey died in the process. A rounding of Cape Horn became a sailor's

most feared and cherished passage, so much so that those who rounded the cape called themselves "Cape Horners," and the title traditionally came with benefits, such as sporting a gold hoop earring in the ear that passed closest to the horn when looking forward on one's vessel. Another benefit was said to be the ability to urinate into the wind.

Seafaring history is full of romantic notions, highlighting the beauty of the sea and the freedom of a voyage under sail. Yet that history is also littered with tragedy, hardship, disease, and fear. By the mid-nineteenth century the marine industry was faced with a growing demand for fast sailing ships. In Europe and the United States the growing thirst for tea from China placed an enormous premium on the first and freshest cargoes of the year to reach London and New York. The discovery of gold in Australia and California and the explosion of immigration and economic growth also had shipping companies scrambling to build vessels that could shorten the time taken for long voyages from eastern Europe to the United States. In response, engineers attempted to develop faster yachts. The clipper ship was the product of such efforts.

Types of Boats

Carbon-fiber boats are the modern equivalent of the clipper speed machines. They are graceful and swift, able to exceed the speed of the wind. Round-the-world races are usually raced in monohull yachts of 18 meters in length or more. However, these boats vary greatly in shape and size because their designs are dependent on whether they are being raced solo or crewed or whether they are taking the traditional east-about route as opposed to the west-about route, which goes against the prevailing winds and currents.

Steel-hulled yachts "punch" their way around the world against the prevailing winds and currents on an east-west course. On the swifter carbon-fiber, single-hulled craft, solo and fully crewed sailors chase the low-pressure weather systems, riding the breeze like a surfer on a wave, exploring the limit of control. Yachts competing in round-the-world races with stopovers at key ports also have a design that is different than that of yachts competing in nonstop races. Many races permit short stops in places such as South Africa, Australia, and South America. Such stops allow crews to push their own limits, as well as those of their tools, with the knowledge that they have the chance to regroup and repair broken equipment at the next stop. Nonstop racers do not have this luxury, so their boats are built not only for speed but also for endurance so that they can finish the "marathon" of circumnavigation.

The evolution of the multihull yachts, the fastest passage makers ever to grace the vast oceans, will mean faster and faster record times.

Extreme Environments

The Southern Ocean, which round-the-world sailors must cross, is an extreme environment. Given its location at the bottom of the world with its southern boundary at the ice continent of Antarctica, the Southern Ocean is continually lashed by strong, cold storm systems that create swells of a dramatic scale. These systems travel west to east with hurricane-force winds that can reach speeds of 60–80 knots (111–148 kilometers per hour) and that do not disperse over the thermal warmth of land. Plus, the wave patterns continue to grow in mass and speed without a shore to break their stride and can build to more than 30 meters in height. The Southern Ocean is so remote and so hostile that when sailors enter the latitude of 40 degrees south they leave behind the element of security. A sailor's fastest passage through this ocean—described as "without law and without God"—often involves weeks in subzero temperatures. A lone sailor's greatest chance of rescue is, at best, three days away.

This ocean has broken the bravest of hearts and the

Solo Ocean Racer

She came racing down the craggy sea
Like a deer over shale, sure footed
Wary of sliding into vaulted space
Where providence was a trench and
Deliverance a defile of frantic
Ocean forty foot high and laden.

Then gifted space and channel of hope
She hitched her heart to a star nailed
On a shimmering dome
This lone yachtswoman who rode
Destiny like a valkyrie a thousand
Waves beyond Valparaiso.

Robin McConnell

---

strongest of personalities. To survive it a yacht sailor must prepare for the unknown. The few who prepare well can find incredible inner strength in the face of danger. Indeed, driving a yacht hard in storm-force winds and huge seas at night with a minefield of icebergs ahead takes tremendous courage and focus.

Focus, however, is difficult to maintain in an environment with numerous distractions, including the bone-chilling cold from wet apparel and the sound of the wind and sea screaming around the boat. In the darkness of night, steering around the powerful mass of huge, rolling, white wave crests demands the helmsman's full attention. The mast and rigging groan under the strain. In these circumstances the boat reaches speeds that demand immediate calculation and response from brain-to-hand movement. One false move, and the yacht could spin out of control. Bodies ache from continually bracing against the lurching movement of the boat or the force of a mass of water racing down the deck, trying to drag the sailor into the cold sea. Adrenaline is a great aid in such an environment. There is an art to harnessing discomfort and fear and producing a motivation so strong that the mind develops complete concentration on one goal: survival.

Cape Horn

At the southernmost tip of South America lies Cape Horn—a sailor's Mount Everest. This cape remains the most respected maritime landmark because of navigational and environmental difficulties, and earning "the right to round" it is hard-fought. Here enormous driving seas and storm-force winds funnel through a relatively narrow gap (just 430 nautical miles [796 kilometers] separate Cape Horn and the Antarctic Peninsula to the south) named "Drake's Strait." The seabed rises suddenly in this gap, increasing the wave size and forcing waves to break. These killer waves collide with an acceleration of the storm-force winds, which increase in strength as they sweep along the Andean glaciers, creating a cauldron of water known as "the graveyard of the sea."

North Atlantic

Although danger in round-the-world yacht racing is not exclusive to the Southern Ocean, it is typically associated with the older oceanic regions. The North Atlantic, dividing North America and Europe, is another treacherous body of water. It lies beneath an upper-level jet stream of strong winds that is a common source of powerful storm systems that sweep west to east. This ocean has a dangerous mixture of varying sea temperatures fed by strong currents north and south of the Grand Banks (scene of the film and book *The Perfect Storm*). The mixture of currents produces a huge expanse of water that is frequently draped in a dense fog that renders a sailor blind and distorts sound waves. Often a sailor hears the churning of a ship's engine, but the direction that the sound is coming from is greatly distorted under the acoustic blanket. Ice is another danger in this ocean.

The North Atlantic has been responsible for some of the world's most famous maritime disasters. The *Titanic* sank after it collided with an iceberg in 1912. In 2006 the North Atlantic made headlines again when a crew member of a yacht competing in the Volvo Ocean Race was dragged into the sea by water sweeping across the deck. This incident was a sharp reminder to sailors that offshore racing can be deadly.

Warmer Waters

Sailing in the warmer waters of the Atlantic, Pacific, and Indian Oceans carries a different set of risks. Piracy remains a danger. Pirates no longer sport a parrot on one shoulder or a patch on one eye, but they do still sail armed with fast vessels, high-tech equipment and weapons, and have the same intention of yesteryear—to board a vessel, steal its bounty,

and sell that bounty on the black market. The number of reported acts of piracy has declined over recent years, but the number of deaths related to piracy has increased. On 6 December 2001, New Zealand sailing legend Sir Peter Blake was shot and killed by pirates while waiting to clear customs at the mouth of the Amazon River. Sir Peter had received his knighthood for his services to sailing by winning the Whitbread Round the World Race (now the Volvo Ocean Race) and the America's Cup for New Zealand. Blake was the second skipper, after Peyron, to receive the Jules Verne Trophy when he co-skippered the yacht *ENZA* around the world in just less than seventy days.

Technology

In recent years round-the-world yacht racing has captivated a global audience. Technological developments such as satellite communications enable the drama of such races to be communicated to a worldwide audience almost instantaneously. Successful sailors return to a hero's welcome because their journey has been shared by thousands every wave of the way. Modern technology has created a virtual stadium for offshore yacht racing. This was demonstrated when Ellen MacArthur set the solo, nonstop, round-the-world record by crossing the finish line on 7 February 2005. Hundreds of thousands of viewers followed her progress via the Internet, reading her latest e-mails, seeing the latest video and photographs from onboard. This public support of her record attempt spilled into the media—the story was featured on the front page of national newspapers, and television networks around the world reported on the story. With such technological developments, offshore sailing is no longer "out of sight, out of mind."

The clothing worn by sailors, as well as their food supplies, has also developed. Heavy exposure to the elements can lead to frostbite and hyperthermia, thus the warmest, but lightest, clothing is essential. Food is critical in a world where weight hinders performance. Offshore sailors tend to rely on a diet of freeze-dried food, much of which was developed in pioneering space programs.

Racing around the world is a journey of endurance and danger, but the rewards are extraordinary. Although the history of round-the-world yacht racing is littered with death and injury, most seafarers say the beauty that lies beyond the horizon calls them back time and time again.

Nick Moloney

Further Reading

Barcelona World Race. (2007). *Two crew, non-stop—a new concept in world racing.* Retrieved February 1, 2007, from http://www.barcelonaworldrace.com/en/

Bareboats, BVI. (2006). *Yacht chart glossary.* Retrieved February 1, 2007, from http://www.bareboatsbvi.com/yacht_charter_glossary.html

Offshore Challenges. (2007). Retrieved February 1, 2007, from http://www.offshorechallenges-sailingteam.com/#

Volvo Ocean Race. (2006). Retrieved February 1, 200,7 from http://www.volvooceanrace.org/index.aspx?bhcp=1

Werth, Lee F. (1987). The paradox of single-handed sailing (Case studies in existentialism). *The Journal of American Culture, 10*(1), 65–78.

Scuba Diving

Scuba divers use the self-contained underwater breathing apparatus (SCUBA) that gives the sport its name to sustain their lives in an otherwise lethal environment. Because the physiological effects of diving are still not completely understood, the vital tables that determine the depth and time limits of a given dive are based on statistical analysis and theoretical models. As a result divers can dive well within the limits of the tables and still suffer the decompression sickness that the tables are intended to prevent. Apart from the physiological risks of breathing under water, scuba equipment and the aquatic environment pose other dangers. Divers inhabit a distinct subculture, with its own language, symbols, and customs, which crosses other linguistic and cultural barriers.

However, the diving community has tried to avoid the "extreme" label for a number of reasons. Scuba diving has a remarkable safety record, one that has allowed the sport to remain self-regulated in many nations despite the dangers. Children, the elderly, and the physically challenged all participate in scuba diving. Although the sport is exciting on many levels, it should never provoke fear from a participant. After a diver leaves the surface, he or she depends on the finite amount of life support provided by the scuba unit. The alien environment and the narcotic effect of breathing under high pressures can rapidly amplify stress into potentially dangerous panic. For those reasons divers attempt to minimize the impact of anything that increases breathing rates or stress levels. Divers also depend on each other for mutual safety under water. Those who deliberately seek danger or who fail to respect the safety and environmental concerns of the diving community are strongly discouraged from scuba diving. Those who are willing to accept the risks of scuba diving and manage them appropriately are rewarded by a sport that takes them to the extremes of human activity and exploration.

Origins

Effective systems for preserving human life under water for extended periods were not developed until the nineteenth century. In the 1869 novel 20,000 *Leagues Beneath the Sea*, French science-fiction author Jules Verne hypothesized that a recently introduced French commercial diving system that pumped air from the surface into a tank carried by a diver and then used a demand valve to supply the diver from the tank could be further modified. By eliminating the first portion of that system and personally carrying all of the required air, a diver could freely interact with the marine environment. A series of experiments over the ensuing decades produced successful rebreathers, devices that filtered divers' exhalations and replenished their oxygen levels in a continuous breathing loop. Although useful in military and commercial applications, this technology remained too complex and hazardous for recreational use.

Two French inventors, engineer Emile Gagnan and free diver Jacques-Yves Cousteau, resolved that difficulty in 1943 with a mechanism similar to the one described by Jules Verne. A demand valve attached to a tank of compressed air allowed the diver to breathe comfortably despite the pressure of the surrounding water. Although the earlier rebreather technology can also be described as a "self-contained underwater breathing apparatus," the term and its acronym, *SCUBA*, properly refer to the mechanism designed by Gagnan and Cousteau. In combination with fins worn on the feet to aid propulsion and goggles to allow the eye to focus underwater, scuba provided access to the underwater world.

Scuba equipment and training methods were comparatively crude in the early decades of the sport. The limited training available was largely based on military models, emphasizing physical skills, emergency procedures, and risks. Equipment was awkward and uncomfortable, with relatively little provision for the diver's safety. As a result the sport was largely male-dominated and widely regarded as dangerous. Improvements in scuba training and equipment gradually changed that reputation as the sport expanded, and competition produced numerous manufacturers and training organizations. In the 1970s the growing dive industry started producing equipment specifically for female divers, who began embracing the sport as it abandoned adversarial training techniques. Specialized dive resorts began to appear around the world, soon joining forces with a larger movement toward eco-tourism. By the end of the twentieth century participation in scuba diving approached gender neutrality, with safe and comfortable equipment and easily accessible training.

As scuba diving became more popular, divers continued to push the boundaries of the sport. Some explored new geographic areas. Others developed new equipment and techniques as they exceeded the limits of what the dive industry came to define as "recreational" diving. A diver exceeding those limits enters the hazardous realm of "technical" diving, a term that recognizes the greater demands such activities place on a diver's knowledge, skills, and equipment. Technical divers have contributed to the safety of the entire diving community as the lessons they learn are applied to recreational diving. They have also paid a heavy price for those lessons. The boundary between recreational and technical diving is defined by important safety factors, including the ability to ascend directly to the surface without stopping in the event of an emergency. As a result, technical diving is far more dangerous than recreational diving.

Recreational Diving

Various training agencies employ their own definitions, but recreational scuba diving can be generally defined as the ability to ascend directly to the surface without stopping from any point in the dive while breathing compressed air from a scuba tank. That definition places a number of limits on a diver. A diver exceeding those limits enters the realm of technical diving.

The necessity of a direct ascent means that a recreational diver cannot allow any significant barrier between himself or herself and the surface. Entering a shipwreck, exploring a cave, or diving below a frozen surface makes a direct ascent impossible, and such activities are beyond recreational diving. Those barriers are fairly obvious.

Another barrier that can come between a diver and the surface is invisible. As a diver breathes air under pressure her body absorbs nitrogen. In addition to a dangerous narcotic effect referred to as "nitrogen narcosis" or "rapture of the deep," this nitrogen poses a threat as the diver surfaces. Ascending more rapidly than the nitrogen can be released produces bubbles in the diver's body, just as bubbles are released in a quickly opened carbonated drink. The resulting "bends," properly known as "decompression sickness," can be fatal. Dive tables estimate the amount of time a diver can spend at a given depth and, when required, identify one or more stops that the diver must make during ascent to allow the excess nitrogen to be exhaled and avoid decompression sickness. Those required decompression stops are also a barrier to direct ascent.

Overhead Barriers

Even a seemingly small physical barrier between a diver and the surface can turn a small problem into a potentially fatal crisis. If a diver encounters a layer of silt-filled water in the open, she has only to rise above it to see again. If the same problem occurs inside a cavern or small wreck, she must find her way despite the loss of visibility until she can return to open water. If she needs to see to find an exit, an otherwise minor annoyance becomes life-threatening. In an "overhead environment" the diver must be able to resolve any immediate problem and move beyond the barrier to ascent before the surface provides a potential refuge.

Technical divers, particularly those involved in shipwreck and cave diving, have developed a number of techniques and an array of tools for dealing with overhead environments. These techniques include the use of guidelines and redundant equipment to ensure that divers can resolve critical problems and find their way back to the surface. Equally important is the technical diver's training and experience. A diver properly prepared for such diving will have planned and practiced for all conceivable emergencies, including many that are not encountered within the limits of recreational diving. A technical diver must be far more knowledgeable and proficient in all aspects of diving than a recreational diver.

Decompression

The invisible barrier represented by a required decompression stop illustrates the gap between recreational and technical diving. Recreational dive tables indicate the point at which a diver can no longer ascend without stopping to exhale accumulated nitrogen—to decompress. Determining the proper depth and duration of such decompression stops is more complex, despite the widespread availability of computers to handle such calculations after the 1980s. And with finite life support and a dynamic environment, simply knowing what decompression stops are required does not necessarily enable the diver to make them.

Technical divers must be able to complete required decompression stops even in the event of an equipment failure or other emergency. This requires careful planning, multiple tanks, stringent monitoring of breathing rates and remaining supplies, and close cooperation between divers. It also means that the diver must be able to carefully control his depth for prolonged periods despite currents, waves, stress, and discomfort. The diver must be able to operate the greater amount of equipment that technical diving requires, even under emergency conditions. Perhaps most challenging of all, the technical diver must control the natural instinct to flee to the surface, even if it is only 3 meters away, if something goes wrong before all required decompression is completed. Doing so risks injury or death.

Mixed Gases

Seeking to minimize the need for decompression stops, to accelerate the decompression process, and to overcome problems such as nitrogen narcosis that result from breathing under greatly increased pressure, technical divers rarely breathe air. Nitrogen makes up approximately 79 percent of air and constitutes a major problem for both recreational and technical divers. Oxygen makes up approximately 21 percent of air and presents both benefits and risks to divers. Technical divers routinely alter the proportions of those gases in their tanks, sometimes adding other gases, to optimize what they breathe for a specific dive. This process requires considerable knowledge of physics, physiology, and equipment and is one of the reasons that this type of diving merits the "technical" label.

The benefits of such tailored gas mixes are substantial. The most common type of mix, oxygen-enriched air, has even been embraced by recreational divers in a strictly limited fashion because the lower percentage of nitrogen increases safety and allows a diver to spend greater time at relatively shallow depths without requiring a decompression stop. However, the more a mix differs from standard air, the greater the risk it carries. A technical diver may carry several gas mixes on a single dive. Each mix offers benefits within a certain depth range but may be harmful or even fatal outside that range or on the surface.

Oxygen itself becomes toxic at high pressures, just as nitrogen becomes increasingly intoxicating. Because helium is not as intoxicating as nitrogen and both enters and leaves the body faster, technical divers often add helium to those two gases to produce "trimix." The percentage of oxygen in trimix can then be lowered to avoid toxicity problems at depth, occasionally to the point that the resulting mixture cannot sustain life on the surface. The diver therefore uses a travel gas, air or oxygen-enriched air, to descend until the trimix can be safely breathed. Upon ascent, elevated levels of oxygen in the oxygen-enriched air, or even pure oxygen in very shallow water, can be used to more rapidly flush the accumulated nitrogen and helium from the diver's body. A technical diver may carry three or more gas mixes, none

Scuba divers exploring the wreck of "El Mina" in the Red Sea. Source: istock.

of them simple air, on a dive. Others employ sophisticated rebreathers that continually recirculate their breath and optimize the mixture of gases within it, exchanging efficiency for still another layer of complexity and risk.

Because of the need to deal with overhead environments, decompression, and multiple tanks containing different breathing mixes, technical divers carry far more equipment than recreational divers. A recreational diver with a single tank and minimal gear for a warm-water dive may carry 22 kilograms of equipment. A technical diver with multiple tanks and required safety equipment can easily carry twice that weight and may well be unable to walk out of the water under the weight of the equipment for a particularly demanding dive.

Culture

Divers share a subculture that has evolved with the sport. Hand signals that developed to communicate vital information underwater even provide a common and relatively uniform means of crude communication between divers who share no other language. The shared experience of exploring the underwater world and the specialized terminology that describes it form another bond. More importantly, scuba divers have a mutual interest in maintaining a sense of community that cuts across other cultural, socioeconomic, and ethnic distinctions.

Diving is an inherently social activity. Divers are encouraged to make each dive with a buddy for mutual safety and enjoyment and to share knowledge with other divers for the same reasons. The resulting social ties extend from buddy teams through small groups or formal clubs to embrace the entire diving community. Reinforcing that tendency is the fact than only another diver can help a diver in trouble beneath the water. In many areas divers may have greater knowledge of the proper diagnosis and treatment of diving-related injuries than do emergency medical personnel. It is therefore in each diver's self-interest to encourage the development of skills, knowledge, and cooperation throughout the diving community.

Bonds are even closer among the minority of scuba divers who participate in technical diving. The small size of the technical diving community ensures both greater mutual interdependence and, where disputes arise, greater internal turmoil than can be found within the recreational diving community. Although they can be depended upon to support each other and the sport in general, enthusiasts

for particular types of technical diving have been known to form rivalries, and occasionally bitter disputes have emerged. Groups of cave divers in Florida and the Yucatan, contending over various records and safety issues, for example, have reportedly not always gotten along despite similar interests and overlapping membership. Within the United States the wreck-diving and cave-diving communities have long indulged in arguments over technique and procedures.

One aspect of the diving subculture that takes many new divers by surprise is its apparent disregard for some standards of modesty and polite behavior. Changing clothes on a small boat or in a remote location, for example, can present challenges to modesty, and divers often require assistance in putting on or taking off form-fitting wetsuits. The common use of saliva to prevent a diver's mask from fogging can cause a group of otherwise well-mannered divers to indulge in a display of spitting that would be unacceptable in most company.

Divers may also display a fascination with bodily functions and the personal behavior of others that can come as a shock to the uninitiated. Motion sickness, for example, is a common problem for divers. It is possible to vomit through a scuba regulator, but in many circles etiquette demands that the sick diver alert nearby divers carrying cameras before doing so. Small fish swarming for the unanticipated meal often provide excellent photo opportunities. Proper diet and hydration are important safety precautions before a dive, just as alcohol is a potential risk factor, so divers take note of and occasionally comment upon what their fellows consume. Similarly, decompression sickness may be first indicated by minor muscle pain, loss of sensation, altered mental state, and a number of other subtle signs, and the afflicted diver often loses the ability to rationally evaluate the problem. So attentive divers inform each other or inquire about such personal matters. Divers who smoke or expose other divers to smoke before a dive, despite the negative effect that tobacco smoke has on a diver's ability to metabolize oxygen and exhale nitrogen for hours afterward, can also expect reactions that would not be considered polite elsewhere.

Competition

Whereas divers do struggle to be the first to explore a new location or reach some other goal, competition in the actual act of diving is highly discouraged. Asking the simple question, "What's the deepest you've been?" is a taboo to many divers because it opens the door to quantitative competition in a sport where the challenges and rewards of each dive are unique. Whereas scuba equipment is used to aid obscure activities such as human-powered submarine races or to provide safety support for other forms of sport, organized competitive events in scuba diving itself are almost unheard of because of the dangerous element that competition introduces to a sport that emphasizes safety and risk management above all else.

This does not mean that scuba divers are not competitive in their sport. Any discussion among divers is likely to include a subtle competition over distant locations visited, rare marine life encountered, and mishaps survived. Within the subculture of scuba divers these discussions determine status and, more importantly, share experiences and form bonds within a community defined by the unique perspective the sport provides.

Jeffery A. Charlston

See also Cave Diving; Ferreras, Pipin; Free Diving; Open Water Swimming; Streeter, Tanya

Further Reading

Chowdhury, B. (2000). *The last dive: A father and son's fatal descent into the ocean's depths.* New York: HarperCollins.

Global Underwater Explorers. http://www.gue.com

International Association of Nitrox and Technical Divers, http://www.iantd.com

Lippman, J. (2006). *Deeper into diving,* 2d. edition. New York: Aqua Quest.

McMurray, K. (2001). *Deep descent: Death and diving the* Andrea Doria. New York: Pocket Books.

Wienke, B. (2001). *Technical diving in depth.* Flagstaff, AZ: Best.

Shaw, Phil

In 1997 Phil Shaw (b. 1974), a resident of Leicester, England, was an information technology administrator in a knitwear factory with a passion for rock climbing. One evening he returned home filled with the desire to head to the mountains for an evening climb. Unfortunately, a pile of clothes needed ironing. When his roommate, fellow climber Paul Cartwright, returned home that evening, Cartwright found Shaw in the back garden practicing climbing moves while ironing—or "extreme ironing," as Shaw called it.

Shaw learned to iron from his mother, a woman who adhered to traditional values. Following her guidance,

Shaw's technique in ironing, both on mountains and in the home, is to begin with the sleeves because they are the most difficult. He then irons the collars and the back, saving the front for last because that is the part of the shirt seen by the most people.

Shaw and Cartwright (nicknamed "Steam" and "Spray," respectively) began developing techniques for the new sport in their back garden and soon recruited friends and others. They formed the Extreme Ironing Bureau to promote the sport. In 1999 they, along with a fellow ironist known as "Short Fuse," launched a worldwide tour, promoting the sport in the United States, Fiji, New Zealand, Australia, and southern Africa. After teaming up with German extreme ironists, the Extreme Ironing Bureau expanded to form Extreme Ironing International and the German Extreme Ironing Section.

In 2002, as captain, Shaw led the British Extreme Ironing Team to gold and bronze medals in the first Extreme Ironing World Championships, held in Munich, Germany. Since then Shaw has continued to promoted the sport. A film about extreme ironing, *Have Fun, Look Tidy,* was shown at the Munich Film Festival, and his book, *Extreme Ironing,* was published in 2003.

Shaw sums up the sport and his attitude toward it this way: "Extreme ironing is the latest danger sport that combines the thrills of an extreme outdoor activity with the satisfaction of a well pressed shirt."

Beth Pamela Skott

Further Reading

Pearson, H. (2006). In their element. *Eastern Airways Magazine.* Retrieved August 9, 2006, from http://www.easternairways.com/files/e-mag.pdf

Shaw, P. (2003). *Extreme ironing.* London: New Holland Publishers.

Simon, S. (2004, September 18). *Extreme ironing: Pressing shirts on the edge* [Radio broadcast]. National Public Radio. Retrieved August 9, 2006, from http://www.npr.org/templates/story/story.php?storyId=3925257

Skateboarding

Skateboarding involves riding a board that has three main components: the board, four wheels, and two axles and suspension elements called "trucks." Although the technology of those components has evolved to allow for an expansion of techniques, skateboarding has remained a youth-oriented sport. It was originally associated with surfing, but other popular cultural associations have included punk rock music in the late 1970s and early 1980s and grunge and hip-hop music in the 1990s.

Skateboarders perform on sidewalks and handrails, in parking garages and pools, and on ramps. Part of the appeal of skateboarding is the fact that there are no conventional boundaries; no formal field of play, no sidelines, no rules, and no time limits exist. In fact, skateboarding is defined by the participants' ability to create new tricks in a variety of places. Because the sport has been informal, commonly valuing aesthetic movement along with risk taking, participants are often portrayed as avant-garde or outsiders.

Skateboarding began in southern California in the 1950s, and its initial popularity occurred in the early 1960s when skateboards were first mass produced. Since then skateboarding has become a global phenomenon and has gone through many cycles of popularity. The sport has been shaped by key stakeholders, including the participants, promoters, media, local governments, and the youth culture industry. These stakeholders have at times worked together, whereas at other times they have been in conflict.

A Brief History

The 1960s brought the initiation of skateboarding's identity as a unique sport, breaking away from images of related children's toys such as rollerskates and scooters. Skateboards were flat and made of wood, the wheels were made of clay. At this time skateboarding was practiced on the ground; there were few aerial moves. Most tricks, such as handstands and spinning moves, were called "freestyle" and had a variety of gymnastic qualities. Slalom was also popular. Few publicly sanctioned places to skateboard existed; participants used paved streets, parking lots, playgrounds, and sidewalks. Some used drained pools but focused primarily on maneuvering on the surfaces as opposed to becoming airborne.

Although the first skateboards were made by rollerskate companies, the surfing industry made the strongest impact on creating and promoting the sport. For example, surf industry leader Hobie Alter worked with a surf shop and a rollerskate company to sell boards and their components as a complete set. Alter then promoted skateboarding by linking exhibitions with the tour of the classic surf film, *The Endless Summer*. In addition, the first skateboard magazine, *Surf Guide*, was established by Surfer Publications. And Larry Stevenson, a publisher of *Surf Guide*, formed a skateboard

company, Makaha, and sponsored a team to help promote the business. Participation was increasing, and skateboarding was on the popular culture map, as evidenced by Jan and Dean's 1964 hit song, "Sidewalk Surfin'," and *Life* magazine's 1965 cover photo of Pat McGee, the national girls champion, performing a handstand while riding her board. Contests even received national television coverage in the United States. This initial stage of development shows how the key stakeholders worked together to promote the sport.

However, by 1966 this first boom was over. One of the main reasons was the inherent danger of the sport and the injuries that resulted. Medical associations issued statements about injury rates and condemned the sport. Owners of property were concerned about their legal responsibilities and the damage that skateboarders might cause to their property. The sport declined at the end of the decade.

1970s

In the early 1970s another wave of popularity occurred, partly because of improved equipment and a growing infrastructure of parks. The technological innovation of polyurethane wheels for skateboards provided a smoother and, importantly, safer ride. At this time kicktails (where the board is turned up at the back end) became more common, and boards were long and skinny, suited to slalom and freestyle skateboarding. Fiberglas and aluminum boards became popular because they were sturdy and provided flexibility for carving. In the early to mid-1970s females were most integrated into the sport. Ellen Oneal, Peggy Oki, Vickie Vickers, and Ellen Berryman were commonly featured in contests. In the mid-1970s privately funded skateboard parks emerged. These parks included gradual variation of terrain and pool-like "bowls." Technology continued to improve, giving skateboarders more control and ability to skate the pools.

The mid-1970s brought a style shift from the 1960s freestyle to a more aggressive style that featured surfing-like moves. Tony Alva, Jay Adams, and Stacy Peralta were at the forefront of this style, which was made famous by the movie *Dogtown and Z-Boys* in 2001. The 1970s also brought increased commercial interest and support; corporations sponsored skateboarders, competitions became more common, and the number of skateparks increased. Popular appeal was strong, as exemplified by the release of a mainstream movie, *Skateboard*, starring U.S. teen idol Leif Garrett. However, by the end of the 1970s skateboarding hit another low, and most of the skateparks closed because of the cost of liability insurance. Most participants were forced to go back to the streets or to backyards, where they constructed ramps to retain some of the park features.

1980s

Skateboarding took a significant turn in the 1980s in its style, culture, and global reach. After a lull in the early part of the decade, skateboarding was booming globally by the end of the decade. The ramp and aerial styles were most popular until the end of the 1980s, when "street" style became prominent. Street style emerged from freestyle but was modified to blend with the urban landscape. Rodney Mullen's career exemplifies the transition from freestyle to street style.

The ollie move was the technical invention that significantly changed both street and aerial or vertical (vert) styles. Alan Gelfand originated the ollie in the late 1970s, but it was not widely used until the 1980s. The ollie enables a skateboarder to propel the board off the ground. With this move skateboarders could "jump" onto a variety of objects. Freestyle evolved aerially and was used on the street as well as on ramps and in pools. On the streets skateboarders were jumping onto objects such as handrails or parking blocks and then sliding their boards on them. Mark Gonzales and Natas Kaupas were key figures in creating the street style of the 1980s. This period also brought the development of aerial vertical skateboarding (as exemplified by Christian Hosoi and Tony Hawk), which takes place on (and above) ramps, halfpipes, and pools.

Skateboarding's culture changed to include not only the California beach and surf scene, but also the urban punk lifestyle. The cultural turn toward a punk, underground, and urban orientation affected female participation. Participation rates dropped, and the specialist media did not cover those females who were participating. Not until the late 1990s did females become visible again. These cultural trends were reflected in the two magazines that were established in this decade. In 1981 *Thrasher* magazine was started by Fausto Vitello, who worked in the skateboard manufacturing business and wanted to create a magazine dedicated to the "core" participants. *Thrasher* was associated more with punk, as indicated by the motto "Skate and Destroy." Topics ranged from featured skaters, new moves, and global places to skate to music and the social lives of skaters. In 1983 *Transworld Skateboarding* was founded by Larry Balma. *Transworld* was a glossy magazine whose audience was broader and whose content was less likely to offend. These two magazines are still the most popular today. At the local level many skaters created neighborhood magazines, called "zines," which were distributed at local skate shops.

Videos also became prominent during this time. Initially they featured skateboarders performing tricks and were used to sell products, but they evolved to include storylines and became a means of transmitting culture. In turn skateboarders began using videos to document their local scene. Videos remain a primary means of artistic expression and communication among skateboarders.

The 1980s skateboard industry was dominated by a few large corporations. Powell Peralta was one of those corporations whose talent and media savvy made a significant cultural impact. It was started in the 1970s by George Powell. Later he signed on legendary skater Stacy Peralta. One of the products they created and sold was a wheel that had a whitish color, so it was called "Bones." Peralta put together a group of skateboarders for the company team called "Bones Brigade." The team included top talent of the 1980s, such as Rodney Mullen, Tony Hawk, Steve Caballero, Lance Mountain, and Tommy Guerrero. One of their videos, *Search for Animal Chin*, not only showcased the skaters' skills, but also created a storyline that represented intrinsic motivation as the ideal of skating. In addition, Powell Peralta employed talented artists to develop its graphics, some of which, such as the skull peering out of a torn cloth, became iconic.

At the end of the decade skateboarding was extremely popular (the number of participants wasn't matched again until the turn of the century). The European championship was established, and several international competitions were held. Munster, Germany, held one of the most internationally vibrant skateboarding competitions throughout the late 1980s and 1990s.

Such global success brought profits to the dominant corporations. However, an internal struggle began to surface, and a growing backlash against those corporations boiled over as many skateboarders pointed to monopoly-like practices. One rallying cry of the late 1980s and early 1990s was to "keep it real" and not to "sell out" to commercialization. Frustrated, some of those skateboarders went on to create their own companies. However, another lull in popularity occurred during this time, primarily because of the worldwide economic recession. At the end of the 1980s skateboarding went through tough times with serious internal divisions, a sharp decline in the number of participants, and the infamous reputation as slacker punks for those skateboarders who did participate. Few observers could have predicted that in ten years skateboarding would be a powerful and positive cultural symbol.

challenged the status quo of the 1980s. He created World Industries, and soon after many skateboarders followed suit and started their own companies. Rocco and his World Industries defied many of the 1980s traditions; in particular he employed self-deprecating humor and developed cartoon graphics that are now rather common. Rocco also founded a magazine to compete with *Thrasher* and *Transworld*. *Big Brother* was introduced in 1992 and was notorious for its "sex, drugs, and rock 'n' roll" content. It was commonly sold with privacy wraps, and in 1997 Larry Flint Publishers took it over. A creative, combative, and controversial edge was brought forth in the early 1990s, expressed in the art and media of skateboarders.

X Games and Lifestyle Branding

Two developments that significantly affected the direction and popularity of skateboarding were the X Games and lifestyle branding. The X Games, developed in 1995 by all-sports cable channel ESPN, were an attempt to reach a young and hip male audience by providing an "Olympics" of extreme sports. The nature and scope of the sports included have evolved. For example, a winter version and several international and regional X Games, such as the Asian X Games, have been added. In skateboarding the X Games have featured high-flying ramp skating. Skateboarders such as Tony Hawk were given an ideal platform to showcase their talent. Hawk is now one of the most sought-after athletes for endorsements.

Lifestyle branding was also crucial in catapulting skateboarding onto the popular culture stage. Skateboarding was used in marketing campaigns as a central symbol of "cool." Unlike the 1980s, when the business strategies of skateboard corporations focused on promotion of products, the 1990s brought an integration of a variety of teenage products and activities such as music, movies, fashion, video games, and sports. For example, corporations that produced video games created a holistic lifestyle in their representation of skateboarding by incorporating music and fashion. Recently *Thrasher* magazine sold the rights to its motto, "Skate and Destroy," for the title of a skateboarding video game. Global media companies have become explicit in their use of skateboarding to sell a variety of other products. Disney is one example. It owns ESPN, which owns the brand "X Games." Disney produces other media, including the movie *Ultimate*

A young male skateboarder doing a nose-grab air.
Source: istock/Christian Carroll.

1990s

Not only did skateboarding rebound in the 1990s, but also it became one of the most powerful symbols of the hip, independent, and entrepreneurial teenager. Such cultural appeal is shown by the facts that Tony Hawk was one of the most popular athletes, and skateboarding was used to sell everything from soda and fast food to antiperspirant and cars. An overview of the dynamic changes within skateboarding helps to explain this meteoric rise in popularity.

The 1990s brought a proliferation of companies and the development of a variety of products and styles. For example, three main brands of skate shoes existed in the 1980s, but by the end of the 1990s more than fifty brands existed. Steve Rocco was a leading force in this change as he aggressively

X, and has bought the rights to Tony Hawk's autobiography. MTV has used skateboarders to create the series *Jackass*, which has been developed into two feature-length films. And corporations that originally focused on building and selling skateboard products have expanded into media and music. Some have branded everything from perfume to bed sheets. By incorporating various products under a lifestyle brand, corporations are able to sell more products to a broader audience. Skateboarding provides a primary means for conveying a cool brand image.

This broad-based appeal created new dynamics within skateboarding. The sport has certainly become more mainstream, more financially profitable, and more formally organized. Some of the older skateboarders bemoan these changes, but younger skateboarders tend to embrace the benefits of this popularity. This dynamic can be seen in Nike's presence in the market. In the late 1990s Nike tried to enter the skateboarding footwear market. It used a clever ad in which it acknowledged the absurdity of the illegal status of skateboarding in pubic spaces. The ad showed athletes in traditional sports being chased and harassed by police and then shifted by asking the viewer to consider what if every athlete were treated like a skateboarder. Although the ad was well received, skateboarders rejected Nike shoes. Skateboarders still had enough desire to maintain an alternative image that they did not want to support the icon of mainstream sports. Now the taboo against Nike no longer exists—Nike sponsors a team of professional skateboarders and sells its shoes. Market analysts give credit to Nike's strategies but suggest that the current target audience tends to embrace corporate presence in its leisure time.

Skateboarding Scene

The proliferation of styles and the increased numbers of participants have made the skateboarding scene quite dynamic. Street and ramp skateboarding remain most popular, but long boarding and its slalom style have been revived (BMW even developed a high-tech long board). Along with formal competitions, spectacularized single events have emerged. Examples are Danny Way's using a huge vert ramp to jump the Great Wall of China in 2005 and Tony Hawk's creating a traveling show of athletes called the "Boom Boom Huckjam." In addition, many variations of the skateboard, including the mountain board and the sand board, have been introduced.

As noted, some skateboarders have embraced the commercial success and mainstreaming of the sport, whereas others have had concerns and have used various media to mock the latest commercial trends. During the 1990s many subgroups thrived simultaneously on the skateboarding scene, reflected in the creation of several magazines (most of which have since folded) that represented different lifestyle components of skateboarding. Many practitioners still celebrate the artistic and creative aspects of skateboarding. Mark Gonzales and Ed Templeton are practicing artists who directly associate their inspiration from skateboarding urban environments.

Female skateboarders came back onto the scene largely because of the advocacy of a core group. Because of their marginalization by niche magazine coverage and at many competitions, women organized their own tour, the All Girl Skate Jam, and created niche magazines and web sites. Cara Beth Burnside was the first woman to have a signature shoe and continues to be one of the top vert skaters, along with Holly Lyons, Mimi Koop, and Karen Jonz. The dominant street skater, Elisa Steamer, has been featured in Tony Hawk's video game. Vanessa Torres and Amy Caron are also leading street competitors. Their male counterparts in street style are Jamie Thomas, Chad Muska, and Eric Koston. Besides Tony Hawk, other successful vert competitors are Colin McKay, Sandro Dias, Bob Burnquist, and Shaun White.

The 1990s brought the establishment of several professional organizations. World Cup Skateboarding was developed from the 1980s National Skateboard Association. World Cup promotes competitions and provides rankings of professionals and amateurs. Many countries, such as Japan, England, and Scotland, have their own associations. The International Association of Skateboard Companies was founded has been working for several years to promote the sport globally. One of its successes was changing the legal status of skateboarding to relieve the liability burden. In turn the number of new skateboard parks in the United States increased significantly in the 1990s.

Skateboarders also began to organize to negotiate labor issues with the sponsors of contests, such as media and governing bodies. In 2002 skateboarders nearly boycotted the X Games because of perceived inequities in shares of the profits. In 2005 women skateboarders organized and worked with the Women's Sports Foundation to negotiate with the X Games to win prize money parity with male skateboarders.

Skateboarding has evolved from a children's pastime to an international sport and cultural symbol of cool. The technology and skill sets have evolved to create a variety of ways to skateboard. Today skateboarding is a multifaceted sport and culture incorporating leisure, artistic, and competitive orientations.

Becky Beal

See also Dogtown and Z-Boys; Extreme Media; Gender; Hawk, Tony; Mullen, Rodney; Surfing; White, Shaun; X Games

Further Reading

Beal, B., & Wilson, C. (2004). "Chicks dig scars:" Commercialisation and the transformations of skateboarders' identities. In B. Wheaton (Ed.), *Understanding lifestyle sports: Consumption, identity and difference.* London: Routledge.

Borden, I. (2001). *Skateboarding, space & the city: Architecture and the body.* Oxford, UK: Berg.

Brooke, M. (1999). *The concrete wave: The history of skateboarding.* Toronto, Canada: Warwick Publishing.

Davis, J. (1999). *Skateboard roadmap.* London: Carlton Books.

Ski Jumping

Ski jumping—and especially its most spectacular form, ski flying—involves jumping and flying through the air on skis from large jumps or ramps specially built for this purpose. One competes primarily for distance but also for style. The distance jumped is measured from where the jumper leaves the snow to where he or she makes a standing landing down the hill. Ski jumpers travel along the run-in, toward the jump, at speeds of approximately 90 kilometers per hour. Then, soaring off the end of the jump, they must find an optimal floating position to give maximum uplift. After three to five seconds in flight, a jumper must then make a controlled landing. In September 2006 Bjørn-Erik Romøren of Norway set a world record when he ski jumped 239 meters. Janne Ahonen of Finland jumped 240 meters, but he did not manage to stay on his feet upon landing. Hence, his jump could not be recognized.

Ski jumping represents the height of skiing prowess, particularly in traditional skiing areas such as Finland, Austria, Germany, Norway, Slovenia (formerly part of Yugoslavia), and the Czech Republic, where the sport attracts many spectators. The annual ski flying events in Planica, Slovenia, are attended by approximately one hundred thousand spectators.

History

Historically ski jumping was associated with everyday transportation in the Norwegian winter environment. Rather than being a test of acrobatic skills by daredevils, ski jumping derived from, and was meant to foster, practical skills in mastering snow-covered, natural, downhill terrain. Nordic skiing traditionalists would never have conceived of their sport of ski jumping as an extreme sport. However, jumping over snowy natural terrain eventually developed into jumping on specially constructed jumping hills. Because of this practical and ideological background, discussions of how the sport should be performed have been a steady companion of ski jumping.

As early as the mid-nineteenth century Norwegian immigrants brought ski jumping to North America. In the late nineteenth and early twentieth centuries ski jumping was also introduced to European regions where the winter climate and landscape favor the sport, including Austria, Germany, Switzerland, France, and Italy. Shortly afterward Czechoslovakia, Poland, Yugoslavia, and Japan also began experimenting with ski jumping. As ski jumping was transplanted to new settings, the sport experienced cultural and ideological changes. In North America, for example, emphasis was put on setting world records for the longest ski jump.

Although distance has always been of utmost importance, points are also awarded for style. Demonstration of style and control while in the air and upon landing is essential in ski jumping. The longest jump is not always judged as the best or most technically correct.

Ski-jumping pioneers, including the Ruud brothers from Kongsberg, Norway (Birger Ruud being the most legendary) and Alf Engen of the United States, were athletes who were trained in gymnastics and who liked to challenge themselves to push the boundaries of the sport. They experimented with different jumping techniques and styles. For example, they attempted to perform somersaults in flight and tried to perform two and three at the same time. However, as the International Skiing Federation (FIS) took control of the sport, and as the sport was added to the 1924 Winter Olympic program, ski jumping gradually became more regulated. Competition procedures, profiles of the hills, and equipment (i.e., skis and jumpsuits) must follow regulations set by the FIS. However, the dynamics of competitive ski jumping, and particularly the continual quest for greater distances, have led to the construction of bigger and bigger hills, enabling more flight time and greater distances to be achieved.

The concept of world records in ski jumping was initially opposed by the FIS, which maintained that ski jumping is not solely about distance and that the record-seeking mentality conveys a misconception of the sport's founding values. For many years the FIS did not officially recognize a world record in ski jumping. However, after being pressed to accept that ski flying is not a passing fad and that records are popular among spectators, the FIS reluctantly agreed to recognize the longest jumps. Nonetheless, the FIS sought to counteract what it saw as an unhealthy tendency to build constantly larger hills. For example, in an attempt to discourage the development of so-called mammoth hills, between 1987 and 1994 the FIS refused to recognize any jump longer than the 192 meters achieved by Poland's Pjotr Fijas.

This policy, however, was mostly in vain. Long jumps were unofficially recognized and followed with much interest. This was especially true in the less "traditional" skiing nations (i.e., outside of Scandinavia), where length proved to be at the core of ski jumping's popularity. In the early 1930s jumpers at special events started landing at distances greater than 90 meters. This was an impressive feat, considering that the longest jumps in Olympic competitions rarely exceeded 70 meters. The magic limit of 100 meters was broken in 1936 in Planica, Slovenia, when the Austrian Sepp Bradl planted his skis at 101 meters. Nearly seventy years later Toni Nieminen of Finland completed the first jump of more than 200 meters (203 meters) in 1994; this feat also took place in Planica.

Planica has continued to be a key destination, hosting many of the longest jumps in history. Kulm, Austria; Oberstdorff, Germany; Vikersund, Norway; and Harrachow, Czech Republic, have, however, occasionally challenged Planica's dominant position by modernizing and rebuilding their hills. However, the Slovenian site has managed to increase its hill size continuously to remain the world's supreme ski-flying destination. The first world championship was held there in 1972. Since then this event has been held nineteen times at the five big hills in this region

With the ever-increasing size of the ramps jumped from, the safety of jumpers is crucial. Big hills are not built with a profile that gives jumpers enormous height during their flight. In fact, successful ski jumpers tend to stay within a few meters of the ground. Under perfect conditions light headwinds provide the desired uplift and allow jumpers to float along with their skis almost touching the snow. The jumpsuit and the skis also are factors. Their shape and

A ski jumper soars in front of a green forest. Source: istock/Bernd Klumpp.

consistency can influence the length of the jump, and strict regulations have been imposed on size, form, and materials. Other factors that are regulated are the relationship between the height of a jumper and the length and breadth of the skis and the jumper's weight. Such regulations were introduced to eliminate "anorectic" conditions among jumpers.

However, modern ski jumping clearly favors jumpers who have floating properties (i.e., a relatively large floating surface relative to weight). Regulations were introduced not to give slim athletes in oversized jumpsuits an advantage. Nevertheless, the ideal body type for ski jumping has changed during the last fifty years. The current ideal body type favors the tall, broad, yet light jumper. Women often participate at equal levels with men. Thus, ski jumping also offers an interesting discourse in gender stereotypes and expectations.

During its first hundred years ski jumping was an entirely male domain. It was considered a sport for the tough, athletic, and daring man. Accordingly, women were prevented from taking part in competitive ski jumping until recently. In 2003 Daniela Iraschko of Austria jumped 200 meters in Kulm (just nine years after the first man). Although no women's division exists in Olympic ski jumping, the FIS added ski-jumping competitions for women in 2004. The inclusion of women has led to a transformation of ski jumping from a male-dominated sport to one focused solely on weight, body shape, skill, and technique.

Giants of the Jump

Matti Nykanen of Finland was one of the most successful jumpers after World War II. He won nineteen Olympic medals and world championship titles. Another standout athlete was Birger Ruud of Norway. Birger was one of three brothers, all of whom were successful jumpers with at least one Olympic gold medal or world championship title. Indeed, a Ruud brother stood on every Olympic ski-jumping podium between 1928 and 1948. The brothers also won seven out of ten international titles between 1928 and 1938. However, of the three, Birger was the most outstanding. He won the last two Olympic gold medals before World War II (1932 and 1936) and came back sixteen years after his first win to capture a silver medal in the 1948 St. Moritz Olympic Games. He also won the downhill race—which counted as a part of the Alpine combination—in Garmisch-Partenkirchen, Germany, in 1936. Another modern champion was the German Jens Weissflog, who won gold and silver medals in the 1984 Games (representing the German Democratic Republic)

and came back after a ten-year Olympic medal drought to win another gold medal at the 1994 Games at Lillehammer, Norway. His achievement was all the more impressive because ski jumping in the meantime had gone through a virtual revolution in the shift to the V-style.

Technical Developments

Norms and rules of evaluation in ski jumping have changed considerably during the years. As the hills grew, more aerodynamic styles became popular among jumpers. The last significant innovation was the V-style, which was introduced by the Swede Jan Boklöv in 1986. Rather than jumping with the skis parallel, Boklöv spread his skis in a V-shape (as seen from behind). Although Boklöv's style was ridiculed by traditionalists and punished by the style judges, the V-style quickly became (and remains) the dominant style in competitions. The Telemark landing, with bent knees, one foot ahead of the other, has remained mandatory.

Although the technological and cultural aspects of ski jumping will continue to change as athletes strive for longer distances on bigger jumps, one fact will remain: In ski jumping the bottom of the hill, not the sky, is the limit.

Matti Erik Goksøyr

See also France; Skiing

Further Reading

ESkiJumping.com. (2006). *Everything about ski jumping.* Retrieved Feb. 1, 2007, from http://www.eskijumping.com/

International Olympic Committee. (2006). *International Olympic committee—sports.* Retrieved Feb. 1, 2007, from http://www.olympic.org/uk/sports/programme/history_uk.asp?DiscCode=SJ&sportCode=SI/

International Ski Federation. (2006). *Ski jumping.* Retrieved Feb. 1, 2007, from http://www.fis-ski.com/uk/disciplines/skijumping.html

Ski Jumping USA. (2006). *US ski jumping history.* Retrieved Feb. 1, 2007, from http://www.skijumpingusa.com/

Women's Ski Jumping. (2006). *Women's ski jumping USA.* Retrieved Feb. 1, 2007, from http://www.womensskijumpingusa.com/news.htm

Skiing

The term *extreme skiing* was coined in the 1970s to describe the practice of skiing steep slopes in wild terrain. However, the term lacks precision given that levels of risk associated with the pursuit remain subjective.

Skiing, From Above

With the prevalence of ski resorts, skiing has become a far more accessible sport than it used to be, leaving some skiers searching for a bigger thrill. But, as the extract below indicates, extreme enthusiasts are finding that there are ways to get away from the resort slopes to find their thrills.

Heli-skiing Takes the Country by Copter

The harsh chop of the helicopter blades cuts through the silence as the craft lifts away from a mountaintop in British Columbia, Canada. Deposited on the peak and surrounded by hundreds of miles of pristine snow are a small band of heli-skiers.

Helicopters transport skiers to the tops of otherwise inaccessible mountains, many of them in northern Canada and Europe. Once at the top, the small group skis down through untouched snow.

"Your first experience... is a bit overwhelming because you think what have I got myself into? It's all kinds of conditions, and there are always challenges," says John Baker. "That is the nature of open-mountain skiing. You develop a wide variety of skills."

It is not without risk, however. Avalanches can roar down with little or no warning, crushing and burying skiers and snowboarders in their wake. In January 2003, for instance, snowboarding champion Craig Kelly was among seven people killed in a massive avalanche near Revelstoke, British Columbia, an area where heli-skiers frequent.

The dangers notwithstanding, Marty von Neudegg said heli-skiing is a unique adventure. "The whole experience is really sensory," said von Neudegg. "The vast terrain, silence of the mountains, the sensation of being in deep snow, it's like skiing in a cloud."

Source: Trickey, H. (2004, Jan. 21). *Heli-skiing takes the country by copter.* Retrieved February 1, 2007, from http://www.cnn.com/2004/TRAVEL/01/21/sprj.ski04.heliskiing/

The Pioneers

The emergence of extreme skiing is often associated with the Swiss, Sylvain Saudan (b. 1936), who in 1967 successfully descended the couloir Spencer (Blaitière, France) and a year later the couloir Whymper (L'Aiguille Verte, France). He is generally recognized as the first to ski down slopes of more than 55 degrees inclination.

However, some Alpinists had already achieved such feats. In 1935 the Austrians Krüler, Schindelmesiter, and Schlager descended the north face of the Fuscherkarkopf (Austria); in 1941 Émile Allais and André Tournier skied le glacier du Milieu (L'Aiguille d'Argentière, France). Thus, most of them did not consider steep slope skiing as a practice independent from Alpinism. By occasionally using guides or helicopters to take his equipment up, Saudan distinguished himself from other contemporary pioneers such as Patrick Vallençant (1946–1989) and Heini Holzer (1945–1977), who continued to champion the ethics of Alpinism and attach more importance to the climb. By emphasizing the difficulty involved in descending rather than in climbing, Saudan gave birth to a new practice; at the same time he precipitated a number of controversies. In fact, Alpinists consider that descending can't be achieved without climbing. For them this is an ethical issue. Indeed, the use of helicopters to transport skiers and snowboarders to different peaks remains a subject of much controversy.

During the seventies extreme skiers conquered many landmarks: In 1971 Cachat-Rosset skied down the northeast slope of Les Courtes (France); in 1978 Vallençant skied the southwest and north faces of Huascarán (6,750 meters), in Peru; and in 1982 Saudan skied the first 8,000 meters of the Hidden Peak, Pakistan. These achievements drew important media coverage and captured the public's attention. In the 1980s commercial interests hoped to capitalize on the public's growing interest. Yet, extreme skiing remained a minority pastime until the 1990s at which point it became more mainstream.

The Mainstreaming of Extreme Skiing

In the 1990s the ski industry faced a sharp decline as skiers turned to snowboarding. To limit this trend, designers came up with parabolic skis based on the technical speci-

A backcountry skier makes a sharp turn coming down a steep hill. Source: istock/Jon Faulknor.

fications of snowboards. This flattened the novice skier's learning curve, making turning easier and improving access to powdery snow. With parabolic skis came the concept of freeriding, which opened up natural, unmanaged spaces, previously open only to snowboarders, to a new generation of skiers. This type of skiing was further popularized by world champion Craig Kelly.

While the invention of freeride skiing precipitated the development of extreme skiing, freeride skiing and extreme skiing are two different entities and usually appeal to different kinds of skiers. While freeride skiing involves a level of unrecognized risk (e,g., avalanches), the level of assumed risk is less than the level presented by extreme skiing, where fatal risk is present on every run.

The Media, Competitions, and Organizations

In the late 1980s and early 1990s, producers such as Warren Miller and Greg Stump began to put out films dedicated to extreme skiing. Some of their productions became international hits (e.g., *The Blizzard of AAHHH's*, 1988) and contributed to the increasing popularity of the sport. The skiers featured in these films quickly became international celebrities (e.g., Glen Plake, Scot Schmidt,

Mike Hattrup), and as skiing "celebrities," they added a new dimension to advertising extreme skiing and its commercial sponsors.

The first competition took place in 1991 at the World Extreme Skiing Championship (WESC) in Valdez (Alaska); a year later the U.S. Extreme Free Skiing Championship was staged in Crested Butte (Colorado). These competitions also produced new legends, like Doug Coombs (1957–2006) and Kim Reichhelm (b. 1960), who won the first WESCs in the male and female categories respectively.

In 1996 extreme skiers formed the International Free Skiers Association (IFSA). The IFSA aims to spin off from the Fédération Internationale de Ski (FIS) and to bring together freeskiers and those who ski in half-pipes and other manmade obstacles (IFSA 2006). With the introduction of competitive extreme skiing, skiers are now evaluated on five criteria during their course (IFSA, 2006): (1) line choice: high scores are given for choosing difficult routes, determined by steepness, exposure, air, snow, and course conditions; (2) aggressiveness: this is defined as the energy with which a competitor descends a chosen line; (3) technique: skiers are judged on style and turn quality; (4) fluidity: this criterion includes continuity, pace, and smooth transitions between sections of the course; and (5) control: any loss of control will result in a lower score.

At the same time, with the introduction of organized

competition, the term *extreme skiing* has been largely abandoned in favor of *freeskiing* or *big mountain skiing*. This development is not only a change of vocabulary, it also symbolizes a change in the practice and state of mind of the athletes. The objective becomes less of doing first descents in couloirs nearing 60 degrees of inclination where a drop is synonymous with death, but more of competing against other skiers in less dangerous terrains, where jumps and maneuvers are the common denominator.

Over time sponsors and organizers of competitions have influenced the evolution of the discipline, particularly with respect to reducing deaths and injuries during competitions. These changes have come due in large part to the risk of bad publicity these misfortunes can bring to the sport.

Community Values

The development of extreme skiing parallels the transformation of sport in general and skiing in particular. Inspired by the American counterculture of the sixties, many skiers began questioning the traditional values of the sport such as competition and other practices relating to rigid technique and performance. They began to subscribe to notions of freedom, creativity, aestheticism, and hedonistic sensation. Risk too became to be seen as a way to increase pleasure (Stranger 1999). Risk now occupies a central place in extreme skiing even if it is seldom acknowledged as such. While many outsiders equate risk with suicidal impulses, extreme skiers insist that they are in control, even in high-risk situations, and that sensation brings them pleasure (Drouet and Keimo Keimbou 2005; Lyng 1990).

The aesthetic character of the sport provides a leitmotiv. Part of its pleasure derives from the wild landscapes in which extreme skiing takes place. The beauty of the site is characterized by its virginity. Extreme skiers give great weight to the fact that the slopes they use have not already been "marked"—traversed. Skiers also evoke an aesthetic in defining the best way to ski. Short turns are associated with obsolete skiing practice, while wide arcs are synonymous with style (Drouet and Keimo Keimbou 2005). Control then reappears as a theme associated with the beauty of skiing. Extreme skiers can immediately perceive an athlete who is skiing on a slope too difficult for his/her technical skills; the tense skier is said to lack grace. Thus, the technical virtuosity of extreme skiers in the trickiest areas enables them to identify the best skiers, and it is those skiers who implicitly set the aesthetic standard.

Evolution of Extreme Skiing

Between the appearance of extreme skiing in the 1960s and its commercialization in the 1990s, its practice has changed with regard to the development of equipment, new techniques, and approaches to steeper slopes.

Extreme skiing is also used for commercial interests with athletes representing the products of their sponsors and attracting newcomers to off-piste terrain. In short, extreme skiing, like many other sports, has undergone the process of commodification.

Kévin Vermeir

Further Reading

Drouet, Y., Kemo Keimbou, D-C. (2005). Comment devient-on FREE-RIDER? Une approche socio-anthropologique [How does one become a free-rider? A socio-anthropological approach.] *Society and Leisure*, 28(1), 67–88.

International Free Skiers Association. (2006). Retrieved February 1, 2007, from http://www.freeskiers.org

Kay, J., & Laberge, S. (2003). Oh say can you ski? Imperialistic construction of freedom in Warren Miller's *Freeriders*. In R. Rinehart and S. Sydnor (Eds.), *To the extreme: alternative sports, inside and out* (pp. 381–398). Albany: State University of New York Press.

Lyng, S. (1990). *Edgework*: A social psychological analysis of voluntary risk taking. *American Journal of Sociology*, 95(4), 851–886.

Stranger, M. (1999) The aesthetics of risk. A study of surfing. *International Review for the Sociology of Sport*, 34(3), 265–276.

Skin Diving

See Free Diving

Skydiving/Skysurfing

For many people, jumping out of a "perfectly good airplane" at 3,800 meters, freefalling toward Earth at 200 kilometers per hour for sixty seconds, and then deploying a parachute ten to twelve seconds before impacting the Earth exemplifies extreme sport. Once primarily the purview of military personnel and stunt performers, skydiving has recently entered the mainstream of extreme sport. Marketed as an adventure sport and popularized in advertising campaigns, music videos, and feature films, skydiving has evolved into a sport that millions of people try once and that hundreds of thousands take up on a regular basis.

History

As with many risk activities, the exact genesis of parachuting is a topic of debate. Although Italian painter, sculptor, architect, and engineer Leonardo da Vinci is commonly thought to be the originator of the modern concept of parachuting, other sources suggest that Fausto Veranzio produced the first sketch of a parachute, entitled *Homo Volans* (flying man), in 1595. Meanwhile, Chinese legend suggests that Emperor Shun (2258–2208 BCE) performed the first parachute descent. Whatever the source of the concept, parachute descents from aircraft did not develop until the late eighteenth century. Another century and a half would pass before recreational skydiving as we now know it emerged.

The first parachute descent from an aircraft was made by André Jacques Garnerin, who jumped from a gas-filled balloon above Paris in October 1797. Initially most balloonists balked at the idea of taking a parachute with them for two reasons: the "unnecessary" weight and the idea that carrying one implied a lack of faith in their balloon. Without initial general acceptance as a useful item of safety equipment, the parachute found a more receptive audience with the entertainment-seeking public and the military and, as a result, gained a degree of legitimacy. With the advent of fixed-wing flight at the beginning of the twentieth century came new problems for parachutists. These included the speed of the aircraft, the opening shock of the parachute, and the lack of an apparatus attached to the aircraft from which a parachutist could safely deploy a parachute. Furthermore, with the new technology came a renewed objection on the part of aviators for the use of parachutes as safety devices.

World War I was a turning point for parachuting. Military involvement in parachuting affected the development of the sport in a number of ways. One effect was an increased demand for equipment. This demand led to important technological advances. For instance, in an effort to come up with a parachute suitable for use by military pilots, Leslie Irvin and Floyd Smith designed, built, and tested the first practical manually operated parachute in the United States. After demonstrating the suitability of the equipment by performing a freefall jump (a jump in which one's parachute is opened manually after a delay following exit from the aircraft) in 1919, Irvin received an order from the army for three hundred parachutes. The military provided such an immense demand for equipment that the few manufacturers employed were unable to meet the demand until 1942. Perhaps the defining moment for the legitimation of parachuting came in the spring of 1941. The German capture of the island of Crete was the culmination of the successes and the technological advances by the military in parachuting. With the foundation laid by the experiences of stunt jumpers and military personnel, in the post–World War II period parachuting gained popularity as a sport in Western societies.

Technical Issues

Skydiving is perhaps most accurately referred to as "sport parachuting," in part to reflect the fact that it includes both one's time in freefall (i.e., the time between leaving the aircraft and deploying one's parachute) and one's time underneath a parachute. Nevertheless, both practitioners and members of the general public tend to refer to the sport as "skydiving." Generally, skydiving takes place at a drop zone (DZ), a facility with authorization for parachute jumps. In addition to regular jumps, many skydivers attend events called "boogies." Boogies are special events hosted by one DZ to draw jumpers from surrounding DZs for jumping and partying. They range from the relatively small, which draw jumpers from only a few drop zones, to large international boogies such as the World Freefall Convention, which draws thousands of skydivers every year.

The central item of skydiving equipment is a "rig," a container system housing two parachutes: a main and a reserve. In the case of a malfunction of the main, a jumper may or may not jettison it (depending on the type of malfunction) before deploying the reserve. Rigs may also be equipped with an apparatus known as an "automatic activation device" (AAD). Various designs of AADs (e.g., timer, barometric) have been around since the 1950s, with all but the earliest models designed to automatically deploy the reserve if a jumper is too close to the ground and still falling too quickly. (Before the arrival of the Sentinel in 1959, AADs were armed just prior to exit and set to fire the main after a delay. If the main had already been deployed, the device still fired.) Initially AAD technology was somewhat suspect, with early models sometimes activating at inappropriate altitudes. An unexpected reserve deployment at an inopportune time can result in one jumper colliding with another jumper or having one's main and reserve canopies deployed at the same time, both potentially dangerous situations. As such, most experienced jumpers initially avoided AADs. Since the late 1980s, however, more precise and reliable models of AADs have been developed and have become popular.

Perhaps the most significant technological innovation to shape modern skydiving was the rectangular ram-air parachute, introduced in the late 1960s and refined in subsequent decades. In contrast to a round parachute that simply slows descent (leaving a jumper largely at the mercy of the winds), the ram-air parachute is a self-inflating design shaped somewhat like an airplane wing and allows for accurate steering and softer landings. This innovation changed the sport dramatically. The advent and development of this canopy technology made jumpers canopy pilots rather than captives of the wind. In addition, this innovation laid the foundation for numerous advances in canopy technologies from the late 1980s on. Modern high-performance canopies (many of which are elliptical rather than rectangular) are capable of previously unimaginable ground speed and responsiveness while still allowing for safe landings. Many observers suggest, however, that these canopies also reduce the skydiver's margin for error. Interestingly, some controversy exists within the skydiving community as to the suitability of such high-performance canopies. Many jumpers enjoy generating high speeds by doing a maneuver often called a "hook turn" or a "swoop." This maneuver involves initiating a turn just prior to landing so that the canopy dives toward the ground. As the parachute planes out of this dive, the canopy achieves an increase in ground speed. The parachutist "surfs" just inches above the ground for some time and then uses the "brakes" to "flare," slowing the parachute for landing. If performed skillfully, a hook turn can result in a spectacular approach and a soft and safe landing. A number of serious injuries and deaths, however, have resulted from improperly executed hook turns.

Skydiving Community

Surveys indicate that 85 percent of skydivers are men and that the majority of jumpers are between thirty and forty-nine years of age. Further, there is a skew toward the upper middle class in terms of income and education. This skew can be explained by the fact that serious involvement in skydiving requires considerable investment of time and money. Globally, skydiving is much more prevalent in developed societies, with approximately 40 percent of jumpers residing in the United States.

The Longest Leap

Air Force Association's Air Force Magazine *reports on the first supersonic skydive, first completed in 1960.*

Aug. 16, 1960, was set for the ultimate test. Kittinger rode a four-and-a-half-foot open gondola to 102,800 feet. The ascent, through temperatures that fell to 94 degrees below zero, took an hour and a half. Failure of his life-support system above 60,000 feet would have meant almost instant death.

With that and other hazards in mind, he stepped out of the gondola and plunged through the stratosphere, reaching supersonic speed in the rarified atmosphere. Between 90,000 and 70,000 feet, he experienced great difficulty in breathing. At about 50,000 feet, his free-fall speed had dropped to 250 miles an hour in the denser atmosphere. He was suffering extreme pain in his right hand that was caused by partial failure of pressure in that glove during the ascent.

After he had fallen for four minutes and thirty seven seconds, Kittinger's main chute opened, and some eight minutes later he landed at the White Sands Missile Range in New Mexico with no permanent injuries but with three world records: the highest open-gondola balloon ascent, the longest free-fall, and the longest parachute descent. He was also the first man to go supersonic in a free-fall. Kittinger had proved that man could function in near-space and that parachuting from very high altitudes was feasible.

By John L. Frisbee

Source: Air Force Association. *Air Force Magazine.* Retrieved July 1, 2006, from http://www.afa.org/magazine/valor/0685valor.asp

A 2003 report by the International Parachuting Commission (IPC) indicates that, between 1989 and 2002, between 285,000 and 417,000 jumpers worldwide performed between 4.59 million and 6.87 million skydives each year. Because not all countries submitted data for each year, these estimates are slightly conservative. From these same data the IPC concluded that during this time roughly 4,500 jumpers performed seventy-six thousand skydives for every one fatality. In addition to these fatalities, as well as those that might not have been counted in this report, numerous injuries in skydiving were reported. Because these injuries tend to be underreported, it is impossible to accurately assess the rate of injury in the sport.

During the past decade and a half more experienced jumpers (as a percentage of all fatalities) have been dying. In 1990 expert skydivers (those with more than 250 freefalls) accounted for 33 percent (23 of 70) of all skydiving fatalities, according to the IPC. In contrast, in 2002 expert skydivers represented 60 percent (44 of 72) of all fatalities. Researchers and jumpers also have noted more landing mishaps as the cause of skydiving fatalities. In 2002, for example, of the seventy-three fatalities for which the IPC has data, thirty-eight (52 percent) could be attributed to "fast canopies" or "other landing errors." Because jumpers generally gain a certain amount of experience in the sport before attempt-

ing these high-performance landings, these two findings seem to be related.

Subdisciplines

A jumper has a certain amount of time in freefall, usually between thirty and sixty seconds, to perform as many maneuvers as possible before the time comes to activate his or her parachute. Jumpers can pursue a number of subdisciplines in freefall.

For many recreational and competitive jumpers, freefall time is used for formation skydiving (FS), often referred to as "relative work" because jumpers fly relative to one another, making particular formations with their bodies in freefall. An FS jump is generally referred to as an "X-way." A two-person jump is a two-way, a four-person jump is a four-way, and so on. As abilities and techniques developed, progres-

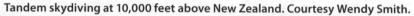

Tandem skydiving at 10,000 feet above New Zealand. Courtesy Wendy Smith.

sively larger freefall formations became possible, building up to 50-ways in the late 1970s and a world-record 400-way in 2006 over Udon Thani, Thailand. At the same time competitions (primarily in 8-way and 4-way) developed around the number of set formations a team could complete in a given time period.

During the mid-1980s the discipline of freeflying developed out of the experiments of a group of jumpers (called the "freefly clowns") with nontraditional freefall positions and has become popular. Whereas relative work is performed almost exclusively belly-to-Earth (a stable freefall position), freeflying is performed in sitting, head-down, and standing positions, among others. Advocates suggest that freeflying expands the possibilities of movement in freefall and thus allows for more creativity and flow.

Another subdiscipline is skysurfing, which involves freefalling while attached to a surfboard-like apparatus. The board is generally the size of a snowboard, demands a particular set of skills related to control over various body positions in freefall, and also necessitates specifically designed safety equipment. For example, there is a cutaway cable so that a jumper can jettison the board in the event of trouble. Skysurfing has proven to be a marketable form of skydiving, having been featured in numerous popular culture outlets and for a time included in the ESPN X-Games.

Some people consider BASE (building, antenna, span, Earth) jumping (also known as "fixed object jumping") to be a subdiscipline of skydiving. Although skydiving and BASE jumping share some technical elements, they also have numerous elements of divergence.

"Pond-swooping" is a discipline that has only recently developed. Participants perform an aggressive swoop as they approach the landing area, then glide across a small body of water, aiming to travel a great distance just inches above the water before touching down on land. In competition, points are awarded for such aspects as greatest distance, style, and degree of technical difficulty. Competition began in the late 1990s, and the sport has since been formalized, with the Pro Swooping Tour conducting events in which competitors vie for tens of thousands of dollars in prize money. Swooping has been featured in numerous media outlets, including *Sports Illustrated*, the *Today Show*, and the Outdoor Life Network.

Since the 1930s a small number of jumpers have experimented with various configurations of "wings" to be worn in freefall. Between 1930 and 1961 seventy-two of the seventy-five "birdmen" working on these wings died in the attempt. More recently, Patrick de Gayardon, an experienced French jumper, developed a wingsuit that revolutionized this type of skydiving. Although de Gayardon died in 1998 because of a rigging error as he was working on a modification of the suit, he laid the foundations for the subdiscipline that has come to be called "skyflying." Highly experienced jumpers can now slow their vertical descent to below 40 kilometers per hour and cover great horizontal distances as well. This slowed fall rate means that jumpers spend longer in freefall—often between one and three minutes. Modern wingsuits use ram-air technology, and many people argue that skyflying is the closest thing to pure human flight that anyone has achieved.

Some jumpers engage in a discipline of skydiving in which freefall is not at all the point. In canopy formation skydiving (CFS)—often called "canopy relative work" or "CRW"—jumpers construct formations with each other after they have deployed their parachutes. As in formation skydiving, jumpers in CFS may try to construct many formations in one jump or build large formations. The current record for the largest formation is an 85-way, set in 2005 over Lake Wales, Florida.

Training and Competition

In recent decades, with more people taking up skydiving, training practices have been formalized. One popular way for jumpers to begin in the sport, for instance, is to perform a "tandem jump." In a tandem jump senior instructors wear a special rig designed to carry two people. He or she attaches a novice to him/herself and the rig with a harness and is ultimately in charge of the operation of the parachute equipment, helping the novice to deploy the parachute and land safely. Another popular way to get started in the sport is to perform a "static-line" jump or an "instructor-assisted deployment" (IAD). Although these methods have slight differences, they are substantially similar in the sense that a student jumper performs the jump on his or her own, but an instructor is responsible for deploying the student's parachute as the student leaves the aircraft. Another popular method to train students goes by various names, including "accelerated freefall" (United States, Australia, United Kingdom) and "progressive freefall" (Canada). This method is particularly common at DZs with large aircraft (larger aircraft are generally unsuitable for static lines or IADs, and they provide more altitude for longer freefalls). With this method, students progress quickly to lengthy freefall jumps, accompanied by one or two experienced instructors who offer corrections to body position, help develop awareness in freefall, and provide help in parachute deployment if necessary.

After becoming proficient at basic skydiving skills (e.g., stable freefall position, parachute deployment, basic safety procedures), novice parachutists continue to follow progression guidelines toward higher levels of proficiency in various areas of the sport before they are permitted to participate in jumps demanding these skills (e.g., night jumps, formation skydives).

Skydiving competitions date back to at least 1930, when jumpers gathered in Russia to demonstrate who could land closest to a target on the ground. The Fédération Aéronautique Internationale (FAI) sanctioned the World Parachuting Championships in 1951, with events being added as subdisciplines have been developed. The most recent discipline to be added to major competitions is freeflying, sanctioned in 2000.

The Sky's the Limit

Is skydiving an extreme sport? This question is difficult to answer primarily because of the recent technical innovations and the variety of ways to engage in the sport. Together these factors have changed the face of skydiving dramatically in the last forty years. In the 1960s and into the 1970s, for example, jumping equipment was heavy, landings were routinely hard under round parachutes, and numerous serious injuries and deaths resulted from situations in which jumpers failed to deploy a parachute in time for it to fully inflate. These days, however, people commonly perform their first jumps (either solo or tandem) under large rectangular parachutes equipped with AADs, performing soft, accurate landings. Moreover, modern canopy technologies, AADs, and training protocols seem to have dramatically decreased the hazards of the sport for many recreational jumpers. However, despite these advances in technologies, many people argue that skydiving remains "extreme." Even for those jumpers practicing a relatively mainstream version of skydiving, the risk is so dramatic that it would be difficult to argue otherwise.

Moreover, recent innovations create opportunities for jumpers to push the envelope in ways that would have been difficult to envision only twenty years ago. For jumpers pioneering these innovations, skydiving is definitely an extreme sport. Jeb Corliss and Luigi Cani, for example, are developing the skills and technologies to attempt to land a wingsuit

without the use of a parachute. Many of skydiving's most important innovations have been driven by participants' thirst for new adventures and achievements. Although skydiving appears to have become less extreme for those who do it as a one-time adventure and perhaps for those who pursue relatively mainstream versions of the sport, it remains, for many, the most extreme of sports.

Jason Laurendeau

See also BASE Jumping

Further Reading

Celsi, R., Rose, R., & Leigh, T. (1993). An exploration of high-risk leisure consumption through skydiving. *Journal of Consumer Research*, 20(1), 1–23.

Fensch, T. (1980). *Skydiving book*. Mountainview, CA: Anderson World.

Greenwood, J. (1978). *Parachuting for sport* (2nd ed.). Blue Ridge Summit, PA: Tab Books.

Horan, M. (1979). *Index to parachuting 1900–1975*. Richmond, IN: Parachuting Resources.

Huston, J. (1972). *Out of the blue*. West Lafayette, IN: Purdue University Studies.

International Parachuting Commission. (2003). *2002 IPC AAD survey report*. Lausanne, Switzerland: Fédération Aéronautique Internationale.

International Parachuting Commission. (2003). *2002 IPC safety survey report*. Lausanne, Switzerland: Fédération Aéronautique Internationale.

Laurendeau, J. (in press). "He didn't go in doing a skydive": Sustaining the illusion of control in an edgework activity. *Sociological Perspectives*.

Laurendeau, J., & Gibbs Van Brunschot, E. (2006). Policing the edge: Risk and social control in skydiving. *Deviant Behavior*, 27(2), 173–201.

Lyng, S., & Snow, D. (1986). Vocabularies of motive and high-risk behavior: The case of skydiving. In E. Lawler (Ed.), *Advances in group processes: Theory and Research*, Vol. 3. (pp. 157–179). Greenwich, CT: JAI Press.

Miller, W., & Frey, J. (1996). Skydivers as risk takers: An examination. *Humanity and Society*, 20(4), 3–15.

Poynter, D., & Turoff, M. (2000). *Parachuting: The skydivers' handbook* (8th ed.). Santa Barbara, CA: Para Publishing.

Pro Swooping Tour. (n.d.). http://www.proswoopingtour.tv/

United States Parachute Association. (n.d.). 2005 skydiving review. Retrieved July 7, 2006, from http://www.uspa.org/about/images/mem survey05.pdf.

Snowboarding

When a sixteen-year-old male snowboarder traveling at an estimated 60 miles per hour collided with, and killed, a twenty-nine-year-old female skier in February 2005, the incident grabbed headlines across America and stirred considerable debate. Many contributors to the argument reinforced stereotypes of snowboarders as drug-addled, careless brats who are anti-social to the point of posing a danger to skiers. Indeed, snowboarding has been labeled a "radical," "risky," and "extreme" pursuit since its inception. But today, with more than 18.5 million snowboarders worldwide, and participants ranging from five to seventy-five years of age, the notion of snowboarding as extreme seems obtuse. Jake Burton, owner of the world's largest snowboarding company agrees, noting that "there [are] a lot of people that snowboard in a fairly conservative manner" (cited in Wheaton 2004, 4). Nonetheless, with more than 75 percent of American snowboarders under the age of twenty-four, and males constituting approximately 70 percent of all boarders, it is no wonder that stereotypes continue to abound.

Snowboarding is commonly understood as a dangerous activity enjoyed mostly by daredevil, risk-taking, adrenaline-seeking youths. Certainly, there is an element of risk involved, but in most cases risk is a subjective calculation that individuals make in the context of their ability. For example, a sign at an Austrian resort that reads, "Runs are extremely dangerous. 70 degree slope. One fall could result in loss of life," might petrify some boarders while exhilarating others. According to a recent study, snowboarding is the third riskiest sport behind boxing and tackle football. Another study shows snowboarders are more than twice as likely as skiers to sustain serious fractures, become concussed and lose consciousness, dislocate joints, and have their teeth knocked out. While advanced snowboarders traveling at high speeds and trying dangerous maneuvers such as jumps and other aerial tricks are at risk of serious injuries, including trauma to the head, neck, and abdomen, beginner snowboarders are the most frequently injured. Falling is the lead cause of injury; thus it is understandable that almost one-quarter of all snowboarding injuries occur during a person's first experience, and almost one-half occur during the first season. The majority of these injuries, however, tend to be minor, including wrist, ankle, and knee sprains and fractures. Colliding with a tree is the most common cause of severe injury, but such occurrences are rare. The risk of fatality for snowboarders, calculated at 0.000000231 per snowboarding day, is in fact lower than that for skiers. According to the National Ski Areas Association, in terms of the average number of deaths on the slopes, snowboarding is significantly safer than bicycling or swimming.

So what is so extreme about snowboarding? While snowboarding might not be an overly dangerous activity for the majority of participants, the term extreme has relevance in three distinct ways. First, snowboarding's countercultural roots and irreverent lifestyle contributed to the general public's perception of the activity and subsequent extreme labeling. Second, in the late 1990s television and corporate sponsors recognized the huge potential in snowboarding to tap into the young male market and thus went to great lengths to portray snowboarders as extreme in their perilous approach to the activity and in their personas. Third, big mountain snowboarding, which exposes the individual to the raw power of the natural environment, including gale-force winds, subzero temperatures, 60-degree slopes, ice, rocks, slides, avalanches, cliffs and crevasses, is undeniably extreme.

Alternative Youths on Board

Snowboarding as we understand the activity today emerged in the late 1960s and 1970s in North America. The early pioneers embodied the idealism of the counterculture and, in direct contrast to skiing, which was an expensive and bourgeois sport framed by a strong set of rules of conduct, embraced snowboarding as a free, fun, cooperative, and individualistic activity. In comparison with skiers, snowboarders were typically younger, less educated, single, male, low-income earners or students. Summarizing the cultural differences during this period, Duncan Humphreys explains that whereas "skiing embodied technical discipline and control," snowboarding "embodied freedom, hedonism and irresponsibility" (Humphreys 1996, 9). Indeed, as part of the new leisure movement, snowboarders subscribed to antiestablishment counterculture values and do-it-yourself philosophies. Ben, an early snowboarder, describes the antiestablishment mentality among snowboarders as "ruining all the fixtures at resorts, rails and running into skiers and telling them to screw off…" (Anderson 1999, 68). Jake Blattner, an early professional snowboarder, recalls the do-it-yourself mentality prevalent in early snowboarding culture: "We cut the noses off our boards. It was just to see what would happen. It was like being your own board manufacturer instead of having to rely on some company to make something how you want it. There were no boards being made for what we wanted to do…so we took matters into our own hands" (cited in Howe, 1998, 86).

However, Terje Haakonsen, a snowboarder of legendary status, best captures the countercultural ideology of boarders when he described snowboarding as about making "fresh tracks and carving powder and being yourself" rather than "nationalism and politics and big money" (Lidz 1997, 114). Snowboarding was in the words of cultural commentator Jamie Brisick "an expansion of surfing and skateboarding, a way to explore different terrain with the same mind-set" (Brisick 2004, 69).

The long history and acceptance of skiing as a legitimate pastime and sport bestowed skiers with social authority on the mountain. Snowboarders challenged skiers' power. Thus, ski resorts initially banned snowboarders. Owners, managers and their skiing clientele defined the snowboarding cohort as "13–18 year olds with raging hormones" who liked skateboarding and surfing (Hughes 1988). Negative images of surfing and skateboarding from the 1970s contributed to the public dislike and distrust of snowboarding. David Schmidt, the national sales manager for Burton Snowboards, says that "most people visualize[d] snowboarders as a bunch of skate rats who are going to terrorize the mountain" (Nelson 1989). One running joke among skiers went: "What's the difference between a boarder and a catfish? One is a bottom-dwelling, disgusting, rejected muck sucker and the other is a fish" (Coleman 2004, 206). But while bans made participation difficult, they did not stop determined and passionate devotees.

Modern competitive snowboarding began in 1981 with the first American national titles held at Suicide Six (Vermont). The next year, the resort hosted the first international snowboard race. Snowboard competitions later in the 1980s embodied an inclusive ideology. Tina Basich recollects one of the first regional competitions in 1986 in which everybody, from both genders, competed together. Snowboarding historian Susanna Howe describes these events as "cultural hotbeds" that effectively ironed out any notions of social stratification. Everyone, she adds, was "drunk and disorderly" (Howe 1998, 41). Early snowboard competitions were poorly organized and, in keeping with countercultural traditions, privileged fun over serious competition and individualism.

It was not until 1983 that Stratton Mountain (Vermont) became the first major ski field to open its piste to snowboarders. Others quickly followed. Skiing had reached a growth plateau and snowboarding offered ski fields a new youth market and ongoing economic prosperity. In the words of one cultural commentator, snowboarding was the "biggest boost to the ski industry since chairlifts" (Hughes 1998). Nevertheless, by 1988 snowboarders comprised only 6 percent of the ski resort population. Negative media coverage influenced the mainstream's opinion of snowboarding, and its followers, during this period. For example, *Time* magazine that year declared snowboarding "the worst new sport." Certainly, the distinctive personalities and styles embodied by early professional snowboarders Damion Sanders and Shaun Palmer contributed to the general public's dislike and distrust of snowboarders.

Damian, the younger brother of Avalanche founder Chris Sanders, was "perhaps the most visible poster boy of snowboarding's 'radical,' 'extreme' image. He embodied this with everything from clothing to riding style, Spiky hair and Day-Glo head bands; every flashy mutation of the board

The Journey

The following is an account of what was running through author Megan Popovic's mind as she tried out an extreme sport for the first time. Popovic decided to try snowboarding as part of her graduate research on the topic.

I'm staring up the mountain that I know I must climb and yet I am frozen with fear and self-doubt. I can hear my mentor's motto whispering in my mind, "it is the process instead of the end-result which defines one's character," and question whether I have the skills to tackle the ride. I begin to move. The journey to the top is filled with pitfalls and periods of wonderment as I gaze up to where I am headed and then turn around to observe the path

I have made. It is a world that was unknown to me not too long ago, and yet through immersing myself in the culture, I am in awe with the freedom and individuality engrained within the essence of the sport. Step-by-step I reach the top, overwhelmed with pride and speechless from the vast view at this pinnacle of my young life. I take a breath, allow the present-moment to permeate my body, and then set off with my feet grounded to the earth and the wind blowing through my hair.

Such was my experience completing a Master's thesis on snowboarding.

Megan Popovic

garb was 'extreme.' Huge cliffs, over-extended postures, gritted teeth, and clenched fists were signs of aggression and in vogue [among boarders]" (Howe 1998, 70). Voted the "most extreme snowboarder" in an early *Transworld Snowboarding* magazine rider roll, Sanders explains that "the wilder I was the better they [boarders] like it" (cited in Howe 1998, 73).

Shaun Palmer further epitomized the rebellious image of snowboarding; he was foul-mouthed and "would drink and do drugs all night, and win half-pipe contests in the morning" (Howe 1998, 78). Palmer was essentially snowboarding's "first real bad boy." He was, according to snowboarding historian Susana Howe, "cocky, rude, and couldn't lose a contest between 1988 and 1990. While he was at it, he created some of the most lasting images in the history of snowboarding. When people remember those days of competition, they inevitably get a sparkle in their eye, and mention some crazy thing that Palmer did: jumping out a hotel room window, throwing a snowboard into a sacred Japanese bath, flinging a hot dog at a contest organizer, the stories go on and on, and they shaped the image of what it meant to be a real, hardcore, snowboarder" (Howe 1998, 70). Palmer's constant bravado, athletic prowess and belligerent and hedonistic lifestyle combined to create a cultural ideal that appealed to many youths seeking an "alternative" identity.

Significant change occurred in the late 1980s and 1990s. The convergence of several factors contributed to the escalating number of snowboarders. More ski resorts opened their pistes to snowboarders, the mainstream media started reporting favorably on snowboarding culture, and snowboarding magazines (e.g., *International Snowboarder Magazine, Transworld Snowboarding, Snowboarder, Blunt*) and films (e.g., *Snowboarders in Exile, Critical Condition, Totally Board*) communicated positive images, attitudes, and styles across the whole culture. Technological advances and an increasingly competitive market also provided participants with a cheaper and wider variety of equipment. Economic growth in the associated cultural and manufacturing industries and institutionalization accompanied growing numbers of participants. Television and corporate sponsors also started to identify the huge potential in extreme sports as a way to tap into the young-male market, and mainstream companies began appropriating the alternative, hedonistic, and youthful image of the boarder to sell products ranging from chewing gum to vehicles.

Institutionalization and commercialization angered many snowboarders: Some overtly resisted the process. For this group competitive boarding stood in symbolic juxtaposition to "soul boarding." For example, in 1990 world champion snowboarder Craig Kelly retired at the peak of his career from the competitive circuit that he likened to prostitution. As he put it: "Snowboarding is something that I think should be done on your own terms. Society is full of rules, and I use the time I spend in the mountains as an opportunity to free myself of all constraints.... I decided that competing on the World Tour restricted the freedom that I found with snowboarding in the first place" (cited in Reed 2005, 54).

Debates over the institutionalization process in snowboarding came to the fore in the lead-up to the 1998 Winter Olympics. The loudest voice of opposition came from Terje Haakonsen who refused to enter the games because he believed, quite correctly in the eyes of many, that the International Olympic Committee comprised a group of Mafia-like officials and that the event was tantamount to joining the army. Haakonsen refused to be turned into a uniform-wearing, flag-bearing, walking logo. Other snowboarders expressed similar sentiments. Morgan Lafonte from the United States, for example, declared that "the Olympics are way too big" and will mold snowboarding into its image (cited in Howe 1998, 151). Some boarders, however, embraced these changes. American snowboarder Jimi Scott wanted to "be the first snowboarder to win a gold medal and be written into the history books" (cited in Howe 1998, 151). In his biography professional snowboarder Todd Richards explains that while "half of the companies and riders were looking forward to the Olympics as the ultimate forum that would legitimize the sport," the other half "didn't give a damn about the Olympics because it reeked of skiing—a stuffy by-the-books sport with an attitude that was the kiss of death for snowboarding's irreverent spirit" (Richards 2003, 135). Nonetheless, he conceded that "finally snowboarding is becoming lucrative." Debates among snowboarders over the commercialization process in general, and the 1998 Winter Olympics more specifically, illustrate the growing divisions and cultural fragmentation within the broader snowboarding culture during this period.

The Mainstreaming of Extreme

Inevitably, incorporation continued regardless of the contrasting viewpoints of boarders, and snowboarding increasingly became controlled and defined by transnational media exposure like ESPN's X Games and NBC's Gravity Games. According to Todd Richards: "The X Games marked the end of one era but simultaneously gave birth to a whole new world of possibilities. It was sort of sad to say good-bye to being a bunch of misunderstood outcasts. A lot of joy was derived from the punk-rock-spirit, and once the masses join your ranks...its over. The image had already begun to change, but the X Games put the icing on the mainstream cake" (Richards 2003, 182).

In 1998 ESPN beamed the X Games to 198 countries in twenty-one languages. The incorporation of snow-boarding into the 1998 Winter Olympics, video games including Playstation's Cool Boarders and Shaun Palmer Pro-Snowboarder, and blockbuster movies such as *First Descent* (2005) helped further expose the sport to the mainstream. According to a Leisure Trends survey, 32 percent (nearly 92 million people) of the United States population watched the 2002 Olympic's snowboarding half-pipe competition in which Americans won gold (Ross Powers), silver (Danny Kass), and bronze (J. J. Thomas) in the men's event (this was the first U.S. Winter Olympic medal sweep since 1956) and gold (Kelly Clark) in the women's event. Of those viewers 18.6 million Americans said they wanted to try snowboarding.

As snowboarding became popularized and incorporated into the mainstream, it adopted many of the trappings of traditional modern sports: corporate sponsorship, large prize monies, rationalized systems of rules, hierarchical and individualistic star systems, win-at-all costs values, and the creation of heroes, heroines, and in the words of Mike Messner, "rebel athletes who look like walking corporate billboards" (Messner 2002, 178). Unlike earlier generations many current boarders embrace commercial approaches or, in the more colorful words of professional snowboarder Todd Richards, "milk[ing] it while it's lactating" (Richards 2003, 178). Professional snowboarders including Shaun White, Danny Kass, Todd Richards, Tara Dakides, Gretchen Bleiler, Lindsey Jacobellis, Kelly Clark, and Hannah Tetter have benefited from the recently commercialized form of snowboarding. They have achieved superstar status within the culture, attracting corporate sponsors including Target, Visa, Nike, Mountain Dew, Campbell's Soup, and Boost Mobile. Some earn seven-figure salaries. But with major corporate sponsors offering large prize monies, the focus of many boarding competitions is no longer fun; extreme forms of individualism and egocentricity prevail. Olympic silver medallist Gretchen Bleiler believes the "industry pressure" and "ultra-high" level of snowboarding ability are creating an "extremely competitive" atmosphere in snowboarding, and decries a younger generation who, in their hunger to

win, are "changing the overall feel at the top of the half-pipe" (cited in Sherowski 2003, 146).

In this hypercommercial context of the X Games, Gravity Games, and prime-time television exposure, new competition formats and boarding disciplines that lend themselves to television coverage emerged, including boarder-cross, slope-style, and big-air competitions. These events are spectacular with crashes virtually guaranteed. This was certainly true when professional snowboarder Tara Dakides attempted to perform a spectacular big-air stunt live on *The Late Show with David Letterman* in February 2004. The producers built a massive wooden ramp outside the studio in the middle of New York's 53rd Street and then covered it in snow. It was supposed to launch Dakides over a 20-foot gap. But various factors including lack of building materials, warm weather melting the snow, and the pressure of a big-time production diminished Dakides chances of successfully completing the stunt. In her own words: "I wasn't aware of it, but the snow on the run-in was soft [and] when I went to turn I sunk to the wood....I went off in a direction that I knew was bad. Before I even took off, I was like, 'Oh Shit!' You hear it clear as day on the tape. I was already committed, so I went for it [the 360-degree rotation], but I knew I was in trouble. I came around and all I saw was concrete. I didn't even see the cameraman I hit" (cited in Roenigk 2004, para. 11). In front of a stunned crowd and live national audience, Dakides fell on the asphalt from an estimated height of 25 feet, was knocked unconscious, and split her head. The event was covered by every major American newspaper and became the lead story on local news programs across the country, thus reinforcing the "extreme" nature of snowboarding and snowboarders.

Despite the increasing professionalism at the elite level, residual traces of snowboarding's countercultural past remain. Top snowboarders must not appear to take the activity too seriously; they must maintain a marketable image that is part snowboarding larrikin and part professional athlete. In interviews professional snowboarders frequently emphasize their hedonistic and party lifestyle, disregard for authority, heterosexual pursuits, and high jinks. For example, in *Snowboarder* magazine, professional snowboarder Romain DeMarchi reveals that he has a "bad boy image" for being "a hard-core partier" and admits he has been arrested four times. DeMarchi is very aware of the economic value of a distinctly "extreme" personality that makes links to snowboarding's history of rebellion: "People say, 'Ah, Romain's the wild guy, he's going to go out and rage his ass off and be a f—ker and a dickhead!' But you know, who cares if these things are said? People label

A snowboarder going big high above the half pipe. Source: istock/Jason Lugo.

me as crazy, and it's good for me. It sells, so the sponsors use it and the magazines use it" (Bridges 2004, 101).

Arguably the most professional competitive snowboarder, Olympic half-pipe gold medalist Shaun White downplays the professionalism of snowboarding in an interview with *Rolling Stone*: "We are still the dirty ones in the bunch, the sketchy snowboard kids. I don't think I'd have it any other way" (Edwards 2006, 45). Of course, neither would the corporate sponsors who have profited enormously from the commodification of snowboarding's perceived irresponsible and uncontrolled image.

The mainstream exposure of snowboarding had a significant influence on cultural demographics. Snowboarding attracted an influx of participants from around the world, and from different social classes and age groups. Snowboarding has seen a 385 percent increase in participation between 1988 and 2003, and it is one of America's fastest growing sports. But the influx of new participants during

the late 1990s and early 2000s fueled struggles within the snowboarding culture between insiders and newcomers, and various subgroups. Andy Blumberg, editor of *Transworld Snowboarding*, explains that "once united we seem today divided" (Blumberg 2002, 16). Core participants include males and females whose commitment to the activity is such that it organizes their whole lives. According to snowboarding journalist Jennifer Sherowski: "Not everyone who rides a snowboard is a snowboarder, but for those who do bear this illustrious title, it's an undeniable way of life. High school ends, and the road starts calling—off to mountain towns and the assimilation into weird, transient tribes full of people who work night jobs cleaning toilets or handing you your coffee in the early mornings, all so they can shove a fistful of tips in their pocket and ride, their real motives betrayed by goggle tans or chins scuffed by Gore-Tex. In this world, people don't ask what you 'do,' they ask you where you work—knowing that what you do is snowboard, just like them, and any job you might have is simply a means for it" (Sherowski 2005, 160).

Snowboard instructor, park crew, journalist, photographer, competition judge, coach, event organizer, and semi-sponsored snowboarder, are among the jobs held by passionate snowboarders committed to the lifestyle rather than the economic rewards. In contrast to core boarders, snowboarders who are less committed—including male and female novices, poseurs, or weekend warriors—have lower cultural status. Rather than demonstrating commitment via participation, poseurs display what Becky Beal and Lisa Weidman call a "prefabricated version" of a snowboarder by consciously displaying name-brand clothing and equipment. Although taste and style play an important part in constructing a distinctive snowboarding identity, members cannot buy their way into the core of the culture. As *New Zealand Snowboarder* magazine puts it, respect has "to be earned, usually with a lot of blood, sweat and tears" (May/June 1995, 9).

Various identities, and preferred styles of participation (e.g., free riding, free-styling, and alpine) exist within this core group. Freeriders prefer to hike, ride a snowmobile, or pay for a helicopter ride, to access remote backcountry terrain, where they might drop off rocks or cliffs, ride down chutes, and snowboard in powder and among trees. Others, including freestyle boarders, prefer to ride the more accessible, yet typically crowded, ski resort slopes. Freestyle riding, which includes snowboarding on man-made features such as half-pipes and terrain parks, is currently the most popular form of participation. This style rests on creative and technical maneuvers (e.g., spins, grabs, inverts), many of which have their roots in skateboarding. In response to this trend, the typical ski resort invests in equipment and personnel to create and maintain features such as terrain parks and half-pipes to attract snowboarding patrons. Some core snowboarders also enjoy "jibbing," a sub-style of freestyle snowboarding that involves performing various skateboarding inspired maneuvers on obstacles including trees, stumps, and rails. Jibbing in urban environments has also become a popular activity among core boarders; jibbers locate a handrail (e.g., down a flight of stairs outside a school, hospital, mall. etc.), shovel snow at the top and bottom of the rail (to create a run-in and landing), and then perform technical maneuvers while jumping onto, sliding down, and jumping off the rail. Alpine, another style of participation, privileges speed and carving over jumping or jibbing, but it is the least popular style among core snowboarders who tend to dismiss participants as skiers on boards. Simply put,

styles of participation are constantly evolving, boarders are continually creating new and more technical maneuvers, and snowboarding companies and ski resorts are going to great lengths to cater to the diverse demands of participants. A recent example is the production of snow-skates (skateboards for the snow) and the creation of specially built snow-skate parks at many major ski resorts.

Different styles of snowboarding participation carry different sets of risks. Freestyle snowboarding is often portrayed as the most aggressive and perilous style of snowboarding. While serious injury can and does occur in these artificially constructed playgrounds, risk tends to be more perceived than real. Terrain parks and half-pipes are carefully constructed and maintained by trained professionals, they are positioned within the boundaries of the ski resorts, rules and regulations are signposted and policed by resort employees, and, if injury should occur, the ski patrol and medical facilities are only minutes away. Jibbing in urban environments carries a new set of risks, including arrest by police and the physical consequences of falling on concrete steps or metal railings. But big mountain snowboarding is undoubtedly the most risky style of participation.

Big Mountain Snowboarding: The Meaning of Extreme

It is in relation to riding big mountain terrain that the term *extreme* has most relevance in snowboarding. Big mountain riding is, in the words of Susanna Howe, "downright dangerous: avalanches, sluffs, helicopter crashes, crevasses, rocks, and exposure to the elements take their toll on those who aren't prepared or aren't lucky" (Howe 1998, 143). Big mountain riders tend to be physically taller and more powerful than freestyle snowboarders. With their greater strength they are able to ride longer and stiffer boards. Many big mountain riders are mountaineers who spend years learning about snow conditions, weather patterns, emergency techniques, and rock climbing. While big mountain riding is rarely a competitive endeavor, the world's best big mountain riders do put their skills to the test in the annual Xtreme Verbier (Switzerland) contest held on the infamous Bec des Rosses, a dauntingly steep and frighteningly jagged rock face standing at 3,222 meters. Prior to the event contestants must study the mountain face with binoculars and choose their line. On the day of the competition, they hike for over an hour to the summit and then, one by one, ride down "the

Bec" in an attempt to qualify for the podium. Not only must they make it down the face alive (which would be a challenge for even the most experienced boarder), the riders are also judged on the "steepness, exposure, snow conditions, difficulty of terrain, obstacles, jumps, control, falls, continuity, pace, smooth transitions, style, technical ability, and energy" of their 500-meter vertical descent.

Death is a very real threat in big mountain riding. Shaun White described his first experience snowboarding in Alaska—"the fabled North Shore of snowboarding"—as follows: "It was really intense out there. Everything seems to be about dying out there. 'Oh man, you go over the falls there and you're dead.' 'Don't set that off, or you're dead.' 'You're gonna die here.' 'Oh, that's death for sure.' Even getting ready to go up the mountain is sketchy. I'm wearing peeps [avalanche transceiver], I have their gnarly backpack survival kit with a shovel and probes and all this stuff in it, and then I'm wearing a harness. I'm like, 'why do I need a harness?' They go, 'Dude, if you fall in a hole and you're dead we have to use it to drag you out.' What? I don't want to deal with that! Are you kidding me? I thought knee surgery was bad, I don't want to die!" (Bridges 2005, 88).

While White clearly ventured out of his comfort zone, other boarders, more confident in their abilities and knowledge, are excited by the challenges of big mountain riding. "There's always a chance to die, but you don't go out and try to kill yourself," says legendary big mountain rider Tom Burt. "[T]o say that what I do is the most dangerous aspect of snowboarding... well, it's a relative thing because of ability, training, and experience." Big mountain riding clearly divides the men from the boys. Furthermore, while a few women are big mountain riders (e.g., Julie Zell, Victoria Jealouse, and Tina Basich), the activity continues to be heavily dominated by men.

Whether performing a corked backside 720 over an 80-foot jump in a terrain park or completing a first descent in Alaska, snowboarders earn prestige and respect from their peers through displays of physical prowess and courage. *Transworld Snowboarding*'s introduction to professional boarder Roman De Marchi highlights the value of such traits in gaining cultural status: "How many people do you know who live life like there's no tomorrow? He'll look at something and say, 'I'm gonna do that. Get out your camera.' And everyone else will be like, 'are you fking nuts? Shit that doesn't look doable,' he'll stomp it nine out of ten times... his riding is going bigger, harder, and gnarlier then everybody else's." (Muzzey 2003, 126)

Many male snowboarders accept injury and risk taking as part of the core snowboarding experience. The following interviews by two core boarders illustrate the reckless relationships many boarders have with their bodies: "In the 2002 X Games at Whakapapa [New Zealand ski resort], I was competing. I came down to the med[ical] bay, I had 4 cracked ribs and a twisted knee and I was the least injured guy there; fractured skulls, massive back injuries, guys with their calves ripped open, you name it. It was crazy. I was just like, 'give me my two Panadols [painkillers] and I'll be on my way.' *Accidents happen aye*"; "I fractured my radial head in my elbow this season jumping off a 30ft cliff [in Whistler, Canada]. Putting my hand down straight, the impact rammed my radius into my humerus chipping the end off it. But it only had me out for 28 days."

Like their male counterparts, female riders embody the cultural values of courage and risk taking and experience their share of injuries. Tara Dakides has fractured her back, dislocated elbows, and torn ligaments in both knees. Big mountain rider Victoria Jealouse once found herself caught in an avalanche above a 1,000-foot chute with car-size rocks in the middle and house-size rocks at the bottom. To survive she had to "do two back-flips and then cling on some rocks to avoid falling in" (cited in Ulmer and Straus 2002). While snowboarders who are prepared to risk it all receive the most media coverage (in advertising, editorial, and video) and cultural respect, few participants embody this attitude to risk. Snowboarders, particularly professionals wanting to prolong their careers, are increasingly taking safety precautions. For example, many freestyle snowboarders have taken to wearing helmets and body armor (extensive lower- and upper-body padding) in terrain parks and half-pipes, and free riders are wearing avalanche transceivers, probes, and shovels in case of an emergency.

Nevertheless, snowboarders do not always avoid death; on the contrary, for some it is the object of a strong unconscious attraction. For example, a recent trend among "passionate snowboarders" is to hike into the backcountry and provoke an avalanche to ride: The boarder who "surfs" the avalanche the longest is the "winner." Those who drown obviously lose. Another trend is extreme terrain parks built by ski resorts eager to attract the elite snowboarding patron. A direct consequence is increasingly severe injuries. Ste'en Webster, editor of *New Zealand Snowboarder* magazine, observes that the "consequences of pushing your limits have changed... we never used to do jumps that could kill you ... people are dying now" (personal communication, 2005).

An American snowboarding cinematographer also sees the sport "becoming more and more dangerous because people have to keep pushing the limits to get *more recognition*. . . . kids don't *respect* anything if someone's not going 100 feet [size of jump] and doing a 1080 [degree spin]; it is way harder to *get noticed*. I think a lot of these guys [professional snowboarders] are taking these risks with confidence, but who is going to suffer is the kids that think to be good they have to do the craziest thing ever, and eventually that is going to catch up. . . . I think more people are going to start dying soon" (personal communication, 2005). The recent deaths of several top snowboarders, including Craig Kelly, Jeff Anderson, Tristan Picot, Line Ostvold, Josh Malay, and Tommy Brunner, certainly sent "shockwaves of grief" through the snowboarding community.

While television and corporate sponsors attach the moniker extreme to all snowboarding in an attempt to sell products, personalities, and events, the relevance of the term is remarkably limited to a minority of participants in a minority of styles.

Holly Thorpe

See also Alaska; Dakides, Tara; Extreme Media; France; Gender; Haakonsen, Terje; Kelly, Craig; Whistler; White, Shaun; X Games.

Further Reading
Anderson, K. (1999). Snowboarding: The construction of gender in an emerging sport. *Journal of Sport and Social Issues*, 23(1), 55–79.
Basich, T., with Gasperini, K. (2003). *Pretty good for a girl: The autobiography of a snowboarding pioneer*. New York: HarperCollins.
Beal, B., & Weidman, L. (2003). Authenticity in the skateboarding world. In R. Rinehart and S. Sydnor (Eds.), *To the extreme: Alternative sports, inside and out*. Albany: State University of New York Press.
Blumberg, A. (2002, January). Launch. *Transworld Snowboarding*.
Bridges, P. (2004, November). Romain DeMarchi. *Snowboarder Magazine*, 94–105.
Bridges, P. (2005, August). The next Shaun White. *Snowboarder Magazine*, 82–93.
Brisick, J. (2004). *Have board will travel: The definitive history of surf, skate and snow*. New York: HarperCollins.
Coleman, A. G. (2004). *Ski style: Sport and culture in the Rockies*. Lawrence: University Press of Kansas.
Edwards, G. (2006, March 9). Attack of the flying tomato. *Rolling Stone*, 43–45.
Howe, S. (1998). *(SICK): A cultural history of snowboarding*. New York: St. Martins Griffin.
Hughes, K. (1988, March). Surfboarding shifts to the ski slopes and cultures clash. *The Wall Street Journal*. Retrieved March 10, 2003, from http://global.factiva.com/en/arch/display.asp
Humphreys, D. (1996). Snowboarders: Bodies out of control and in conflict. *Sporting Traditions*, 13(1), 3–23.

Lidz, F. (1997, December). Lord of the board. *Sports Illustrated*, 87, 114–119.
Messner, M. (2002). *Taking the field: Women, men and sports*. London: Minnesota Press.
Muzzey, J. (2003, April). Romain De Marchi. *Transworld Snowboarding*, 126–139.
Nelson, Janet (1989, January 29). Snowboarding: Riding the bank sideways. *New York Times*.
Richards, T., with Blehm, E. (2003). *P3: Pipes, parks, and powder*. New York: HarperCollins.
Roenigk, A. (2004, February 17). Tara Dakides talks, part one. Retrieved February 14, 2007, from http://expn.go.com/expn/story?pageName=040211_tara_dakides
Sherowski, J. (2003, November). Women on the verge: The future of female supershredding is now. *Transworld Snowboarding*, 146.
Sherowski, J. (2005, January). What it means to be a snowboarder. *Transworld Snowboarding*, 160–169.
Thorpe, H. (2004). Embodied boarders: Snowboarding, status and style. *Waikato Journal of Education*, 10, 181–202.
Ulmer, K., & Straus, A. (2002). Action figures: the girls of extreme sports. Retrieved May 10, 2004, from http://www.maximonline.com/sports/girls_of_extreme_sports/dakides.html
Wheaton, B. (Ed) (2004). *Introduction. Understanding lifestyle sports* (pp. 1–28). London: Routledge.
Williams, P. W., Dossa, K. B., and Fulton, A (1994). Tension on the slopes: Managing conflict between skiers and snowboarders. *Journal of Applied Recreation Research*, 19(3), 191–213.

Sociology of Risk

Commentators sometimes claim that extreme sports involve a shift from taking risks in order to achieve a goal, to risk taking "for it's own sake." However, this claim is not strictly true. Participants engage in even the basest risk-taking leisure activity, such as bungee jumping, because they expect to get something out of it; they do it for the thrill, feelings of conquest, prestige. Risk-taking activities that are structured enough to come under the banner of "extreme sports" involve meanings significant enough for participants to dedicate considerable time and resources to them.

The way people think about risks and the meanings that people attribute to risk-taking activities are socially constructed, and so the broader social and cultural environment in which extreme sports have come to flourish is fundamental to understanding this phenomenon. What are some of the key elements of contemporary social change and the ways in which these elements may be linked to current trends and modes of risk-taking leisure?

Social Change

Social theorists say we are in the midst of significant social change. Some theorists say that this period of change is as significant as the earlier transition from traditional society to modern industrial society. That process of modernization was characterized by a challenge to enduring traditional knowledge and social formations by the logic of scientific rational calculation. The modern society that emerged involved an endless cycle of rational calculation, resulting in constantly evolving processes of social and cultural change, based in particular on imperatives toward specialization and differentiation in work and social formations, the proliferation of bureaucratic organizations, the spread of industrial capitalism, and the rise of individualism. Some people have described the extent and nature of contemporary social change as an inevitable consequence of contradictions inherent in the logical unfolding of these modern imperatives.

For the sake of simplicity, the term *postmodern* (and its extensions) is used here as an umbrella term to cover all *post*modern (beyond modern) and *neo*modern (new modern) theoretical approaches to social change, such as *advanced capitalism, late modernity,* and *liquid modernity. Postmodernization* is therefore used here to describe the current transition from the modern to a postmodern/neomodern society. As Kumar points out, much of the difference between these approaches hinges on emphasis and terminology. Although considerable debate centers around the trajectory, causes, and implications of these current trends, a reasonable level of agreement exists as to their nature. Key elements include (1) a weakening of modern social categories, such as class, gender, and the distinction between the public and private and the political and religious spheres; (2) the infiltration of the economy into almost all aspects of our daily lives; (3) a weakening of the all-pervasive (at least symbolic) dominance of rational calculation and a decline in the authority of knowledge and institutions based on it; and (4) a level of individualization whereby each person is involved in the deliberate and ongoing construction of his or her own identities and social formations.

The traditional, modern, and postmodern categories are theoretical constructs used to describe particular modes of society characterized by different social formations and orientations. Although they are sometimes used to refer to an era, they coexist, with each more or less *residual, dominant,* or *emergent.* For example, *residual* forms of traditional religious belief have survived the *dominant* scientific rationalism of modernization. Traditional and modern modes

will be integral to any *emergent* postmodern future, if only in some stylized simulation. A related construct—the "ideal type"—is a hypothetical example of something that belongs to a theoretical category, that is, it embodies key characteristics of the category. Of course, the "real world" is never so obliging as to fit perfectly into any of these categories or types.

Link with Extreme Sports

The current increase in participation and diversification of risk-taking leisure forms has emerged along with the transition toward postmodernity in the way that sports such as rugby did during the modern industrial period. However, while the current proliferation of extreme *sports* is new, risk-taking *leisure* is not. The early forms of many modern sports—football, for example—were dangerous. What stimulated their evolution into modern sports was a conflict between what Elias and Dunning (1986) called a "quest for excitement" and the more powerful rational imperative (and its inherent logic of risk management) that led to modern sport being characterized by the "controlled decontrolling" of emotions, violence, and danger. What characterizes the new postmodern forms of risk-taking leisure is a challenge to the *dominant* mode of rational risk management by an *emergent* aesthetic sensibility that embraces risk. Whereas modernization is characterized by risk minimization, postmodernization unleashes the thrill-seeking beast.

A postmodern understanding of risk-taking leisure has its roots in the work of one of sociology's "alternative" founding scholars around the end of the nineteenth century. Georg Simmel of Germany focused on what he saw as an inherent aesthetic reaction to the stifling imperative for rational calculation that increasingly governed life in modern industrial society. He described one of his ideal social types—"the adventurer"—as someone who abandons himself to the "powers and accidents of the world, which can delight us, but in the same breath can also destroy us" (Simmel 1971, 193). Simmel said the adventurer is like an artist who can experience the "secret unities" that are lost within the world of rational calculation. For Simmel risk-taking leisure activities, such as mountaineering, were a means of self-transcendence.

An ideal type modern approach to risk-taking leisure is to manage the risk through regulation, training, accreditation, codification of the activity as a sport, and establishment of a controlling body. This trajectory would lead to the professionalization of the sport and its integration into the wider economy. Resistance to these modernizing processes represents an aesthetic sensibility in opposition to the rational imperatives of modernity, an opposition Simmel believed was inherent in modernity and is now considered to be a key driver of postmodernization.

Earlier work on youth subcultures used the categories of *incorporation* and *resistance* to study the imperatives toward being subsumed by the dominant (or parent) culture and the opposition to this that the subcultures represented. In contemporary risk-taking leisure subcultures this dynamic is still evident, particularly in the tension between imperatives to *incorporate* the activity into a sporting format and *resistance* to such incorporation in favor of maintaining an unregulated play orientation. However, what constitutes the dominant culture is increasingly problematic with the progress of postmodernization, and as a result the concept of subculture has also been questioned. A well integrated and coherent ideal type modern mainstream operates on the basis of mutual interdependence. Today's postmodernizing mainstream is more accurately characterized as a fluid conglomeration of cultural tensions, fleeting and intense moments of sociality, and the all-pervasive and erratic forms of "disorganized capitalism" (Beck, Giddens, and Lash 1994, 200–9), held together more by constant motion and surveillance than a sense of interdependence. Although the relationship between subcultures and the more ephemeral dominant culture is now clearly more complex, a subculture's existence remains contingent on resisting subsumption by the dominant culture and maintaining cultural integrity in the distinction between it and the dominant culture.

The processes of postmodernization are so fragmented and unpredictable that no single ideal type postmodern approach exists. However, it can be divided into two broadly distinguishable trajectories—*mainstream* and *oppositional*. An ideal type *mainstream* trajectory involves the appropriation of the subculture's symbolic culture for mainstream markets (including images of the activity, lifestyle, argot, tastes, and fashion), both as a marketing tool (used to sell anything from soft drinks to prestige cars) and as a commodity (fashion and style consumed in the construction of depthless and transient postmodern identities). The activity will be transformed into a form of entertainment for the mainstream media or a packaged experience for the adventure tourism market, where consumers share fleeting moments of "real" life and sociality. This process is essentially an extension of the logic of modern capitalism whereby the activity is no longer of any real consequence, apart from its potential economic value. The activity is therefore manipulated and exploited to maximize the monetary return for the sport, media, and other culture industry players. The

The warning sign is one mechanism used by society to control risk. Source: istock/John Archer.

term *extreme sport* itself is a product of this process, as it gained popular currency through the made-for-cable television sporting event, the X Games.

In an *oppositional* trajectory the participants resist this appropriation by the dominant culture, resist efforts to codify and turn the activity into a sport, and resist the imposition of any controlling bureaucracy. Here we see the extension of the inherent resistance to modernity's rationalizing imperatives that Simmel discussed. A key difference here is that postmodern mainstreaming activities supply volatile and fragmented niche markets through the unstable, even chaotic, processes of "disorganized capitalism" rather than operating within a more integrated modern industrial society. Although both the mainstream and oppositional postmodern trajectories involve an aesthetic reflexivity (consideration based more on emotional response than rational calculation), reflected in the desire for sensation and thrills, the mainstream arena operates largely on the surface, where meaning, sociality, and even identity are transient. Here risk taking involves fleeting experiences of thrill seeking such as "running" red traffic lights, using drugs, being sexually promiscuous, and adventure tourism. The oppositional approach values not only the sensation and thrills inherent in the risky leisure experience, but also the freedom to pursue that activity unimpeded by controls imposed from "outside." For these participants, being as free as possible from regulation and manipulation by "outsiders" is essential if they are to maintain the integrity of their core activities, which are central to what defines their subcultures and their distinct forms of sociality. Even those participants caught up in the commercialization and sportization of their activities often express an ambivalence about what they are involved in. This is exemplified by a professional windsurfer: "Competition doesn't promote good sailing, it doesn't promote talent—it promotes companies. I'm not into that" (Mark Angulo quoted in Rinehart and Snydor 2003, 80).

A common feature of risk-taking activities is that they involve consumption in the form of performance technologies, access to arenas, and other cultural items. The more participants rely on the dominant culture to provide these goods and services, the more the participants are open to manipulation, exploitation, and incorporation. Resistance has developed through combinations of: 1) grass-roots industries that emerge and operate to a significant extent within subcultural economies; 2) reliance on consumer power to ensure that "outsider" suppliers do the right thing; and 3) adapting meanings and practices to exploit what the dominant culture has to offer.

Risk Perception

Clearly the perception of risk differs between individuals. What is terrifying for one might be exciting for another. In regards to risk-taking leisure, individuals' perceptions of risk are primarily constructed within their more or less distinct risk-taking leisure subcultures. The different ways by which risk is perceived and addressed by different subcultures—and between different sectors of the same subculture—reflect different modern and postmodern modes and orientations.

The ideal type modern approach to risk-taking leisure includes a bureaucratic governing body that provides a dialogue (for some even a policy) of risk assessment and risk management aimed at risk minimization. Risking your life in pursuit of leisure is not, on the surface at least, a rational act. A common approach is to deny that any significant risk exists, and people often bring pseudo-statistical arguments to bear in support of this denial. For example, participants might claim that they are more likely to die while driving a car to the activity than while participating in the activity itself. Similarly, participants argue that given the proper training and safety procedures, risks are minimized to an acceptable level. Deciding whether a risk is acceptable within this rational paradigm involves a weighing of the risk and potential injury against the potential benefits. Benefits often cited to justify risk-taking leisure include character building, self-knowledge, catharsis, status, prestige, honing of reflexes and skills, team building, health and fitness, public service, and money.

Bureaucratic governing bodies, whether less formal clubs or professionally staffed national associations, are not only key to risk management and minimization, but also to the discourse about risk that stems from their instrumentally rational approach. Typically, the more established and bureaucratic the body, the more entrenched and pervasive the risk management and associated rhetoric will be. Some older risk-taking sports such as skydiving, scuba diving, and motor racing, with their systems of training and accreditation, represent their activities as "safe" so long as participants are properly trained and follow all the safety guidelines. In fact, a participant may even fail to consciously acknowledge the activity's risk of causing injury as the risk is subsumed within the dominant discourse of risk management.

A consequence of this myth of safety is that whenever deaths or injuries occur, people place primary blame on human error (echoing the U.S. Occupational Safety and Health Administration mantra "There is no such thing as an accident"). In this way the public and participants are led to the conclusion that an accident could have been avoided if only the blameworthy person(s) had followed the guidelines.

> [I]t was human error, it was a mistake. I feel good about it, because it was not equipment failure. (Skydiver commenting on the death of a fellow club member in a skydiving accident, in Celsi et al 1993, 19)

This helps maintain the illusion that the activity can be made safe, and any nagging doubts that might arise can be assuaged and buried through the communal ritual inquest, blaming and reinforcing (or redefining) the boundaries of safe and unsafe (i.e., "deviant") behavior. The process reinforces not only the myth of safety, but also the solidarity of fellow risk-takers.

The postmodern paradigm embraces an activity for more intrinsic values rather than for the benefits that might flow from participation.

> Even if there was no transfer to my daily life I would carry on doing solo [climbing] just for the pleasure of this feeling of freedom and the unique or even extreme sensation that goes with climbing without safety equipment. (solo climber in Le Breton 2000, 4)

The trend toward a postmodern sensibility can be seen in the justification that participants now overwhelmingly provide for their involvement in risk-taking leisure—they do it for the thrill. This is not to say that people who participated in risk-taking leisure in the 1950s (e.g., surfing, mountaineering) were oblivious to moments of intense thrills but rather that their justification for participation was typically couched in terms of more socially acceptable outcomes. The emergent aesthetic reflexivity leads to participants recognizing and emphasizing the intrinsic value of the embodied experience. Although other benefits—such as fitness and self-confidence—may be appreciated, they are much less likely to be presented as the primary motivation for participation.

The postmodern approach to risk and its role in leisure activities lead to a different understanding of injury and death. In this environment risk is consciously recognized (maybe even exaggerated), and risk taking is celebrated as an integral part of the activity. Those participants who suffer the consequences achieve status and prestige, and if they die they are fallen heroes.

> We miss all those fallen freeriders [extreme skiers] and what they stood for and what they accomplished. Their adventures have inspired a lot of other skiers to try and go for even more freedom with even steeper descents. (quoted from the ski film *Freerider* in Rinehart and Sydor 2003, 392)

In this way death and injury also reinforce solidarity within these groups, but through a process very different to that of the modern paradigm. Risk assessment still takes place within a postmodern environment; however, this rational process is mediated through an aesthetic sensibility (i.e., one that embraces the subject's desire to engage in the activity), and the modern rational step to risk minimization is now problematic. People have described risk-taking leisure as addictive, and participants often feel the need to increase the level of risk in order to achieve the same intensity of thrill.

> You know it's an addiction and it's a way of life, you know. If they [family] can't cope with that, then they're really not worth bothering with. (Stephanie, windsurfer in Rinehart and Sydnor 2003, 88)

Adding Commerce to the Mix

Adventure tourism is an example of a modernist approach to participating in otherwise typically postmodern risk-taking activities, such as bungee jumping, canyoning, whitewater rafting, paragliding, tandem skydiving, tandem hanggliding, and mountaineering. Clients are persuaded to have faith in the tourism company, trusting that it has the experience, skills, resources, and knowledge to provide a thrilling but ultimately safe experience. The company takes the place of the modern risk-taking sports bureaucracy, adopting the same rational risk-management rhetoric. Here, though, the imperatives of risk minimization are overlaid by the imperatives of commerce. As well as the need to attract clients, the latter imperatives include the need to be seen to comply with government safety regulations and the need to qualify for the relevant insurances (at affordable rates).

Adventure tourism clients do not commit themselves to the activity in the way that "authentic" risk-taking leisure participants do. Although these clients display the postmodern aesthetic in their thirst for "real" experience and thrills, they are consuming a packaged experience rather than going through the longer-term processes of acquiring the physical, social, and cultural knowledge and skills involved in a commitment to risk-taking leisure and subculture membership.

Although the dominant culture functions to minimize the danger involved in risk-taking leisure, risk taking within the controlled environment of professional sports and the entertainment industry has long been considered more acceptable. Here risk-minimization imperatives go hand-in-hand with the promotion of the excitement inherent in the risks and the potential spectacle of their realization. The most obvious example of this is in the motor sports industry. Professionalism in sports has the potential to push risk taking to higher levels than might otherwise be the case in order to get the exposure needed to satisfy sponsors and media audiences. The mainstream media coverage of extreme sports is typically different from that of the subcultural media. At the extreme ends of this dichotomy the former will frame an event in terms of "conquest," "competition," "challenge," "sporting prowess," "spirit of adventure," "courage," and so forth, whereas the latter will emphasize hedonistic freedom and thrills, and through their unique visual aesthetics, members of the insider audience share in the sublime nature of the experience. The former is a modern, objective, rational, sports-style commentary aimed at a general audience; the latter is a postmodern, subjective, aesthetic, pornographic style (i.e., it affects a desire in insiders to indulge in the activity) and is aimed at subcultural insiders; e.g., "One interviewee described the image of a perfect wave as '...like a beautiful woman lifting her skirt'" (Stranger 2001, 193). The former promotes risk-taking as a spectacle emphasizing the superhuman skill and courage of the practitioners as "a breed apart," whereas the latter is an integral part of the dynamic of desire and indulgence that promotes participation in risk-taking for insiders and is central to risk-taking leisure lifestyles and culture.

Identity

For scholars such as Ulrich Beck, contemporary society is characterized by the need for people to be ever vigilant in their approach to risk management. In this "risk society" people are also conscious of the ever-present potential for large-scale disasters that they cannot prevent or even predict or detect, such as radiation poisoning, germ warfare, chemical pollution, pandemic disease, terrorism, and the consequences of global warming. For some scholars risk-taking leisure is a response to the anxieties inherent in such

a world where risks are ever present but where individuals feel powerless to confront and conquer them. Risk-taking leisure is said to provide proof to the participants that they have what it takes to survive in this world. Similarly, the act of voluntarily facing and overcoming risks is described as a cathartic experience.

Notwithstanding the cathartic and confidence-boosting potential of risk-taking leisure, these perspectives largely ignore the thrill-seeking motivation of participants. The fact that most participants articulate their reasons for participation in terms of the thrill is significant. In particular it represents a move from a modern rational reflexivity to a postmodern aesthetic reflexivity.

In a postmodernizing world of uncertainty, fragmentation, and rapid change, one of the complications of increased individualization is that the freedom/imperative to choose our own path in life is coupled with a lack of authoritative direction as to which path to choose and no certainty as to where any path might lead. As a consequence, this era of do-it-yourself identity construction is said to result in a crisis of identity. People find alternative sources of guidance through a myriad of social formations and cultural orientations, ranging from the more stable and traditional (such as established religions) to the transient and experimental (based on fashion, style, taste, and desire).

A mainstream postmodern scenario emphasizes the way individuals simply purchase the symbols of any number of different identities and the depthless, fragmented, and transient nature of these identities. Risk-taking leisure subcultures provide a wealth of choice for identity shoppers in the postmodern "archive of styles" (Crook, Pakulski, and Waters 1992, 36). However, a clear distinction exists between the identity shopper whose surfing lifestyle consists of wearing a Quiksilver (a maker of wetsuits and other surfing accessories) T-shirt and hanging out with other pseudo-surfer dudes at their local Hawaiian bar on Saturday nights and the surfer whose life revolves around the activity of searching for and riding waves. The latter is an example of an oppositional postmodern alternative to the former transient mainstream postmodern identity.

Flow theory provides a psychological framework that can be adapted to explain the apparent addiction some participants have to the thrill of extreme sports.

> Whenever we are fully functioning, involved in a challenging activity that requires all our skill, and more, we feel a great sense of exhilaration. Because of this we want to repeat the experience. But to

feel the same exhilaration again, it is necessary to take on a slightly greater challenge, and to develop slightly greater skills. (Csikszentmihalyi & Csikszentmihalyi 1988, 367)

By equating risk with challenge, we can see that too much risk may scare participants into inaction or cause them to fail and suffer unacceptable consequences. Too little risk means no significant challenge, and therefore no thrills. The right amount of risk will challenge the participants' psychological and physical ability to the point where they no longer have the psychic capacity (no time to think) to distinguish between themselves, the activity, and their immediate environment. The thrill involved in these moments where participants become one with their world of activity, is described by scholars as *transcendent, ecstatic, sublime, optimum* or *peak* experience.

> That's when a marvellous phenomenon takes place, an awareness of those moments when the individual surpasses himself and attains a state of fulfilment that is sheer bliss. I live this experience with such intensity that I've made it my life goal and I would like to share it with others. (Le Breton 2000, 9)

The addictive quality of the experiences is said to come from the desire of the self to continue to experience the "true self" because the experience is of the "I" unmediated by the ego. The more experienced practitioners become, the more difficulty they have in adequately challenging their skills to achieve these states. Consequently, these practitioners often describe the need to increase the level of risk in order to achieve the desired intensity of experience.

> The level's always growing as to what's BIG. What's big is what's going to get me that feeling . . . But still, I'm not out there because of this challenge with fear. It's fun. I love it. (Stranger 1999, 268)

The desire to replicate the experience and the fact that it becomes more difficult to achieve are the basis for commitment. The knowledge that others share in the same ecstatic experience and desire is the basis for community in the form of risk-taking leisure subcultures. These subcultures provide the frameworks for the creation of meanings and sociality that support core practitioners in their search for ecstatic moments that may be achieved only a few times a year. They are therefore more stable and enduring than the transient "neo-tribal" (Maffesoli 1996) configurations that emerge and disperse around activities that require no significant commitment over time.

This kind of transcendent experience is most apposite in a postmodern world where the social fabric that cocooned us from such experiences in the past is so fragmented and dislocated from any meaningful anchorage in a tradition or common worldview. In other words the breakdown in the authority of institutions that gave direction and defined the world we experience means that we are now open to socially un(der)mediated experiences. Here new meanings and meaningful interactions emerge around what would previously have been dismissed as hedonistic and self-centered thrill seeking.

The most dominant subtheme in the area of identity and extreme sports is the issue of gender. The postmodern breakdown of social categories has included the blurring of gender boundaries and the emergence of multiple modes of femininity and masculinity. For both sexes this represents a broader spectrum of opportunities, but, as outlined above, with this comes a lack of any overarching authoritative guidance.

Some scholars suggest that the loosely configured and play-oriented nature of risk-taking leisure provides an environment in which the boundaries between the sexes can be broken down. On the surface at least, this appears to be the case, with increasing participation by females in once almost exclusively male spheres of activity, displaying what are traditionally considered masculine qualities of courage and bravado. The problem with the open and informal nature of postmodern formations is that they include the widest possible range of outcomes, from reactionary to revolutionary. Accordingly, risk-taking leisure has been described as an enclave for dominant masculinity where participants prove their manliness with displays of courage and strength. Others suggest that these activities provide an arena in which participants not only affirm their maleness, but also reassert the dominant position of masculinity in opposition to the feminine. These approaches focus on the fact that it is predominantly males that participate in extreme sports, and they point to examples of sexism, homophobia and misogyny within the different subcultures. Others point out that while this kind of behaviour is evident, it is not necessarily dominant, and that it may be concentrated within subsections and particular demographic groups or locations of subcultures, simply reflecting the particular cultural backgrounds of these participants and not an inherent feature of the subculture.

Running of the Bulls, San Fermin Festival, Pamplona, Spain

Every year, starting on July 6, the famous running of the bulls takes place in Pamplona, Spain. The event brings together thrill seekers from across the globe who run the half-mile course through Pamplona's cobbled city streets. The run is dangerous, and several deaths have occurred over the years. TotallySpain.com has compiled the following recommendations for anyone who wants to try outrunning Pamplona's bulls.

For those crazy folk who choose to take part in the challenging run then there are a number of basic guidelines to be followed.

- It is forbidden to run if [you] are under 18.
- Never, ever run if you are drunk or excessively tired.
- Do not carry items such as cameras, videos, backpacks, etc...They'll get damaged or impede your exit. Unsuitable clothing or footwear is forbidden.
- You must enter the route at an official gate either at the Plaza Consistorial or at the Plaza del Mercado. Gates close at 7:30 A.M.
- Never stand still during the run.
- While running you must be sure to look all around you. Up ahead for other runners who might trip you and behind for the bulls. This is not a race and you won't be able to run the entire route so have in mind beforehand a spot where you plan to exit. The bulls run very fast and will be ahead of you before you know it.
- Do not try to touch the bulls or catch their attention as a distracted bull may decide to break from the herd. A lone bull is extremely dangerous and much more likely to attack. Also the drovers, who carry very large poles, do not tolerate messing and freely whack offenders.
- If you should fall there is one and only one thing to do. Stay down and cover your head. When all the bulls have passed someone will tap you on the shoulder to let you know you're safe. It was by attempting to stand up that Peter Mathews Tasio was fatally gored. You may receive some bumps and bruises but that should be all.
- If you happen to run the last section of the route into the bullring then upon entering the ring spread out to the sides and let the drovers do their work of sidling the bulls into the pen. There will be a lot of runners in the ring and again a distracted bull can cause serious danger.

Source: http://www.in-spain.info/special-features/running-of-the-bulls-pamplona-spain.htm

Even amongst some major subcultures that have been described as enclaves of discriminatory behaviour—such as surfing, windsurfing and climbing—the rate of female participation has been steadily increasing. Many women are gaining access through the modern gateways of formal schools and organized sporting events. The extent to which these gateways are used is influenced by the culture industries that have begun targeting young women in promotional campaigns, using images of them as active participants rather than passive hangers-on, and thereby promoting an expansion of their markets. However, the promotion of these activities as competitive sports is problematic, in that such sports typically entail sex segregation and all the inherent symbolism of male superiority and domination.

But increasingly women are participating in risk-taking leisure at a level that would only recently have been considered the domain of elite men. They demonstrate the same level of commitment and talk about their reasons for participating in the same thrill-seeking terms as their male counterparts. According to World Champion surfer, Pam Burridge:

If you get an incredible barrel [a large "hollow" wave] you just scream...it's an overwhelming exhilaration.... The chase for dangerous waves and challenging situations, for power, pushing the limits . . . the risk factor; it's very important. You feel stoked [thrilled] when you have nearly been killed . . . it's weird. (Stranger 2001, 117)

Because risk taking and commitment are two of the key factors in status ascription, and because so many of the activities involve an individual challenge rather than a competition between competitors (at least in the oppositional, play-oriented environment) it will become increasingly difficult for men to dismiss women's achievements in the way that they might in the sex-segregated sporting environment. An approach that gives more consideration to the account these women give of their experiences sees their participation as exemplifying a postmodern increase in the diversity of femininities, and a breakdown of traditional gender boundaries.

In Brief

Modern sports have been described as a quest for excitement, an attempt to escape mundane modern rational life. However, the escape was always an illusion, a controlled outing. The risks involved were minimized by the rational ordering processes that the participants sought to escape, and their participation was justified in terms of socially acceptable, rational outcomes.

Risk-taking leisure is also described as an escape attempt, but it is an attempt to escape from the anxieties and anomie of our contemporary world. The same imperatives that minimized risks in modernity still operate, but resistance to them is inherent in the emergent aesthetic mode, and so the ecstatic thrills of risk-taking leisure are embraced. The knowledge that others share a commitment to the pursuit of these experiences is the basis of new social formations.

In his book *Future Shock* Alvin Toffler claimed that the U.S. surfing subculture of the 1960s was "a signpost pointing to the future" (Toffler 1970, 263). Surfing and other risk-taking leisure subcultures are not so much adaptations to a changing society as agents of that change, engaged in a dialectical relationship with the dominant culture. Through the dominant culture's appropriation of their symbolic culture, risk-taking leisure activities have functioned like hosts to a postmodern virus. Absorbed through the insatiable consumerism of the mainstream, their style, aesthetic sensibility and ethos (distinguishing character,

sentiment, moral nature, or guiding beliefs) proved apposite to the uncertainties that define postmodern times. Living in the moment and adapting to unexpected risks and opportunities as they emerge are no longer considered irresponsible or hedonistic; they're practically a prerequisite for success.

Mark Stranger

See also Body and Extreme Sport, The; Commercialization; Extreme Media; Gender; Injury; Meaning of Extreme, The; Media and Extreme Sport; X Games

Further Reading

Bauman, Z. (1992). *Intimations of postmodernity*. London: Routledge.

Bauman Z. (2000). *Liquid Modernity*. Oxford, UK: Blackwell.

Beck, U. (1992). *Risk society: Towards a new modernity*. London: Sage.

Beck, U., Giddens, A., & Lash, S. (1994). *Reflexive modernization: Politics, tradition and aestheticization in the modern social order*. Cambridge, UK: Polity Press.

Celsi, R., Rose, R., & Leigh, T. (1993, June). An exploration of high-risk leisure consumption through skydiving. *Journal of Consumer Research, 20*, 1–23.

Cohen, S., & Taylor, L. (1992). *Escape attempts: The theory and practice of resistance to everyday life* (2nd ed.). London: Routledge.

Crook, S., Pakulski, J., & Waters, M. (1992). *Postmodernization: Change in advanced society*. London: Sage.

Csikszentmihalyi, M., & Csikszentmihalyi, I. S. (Eds.). (1988). *Optimal experience: Psychological studies of flow in consciousness*. Cambridge, UK: Cambridge University Press.

Donnelly, P. (1993). Subcultures in sport: Resilience and transformation. In A. G. Ingham & J. W. Loy (Eds.), *Sport in social development: Traditions, transitions, and transformations* (pp. 119–145). Champaign, IL: Human Kinetics Publishers.

Douglas, M. (1992). *Risk and blame: Essays in cultural theory*. London: Routledge.

Elias, N., & Dunning, E. (1986). *Quest for excitement: Sport and leisure in the civilizing process*. Oxford, UK: Blackwell.

Ford, N., & Brown, D. (2006). *Surfing and social theory: Experience, embodiment and narrative of the dream glide*. London: Routledge.

Giddens, A. (1991). *Modernity and self-identity: Self and society in the late modern age*. Cambridge, UK: Polity Press.

Hall, S., & Jefferson, T. (Eds.). (1976). *Resistance through ritual: Youth subcultures in post-war Britain*. London: Hutchinson.

Hebdige, D. (1991). *Subculture: The meaning of style*. London: Routledge.

Huizinga, J. (1949). *Homo ludens: A study of the play-element in culture*. London: Routledge & Kegan Paul.

Kumar, K. (1995). *From post-industrial to post-modern society: New theories of the contemporary world*. Oxford, UK: Blackwell.

Lash, S. (1990). *Sociology of postmodernism*. London: Routledge.

Lash, S. (1993). Reflexive modernization: The aesthetic dimension. *Theory, Culture & Society, 10*(1), 1–23.

Lash, S., & Friedman, J. (Eds.). (1992). *Modernity and identity*. Oxford, UK: Blackwell.

Le Breton, D. (2000). Playing symbolically with death in extreme sports. *Body & Society*, 6(1), 1–11.

Maffesoli, M. (1996). *The time of the tribes: The decline of individualism in mass society.* London: Sage.

Maslow, A. (1970). *Religions, values, and peak-experiences.* New York: Viking Press.

Midol, N., & Broyer, G. (1995). Towards an anthropological analysis of new sport cultures: The case of whiz sports in France. *Sociology of Sport Journal*, 12, 204–212.

Muggleton, D., & Weinzierl, R. (Eds.). (2003). *The post-subcultures reader.* Oxford, UK: Sage.

Rinehart, R. E., & Sydnor, S. (Eds.). (2003). *To the extreme: Alternative sports, inside and out.* Albany: State University of New York Press.

Rojek, C. (2000). *Leisure and culture.* London: Macmillan.

Simmel, G. (1971). *Georg Simmel on individuality and social forms* (D. N. Levine, Ed.). Chicago: University of Chicago Press.

Stranger, M. (1999). The aesthetics of risk: A study of surfing. *International Review for the Sociology of Sport*, 34(3), 265–276.

Stranger, M. (2001) *Risk-taking & postmodernity: Commodification & the ecstatic in leisure lifestyles—the case of surfing*, PhD thesis, University of Tasmania (monograph forthcoming).

Thrift, N. (2000). Still life in nearly present time: The object of nature. *Body & Society*, 6(3–4), 34–57.

Toffler, A. (1970) *Future shock*, New York: Random House.

Wearing, B. (1996). *Gender: The pain and pleasure of difference.* Melbourne, Australia: Longman.

Welsch, W. (1997). *Undoing aesthetics.* London: Sage.

Wheaton, B. (Ed.). (2004). *Understanding lifestyle sports: Consumption, identity and difference.* Abingdon, UK: Routledge.

Spirituality

Many extreme sports emerged during the 1960s and 1970s as distinct endeavors, rooted in the counter-culture movement. Indeed, many of their adherents were from the American West, and some had been previously involved with the LSD and Eastern guru movements. These adherents found in extreme sports and in meditation more authentic experiences than they previously had with drugs. In contrast to traditional sports, extreme sports embody a new outlook: They tend to be solitary rather than team activities in which rules are loosened and competition is largely against oneself rather than against others, and their character is often youthful and rebellious.

Many of these characteristics of extreme sports (e.g., the tendency to be solitary, the loosening of rules) and the natural environments in which they are engaged (e.g., mountains) are conductive of spiritual experiences. Indeed, participants in extreme sports often describe their experiences as constituting spiritual and transcendental elements. For example, describing the feelings she gets from climbing, one participant says, "There is this feeling of . . . accomplishment. It just feels good . . . like magic or something" (Bane 1998, 164), and, according to a surfer, "the ocean itself gives you spirituality" (Mendelsohn 2004).

An operational definition of *spirituality*, even though it may seem limited, focuses on feelings of connectedness to a higher power, on beliefs and their integration into everyday life, positive inner affective states, and personal growth. Here we understand spirituality as a feeling of connectedness to the uncanny reality beyond one's rational understanding, be it God or an unnamed power. Note that this reality falls outside the categories of "external" and "internal" because it is expressed as an inner feeling but also experienced as an outside phenomenon: Its essence partakes of both natures.

The spirituality of extreme sports is a spirituality of seeking, as differentiated from the spirituality of dwelling. The latter includes specific beliefs and practices and centers around a particular community. In contrast, personal choice is dominant in the spirituality of seeking, and the sacred is sought within the ordinary. More specifically, the spirituality of seeking in extreme sports is a particular expression of the quest to overcome human limits that comes from the awareness of the gap between our inner universes and the way the human condition looks from outside. Since the most ancient times we have struggled to go beyond the limitations of our existence. Capturing the appeal of such transcendental experiences, the Russian poet Alexander Pushkin wrote:

> There is rapture in the bullet's flight
> And on the mountain's treacherous height
> And on a ship's deck far from land
> When skies grow dark and waves swell high,
> And in Sahara's blowing sand
> And when the pestilence is nigh
>
> All, all that threatens to destroy,
> Fills mortal hearts with secret joy—
> Perhaps it bodes eternal life!
> And blest is he who can attain
> That ecstasy in storm and strife!
> (Pushkin 2000, 101)

The work of other artists also alludes to the fact that sportspersons and adventurers have had spiritual experiences for a long time. In the 1930s, for example, the Russian

A woman practicing yoga as the sun sets. Source: istock.

poet Marina Tsvetaeva wrote in her *Memories* on the spirituality of mountain climbing as expressed by her younger contemporary, a poet-mountaineer, in his poem "Belladonna." Ernest Hemingway in *The Sun Also Rises: Fiesta* also depicted the spirituality of a matador who risks living on the edge—dangerously but authentically. However ancient, this quest for transcendental experiences is also apparent in contemporary culture in which individuals continue to search out new ways of pushing personal limits and overcoming the boundaries of the human. Today the quest is expressed in the interest in self-knowledge, mystical traditions, and other practices, among which are extreme sports.

Spiritual Experiences in Extreme Sports

Many people engaged in extreme sports seek out risk. They make conscious choices to put themselves on the edge of danger, which can sometimes lead to having transcendental experiences, popularly described as being in the "zone" or "flow," to feeling fully connected to natural forces, or to getting to a place where "magic" happens. Extreme sports often provide practitioners with the opportunity to push their physical and mental limits. As one participant writes, extreme sports allow the individual "to stretch the limits of

what you think you can do—that is, pushing what seems rationally possible" (Bane 1998, 28). Participants in extreme races often report intense emotions and significant shifts in understanding of self, which can lead to transcendental experiences: "You're being pushed to the mental and physical limits. Strange things happen to your brain. It's like every emotion you ever had—love, hate, fear, anger, all of them—at one time or another out here, they all come out" (Bane 1998, 40).

One curious aspect of spiritual experiences is that they are not guaranteed. The presence of all external conditions—risk, extreme physical effort, deprivation, fanatical striving toward a goal—does not always lead to such experiences. Under the same circumstances a spiritual response may or may not occur. In fact, the deliberate search for such experiences has revealed how rarely they actually occur. Spiritual experiences are not limited to one kind of sport. Although high altitudes (e.g., in mountain climbing, delta flying, or hiking) seem to increase their frequency, spiritual experiences do occur in other kinds of extreme sports (e.g., adventure racing, running, kayaking, surfing, snowboarding).

The kinds of spiritual experiences that occur in extreme sports (aside from more physical consequences such as the achievement of optimal levels of athletic performance) are those associated with the effects of risk and physical/sensory

deprivation. These experiences can be organized into three main categories:

- Experiencing altered states of mind in which performance goes beyond the ordinary limits. These states include overcoming the ordinary ego and feeling deeper oneness with the larger whole of reality. The experience is never complete but includes the feeling of access to superior power and wisdom.
- Experiencing a meaningful coincidence (also known as "synchronicity") such that a potentially fatal situation might be avoided.
- Seeing visions and having feelings of presences and/ or phantom companions.

We will first address these three experiences respectively and then consider their neurophysiological, philosophical, and psychological interpretations.

Altered States of Mind

Altered states of mind in extreme sports are the subject of Rob Schultheis's *Bone Games*, in which he describes how, while mountain climbing, he fell and found himself only inches from certain death. He had to climb away from the place where he had fallen before nightfall because he could not survive the night there. In this situation he suddenly started climbing on a level of performance that he had previously considered impossible. He said, "What I am doing is absolutely impossible, I thought. I can't be doing this. But I have the grace, the radiant mojo, and here I am!" (Schultheis 1996, 11).

According to Schultheis , his performance in that situation went far beyond his limitations, which he knew well. The feeling of fear and fatigue was overpowered by confidence; he felt "full of insane joy" and experienced a feeling of soaring and lightness in the body. Moreover, his feeling of self had radically changed: "It was just too different from my everyday self, and I have never seen its like before, nor have I seen it since ... The person I became ... was the best possible version of myself, the person I *should have been* throughout my life. No regrets, no hesitation, there were no false moves left in me" (Schultheis 1996, 12).

The experience for Schultheis was permeated with sublime confidence in his own abilities—he believed he simply could not and would not fail. This example corresponds to the idea of U.S. psychologist and philosopher William James that *faith itself creates reality*. In other words, Schul-

theis's feeling of confidence triggered a level of athletic performance far beyond his personal limits, which allowed him to escape from a dangerous situation: His confidence saved his life. His emotional response to this experience was sublime and ultimate joy.

Another example of altered states of mind in extreme sports is hearing sublime music. Rarely, however, can individuals recapture the music after it has occurred.

Adventurers tend to equate experiences of altered states of mind with the Zen Buddhist concept of *satori* . These experiences are preceded by desperation and helplessness—a new, sublime identity emerges after the original identity is suppressed by such circumstances. The transformation is temporary: A few weeks later one returns to one's ordinary mind. The experience, however, stays forever in a subtler manner. Interestingly, not only participants in extreme sports or adventurers experience such altered states of mind. The geologist Albert von St. Gallen Heim collected similar experiences, recorded in his interviews, with accident survivors. The survivors mention sudden enormous increases in mental activity and lightning speed of action during their accident.

Meaningful Coincidences

The second type of spiritual experience in extreme sports is meaningful coincidences (i.e., *synchronicity*). For Schultheis a meaningful coincidence could be the fall of an owl's feather a few minutes after he had asked for support or the unusual behavior of birds or other animals, whose actions seemed to be reactions to the adventurer's state of mind. For instance, a climber who had made an intuitive "agreement" with a particular mountain observed a ritual-like behavior by four or five types of mountain birds immediately thereafter. Such coincidences offer inspiration and psychological support to adventurers, whereas in other cases intuitive messages from meaningful coincidences have been credited with saving lives by warning people about approaching avalanches or rock falls. Of course, such occurrences will always be subjective experiences, the meanings of which will be read differently by individuals in various situations.

Phantom Companions

The third type of spiritual experience in extreme sports is having visions of phantom companions or hallucinatory helpers, which take the form of people or spirits who provide practitioners with energy, instinctive wisdom, or encouragement. Accident survivors report such helpers particularly frequently. This "phantom companion phenomenon" also appears in the reports of Himalayan climbers and Arctic and desert explorers. Rob Schultheis, for example, described a phantom Indian who helped him restore his balance while crossing a stream when a fall would have been fatal. Schultheis explains such visions as unconscious compensations for loneliness, from which climbers and adventurers often suffer. However, a similar phantom companion was reported in the German poet, novelist, and painter Herman Hesse's childhood , when he was not lonely. The Swiss psychiatrist Carl Jung viewed phantom companions as projections of the "Self." This view seems more satisfactory because accident survivors who have visions are not necessarily lonely.

Interpretations of Spiritual Experiences

Despite being a relatively new area of academic interest, spiritual experiences in extreme sports are beginning to attract interpretation from various fields, including neurophysiology, anthropology, psychology, and philosophy.

Neurophysiological

Researchers have conducted several studies in an attempt to provide biochemical explanations for spiritual experiences in extreme sports. These experiences, also called "peak" (by Abraham Maslow) or altered (by today's psychologists), can be defined as feelings of intense happiness, connected with feelings of ultimate truth and interconnectedness of all things. They are usually accompanied by a sense of widened awareness, and increased control over one's body and emotions; Maslow sees them as self-validating. These experiences refer to the altered states of mind. Peak and altered experiences are said to correlate with the production of various hormones, which can be roughly divided into the endogenous opiates and analgesics on the one hand and those that increase alertness and speed of response on the other hand. Another physical response to stress is hypoxia (deficiency of oxygen consumption by the brain, which can be caused by heavy effort), which increases carbon dioxide levels, consequently producing lactic acid and playing a role in altered states of mind. Many extreme sports are prac-

ticed on high altitudes, and some researchers suggest that high altitudes have an effect on the functioning of certain brain areas that are linked to altered body perception and mystical experiences.

The question is whether spiritual experiences are a product of our biological constitution or a genuine account of reality. Mystical experiences clearly have neurophysiological elements, yet the content of these subjective experiences cannot be reduced to brain chemicals alone. Spiritual experiences are not predetermined by any particular external circumstances, which demonstrates their free nature. Even though the study of the physiology of mystical experiences is a valuable contribution, we should be cautious of reducing spiritual experiences to mere neural processes because to do so ignores the broader environmental and social context within which such experiences occur as well as psychological dimensions.

Psychological

Sports psychologists have established a positive correlation between experiencing spirituality (beliefs and feelings) and being in "the zone" of optimal athletic performance in team sports (Dillon and Tait 2000, 91). Although spiritual and transcendental experiences during sports and exercise are an area of interest among some contemporary sport psychologists, the area is not new among psychologists. Various thinkers, including William James, Sigmund Freud, Carl Jung, and Abraham Maslow, have interpreted mystical experiences. Jung, for example, postulated that behind the ego—the fragile and limited center of consciousness—lies the unconscious subject of the entire psyche, called the "Self." The Self most frequently remains in its latent state, but under extreme circumstances, when the ego does not hold its function any more, the Self emerges and provides superior mind-body integrity. The emergence of the Self explains the sudden increase in mental alertness and physical speed in subjects who make extreme physical efforts under risk and deprivation. Indeed, the Self is in charge of the entire psycho-physical wholeness, which is vaster and far more powerful than the limited area of the individual ego consciousness.

Extreme sports can involve situations in which participants must struggle for survival, and thus such situations share some important characteristics with the mystical and spiritual experiences described in earlier psychological studies. These characteristics are hyperarousal, sensory overload, strenuous effort, exhaustion, food restriction, and hypoxia. Under the circumstances of extreme sports, hyperarousal and accompanying conditions are sometimes followed by the silencing of the mind when the ego as regulatory center is loosened (albeit preserved) and gives up control to the body-mind unity of Self. The reports of adventurers suggest that this new regulatory center is superior in situations of struggle for survival. "Going with the flow" or "being in the center," according to some participants in extreme sports, has saved the lives of people in extraordinary situations. According to anecdotal evidence, thinking is faster, muscles are stronger, reaction is almost instantaneous, and alertness is extraordinary, and thus some researchers have suggested that, in at least some cases, altered states of mind do not only *feel* superior (because of ecstasy and euphoria) but also actually *are* superior in the objective terms of athletic performance and survival capacity.

Philosophical

In assessing the role of spirituality in extreme sports, the two trends of reductionism (an attempt to explain wholes solely in terms of their parts) and integral thinking (which considers that a whole exceeds any sum of its parts) are pitted against each other. The reductionist viewpoint either dismisses spiritual experiences as nonsense or insanity or, in a more contemporary version, seeks to explain them exclusively in terms of neural functioning and brain structures. Illusions are reduced to misperceptions generated by neural structures in the absence of external output.

The comprehensive or integral thinking approach to spirituality in extreme sports was introduced by William James and Aldous Huxley and further developed by contemporary scholars such as Carl Pribram. They were committed to viewing the brain as an entity that *transmits* rather than *generates* mind functioning: Pribram even compares the brain with a television set. Adapted to the pragmatic purpose of orientation and survival in the physical world, the brain usually transmits only useful and relevant information. However, in extreme circumstances, this information is insufficient, and larger "doors of perception" are opened, making it possible to access authentic reality via mystical experiences (Huxley 1990, 87). Scholars are continuously developing arguments for and against the reductionist and comprehensive approaches, to which the study of extreme sports has also contributed.

Even though spiritual experiences have long been attributed to outstanding achievements in the arts and sciences, only recently have explanations been extended to include extreme sports. Far from being disorienting, spiritual

Gods and Games

Sports can be approached with the same fervor as religion, but how else are they similar? Below is an excerpt from an essay examining the link between sports and religion.

Is sports a religion? Is religion a sport?

After organized worship, athletic competition is perhaps the oldest communal impulse known to mankind, and today sports and religion mirror each other as never before, experts say. Religion seems to be becoming more prominent than ever in the sporting world, and arenas are a virtual pulpit. Athletes routinely thank God for their victory or use their post-game interviews as an opportunity to witness to their faith. Post-game prayer circles are regular features, and athletes wear expressions of their faith on sweatbands and protective gear.

NASCAR races, heavyweight boxing bouts, professional golf tournaments and even poker games have become forums for faith. But more than ever before, scholars, religious leaders, and the general public are wondering whether the intimate connections between religion and sports are such a good thing. Does invoking God on behalf of one's team cheapen the tradition of prayer? Is religion in America taking on the uglier aspects of hyper-competitive sports in a race for converts? Experts say the symbiosis between religion and sports shows how deeply religion is embedded in American culture, and vice versa.

Source: Religionlink.org. Retrieved February 2, 2007, from http://www.religionlink.org/tip_050118a.php

experiences in extreme sports have the potential to enhance athletic performance and perhaps even save lives.

Relationships of Participants to the Environment

Many extreme sports take place in beautiful wilderness and natural environments, including forests, mountains, waterfalls, and oceans. Participants in such sports regularly express feeling "at one" with their environment. Indeed, knowledge of the environment and the ability to interpret conditions are often essential elements in extreme sports (e.g., surfers must read waves and position themselves accordingly; backcountry snowboarders and skiers must be acutely aware of snow conditions). Furthermore, the forces of the natural environment, be they the rapids for kayakers, the air currents for hang gliders, or the rock face for climbers, are often the "other player" in the "game" of extreme sports. Thus, for many the beauty and unity with the natural environment are essential parts of the experience. "Spirituality is watching the sun rise as you catch a wave," said one passionate surfer (Mendelsohn 2004). A climber also reported aesthetic enjoyment of nature:

> The woods were incredible that morning! Moss clung to the boulders and the pine branches, which hung low to the ground, still had the bright green of summer, even though it was close to Fall Equinox. There is something magical about woods, with the smells of fall in the air, the moist, crisp atmosphere, and sunlight twinkling through the branches. That sense of magic in the air set the tone for us as we set off to climb the highest peak in Colorado, with a sense of adventure and awe. (Chandler 1997)

It is not a big leap from having aesthetic appreciation while observing such surroundings to experiencing a sense of spiritual unity while climbing, canyoning, or delta flying in the same environment:

> The view was breathtaking, and I became increasingly aware of how connected I felt to each moment, and to all that surrounded me. The expansive feelings of interconnectedness with all life forms continued with each breath, whether it was laboured or eased, throughout the entire climb.... The summit

of Mt. Elbert is awesome!... It is difficult to find words that adequately express the feelings I had while looking at the world from that summit. I felt incredibly insignificant compared to the awesome land I was seeing, and at the same time felt completely part of the whole. The vastness of the planet we live on and take for granted takes on a whole new meaning when viewed from a mountaintop. Truly, I fell in love with Tara, our beloved earth, again as I sat on the summit ... (Chandler 1997)

Intense feelings of awe and unity with nature and the experience of nature as sublime are often integral to the spirituality of extreme sports. More extreme sports are practiced on mountains than anywhere else, and certain spiritual phenomena occur there more frequently or in a particularly strong way. Mountains were also important to the founders of the three major monotheistic religions—Jesus, Abraham and Mohammed.

The Future

Many participants in extreme sports report spiritual and transcendental experiences. Arguably, the spiritual dimension of extreme sports sets them apart from traditional sports. Although the latter are not deprived of spirituality, transcendental experiences seem to be reported more frequently by participants in extreme sports in natural environments, especially those engaged in at high altitudes (e.g., mountaineering). Although people have proposed various neuro-physiological, psychological, and philosophical interpretations of these experiences, as yet no single simple explanation exists. Spirituality in extreme sports remains a mystical and subjective experience. Nonetheless, as more participants engage in extreme sports and more anecdotal evidence is amassed, more research surely will be conducted on this topic.

Tatjana Kochetkova

Further Reading

Appleton, J. (2005). What's so extreme about extreme sports? Retrieved December 11, 2006, from http://www.spiked-online.com/Articles/0000000CAD26.htm

Arzy, S., Idel, M., Landis, T., & Blanke, O. (2005). Why revelations have occurred on mountains? Linking mystical experiences and cognitive neuroscience. *Medical Hypotheses, 65* (5), 841–845.

Bane, M. (1998). *Over the edge: A regular guy's odyssey in extreme sports.* London: Guersney Press.

Chandler, T. (1997). An integrated body-mind experience ... or the zen of mountain climbing. Retrieved December 11, 2006, from http://skdesigns.com/internet/articles/spirituality/chandler/climbing/

Dillon, K., & Tait, J. (2000). Spirituality and being in the zone of team sports: A relationship? *Journal of Sport Behaviour*, 23(2), 91–100.

Evola, J. (1998). *Meditations on the peaks: Mountain climbing as metaphor for the spiritual quest*. Rochester, VT: Inner Traditions.

Fries, D. S. (2002). Opioid analgesics. In D. A. Williams & T. L. Lemke (Eds.), *Foye's principles of medicinal chemistry* (5th ed., pp. 247–269) Philadelphia : Lippincott Williams & Wilkins.

Grof, S. (2000). *The psychology of the future*. Albany: State University of New York Press.

Huxley, A. (1990). *The doors of perception and heaven and hell*. New York: Harper & Row.

James, W. (1956). *The will to believe, human immortality*. New York: Dover Publications.

Jamison, N., Moslow-Benway, M., & Stover, N. (Eds.). (2005). *The thrill of victory, the agony of my feet: Tales from the world of adventure racing*. New York: Breakaway Books.

Krippner, S., Etzel, C., & Stephen, J. L. (Eds.). (2000). *Varieties of anomalous experience: Examining the scientific evidence*. Washington, DC: American Psychological Association.

Mendelsohn, A. (2004) Wave-riders reflect on the spirituality of surfing, Retrieved December 11, 2006, from http://www.surfingrabbi.com/sentinel-article.htm

Messner, R. (2001). *The second death of George Mallory: The enigma and spirit of Mount Everest*. New York: St. Martin's Press.

Muir, J. (1997). *Nature writings*. New York: Penguin Books.

Newberg, A., D'Aquili, E., & Rause, V. (2001). *Why God won't go away: Brain science and the biology of belief*. New York: Ballantine Books.

Pushkin, A. (2000). A feast during the plague. In N. K. Anderson (Trans.), *The little tragedies*, pp. 95–107. New Haven, CT: Yale University Press.

Rhawn, J. (Ed.). (2002). *Neurotheology: Brain, science, spirituality, and religious experience*. San Jose, CA: University Press.

Roy, L. (2001). *Transcendent experiences: Phenomenology and critique*. Toronto, Canada: University of Toronto Press.

Schultheis, R. (1996). *Bone games: Extreme sports, shamanism, zen, and the search for transcendence*. New York: Breakaway Books.

Tart, C. T. (1975). *States of consciousness*. New York: E. P. Dutton.

Wilber, K. (2000). *Integral psychology: Consciousness, spirit, psychology, therapy*. Boston: Shambhala.

Wuthnow, R. (1998). *After heaven: Spirituality in America since the 1950's*. Berkeley and Los Angeles: University of California Press.

Stamstad, John

John Stamstad (b. 1966) is a freelance photographer and professional ultramarathon mountain biker. As the only solo participant in the original twenty-four-hour mountain bike race—the 24 Hours of Canaan in Canaan Valley, West Virginia—Stamstad helped to define the sport of solo ultramarathon mountain bike racing. Subsequent victories in many of the world's most challenging races have ensured Stamstad's legacy as a pioneer of endurance mountain biking.

Growing up in the college town of Madison, Wisconsin, Stamstad commuted to work at his father's business by running each way. A fractured femur forced him to begin cycling as a way to recuperate from his injury. He quickly gravitated to long-distance bicycle touring, often riding as many as 320 kilometers a day. In 1986 Stamstad caught the racing bug and entered his first race—the 885-kilometer bicycle race across the state of Missouri. He moved to Cincinnati to pursue a career in photojournalism, doing freelance work for local magazines, before turning his attention to mountain bike racing full-time. Stamstad then won the most difficult off-road races in the world, including the twenty-four-hour Montezuma's Revenge wilderness mountain bike race, which climbs 4,350-meter Gray's Peak in Colorado, and the Alaskan Iditasport race along the tundra of the Iditarod trail (where Stamstad has never been beaten in eight attempts). He also holds the Ultra-Marathon Cycling Association twenty-four-hour off-road world record of 566 kilometers. In 1996 Stamstad was the first person to ride the 24 Hours of Canaan solo when, against the rules, he entered the relay race under four variations of his name. The next year a solo category was created, and twenty-four-hour solo racing has grown in popularity since.

As Stamstad became more frustrated with the commercialization and growing popularity of twenty-four-hour events, he began looking for more extreme events, often creating an event if one did not exist. In 1999 Stamstad set out on his biggest challenge yet—an unassisted ride along the 4,000-kilometer Great Divide mountain bike trail. Relying only on the gear he could haul on his handlebar-mounted pack, Stamstad covered the distance—and almost 61,000 meters of vertical climbing—in eighteen days, averaging 225 kilometers a day.

In 2000 Stamstad was inducted into the Mountain Bike Hall of Fame and officially retired from endurance mountain bike racing. He moved to Seattle, Washington, and founded Singletrack Ranch, an off-road mountain bike camp for enthusiasts. However, Stamstad did not rest on his laurels; in 2005 he successfully completeed an unsupported solo ride along the 339-kilometer John Muir Trail in California.

Matthew A. Masucci

Further Reading

Balf, T. (1996, September). That which does not kill me makes me stranger. *Outside Magazine, 21*(9), 32–35.

Koeppel, D. (1999, November). The long, strange and incredibly bonked-out ride of John Stamstad. *Sports Afield, 222,* 70–75.

Martin, S. (1995, June). Trying to find the one the breaks me: Interview with John Stamstad. *Bicycling, 36,* 60–64.

Stamstad, J. (2006, July). Heart of the matter. *Trail Runner Magazine, 40,* 38–44.

Streeter, Tanya

World champion free diver Tanya Streeter (b. 1973) was raised on Grand Cayman Island by her British mother and American father and spent her childhood snorkeling in one of the Caribbean's most popular diving destinations. However, she remained unaware of the sport of free diving until she was twenty-five years old. She then made up for lost time, launching a career as an athlete, environmentalist, and spokesmodel.

As a child Streeter recognized that she could hold her breath longer and dive deeper than others but was not introduced to competitive free diving until 1997. A few months later she began to set records for both genders in a variety of events. In 1998 she broke the U.S. record for saltwater constant ballast diving with a plunge to 53 meters, ascending and descending entirely under her own power. That year she also broke the women's world record for no-limits free diving by riding a weighted sled down to 113 meters and rocketing to the surface beneath an inflated lift bag. She also broke the world record in saltwater constant ballast when she propelled herself to 67 meters. Streeter concluded her first year of competitive free diving by establishing a world record for freshwater constant ballast with a dive to 57 meters—the first time a woman had claimed that title.

She continued to set records as the combination of talent and training allowed her to hold her breath for more than six minutes. By late 2003 she held the world record in every category of free diving recognized by the governing body Association Internationale pour le Developpement de l'Apnee (International Association for the Development of Apnea).

Streeter also has emerged as a spokesperson and role model for free diving, which she regards as less extreme and less risky than scuba diving. She also has emerged as an ambassador for the aquatic environment. Aided by endorse-ments from companies such as wetsuit maker Yamamoto, Tag Heuer watches, and Red Bull energy drinks. Streeter has hosted several British Broadcasting Corporation educational programs that combine marine education and advocacy of her sport.

She declines much of the credit for her athletic achievements, pointing out that she is in fact part of a large team of trainers and safety divers who work together to maximize her achievements. She regards competitive free diving as a team sport, insists that she would not dive without her team, and does not cancel scheduled dives for personal reasons. This attitude is noteworthy in a sport in which the athlete's mental state primarily determines performance and safety.

Jeffery A. Charlston

See also Free Diving; Gender; Scuba Diving

Further Reading

Pelizzarri, U., & Tovaglieri, S. (2004). *Manual of freediving: Underwater on a single breath.* Naples, Italy: Idelson Gnocchi.

Sipperly, D. & Mass, T. (1998) *Freedive!* Ventura, CA: Blue Water Freedivers.

Tanya Streeter. (n.d.). Retrieved February 16, 2007, from http://redefine yourlimits.com

Strength

Strength is the capacity to move a load. A load may be an object, as is the case when a person lifts a massive stone, or it may be the human body, as is the case when an athlete does a pushup. The Russian fitness instructor Pavel Tsatsouline identifies three types of strength. (1) Extreme sports that require a single, maximum effort call on maximum strength. A ski jumper or bungee jumper who springs into the air in a single thrust displays maximum strength. (2) Extreme sports that require a sudden burst of strength demand explosive strength. The mountain biker who surges up a short hill displays explosive strength. (3) Extreme sports that demand a sustained effort over a long duration call on strength endurance. The triathlete displays strength endurance throughout the course of an event.

Extreme sports emphasize individual accomplishment rather than team play and have an ethos (distinguishing character, sentiment, moral nature, or guiding beliefs) that celebrates the counterculture rather than validates tradi-

tional norms. However, the triathlon, for example, reveals another aspect of extreme sports in calling forth an extreme effort from an athlete. One cannot participate in a triathlon halfway; an all-out effort over the course of several hours is necessary to finish the event. The triathlon demands extreme strength endurance. In this regard "extreme" means "maximum." Extreme sports push an athlete to the limit of strength.

Science of Strength

People in antiquity understood strength through myth. Samson, Hercules, and other mythological figures embodied the ideal of strength. In modernity the myths of antiquity ceded ground to science, particularly to the study of the action of muscles. In his *Fabric of the Human Body* the Flemish physician Andreas Vesalius in 1543 cataloged the body's roughly six hundred muscles in a series of striking drawings. In the eighteenth century the Italian physician Luigi Galvani demonstrated that electricity causes a muscle to contract or shorten. Contemporary science holds muscle contraction to be an electrochemical process. A nerve carries electricity in the form of ions, molecules with a chemical charge. The charge is an electrochemical signal that ripples down the length of a muscle fiber and causes its filaments to slide past each other, contracting the muscle. In moving an object a muscle may contract some or all of its fibers, although, of course, only by contracting all fibers can it move the heaviest load.

In contracting, a muscle does not move a load directly but instead moves a bone to which it attaches. Every muscle has two attachments: origin and insertion. The origin anchors a muscle in place and is the attachment to a bone that does not move. The insertion, on the other hand, is the attachment to a bone that a muscle moves by contracting. The point of insertion is one factor, along with the number of muscle fibers, their composition as fast and slow twitch, their thickness, and the age of an athlete, that determines strength. As with the number of muscle fibers and their composition, heredity determines a muscle's point of origin and insertion. As important as training is, heredity limits how strong a person can become.

As the foregoing suggests, a muscle is not a homogeneous bundle of fibers. Some fibers contract faster than others, hence the designations "fast" and "slow" twitch fibers. These types of fibers are not equivalent in strength because the faster a muscle contracts the stronger it is. A muscle

with only fast twitch fibers is, all other factors being equal, nearly twice as strong as a muscle with its fibers evenly divided between fast and slow twitch.

Consider how muscles work the quadriceps, a group of four muscles in the front of the thigh. The extreme cycling sports place heavy demands on the quadriceps, making them an apt choice as an example. The quadriceps anchor to the ilium and femur and insert at the tibia. In contracting the quadriceps pull the tibia and thus the lower leg forward. In concert with other muscles of the thigh, lower leg, and buttocks the mountain biker uses the quadriceps to push the lower leg down along the curve of the pedals. The movement of the quadriceps in this instance is quick, even explosive in short bursts. One might imagine the quadriceps operating on the thigh and lower leg as though the two were a type of lever and as though the knee were the fulcrum about which the lower leg pivots. In contracting, the quadriceps straighten the knee, bringing the lower leg roughly parallel with the thigh. At the point of extension the lower leg and thigh form a 180-degree angle, and the quadriceps will have contracted to their shortest length.

Strength is a function not only of the number of fibers a muscle contracts and of the composition of fibers as fast or slow twitch, but also of the size of a muscle. The larger the muscle, the heavier the load it can move. Two factors determine the size of a muscle: the number of fibers and their thickness. As we have seen, heredity fixes the number of fibers; despite a misconception to the contrary, exercise cannot increase the number of muscle fibers. Nutrition and exercise can, however, thicken the fibers, thereby strengthening an athlete. In addition to diet and exercise, age affects the thickness of muscle fibers. Athletes at their peak can, through training, retain strength with little or no decrease into their forties. During their fifties, however, strength diminishes as they lose muscle mass. Not only do muscle fibers thin in this instance, but also the number of fibers decreases. The loss in the number of fibers makes irreversible this diminution in strength and explains why athletes are capable of peak performance for only a brief duration of their lives.

The central nervous system also affects a person's strength. In lifting a heavy object or performing a sport that requires strength, the nerves recruit muscle fibers. In repeating a strength activity nerves learn to recruit more fibers. The increase in the recruitment of fibers causes athletes to gain strength even if their muscles do not enlarge. The recruitment of increasing numbers of fibers accounts for much of the strength gains in women and children, whereas

Arnold Schwarzenegger

Arnold Schwarzenegger is known as the Hollywood actor who played tough-guy roles in The Terminator *movies and* Conan the Barbarian, *and earned later fame becoming the governor of California. But, before the acting and politics, Schwarzenegger was a world-renowned bodybuilder, and had his own thoughts on the extreme nature of the physical training needed to reach the height of bodybuilding fame he achieved.*

There are various ways of assessing strength. If I can lift 300 pounds and you can lift only 250, I am stronger than you in one-rep strength. However, if you can lift 250 pounds ten times and I can only lift it eight times, that is a different kind of strength; you would be surpassing me in muscular endurance—the ability to continue to be strong over a series of movements.

To shape and develop the body, it is necessary to do a lot of the "endurance" kind of training—plenty of sets and reps. But I also believe that, unless you include low-rep, strength training, you will never achieve the hardness and density necessary to create a truly first-class physique.

In the days of John Grimek and Clancey Ross, virtually all bodybuilders trained for power. Although most of them lacked the total refinement that top bodybuilders have today, they were extremely strong, hard, and impressive physical specimens.

Source: Arnold Schwarzenegger. *Encyclopedia of Modern Bodybuilding.* New York: Simon & Schuster, 1985.

ing a sport and draws on this memory to decide how many neurons to stimulate and thereby how many muscle fibers to recruit. Practice—lifting weights for several months or even years, for example—does more than enlarge muscles. It codifies in the memory how many neurons to stimulate so that athletes gain strength both in their muscles and through memory, hence the connection between mind and body.

Extreme athletes who have enlarged their muscles to the maximum and recruited the maximum neurons for an event may appear to be at the limit of strength. However, recall that strength is the capacity to move a load. An athlete who can lighten the load increases strength relative to the load. Because many extreme sports—climbing and mountain biking, for example—use the body as the load, athletes who lower their weight increase their strength relative to weight. However, this reduction in weight is self-defeating if it comes at the expense of muscle. The extreme athlete can only benefit by losing fat. The imperative to be both strong and lean is evident in triathletes, many of whom have little fat, being something akin to muscle-powered skeletons.

Differences in Strength

Perhaps because of conceit humans tend to believe themselves exceptionally strong. We glorify the athlete who possesses abundant strength as though this quality distinguishes us from other animals. In fact we set ourselves apart from the rest of animal life by our comparative weakness. Insects can drag along the ground objects several thousand times their weight, whereas we can manage an object just 60 percent our weight. Among the primates humans fare little better. A 54-kilogram chimpanzee is on average three to five times stronger than a man. Even among hominids humans cannot boast great strength. Members of a long line of prehumans—*Australopithicus robustus, Australopithicus boisei, Homo erectus,* and *Homo neanderthalis*—all had thick bones and wide slots for the origin and insertion of tendons, making clear that they had larger muscles and were stronger than are modern humans. Cro-Magnon, the earliest modern people of Europe, were more robust than we are. Paleoanthropologists class modern humans as the gracile (slender) hominid. Simply put we have less muscle and are surely weaker than were our closest hominid kin.

Humans' comparative lack of strength does not prevent men from boasting greater strength than women. Men are on average 33 percent stronger than women because of dif-

men gain much of their strength by enlarging their muscles. The nerves stimulate muscles to contract at the neuron, the nerve cells that contact a muscle. Neurons differ in the number of muscle fibers they contract. A neuron that contacts a muscle of the eye contracts as few as ten fibers, whereas a neuron in the calf contracts some two thousand fibers.

Neurons contract few or many fibers for an activity. Recall that the heavier the load, the more fibers a neuron contracts. This recruitment of fibers depends on memory. The brain stores the experience of lifting an object or perform-

ferences in the amount of muscle in men and women. These differences are greater in the upper body, where men are twice as strong as women. Closer to equivalent in the lower body, women are 75 percent as strong as men. Although these differences are rooted in biology, the exaggerated notion that women are weak and frail dates from the Victorian era and persists among the unenlightened today. This notion of women as the weaker sex is pure fiction. Where muscle mass is equivalent women are as strong as men. To put the matter another way, a muscle fiber has the same strength in women as in men. At the level of the muscle fiber the distinction between male and female disappears.

Testosterone, a hormone synthesized from cholesterol and secreted by the testes, accounts for the disparity in muscle mass and thereby strength between men and women. Testosterone stimulates the synthesis of protein into muscle and inhibits the breakdown of protein. The higher the concentration of testosterone is in the body, the larger the muscles and the stronger the athlete. At puberty the testes begin secreting testosterone, signaling a capacity to build strength that continues into early adulthood. Heredity fixes the amount of testosterone and so, as with other hereditary factors, limits how strong an athlete can become. Because humans have genetic diversity, they have a range of testosterone levels. Some men have ten times as much testosterone as others, and women have little, a fact that explains why women are on average weaker than men. Testosterone attaches to muscle fibers at testosterone receptor sites. A testosterone molecule, having attached to a site, signals the muscle fiber to thicken by adding protein to it. As with testosterone, heredity fixes the number of receptor sites. All other factors being equal, athletes with a large number of sites will build more muscle and be stronger than those with few sites. Curiously, testosterone and testosterone receptor sites do not go hand in hand. An athlete may produce much testosterone but have few receptor sites, whereas another athlete may produce little testosterone but have many sites. The athlete lucky enough to have inherited large amounts of both stands the best chance of building muscle and strength quickly and to a high degree.

As is self-evident, differences in strength affect the outcome of an extreme sport. Consider two mountain bikers, one of whom is stronger than the other. The stronger athlete will be able to pedal a higher gear than will the weaker one. If the cadence of pedaling is equal between the two, the stronger athlete, by virtue of pedaling a higher gear, will be faster than the weaker one. A 10 percent difference in strength will allow the stronger mountain biker to cover a thirty-minute stretch of terrain three minutes faster than the weaker mountain biker.

Strength Exercises

According to Greek myth the athlete Milo of Croton as a boy lifted a calf every day, continuing this exertion until both he and the calf had grown into adults. Although fiction this story dramatizes the ability of humans to build strength. By one estimate men and women can increase strength 30 to 60 percent through exercise. Coaches and athletes distinguish between two types of strength exercises. Isometric exercise tenses muscles but prevents their contracting through a range of motion. Two wrestlers who push against one another, neither yielding an inch, perform isometric exercise. Isotonic exercise, on the other hand, allows a muscle to contract through a range of motion. Should one wrestler gain the advantage and force his opponent to the ground he will have transformed the stasis of what had been an isometric exercise into an isotonic exercise. Because most extreme sports require motion they are isotonic by nature, leading athletes to favor isotonic exercise in building strength.

Weight training is perhaps the most popular form of isotonic exercise. Human performance writer Chris MacNab cites weight training as the most important type of conditioning an extreme athlete can do. Milo's exertions were a form of weight training, although today athletes use barbells, dumbbells, and machines rather than livestock. Barbells and dumbbells, unsupported by any apparatus, are free weights. Alternatively an athlete may use a machine or apparatus that steadies a weight through its range of motion. One school of thought holds that free weights are superior to machines because free weights require an athlete to balance a weight while lifting it, a skill he cannot develop on a machine. On the other hand, one might assert that a machine is a safer means of building strength because an athlete cannot drop a machine on himself, whereas he can drop a free weight on some part of his body, risking injury. Rather than free weights or machines an athlete may use the body as the load, as a climber does in ascending a mountain, to build strength.

Controversy fires the issue of how many repetitions of an exercise an athlete should perform. One line of reasoning asserts that only the performance of a single repetition goads an athlete to recruit all fibers of his muscles in moving a load. Only a single repetition can therefore stimulate the development of maximum strength. A second line of reasoning counters that such exercise does not replicate the reality of competition. The bicycle motocross (BMX) racer does not pedal his bicycle once but hundreds, perhaps even thousands, of times during a race. Better, according to this line of reasoning, to build strength through multiple repetitions of an exercise.

An increase in strength entails an increase in muscle mass, and yet this increase in mass may be a mixed blessing for some extreme athletes. On the one hand, strength helps extreme athletes endure the rigors of competition, but, on the other hand, several extreme sports—mountain biking, climbing, and the triathlon are examples—use the body as the load. Any extra weight has the potential to slow athletes in these sports. The tradeoff between strength and mass is difficult to evaluate. Extreme athletes tend to compromise between strength and muscle mass by using light weights for many repetitions to build strength with a minimum of muscle bulk.

Schedules for how often to lift weights for strength abound. MacNab recommends three days per week for extreme athletes. By alternating each day of strength training with a day of rest, an athlete gets two days off after the third day, a convenient schedule when the three days are Monday, Wednesday, and Friday. By alternating days the athlete has time to recuperate between sessions. Another popular schedule is the four-day routine in which an athlete trains the upper body two days per week and the lower body another two. A common distribution of training by the four-day routine is the upper body on Monday and Thursday and the lower body on Tuesday and Friday. Whatever the schedule, as athletes strengthen they should add weight to their regime. MacNab recommends small increases of one to three pounds per exercise. Because extreme sports demand strength from a large number of muscles MacNab recommends strength-training exercises that use multiple muscles. The squat, for example, strengthens the quadriceps, the lower legs, the buttocks, the core, the shoulders, and the neck.

Although both men and women can increase strength by lifting weights, sexism persists, as we have seen, among the unenlightened advocates of strength training who believe women sacrifice femininity in building strong muscles. According to this school of thought women who lift weights for strength bump up against the biological limit of their delicate physique and can manage only light weights. This rationale errs in defining strength as a male attribute. In contrast to this sexism a balanced perspective acknowledges strength as a gender-neutral attribute in recognition of the fact that both women and men have an innate capacity to build strength and muscle mass.

Avoiding sexism, some women have joined gyms that cater only to women. Curves, for example, since 1979 has opened its gyms only to women and now has more than nine thousand gyms worldwide. The Curves formula combines strength training and nutrition with an emphasis as much on athletes' growing strong as on their maintaining proper weight for their age and height. Perhaps more than traditional gyms, Curves promotes camaraderie among its members. Its success suggests that women want more than strength from their training.

In addition to sexism, a second type of error conflates weight lifting and strength training despite the fact that not every athlete lifts weights to increase strength. Bodybuilders, for example, lift weights without regard to strength. Their sole object is to sculpt their physiques, building muscle and reducing fat to the point of being "ripped," the term for extreme muscle definition. As important as strength is to many athletes, bodybuilding underscores the fact that most athletes do not seek strength as an end in itself but rather as a means of enhancing performance.

Despite the benefits of strength training some coaches steer their athletes away from it for fear that their charges will become bulky and slow. This image harkens back to the notion that bodybuilders are all show and no substance. They cannot, according to this notion, run fast, jump high, or perform any athletic event well. The prevailing opinion, however, is that athletes who gain strength also gain speed and power.

Nutrition and Drugs

Extreme sports, in their demands on an athlete, magnify the importance of nutrition. Several extreme sports, such as open-water swimming and the triathlon, demand strength endurance. The athlete in these sports burns more than one thousand calories during competition, making it essential that extreme athletes eat a diet rich in carbohydrates, a type of sugar or starch that muscles burn during practice and competition. The muscles store carbohydrates as glycogen, which then serves as a reserve on which athletes can draw during the rigors of their sport.

In addition to carbohydrates, extreme athletes need protein to build muscle. The word *protein*, from the Greek *protos* for "first," suggests the importance protein has long had in the diet. Indeed, some athletes are guilty of exaggerating the value of protein, believing that if 100 grams of protein will add 1 gram of muscle, then 200 grams of protein will add 2 grams of muscle. The advertisers of protein powder, in an effort to increase sales, promote this fallacy, and muscle magazines carry articles that lavish praise on high-protein diets. The body cannot, of course, absorb protein ad infinitum. An athlete needs only 1 gram of protein per kilogram of body weight per day. Anything above this amount passes through the body. Even when the diet is optimal most protein does not build new muscle but instead replaces muscle that the body has metabolized. The fraction of protein that builds new muscle does so by thickening muscle fibers rather than by making new fibers.

Some athletes resort to taking anabolic steroids, a class of chemicals that mimics the male hormone testosterone, to build muscle and strength beyond what exercise and diet alone can achieve. The number of athletes worldwide who use steroids may be impossible to gauge, although one estimate puts the number at 1 million in the United States and at $10 million in annual sales on the black market. The use of steroids allows an athlete to boost strength 5 to 10 percent in six weeks, although after an athlete is off steroids his strength returns to the baseline in another six weeks. The transient nature of this strength gain may tempt athletes to take steroids for months or even years, but at a price: Long use increases the risk of liver damage, heart disease, and cancer. These risks have led several governing boards to ban the use of steroids. Public exposure of steroid use tarnishes athletes, prompting the charge that they seek an unfair advantage in competition.

Extreme Sports and Extreme Strength

Whereas weight training is a tool of extreme athletes, competitive weightlifting and bodybuilding are extreme sports, according to sportswriter Bill Lund. Competitive weightlifting makes extreme demands on an athlete's strength. More than in any other extreme sport, strength is the decisive factor in weightlifting. Although technique plays a role in the success of a weightlifter, technique is secondary to strength. Weightlifting requires a combination of maximum strength and explosive strength to move a weight. The best weightlifters are not merely strong in a conventional sense; they have an explosive ability to thrust a weight over the desired trajectory. The extreme weightlifter manifests strength as a combination of power and speed.

The desire of weightlifters to pit their strength against one another has culminated in several strength competitions, each with its own traditions and events. The Scottish Highland Games claim to be the oldest strength competition at one thousand years. The seven events include the familiar

A man exercising to increase balance. Source: istock/Nicholas Monu.

hammer throw and shot put, but others are unique. The caber throw challenges participants to hoist an 86-kilogram tree trunk, balance it during an 18-meter run, and toss it for distance and accuracy: The trunk must align parallel to the participant's line of approach for full points. The event that makes explicit the competition's ethos is the lifting of massive stones, the "manhood stones," language that affirms the old prejudice that strength is solely a masculine trait.

The Basques have their own stone-lifting contest in Ustaritz, France. Contestants hoist a stone around which the tribal elders once met. Basques believe that the stone lift commemorates their Druid origins and so is more than a strength contest. Basques believe the stone is a religious symbol. The men who hoist it demonstrate through their strength that the gods favor them. In this sense the stone lift affirms strength as a divine attribute.

Since 1977 Universal Studios in the United States has hosted the World's Strongest Man competition, which draws inspiration from the games in Scotland and France but which belongs to the machine era of Henry Ford and the Wright brothers. Contestants forgo the lifting of stones and the tossing of tree trunks and instead try to pull a Boeing 747 along a runway. Another event challenges contestants to lift a tire from a semitrailer. The competition pits man against machine in the tradition of John Henry. In this respect it is less a world event than a U.S. event in its ethos.

More than other extreme sports, bodybuilding has an ambivalent relationship with strength. The bodybuilder works to increase the size of muscles, and this increase necessarily increases strength. At some gyms bodybuilders challenge one another in impromptu strength competitions and take pride in their strength. Indeed strength seems to be an affirmation of a bodybuilder's self-worth.

Yet, as we have seen, bodybuilders do not train to increase strength. Any gains in strength are secondary to the primary goal of sculpting their muscles. The bodybuilder wins or loses a competition on aesthetic grounds, not on strength. Bodybuilding is one of the few extreme sports that rewards competitors regardless of strength. Victory goes to the bodybuilder whom judges deem the most pleasing to the eye. Large muscles and minimal fat rather than strength win competitions. The bodybuilder must be ripped.

Place of Strength in Extreme Sports

The extreme cyclist, as we have seen, needs strong quadriceps to power her bicycle. Beyond these muscles, the ex-

treme cyclist needs a strong core to absorb the shock of uneven terrain or to provide the surge of strength necessary to propel a bicycle into midair. The extreme cyclist needs explosive strength for short bursts of activity. The BMX cyclist who leaps from a ramp in an acrobatics of agility displays explosive strength. The mountain biker who negotiates a ten-mile trail needs explosive strength to climb short hills as well as strength endurance to cover the entire course. Extreme cycling sports therefore require athletes to develop both explosive strength and strength endurance and to develop these types of strength in a large number of muscles.

A variant of extreme cycling is the triathlon, which requires participants to swim, cycle, and run in order to complete the event. Perhaps the most extreme example of this sport is the Ironman triathlon in Hawaii, which since 1978 has included a 3.8-kilometer swim in the Pacific Ocean, a 180-kilometer bicycle race, and a traditional marathon (26.2 miles/42.1 kilometers). The duration of these events is not the only challenge to athletes. Temperatures soar to 90° Fahrenheit, humidity reaches 85 percent, and wind surges as much as 96 kilometers per hour, forcing participants to battle the elements as well as the terrain and ocean. The Ironman triathlon and events like it require strength endurance from all muscles in the body. The cycling and running portions of the triathlon demand strength endurance from the thighs, lower legs, buttocks, and core. The swim portion calls on athletes to display strength endurance in all these muscles along with the muscles of the shoulders and arms. The triathlete must display all-around strength in order to excel.

The climbing sports likewise require all-around strength. The most extreme climb is Mount Everest (8,850 meters), although many shorter summits are scarcely less taxing. Extreme climbers also scale the artificial climbing walls at gyms. Extreme climbing demands strength from the legs, the core, the buttocks, the shoulders, and the arms. In its duration an extreme climb makes the heaviest demand on strength endurance, particularly where oxygen diminishes at high altitude. The observer who assumes that all the rigors lie in the ascent of a mountain or an artificial climbing wall might reflect on the demands of the descent because an athlete must retrace her route when she is no longer fresh but rather tired from the ascent. In this respect the descent, rather than the ascent, makes the greater demand of strength endurance.

A defining feature of extreme sports is the demand they place on multiple muscle groups. Open-water swimming, for example, demands strength from muscles in the legs, arms, shoulders, and core. Moreover, these demands are simultaneous: The open-water swimmer uses all the listed muscles at the same time and without respite. Accordingly, open-water swimming taxes the strength of multiple muscles to an extreme degree. BMX cycling likewise demands the strength of multiple muscles. The primary demand is on the quadriceps, but the core and shoulders must also be strong to maneuver the bicycle and to absorb the shock of jumps.

Noteworthy, too, are the extreme sports that place heavy demands on the muscles of the legs. Extreme cycling sports, although demanding all-around strength, make the heaviest demands on the quadriceps. In-line skating, roller hockey, skateboarding, snowboarding, and speed skating all tax the muscles in the legs. In these sports strength is anchored in the legs and core and radiates outward to other muscles in the body. The strong in-line skater will take longer strides, pushing more vigorously through each stride than will the weaker in-line skater. The ability of the strong speed skater and roller hockey player to take long, powerful strides will translate into greater speed than a weaker athlete can generate.

Strength is a safeguard against injury. The extreme athlete who has strong, thick muscles will absorb the rigors of competition better than will a weaker extreme athlete. The shock of competition in BMX cycling demands strength in the muscles and tendons, particularly in the quadriceps, to avoid injury. The bungee jumper as well needs strength in the core to absorb the force of the recoil at the bottom of the descent. A strong surfer is less likely than a weak one to suffer injury in the course of wiping out at the end of riding a wave.

These examples underscore the fact that extreme sports make extreme demands of muscles. Extreme sports demand strength from all muscles in the body and the perseverance to be strong over long durations. Extreme sports demand extreme strength, whether explosive strength, strength endurance, or a combination of the two.

Toward the Limits of Strength

Although one may be tempted to believe otherwise, humans cannot increase strength without limit. Even now, with performance in strength events inching upward or holding constant, we may be near the maximum. Counterintuitive as it seems, the quest for maximum strength diminishes the role that strength plays in separating winners from losers as athletes approach the maximum. Near the maximum little separates elite athletes, all of whom possess roughly equal strength. The athlete who gains some small advantage finds

himself only infinitesimally stronger than his rivals, all of whom are bumping up against the same strength ceiling.

With little to differentiate elite athletes in strength, the focus of training may shift away from building the last iota of strength to extending strength at a high level over the course of a career. An athlete who retains her strength into her forties may add a decade to her career and reap the earnings from longevity. Whether athletes will desire such longevity is open to question. Elite athletes command lucrative pay in some extreme sports, are financially secure after a few years, and do not need to compete long years for their sustenance. Yet, longevity is essential if an athlete hopes to set records and secure his or her place in the history of extreme sports. Other athletes compete not for money but rather for the adrenaline rush that extreme sports provide. For them the maintenance of strength over time gives them the ability to extend their competitive years and the joy they derive from extreme sports. For these athletes extreme sports are a passion and the maintenance of strength a means of enjoying their passion over a long career. By their nature extreme sports seem to demand that athletes develop and maintain strength as a means of prolonging the high they receive from sports.

Christopher Cumo

Further Reading

Ebben, W., & Jensen, R. (1998). Strength training for women: Debunking myths that block opportunity. Retrieved February 22, 2005, from http://www.physsportsmed.com/issues/1998/05may/ebben.htm

Feinber, B. (1993). *The musculoskeletal system*. Langhorne, PA: Chelsea House.

Kumar, S. (2004). *Muscle strength*. Boca Raton, FL: CFC Press.

Lund, B. (1996). *Weight lifting*. Mankato, MN: Capstone Press.

MacNab, C. (2004). *Extreme sports*. Broomall, PA: Mason Crest Publishers.

Serafini, A. (1981). *The muscle book*. New York: Arno.

Sprague, K. (1996). *More muscle*. Champaign, IL: Human Kinetics.

Tomlinson, J. (1996). *Extreme sports*. New York: Smithmark.

Tsatsouline, P. (2003). *The naked warrior*. St. Paul, MN: Dragon Door Publications.

Williams, M. (1989). *Beyond training: How athletes enhance performance legally and illegally*. Champaign, IL: Leisure Press.

Surfing

In the popular imagination surfing is a classic extreme sport. Every surfer seemingly confronts collapsing walls of water, violent turbulence, frenzied sharks, and either razor-sharp coral heads or boulder-strewn reefs. Stories, films, and photos reinforce these popular images. A picture of Jay Moriarty free-falling down the face of a 6-meter wave at Maverick's (northern California) in December 1994 appeared in the *New York Times*; NBC's *Nightly News* showed footage of the wipeout. Laird Hamilton's ride across a 5.4-meter wall at Teahupoo, Tahiti, in August 2000 received front-page coverage in the *Los Angeles Times* and won the Action Sports Feat of 2000 Award at the annual ESPN Action Sports Awards. The international media reported the shark attack on thirteen-year-old surfer Bethany Hamilton at Ha'ena, Hawaii, in October 2003. Hamilton, who lost her left arm just below the shoulder, subsequently appeared on the *Oprah Winfrey Show* and gave interviews to *Glamour* magazine and *Entertainment Tonight*.

However, contrary to these images and anecdotes, surfing is a particularly safe sport with a rate of injury no higher than that of fishing. The average surfer incurs four injuries (deep cuts, sprains, fractures, and so forth) every one thousand days of riding. Most injuries happen in waves of less than 1.2 meters as a result of surfers colliding with their own surfboards or the ocean bed. Shark attacks, drownings, and deaths are rare. Of course, this rarity, paradoxically, draws media attention that fuels the popular imagination of a wildly dangerous pastime. Such media attention certainly was drawn during the mid-1990s when a spate of accidents involved the deaths of three big-wave riders. Mark Foo drowned on 23 December 1994, after wiping out on a 4.5-meter wave at Maverick's. A few years earlier he had prophetically warned those seeking "the ultimate thrill" that they may "pay the ultimate price." Donnie Solomon died at the shrine of big-wave riding—Waimea Bay, Hawaii—one year to the day after Foo's death. Todd Chesser drowned at Outside Alligators, a reef west of Waimea Bay, on 13 February 1997.

Given surfing's relatively good safety record, the label "extreme" would appear a misnomer. However, the label is valid in two distinct senses. First, surfing fits the "extreme" label by virtue of its irreverent culture and associated lifestyle. Second, big waves are violent masses of water that break ferociously; typically they explode in shallow water overlying coral heads and lava rocks. Surfers who ride these waves risk having their bones smashed and their flesh torn open.

Irreverent Culture

Although "rediscovered" at the turn of the twentieth century, the ancient Polynesian art of surfing did not become popular until the mid-1950s. Technology was the initial obstacle to the development of surfing. Made of solid wood, early surfboards were heavy and impossible for all but the highly skilled to ride. In the 1950s California surfers produced shorter, lighter, and highly maneuverable boards made of balsa wood. These Malibu boards made surfing more accessible, and the activity burgeoned in California. Anthropologist John Irwin estimates that the surfboard-riding population of southern California grew from five thousand in 1956 to one hundred thousand in 1962. Assisting the diffusion of surfing were Hollywood surf films (such as *Gidget* and *Muscle Beach*), "pure" surf films made by devotees (*Slippery When Wet, The Big Surf, Surf Trek to Hawaii*), and specialist surfing magazines (*Surfer, Surfing, Surfing World*).

Many young surfers adopted an irreverent, hedonistic culture and drew critical comment from their elders, members of a generation whose life perspectives were forged in depression and world war. Social commentators in the 1950s and early 1960s condemned surfing as an indolent, wasteful, selfish, and institutionally unanchored pastime. Surfers' corporeal style, the "trademark" of which was long bleached hair, irreverent argot, humor, and rituals, and nomadic lifestyle, rendered them socially irresponsible. Bruce Brown, producer and director of *The Endless Summer*, remembers well parents and nonsurfing peers chiding him for "wasting time" and urging him to "do something useful." As a boy, Greg Noll, who became a professional surfer, recalls one particular exchange with a school principal:

> What do you guys do down there at the Manhattan Beach Surf Club? What are your goals, what do you want to become?" I told him that I wanted to surf, I wanted to make surfboards, I wanted to go to Hawaii, I wanted to see the world and have a good time. From the principal's point of view, that qualified me as most likely to end up a beach bum and never amount to shit. (Noll and Gabbard 1989, 31)

In Australia, where surfing culture developed quickly behind California, surfers also attracted bad publicity. One observer referred to surfers as "useless": They "cruise from beach to beach looking for the best surf" and "pay no rates or fees of any kind, frequently not even parking fees." Another denounced "long-haired" surfers who "took over footpaths for their boards, public toilets for changing rooms, made unofficial headquarters of public facilities," and made "rude" and "foul" remarks to girls.

Fieldnotes from a Remote Desert Surfing Location in Australia

This evening the pounding of the shore break (which is considerably smaller than the waves on the reef) makes the walls of the tent shake.... [In the morning] I will travel to Big Reef break where the surf will be a bit bigger, much hollower and apparently twice as powerful.

The sound of the big sets breaking on the shore in front of my tent scares me; and there are plenty of reasons why it should.... I could be seriously injured or even killed. So why even consider it?

Prestige...Conquest...Aesthetics—I really want to experience the exhilaration and the visual spectacle that comes with being inside a barrel that large and travelling that fast. Above all else I want to dance this dance and I want to do it well. It's not just 'because it's there,' these waves may well be the most terrible and beautiful I will ever see; to ride one of them has spiritual connotations.

More than anything this last factor is pushing me to overcome the fear and accept the experience on offer. But I don't expect to get much sleep listening and feeling the pounding of the swell and mulling over my responsibility as a father; without doubt the biggest pull in the other direction. I am afraid of the surf but when I was young and single that fear was easily converted into the adrenalin of a challenge readily accepted. Now it seems selfish to risk the prospect of my wife and kids witnessing my foolish death or dealing with any large-scale injury.

Source: Stranger, M. (2001). Risk-taking & Postmodernity: Commodification and the Ecstatic in Leisure Lifestyles—The Case of Surfing. Unpublished PhD Thesis, University of Tasmania p. 197.

Surfing into the Mainstream

In the early 1960s some surfers attempted to negotiate a more acceptable cultural style and expression by defining themselves as sportspersons. Concomitantly they established new regional and national associations and organized competitions to take surfing into the mainstream sporting world. Initially they appeared to have succeeded. Hoppy Swarts, the inaugural president of the United States Surfing Association, noted with pride that competitions had "helped develop a new image with the public—the public has come to respect our surfers in the same way as they respect other athletes." A Sydney, Australia, newspaper echoed Swarts's sentiments, praising surfers' new found "maturity" since they had formed an official body. Big business and vested political interests flocked to surfing. Sponsors of the first official world surfing championships at Manly Beach, Sydney, in May 1964 included Manly Council, Ampol (Petroleum), and TAA (Trans Australian Airlines). They were blunt about their motives: "Manly will get a lot of publicity from international television coverage of the event," said Mayor Bill Nicholas. The championships were a phenomenal success—an estimated crowd of sixty-five thousand watched Australian

Bernard "Midget" Farrelly win the crown. A senior Ampol representative described surfing as "the fastest-growing sport in Australia" and pledged his company's ongoing support.

However, organized competition required formal rules, and codification was no simple matter with surfing styles reflecting regional variations, particularly between California and Australia: Australians sought waves to slash and conquer, Californians sought waves for artistic expression. Debate over style fueled dissension over judging methods and scoring and led to accusations of corruption, cronyism, and nepotism. The result was a significant decline in competitive surfing during the late 1960s.

The counterculture also influenced this decline. An amalgam of alternative, typically utopian, lifestyles and political activism, the counterculture emphasized self-realization and encouraged individuals to pursue their dreams through a distinctive "new left" politics that embraced antiauthoritarian gestures, iconoclastic habits (in music, dress, language, and lifestyle), and a general critique of everyday life. Soul-surfing—riding waves for "the good of one's soul"—articulated this new politics and conjoined surfing with the counterculture. Soul-surfers scorned organized surfing as a form of institutionalization. Kimo Hollinger captures the general animosity toward competitive surfing. He was at Waimea Bay when a contest began:

> The kids started paddling out with numbers on their bodies. Numbers! It was incongruous to the point of being blasphemous. I wondered about myself. I had been a contestant and a judge in a few of those contests when it all seemed innocent and fun. But it never is. The system is like an octopus with long legs and suckers that envelop you and suck you down. The free and easy surfer, with his ability to communicate so personally and intensely with his God, is conned into playing the plastic numbers game with the squares, losing his freedom, his identity, and his vitality, becoming a virtual prostitute. And what is even worse, the surfers fall for it. I felt sick. (Hollinger 1975, 40)

Under the influence of the counterculture soul-surfers applied increasingly esoteric interpretations to surfing: Waves became dreams, playgrounds, podia, and even asylums, and the search for perfect waves became an endless pursuit. Surfing signified self-expression, escape, and freedom. Australian surfer Robert Conneeley described surfing as "the ultimate liberating factor on the planet"; fellow traveler Ted Spencer claimed that he "dance[d] for Krishna" when he surfed; and former world champion-turned-soul-surfer Nat Young believed that by the simple virtue of riding waves, surfers were "supporting the revolution."

The tabloid media, however, found no merit in a youth-led social revolution. It accused surfers of being long-haired, unwashed, undisciplined, indulgent, and decadent. Sydney's *Sun-Herald*, for example, called them "jobless junkies."

Ultimately the counterculture was unsustainable. Yippie leader Jerry Rubin's words, "people should do whatever the fuck they want," could not reconcile alternative independence with an interdependent society. Yet, the counterculture did contribute to the development of professional surfing: Its work-is-play philosophy encouraged one group of surfers to establish a professional circuit in the belief that it would offer them an economic avenue to eternal hedonism.

Today surfing is a widely organized and accepted sport. Surfers compete for honors, as amateurs and professionals, at every level: school, university, city, region, national, and world. Yet, most surfers subscribe to the irreverent culture of the early founders; the same culture also firmly underpins the multibillion-dollar surfing industry. Consistent with this culture, surfers continue to question the place of competi-

tion and professional surfing in particular: Manicured images portrayed by professional surfers to win broad public appeal simply do not resonate with a culture that marches to a different beat and that shuns institutionalism in all its guises. "As soon as those assholes in the seventies tried to turn 'surfing the artform' into 'surfing the sport' surf culture suffered," complains Kit, a correspondent who echoes the sentiments of thousands and illustrates an "extreme" cultural perspective.

Big-Wave Riding

Although injury statistics reveal surfing to be a comparatively safe sport, its record rests more on the fact that the overwhelming majority of participants do not venture into big waves. Indeed, when the big waves arrive excuses pour forth to explain the absences—"doctor's appointment," "collecting the kids," "work commitments," "family engagements." Big-wave rider Ken Bradshaw observes that "the crowds on the beach may have increased" during the last half-century, "but the number of guys in the water on a big day has stayed about the same." Similarly, although their numbers escalated during the late 1990s, few women venture into big surf. Among the better-known exceptions are Linda Benson, Betty Depolito, Maria Souza, Layne Beachley, and Sarah Gerhardt. Referring to Waimea Bay, Bradshaw notes that the only time crowds appear is when the waves break under 5.4 meters:

> That's when guys who want to say that they've surfed Waimea go out. They sit in the bowl area for a 15ft wave and end up in everyone's way when a set comes through. At 18–20ft, the second reef starts to pump and the crowd splits up. You get maybe 20 guys hustling for it. The first set that hits 25ft, that's it. You're suddenly down to six or eight guys. It's that first big dark one that clears it out real fast. (Noll and Gabbard 1989, 146–147)

Although most explanations of the contemporary surge in extreme sports focus on individual temperaments and the apparent psychological need for some people to find meaning by risking their lives, Bradshaw's comments alert us to sociological factors.

Big-wave riders are surfing's warrior caste; riding giant waves bestows the greatest prestige. Indeed, regardless of the era and performance in organized competitions, surfers have always reserved the most prestige for those who show excess courage in big waves. Ancient Hawaiian legends, for example, recount the big-wave riding feats of Kelea, Mamala, Hauailiki, Umi-a-liloa, and Holoua. When the first wave in a set of tsunamis washed Holoua, his house, and all of his belongings out to sea, Holoua pulled a plank from the side of his house. He used it to ride the next wave in the set, at 15 meters, back to the shore.

Prestige is a resource in all sporting cultures, and it is a resource for which competition is intense. Although the primary function of a culture is to build social consensus, this consensus does not eliminate competition for prestige. On the contrary, competitors who continue to compete are the building blocks of cultural groups. Among surfers competition for prestige involves displays of physical prowess and courage in big waves, and it can often lead to extreme situations, as oceanographer and big-wave rider Ricky Grigg has noted. Grigg was a member of the first small group of surfers in the modern era to ride the giant waves on the North Shore of Hawaii's Oahu, and he recalls the competitive spirit and behavior that it evoked: "You got damn scared at times. You got so scared you needed each other to do what you were doing. I've been real scared at Waimea... I've taken off on waves at Waimea that I probably wouldn't have, had [my peers] not been watching" (Noll and Gabbard 1989, 146).

Although all surfers intrinsically know that, in the words of surf-film cinematographer Bruce Brown, "It takes a lot of guts to go out there when the waves are breaking bigger than a house," many of the dangers are not immediately apparent, especially from the shore. For example, nearly all big rideable waves break on reefs, the depth of which is not always easy to decipher. Former world champion Nat Young describes the acute sense of alertness and skill needed to ride waves that break on shallow coral reefs. The surfer must always focus well ahead looking for the dreaded "hidden bowl" marking shallower water: "Sometimes it's a boil in the face of the wave, at others there's no sign at all, the wave just sucks out, revealing dry reef. [B]ut one thing is for sure, on every wave I know the bowl is lying there waiting to rip my head off if my timing isn't absolutely perfect. It's a fine line: a heavy wipeout or a perfect backdoor tube" (Young 1998, 395).

Deep holes formed by coral polyps also pose dangers, as skilled waterman and pioneer big-wave rider José Angel can testify. Surfing in 4.5-meter surf at the famed Pipeline, Hawaii, in 1967 Angel wiped out and was "blasted" into a pitch-black vertical cavern with an overhanging lip. Disoriented, he searched in vain for the exit. Angel escaped only when a subsequent wave broke particularly hard on the reef, and the release of energy literally ejected him from a potential coral coffin.

Being caught in the impact zone of a big breaking wave and being churned by its turbulence like a ragdoll in a washing machine are no less hazardous than being pitched into a serrated coral head. Big-wave rider Greg Noll compares entanglement in a collapsing 7.6-meter wall of water with "going off Niagara Falls without the barrel." He estimates the chances of drowning at "about 80 percent." After wiping out at Maverick's in 1994, Jay Moriarty spoke of having his "skin ripped from my bones." However, Moriarty also considered himself fortunate: "Luckily the force of the wave pushed me so deep that I struck the reef and realized which way was up. Otherwise I don't think I would have made it

A drop-knee bodyboarder in a tropical barrel in Puerto Escondido, Mexico. Source: istock/Ian McDonnell.

to the surface to get a suck of air before the next wave hit" (Warshaw 2000, 14–15).

Briece Taerea was not so fortunate. Confronted by a 7.6-meter wall of water at Teahupoo in April 2000, he tried to push through its face. However, the wave at the world's most challenging and dangerous reef was too thick. It sucked him backward and rammed him into the marine floor, breaking his neck and back. Taerea died two days later.

Tow-in Surfing

No matter how experienced, all surfers must deal with "closeout sets"—waves that break just in front of a surfer paddling toward the takeoff zone. Surfers commonly face this hazard at the conclusion of a ride, especially if they ride a "smaller" wave early in a set. For Brock Little, who established his credentials as a big-wave rider as a teenager, the turbulence created by closeout sets at Waimea invokes genuine fear: "When I kick out on a wave and the one behind closes out, that doesn't *really* scare me—one wave it's cool, but when it's a full-on powerful set, six or seven waves on top of your head and the rip takes you anywhere, that's the scariest" (Long 1999, 83–85).

More recently the dimensions of big-wave riding have been radically redefined. Using finely tuned jet skis, devotees are towing each other, like water skiers, into ocean waves that produce 12-, 15-, and even 18-meter faces. In addition to narrow surfboards and cushioned straps for riders' feet, tow-in equipment includes a battery of safety equipment from neck braces to hospital-grade oxygen.

In the quest for prestige and honor, tow-in surfing has sparked intense debate. Critics call tow-in surfers "phonies" and label the activity "cheating." They charge that without a "takeoff and drop" the tow-in brigade evades the most dangerous part of surfing. Former world champion Sunny Garcia laments that surfers "who have never even paddled into a 10ft wave let alone a 20ft wave are now on 50ft and 60ft waves. Every average Joe who can stand up on a board can get towed into a really big wave and claim to be a big-wave surfer ... but I would say about 50 to 75 per cent ... are just kooks" (Bradley 2005). Laird Hamilton, the undisputed king of tow-in surfing, disagrees. Towing in, he says, equates to "high performance and efficiency." It allows surfers to get deeper into the tube (the cylinder formed between the wall of the wave and its spitting lip), and foot straps enable them to "do a bunch of slick stuff." Moreover, towing allows surfers to "ride the wave twice as far and be back to catch another wave" quickly. Thus, it is "totally superior" with respect to both physical exertion and the actual time spent riding.

Towing-in has, however, changed the nature of relationships between surfers by introducing support teams and teamwork. Traditionally surfers emphasized their individuality and relied totally on their own skills. They never ex-

---

Surviving a Wipe-out

In the middle of the ocean, with waves crashing overhead, it is important to be conscious of the dangers, and how to avoid them.

- When falling try to put some distance between you and the board so it doesn't hit you.
- Take a good breath before you hit the water—you could be under for some time.
- As you go under curl up your body and use your arms to protect your head and face as you may get hit by the board, or collide with rocks, coral, sharks teeth or other solid stuff. Exhaling slightly can help prevent the water (at high pressure) from entering your nostrils. It's probably a good idea to keep your mouth shut and teeth clenched

as this will prevent you from cutting your tongue and if your head or jaw takes a big klonk.

- Keep you[r] eyes closed initially, but it might be useful to open them when things calm a bit so you know which direction to swim up to the surface.
- When surfacing quickly grab your leash, find your surfboard and if the surf is crashing get the hell out of there!
- If you are injured or need assistance signal for help immediately and **stay with your surfboard!**

Source: http://www.doctordanger.com/surfing/surfingTips SurviveWipeout.html

pected anyone to look after their interests. Indeed, when Mark Foo drowned after wiping out on a relatively small 5.4-meter wave at Maverick's, his body floated for two hours before being discovered, despite the fact that a photographer captured his last wave and wipeout on film. Of course, even if a surfer is in trouble, peers are not necessarily in a position to help. Close friend and Makaha lifeguard Richard "Buffalo" Keaulana tracked Noll's movements in the water after he wiped out in 7.6-meter surf in 1969. "Good ting you wen make 'em Brudda," Keaulana told Noll as he crawled out of the water, "'cause no way I was comin' in afta you. I was jus goin' wave goodbye and say 'Alooo-ha'" (Noll and Gabbard 1989, 146–147). By contrast, assistance is a critical ingredient of tow-in surfing. Hawaiian surfer Gerry Lopez describes the impact zone at the popular tow-in location of Peahi, Hawaii, as "nauseating." "Taking a hit out there," he says, "could mean dismemberment." In short, the survival of surfers trapped in the impact zone at Peahi depends on their partners driving through on jet skis—risking their own lives and equipment—to collect them. However, even when partners are present, events can go wrong. Michael Willis was about to be collected in the face of a monster wave when his partner stalled the jet ski. Somehow the tow rope, which was drifting in the water, wrapped around Willis's right leg. The wave crashed over the driver and Willis and dragged the latter, now attached to the ski, some 400 meters. As the wave dragged Willis and the ski, the rope progressively tightened and cut deeper into his leg muscle. Willis was lucky; the injury confined him to crutches for just two weeks.

Towing-in has expanded the boundaries of extreme surfing, allowing surfers to circumvent the physical forces that prevent them from paddling into waves higher than 9 meters. (At this height the water traveling up the face of the wave moves faster than surfers can paddle.) However, as the critics of towing-in remind, the concept of extreme is also deeply rooted in the culture of surfing and the surfer's quest for prestige.

Douglas Booth

Further Reading

Blakey, A., Dart, W., & Ridgway, N. (1995, October). 25 heavies. *Tracks*, 67–81.

Booth, D. (2001). *Beach cultures: Sun, sand and surf in Australia*. London: Frank Cass.

Bradley, G. (2005, October 25). Surf sessions show off Sunny's side of life. *New Zealand Herald*, p. D13.

Carroll, N. (1997, December 6). Yikes! Good weekend [Supplement]. *Sydney Morning Herald*, pp. 23–27.

Finney, B., & Houston, J. (1996). *Surfing: A history of the ancient Hawaiian sport*. Rohnert Park, CA: Pomegranate Artbooks.

Foo, M. (1991). Waimea Bay. In N. Carroll (Ed.), *The next wave: A survey of world surfing* (pp. 144–145). Sydney, Australia: Angus & Robertson.

Grigg, R. (1998). *Big surf, deep dives and the islands*. Honolulu, HI: Editions Limited.

Grissim, J. (1982). *Pure stoke*. New York: HarperColophon Books.

Hollinger, K. (1975, August/September). An alternative viewpoint. *Surfer*, 38–40.

Irwin, J. (1973). Surfing: The natural history of an urban scene. *Urban Life and Culture*, 2(2), 131–160.

Jarratt, P. (1997). *Mr. Sunset: The Jeff Hakman story*. London: Gen X Publishing.

Jenkins, B. (1997). Laird Hamilton: 20th century man. *The Australian Surfer's Journal*, 1(1), 84–121.

Jenkins, B. (1999). *North Shore chronicles: Big wave surfing in Hawaii* (2nd ed.). Berkeley, CA: Frog.

Kampion, D. (1997). *Stoked: A history of surf culture*. Los Angeles: General Publishing.

Kirsop, K. (1991). Sunset Beach. In N. Carroll (Ed.), *The next wave: A survey of world surfing* (pp. 130–131). Sydney, Australia: Angus & Robertson.

Long, B. (1999). *The big drop*. Helena, Montana: Falcon.

Lyon, C., & Lyon, L. (1997). *Jaws Maui*. Maui, HI: Peter Cannon.

Noll, G., & Gabbard, A. (1989). *Da Bull: Life over the edge*. Berkeley, CA: North Atlantic Books.

O'Keefe, J. (1999, Winter). Surfers of the new millennium. *The Australian Surfer's Journal*, 42–59.

Renneker, M., Star, K., & Booth, G. (1993). *Sick surfers ask the surf docs & Dr. Geoff*. Palo Alto, CA: Bull Publishing.

Warshaw, M. (2000). *Maverick's: The story of big-wave surfing*. San Francisco: Chronicle Books.

Wolf, D. (2000). *Sleeping in the shorebreak and other hairy surfing stories*. Manhattan Beach, CA: Waverider Publications.

Young, N. (1998). *Nat's Nat and that's that*. Angourie, Australia: Nymboida Press.

Tenzing Norgay

See Hillary, Sir Edmund and Tenzing Norgay

Triathlon

In a triathlon athletes compete sequentially in three events. The Olympic distance triathlon includes a 1,500-meter swim race, a 40-kilometer bike race, and a 10-kilometer foot race, but triathlons may include events that have a range of other distances, with anything from a 50-meter to a many-kilometer swim distance and similar variations over the other two events. Triathlons may be held informally over much shorter or much longer distances, in different order of events, or include other individual sports, such as kayaking, in-line skating, skiing, or mountain biking. Despite the mainstream status that the triathlon occupies in many communities today, both the original concept and certain contemporary variants of the triathlon make it an extreme sport.

The first triathlon was staged in 1974. Organized by the San Diego Track Club, the triathlon presented a challenge for those athletes who had already conquered the 42-kilometer marathon road running event and who sought to extend their limits of physical exertion. This triathlon took place during the height of the fitness and running boom that made many previously nonathletic people realize that they could accomplish feats thought to be on the extreme end of the human potential. Completing a marathon, which at least in legend ended in the death of Pheidippides, the Greek messenger, was celebrated not only as evidence of competitive sporting ability, but also as a personal victory and an individual fulfillment: an epiphany. With the multiplication of marathons, joggers and runners flocked to the starting lines; the feat of finishing paled by its banality. The triathlon logically replaced for many the challenge previously presented by early road running.

Although the first triathlon in San Diego's Mission Bay may have consisted of only a 6-mile (9.6 kilometers) foot race, a 5-mile (8 kilometers) bike race, and a 500-yard (457 meters) swim race, rapidly the idea of making the triathlon more testing led to longer triathlons and greater challenges. John Collins, a U.S. naval officer posted in Hawaii who had participated in the inaugural Mission Bay triathlon, launched the first Ironman triathlon in 1978: a 2.4-mile (3.8 kilometers) swim race, a 115-mile (185 kilometers) bike race, and a 26-mile (41 kilometers) foot race around Oahu Island. At the time, the Waikiki Swimmers and the Mid-Pacific Road Runners were engaged in a debate about whose club members were the fittest sportspeople. In an attempt to settle the debate, Collins merged three events that were considered the pinnacle of endurance contests on the island—the Waikiki Rough Water Swim, the Around Oahu bike race, and the Honolulu Marathon. The resulting event, which later moved from Oahu to Hawaii Island, is the Ironman Triathlon, a 3.8-kilometer swim race, a 180-kilometer bike race, and a 42.2-kilometer foot race.

For some athletes even the Ironman did not present enough challenge. The first *double* Ironman was held in 1985 in Huntsville, Alabama, and a *triple* Ironman was held at Fontanil, France, in 1988. These long races are referred to as "ultratriathlons" and may be two times, three times, or even ten times the length of the Ironman Triathlon. The decatriathlon, held in Monterrey, Mexico, features a 38-kilometer swim race, an 1,800-kilometer bike race, and a 422-kilometer foot race. Since the first event in 1985, almost two thousand athletes have participated in events ranging from the ultratriathlon (7.6-kilometer swim race, 360-kilometer bike race, and 84.4-kilometer foot race) to the double-deca ultratriathlon, which features a 76-kilometer swim race, a 3,600-kilometer bike race, and an 844-kilometer foot race. The International Ultra-Triathlon Association (IUTA), established by ultratriathlon race organizers and participants in 1995 to ensure the safety and standards of the contests, has fifteen events on its annual program, all exceeding the Ironman distance by multiples of two to twenty. The organization has no more than sixty members and elects a president, a vice president, and a treasurer, for a four-year term. The IUTA is funded by subscriptions from the race organizers.

Governing Bodies

Whereas the early triathlons may have been spontaneously organized fun events, staged without codes, standards, or expectations, some forms of the sport were institutionalized in a relatively short time. By 1988 the International Olympic Committee (IOC) convened a meeting of national triathlon federations in Stockholm to establish a working committee on triathlon. This meeting led to the first Congress of the International Triathlon Union (ITU) the following year

Competitors in a surf
Iron Man race enter the
water at full pace. Source:
istock/Flavia Bottazzini.

in Avignon, France. The first world triathlon championships were organized by the ITU in August of the same year. Mark Allen from the United States and Erin Baker of New Zealand won the elite men's and women's events. World championships have been held every year since, and the triathlon held its Olympic debut in 2000 at Sydney, Australia, one of the strongest competing countries in the sport, with numerous world championship teams and individuals. Australia was the only country to host more than three world championships in the first eleven years of the ITU's existence.

The Ironman, however, does not fall under the ITU umbrella. Well before creation of the ITU, the organizers of the Ironman had already established rules, qualifying races, and performance standards. Under the eye of Collins's successor, Valerie Silk, the Ironman had grown into an international event with the prestige of a world championship label. The notion of "ownership" is important in the history and current status of the Ironman. Its institutionalization was the result of commercially driven interests. Today the Ironman "belongs" to the World Triathlon Corporation (WTC), and its name is a registered trademark. Ironman competitions around the world are licensed by the WTC; they operate outside of the ITU's sanctions, rules, and scrutiny. The ITU and WTC have engaged in regular legal and political confrontations over the legitimacy of the world

championship title and over the commercial rights to the triathlon. Individual triathletes, however, participate, without penalty, in both WTC and ITU events; however, the ITU has regularly threatened to ban those athletes who compete in WTC events from the ITU world cup or world championship events. Although this threat has been vociferously expressed by ITU president Les McDonald, he has not had the clout to enact it. The athletes' capital has been too great to enable their exclusion.

The Event

Although the triathlon was initially an improvised competition, it is now highly codified, with a specific order of events, and strictly enforced regulations about each event of the race and the transitions between events. Although there has been much experimentation with the order of events, in ITU-sanctioned triathlons, the swim race comes first, followed by the bike race and then the foot race. Swimmers complete their designated course—usually in open water and sometimes in surf—and then run up the beach to the transition area. In the transition area they shed their wetsuits, don their bicycle helmets, and take their bikes, which were set up prior to the start, usually hanging by the seat or the handlebars on a specially designed rack. They cannot take their bikes off the racks prior to fastening their helmets, nor may they mount their bikes before they leave the transition area. Once outside of the transition area, they mount their bikes, wiggle their feet into specialized cycling shoes that are fastened onto the pedals, and proceed to the bike segment.

The bike segment may or may not allow drafting. *Drafting* refers to riding in the slipstream of the leading competitor or competitors in a group of cyclists. Most elite-level triathlon competitions allow drafting because enforcing drafting rules is difficult and also, perhaps, because it creates a more television-friendly race, with groups of competitors to follow, ostentatiously engaged in fierce competition, rather than individual cyclists spread out in isolation over a long stretch of road. However, much debate exists about whether draft-legal racing is good for the sport. Drafting provides a distinct advantage to the cyclist who is in the slipstream and enables him or her to exert far less energy than the cyclist who is leading. As a result, the drafter will arrive at the final leg of the triathlon fresher and able to run faster. Many triathlon enthusiasts believe that drafting turns the triathlon into a "runner's race," where less-adept cyclists benefit from the practice and win with superior running ability. A draft-free race requires participants to cycle on their own and in theory, at least, reflects ability across all three subspecialties. The Athens 2004 Olympics resolved the problems of transforming a draft-legal event into a runner's race by a cycling course that was sufficiently arduous to prevent triathletes from "catching a wheel" unless they were expert cyclists in their own right. All elite-level ITU triathlon races allow drafting.

In many draft-free races, drafting is nonetheless the rule, and "draft busters" on motorcycles will attempt to catch and penalize triathletes who are closer than 5 meters from the back wheel of the bike in front of them or less than 2 meters from a bike on either side. Disciplinary actions for triathletes caught drafting in a draft-free race can range from time penalties to disqualification; often, however, the culprits are not caught and gain a strategic advantage over the nondrafters in the field.

At the conclusion of the race, the triathletes dismount their bikes and enter the transition area again. There they "rack" their bikes or return them to the special support structures, remove their helmets, exchange cycle shoes for running shoes, and take off for the foot race. Participants typically describe the unbearable feeling of heavy legs after cycling as being one of the most difficult obstacles to completing a triathlon. World-leading triathletes may nonethe-less run times that challenge those of national-caliber road runners despite the fatigue of the previous two events.

One of the particularities of the ITU triathlon movement is that participants are placed either in an elite, or open, class or in age-group categories, even in official championship events. At the founding meeting of the ITU in 1989, strong representations by the United States, Canada, Great Britain, Australia, and New Zealand countered European opposition and established the inclusion of age-group representation in the world championships. Although countries may send a certain number of elite triathletes to compete in the world championships, they are also entitled to send up to twelve athletes in each five-year age bracket from sixteen to seventy and beyond. This entitlement opens the experience of international competition, with the accompanying pomp and circumstance, to a wide range of participants. The athletes and the countries they represent take these events seriously and vie for selection competitively. The world championship events include a parade of nations and a closing ceremony, as do other multinational championships. Age-group racing is normally draft free, whereas elite racing is more likely to allow drafting.

Training

Part of the extreme nature of the triathlon is the sheer volume of training that even recreational triathletes undertake. Training for the triathlon is more time consuming than for most other sports. A serious amateur triathlete may train twenty-five hours a week, whereas an Ironman triathlete can train upward of forty hours a week. Training typically involves two- and sometimes three-a-day workouts. A triathlete is likely to spend most of the week practicing the individual sports on their own, swimming, for example, in the morning and running or cycling in the afternoon. Sometimes, however, stacked practice is vital, incorporating at least two of the sports in combined practice, with a composite session of swimming and cycling, cycling and running, or swimming and running. These sessions are often technically difficult and time consuming but invaluable in training the triathlete for race conditions.

The triathlete will also practice transitions, or the skill of changing sports and equipment. Notably, the transition from swimming to cycling is important to master. Shedding the wetsuit and getting on the bike in a speedy manner are vital for the triathlete, particularly in a drafting race. A slow transition can lead the triathlete to miss a pack of cyclists

Triathlon Training

The surreal hills
shoulder sky
purple
beyond this grey day
brooding
and a lone runner
hunches sky
to his earthbound
body
muscles tight
wound and holding
at the 10 k turn.

Robin McConnell

whose numbers offer a much better drafting opportunity and a certain advantage to cycling in isolation. The transition from the bike race to the foot race is also strategically important because it can convey a needed advantage at a psychologically and physiologically draining point in the race.

Down the Road

The triathlon has reached an important point in its history. The International Olympic Committee consolidated the institutionalization of the short version of the race by not only including it in the Sydney 2000 Olympic Games, but also by staging it in the prominent position of the first Olympic event of the millennium, bringing the triathlon firmly into the public eye. In countries such as New Zealand, which claimed the gold and silver medals in the triathlon at the Athens 2004 Games, a children's triathlon series brings out fields of up to two thousand children in all of New Zealand's major cities. However, the sheen of the Olympic medal with respect to its ability to stimulate interest in the sport by the community is by no means assured for eternity because its inclusion in the Games is up for review, as is that of other new sports.

The triathlon has evolved from an improvised non-specialist event to a highly codified, institutionalized, and commodified event. The consequences of this evolution will influence the future of the event. On one hand, the triathlon is recognized by many institutions, both public and private, as worthy of support. Substantial amounts of money are now available in many countries for the promotion of the sport and the development of athletes. The professional triathlon tour provides a wide range of triathletes with their living. The visibility of the triathlon makes the triathlete an attractive billboard for the corporate world; cameras, wetsuits, automobiles, nutritional supplements, and breakfast cereals are among the sponsors of triathletes and triathlon events. Triathletes spend a great deal of money on their sporting gear because they require equipment for three sports, rather than for just one. Many triathletes are "gadget freaks," keen to acquire the newest and the most enticing pedals, goggles, and racing shoes. Because of the age-group feature, many older triathletes, with larger disposable incomes than the typical teenager or young adult, will acquire goods that bicycle, running shoe, and swimwear manufacturers are delighted to produce and promote.

On the other hand, wrangling between the ITU and the professional athletes' union underlines the fact that the codification of the sport may also come at a cost. Athletes have complained that the governing body of the sport is not attuned to their needs but rather is concerned with impressing the IOC and corporate sponsors at the expense of the athletes.

Furthermore, the bickering between the WTC and the ITU often resembles a turf war. Recent legal action by the WTC claimed that the ITU had attempted to monopolize the commercial side of the sport. However, although accusing the ITU of using its gatekeeper role in the Olympics to benefit its commercial interests, the WTC nonetheless is a commercial enterprise that makes its own profit from "ownership" of the Ironman Triathlon. Entry to the event is strictly regulated and expensive. An event that started as an endurance contest between friendly rivals is now an article for consumption, ostensibly offered as the greatest physical challenge available. The Ironman is more than just an event, however, with producers of a wide range of objects paying royalties to the WTC in order to gain access to the Ironman tag. From nutritional supplements to watches, breakfast cereals, clothing, wetsuits, and video games, Ironman branding is prominent among products geared to convey the image of unfaltering strength and endurance. Entry into an Ironman event may cost as much as four hundred dollars.

The ITU has recently started a movement to try to reappropriate the longer distance events, which WTC has dominated by declaring itself their governing body, organizing its own series of events called the "long distance world tour" and passing a resolution at the ITU World Congress in 2005 that ITU member federations (national governing bodies) would not sanction any event attached to the WTC. The rationale for this resolution was that the World Triathlon Corporation did not recognize the ITU as the world governing body for triathlon, was developing property that was in conflict with ITU property (e.g., long- and Olympic-distance world championships, with their own set of rules), was a profit-driven organization, and did not follow World Anti-Doping Agency (WADA) rules.

The resolution was unlikely to stand up to legal scrutiny, should the WTC decide to take the matter further. A previous agreement in 1998 between the two organizations stipulated that the "ITU shall not in any way influence nor adopt any rule or policy, whether written or unwritten, prohibiting the issuance of a sanction by any member national federation to World Triathlon Corporation or any of its Ironman races" (Elford 2005). And indeed the WTC led the ITU to settle out of court, revoking the resolution.

It is difficult to know how the sport will evolve. It is at a juncture where institutional recognition may carry away the spontaneous challenge that triathlon initially offered its participants. In both New Zealand and Australia, where triathlon is a highly visible sport, large numbers of triath-letes are loathe to join clubs or pay dues to national governing bodies. For them the triathlon is a lifestyle recreational sport; they are not concerned with rules, sanctioning is a burden, and championships are not a focus. Although institutionalization intends to promote the sport in order to enhance participation, the very fact of structuring the triathlon experience may be at the heart of its demise. Adventure sport, multisport and off-road running, and cycling events remain attractive alternatives for lifestyle triathletes. Furthermore, the very demystification that caused marathoners to head off toward greater challenges may be a similar source of disenchantment for triathletes. Now that everyone can "have a go," the triathlon may lose some of its appeal.

Annemarie Jutel

Further Reading

Elford, C. (2005). WTC-ITU agreement appears to void recent ITU resolution. *Triathlete*. Retrieved July 21, 2006, from http://www.triathlete mag.com/story.cfm?story_id=10910&pageID=1728

International Triathlon Union. (2006). Retrieved July 13, 2006, from www.triathlon.org

International Ultra Triathlon Association. (n.d). Retrieved July 14, 2006, from www.iuta.com

Ironman Series. (2006). World Triathlon Corporation. Retrieved July 13, 2006, from www.ironman.com

Ultimate Fighting

U ltimate fighting is a genre of combat sport that generally involves two competitors who use a combination of ground-based wrestling and jujitsu as well as standup striking skills to knock out or submit their opponent. This genre, although increasingly popular in the United States, Japan, the United Kingdom, and Australia, is often mired in controversy because of the public perception of extreme violence and brutality, which led U.S. Senator John McCain to brand the sport "human cockfighting." Although many organizations worldwide promote what are known as "mixed martial arts" (MMA) contests, a U.S. organization, the Ultimate Fighting Championship (UFC), perhaps more than any other helped to introduce this extreme sport to the masses.

Ancient Roots

So-called no-holds-barred fighting competitions have been held since at least the seventh century BCE. In ancient Greece the *pankration*, regarded as one of the first "fighting systems" and the precursor of the modern sport of MMA, was a combination of standup striking and ground-based wrestling that employed a number of sophisticated joint locks. *Kato pankration* was added to the thirty-third Olympiad in 648 BCE and was said to have been founded by the mythical hero Theseus, who used a combination of boxing and wrestling to defeat the Minotaur in the Labyrinth.

No gloves or hand wraps were used in the original contests, and the only prohibited actions were eye gouging and biting. Despite the fact that knockouts were common because of the legality of striking and kicking while standing and while both competitors were on the ground, the majority of contests ended when one person choked, strangled, or submitted his adversary with a joint-lock hold. However, the contemporary mixed martial arts and in particular the Ultimate Fighting Championship can trace their more recent lineage to the streets of Brazil.

Brazilian Connection

UFC began in Brazil when Carlos Gracie, the descendent of Scottish immigrants, began teaching a modified version of traditional Japanese jujitsu and adapted it to feature ground-based grappling and efficient submission holds such as chokes and joint locks. The Gracies were a wealthy family who relocated from Scotland to Brazil in the late 1800s and helped to arrange the settlement of Japanese immigrants in Brazil. To show his appreciation for helping to settle his fellow countrymen and women, former Japanese jujitsu champion Mitsuyo Maeda offered to teach Gastão Gracie's eldest son, Carlos, jujitsu. Carlos and his brother Helio are credited with modifying traditional jujitsu to capitalize on leverage rather than strength. Moreover, these modifications were found to be more effective in "free-fighting" contests, dubbed "*vale tudo*," which were often conducted between martial arts academies of various styles. Through a series of promotions and the success of the slightly built Helio, the Gracie name would become synonymous with the hybrid form known as "Brazilian jujitsu" (BJJ).

By the late 1980s, having moved to the United States, Helio's son Rorion, in an attempt to expand and market the Gracie fighting system, issued a series of challenges in martial arts magazines. In an article in a 1989 issue of *Playboy* entitled, "Bad," he offered money to any challenger who could beat one of his brothers in a no-rules fight. Shrewdly, Rorion Gracie began videotaping these fights, which often pitted various martial arts disciplines against Gracie jujitsu. Rorion Gracie marketed the videotapes, entitled *Gracies in Action*, which demonstrated the superiority of the Gracie system to the flashy-yet-ineffective martial arts styles that were popular in the United States at that time.

Ultimate Fighting Championship Is Born

Rorion Gracie had an idea to promote the Gracie style of jujitsu in the United States modeled after the anything-goes, style-versus-style *vale tudo* contests popular in Brazil since the 1950s. His idea evolved into the Ultimate Fighting Championship, an organization that held its inaugural contest in Denver, Colorado, in 1993. Billed as a battle of various fighting styles, including karate, kickboxing, judo, standup striking, wrestling, and jujitsu, the contest was ultimately a vehicle to showcase the Gracie system of fighting. The early UFC promotion used the catch phrase, "There are no rules!" to differentiate it from boxing, full-contact karate, and other "mainstream" combat sports of the day. Although this marketing ploy initially helped to generate interest and eventually pay-per-view (PPV) showings that would rival

Ultimate Fighting Championship Fouls

The list of fouls in Ultimate Fighting bouts are listed below. Committing any of these fouls can result in lost points, and other penalties.

Fouls

1. Butting with the head.
2. Eye gouging of any kind.
3. Biting.
4. Hair pulling.
5. Fish hooking.
6. Groin attacks of any kind.
7. Putting a finger into any orifice or into any cut or laceration on an opponent.
8. Small joint manipulation.
9. Striking to the spine or the back of the head.
10. Striking downward using the point of the elbow.
11. Throat strikes of any kind, including, without limitation, grabbing the trachea.
12. Clawing, pinching or twisting the flesh.
13. Grabbing the clavicle.
14. Kicking the head of a grounded opponent.
15. Kneeing the head of a grounded opponent.
16. Stomping a grounded opponent.
17. Kicking to the kidney with the heel.
18. Spiking an opponent to the canvas on his head or neck.
19. Throwing an opponent out of the ring or fenced area.
20. Holding the shorts or gloves of an opponent.
21. Spitting at an opponent.
22. Engaging in an unsportsmanlike conduct that causes an injury to an opponent.
23. Holding the ropes or the fence.
24. Using abusive language in the ring or fenced area.
25. Attacking an opponent on or during the break.
26. Attacking an opponent who is under the care of the referee.
27. Attacking an opponent after the bell has sounded the end of the period of unarmed combat.
28. Flagrantly disregarding the instructions of the referee.
29. Timidity, including, without limitation, avoiding contact with an opponent, intentionally or consistently dropping the mouthpiece or faking an injury.
30. Interference by the corner.
31. Throwing in the towel during competition.

Source: Ultimate Fighting Championship. Retrieved Feb. 8, 2007 from http://www.ufc.com/index.cfm?fa=LearnUFC.Rules

---

those of boxing and professional wrestling in the mid-1990s, the brand was marked as a brutal oddity.

With the growing success of videotape sales and the increasing numbers of students whom Rorion Gracie was teaching in his converted California garage, interest picked up after the publication of the *Playboy* article. In fact, with the success of the "Gracie Challenge" Rorion Gracie was able to open a new school in Torrance, California. The *Playboy* article intrigued Art Davie, an advertising agency employee, and he tracked down Rorion Gracie at his new school to pitch a promotion idea. The meeting resulted in Davie quitting his job at the advertising agency and going to work for the Gracies to broker a deal that would capitalize on the growing interest in BJJ. The idea of putting on a tournament showcasing the superiority of Gracie jujitsu suited Rorion Gracie's larger plan of promoting Gracie academies throughout the United States. Davie began shopping the idea for a tournament tentatively called the "War of the Worlds" with little success until he met with executives from Semaphore Entertainment Group (SEG). Despite limited knowledge of martial arts, president and *King Biscuit Flour Hour*–creator Bob Meyrowitz trusted his staff and approved the project because SEG had been looking for a new pay-per-view event.

The inaugural UFC contest was notable for its lack of professional presentation. Although the presentation featured as commentators NFL star Jim Brown, karate champion Bill "Superfoot" Wallace, and former kickboxing champion Kathy Long, their lack of familiarity with this novel contest left them struggling to make sense of what they saw. The rules for the first UFC were simple: no biting and no eye gouging. There were no weight classes, no gloves, no time limits, and no judges. Twenty-six seconds into the first bout, Dutch kickboxing champion Gerard Gordeau had knocked down 185-kilogram sumo champion Teila Tuli and, according to Rosenberg's *Los Angeles Times* account, "sent a tooth flying and blood pouring from his mouth" with a savage kick (Rosenberg 1993, F-1). Although the contest appeared chaotic and barbaric to many outsiders, the matchups were carefully controlled by Gracie and SEG. Because the larger aim of the tournament was to demonstrate the superior fighting technique of the Gracie system, it was important to ensure that Royce Gracie, the smallest competitor in the contest, would be able to showcase his Brazilian jujitsu skills.

Political Backlash

Despite eventual rule changes and the financial success of the UFC, public scrutiny was growing because of the violent nature of the sport. U.S. Senator John McCain of Arizona, then chairman of the Senate Commerce Committee, began to exert pressure on cable operators who broadcast the UFC events. Because the sport was constantly mired in controversy, especially after the ban of MMA competitions in New York State, the rationale for cable operators to end the broadcasts seemed, on the surface, quite clear. Indeed, although McCain's publicly stated reasons for pressuring the major PPV providers revolved around violence, as showcased in a debate on no-holds-barred fighting on the *Larry King Live* show in 1995, McCain, himself a vocal supporter of boxing, a major competitor of the UFC, had close family ties to Anheuser-Busch, one of the largest sponsors of boxing in the United States.

Prior to the cancellation, the UFC had generated an estimated 300,000 PPV sales on its more successful broadcasts, and the UFC alone represented approximately 10 percent of all PPV broadcasts. After the McCain-led "boycott," however, the events were available only on the up-and-coming satellite provider DirecTV, and the PPV sales dwindled to a paltry twenty-five thousand. In short, the financial consequences of the UFC being pulled off the air by the major cable pay-per-view operators, In-Demand

and then Viewer's Choice, less than two years after the Larry King broadcast were devastating. In what could be deemed a desperate move, during the 27 July 1997 broadcast of UFC 14, "Showdown," the commentators thanked the fans who stayed with them but urged others to contact their local cable providers in an attempt to get the UFC back on cable TV.

Transitioning into the Mainstream

In many ways the UFC was reborn in 2001 when Zuffa Sports Entertainment bought the struggling promotion. The new UFC owners had big plans to elevate the promotion in the eyes of the public, and they would implement a sophisticated strategy to reposition the brand as a legitimate sporting event. The new owners were Frank and Lorenzo Fertitta, Las Vegas casino owners who had ties to the Nevada State Athletic Commission. Lorenzo, in fact, had served on the commission since 1996 and in 1999 was invited at the request of SEG to attend UFC 21 in Iowa. He was impressed with the professionalism and athleticism that competitors displayed. Upon his resigning from the Nevada State Athletic Commission, the idea to buy out the UFC began to emerge. The Fertitta brothers—along with long-time friend Dana White, who was appointed president, began to plot how to promote the sport. The new business, named "Zuffa" (Italian for "to scrap" or "to fight"), set out on a promotional campaign to educate state athletic commissioners, television cable companies, and the public. By highlighting rule changes—many of which had been implemented by the end of SEG's ownership—including the introduction of rounds, mandatory gloves, weight classes, and the prohibition of head-butting, the UFC hoped to reposition itself as a legitimate sport. The first Zuffa-promoted event took place at the Trump Taj Mahal casino in Atlantic City, New Jersey, on 23 February 1999. Although the event was not broadcast on PPV, that milestone would occur less than a year after Zuffa's purchase.

In the most important business move since Zuffa's UFC buyout, the UFC secured a deal with the Spike TV network in 2004. Spike purchased the rights to air a Zuffa-produced reality-television show, *The Ultimate Fighter* (*TUF*), which featured two teams of relatively unknown fighters vying for a chance to win a UFC contract. The contestants lived in a lavish house and trained under two of the UFC's marquee fighters, Chuck Liddell and Randy Couture. The show not only generated a record number of viewers, but also served as a season-long buildup for the anticipated rematch of Couture and Liddell. Not only was the show a hit for Spike TV (winning the coveted male eighteen-to-thirty-five-year-old audience), but also the fact that an MMA show of any type was available on cable was a coup for the UFC. In five years the brand had repositioned itself through the familiar genre of reality television.

Future of Ultimate Fighting

The popularity of MMA contests is perhaps at an all-time high, as demonstrated by a record-breaking attendance of 18,265 on 10 March 2006 at California's first officially sanctioned MMA event in San Jose. Moreover, the UFC's move toward recognition as a "valid" sport was most recently aided by the hiring of long-time Nevada state athletic commissioner Mark Rattner. In a calculated move, signing Rattner, who served with Lorenzo Fertitta on the Nevada athletic commission, gave the UFC a degree of insider credibility and provided the respected voice that would be necessary to broker sanctioning in the states that currently refuse to allow MMA and UFC contests. The Ultimate Fighting Championship remains on the margins of popular U.S. sporting practices, however, and more often than not the UFC is unglamorously characterized as "barbaric" and "human cockfighting" despite the company's attempts to frame its product as the "new and safer boxing" and the "sport of the future."

Matthew A. Masucci

See also Agon Motif; Gladiator Competitions; *Pankration*; Professional Wrestling

Further Reading

Douthit, R. (Executive Producer). (1995, December 6). *Larry King live* [Television broadcast]. New York: Cable News Network.

Gentry, C. (2005). *No holds barred: Ultimate fighting and the martial arts revolution*. Preston, UK: Milo Books.

Greenhalgh, J. (Producer), & Hyams, J. (Director). (2003). *The smashing machine: The life and times of extreme fighter Mark Kerr* [Motion picture]. New York: Docudrama.

Krauss, E., & Aita, B. (2002). *Brawl: A behind-the-scenes look at mixed martial arts competition*. Toronto, Canada: ECW Press.

Poliakoff, M. (1987). *Combat sports in the ancient world: Competition, violence, and culture*. New Haven, CT: Yale University Press.

Rosenberg, H. (1993, November 15). "Ultimate" fight lives up to name. *Los Angeles Times*, p. F-1.

Shamrock, K., & Hanner, R. (1998). *Inside the lion's den: The life and submission fighting system of Ken Shamrock*. North Clarendon, VT: Tuttle Publishing.

Shamrock, K., & Krauss, E. (2005). *Beyond the lion's den: The life, the fights, the techniques*. North Clarendon, VT: Tuttle Publishing.

Ultramarathon

Ultramarathons are footraces that exceed the standard marathon distance of 42.2 kilometers. Ultramarathons are run on indoor/outdoor tracks, in remote mountains, urban environments, Arctic regions, and deserts and can last for months. The Self-Trancendence 3,100 Mile Ultramarathon is a formidable and extreme event involving 3,100 miles of running on foot continuously for two months in an urban environment, in all types of weather conditions, and through all types of physical and mental ailments imaginable.

The Self-Transcendence 3,100-Mile Ultramarathon, at 4,988 kilometers, is the longest certified footrace in the world. Sponsored by the Sri Chinmoy Marathon Team, it is run in the neighborhood of Jamaica in Queens, New York City. Sri Chinmoy (pronounced "Shree Chin-Moy") was born in 1931 in Bangladesh. He immigrated to Queens in 1964 to work as a philosopher, author, musician, spiritual teacher, and physical fitness guru while establishing spiritual centers in several countries.

A Race Is Born

The predecessor of the race was the Sri Chinmoy 2,700-mile (4,300-kilometer) footrace in 1996. The inaugural Self-Transcendence 3,100-Mile Ultramarathon was run in 1997 and has been run each June–August since on a .5488-mile (.86-kilometer) course around one city block. This distance equates to 5,649 laps. Some runners add thirteen laps to reach 5,000 kilometers (3,105 miles). The time required to finish the race has ranged from 41 days 8 hours 16 minutes as Germany's Madhupran Wolfgang Schwerk, fifty, shattered his own world record in 2006, to 64 days by Suprabha Beckjord, fifty, of Washington, D.C., in 2005. Officially runners must complete the course in less than fifty-one days, but an extension to 60–65 days is occasionally given. The inaugural 2,700-mile race was run in a forty-seven-day time limit.

Race History

Race participation has increased from only two finishers in 1997 to fourteen finishers in 2006. Ed Kelley of California won the 1997 race in 47 days 15 hours. The other finisher was Beckjord, who ran the race in 51 days 2 hours. Beckjord is also the only woman to attempt the race and the only runner to finish the race ten times. In 2006 her time was 60 days 4 hours 35 minutes. She has now run more than 54,000 kilometers around the block in Queens.

In 1998 a Hungarian, Istvan Sipos, beat Ed Kelley; four runners finished the race. Sipos finished in 46 days 17 hours. In 1999 five starters endured intense heat for several weeks. However, the heat did not stop Kelley from claiming his second win with 48 days 12 hours. In 2000 three finishers followed the winner, Finland's Asprihanal Alto, who won with 47 days 13 hours. Alto repeated his win in 2001, again with three other finishers. In 2002 six finishers were led by Schwerk, who set the world record with a time of 42 days 13 hours. Alto finished second but still broke the previous record of 48 days by a few hours. In 2003 Yugoslavia's Namitabha Arsic led seven other runners to the finish. In 2004 Alto won for the third time with a personal best of 46 days 6 hours. Srdjan Stojanovich from Serbia-Montenegro won in 2005 with 46 days 10 hours.

The extreme nature of the race provides an outlet for a small group of motivated, physically adept, and psychologically strong runners. A majority of the runners follow Sri Chinmoy's spiritual teachings. However, one does not have to follow his teachings in order to participate in this or any other Sri Chinmoy–sponsored event.

Spirituality and the 3,100-Mile Ultramarathon

The Self-Transcendence 3,100-Mile Ultramarathon involves a high level of spiritual guidance, fortitude and awareness. Sri Chinmoy is a spiritual guru who practices meditation, vegetarianism and the pursuit of self-transcendence in all aspects of life. Importantly, the Self-Transcendence 3,100-Mile Ultramarathon requires not only physical training and abilities; but a higher, spiritual awakening, as well. The core spirituality of those involved in the Self-Transcendence 3,100-Mile Ultramarathon varies; but many participants are active followers of Sri Chinmoy's teachings. The ultimate spiritual concept for runners in the 3,100-mile ultramarathon, involve the notion of self-transcendence. The role of self-transcendence for the runner is necessary to overcome previous physical or mental barriers. Essentially, self-transcendence is a quality

A trail runner in motion in the Sandia Mountains of central New Mexico. Source: istock.

The Extreme Marathon

In the far North of New Zealand the story is told of the indigenous peoples' Maori chief, Houteawa, and his legendary beach run that is commemorated annually with an international extreme marathon. The story tells of Houteawa's mother asking him to gather some *kumara* (sweet potatoes) for a meal. Houteawa, a descendant of the famed chief Te Ikanui of the Te Aupouri tribe, sought the food nearby but could find none. He then recalled that the enemy tribe, Te Rarawa, had stores of *kumara*. He set out into the enemy territory and eventually stole the food he sought. He was challenged, blocked and chased by the enemy who wanted to capture and enslave him. Houteawa eluded his pursuers and raced down Te Oneroa a Tohe (Ninety Mile Beach) bringing two woven kits of *kumara* to his mother. His amazing run is emulated by runners from various countries who gather in New Zealand to compete in a 60-kilometer ultramarathon race, a 42-kilometer marathon and other races.

Cassie Lynch

that carries runners to the next level of performance by transcending their previous personal achievements.

The Game Is Afoot

The time and distance involved in such a footrace present challenges in obtaining adequate food, water, and rest. All participants are allowed to be on the course from 6 A.M. until midnight. A sleep/rest period is mandatory from midnight to around 6 A.M. Runners are not allowed on the course during that time. Around midnight runners are transported by their crews or Sri Chinmoy staff to nearby apartments for the sleep/rest period. During the day runners are given eighteen hours to "go as they please." This equates to 5.4 kilometers per hour a day for a fifty-one-day finish. Vegetarian meals are provided by the Sri Chinmoy cooking staff three times a day. Runners are also encouraged to bring their own food.

Runners receive snacks and liquids in paper cups as they walk or run around the block. Runners must maintain adequate food intake and normal hydration before, during, and after the race. Proper food and fluid intake is essential for maintenance, performance, and recovery of the body during weeks of running or walking. Consequently, a handler or a crew is essential for the everyday needs of the runners. Each runner must plan a typical day with flexible lap goals, rest breaks, clothing changes, injury assessment and care, sleep breaks, and bathroom breaks and also allow for unforeseen problems. Doctors, physical therapists, acupuncturists, and chiropractors from around the world offer their services to runners for a few days or for the entire race.

A major factor in the race is the summer heat of a concrete, urban environment. Runners do have the luxury of passing under a few trees along the route, but these trees provide only a temporary respite from the heat. Other external hazards include lightning, rain, wind, hail, traffic, and noise. The course surrounds part of a park with a baseball field, a high school, and residential housing with the typical sights and sounds of a New York City neighborhood. Consequently, something is going on almost always to keep the mind alert as long days of running lead to exhaustion.

Planning Is First Step

Running 4,988 kilometers requires months of training, planning, and financial resources. Runners must allow for a two-month leave from their employment. Among the occupations of participants are waiter, woodworker, postal worker, courier, doctor, and gift shop owner. Most participants travel hundreds or thousands of miles to run the race. Runners customarily arrive one or two weeks before the start of the race to buy supplies and familiarize themselves with the area. Runners who apply to run the race are accepted by invitation after staff members review their performances in other multiday running events. Runners accepted in 2006 paid an entrance fee of $1,250.

The only other race of a comparable distance, approximately 3,100 miles, is the Run Across America, which has a longer finishing time of seventy-one days. This race extends from Huntington Beach, California, to New York City. The entry fee was $2,000 in 2004, and each runner spent $8,500–$11,000 on food, clothing, transportation, gear, lodging, shoes, and so forth, making the Run Across America at least two times more expensive than the Self-Transcendence 3,100-Mile Ultramarathon. The Run Across America is not the longest certified race because its running route varies from year to year, depending on weather hazards, road construction, race budget, and other factors.

The cost of food, liquids, clothing, shoes, supplements, and other items also must be factored into planning the Self-Transcendence 3,100-Mile Ultramarathon. Runners typically are equipped with ten to fifteen pairs of shoes, portable music player, hats, vitamins, minerals, supplements, liquids, food, and injury-prevention aids. The biggest expense may be shoes. Runners wear shoes that are up to two sizes larger than normal. A larger shoe accommodates swelling of the feet during the race, caused by an electrolyte imbalance or gravitational edema from long periods of time spent upright on a hard concrete surface. Moreover, shoes succumb to wear on a concrete surface within four to seven days. Again, a runner must plan the entire race to cover every item that may be needed with the aid of the Sri Chinmoy staff and the runner's personal crew.

Injuries

The Self-Transcendence 3,100-Mile Ultramarathon requires a checklist of supplies and strategies to prevent or deal with injuries. A combination of running and walking for up to eighteen hours a day for several weeks puts the human body under a great mechanical, physiological, and psychological stress. Physical ailments include blisters, gastrointestinal problems, chafing, rashes, infection, fever, bloating, edema, shin splints, sore muscles, lethargy, dehydration, hyponatremia, sunburn, heat exhaustion, weight fluctuations, and muscle loss. Runners deal with ailments in different ways and also exhibit different tolerances and susceptibilities to ailments.

The Road to Recovery

The end of the race is as important as the beginning. Runners must take care to recuperate physiologically, mechanically, and psychologically. The transition from running for two months around a city block to returning to everyday life may be challenging. However, most runners have confidence, perseverance, and faith. Postrace regimens should include rest, hydration, and proper food intake. Also, the endocrine system, which is responsible for the body's hormonal function, is sensitive to extreme physical exertion. Some runners have taken endocrine-boosting supplements or other supplements to aid in nutritional recovery, muscle gain, normal hydration, and normal sleep cycles. Up to four weeks should be allowed for recovery. Sleep disturbances are the most common postrace side effects. Also, the immune system may be depressed and susceptible to viral and bacterial infections.

In the Long Run

Despite the distance and time involved, the Self-Transcendence 3,100-Mile Ultramarathon is a rather low-key event with little media coverage and no prize money. Runners receive only a T-shirt, photo, cake, and personal congratulations from Sri Chinmoy himself at the finish line. Runners seem unfazed by the entry fee, the time spent running, the time spent away from employment, the disconnection from everyday life, and the physical, mechanical, and psychological rigors. Runners compete in the race with the notion that the journey will nourish the soul and awaken the spirit while also allowing runners, as the name implies, to transcend the self and their previous running achievements.

Matthew J. Forss

See also Endurance and Performance Training; Long Distance Racing and Pedestrianism; Spirituality

Further Reading

Allison, D. (2003). *A step beyond: A definitive guide to ultrarunning*. Weymouth, MA: UltraRunning Publishers.

Boulton, R. M. (2004). In at the deep end: Rathin Boulton in the 3100: Part 2. *Multiday Running, 1*(2), 34–38.

Boulton, R. M. (2004). My 3100 mile race experience: Part 1. *Multiday Running, 1*(1), 17–20.

Boulton, R. M. (2005). In at the deep end: Part 3. *Multiday Running, 2*(1), 79–84.

Cherns, T. (2003). 3,100 miles around the block. *Ultrarunning, 23*(7), 50.

Essam, P. (2005). Crewing at ultras and multiday races. *Multiday Running, 2*(2), 46–50.

Fallon, K. E. (1999). The biochemistry of runners in a 1600 km ultramarathon. *British Journal of Sports Medicine, 33*(8), 264–269.

Fallon, K. E. (2001). The acute phase response and exercise: The ultramarathon as prototype exercise. *Clinical Journal of Sport Medicine, 11*(1), 38–43.

Firth, A. (2004). Run across America 2004—Race details. Retrieved August 15, 2006, from http://www.runacrossamerica2002.com

Szczesiul, S. (2004). About the 3100 mile race. Sri Chinmoy Marathon Team. Retrieved August 15, 2006, from http://www.srichinmoyraces.org/3100/about3100/

Szczesiul, S. (2004). The eighth annual 3100 mile race: Double your fun. *Multiday Running, 1*(2), 6–11.

Watkins, A. (2004). Chafing—Not if but when. *Multiday Running, 1*(1), 30–31.

336

Valeruz, Toni

Further Reading

Giorgio, D. (Ed.). (2001). *Dimensione sci* (Skiing Dimension). Turin: CDA.

Tonivaleruz.com. (n.d.). Retrieved June 7, 2006, from http://www.toni valeruz.com

Valeruz, T. (2004). *35 anni e più di sci estremo* (35 years and more of extreme skiing). Trento, Italy: Edizioni Osiride.

Perhaps the most famous Italian athlete in extreme sports, Toni Valeruz (b. 1951) helped pioneer extreme skiing in Europe and South America.

Valeruz was born in Alba, a hamlet near Canazei, a mountainous district situated at the borderland between Italy and Austria. Growing up in the Val di Fassa, he was taught by his family to ski at an early age, and he quickly developed a love for the mountains and the challenging terrain at his doorstep. As is common in such regions, his childhood was dedicated to winter sports.

In 1968 he entered extreme skiing by confronting the Marmolada, a group of mountains with peaks reaching 3,342 meters and slopes of 55 degrees. In this challenging terrain Valeruz skied twenty of the most renowned faces. In 1976 he skied in the dangerous eastern face of Cervino, in 1978 Mount Blanc, and in 1983 the Eiger, all of which are more than 4,000 meters high. In sum, he has made first descents on more than fifty of the world's most challenging slopes. Furthermore, at the time of his accomplishments his skis were made of wood and did not have the flexibility and sophisticated technology available today. In 1985 Valeruz skied the Lyscamm, a 1,200-meter mountain with 57-degree slopes, in just five minutes. In the 1980s his fame reached its peak, and he became famous for his technical skills and demonstrations of courage. With the support of his sponsors he traveled to South America, where he conquered many of the most challenging mountains. Supported by Town of Trento expedition, he also descended the western face of Makalù, an 8,100-meter Himalayan peak. Furthermore, in 1997 he descended the northern face of Vernel Mount, in the Val di Fassa (Dolomites, Alps) at 2 A.M. Despite the difficulty of the terrain, he was guided only by the light of the moon.

At the beginning of his career Valeruz met some opposition from people who labeled him a "crazy" risk taker. However, he has argued (and demonstrated) that his feats have been inspired by a love for the mountains, and today he boasts respect and prestige. Today Valeruz is a skiing instructor and leader of challenging excursions. As an instructor he stresses that an extreme skier must learn various techniques, including Alpine skiing, snowboarding, mountaineering, and skiing-mountaineering, as well as a respect for the raw power of the mountain.

Gherardo Bonini

See also Skiing

Venice Beach

Venice Beach and Santa Monica encompass a coastal region of California, west of Los Angeles, south of Malibu, and north of Marina Del Rey. The area of Dogtown, the so-called slums of the affluent west side, played an integral role in the development of modern skateboarding culture.

Although skateboarding was popular in Santa Monica and Venice Beach during the 1950s, after the closing of Ocean Park (a beach-based amusement park located on the old Pacific Ocean pier) in 1956, the sport largely disappeared until the early 1970s. Surfing, however, continued to be popular among local residents. Surfing through the remnants of the old Ocean Park pier, surfers developed a style of tight turns to avoid pilings and prized risky tricks. The area was also famous for its localism. During the 1970s and 1980s, when the waves were poor, local surfers practiced on skateboards, enabled by advances in materials, specifically urethane wheels. The style and tricks of traditional skateboarding had changed little since the 1950s; however, when skating met surfing in Dogtown, the sport was changed, and the popularity of skateboarding was revived.

During the 1970s and 1980s Dogtown became the locus of skateboarding culture. At the center was the Zephyr Surf Shop, a local hangout that integrated street style into surf- and skateboard designs. Eventually the Zephyr surf and skate team—called the "Z-Boys"—became an influence. Bicknell Hill, a steep street located near the beach, became a key spot for the Z-Boys, allowing them to ride asphalt in the style of waves. Some core members of the Z-Boys were Jay Adams, Tony Alva, and Tony Peralta. As these and other Z-Boys developed their skills, skateboarding became a year-around sport, and they sought out more places to hone their skills. Local schools on the west side became boarder hotspots because most tended to have walls of banked asphalt, which were perfect for tricks. Sneaking in to these schools, making late-night runs down the canyon roads, and encountering pedestrian conflicts gave the boarders outlaw status. The outlaw mystique that surrounded boarding intensified when droughts in the late 1970s emptied pools across the area. In particular, the Dog Bowl, named for its canine fans, became a practice site. Sneaking in to ride the pools, ready to flee when the police arrived, skateboarding pioneers developed a host of aerial maneuvers, many of which continue to influence the skills and techniques practiced by contemporary skateboarders.

As a local team, the Z-Boys competed in local events. In 1975 the Del Mar Nationals were held in California, and the Z-Boys emerged as the preeminent performers. As shown in the skateboarding documentary, *Dogtown and Z-Boys*, this event changed the sport forever. Jay Adams, Tony Alva, and Tony Peralta emerged as icons in the culture. Their distinc-

A teenage boy performing a frontside grind on a miniramp section of a skatepark. Source: istock/Christian Carroll.

tive personal and skateboarding styles were communicated via magazines and videos across the broader skateboarding culture, and boarders across the country imitated the Z-Boys style. However, as skateboarding started to become more commercialized, conflict over corporate sponsorship, media hype, and egos contributed to the dissolution of the Z-Boys team. The Zephyr shop closed just months after the Del Mar Nationals, and the team members went their separate ways. Nonetheless, the impact they had on skateboarding remains. Moreover, Venice Beach and Santa Monica remain firmly established in the collective cultural memory as key sites in the development of skateboarding.

Faye Linda Wachs

See also Dogtown and Z-Boys; Skateboarding

Further Reading

Brooke, M. (1999). *The concrete wave: The history of skateboarding.* Toronto, Canada: Warwick Publishing Inc.

Davis, J., & Phillips, S. (2004). *Skateboarding is not a crime: 50 years of street culture.* New York: Firefly Books.

Friedman, Glen E., & Stecyk III, C. R. (2004). *Dogtown: The legend of Z-Boys.* New York: Burning Flags Press.

Vine Jumping

Vine jumping (or "land diving" [*n'gol* or *naghol* in the Sa language of the indigenous people]) is an extreme physical ritual unique to Pentecost Island, one of the eighty-three islands of the nation of Vanuatu in the South Pacific. Pentecost has a population of fewer than ten thousand. Pentecost men jump from a platform atop a wooden tower with vines tied to the tower and around their ankles to break their fall. Some commentators view the Pentecost ritual as a precursor of the sport of bungee jumping. However, no known historical relationship exists between the two, and even in its modern, tourist-driven form, vine jumping differs from bungee jumping in several significant ways.

Little is known of the origin of vine jumping. According to Pentecost mythology it began when a young woman climbed a tall tree to escape her husband's wrath. He climbed up after her, and she leaped to escape his grasp. He leaped after her, and both fell to the ground. She survived because the vines she had tied around her ankles broke her fall. He was killed. The myth is today more important to outsiders who promote vine jumping as a tourist event

Extreme Tourist Attraction

In addition to being an early extreme sport, vine jumping has become one of the main attractions of Vanuatu's Pentecost Island.

This awe inspiring ancient tradition, also known as land diving, is a feat of courage and Stone Age ingenuity that gave birth to modern bungee jumping.

Each year, in conjunction with the yam harvest, giant towers are constructed in the southern villages of Vanuatu's Pentecost Island. The wooden towers themselves are amazing structures; up to 70 feet tall, each of their joints are lashed together with local vines.

Remarkably, not a single nail or any other piece of manmade building material is used. The resulting tower is disconcertingly flexible and sways in the breeze, but is further supported by an elaborate system of vines anchoring it to a hillside.

Throughout the Naghol ceremony as many as 20 divers, clad only in nambas (traditional woven mats wrapped around the loins) will leap from staggered platforms on the tower with carefully chosen and measured vines tied around their ankles. Precision in preparing the vines is of grave importance. Too short and the diver will swing back into the tower; too long and he will slam into earth in an unchecked freefall.

Source: Source Gonomad.com, *Vanuatu's original bungee jumpers.* Retrieved February 1, 2007, from: http://www. gonomad.com/features/0406/vanuatus_original_bungee_jumpers.html

than to the Pentecost Islanders themselves. For the islanders vine jumping is an agricultural ritual meant to ensure an abundant crop of yams, one of the island's staple foods. The ritual is held in villages each year from the time when the yams begin to ripen to when they are harvested. Landing so that one's hair or shoulders touch the ground ensures a bountiful harvest. As important as the divers are, the people who gather below and around the platform chant and dance during the ritual and become quiet only during the actual jump. The jump is managed by older men; younger men and boys are the jumpers.

Diving towers as high as 22 meters are built of wood lashed together with vines. Their platforms are made of branches and leaves. A tower sways in the wind and is often lashed to a hillside to increase stability. Liana vines, which are filled with water to make them pliable and less likely to break, are tied to the tower at one end, and the other end is shredded and tied around a jumper's ankles. The vines are cut to a length such that they break a jumper's fall just before he reaches the ground. The landing area at the bottom of the tower is turned over to soften it, and all rocks are removed.

Correct jumping technique is crucial for survival, and correct behavior is crucial for ritual success. A jumper wears only a traditional woven mat wrapped around his waist. Once on the platform, he crosses his arms across his chest and then raises his hands to signal he is ready to jump. He may at that point share thoughts with the crowd gathered below. The crowd stops chanting, and he then jumps away from the tower in a horizontal position. The horizontal pushoff is the key to a safe jump. If he were to fall straight down he would either slam back into the tower or hit the ground at full force. The vines are cut to add a few extra feet for the horizontal distance from the tower. After the jumper ends his jump, male kin untie the vines and help him to his feet. In a perfect jump the vines jerk the jumper into an upright position just before he reaches the ground. Younger jumpers usually go first, from lower heights, with the highest jumps coming at the end of the ritual.

Vine jumping first drew attention in the West in the 1950s, when a BBC crew filmed the ritual. Since then the ritual has received considerable attention, such that in 1995 the government banned it because it had become too commercialized. However, two sites were established for tourist exhibitions, with men from villages going there to jump. Although vine jumping continues in the villages, it is not open to most outsiders.

David Levinson

Further Reading

Allen, M. (Ed.). (1981). *Vanuatu: Politics, economics, and ritual in island Melanesia.* Sydney, Australia: Academic Press.

Reedy, A. (n.d.). Vanuatu's original bungee jumpers. Retrieved June 14, 2006, from http://www.gonomad.com/features/0406/vanuatus_original_bungee_jumpers.html

Violence

Violence is part of the game in several mainstream sports that have the largest audiences and that generate the most revenue (football, hockey, and boxing). In contrast, the most "mainstream" of the extreme sports (snowboarding, skateboarding, surfing, and motocross) do not require violence as part of the competition. In fact, few extreme sports qualify as contact sports, let alone violent sports.

Although many extreme sports are not violent, extreme sports are unique in at least two key ways that are related to violence. First, many extreme sports are not under the oversight of a commission or league, as are violent mainstream sports such as football (NFL), hockey (NHL), and lacrosse (NCAA). The absence of a commission or league results in a lack of rules; no mechanism exists to investigate violence that gets out of control; and no party has the power to impose penalties when violence occurs. Thus, for example, when a fan-player scuffle broke out at a Detroit Pistons–Indiana Pacers professional basketball game (19 November 2004) that resulted in Pacer Ron Artest assaulting a fan in the stands, NBA Commissioner David Stern reviewed the incident and imposed both monetary fines and a suspension on Artest and others players who were involved in the scuffle. In contrast, if such a scuffle were to take place at a skateboarding competition, likely no governing body would investigate the incident and impose sanctions if necessary.

Second, many extreme sports do not employ a referee or official of any sort who has the power to interrupt player violence. Thus, for example, during a boxing match or a football game the referee has the power to determine that a hit is illegal (below the belt, after the stop of play, and so forth) and can impose a penalty on the offending athlete or in some cases stop the competition and/or eject the athlete from the competition. For example, when boxer Mike Tyson bit the ear of his opponent, Evander Holyfield (28 June 1997), referee Miles Lane stopped the action, and the Nevada Athletic Commission revoked Tyson's license and fined him three million dollars. Thus, where regulation ex-

ists, the governing body will typically continue to investigate the incident and may impose additional sanctions if the incident is egregious enough.

In contrast, no officials are present at many extreme sports events, particularly those that are way out of the mainstream, such as backyard wrestling, a competitive and violent form of TV wrestling without the necessary safeguards. In fact, because extreme sports are highly concentrated among young people, often no adults are present for competitions. Thus, when the violence that is inherent in backyard wrestling gets out of control—including competitors hitting each other with dangerous objects, bouncing each other off of trampolines, and sending competitors head first into concrete—rarely is anyone present to interrupt that violence and impose sanctions on the competitors. Thus, the violence in extreme sports is highly unregulated and, like so many violent crimes in U.S. society, goes unreported. These conditions make tracking violence and ensuring that competitions are conducted safely difficult.

Violence as Turf Wars

One of the triggers of violence by extreme sports athletes is conflicts over the use of social space or "turf." Specifically, violence erupts between groups of athletes participating in different sports when access to the space both groups need to participate is scarce. Two examples—snowboarding and surfing—illustrate:

When snowboarding began some turf wars occurred with skiers. The arguments and violence erupted around who could use the space and what behavior was appropriate for the space. Despite the fact that snowboarding has been around for at least two decades, these turf wars continue. Vaske and colleagues surveyed skiers and snowboarders in Colorado. They report: "Bivariate analyses [examining the relationship between two variables] indicated that skiers reported more unacceptable behaviors by snowboarders than by fellow skiers, and snowboarders also identified more out-group than in-group conflict" (Vakse, Carothers, Donnelly, and Baird 2000, 297)

Similar turf wars have erupted as sports that were once marginal and had relatively few participants have become more mainstream and thus more popular. An example is surfing. Once a relatively marginal sport with just a few local die-hards, surfing has become significantly more mainstream and popular in the last two decades. As Nick Ford and

David Brown write, "The enormous increase in the numbers participating in surfing [has led] to problems of crowding in many urban surfing areas . . . The inherent scarcity of waves in crowded conditions leads to expressions of localism and even 'surf rage'" (Ford and Brown 2006, 32). Such crowding problems have led to "increasing competitiveness and invidiousness (threatening newcomers)" in many surfing locales around the world (Ford and Brown 2006, 78).

Violence by Extreme Sports Athletes

In some cases extreme sports athletes have perpetrated violence off the field of competition. In such cases we can examine patterns of behavior that are associated with the extreme sports culture. For example, in April 2002 two skateboarders in Seattle assaulted Demtri Andrews, who died as a result of the assault: "So while Andrews tried to steady himself, Strano came from behind and trucked him with 'all his might' in the back of the head. (To 'truck' someone is to strike the person with one of the metal trucks on the underside of a skateboard)" (Preusch 2003).

In December 2002 Timothy Strano, twenty-three years old, pleaded guilty to manslaughter and was sentenced to six and one-half years in prison. This case is important because it highlights the type of violence that many people outside of extreme sports associate with these sports and the athletes who participate in them: thug violence.

Extreme sports athletes have committed other acts of violence off the field. In 2002 professional skateboarder Neil Heddings and his wife murdered their two-and-one-half-year-old son, Marcus, by beating him to death in their home. Heddings was found guilty in 2005 and will serve fourteen to fifty years in prison. Legendary skateboarder Mark "Gator" Rogowski, whose career is documented in the film *Stoked: The Rise and Fall of Gator*, provides another example. "Gator" had risen to the top of the skating world and was making big money through competitions as well as endorsements. His name was associated with virtually every type of skating merchandise. In 1991 he raped and murdered a twenty-one-year-old woman and stuffed her body into a surfboard bag. He is serving a life sentence in the California prison system. Although the examples here focus on skateboarders, such acts of violence are not limited to skateboarding culture.

Obviously such violence can be perpetrated by people (mostly men) from all walks of life and those participating in all types of sports. Yet, the examples given are suggestive of the ways in which violence perpetrated by extreme sports athletes is shaped not only by the broader society, but also by the sports cultures themselves.

Culture of Youthful Masculinity

Athletes in some mainstream sports compete as professionals well into their fifties (e.g., golf, NASCAR), and many athletes peak in their late twenties and early thirties; the majority of extreme sports athletes, however, are in their teens and twenties. Therefore, any examination of violence in extreme sports would not be complete without a discussion of youth violence.

Youth violence is a major epidemic in U.S. society today and has been for many years. And although most young people do not commit major crimes such as robbery, burglary, syndicated crime, political crime, and/or white-collar crime, today's youth are more likely to be involved in interpersonal acts of violence such as bullying, sexual harassment, and more recently acts of violence including homicide at school.

Criminologists have argued that, despite the popularity of youth subcultures that are antiadult establishment, young people usually outgrow their participation in such subcultures and in so doing often also "outgrow crime." University of Chicago criminologist Clifford Shaw and his colleague Ernest Burgess in their seminal study of youth crime entitled *The Jack Roller* clearly show that over time young people will typically move on from their penchant for crime and violence.

Extreme sports began outside the mainstream, and even those that have managed to enter the mainstream (such as snowboarding) are still considered by many both inside and outside the sports to be associated with alternative, antiestablishment, punk, heavy metal, and "grunge rock" culture. In particular, many extreme sports athletes have an image that is associated with, among other traits and behaviors, alcohol, drugs, tattoos, nontraditional piercing, and violence. Extreme athletes not only play to these images, but in many cases seem to embrace them. For example, during the 2006 winter Olympics in Turin, Italy, such counterculture images swirled around U.S. skier Bode Miller. In television interviews Miller proclaimed that he had routinely skied "high" after smoking marijuana, and he and others noted that he shares his last name with a popular beer: Miller.

Part of what distinguishes an extreme sport from a mainstream sport is the relationship between on-the-field violence and the culture of violence associated with that sport. The typical pattern in mainstream sports is a direct correlation: The rates of athlete violence off the field are directly related to the level of contact and violence on the field. The highest rates of off-the-field violence by mainstream athletes are among football, basketball, hockey, boxing, and baseball players. Few examples exist of athletes in noncontact, individual sports perpetrating violence off the field. (Tonya Harding's contract beating of Nancy Kerrigan is a notable exception.)

In contrast, in extreme sports violence is perpetrated by athletes who participate in noncontact, individual sports such as skateboarding, snowboarding, and surfing. Just as the violence on the field creates a culture of hypermasculinity among mainstream athletes, a similar culture of hypermasculinity is associated with the extreme sport itself. In his autobiography snowboarder and skateboarder Todd Richards alludes to the culture of hypermasculinity that is embedded in the boarding culture:

> The secret was to pick the weakest animal in the herd and then patiently wait for him to drink himself to oblivion. After he passed out, someone would generally say a prayer to the effect of, "God help him." Then we would move in like hyenas, with magic markers, honey, duct tape, and anything else that was handy. It would begin innocently enough, with a large "idiot" written on the forehead. A moustache would be added. Empty beer cans and beer bottles would be shoved ceremoniously down the victim's pants, honey massaged into his hair, and by the time we'd finished, his entire face, eyebrows, neck, and other exposed skin would be covered in "non-toxic" ink. The coup de grace was duct-taping beer bottles onto both hands. Not like he's holding the bottles, but with the bottles pointing in the same direction as his outstretched fingers. When he'd go to scratch himself, hopefully on the head or the balls, it would be with a thunk. (Richards and Blehm 2003, 176)

Despite being masked as a humorous act, such behavior is not dissimilar from hazing or other initiation rituals prevalent in many mainstream team sports. We see a similar illustration from a skater interviewed by Matthew Preusch. The skater demonstrates that some "skaters" continue to idealize the negative, dangerous image that surrounds them:

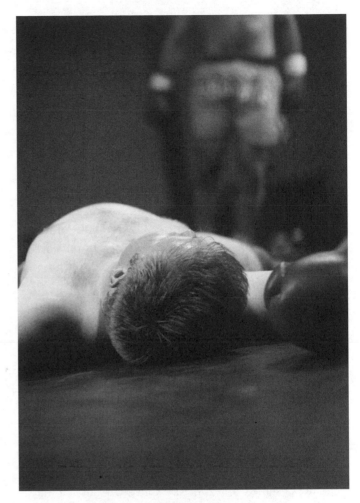

A fighter is knocked out by another fighter during a kickboxing match. Source: Istock/Arlen G. Roche.

Aaron Miles, a 20-year-old hanging outside the show, was convinced it was his key to getting laid. "I think it's cool [that skateboarding is] associated with violence, because it will get us more chicks. And parents will think we're, like, mad violent people and tell their daughters, 'You better not date that skateboarder.' Then girls will want to fuck us." (Preusch 2003)

Violence in Video Games and TV

Another way in which extreme sports are similar to mainstream sports is in the proliferation of video games based on these sports. Just as video games (Xbox, Playstation,

---

Violence

Violence is an integral part of contemporary sports. But how much of it is acceptable? And in what forms?

"Borderline violence" consists of behaviors that violate the official rules of the sport but that are accepted by players and fans alike as a legitimate part of the game. Such behavior—a fistfight in ice hockey or an intentional foul in association football's penalty zone—is rarely subject to legal proceedings and tends to be dealt with by penalties imposed by referees, umpires, or league administrators. A memorable example of this occurred in 1997 when the Nevada Boxing Commission censured and banned heavyweight boxer Mike Tyson for biting his opponent. More-extreme rule infractions—i.e., those that violate not only the formal rules of the sport but also the law of the land—elicit a harsher formal response, especially when the violence results in serious injury. High or late tackles in gridiron football usually create serious outrage and have on occasion led to the strict imposition of a lifetime ban, but recourse to the law in cases of quasi-criminal violence is infrequent.

Source: Maguire, J. (December 6, 2006). *Violence and sports: Ugly but useful.* Retrieved February 1, 2007, from http://blogs.britannica.com/blog/main/2006/12/violence-and-sports-ugly-but-useful/

Nintendo) are based on sports of the NBA, NHL, NASCAR, and NCAA, video games also are based on many of the extreme sports. Among the most popular of all video games are the Tony Hawk skateboarding games. (Tony Hawk is one of the pioneers of skateboarding as an extreme sport.)

Whereas the video games associated with a mainstream sport are designed to mimic the sport, with little time allowed for off-field activities, video games associated with extreme sports are designed around violence that is perpetrated by the game player and is required in order to move to the next level. For example, in the Tony Hawk videos the player has to bury a bully under the snow (*Tony Hawk 3*), break into buildings, and rescue drunk friends from a hotel. As Preusch explains, "not that skateboarding has not had a mixed past: Many skate videos still glorify vandalism and violence" (Preusch 2003).

Movies and television programs also glorify the violence, vandalism, and "bathroom" humor prevalent in many extreme sports cultures. In some cases the actors in the programs and movies are required to engage in unsafe behavior such as excessive drinking or physically dangerous stunts. For example, during the late 1990s, as snowboarding was exploding at Whistler (British Columbia, Canada), passionate boarders Sean Kearns and Sean Johnson created a series of films called the *Whiskey* videos, using the "lifestyle" approach to show what was really happening on and off the snow. These films were a raw mix of snowboarding, skateboarding, inebriation, broken bottles, and broken noses and remain infamous in the snowboarding culture.

The *CKY* (Camp Kill Yourself) videos are a creation of West Chester, Pennsylvania, skateboarders Bam Margera and Brandon DiCamillo. The videos feature Margera, DiCamillo, and their friends and relatives in what they describe as insane "stunts, pranks and acts of fun," interspersed with skating footage of Margera and other pros. A trademark of the skating footage is to show unsuccessful trick attempts immediately followed by the same skater successfully completing the trick.

Perhaps the most mainstream series was *Jackass*, a half-hour television series, originally shown on MTV from 2000 to 2002, in which a group of young men performs violent and dangerous stunts. In an episode called "Poo Cocktail" Johnny Knoxville enters a portable toilet and places 1 kilogram of dog feces on the commode, then locks himself inside. Next a crane lifts the portable toilet with Knoxville inside, spilling the excrement all over the cabin. In an episode entitled "The Vomlette" Dave England swallows raw eggs, onions, sausages, and cheese and then regurgitates the mixture into a frying pan to make an omelet, which he eats.

Mainstream sports have no counterpart to these types of shows. Thus, we see the role in which the media create

and contribute to a culture of hypermasculinity that is embedded in extreme sports.

Much variation exists in the violence associated with mainstream sports. For example, some mainstream sports, such as Olympic boxing, require violence in the same way that some extreme sports, such as backyard wrestling, do. Other mainstream sports—sometimes referred to as "contact sports" or "helmet sports," including football, lacrosse, and hockey—are characterized by more violence on and off the field than are other mainstream sports such as the country club sports of golf and tennis. Although violence is not the goal of helmet sports, it is an inherent part of these sports. Helmet sports are also frequently associated with a culture of violence and hypermasculinity as a result of publicized incidents.

Athletes—mainstream and extreme—sometimes feel a sense of privilege and entitlement. This sense sometimes extends to demanding sex with the women they choose, when they choose, and how they choose. Violence erupts when the demands of privileged athletes collide with the wishes of the women around them. For the women this experience is perceived as, and often meets the legal definition of, rape. The culture of violence, recklessness, and bathroom humor that is associated with some extreme sports is coupled with a sense of status, privilege, and entitlement, at least within the community of extreme sports athletes and enthusiasts. It is not surprising, then, that violence, and especially violence against women, occurs within that culture just as it occurs in other sports cultures and in the larger U.S. society.

Angela Hattery and Earl Smith

Further Reading

Brady, E. (2006, April 7). Duke lacrosse allegations fit mold. *USA Today*, p. 10C.

Carvalho, I., & Lewis, D. A. (2003). Beyond community: Reactions to crime and disorder among inner-city residents. *Criminology, 41*, 779–812.

Cloward, R. A. (1961). *Delinquency and opportunity: A theory of delinquent gangs*. London: Routledge & Kegan Paul.

Ford, N. J., & Brown, D. (2006). *Surfing and social theory: Experience, embodiment and narrative of the dream glide*. New York: Routledge.

Kane, E. W., & Schippers, M. (1996). Men's and women's beliefs about gender and sexuality. *Gender & Society, 10*, 650–665.

Katz, J. (2006). *The macho paradox: Why some men hurt women and how all men can help*. Naperville, IL: Sourcebooks.

Pappas, N. T., McKenry, P. C., & Catlett, B. S. (2004). Athlete aggression on the rink and off the ice: Athlete violence and aggression in hockey and interpersonal relationships. *Men and Masculinities, 6*, 291–312.

Preusch, M. (2003, January 9–15). Skatebording as a crime, in *The Stranger*. Retrieved January 2, 2007, from http://www.thestranger.com/seattle/Content?oid=13041

Richards, T., & Blehm, E. (2003). *P3: Parks, pipes and powder*. New York: Regan Books.

Shaw, C. R., & Burgess, E. W. (1930). *The jack-roller, a delinquent boy's own story*. Chicago: University of Chicago Press.

Smith, E., & Hattery, A. (2005). Violence in sports. In D. Levinson & K. Christensen (Eds.), *Berkshire encyclopedia of world sport* (Vol. 4, pp. 1670–1676). Great Barrington, MA: Berkshire Publishing.

Smith, E., & Hattery, A. (2006, March). *African American male student athletes: Overrepresentation at Division 1A colleges and universities and in deviant and criminal behavior*. Paper presented at the annual meeting of the Drake Group. Indianapolis, IN.

Smith, E., & Hattery, A. (2006). Hey, Stud: Race, sex, and sports. *Journal of Sexuality and Culture, 10*(2), 3–32.

Vakse, J. L., Carothers, P., Donnelly, M. P., & Baird, B. (2000). Recreation conflict among skiers and snowboarders. *Leisure Sciences, 22*(4), 297–313.

Wakeboarding

Imagine yourself holding onto a rope that is tethered to a boat. Imagine going close to 25 miles per hour on the water, simply by holding onto that rope and standing on a board. This is the feeling experienced by anyone who goes wakeboarding.

Wakeboarding is an extreme sport that combines the aspects of three other sports: waterskiing, snowboarding, and surfing. It is similar to waterskiing because the rider is pulled behind a boat using a towline. It is comparable to snowboarding in that the rider is strapped to a board with bindings that lock his or her feet into place. It is like surfing because the waterboarder must then balance weight in order to prevent mistakes and avoid spills.

Wakeboarding is also considered an extreme sport because there are many dangers associated with it that are not associated with any other sport. Proper precautions must be followed in order to maintain safety of the wakeboarder.

Tony Finn, a surfer from San Diego, came up with the concept of the "Skurfer," a wakeboard-type invention, in 1985. He shortened the length of a regular surfboard and had it towed behind a boat. While it was common for people to be towed behind boats on full-length surfboards, this shorter board made for a unique ride.

In the summer of 1985, Finn decided to add straps, called bindings or foot-straps, to his board to prevent the boarder from falling off. This made it easier to maneuver the board. At the same time a man from Austin, Texas, named Jimmy Redmon was developing similar technologies. The bindings make it much easier to perform tricks: One can do flips in the air with the wakeboard attached the whole time. Tony Finn spent a great deal of time promoting the Skurfer. He introduced many people to this exciting new sport; ESPN filmed and broadcasted the Skurfer championships in 1990.

Despite the news coverage, the activity of skurfing continued to face many challenges. Early technologies made participation difficult. The Skurfer was a very thin board that made it extremely difficult to stand, let alone perform maneuvers. Thus, in the early years participation was limited to those few willing to spend the time and energy necessary to develop even the most basic skurfing skills. For the activity to appeal to a broader population, new technological developments were required that would make it easier to learn the sport.

Wakeboarding, like many water sports and extreme sports, is more accessible to the upper middle class, however, unlike some extreme sports, there is no "core lifestyle" identified with the sport. Athletes participate at many levels, from those who dabble in the sport, to those who invest the time and money into becoming an expert.

New Technology

Herb O'Brien was integral to the new technological developments that would ultimately make wakeboarding a much more accessible activity. O'Brien was the successful owner of H.O. Sports, a business that specialized in waterskiing. O'Brien started experimenting with different types of boards, trying to find something that would be easier to use than the Skurfer. In so doing, he developed what is known today as the wakeboard. His wakeboard was compression molded, allowing it to be neutrally buoyant. O'Brien named his invention the Hyperlite, and it was the galvanizing force that led to the increased popularity of the sport. The Hyperlite was much easier to control than the Skurfer. This made it much more popular with Skurfers of average abilities, since it provided them increased opportunities to go out on the water and enjoy themselves, and once they became expert, it made it easier for them to perform tricks. The Hyperlite was neutrally buoyant—not quite sinking, and not quite floating—so it was easier to submerge the wakeboard when performing tricks.

However, Herb O'Brien was not satisfied with his Hyperlite and continued to develop new technologies. He made the board thinner, thus allowing it to carve through the water much like a slalom ski. He also designed the board so that it could break up "water adhesion and gave the board a quicker 'loose' feel and softer landing from wake jumps."

While popular among core enthusiasts, the 1990 version of the wakeboard created by H.O. Sports soon became outdated and was replaced by a newer version created by Jimmy Redmon. In 1993 Redmon designed a wakeboard using "twin-tip" technology, meaning that it had a symmetrical design. The twin-tip board has a fin under both its nose and tail, allowing the rider to use multiple stances (different ways of riding the board) while being able to perform well. In other words the symmetrical design of the Redmon board enabled wakeboarders to ride with either their left or right leg forward and made it possible for boarders to switch between stances while riding behind the boat. In 1989 Redmon created the World Wakeboard Association (WWA). This organization is currently the governing force for wakeboarding and is in charge of establishing the rules of the sport.

Despite the establishment of the WWA in 1989, wakeboarding did not become a widespread professional sport until the early 1990s. In 1992 World Sports and Marketing, a sports promoter from Florida, began hosting professional wakeboarding events. ESPN and ESPN2 showed these exhibitions on television, giving professional wakeboarders national and international exposure. This coverage introduced wakeboarding to a broader audience; the popularity of the sport began to grow quickly.

In 1998 the sport had several further opportunities for growth. Two major series were added to the wakeboarding circuits: the Vans Triple Crown of Wakeboarding and the Wakeboard World Cup. Those two, along with the Wakeboard Tour, are the most highly respected competitions among wakeboarders. Performing well and winning at these events carries high cultural status among boarders.

The number of competitors attending these events and the prize monies available to athletes continue to grow every year, as skill levels improve. Some of the most recent advances for wakeboarding competitions include the different types of courses and additional ways to perform tricks.

The Basics

So what exactly is wakeboarding? Wakeboarding is a sport in which the rider is attached to a boat by a cable and is pulled behind the boat. Beginners tend to use slower speeds with shorter ropes: The speed is approximately 18 miles per hour; the length of the rope between 60 and 65 feet. However, once a rider becomes experienced, she or he begins to travel at faster speeds with longer ropes. Typically, an experienced wakeboarder will travel at speeds of approximately 25 miles per hour, with a role length of about 80 feet. The rider stands on a single board with nonrelease bindings. The rider stands sideways, much like the way one would ride a snowboard, surfboard, or skateboard. Wakeboarding can be done on any body of water big enough to allow a speed boat to accelerate, maneuver, and maintain movement.

The Board

Wakeboards are typically 120–147 centimeters long. They tend to be approximately 45 centimeters wide. They have a concave shape, which is known as a rocker. There are two types of rockers: a continuous rocker, which has a constant curve, and a staged rocker, which has two or more straight parts that are connected in a way that makes it close to a curve.

In wakeboarding a specific type of boat must be used to achieve top performances. The boat should have a tower that stands approximately 2 meters above the water, with the towing cable attached to this tower. The height of the tower makes it much easier for the boarder to perform aerial maneuvers. The boat also has water ballasts that are placed in specific areas to help create a larger wake.

In wakeboarding the rider uses the wake in performing tricks. The wakes themselves serve as a makeshift ramp, allowing the rider to gain air-time and perform technical "tricks" or maneuvers. Tricks are typically done when the rider jumps from one side of the wake to the other.

A professional wakeboarder passes the handle behind his back as he rotates. Source: istock/Jacom Stephens.

Bigger Wake, Better Wakeboarding

In order to participate in wakeboarding, you need a boat creating a wake, and a wakeboard. But to excel at wakeboarding, and to do bigger and better tricks, you need a bigger wake.

Getting a Bigger Wake

Everyone is always asking how to get a bigger wake. There are several things you can do to achieve this depending on your boat arrangement. The simplest thing you can do is getting everybody in the boat to sit or stand in the back. This obviously puts all the weight in the back and forms a bigger wake. If your boat is of any size, this won't work as well. Another common method is using "Fat Sacks." Fat Sacks are large rubber reservoirs that can be filled up with water and placed in the back of the boat. They come in all different sizes so you can fit them in any boat. Other methods include putting cinder blocks in the back, or Tupperware containers filled with cement. Remember though that weighing down just the back might not work. The boat will be going slow and the bow will be way up in the air. So whatever amount of weight you put in the back, put a little in the front to so that the boat is not way off balance. One other thing that no one thinks of is the rope length. You might be too far out and not getting the biggest area of the wake. So play with the rope length and try and get yourself where the wake peaks.

Source: Lifetips.com. *Wakebaording, wakeboarding tips, wakeboarding tricks.* Retrieved Feb. 5, 2007, from http://wakeboard.lifetips.com/cat/60427/wakeboarding/index.html

Language

There are many different terms particular to wakeboarding. For example, there are two different terms for the way of riding the wakeboard: *heel-side cutting* and *toe-side cutting.* Heel-side is where the rider rides toward the wake with the chest facing the boat and the heel-edge of the wakeboard pressed into the water. Toe-side is the exact opposite: The rider rides toward the wake with the chest facing away from the boat, using the toe-edge of the board to help hold position and direction. Each technical trick has a different name: tantrum, backroll, 360, and so on. A rider can perform a trick from either heel-side or toe-side, depending on preference.

A rider performing a tantrum does a back flip over the wake perpendicular to the direction of the board. Doing a backroll requires the rider to do a back flip or a roll over the wake parallel to the board. A rider completing a 360 will spin 360 degrees while jumping over the wake.

Wakeboarding is a freestyle sport, meaning that it gives the competitors the option to perform their choice of tricks in any order. The creative freedom involved in competitive wakeboarding appeals to boarders who like the idea of being able to do what they want, when they want to. The thrill a rider gets when they master new stunts also adds to the appeal. It allows them to express themselves in an enjoyable way.

USA Wakeboarding

USA Wakeboarding, the National Wakeboard League, provides wakeboarders of varying skill levels opportunities to participate in organized competitions. USA Wakeboarding has hosted more than two hundred wakeboard tournaments over the past several years.

Wakeboarding was added to the X Games in 1996, which gave the sport considerable national and international exposure. Indeed, according to USA Wakeboarding's Web site, the sport is now considered the "fastest growing water sport in the world." Some of the most successful competitors in the X Games include Parks Bonifay and Tara Hamilton. Other well-known competitors include Dallas Friday, Danny Harf, Scott Bylery, Darren Shapiro, and Shaun Murray, many of whom are at the forefront of developing new tricks and pushing the sport to new levels.

Wakeboarding's future is promising. With constant improvements in technology, techniques, and tricks and more media exposure, it seems inevitable that wakeboarding will continue to grow as a popular participant and spectator sport.

Melissa Mead

Further Reading

Profile of wakeboarding. (n.d.). Retrieved February 16, 2007, from http://www.usawaterski.org/pages/divisions/wakeboard/history.htm

Wakeboard history. (n.d.). Retrieved February 16, 2007, from http://www.stokecity.ca/history.shtml

WakeBoarder.com. (2005). Retrieved February 16, 2007, from http://WakeBoarder.com

Wakeboarding Online. (2007). Retrieved February 16, 2007, from http://wakeboardingmag.com

Wakeskating

A subculture is a group of persons with beliefs and behaviors that differentiate them from their larger culture. However, as subcultures often become adopted by mass society, this adoption provokes a constant state of subcultural evolution, and some of the best examples come from extreme sports. Extreme sports continue to broaden their range of inclusion with each passing season, and new extreme sports emerge as a result of modifications to existing extreme sports. Wakeboarding, for instance, was initially developed by individuals seeking to combine surfing style with waterskiing technologies.

Wakeboarding has become one of the most popular alternative water sports, especially of the tow-rope variety. Recently, though, an explosion in popularity has surrounded another modification to this sport. The foundations of wakeboarding have been transformed to incorporate elements of skateboarding. Appropriately, this sport variation is referred to as "wakeskating." By definition a wakeskate is a smaller wakeboard without bindings. As simple as this difference may sound, the sport itself is quite complex. The aggressive "edge-and-huck" approach (where the wakeboarder pulls away from the wake of the tow) to wakeboarding has allowed wakeboarders to perform more impressive tricks not found in wakeskating. Instead, fluidity and composure are essential components, and because of the basic nature of the sport, style is important.

Pioneers

The birth of wakeskating can be traced to the mid-1990s in Orlando, Florida, when wakeboarding was just beginning to be embraced by the masses. Wakeskating was born in part out of the desire for a "change of pace" some professional wakeboarders were looking for, something to break up the repetition of daily practices. For one professional rider in particular, the urge to take the bindings off his board and ride it without being physically attached resulted in a variant of wakeboarding. Scott Byerly not only removed the bindings from his board, but also modified his wakeboard by cutting down the nose and tail to make it shorter and applied grip-enhancing material called "Astrodeck" to the

Rail sliding the Virgin River on a wakeskate. Source: istock/Jordan Shaw.

surface. In doing this, he created what is popularly considered to be the original wakeskate.

Although the notion of skateboarding on water was primarily inspired by Byerly, similar developments were taking place in snowboarding culture during this period. The snowskate, a skateboard for snow, was also developed in the mid-1990s. The wakeskate and the snowskate are examples of the cross-pollination of styles and technologies between the board sports of skateboarding, snowboarding, and wakeboarding.

Although Byerly is considered to have planted the wakeskate seed, another professional wakeboarder, Thomas Horrell, ensured that wakeskating had the opportunity to grow. Horrell is considered to be the founder of wakeskating because of his initiative to produce authentic eight-ply wood wakeskates. Since the inception of his company in 1999, team riders and product designers at Cassette Wakeskates have conceptualized ideas that result in progressive wakeskates. The influence of a wakeskate-specific manufacturer such as Cassette prompted prevailing wakeboard companies such as Hyperlite and Liquid Force to produce wakeskates themselves. Simultaneously, passionate wakeskaters, particularly team riders, ensure the development of new wakeskating technologies by spending many hours on the water to test the limits and possibilities of the latest products.

Equipment

Since the original flat, wooden deck of the first wakeskate, boards have undergone considerable technological developments. Pioneers experimented with various levels of concavity to facilitate skateboarding-inspired "flip tricks" and asymmetrical shapes to offer more one-directional riding. Furthermore, composite boards have been introduced because they do not distort in shape in comparison with some of their wooden counterparts. Recently, though, one of the most unique wakeskate design variations was the brainchild of the Cassette team. In 2005 it introduced the bilevel wakeskate—the first two-tiered wakeskate. Cassette riders found that using the surface of the water to get more "pop" was inefficient. Achieving good pop is necessary to perform an "ollie," a skateboarding-inspired maneuver that enables the wakeskater to perform tricks above the surface of the water. Cassette riders and designers recognized that getting more pop is critical for the advancement of the technical aspects of this sport, and thus they experimented with ways

to use the leverage of the board. The result was the bilevel wakeskate, a combination of a flat deck on the bottom and a contoured deck like a skateboard on the top. The two boards are mounted together where trucks would be on a skateboard in order to keep the two decks separated. While some riders have experimented with the bilevel wakeskate, many prefer the simple eight-ply wooden wakeskates.

Wakeskates range from 100 to 120 centimeters in length. With considerably less surface area than wakeboards, wakeskates have less stability on the water. Because the skater is not physically attached to the board by bindings, the "attachment" must come from the skater's "feel" for the board. Riding without bindings provides the wakeskater with a more natural sensation than being strapped to the board. This being said, wakeskating requires a skater to master the fundamental technical elements of riding, such as edge control and timing, before any progression can occur. Participants must employ calculated movements and maintain a certain degree of balance and composure while riding a wakeskate because there is little room for error and even less room for recovery.

The elimination of physical attachment to the board creates new challenges, but such challenges are what make the sport appealing to participants. This simple-yet-difficult paradox attracts riders from various sporting backgrounds, and wakeboard experience is not a prerequisite for wakeskating. Many skateboarders, for example, have transitioned from the concrete and metal obstacles of inner cities and skateboard parks to become successful wakeskaters. The cost of wakeskating can be much less than that of wakeboarding, which has been considered by some people within the alternative sports culture as an elitist sport. Not only does wakeskate equipment cost less (boards range from US$50 to US$250), but also less emphasis is placed on having access to an expensive wakeboard-specific boat. Nonetheless, many wakeskaters are also passionate wakeboarders and often ride behind wakeboard boats. However, the sport can be performed behind any type of boat or jet ski. Indeed, even an automobile driving beside a small area of water can be used to pull a wakeskater.

Competitions

Since the late 1990s wakeskating has grown in popularity such that wakeskate competitions have been included on the Pro Wakeboard Tour. However, wakeskating has often been the exhibition sideshow to more spectacular wake-

From Plywood to Polycarbonates

Though wakeskating is done by using a thin piece of plywood board the technology that has developed in this extreme sport is way more specialized than just plywood. Here is an advertisement for a wakeboard re-released in 2007:

Sattelyte Heartbreaker 41″ (re-released for 2007)

Our riders and shops wanted to see wider nose and tails, deeper concave for better board feel, higher elevated kick tails, and durability. All these features are visable in Sattelyte's 07 line up. One of the biggest improvements is the PBT base. The PBT allows for a stronger base resulting in longetivty for your board and its slick nature is awesome on rails. To tie it all together Sattelyte chose to go with more organic yet edgy graphics, that really suited the overall feel of the line and team. Quality product designed and developed by riders. Carried over from the success of last season, the Heartbreaker makes its second appearence. Its still breaking hearts everywhere, so beware ladies . . . this deck come[s] with a warning sign. If you love your boyfriend you may want to hide his credit card.

Size: 41″
Waist width: 15.5″
Nose/Tail: 12″
Rocker: 2.10″
Weight: 8.25 lbs

Source: Wakeskate World (2007). Retrieved Feb. 1, 2007, from http://www.wakeskateworld.com/

board events that receive greater attention from spectators, the media, and corporate sponsors. However, recently the influence of one competition in particular has laid the foundation for future wakeskate-specific events to build upon.

In 2004 the first annual Byerly Toe Jam was held at The Projects wakeboard and wakeskate park in Orlando, Florida. On 35 hectares of land with three private lakes, this wake park and camp is protected from wind by surrounding forests and offers one of the best locations to hold a wakeskate contest. Ten of the best wakeskaters were invited, and a handful of other riders qualified to participate. The Byerly Toe Jam competition embraced three disciplines: boat, rail, and winch. The boat discipline involves athletes performing tricks while being towed behind boats, rail events involve performing tricks on rails, boxes, and other objects in the water, and winch events are typically single-trick events, where the rider is towed in a small inland pool by a mechanical winch, allowing spectators to get closer than open water events allow.

The Toe Jam now attracts many of the world's best wakeskaters and has inspired the organization of other wakeskate-specific events. As the number of competitive riders continues to increase, more contests probably will focus on wakeskating, and instructional camps such as The Projects will offer programs exclusively for wakeskaters. When wakeboarding was growing in popularity during the late 1980s, waterskiers argued that it was "just a fad" that would fade in time. However, wakeboarding continues to thrive. In a similar way wakeskating—initially an alternative sport for passionate wakeboarding participants—is growing in popularity, and the institutionalization and commercialization of wakeskating are well under way. Although devotees will continue to push the technical and physical limits of wakeskating, it is difficult to know how long this sport will hold the attention of extreme sports enthusiasts searching for the newest variant to master. Eventually a passionate participant seeking new challenges probably may develop the next "alternative" variant of rope-tow board sports, but until then, wakeskating remains a new sport that is beginning to climb the ladder of popularity and commercial recognition.

Dane Bourgard

See also Skateboarding; Wakeboarding; Waterskiing

Further Reading

Alliance Wakeboard Magazine. Retrieved December 1, 2006, from http://www.alliancewake.com/default2.aspx?pg=article

Wakeskating.com. (n.d.). Retrieved February 16, 2007, from http://wakeskating.com

What Is Wakeskating? (n.d.). Retrieved December 1, 2006, from http://www.stokecity.ca/whatiswakeskating.shtml

Waterskiing

From its creation in 1922 by Ralph Samuelson, waterskiing was an extreme sport. Local people were captivated as they watched Samuelson experiment with different types of skis, boat speeds, and variations on Lake Pepin in Minnesota. After much trial and error, Samuelson invented water skis, as well as the first water-ski jump, during a time when waterways and boats were used mainly for shipping and transportation.

As the popularity of waterskiing spread across the United States, the sport evolved from a recreational sport to a competitive sport. Ski shows gained popularity in the 1930s and exposed people from Chicago to Atlantic City to the new sport. By the end of the decade a national governing body, American Water Ski Association (AWSA), was formed and organized the first U.S. national water-ski championships.

The 1940s brought the creation of variations of waterskiing, including barefoot skiing by A. G. Hancock and Dick Pople Jr. During this time the sport spread to the world stage, and the first World Water Ski Championship tournament was held in France in 1949. By the 1950s water-ski jumpers were reaching distances of more than 30 meters, AWSA had begun publishing *Water Skier* magazine, and the Masters Water Ski Tournament was begun in Callaway Gardens, Georgia.

The sport that Samuelson created is now a global and multibillion-dollar industry, with numerous disciplines and many participants. The national governing body of waterskiing, USA Water Ski, reports 10,968 members in the water-ski sport division, 796 in the barefoot division, and 374 in the hydrofoil (airchair) division. AWSA changed its name to USA Water Ski when the organization began receiving funding as a member of the U.S. Olympic Committee.

The International Water Ski Federation (IWSF) is the international governing body of water sports. The IWSF

A water skier in a lake. Source: istock/Trevor Allen.

regulates three-event skiing, as well as cable ski, barefoot, wakeboard, ski racing, and disabled waterskiing. Ninety countries are members of the IWSF. Each country also operates its own national governing body for water-ski sports. To date 52,000 competitors and 3 million participants are registered with the IWSF throughout the world.

Competitive Waterskiing

Today waterskiing is even more extreme. Athletes are towed at fast speeds behind boats with supercharged engines and attempt daring maneuvers that most people could not fathom doing even on dry land. Water skiers perform tricks, launch into the air off ski jumps, and swerve around buoys while being pulled behind a tow boat that is traveling in excess of 48 kilometers per hour.

Competitive waterskiing consists of three events: jumping, slalom, and trick.

Jumping

Jumping, considered by many to be the most dangerous event, combines the element of speed with precise timing and body position while the skier is being launched off a jump ramp. Skiers have three attempts to jump as far as they can, with the highest scoring jump counting. During the jump event a skier uses boat power and technique to gain even more speed, which means that a skier can be traveling close to 160 kilometers per hour when hitting the jump ramp. When the skier approaches the ramp at this speed and is able to maintain a stable body position, there is the potential to soar considerable distances. Some experienced ski jumpers can travel more than 60 meters.

The speed at which the skier is traveling, combined with the attempt to hit a stationary object while traveling across water and then launching into the air, makes the potential for injury high. Small errors can produce disastrous results for a skier. Hitting the ramp in an undesirable position can cause the skis to slip out on the ramp, causing a skier to fall in a backflip motion or to be thrown forward and propelled toward the water head first. The speed of the skier leaves little room for error and almost no time for recovery. Skiers say that crashing is like falling out of the sky. Moreover, hitting the water can feel like hitting concrete. Broken bones, especially ribs, and torn ligaments in the lower body are not uncommon injuries from the impact of a bad crash.

By the mid-1990s jumpers were looking for ways to ad-

vance their equipment in hopes of attaining even greater distances. Until this point the average length of jump skis was 182 centimeters. The skis used by jumpers today are 213 to 238 centimeters long and are designed to sustain flight for as long as possible. The tips of the skis are slightly twisted outward to increase the amount of surface area exposed to airflow. By using technology from the aviation industry, jumpers were able to increase the lift off the ramp and remain in the air longer.

The longer skis resulted in increased distances for jumpers, but the length of the skis also brought an increased risk of injury. The extra length and surface area allow a jumper to accelerate quickly, resulting in the skier contacting the ramp with a greater speed. When a skier is traveling at higher speeds and is out of control, hitting the water on the head, back, or side (rather than landing standing up on the skis) can cause many injuries. Often the skis stick in the water and stop moving while the body continues to travel forward in a twisting motion. This phenomenon, in conjunction with the force of hitting the water, can cause injuries such as hip dislocation, torn ligaments in the knee, concussions, and broken ribs. Experienced skiers are often able to minimize the injury potential of a crash by rolling while in the air into a position such that they will hit the water on their back rather than face. To do this, skiers must not let go of the handle and must use the tension of the rope to move the body around. Although hitting the water in this position is still painful, it protects most vital organs and positions the skis so that they don't catch in the water and place extreme stress on the lower body.

In a 15 July 2006 telephone interview, professional jumper Scot Ellis describes a jump crash as "the most violent 5 seconds of your life." According to Ellis, "The impact seems to hit your entire body at once, you have no idea where you are, and it doesn't even feel like you're in the water—am I up side down, right side up? You cannot see anything, and it feels like your getting pulled in every direction. As you start to slow down, you open your eyes but you're under water. Your right arm can't move cause of the sling, you panic to get air, but you can't breathe, because the wind has been knocked out of you. You try to take a breath, but it feels like two people are standing on your chest."

On every jump great forces are placed on the entire body while it is being towed behind the boat. Studies have shown that during the initial deep-water start alone, the forces acting on the body are equal to one and one half times the skier's weight. When skiers are traveling behind the boat during the slalom and jump events and resisting the pull of the boat, forces are at least two to three times the weight of the skier.

To counter the forces acting on the body, skiers wear back braces, knee braces, and gloves. During the jump event an arm sling is also worn. The arm sling keeps the skier's right arm close to the body while the skier cuts to the jump ramp. Jump helmets have evolved over the years from a design covering just the top of the head to a design with full-face protection. Helmets today feature high-impact foam that absorbs the impact forces during a crash and prevent brain and head trauma. The full-face helmet covers the ears, jaw, mouth, and nose and offers considerably more protection than the original design.

The jump event, although dangerous, is a spectator favorite. At major tournaments such as the U.S. Masters, Pro Tour events, and World Cup events crowds are always attentive when jumpers line up to hit the ramp. When conditions are good, a jumper has the potential to fly great distances. Currently the men's world record is 73 meters by Freddy Kreuger of the United States. The women's record is 56.6 meters by Elena Milakova of Russia.

Slalom

During the slalom event a skier attempts to attain the speed required to reach a given width on the boat, to go around the turn buoy while maintaining the desired direction behind the boat, and then to abruptly slow to turn. During slalom, the skier is required to maneuver through a course of six buoys that are set a specific distance from the pat of the boat. After going around all six successfully at the maximum speed allowed, the rope is shortened in predetermined increments. This shortening process continues until the skier either falls or misses a buoy. As the rope gets shorter, the skier has more difficulty obtaining and controlling speed to get around the turn buoy, or turn ball, because the forces on the body are greater. The speed that a slalom skier reaches makes falls dangerous. Although slalom skiers are closer to the water than jumpers, slalom skiers have little time to brace for the impact. Slalom skiers do not wear helmets. They wear a padded vest for floatation and sometimes a back brace.

Trick

Trick skiing, although performed at much slower speeds than are slalom and jumping, is dangerous. The object is to complete as many tricks as possible in two twenty-second passes. Trick skiers often wrap the rope around their body or perform turns and wake jumps with one foot harnessed in the handle. The rope is attached to a release so that in the event of a fall the skier will not be dragged behind the boat. Often skiers fall down within a split second when the edge of a ski catches the water, leaving their fate entirely in the hands of the release operator. When a ski catches an edge the ski stops moving, but the skier's momentum causes the skier to continue to twist. This situation, coupled with a late release, can result in injury to a knee, leg, or hip. Spiral fractures of the femur, as well as torn ligaments in the knee, are common injuries for trick skiers.

Lifestyle

Skiers' commitment to the sport often takes precedence over everything else in life. During the season, when the quality of the training set, or one ski session, is essential, a skier may be on the water just after sunrise, taking advantage of the calm, quiet conditions before the lake (or river) is overrun with boats and other people. An ideal training set includes four to six jumps, ten to twenty minutes practicing certain tricks, or six to eight slalom runs. Many skiers, finding the public waterways more crowded with each year, build their own private lake for waterskiing. These artificial bodies of water are generally costly to build but offer the skier pristine training conditions any time of the day, without the hassle of busy public waterways. The most committed skiers may purchase land and dig a ski lake rather than buy a house or upgrade living conditions because skiing is their highest priority.

Barefoot Skiing

Barefoot skiing (barefooting) caught on in Australia quicker than it did in the United States. Although the skiers of Cypress Gardens in Florida first skied on bare feet in 1947, the Australians began organizing tournaments and moving the sport from a recreational level to a competitive one. By 1960 the Australian Water Ski Club was formed and three years later held the first Australian National Championships. The Australians, including Garry Barton and John Hacker, introduced numerous tricks, such as the backward deep-water start, stepover back to front, and the backward flying dock start.

Modern Barefoot Skiing

The speed and danger of barefoot skiing make it an extreme sport. In order for skiers to glide across the water on

bare feet, the boat must travel at considerably faster speeds than for other water sports. Typically a barefoot skier is towed behind the boat at speeds of 48 to 72 kilometers per hour. Falls at such speeds are not only inevitable, but also dangerous. Barefooters wear protective gear, but much of this gear was not introduced until the 1990s. In an effort to reduce injuries from falls, barefoot coaches stress the proper technique while falling. A slight turn of the head can leave a barefooter with a ruptured eardrum. Rather than attempt to shield one's face with the hands, which can produce a black eye, coaches instruct skiers to leave the arms and hands where they are when the skier lets go of the rope and simply tuck the chin to the chest and roll forward. Barefooters often practice this maneuver at slow speeds off the boom, a bar that extends out the side of the boat approximately 1.5 meters. Learning the proper way to fall and enter the water can extend the barefooter's career and aid in avoiding injury.

Barefoot Competition

Barefoot competitions feature the same events as three-event waterskiing: slalom, trick, and jump. However, slight variations in each make the events unique to barefooting. The slalom event is run in a course without any buoys, and a skier earns points for each successful crossing of the boat's wake. Skiers must move from the outside of the first wake wave and across to the outside of the second wake wave as many times as possible within the fifteen-second time limit. They have the option to ski on one foot or two feet and face either forward or backward. Keith St. Onge of the United States, with 20.6 points, holds the world record for men in this event; Nadine De Villiers of Russia holds the world record for women with 17 points.

The trick event in barefooting is similar to that in traditional waterskiing. Skiers have fifteen seconds to complete as many tricks as they can. Each trick performed is scored a certain number of points.

The jump event uses a much smaller ramp than a waterski jump, and the boat speed is faster. The top edge of the jump is a mere 45 centimeters off the water, whereas a traditional ramp is from 1.5 to 1.8 meters off the water. The boat travels at 64 kilometers per hour or faster (compared with the 56 kilometers per hour that jumpers with skis use), making this event extremely dangerous. When Australians practiced barefoot jumping in the late 1960s and 1970s, it was high risk. At that time skiers did not wear helmets or the padded wetsuits that are standard equipment today.

Although the exact history of the jump event is not clear, popular belief is that the first few skiers to attempt barefoot jumping were paralyzed from falling on the ramp.

Airchair

The sport of airchair was developed through hydrofoil technology, which was initially used for boating in the early 1900s. The towed hydrofoil was developed about 1960 by Walter Woodard, an aeronautical engineer. Then came hydrofoil water skis, as well as a hydrofoil surfboard and hydrofoil catamaran. The hydrofoil, with the struts and wings attached under the surface of the water, allows the skier to slice effortlessly through rough water and waves. The concept was developed throughout the 1970s to include a hydrofoil knee-board. The seated hydrofoil, or airchair, was developed in 1984.

Water Skiing on Lake Rotorua

In touchstone of memory
we all have days that settle
on the heart like oil upon water.

The perfect curve of body
skinned in spray is mine,
the arc of a jump start

Overture of single ski
and orchestrated boat
to whip rope into sinew

Breaking-in a bucking wake
before body skims
to exult over depths

Unfathomed by reason.
Even the cottage seemed perfect
that night as the fire painted

spectating walls and old songs
tapped wellsprings in
delectable time.

Robin McConnell

The skier controls the hydrofoil by leaning either forward or backward to get the foil to move up or down. Experienced skiers are able to time the lean and ride the foil up to the top of the wake or even a large wave and launch 6 meters or more into the air. Airchair riders are known for the height they achieve during tricks, and because of this height riders are able to perform almost every flip variation possible. At the initiation of the sport, numerous injuries were reported as a result of riders falling off the hydrofoil skis or the airchair and landing on the metal foil piece. In the mid-1980s, as a safety precaution, Mike Mack, who developed the sport, devised a seat-belt-like device to strap the rider to the chair. The "Mack Strap," as it was called, along with a heel strap, secured riders to the board, advanced the sport, and increased safety.

Airchair competitions, called "fly-ins," are a popular way for riders to perform tricks and impress a crowd. The goal of such competitions is for riders to attempt big-air tricks with maximum style. Riders are awarded points for each trick they complete, with extra style points awarded for grabs or tweaks at the discretion of judges. Grabs are done when the rider is in the air and takes one hand off the rope handle and grabs part of the board, or air chair, for a brief moment. They make the trick more difficult. Tweaks are small movements in the air, bringing the board sideways or otherwise off axis, before returning to the starting position for the landing. To date 374 airchair riders are registered with USA Water Ski.

Waterskiing Sports in the Twenty-first Century

Waterskiing, barefoot skiing, and airchair continue to grow in popularity. Each year advances in equipment and tow boats allow skiers to go faster and higher and to perform more technical maneuvers. These advances are constantly expanding the limits of the sport. As a result, the level of risk is also increasing. Athletes, as they strive to be the best, are constantly reminded just how extreme the sports are. When everything goes right, incredible results are achieved, but if something goes awry, disastrous consequences can occur.

Audrey S. Lundy

See also Wakeboarding

Further Reading

American Water Ski Educational Foundation. (n.d.). AWSEF Hall of Fame. Retrieved August 11, 2006, from http://www.waterskihalloffame.com

Athalwin Ziemer, G. (2005). *A daredevil and two boards: Ralph Samuelson, the Lake Pepin pioneer who invented water skiing.* Madison, WI: Hunter Havlerson Press.

Atkinson, S. (2004). Thrills and spills—45th Chevy Masters. *The Water Skier, 54*(4), 26–30.

Barefoot Central. (n.d.). Retrieved August 11, 2006, from http://www.barefootcentral.com

Barton, R. (2000). The merge. *Waterski Magazine, 22*(9), 21.

Benoist, B. (2004). Barefoot backward baby—Six baby steps to a back deep. *Waterski Magazine, 26*(7), 78–80.

Bleyer, J. (2006, July 28). Barefoot waterskiing: Putting your wet foot forward. *New York Times, retrieved from www.nytimes.com.*

Bowers, L. (2004). Winning grin. *Waterski Magazine, 26*(3), 112.

Favret, B., & Benzel, D. (1997). *Complete guide to water skiing—Slalom tricks jump.* Champaign, IL: Human Kinetics.

Finlayson, T. (2006). Point of view. *Waterski Magazine, 28*(4), 68–69.

Finlayson, T. (2006). Turning point: Four tips for getting back to the handle with the least resistance. *Waterski Magazine, 28*(7), 72–73.

Gleason, C. (2005). Barefoot endurance NASCAR style. *Waterski Magazine, 27*(2), 80–82.

Hagerdorn, A. (2004). Boys will be "nasty boys." *Waterski Magazine, 26*(2) 52–59.

Keverline, J. P., Englund, R., & Cooney, T. E. (2003). Takeoff forces transmitted to the upper extremity during water-skiing. *Orthopedics, 26*(7), 707–710.

Kreuger, L. (2004). Learning to jump. *The Water Skier, 54*(4), 38–39.

McDonald, P. (2003). Barefoot 411. *Waterski Magazine, 25*(2), 87.

McDonald, P. (2006). The (almost) complete guide to footing. *Waterski Magazine, 28*(4), 90–92.

Roberts, S. N., & Roberts, P. M. (1996). Tournament water skiing trauma. *British Journal of Sports Medicine, 30*(2), 90–93.

Ross, D. (2000). The return. *Waterski Magazine, 22*(9), 42–43, 84.

Scarpa, R. (1999). Coaches corner. *Waterski Magazine, 21*(5), 104.

Sullivan, C. (2006). The swing of slalom. *Waterski Magazine, 28*(4), 66–67.

Tauber. C. (2004). How you can win them all. *Waterski Magazine, 26*(7), 48–55.

Tauber. C. (2006). The evolution of slalom. *Waterski Magazine, 28*(4), 70–77.

USA Water Ski. (n.d.). Retrieved August 11, 2006, from http://usawaterski.org/index1.html

Woodling, L. (2005). The playboy. *Waterski Magazine, 54*(4), 62–69.

Whistler

The village of Whistler, Canada, is the mecca of snowboarding. Every year thousands of snowboarders from across the globe travel to Whistler to live and breathe snowboarding for the season; some don't ever leave. Located less than two hours north of Vancouver, Whistler is home to some of the world's best snowboarding terrain. Two mountains, Whistler and Blackcomb, rise 1,600 meters out of the

Aboriginal Participation

Whistler, British Columbia, is the site of the 2010 Winter Olympics, which is again drawing attention to where extreme sports are performed. Events, especially those the magnitude of the Olympics, can have a huge impact on the environment, economy, and in this case, the traditional lands of Canada's aboriginal populations.

For the first time in Olympic history, Aboriginal participation is a specific function of an Olympic and Paralympic Games organizing committee. We invite all the Aboriginal people of this country to share their culture with the world.

We are encouraging Aboriginal people from British Columbia and across Canada to participate in as many areas of the 2010 Winter Games as possible: as athletes, volunteers, employees, entrepreneurs, artists and performers, spectators and cultural ambassadors.

We are working with the Lil'wat, Musqueam, Squamish and Tsleil-Waututh First Nations—known as the Four Host First Nations—on whose traditional lands the Games will take place—as well as other First Nation, Inuit and Métis groups throughout Canada in the planning and hosting of the Games.

We are working to:

- Encourage greater Aboriginal participation in sport, identify and develop talented Aboriginal athletes, and support the development of Aboriginal coaches and leaders
- Provide opportunities for Aboriginal people to find jobs, win contracts and promote Aboriginal tourism throughout Canada
- Recognize and celebrate Aboriginal history, arts, culture and languages
- Promote awareness and understanding of the diversity, talents and contributions of Aboriginal peoples in Canada

Source: Vancouver 2010 (2006) *Vancouver 2010—Aboriginial participation.* Retrieved Feb. 1, 2007, from http://vancouver2010.com/en/Sustainability/AboriginalParticipation

---

valley and offer more than 3,200 hectares of ridable terrain. The average annual snowfall is 9.14 meters, and boarders have access to thirty-three lifts and more than two hundred marked runs.

The two mountains also provide snowboarders with five terrain parks, with some jumps exceeding 30 meters, as well as three halfpipes. The two mountains win the *Transworld Snowboarding* Resort Poll year after year because they offer "the complete snowboarding experience on-hill and off—from the perfect corduroy cruisers; long, challenging tree runs; sheer cliffs; and quality of snow, to the epic kickers, rails, and superpipe, as well as the restaurants, hotels and nightlife in Whistler Village" (Fast, 2005, p. 24). The area is also famous for its natural terrain, the preferred playground of free-riders.

Many hardcore snowboarders also own snowmobiles, which they use to access thousands of acres of backcountry terrain. In fact, many magazine photos and much film footage featuring professional snowboarders "going big"—on cliffs and jumps and among powder and trees—are shot in the Whistler backcountry. Snowboarding in summer is also an option. Freestyle snowboard camps, held in terrain parks and halfpipes built on the high alpine (2,300 meters) glaciated snow on Blackcomb Mountain, are popular among young boarders on their summer holidays.

However, terrain isn't Whistler's only attraction. The resort population also likes to party, as it shows during the ten-day annual World Ski and Snowboard Festival, which in 2006 attracted more than 250,000 visitors. The big-air event, where many of the world's best snowboarders and skiers competed for more than $100,000 in cash and prizes, drew a crowd of eighteen thousand. Further illustrating its international cachet, Whistler, with Vancouver, will host the 2010 Winter Olympic Games. Snowboarders no doubt will attend in full force.

Holly Thorpe

Further Reading

Fast, A. (2005, January). Best overall resort: Whistler/Blackcomb. *Transworld Snowboarding 2005 Resort Guide,* 24.

Fast, A. (2005, January). Gangs of B.C. *Transworld Snowboarding,* 254–267.

Huffman, J. (2006, January). 2006 Resort poll: Who's on top? *Transworld Snowboarding, 19,* 131.

White, Shaun

Shaun White (b. 1986) is an Olympic halfpipe gold medalist, eight-time Winter X Games medalist (six gold, two silver), Summer X Games medalist (silver), professional snowboarder, and skateboarder. Growing up in Carlsbad, California, young White took to skateboarding not long after he could walk and started skiing shortly thereafter. Following in his older brother Jesse's footsteps, he started snowboarding when he was only six; he was performing jumps landing them successfully on the same day. According to Jesse, just as "Mozart was supposed to play piano," it was "that kind of deal for Shaun" (Edwards 2006, 44).

White's family was "supportive and tight-knit," and every weekend during the winter his parents drove three hours to the ski areas near Big Bear Lake, California. He started competing—and winning—at age seven. In addition to dominating junior competitions, he appeared in a number of snowboarding films. With sponsorship from Burton Snowboards, White turned professional at the 1998 U.S. Open at age twelve. He was the sport's first prodigy and was nicknamed "Future Boy" for his potential impact on snowboarding.

Indeed, White, with his huge amplitude, technical abilities, and style, has been an undeniable force in halfpipe, slope-style, and big-air competitions. For example, he has won four consecutive gold medals in the X Games slope-style event (2003, 2004, 2005, 2006) and two gold medals in the halfpipe (2003, 2006). In the 2005–2006 season White, at nineteen, became the most successful snowboard competitor in history with twelve consecutive wins, including two X Games gold medals, an Olympic gold medal in the halfpipe, and victory in the U.S. Open halfpipe and slope-style championships. Skateboarding legend Tony Hawk describes White as "one of the most amazing athletes on the planet. He's got his own style—plus he can do tricks five feet higher than everyone else" (Edwards, 2006, p. 43). With his successes, White has gained eminence in the culture. During the 2002–2003 and 2005–2006 seasons he received the most snowboarding print coverage (editorial and advertising). Furthermore, he was the first snowboarder since Terje Haakonsen of Norway to be the subject of a full-length video. *The Shaun White Album* (2004) showcases White's snowboarding and skateboarding skills. White also starred in the film *First Descent* (2005), which featured him performing in halfpipes and on jumps of 28 meters in the backcountry as well as riding death-defying lines in Alaska.

As a skateboarder White was only thirteen when he started touring with Tony Hawk's Boom-Boom Huck Jam demo tour during the summer; Hawk has been a supporter ever since. White rode his skateboard "strictly for fun" until the 2003 Slam City Jam skateboarding event in Vancouver, Canada, where he joined the professional ranks. In 2005 he won a silver medal in the vert ramp skating competition at the Summer X Games, becoming the first extreme athlete to win a medal in both Winter and Summer Games. That year he won his first skateboarding gold medal at the Dew Action Sports Tour. In the words of cultural commentator Rob Reed, "By pushing the envelope in both snowboarding and skateboarding, White has established himself as an action-sport figure beyond compare" (Reed, 2005).

This assessment is particularly true in the eyes of corporate and television sponsors. In addition to endorsing Burton, Oakley, and Volcom, White endorses Mountain Dew, Sony Playstation, and Target, appearing in television commercials and sporting their logos. White's Olympic success propelled him even further into the public eye. His performance grabbed headlines across the country, and he made numerous guest appearances on television and radio talk shows. He was featured on the cover of *Rolling Stone*, which declared him "the coolest *kid* in America," and Ubisoft quickly signed White to a video games sponsorship. His signature video game is expected in 2007.

According to *CNN Money*, "Experts in the field generally point to snowboarder Shaun White as the one breakout star of these Games in terms of endorsement potential. His gold medal win, coupled with his personality, his now famous bright red hair and his memorable nickname—the Flying Tomato—all give him a great profile. He did everything right in Turin. He was even crying on the medals stand. He lived up to the hype. He's clearly comfortable on camera. You'll see a lot of him" (Isidore 2006). Similarly, ESPN.com declares White "one of the biggest financial winners from the Games" (Rovell 2006). White exemplifies the meaning of "extreme," not only in his ability to perform gravity-defying maneuvers in halfpipes and terrain parks, but also in the appeal of his "alternative" image to sponsors and the public.

Holly Thorpe

Further Reading

Bridges, P. (2005, August). The next Shaun White. *Snowboarder Magazine*, 82–93.

Curly, K., & Harrison, K. (Director/Producers). (2005). *First descent: The story of the snowboarding revolution* [Motion picture]. United States: Universal Pictures.

Edwards, G. (2006, March 9). Attack of the flying tomato. *Rolling Stone*, 43–45.

Isidore, C. (2006, February 13). Advertisers going to X-tremes. Retrieved February 16, 2007, from http://money.cnn.com/2006/02/13/commentary/column_sportsbiz/sportsbiz

Reed, R. (2005). *The way of the snowboarder*. New York: Harry N. Abrams.

Rovell, D. (2006). The flying tomato. Retrieved February 16, 2007, from http://sports.espn.go.com/espn/blog/index?name=rovell_darren&month=2&year=2006

Shaunwhite.com. (n.d.). Retrieved July 20, 2006, from http://www.shaunwhite.com/home.html

The White Album. (n.d.). Retrieved July 20, 2006, from http://www.theshaunwhitealbum.com/

Whiteness and Extreme Sports

What is the relationship between whiteness and extreme sports? We would be wrong to assert that extreme sports are simply "white sports," that is, that extreme sports are created and performed exclusively by white people for white audiences. Such an assertion becomes especially erroneous when we acknowledge the increasingly global character of many extreme sports. Take, for example, the extreme sport of skateboarding, which today is performed by youths of color across the globe.

However, we would also be wrong to ignore how extreme sports in the United States are performed mainly by white male youths for a largely young white male demographic (the coveted twelve-to-thirty-four-year-old male audience). We would be wrong not to notice how the most visible icons of extreme sports, those athletes who have also become some of the wealthiest members of this sporting culture, such as Tony Hawk, Mat Hoffman, Dave Mirra, Bob Burnquist, and Bam Margera, are all youthful white men. We would be wrong to fail to see how the rapid mainstreaming of extreme sports since the creation of the cable-televised X Games (first called the "Extreme Games") in 1995 was enabled by the economic and cultural interests of a group of wealthy business and media leaders who are also largely white and male. Further, we must see how the public images and media stories that U.S. culture produces about extreme sports and its participants feature white in-dividuals while popularizing values such as individualism, self-reliance, and male exclusivity and dominance, which historically, and too often today, are the ideological means through which white people claim that race is no longer a limiting barrier in U.S. society after the civil rights movement of the 1950s and 1960s. In other words, stories such as the ones told about extreme sports and its participants, which celebrate individualism and self-reliance and feature white men, even though such stories appear to be race neutral, ultimately reproduce the social power of white people as a group and construct white perspectives and experiences as the "normal" U.S. perspective and experience.

Critical Study of Whiteness

A discussion of the relationship between whiteness and extreme sports must begin with a discussion of the recent history of scholarship on race in the United States. In the 1990s scholars of race not only broadened their field of inquiry to include the study of the systemic processes of racism that affect the everyday lives of, and social opportunities available to, people of color, but also began to recognize and study how many of the social processes of racism simultaneously create a multitude of social privileges for those who are considered to be "white" within various periods of history. This interest in studying whiteness also emerged in the mid-1990s when historically marginalized groups such as people of color, women, and gays and lesbians illuminated and publicly criticized the social, economic, political, and psychic privileges that white straight men take for granted in the United States. Thus, the critical study of whiteness was born.

This critical examination of whiteness is predicated on the idea that no biological imperative exists to categorize people according to their so-called race. Instead, racial scholars have investigated the origin of the use of ideas about race to reveal race to be a social construct that gives value to a person's skin color among other phenotypic (relating to the observable properties of an organism that are produced by the interaction of the genotype and the environment) features. This choice of understanding race as a social construct rather than a biological imperative is not an arbitrary one. Rather, it is based on, and supported by, historical and contemporary cross-cultural evidence that demonstrates that the meanings attached to so-called races and the number of racial categories that exist vary considerably from one culture to another and across history. This constructionist view of race asserts that the meanings given to particular racial groups are grounded more in the interests of producing and maintaining white dominance and social control of racial minorities than in systematic, empirical evidence of the actual behaviors of members of these marginalized groups. However, this view simultaneously emphasizes how race cannot be completely dismissed as a social fiction either because ideas about race are made to matter in order to create racial hierarchies. These racial hierarchies enable whites to occupy a social position where they are regarded as superior to all other racial and ethnic groups. Further, because white elites occupy positions of power in U.S. society, in order to mask their power they promote the idea of white culture as the unmarked racial center of Western civilization. Finally, these "fictions of race" are used to construct social structures within U.S. institutions such as the media, sports, family, and medicine, which produce material hardships and violences against all those people not considered to be "white" at that time in history.

Social System

What exactly do we mean by "whiteness"? Some ambiguity exists in how whiteness is defined in this emergent body of research. However, a good starting point for developing a basic understanding of whiteness is to conceive of it as a social system built by those who are considered to be white at a given time in history in order to provide social advantages to all those who are considered to be white. An important strain of research on whiteness has revealed that who is considered to be "white" differs from one moment in history to another as well as from one culture to another. Again, we must keep in mind how this mode of thinking about race is predicated on the idea that race is socially constructed and not a natural biological category. Thus, a person's skin color (whatever its hue or shade) signifies only a particular racial meaning within the racial ideologies of that culture. The racial meaning associated with that same person would change if a person from another culture with another set of racial ideologies were to read her racial identity.

Whiteness as a social system is established and maintained when "whites" garner the power to construct the social institutions and cultural life of a society in ways that give the greatest value to those social acts and relations that ultimately serve the social, political, and economic interests of those particular "white" people. In democratic

societies such as the United States, the establishment and reproduction of whiteness as a social system are made easier when those considered to be white make up a numerical majority. At times in history (such as the present) when those considered to be "white" have had their majority status challenged by an influx of racial "others," those who make up the "white" category often induce some people once considered to be "nonwhites" to suppress their racial/ethnic identities and be remade as "whites" by granting them fuller (but not always full) access to the social, economic, and political privileges of being considered "white." This social transformation of "nonwhites" into "whites" enables the re-creation of a new white consensus that allows the social privileges of being white to be maintained in the face of challenges to white supremacy in the United States from racial "others."

In a society dominated by whiteness, "white" people control the economic, political, social, and cultural institutions of that society and promote their worldview and social norms as the authentic, legitimate, and seemingly natural viewpoint and way of being and knowing within that society. This dual process of naturalizing and universalizing white values, ideologies, and social norms to determine what it means to be authentically American marginalizes the experiences and voices of those who are considered people of color, along with ostensibly making them second-class citizens. As the representations of white people as most authentically and legitimately American (relative to people of color) are repeatedly forwarded as a "fact" that is taken for granted, many white people can have difficulty discerning how such representations are used to establish and maintain a culturally dominant position in U.S. society for those who are considered white. Many white people also can have difficulty seeing how these images of whites as the embodiments of America, which are often cast in positive, inspiring, patriotic rhetoric, come at the expense of people of color who are then perceived as nonauthentic or, in the common vernacular, "not really American." These types of insights are a key part of the critical study of whiteness.

Drawing on the work of scholars such as W. E. B. Du Bois, James Baldwin, Toni Morrison, David Wellman, and bell hooks, as well as the more contemporary work of George Lipsitz, Abby Ferber, David Roediger, Ruth Frankenburg, and C. Richard King, the best of this scholarship conceives of whiteness as a complex set of systemic social forces that provides a number of "material, symbolic, or psychological" privileges to those who are considered to be white over those considered nonwhite at a given time in history (Feagin

2001, 175). Research on whiteness seeks to illuminate the complex social processes through which social, cultural, economic, political, and psychological advantages are produced through the institutions of U.S. society and accrued in the everyday experiences of most white people in the United States.

"White Positionings"

One goal of research on whiteness is to make visible the ways in which the worldview, social norms, and economic and political interests of particular groups of white people become established as the seemingly naturally occurring, unraced, "normal" views and material interests of "the American people" or as the unspoken social norms of U.S. culture. This research has exposed the ways in which whiteness has historically acted as the unraced, normative center of the racialized world. By exposing the "seeming transparency of white positionings" (Frankenburg, 1997, 1) in U.S. culture, one learns to see the monumental, yet usually overlooked—by white people, at least—ways in which race structures the lives of all Americans regardless of their racial or ethnic identities.

Another goal of this research is to identify and explain the complex ways in which white privilege is produced, reproduced, and legitimized through media discourses, cultural practices, and institutional decisions (i.e., social policies) that take place every day in U.S. society and rarely, if ever, explicitly mention race or, for most whites, seem to be about race. This research seeks to interrupt the tendency of most white people not to understand these aspects of their everyday social lives as fundamentally racial phenomena.

What social and political conditions led to the creation and rapid popularization of extreme sports during the mid- to late 1990s in the United States?

"Extreme sports" were created and became popular during the 1990s. At this time a number of formerly marginalized sports that had no apparent connection, such as skateboarding, BASE (building, antenna, span, Earth) jumping, street luge, BMX bicycle riding, and the Eco-Challenge (a multiday, expedition-length adventure race), were brought together to create the category of "extreme sports." These sports were united by a shared investment by the participants in risk taking, thrill seeking, individual progression, and a consciously resistive, outsider identity relative to the organized sports establishment. At first extreme sports were represented as the unusual sporting preferences

---

Changing Demographics

As part of a concerted effort to attract a wider range of people to its slopes, Vail Resorts in Vail, Colorado, has started a program that provides lift tickets to minority children in the community. The following is an excerpt from Edward Stoner's report on the program in the Vail Daily *newspaper.*

Changing population

For each of the previous two years, Vail Resorts offered about 2,500 skiing scholarships to minority-group children from the Front Range through the Denver-based Alpino program. The company decided to take the program in-house this year.

"(Alpino) really got us started down the right path," said Dee Byrne, director of Vail Ski and Snowboard School.

With minority groups making up a larger percentage of the nation's population, Vail Resorts recognizes the need to appeal to those groups, Byrne said.

"As the demographics in the United States change and the population becomes more mixed, we need to make sure we're reaching out to citizens of all colors as a sport in order to sustain participation in the future," she said.

A big part of that is including workers in the community who do not ski, Byrne said.

"We've got a whole community at the base of these ski resorts we're not tapping into," she said.

The perception that Vail and Beaver Creek only cater to wealthy, out-of-town clients troubles her, she said.

Source: Vail Daily. (2007, January 21). Vail Resorts offers free lift tickets to minorities. Retrieved Feb. 1 2007, from http://www.vaildaily.com/article/20070121/NEWS/101210058&SearchID=73270812196032

of the so-called Generation X. However, during the late 1990s the public image of extreme sports conspicuously shifted. In this public-image makeover, pushed aside were the Generation X skateboarders and BMX riders previously featured in most stories about extreme sports.

These young white males of Generation X were replaced in media stories by mainly white men (with a few women) in their thirties and forties who were portrayed as exploring new U.S. frontiers in the sky through sky surfing and in the wilderness by participating in BASE jumping and the Eco-Challenge. These rough-and-tumble masculine white men were represented as having much in common with U.S. pioneers, who were valorized for heroically conquering new frontiers in order to establish the United States. In short, this media makeover of extreme sports and its practitioners offered an unmistakable white-dominant, male-centered, U.S. national genealogy that began with the country's founding fathers and ended with extreme sportsmen. This peculiar way of telling a story about extreme sports—which appeared in *Time* and *U.S. News & World Report* cover stories—demonstrates how stories about extreme sports were used to promote particular ways of imagining the United States and its citizenry.

These white-exclusive, male-centered stories about the United States, told through these stories about extreme sports, emerged at a time when other alternative stories about the United States as being increasingly tolerant and embracing its newfound cultural diversity were being told. In the realm of sports perhaps the most prominent version of this narrative celebration of a new multicultural United States was stories featuring golfer Tiger Woods. Stories about Woods emerged at approximately the same time when extreme sports were wholeheartedly embraced and gained a foothold in the U.S. mainstream (especially in advertising, where they were used to sell everything from cars to clothing to snack food to soft drinks). Yet, while stories of Tiger Woods were employed by white America to proclaim its color blindness to race and its embrace of racial and ethnic difference, stories about extreme sports subtly told a different story about race and racial tolerance by white America. These stories implicitly revealed a strong anxiety about the United States' emergent cultural diversity and a concomitant desire to recover white culture—and particularly white men's position in U.S. society—as the authentic and legitimate representative of U.S. culture. This anxiety and this desire can be seen in the way in which white men, to the exclusion of people

of color and largely women, were prominently featured in stories about extreme sports.

Extreme Sports as Cultural Site

So, one way in which we can read extreme sports as a cultural site involved in promoting the interests of white people is that media discourses about extreme sports showcased images of white people as representatives of the United States, as white people were exclusively pictured as the ones participating in this new sporting activity supposedly taking over the United States during the late 1990s.

Another way in which we can understand extreme sports as a cultural site involved in the reproduction of the United States' white-dominant society is by noting how popular discourses about the sport promote a set of ideas which often obscure and deny the existence of racial inequalities in contemporary U.S. society. Specifically, stories about extreme sports that cast the white male participants as the descendants of psychologist and philosopher William James and U.S. cowboys promoted ideas of individualism and self-reliance along with a racial color blindness, which together are often the ideological ingredients used to overlook and deny racial asymmetries of power today.

Finally, as cultural diversity, white privilege, and white identity were made visible to white America, white people developed a number of ways to disavow their investment or connection to white privilege, even as they reaped its rewards daily. During the 1990s a number of whites made various claims to marginality, as George Yudice put it. In other words, in the face of public criticisms of white privilege, a sizable number of white people sought to define themselves as economically unprivileged and more connected to the social margins than the privileged white mainstream. The term *white trash*, as a mainly derogatory label for poor white people, became popular in U.S. popular culture. Many whites frequently downplayed the security or comfort of their economic position, or they claimed working-class, poor, or "white trash" roots. Through his origins in Arkansas and a divorced family, even President Bill Clinton was repeatedly lampooned as "white trash," particularly through his nickname, "Bubba." Also, *Roseanne*, which featured the travails of a seemingly dysfunctional, working-class, white family, was the popular TV show of the era.

From this 1990s U.S. context of pervasive criticisms

of white privilege and disavowals by many whites, extreme sports were portrayed in the media as an imaginary solution to the increased visibility of white racial identity and the new public exposure and critique of white privilege. This portrayal occurred in a couple of ways. First, as a sporting culture in which virtually all of the participants were white, many extreme sports provided a safe haven for white participants where they could escape feelings of anxiety and uncertainty that they often felt in this new era of multiculturalism and cultural diversity. Their feelings of comfort and certainty were a result of the way in which extreme sports offered a cultural space where whiteness was the unquestioned social norm (in the absence of people of color). Second, because extreme sports were first thought of as sporting activities marginalized by the traditional mainstream sports of baseball, football, and basketball, extreme sports offered participants a seemingly authentic "outsider" identity that seemed to mark them as disconnected and different from mainstream athletes and the white U.S. mainstream that idolized them.

An example of the way in which some extreme sports participants cultivated an economically unprivileged and socially marginalized identity is representations of skateboarders in skateboarding magazines as well as in the films *Dogtown and Z-Boys* and *Lords of Dogtown*. Through these sorts of representations of these seemingly poor or socially disadvantaged white extreme sportsmen, white privilege is difficult to apprehend. Countless images and stories of young white men who either come from working-class and poor backgrounds or have a sartorial style that symbolizes their supposed distance from white privilege make it difficult for many whites to contemplate the existence of racial privileges for white people in U.S. society.

Beyond sports we could see a similar strategy for representing whites in popular films of the era such as *8 Mile*, *Fight Club*, *Forrest Gump*, and *Good Will Hunting*. Or, as some cultural critics have argued, images and stories of economically unprivileged whites became popular in the 1990s as a way of attempting to disavow the existence of whiteness. Because if all white people are said to be automatically privileged in a white-dominant society, then identifying some whites who appear as socially and economically unprivileged is a way in which whites who secretly wish not to acknowledge white racial privilege could claim it does not exist.

Thus, the relationship between extreme sports and whiteness is that the former's creation and popularization were a product of a historically specific crisis of white dominance and normalcy in U.S. society during the mid- to late 1990s with the rise of cultural diversity initiatives and the new U.S. cultural ideal of multiculturalism. Not only can extreme sports be read as a response to this crisis, but also, particularly in the media stories told about this sports formation, extreme sports served as a cultural means through which white dominance could be restored ironically through the promotion of stories and ideas that implicitly denied and disavowed the existence of social and economic white privilege.

Kyle Kusz

Further Reading

Brayton, S. (2005). Black-lash: Revisiting the white Negro through skateboarding. *Sociology of Sport Journal*, 22(3), 356–371.

Feagin, J.R. (2000). *Racist America: Roots, current realities, & future reparations*. New York: Routledge:

Frankenburg, R. (1997). *Displacing whiteness: Essays in social and cultural criticism*. Durham, NC: Duke University Press.

Heino, R. (2000). What is so punk about snowboarding? *Journal of Sport and Social Issues*, 24, 176–191.

hooks, b. (1992). *Black looks: Race and representation*. Boston: South End Press.

Humphreys, D. (1997). 'Shredheads go mainstream'?: Snowboarding and alternative youth. *International review for the sociology of sport*, 32(2), 147–160. London: Sage Publications

Kincheloe, J., Steinberg, S., Rodriguez, N., & Chennault, R. (Eds.) *White reign: Deploying whiteness in America* (pp. 3–30). New York: St. Martin's Press.

King, C.R. & Springwood, C.F. (2001). *Beyond the cheers: Race as spectacle in college sport*. Albany: State University of New York Press.

Kusz, K.W. (2001). 'I want to be the minority': The politics of youthful white masculinities in sport and popular culture in 1990s America. *Journal of Sport and Social Issues*, 25(4), 390–416.

Kusz, K. (2003). BMX, extreme sports, and the white male backlash. In R. Rinehart & S. Sydnor's (Eds.), *To the extreme: Alternative sports inside and out*. Albany: State University of New York Press.

Kusz, K. (2004). Extreme America: The Cultural politics of extreme sports in 1990s America. In B. Wheaton (Ed.), *Understanding lifestyle sports: Consumption, identity, and difference*. London: Routledge.

Kusz, K.W. (2006). Why be a 'Jackass'?: Media images of young white men in new millennium America. In S. Spickard Prettyman & B. Lampman (Eds.), *Learning culture through sports*. Lanham, MD: Scarecrow Press.

Lipsitz, G. (1998). *The Possessive investment in whiteness: How white people profit from identity politics*. Philadelphia, PA: Temple University Press.

Pfeil, F. (1995). *White guys: Postmodern domination and difference*. London: Verso.

Rinehart, R. (2000). Emerging arriving sport: Alternatives to formal sport. In J. Coakley & E. Dunning (Eds.), *Handbook of Sport Studies*. London: Sage.

Roediger, D. (1994). *Towards the abolition of whiteness: Essays on race, politics, and working class history*. London: Verso.

Whitewater Kayaking and Canoeing

Canoeing and kayaking are sports that have a variety of disciplines. Canoeing, in which participants sit or kneel on seats and use single-bladed paddles, is often called "Canadian canoeing" because of Canada's early promotion of international racing. Kayaking, in which participants use double-bladed paddles, is known as *kanusport* in some countries and is one of the fastest-growing activities globally. According to recent surveys, 11.78 and 6.9 million Americans participate in canoeing and kayaking at least once per year respectively, and there are almost two million paddlers in Britain. While most take to the water in inland rivers (86 percent), the sea, lakes and reservoirs, canals and artificial white-water sites are also used. With so many different types of locations it is not surprising that canoe and kayak styles vary widely, ranging from relaxing recreation to extreme sport. Different styles of participation inevitably carry different sets of risks.

According to a recent study, the overall risk of injury from canoeing and kayaking is 4.5 injuries for every 1000 days paddled (in comparison, the risk of injury from Alpine skiing and windsurfing is 3.2 per 1000 days and 1 per 1000 days, respectively). The most common injury sites are the back and the upper limb (shoulder, wrist/hand and elbow/forearm). Indeed, shoulder dislocation is seen in approximately 6 percent of paddlers. Furthermore, head and facial injuries are not uncommon and can be serious or even fatal. Canoeing and kayaking consistently rank second to motor boating in contributing to water-related sports deaths in the United States. One study even found 1 in 10 competitive paddlers had experienced a near-drowning event in their careers. According to recent research, alcohol is a factor in 25 percent of canoeing deaths, and most fatalities involve some combination of inexperience, hazardous water or weather. Perhaps in response to such statistics, the American Canoe Association has recently produced a safety publication with tips for canoeists emphasizing the importance of wearing personal flotation devices (lifejackets), minimizing movement in the vessel, avoiding extreme weather, not getting drunk and using appropriate safety equipment (e.g., hard hat when in white-water).

History

Canoes and kayaks still show the traditional lines of a Greenland Inuit kayak or Aleutian umiak, a Maori (relating to a Polynesian people native to New Zealand) dugout, or a Native American birch-bark canoe because the designs

Kayaker padding against the strong flow of water. Source: istock/Brian Jenkin.

that allowed paddlers to handle challenging conditions more than five thousand years ago are still relevant today. The traditional lines bring a sense of tradition to paddle sports, appreciated by many modern paddlers regardless of whether they are racing in sleek, modern craft or touring inland waterways in more stable designs.

The peoples of indigenous cultures in North America, Greenland, Scandinavia, and the former Soviet Union used canoes and kayaks. Builders stretched the skins of seal, walrus, or caribou around wooden frames and fastened them with sinew, baleen (a substance found in plates that hang from the upper jaws of baleen whales), bones, or antlers. Later, the presence of metal tools and toggles in North American boat construction indicated contact with European explorers. Ingenious crafters, the Inuit peoples used local materials to develop a variety of functional designs for different conditions, each of which could handle different types of water and activities.

Kayaks (from the Inuit word *qayak*) were traditionally used to hunt sea animals, including large mammals such as walruses and whales. The kayaks were relatively small, often ranging from 3.6 meters to 4.8 meters, which made them highly maneuverable for chasing prey. Because only men hunted in these societies, the kayak has been associated primarily with men until recent history.

The Inuit umiak (canoe) was a large, undecked skin boat of 7.6 meters to 12.1 meters used to carry large groups of people and heavy loads of cargo. Sometimes also used for hunting, it could be paddled, rowed, or sailed long distances. In Greenland the umiak came to be defined as the women's boat because women used them when they handled the transport of communities of people to new settlements. The umiak is believed to be the oldest working boat. Rock paintings in Norway from 5000 BCE show illustrations of what some archaeologists conclude to be open skin boats, although this conclusion is controversial. Some experts believe that the elk figureheads etched onto these boats were a link between land and sea and provided a means for humans to enter the lower spirit world. Similar seaworthy craft are also believed to have aided Asian peoples in their migration to the New World.

Rise of Recreational Racing

Scholars generally believe that canoe races and regattas predate recorded history and figured prominently in the rituals of ancient cultures. Thanks to John MacGregor mod-

ern racing emerged in Great Britain with royal approval in the 1870s, and the military used canoe racing for training throughout the British empire. The American Canoe Association formed in 1880 as an international organization and awarded three honorary memberships to important non-American men such as John MacGregor and Worrington Baden-Powell, the brother of the Boy Scout founder, Robert Baden-Powell. Many ACA members preferred canoe sailing races in decked boats, which looked more like kayaks, rather than the open Canadian canoe. War canoes created a new class of racing in which teams of twenty people or more propelled a large boat, and boys and girls at summer camps quickly embraced this team event. Outrigger canoe racing, initially for men, began in the Hawaiian islands and quickly grew more competitive.

By the turn of the twentieth century racers experimented with the high kneel position of modern "sprint" canoeing for greater leverage against the paddle, and the greater speed made the high kneel the favorite racing position for flatwater despite its instability. After World War I canoeing and kayaking expanded so greatly that the era has been called their "golden age." Men first competed in sprint canoeing and kayaking as demonstration sports in the Olympics in 1924 in Paris and as full medal events in 1936 in Berlin. The onset of World War II stalled the expansion of international racing, but later manufacturers converted the war technologies of aluminum and fiberglass to create a wealth of new canoe and kayak designs. The post–World War II popularity of whitewater paddling in western and eastern Europe and former Soviet bloc countries contributed to the 1972 entry of slalom racing at the Munich Olympics, but it has appeared in only four subsequent Olympics because of the expense of creating artificial whitewater facilities.

The International Canoe Federation (ICF), the international governing body for paddle sports, recently approved canoe water polo for men and women as an international event. In this event two teams of kayakers in highly maneuverable boats attempt to score goals by passing a ball. National governing bodies within each country develop training and racing opportunities for athletes, often in conjunction with local clubs and private schools that have traditionally supported the development of canoe and kayak racing.

However, other forms of racing continue to emerge, often as non-Olympic events. Marathon racing in kayaks and open canoes tests paddlers on 8-kilometer to multiday courses. Whitewater freestyle or rodeo competitions require paddlers to execute technically difficult moves on holes and waves. Flatwater freestyle is sometimes called "canoe ballet."

In it competitors create a dance choreography set to music. Dragon boat racing, similar to war canoe racing, involves teams of twenty-two people. The colorful nature of competition is a reflection of canoeing's and kayaking's enduring popularity among a variety of nations and cultures. It is important to note, however, that competition is not always at the fore of participation. Arguably, the essence of many forms of participation, particularly the more extreme styles (e.g., creeking, freestyle), is having fun, playing and/or performing for one's peers. According to one cultural commentator, "kayaking's new wave is more interested in heading out to the planet's roudiest rivers, HD camera in hand, than in beating each other in a points game" (Reimers, 2005, p. 134).

Nature of the Sports

Many variations of canoeing and kayaking have emerged to offer many opportunities to paddle. Some variations have been accepted as Olympic sports, and many countries have local, regional, or national championships that allow many levels of competition. The International Canoe Federation recognizes the following six disciplines.

Flatwater

In flatwater sprint racing athletes compete head to head on calm bodies of water in 500- and 1,000-meter distances. The events require speed, strength, and endurance. In the Olympics, women's events were added at London in 1948. However, women compete only in kayaking, not in canoeing, in single, double, and four-woman kayaks in 500-meter races. The four-woman kayak event was added in 1984.

Olypmic sprint races begin with qualifying heats, and the eight fastest qualifiers advance directly to the semifinals. The rest compete in a second-chance round known as a *repechage* (French for "fishing again"), and the four fastest boats advance to the semifinals. The top six semifinalists take part in the final, whereas the other six take part in a petit-final to determine seventh through twelfth places. Soviet and German women dominated in the early years, whereas more recently a variety of nations has been represented at the winner's podium.

Slalom

In the slalom single kayakers negotiate a course of twenty-five hanging poles called "gates" over stretches of white-water rapids 300 to 600 meters long. Kayakers attempt to negotiate as quickly as possible the gates in designated upstream-facing or downstream-facing positions. Kayakers try to complete the course without accruing penalties from touching gates (two seconds) or missing gates (fifty seconds). Only men compete in the canoe classes, kneeling in decked boats that resemble kayaks. C-1 (singles) and C-2 (doubles) races are challenging because each canoeist uses only one blade.

The challenge is to be fast and clean through the gates in frothy whitewater, creating an exciting spectator sport. Paddlers take two runs down the course, and both runs are added together for the final score. Women paddle the same whitewater stretch as men in kayaking classes, although the gates may be placed differently. Development of a slalom site can be difficult and expensive if a natural whitewater site is unavailable. However, the sport has spread beyond hosts in mountainous countries known for their steep rivers to urban hosts that have invested in artificial whitewater parks. Slalom is an intermittent demonstration sport in the Olympics.

Wildwater

Wildwater racing is downriver sprinting in either kayaks or decked canoes through whitewater. One of the smallest disciplines, wildwater racing requires that paddlers find the fastest current and negotiate challenging obstacles on a sharply descending river in a race against the clock. The first world championship in France in 1959 featured long races of fifty minutes or more, and the trend through the years has been to shorten distances to enhance spectator interest and reduce the expense of managing long river courses. In 1988 the ICF created two racing classes: classic and sprint. The classic race distances are 4 to 6 kilometers, and the sprint race distances are 500 to 1,000 meters. Men's classes include K-1, C-1, and C-2; women race in K-1; mixed teams (man-woman) compete in C-2. Wildwater racing is currently a non-Olympic event.

Marathon

Canoeing over long flatwater distances is known as "marathon racing" and has enjoyed popularity in Europe with the Kronberg race in Denmark, the Devises in Great Britain, the Sella Descent in Spain, the Liffey Descent in Ireland, and the Tour du Gudena in Denmark. More than twenty national federations sponsored national championships by

Canoe Races

Canoe Sailing

With roots in Polynesian exploration, canoe sailing emerged as a racing discipline in Great Britain through John MacGregor's efforts in 1866 to establish the Canoe Club, which later became the Royal Club. Within twenty years the New York Canoe Club had established an international sailing cup, and U.S. participants had experimented with sliding seats and hiking boards to sit outside the canoe to control the rudder and sails, much to the disdain of British sailors who did not allow such practices. Scandinavians and Germans created entirely different specifications before World War II, and the ICF was challenged to establish hull, sail, and rigging designs acceptable to many countries for the first world championship in 1961. Canoe sailing is currently a non-Olympic sport.

Dragon Boat Racing

A dragon boat resembles the classic Chinese vision of a dragon: At the bow are an oxen's head, deer antlers, and the mane of a horse; the body has the scales of a python; a hawk's claws are represented by canoeists with single-bladed paddles; and at the stern are the fins and tail of a fish. Usually twenty paddlers propel the large dragon boat with a drummer and helmsman. They often race head to head with another boat over various distances where strength and endurance must be married with team unity and spirit to paddle well to the rhythm of the drum. The ancient Chinese originally used the dragon boat in religious events and later in honor of a beloved patriotic poet. Dragon boat races were a symbol of patriotism long before a 1976 festival in Hong Kong began a new era of modern competition. Now more than 20 million Chinese compete in dragon boat racing, which has spread to western and eastern Europe, where fifty thousand people compete. Dragon boat racing is not yet an Olympic sport, but it organizes world and continental championships.

Laurie Gullion

1976, and they proposed to the ICF that marathon racing become a sanctioned event, initially for K-1 and K-2 men. With international interest in marathon racing continuing to build, the ICF finally approved the first world championship in 1988 with trophies for K-1 and K-2 men, K-1 and K-2 women, and C-1 and C-2 men. Interest surged in the United States, Canada, Australia, and South Africa, and now marathon racing exists on all seven continents. It is currently a non-Olympic event.

Extreme Kayaking

Whitewater kayaking can range from a fun, carefree, leisurely float trip to a challenging, adrenaline-filled sport. The difficulty of a whitewater rapid is graded on an International Scale of River Difficulty ranging from I to VI, with class I being the easiest (essentially moving flat-water), and class VI the most difficult (which is rarely, if ever, run, and then only with a high risk of death). The latter typically include large volume rivers with violent rapids, running ledges, slides, and waterfalls. At the core of the contemporary kayaking culture are a group of (typically) young paddlers that actively seek out the most dangerous and challenging rivers. Among their number is South African Steve Fisher.

For almost a decade, Fisher has been a dominant force in various whitewater disciplines. He has won countless kayak rodeos (see below for description), a bronze medal in the 1999 and 2003 World Freestyle Championships, downriver races at the Gorge Games, in Hood River, Oregon, and the Camel White Water Challenge in Chile. He has also invented, or contributed to the development of more than ten freestyle maneuvers, including the airscrew, flip-turn, and helix (an inverted aerial flat spin). In 2002, however, Fisher moved away from the competitive circuit, complaining that the professional tour was not hosting its events on challenging enough waves. Instead, he focused his energies on "doing missions" or "expeditions"—that is "searching out big water, towering waterfalls, and first descents" (Anders, 2005, p. 38). Indeed, he has made more than two-dozen major first descents, including the Upper Middle Kaweah in California, and the Maykha, in Myanmar. In February

2003, Fisher was among a group of paddlers that made the first descent on Tibet's Yarlung Tsangpo, the world's steepest big-water river, otherwise known as the "Everest of rivers" (Anders, 2005, p. 41). In 2003, *Paddler* magazine named Fisher the "world's best kayaker." According to one cultural commentator, Fisher is the embodiment of 'extreme': "His unofficial moto is "Go big." Whether it's hucking himself off Canada's 87-foot Aguasabon Falls, pioneering the first descent of Tibet's Yarlung Tsangpo, inventing aerial freestyle tricks, or pounding lager, he always takes it a couple of steps beyond his peers," he has a "willing-to-put-it-out-there-on-the-edge attitude" (Anders, 2005, 38). Fisher is among a younger generation of extreme kayakers who engage in various new styles of participation, including creeking, extreme racing, and playboating, with the goal of constantly pushing the boundaries of the sport.

Creeking

Creeking is the extreme version of river-running (a tour down a river, to enjoy scenery as well as experiencing challenging whitewater ranging from short day trips to longer multi-day trips). Creeking typically involves very technical and difficult rapids in the class IV to VI range. While definitions vary, creeking generally involves high gradient (approaching or in excess of 100 feet per mile), and is likely to include running ledges, slides, and waterfalls on relatively small and tight rivers. In 2004 World champion freestyle kayaker and rafter, Nikki Kelly, was part of a team that completed the first successful run of seven of California's classic High Sierra creeks in a single season, "that's a staggering 25,000-plus vertical feet over 184 miles of Class V drops in 53 days" (Livingston, 2005, 79). According to Kelly, "these trips are what kayaking's really all about" (cited in Daley, 2005, 76). To further maximize their access to "big-fast-waves," some extreme whitewater kayakers have taken a page from Hawaiian tow-in surfing, and are using Jet Ski's to pull one another into position (Reimers, 2005, 134). Extreme racing is a competitive form of this aspect of whitewater kayaking.

Extreme Racing

In comparison to whitewater racing which is the competitive version of river-running and involves racing specialized canoes or kayaks down grade II to IV rivers, extreme races are typically held on grade V rivers and include waterfalls and dangerous rapids, beyond the ability of the majority of whitewater kayakers. Extreme races may include mass-starts or individual timed runs, and are held at various international locations including the Nevis in Scotland, the Ulla in Norway, and the Russell Fork, Green River Narrows, Upper Gauley River, Upper Youghiogheny River, and Great Falls of the Potomac in the United States.

Rodeo or Playboating

Rodeo, playboating, or freestyle kayaking, is perhaps the most artistic style of participation, and is said to be the "paddling equivalent of skateboarding or BMX" (Wikipedia, 2006). While the objective of most styles of canoeing and kayaking is to travel the length of a section of river, playboaters tend to stay in one place (a playspot), such as "gnarly waves or holes, which occur when water rushes atop a submerged object, typically a rock or bolder, and forces itself under the calm water on the opposite side, thus pushing the water up into a continuously circulating backwash" (Bailey, 2006, 6). Popular playspots include weirs (e.g., Hurley Weir on the Thames near London; Hawaii-sur-Rhone on the Rhône River, Lyon, France), tidal races (e.g., Skookumchuck Narrows, Canada; The Arches, Malahide Estuary in Dublin, Ireland), big volume rivers (e.g., Gerberator, Baby Face and Horseshoe on the Ottawa River, Canada; The White Nile, Uganda; The Zambezi, Zambia), natural playspots (e.g., The Rbioux wave on the Durance, France; School House Rock "KRH" playhole, California; Kaituna "bottom hole," Rotorua, New Zealand), and man-enhanced playspots (e.g., The Salida playhole, Colorado; The Golden Kayak Park, Golden, Colorado).

In these playspots paddlers work with and against the dynamic forces of the water to perform a variety of maneuvers. These can include surfing, various vertical moves (i.e., cartwheels, loops, blunts), and spinning the boat on all possible axes of rotation. More recently aerial moves have become accessible, where paddlers perform tricks having gained air from the speed and bounce of the wave. Kayaks used for playboating are roughly 6 feet long, lightweight, made from plastic (which is more robust than fiberglass or wood), and generally have relatively low volume in the bow and stern (thus allowing the paddler to submerge the ends of the kayak with relative ease). Competitions for playboating or freestyle are sometimes called "whitewater rodeo" in the United States, but more frequently referred to as freestyle events in the United Kingdom and Europe. One cultural commentator describes these competitions as follows:

Paddlers usually get about 45 seconds to demonstrate to observant judges that they can handle the adversity of the ravenous, man-eating wave with relative ease, performing more tricks, and harder tricks, than anybody else who shows up. The tricks, flaunting such official-sounding names as "McNasty," "Donkey Flip" and "Space Godzilla," are worth point levels that vary by difficulty, combination and quality of execution. Freestyle kayaking is so fresh and dynamic that it even allows riders to introduce undefined tricks to the judges beforehand, giving inventive types a chance to contribute to the continual progression of the sport. (Bailey, 2006, 6)

Simply put, in comparison to traditional canoeing and kayaking competitions where he objective is to obtain the fastest time, competitors in freestyle events are judged on performance in similar ways to skateboarders and surfers. While competitions are gaining popularity among young freestyle paddlers, the element of play is the essence of this style of participation. While freestyle kayaking is often considered safer and requiring less effort than whitewater river running or creeking, this is not always the case.

Competition at the Top

Sprint canoeing and kayaking racers compete each year in world championships as well as in the summer Olympic Games every four years in: kayak singles (K-1), kayak tandem (K-2), kayak fours (K-4), and Canadian singles (C-1), Canadian tandem (C-2), and Canadian fours (C-4). The Olympic performance of Germany's athletes was important to the Nazi leader Adolf Hitler, and Germany had a top-three medalist in eight of the ten canoeing and kayaking events in the 1936 Olympics. Other strong contenders in the early years were Austria, France, Sweden, Canada, and Czechoslovakia. Women were allowed to compete in 500-meter sprints in the Olympics in London in 1948, and in the 1956 Olympics in Melbourne, Australia, the Soviet Union made the medals list.

In 1972 slalom racing entered the Munich Olympics as a demonstration sport but had made only its third appearance during the 1996 Olympics in Atlanta, Georgia, because many host countries cannot offer a whitewater venue.

Australia's Danielle Woodward won a silver medal in slalom racing at the Olympics in Barcelona, Spain, in 1992.

Then the 2000 Olympics in Sydney further inspired Australia to build a multimillion-dollar slalom course, the only facility of its kind in the Southern Hemisphere. This course has enhanced the training of canoeists and kayakers in the surrounding countries and made them a more dominant force in competition.

Governing Body

The ICF, formed in 1924, has governed international canoe and kayak racing since World War II and has 117 national associations as members. Europe leads the way with forty-three associations, Asia has twenty-nine, the United States has twenty-four, Africa has fifteen, and Oceania has six. The ICF is located in Madrid, Spain.

The ICF formed to provide a link between national associations, to organize international competitions in three flatwater events (kayak racing, Canadian canoe racing, and canoe sailing), to promote foreign touring through river guides and tourism materials, and to share educational materials about the disciplines. Now millions of people are involved in a variety of competitive events globally.

The Future

Whereas at one time paddling appealed to only people who also hiked and backpacked, paddling has a much broader appeal today, and women in particular often see it as a way to gain outdoor skills. In Europe and mountainous countries such as New Zealand, kayaking was once the province of competitors and hard-core adventurers who could handle the rigors of steep, alpine rivers. However, more recreational paddlers are discovering the joys of learning to negotiate whitewater. River kayaks are shorter and highly maneuverable boats, and new paddlers require instruction to paddle them safely in swift water. Whitewater schools have joined paddling clubs as important developmental programs for recreational paddlers as well as would-be racers.

An analysis of canoeing and kayaking participants reveals some trends. According to the 2004 "Outdoor Recreation Participation Study" released by the Outdoor Industry Association, kayaking has experienced a 235.7 percent increase in new participants between 1998 and 2003—a gain of 5.7 million people. That increase makes kayaking one of the top three fastest-growing activities behind artificial wall climbing and snowboarding. More than half of the participants—2.5 million—are women. The average age of participants is thirty-one years, and they participate an average of seven days each year. Canoeing declined slightly in participation during the same period, but canoeists still outnumber kayakers with 12 million participants. Of that total, 5.9 million are women who average twenty-six years of age. The 6.1 million men who canoe average thirty years of age. About half of those who canoe also fish, and the average number of days in which they canoe is six days. The most active age group for either activity is children from twelve to seventeen years of age. Surprisingly, members of the next most active group of kayakers are ages forty-five to fifty-four, and in canoeing members of the next most active group are ages thirty-five to forty-four.

Most people paddle on vacations, at summer camps, and on adventure travel excursions. Sea kayaking is experiencing a surge in growth internationally as the result of a general growing interest in adventure travel. The longer, sleeker sea kayaks are easy to paddle and stable and thus offer a secure and rewarding introduction to an outdoor experience. They also allow people to explore such beautiful and exotic locations as sea caves in Thailand, the rocky shores around Great Britain and Norway, the dolphin-filled bays and straits of New Zealand, and the island chains within the United States' Great Lakes.

People who fear being enclosed in a kayak can try sit-on-top kayaks, which seem like modified surfboards and have their origins in surfing cultures along the Pacific Ocean. These kayaks look like the bottom half of a kayak with a seat and foot supports that allow paddlers to control the kayak. Canoes continue to be a sensible option for families, and the larger size of canoes allows people a greater opportunity for wilderness travel for extended periods of time.

The ICF moved sharply away from its original promotion of paddling tourism, but the public has continued to be attracted to the wealth of opportunities internationally and fascinated by the many designs of canoes and kayaks.

Laurie Gullion

Further Reading

Anders, M. (2005). Steve Fisher. In G. Schaffer (Ed.), *Faces outside: The 20 greatest athletes now* (pp. 38–42). New Mexico: Mariah Media.

Arina, E. Y. (1987). *Inuit kayaks in Canada: A review of historical records and construction*. Ottawa: National Museums of Canada.

Bailey, B. (June 2006). Playboating: Kayaking's wild side. *Fitness Plus*.

Bond, H. (1995). *Boats and boating in the Adirondacks*. Blue Mountain Lake, NH: Adirondack Museum/Syracuse University Press.

Daley, J. (2005). Nikki Kelly. In G. Schaffer (Ed.), *Faces outside: The 20 greatest athletes now* (pp. 76–78). New Mexico: Mariah Media.

Eleftheriou, K. (n.d.). Canoeing injuries and kayaking injuries. Retrieved from http://www.sportsinjurybulletin.com/archive/canoeing-kayaking-injuries.html

Endicott, W. T. (1980). *To win the worlds: A textbook for elite slalomists and their coaches*. Baltimore: Reese Press.

Fiore, D. (2003). Injuries associated with whitewater rafting and kayaking. *Wilderness and Environmental Medicine, 14* 255–260.

Ford, K. (1995). *Kayaking*. Champaign, IL: Human Kinetics Publishers.

Gullion, L. (1994). *Canoeing*. Champaign, IL: Human Kinetics Publishers.

Gullion, L. (1999). *A Ragged Mountain Press guide: Canoeing*. Camden, ME: Ragged Mountain Press/McGraw-Hill.

Heed, P., & Mansfield, D. (1992). *Canoe racing*. Syracuse, NY: Acorn Publishing.

Kawaharanda, D. (n.d.). The settlement of Polynesia, part I. Retrieved May 22, 2004, from http://leahi.kcc.hawaii.edu/org/pvs/migrations part1.html

Jennings, J. (2002). *The canoe: A living tradition*. Buffalo, NY: Firefly Books.

Livingston, C. (2005). The magnificent seven. In G. Schaffer (Ed.), *Faces outside: The 20 greatest athletes now* (p. 79). New Mexico: Mariah Media.

Reimers, F. (2005). Young guns. In G. Schaffer (Ed.), *Faces outside: The 20 greatest athletes now* (pp. 133–137). New Mexico: Mariah Media.

Snaith, S. (1997) *Umiak: An illustrated guide*. Eastsound, WA: Walrose & Hyde.

Whitewater kayaking. Retrieved from http://en.wikipedia.org/wiki/Whtewater_kayaking

Windsurfing

Windsurfing originated during the mid-1960s and combined elements of surfing and dinghy sailing. However, claims of who "invented" the sport are still contested, with several North Americans and a British man, Pete Chilvers, staking their claim. Chilvers professes to have launched a windsurfing-type craft off Hayling Island in Hampshire, England, as early as 1958. By 1968 two California surfers, Hoyle Schweitzer and Jim Drake, had asserted their place in windsurfing history by patenting a product called the "Windsurfer" in the United States and Europe. However, court battles between "inventors" proliferated, resulting in the patent being revoked. Without the legal and financial restraints, the industry developed rapidly; by the mid-1970s companies were producing windsurf boards around the Western world, the centers being Europe, North America, Japan, and Australia.

The equipment consists of the windsurf board, which is similar in shape to a wide surfboard and like a surfboard is steered by the feet, and the "rig," which is a sail, mast, and boom (which the surfer holds on to). Propulsion is provided by the power of the wind and in some forms of the sport—wave windsurfing—the power of the wave. The most popular type of windsurfing is fun boarding, which takes place in "planing" conditions and often on boards (short boards) that do not support the weight of the surfer. Planing conditions are those in which the wind is strong enough to lift the board onto the surface of the water so that it skims along the surface at speeds of 32–72 kilometers per hour.

Development

Windsurfing and its subculture expanded rapidly during the 1980s, the catalyst being the evolution of the fun board in the mid-1980s. The fun board was shorter, more maneuverable, and about half the weight of its predecessors. Advances in technology, particularly the development of materials with higher strength-to-weight ratios, resulted in lighter, more efficient, and durable boards and rigs that were easier to use and transport. During this period windsurfing was the fastest-growing sport in Europe, and more than half a million boards were sold worldwide. By the early 1990s windsurfing had reached a period of maturation, despite technological innovations in the 1990s enabling manufacturers to produce boards weighing as little as 5 kilograms. These advances made the sport easier to learn and more exciting for participants and led to the creation of specialist forms of windsurfing such as freestyle, speed sailing, and wave sailing and spawned new sports such as kite surfing.

It is difficult to assess the number of participants in windsurfing because participation takes place in largely unregulated spaces. Furthermore, large-scale surveys that attempt to quantify participation levels tend to use different methodologies and different definitions, for example, often failing to differentiate between those who take part occasionally, such as on multiactivity holidays, and those who are committed participants. Survey data, therefore, need to be treated with caution. With that caveat, data in the United Kingdom suggest that an estimated 640,000 "regular" windsurfers in 1991 were using both coastal and inland waters. Trends suggest that windsurfing benefited from significant increases in participation in the early 1980s, declined steadily through the late 1980s, and rebounded slightly in the early 1990s. Mintel (1998), however, reported a slight reduction in windsurfing in the United Kingdom between 1991 and 1995. The overall decline in windsurfing may indicate a maturing and consolidation of the market, with a higher proportion of expert windsurfers and a lower proportion of casual windsurfers. Furthermore, Church and colleagues (2001) note that the new type of short but high-volume beginner's board that came onto the market in 2001 makes windsurfing easier for beginners and may stimulate demand.

The Windsurfing Culture

Historically, as Bourdieu (1984) has observed, windsurfing, like similar "new sports," originated in North America in the late 1960s and was then imported to Europe by U.S. entrepreneurs. With its roots in the countercultural social movements of the 1960s and 1970s windsurfing has characteristics that are different from those of the traditional "dominant," institutionalized, Western "achievement" sports cultures. The windsurfing culture has a participatory ethos that promotes fun, individualism, and self-actualization. Windsurfing has resisted institutionalization. It has few formal rules and regulations and fewer formal restrictions and exclusion policies than do more traditional sports. Only a minority of participants are active members of organizations and tend not to join windsurfing clubs unless forced into membership to gain access to the water, such as inland lakes, or to join in social activities. Even if they are members of clubs based at one location, many people still windsurf at other locations. More advanced participants, in particular, are quite nomadic, engaging in local "surfaris" to different beaches, searching out the best wind and sea conditions.

The sport has developed its own subculture with its own values and ideologies, lifestyle, argot, and "style" that are distinctive from those of many traditional sports cultures but share some values with similar lifestyle sport cultures, and especially the surfing culture from which windsurfing evolved. Committed windsurfers, like surfers, identify with the role of being a windsurfer, and the activity is central to their lives. However, as the sport has developed, the subculture has become more fragmented, encompassing different forms of the sport with their distinct subworlds and "scenes," such as wave sailors and "soul windsurfers." Yet, despite some differences, these subworlds retain their identity within the subcultural whole and share characteristics, attitudes, and values. A crossover also exists in participation between cognate water sports such as surfing and kite surfing. Like the legendary Hawaiian "watermen" among the elite windsurfing community on Maui, participants such as Robby Naish, Laird Hamilton, Pete Cabrina, Rush Randle, and Dave Kalama have become famous for their involvement in tow-in surfing and/or kite surfing as well as windsurfing.

Is Windsurfing Extreme?

Dant and Wheaton (forthcoming) argue that windsurfing is not an extreme sport in terms of danger or physical risk. Windsurfers have been killed in collisions or drowned at sea, but such incidents are rare. Wave sailing is the form of windsurfing where physical risk is most apparent as windsurfers jump or "loop" (somersault above the water) many meters into the air, which can result in the board and rig falling on top of the sailors. Like surfers, windsurfers search out and ride increasingly large waves, such as at Jaws on the windsurfing mecca of Maui, Hawaii. Yet, despite the risk, serious injuries are relatively rare. Whether sailing for fun or for competition, the majority of participants face little risk of serious injury even through falling off at high speed.

Dant and Wheaton suggest that what is extreme about windsurfing and what makes it fascinating to watch and participate in is the complexity of the dynamic relationship between the sailor's body, the kit of sail and board, the water, and the wind. It "combines material, embodied and subcultural capital in ways that cannot be separated out . . . it is the shared understanding of the windsurfing experience within the subculture of windsurfers that ultimately gives meaning to the distinctive merging of body, kit, environment that makes windsurfing into the 'extreme' sport it is" (Dant and Wheaton, forthcoming).

Windsurfers themselves often reject the label of "extreme," which they tend to see as applied by the mainstream media and marketers. Participants describe windsurfing as a lifestyle rather than a sport. A particular style of life is central to the meaning and experience of windsurfing. Participants seek out a lifestyle that is distinctive, often alternative, and that gives them a particular and exclusive social identity.

Commodity Consumption

The landscape of lifestyle sports is increasingly characterized by a range of global commercial images and interests, and windsurfing is no exception. The expansion of global consumer capitalism is particularly evident in the commodities linked to the sport; an ever-burgeoning industry based on the manufacture of specialized equipment and accessories, ranging from wetsuits, sunglasses, T-shirts, sandals, boards, and jewelry to watches, entices the consumer and has increasingly become part of mainstream fashion. Importers or distributors of the multinationals such as Quicksilver and Oakley exist in many countries, helping to produce standardized products and promotional materials. However, also significant are locally based artisans such as the custom board manufacturers and nationally significant clothing brands.

The centrality of the equipment to the windsurfing experience and culture is illustrated by the ways that participants often chart their own windsurfing careers or histories in terms of their equipment, in particular which boards they have owned. However, status in this subculture is based on windsurfing prowess, "attitude," and commitment, not money spent on the sport. As Wheaton (2000) illustrates, although money is essential to become involved in the sport, economic capital won't lead to subcultural status. For example, whereas less-core windsurfers perceive that having the most up-to-date or the most technical equipment intended for more skilled sailors signifies that they are "real" windsurfers, core windsurfers view that perception as a "novice gaffe"—a mismanagement of the process of identity performance. Those people whose lifestyle revolves around windsurfing and who commit time and effort to the sport (and thus usually have a higher skill level) have a higher status among group members, leading Wheaton (2000) to describe windsurfing as a "culture of commitment."

Windsurfing is popular among participants in many industrialized nations, although the centers are Europe, Australasia, and North America, particularly Hawaii. Maui is home to an international community of windsurfers and for several decades has been the center for innovation in equipment. Nevertheless, contrary to stereotypes of windsurfing that suggest it is a sport practiced only in exotic, warm locations, windsurfing takes place in colder climates. For example, the beaches of northern California and Oregon are popular in the United States. In Europe windsurfing centers include the Atlantic coasts of the United Kingdom, Ireland, and France, the North Sea coastal area of Holland and Denmark, and inland lakes in Germany, Austria, Italy, and Switzerland. Improvements in wetsuit technology have enabled participants to continue going into the ocean year around. The sport is also practiced in less-developed countries, including those of South Africa, South America, and

Windsurfer in Poole Harbour, United Kingdom. Source: istock/Joe Gough.

the Caribbean and Pacific Islands; however, because of the cost and lack of availability of the specialized equipment, travelers, rather than indigenous communities, often constitute the majority of participants.

Interaction between these groups of participants occurs symbolically and directly. Despite the relative dearth of organizations, informal small-group interactions play an important role in retaining the conformity in information and cultural characteristics of the windsurfing subculture and allow members in widespread areas to stay in touch. Travel is an integral part of the windsurfer's lifestyle. "Surf safaris," competitions, car trunk sales, and trade shows encourage links between different nations, groups, and communities. Specialist windsurfing magazines and videos are important subcultural resources and, although produced

nationally, have much wider audiences, which helps in the exchange of ideas such as the latest techniques, equipment, and other forms of insider information.

Windsurfing Competition

In 1984 windsurfing was accepted in the Olympic Games as a class in the yachting events. Women and men competed together, although by 1994 separate women's and men's classes were established. However, for many windsurfing participants the pinnacle is represented by the professional fun board circuit under the auspices of the Professional Windsurfing Association (PWA). Competitions take place in a number of categories, including wave sailing, freestyle, racing, speed sailing, and even the media-driven spectacle of indoor windsurfing. Women have their own sailing fleets in each organization, although numbers of competitors tend to be much smaller.

Robby Naish is acknowledged as one of the greatest windsurfers of all time, with a career that now spans more than twenty years since he won his first world title in 1976 at age thirteen. Naish continued to be at the pinnacle of wave sailing competition into the mid-1990s. Since retiring from PWA competitions, Naish has continued to be influential in the windsurfing industry, founding Naish Board and Sails. Along with other Hawaii-based windsurfers, such as Rush Randle, he became a major influence in the development of kite surfing. Dutch Bjorn Dunkerbeck, who lived in the Canary Islands and competed for Spain, took over from Naish as the king of the PWA circuit, becoming PWA champion twelve times between 1988 and 1999, dominating most disciplines of windsurfing competitions in the 1990s. In recent years the women's circuit has been dominated by Spanish twins Iballa and Diada Ruano Moreno, who, with financial sponsorship, including Roxy, have helped progress women's wave sailing and freestyle.

Recreational windsurfers, however, tend not to engage in formal competitions. For example, the largest competitive windsurfing organization in the United Kingdom, the United Kingdom Boardsailing Association (UKBSA), had only twelve hundred members nationwide in 1994. Furthermore, Coalter and MacGregor report that there were fewer elite young windsurf racers nationally in the late 1990s than in the late 1980s. For many windsurfers formal competition opposes the freedom and ethos of the windsurfing lifestyle. However, competition takes other forms—that of pitting self against the elements and gaining peer respect and subcultural status. As in surfing, big-wave riding has become one of the most revered forms of windsurfing. As Booth outlines, "Big-wave riders are surfer's warrior caste: riding giant waves bestows the greatest prestige" (Booth 2004, 104). Riding big waves—whether on a windsurfer or surfboard—requires "skill, strength, endurance, cunning and courage" (Booth 2004, 104), those forms of physical capital that bestow the greatest subcultural capital or status.

Kanaha

Unless you're an aspiring pro windsurfer or an expert windsurfer, Kanaha is probably the place you should be sailing when you come to Maui.

Kanaha is divided into two main sailing areas. The upwind launch and wave break is known as Uppers, the lower (downwind) launch and break is known as Lowers. Most of the time Lowers tends to be a little bit smaller wave than you'll find at Uppers though it is also often a cleaner, longer and more predictable wave than the breaks at Uppers. Lowers also tends to be a little lighter winds than Uppers most of the time. Look for the yellow lifeguard tower and swimming area. Looking straight out from that is the Lowers break. Launch downwind of the swimming area. Don't even think about venturing into the swimming area, even if you're swimming your gear in.

Just upwind from the break at Lowers, if there's any kind of waves breaking, you should see a wave breaking at an odd angle. This is the "Weird Wave." Avoid it. There's a channel between the break at Lowers and Weird Wave. This is your best bet for getting outside the reef if you're not comfortable sailing through the waves.

Source: Maui windsurfing. (2007). Retrieved Feb. 1, 2007, from http://www.mauiwindsurfing.net/mauiwindsurfing info/info.cfm?info=launches

Identity and Difference

A central question that sociologists have asked about "new sports" cultures such as windsurfing is whether the power inequalities that characterize traditional institutionalized sports cultures, particularly with respect to gender, class, sexuality, and race, are qualitatively and quantitatively different. That is, in the windsurfing culture are existing power relations and patterns of inclusion and exclusion reproduced, or does the sport present a challenge to traditional sporting identities and practices?

Windsurfing and its culture are clearly dominated by men; furthermore, participants are predominantly able-bodied, middle class, white, and, as already noted, tend to be from Western industrialized nations. Windsurfing is an expensive leisure sport, and thus participants tend to need sufficient resources to enable them to purchase the equipment and travel to windsurfing locations. Without the financial means, participants' ability to sustain interest and involvement is limited. Furthermore, windsurfing is a time-consuming sport, which restricts many participants, in particular women.

Despite improvements in both teaching equipment and methods that have made the sport more accessible, the perception persists that windsurfing is a difficult sport to learn and that participation depends on strength and power. The mainstream and subcultural media perpetuate this perception by focusing on young males performing advanced windsurfing, with women often playing the symbolic role of the "beach babe," thus representing windsurfing as the preserve of heterosexual young men. This emphasis on the "hard core" element of the sport functions to exclude all those who are different, "outsiders," and particularly women.

Nevertheless, it is a myth that windsurfing performance requires excessive strength; good technique also re-quires balance, flexibility, and grace. Moreover, involvement in the sport is more varied than media images often suggest. Although elite windsurfers *are* predominantly young men (mostly in their twenties), committed recreational participants tend to be older, with active participants ranging from boys to men in their sixties and older. Likewise, although data suggest that women constitute only 13–30 percent of "regular" windsurfers in countries where data are available, research in the United Kingdom has suggested that women's involvement in the subculture is more complex and contradictory; ranging from those women who do not windsurf but whose partners are involved ("windsurfing widows") to those women for whom windsurfing is a central part of their lives. Women windsurfers of all levels and ages have articulated the freedom, confidence, and independence gained through windsurfing, seeing the windsurfing culture as an important arena for developing a sense of identification or self, separate from other people, and norms of female embodiment. Elite women are continuing to push the limits of this still-developing sport and to challenge the association between elite participation and masculinity. For example, Angela Cochran of the United States became the first woman, and one of only a handful of people of either gender, to windsurf the huge waves at the surf break Jaws on Maui. Some participants argue that women-only environments help women to develop their skills in a supportive, safe, less-heterosexist, and noncompetitive environment. However, for men, too, windsurfing has been seen as a sporting sphere that is less excluding of "other" men (men, for example, who are less skilled or of a different class or ethnicity) than traditional sports cultures

and an important site for the performance of less-macho sporting masculinities.

Belinda Wheaton

See also Gender; Surfing

Further Reading

Booth, D. (2004). Surfing: From one (cultural) extreme to another. In B. Wheaton (Ed.), *Understanding lifestyle sports: Consumption, identity and difference* (pp. 94–109). London: Routledge.

Bourdieu, P. (1984). *Distinction: A social critique of the judgement of taste.* London: Routledge & Kegan Paul.

Church, A. (2001). *Water based sport and recreation: The facts: Report prepared for Department for Environment, Food and Rural Affairs (Countryside Division).* Brighton, UK: University of Brighton Consortium.

Dant, T., & Wheaton, B. (forthcoming). Sailing a board—an extreme sport? *Anthropology Today.*

Profile Sport Consultancy Survey. (1994). *The United Kingdom windsurf report.* Profile Sport Market Consultancy and the Royal Yachting Association.

Tomlinson, A., Ravenscroft, N., Wheaton, B., & Gilchrist, P. (2004). *Lifestyle sport and national sport policy: An agenda for research:* Report to Sport England.

Turner, S. (1983). Development and organisation of windsurfing. *Institute of Leisure and Amenity Management, 1,* 13–15.

Wheaton, B. (2000). Just do it: Consumption, commitment and identity in the windsurfing subculture. *Sociology of Sport Journal, 17*(3), 254–274.

Wheaton, B. (2004). *Understanding lifestyle sports: Consumption, identity and difference.* London: Routledge.

Wheaton, B. (2005). Selling out? The globalization and commercialisation of lifestyle sports. In L. Allison (Ed.), *The global politics of sport* (pp. 140–161). London: Routledge.

Wheaton, B., & Tomlinson, A. (1998). The changing gender order in sport? The case of windsurfing. *Journal of Sport and Social Issues, 22,* 252–274.

Woodward, V. (1995). Windsurfing women and change. Unpublished master's thesis, University of Strathclyde, Glasgow, UK.

Wing Walking

From the time of Leonard da Vinci to the present, human beings have dreamed of mastering the sky. In his autobiography, Charles Lindbergh, the famous aviator, poetically described the act of flying as "living in the strange, unmortal space, crowded by beauty, pierced with danger" (2003). Today, travel by air is a routine part of the everyday lives of people around the world, who have grown accustomed to accumulating frequent flier miles, getting online to purchase e-tickets, and well, retrieving lost luggage.

For all of the allure and convenience that flying affords modern travelers and adventurers, concerns about flying remain much as they were when aviation was in its infancy. Consumers still need to be reassured that the skies are safe and that the risks associated with flying are minimal. The difference a century makes, however, is in the degree to which flying has changed from a novelty experienced by a rare few in the early 1900s to something taken-for-granted and experienced by millions of business travelers alone in the early 2000s. This article provides a brief look at a phenomenon called barnstorming, which helped popularize airplanes in the United States; a glimpse at the wing walkers who helped make barnstorming a sensation; and the state of barnstorming and wing walking today.

Origins of Barnstorming in the 1920s

Although the Wright brothers made the first powered flight in 1903, the prospect of getting into the cockpit of a flying machine was still foreign to most people two decades later. Going aloft in a wooden crate with an engine and wings inspired a mix of awe and admiration as well as suspicion and skepticism.

During World War I (1914–1918), the pioneering efforts of Glenn Curtiss, the Wright brothers, and others would add a new dimension to military tactics, that of the aerial assault. The Curtiss JN-4 biplane, otherwise known as the Curtiss Jenny, was used to train pilots during World War I. One of the enduring images from the Great War was that of the top pilot designated as an "ace" who downed at least five enemy aircraft during combat (Varchol 2004). In the United States, Eddie Rickenbacker, who accumulated twenty-six victories in battle, and others were presented by media as heroes. Through their exploits the public became more familiar with the airplane and its possible uses. However, the idea of a civil aviation industry that affected the lives of people in communities far and wide remained a remote one.

Following World War I, conditions were ripe for the growth of civil aviation. Pilots who had trained in the military returned home with a desire to continue their careers in aviation. The availability of cheap war surplus aircraft made the creation of businesses possible, and the lack of regulations governing flying at that time allowed for surges in creative marketing and experimentation that fueled an explosion in flying activity in the 1920s.

Pilots purchased Curtiss Jenny biplanes from the United States government at much reduced prices. As entrepreneurs, they faced the challenge of appealing to a public at once fascinated with the idea of flight but fearful of it as well. Imagine trying to persuade the average woman or man to leave the ground in a contraption that hardly looked stable when so few had done it and when those who did often met with a fatal end?

Out of the necessity to expose customers to the wonders of flight on a personal level, the rollicking phenomenon of barnstorming was born. In what would be considered today a grassroots marketing effort, pilots traveled around the country, visiting small town after small town, showcasing themselves and their planes for local audiences hungry for entertainment delivered right to their neighborhood by way of the sky.

Aviators negotiated with farmers for the use of available fields as temporary landing strips and runways, thus the term *barnstorming*. Once the detail of where they were going to stage a performance was settled, barnstormers would fly overhead, announcing their arrival in town by dropping leaflets and handbills to a surprised and interested clientele. The advertised air shows and exhibitions were designed to draw customers with promises of daring feats of flying skill and other stunts, including parachuting and wing walking. For a fee pilots also offered rides to spectators.

Pilots or aerialists were often greeted with tremendous enthusiasm from local citizens, many of whom had never seen an airplane up close before. A sense of the warm receptions given to barnstormers can be discerned in the reminiscence of Frank Ellis, a Canadian aerialist. He recalled that as the sound of the plane's engine overhead was heard, the whole town would stop what they were doing to look skyward, and children were released from school so that they too could have a chance to be on hand for the festivities. Following by sight and/or sound, people would leave their homes and workplaces to trail behind the plane as it made its way to the landing site. Ellis described the reaction of local citizens in one town this way, "In 'tin Lizzies,' buggies, and wagons, on horseback, on bicycles, and on foot, first to arrive was a breathless youngster who triumphantly thrust a ragged but precious handbill into the pilot's hand" (Graham, 1930).

Barnstorming performances included a wide range of stunts, contingent on the expertise and nerve of the pilot as well as the wherewithal of the plane. Although many pilots also handled their own tricks, over time, some began to specialize in certain maneuvers, leading to a distinction

between stunt pilots and aerialists. Stunt pilots were more inclined to perform breathtaking spins and dives, including the well-known loop-the-loop and barrel rolls. In contrast aerialists gained notoriety by performing feats outside of the cockpit, such as wing walking, parachuting, and midair transfers from one plane to the other or between a plane and another moving vehicle.

The most organized of the barnstorming acts were the "flying circuses," which employed multiple planes and several stunt people. Arguably the most traveled of the barnstorming acts, the Ivan Gates Flying Circus performed in almost every state in the union and abroad. The Gates enterprise was the first to promote the one-dollar "joy ride." One of the co-owners, Clyde Panghorn, specialized in flying upside-down, earning him a stage name that reflected his area of expertise. "Upside-Down" Panghorn also held the record for changing planes in midair.

Other well known flying circuses were run by Jimmy Angel, whose brother Eddie dazzled crowds with the "Dive of Death," a free fall of 5,000 feet performed at night while Eddie held a pair of big flashlights to aid spectators in viewing his descent to earth . The husband and wife team of Jimmy and Jessie Woods became fixtures on the air show circuit as the Flying Aces Circus. Along with their partner, Vincent "Squeek" Burnett, the Woods's were credited with several innovations including the introduction of pyrotechnics into

their shows and executing what they billed as aerial "dog fights." Burnett pioneered the art of picking up small objects, such as a handkerchief, off of the ground with the tail wire while flying in an inverted position. The influential and visionary William J. Powell, who is credited with carrying on the work of the first African-American aviatrix, Bessie Coleman, organized and ran the "The Five Blackbirds."

Wing Walkers

According to the U. S. Centennial Flight Commission, "If barnstormers were the most exciting daredevils in the late 1920s, then wing walkers were the most extreme and intrepid individuals among them." Considered the "King of the Wing Walkers," Ormer Locklear started his career as a pilot, but the cockpit seemed far too small to contain his considerable energies and spirit. Joining the U. S. Army Air Service in 1917, Locklear endeared himself to his commanding officers by venturing out onto the wing to make minor repairs to the planes he was piloting. Although these were offenses that might otherwise have warranted a court martial, Locklear's superiors noted the effect his behavior had on improving morale among the troops, who harbored their own concerns about the soundness of the Jenny biplanes they were asked to pilot. Thus, Locklear's periodic

Stunt planes with wing walkers. Source: istock/Mark Bond.

Wing Walker Helen Tempest's First Wing Walking Experience

Chalford resident Helen Tempest could be described as a frequent flier. In fact, she flies over a hundred times a years—strapped to the wing of a plane, performing aerobatic feats for enthralled crowds across the globe.

I was strapped to the top wing of a Tiger Moth airplane, we did a press day up near Birmingham, and I was diving round trees and having the most exciting time.

I thought that was the only time I'd get to do it and I can't believe I've been able to turn it into a career.

I'm apparently one of world's most experienced wing-walkers because we fly about 100 shows a year around Europe and throughout the UK, and there re-

ally aren't that many other teams who do that amount of display flying…

…In the last maneuver we undo all our safety harnesses and climb from the top wing down to the front seat below, and perform an arabesque as we go. So you're literally standing on the airplane on tiptoe, on one foot, the other leg trailing behind you, holding on with one hand and waving goodbye to the crowd with the other.

Source: BBC. (2004, March 26) Gloucestershire features. Retrieved Feb. 1, 2007, from http://www.bbc.co.uk/gloucestershire/focus/2004/03/wingwalk.shtml

---

excursions on the wing were encouraged. With imitators following in his footsteps, Locklear gave expression to the art of wing walking.

After his discharge from the service, Locklear would pursue a no less colorful career as a barnstormer. With international star status and appeal, Locklear commanded as much as $3,000 a day for a performance. Drawn to the man who lived by the motto "safety second," crowds flocked to his performances. Despite his apparent disregard for personal well-being, Locklear was more than an adrenaline junkie. In explaining his reasons for being so bold, he stated, "I don't do these things because I want to run the risk of being killed. I do it to demonstrate what can be done. Somebody has got to show the way. Someday we will all be flying and the more things that are attempted and accomplished, the quicker we will get there" (Lussier 2004).

Locklear pioneered a range of maneuvers that would become standard in the repertoire of wing walkers, including handstands and hanging positions. He also helped develop the stunt of hanging from a plane by grasping some object (a rope ladder or trapeze bar) with only his teeth. Locklear also experimented with the midair transfer that Upside-Down Pangborn would later perfect.

Other wing walkers would embellish on the basics explored by Locklear, making their own contributions to the high-risk enterprise in which they were engaged. One of the stunts Locklear did not perform was that of parachute jumping. Charles Lindbergh, who would gain international renown for flying the *Spirit of Saint Louis* across the Atlantic,

started his career as a wing walker, performing a stunt called the "double-jump." This required that the performer wear two parachutes. After takeoff and the release of the first parachute, the jumper would cut it away and continue in free fall after which he would open the second parachute.

Women also distinguished themselves as wing walkers. Bessie Coleman, the first African-American female licensed pilot, was a parachute jumper (Freydberg 1994). Gladys Ingle, whose specialties included transferring from moving planes to other moving vehicles, added the intriguing element of practicing archery when she was out on the wing. Mabel Cody, niece of the Wild West Show impresario, Buffalo Bill Cody, owned her own barnstorming team and took to the wing as well (Hopkins 2000).

Locklear's noble sentiment was realized in part. It is the case that the work of stunt pilots and aerialists did change the mindset of masses of people about flying, making it more accessible as a possibility in their lives. At the same time, Locklear's motto came back to haunt him while attempting a stunt for a movie in August of 1920. A similar fate awaited many of his fellow stunt pilots and aerialists.

Government Regulation and Barnstorming Today

The popularity of air shows peaked in the 1920s when competition spurred aerialists and stunt pilots to perform more and more dangerous tricks. After a rash of highly publicized accidents resulting in multiple deaths occurred, the federal government passed legislation that banned some of the tricks that had made the air shows so popular and required owners to maintain their planes according to certain specifications, an impossible task financially for many.

In some respects, the air shows had been extremely effective as a means of educating the public about flying. Commercial airlines became more popular. As more people traveled by plane or were exposed to those who did, flying was no longer the compelling attraction it had once been. Thus, barnstorming eventually gave way to a wave of jet pilots and astronauts, who served up their own brand of riveting performances.

The traditions of barnstorming and wing walking have maintained their romantic allure over time, however. According to the International Council of Air Shows, 269 events were scheduled during the 2006 season in the United States and countries around the world. Wing walkers and stunt pilots, although regulated much more than in the early years of barnstorming, continue to thrill audiences. This generation's "Mr. Upside-Down," Walt Pierce, makes a living as a barnstormer, while fulltime scientist at the University of Notre Dame, Jenny Forsythe, performs as a wing walker on both monoplanes and biplanes. In southern Faquier County, Virginia, The Flying Circus Airshow offers open cockpit rides, airplane rides, and pilots still perform the loop-the-loop and barrel rolls for appreciative spectators (Chinn 2002).

Ellen J. Staurowsky

Further Reading

Chinn, L. (2002, August 15). A circus in the sky. *The Free-Lance Star.*

Cleveland, C. M. (1978). *"Upside-Down" Pangborn: King of the barnstormers.* Glendale, CA: Aviation Book Company.

Clyde Edward Pangborn Papers. (1918–1958). Washington State University Libraries, Manuscripts, Archives, and Special Collections. Retrieved June 28, 2006, from http://www.wsulibs.wsu.edu/holland/masc/finders/cg112.htm

Cooper, A. L. (1993). *On the wing: Jessie Woods and the Flying Aces Air Circus.* Mt. Freedom, NJ: Black Hawk Publishing Company.

Corn, J. T. (1983). *The winged gospel: America's romance with aviation, 1900–1950.* New York: Oxford University Press.

Courtwright, D. T. (2005). *Sky as frontier: Adventure, aviation, and empire.* College Station: Texas A & M University Press.

Denton, A. E. (1999, October). Attorney/wing walker Cynthia Lebourgeois gives new meaning to "legal eagle." *Louisiana Bar Journal 47,* 200–204.

Freydberg, E. H. (1994). *Bessie Coleman: The brownskin lady bird.* New York: Garland Publishing.

Graham, S. (1930). *Barnstorming to bushflying. Stuart Graham collection.* Retrieved June 28, 2006, from http://collections.ic.gc.ca/sgraham/barn.htm

Harrison, J. P. (1996). *Mastering the sky: A history of aviation from ancient times to the present.* New York: Sarpedon.

Hopkins, E. (2000). Air devils: Sky racers, sky divers, and stunt pilots. Logan, IA: Perfection Learning. International Council of Air Shows. (2006). Retrieved July 10, 2006, from http://www.airshows.org/icas.php

Kazmi, A. (2006, January 17). Wing walker shocks crowd as she "falls" off aircraft. *Gulf News.* Retrieved June 25, 2006, from http://web7.infotrac.galegroup.com

Kingsley, J. (2005, July 24). Girls look up, find new heroines: Women aviators featured at annual airfest at airport. *The Star-Gazette.* Retrieved June 25, 2006, from http://stargazette.com

Lindbergh, C. (2003). *The spirit of St. Louis.* New York: Scribner. (Original work published in 1953)

Lussier, T. (2004). Daredevils in the air: Three of the greats—Wilson, Locklear, and Grace. Retrieved June 25, 2006, from http://www.silentsaregolden.com/articles/aviationstuntmen.html

Powell, W. J. (1994). *Black aviator: The story of William J. Powell.* Washington, DC: Smithsonian Press.

Tessendorf, K. C. (1988). *Barnstormers and daredevils.* New York: Atheneum.

The Flying Aces. (2001). International Council of Air Shows Hall of Fame. Retrieved June 25, 2006, from http://www.icasfoundation.org/hall_fame/2001/hf_flyingaces.htm

U.S. Centennial of Flight Commission. Essay on barnstormers. Retrieved July 8, 2006, from http://www.centennialofflight.gov/essay/Explorers_Record_Setters_and_Daredevils/barnstormers/EX12.html

Varchol, J. (2004). The Great War and the shaping of the twentieth century. Co-produced by KCET/Los Angeles and the British Broadcasting Company (BBC). Retrieved July 8, 2006, from http://www.pbs.org/greatwar/about/index.html

Woodward, T. (2006, June 14). "It's like being a bird," says former wing walker. *The Idaho Statemen.* Retrieved July 8, 2006, from http://web7.infotrac.galegroup.com

X Games

During the last decade of the twentieth century viewership of traditional team sports such as football, basketball, and baseball began to decline among the coveted demographic of eighteen-to-thirty-four-year-old males. Because this audience had access to large amounts of liquid capital, corporate executives sought new ways to capture this audience. The popularity of so-called extreme sports offered one way. Skateboarders, skydivers, snowboarders, and mountain bikers began to appear in advertisements for a variety of products. Mountain Dew, a Pepsi product, shaped its advertising campaign around an appeal to the rebel image of extreme athletes. The campaign and others of its type proved successful, and other corporations began to tap into the winning formula, applying the "extreme" label to as many products as they could.

At the same time, the Entertainment and Sports Programming Network (ESPN), which began operation in 1987, was searching for additional content to fill the airtime of its two sports channels and seeking a way to capitalize on the popularity of extreme sports. ESPN decided to create a made-for-television extreme sports festival called the "Extreme Games." Although ESPN was mocked in many quarters for presenting a festival that featured events that many people did not consider sports, the network's experiment became an instant success and raised the visibility of extreme sports and their culture.

Ron Semiao, then director of programming for ESPN2, conceived the idea in 1993 while searching a Connecticut bookstore for the "*Sports Illustrated* of extreme sports" (Donahue 1998, G2). Semiao didn't find one magazine devoted to extreme sports but rather a host of magazines, each of which concentrated on one sport. He decided that if he could bring together the diverse cultures represented by the magazines he would, in his words, "have a winner" (Donahue 1998, G2).

Semiao, along with executive director Jack Weinert and general manager Chris Stiepock, created the Extreme Games from Semiao's original inspiration, and the first games, held in Newport, Rhode Island, were a success, "averaging 22,000 fans per day and an average television viewership of 307,138 households" (*New York Times* 2004, S1). Following the success of the original effort, ESPN decided to rename the event the "X Games" because the network felt that the word "extreme" had been "completely overused, and [ESPN felt] that X has a mystique to it" (Pedersen and Kelly 1999).

The X Games continued to grow in popularity, both in live audience and television audience, and in 1997 ESPN made the games an annual rather than biannual event and added a Winter X Games to accompany its summer games. Since then the network has created spinoffs, including the Asian, Latin, and Euro games and the X Games Global Championship.

The Original Games

The original Extreme Games featured nine main events: aggressive in-line skating, bicycle stunt riding, bungee jumping, extreme adventure racing, skateboarding, skysurfing, snowboarding, sport climbing, street luge racing, and wakeboarding. Aggressive in-line skating attempts the same kind of tricks of skateboarding, such as grinding (sliding down handrails and other objects), jumps, and acrobatic twists with recovery. In the Extreme Games bungee jumping—jumping off of a tower with elasticized cord attached to the feet, which stops the jumper short of the ground—focused on acrobatic maneuvers after the cord had sprung back. Street luge is an adaptation of the winter sport performed on ice. The luge is a larger version of a skateboard, which contestants lie on while racing downhill feet first. Skysurfing consists of a team of two skydivers, one of whom performs acrobatic moves on a snowboard while the other films the partner's actions for the judges below. Extreme adventure racing consists of contestants racing across a course via various means of conveyance such as bicycles, white water rafts, and their own legs in order to traverse difficult terrain in the fastest time. And snowboarding, using artificial slopes for trick moves, was also included in the Extreme Games.

Over the years the program of sports featured by the games has changed considerably. Bungee jumping was taken from the program because of the difficulty in judging acrobatic content. Extreme adventure racing has likewise been taken from the program, as have barefoot water ski jump, sport climbing, and skysurfing. Their place has been taken by other sports such as motocross, which features acrobatics done with motorcycles, BMX (bicycle motocross) racing, and rally car racing.

The Locales

After being held in Rhode Island in 1995, and 1996, the X Games moved to San Diego for the next two years, then to San Francisco and Philadelphia before settling in Los Angeles in 2003. At each new city attendance continued to grow, peaking at 275,000 and gaining its share of the eighteen-to-thirty-four-year-old demographic in 1999.

The first Winter X Games, in 1997, consisted of various trick skiing contests, snowboarding, snow mountain biking, and motocross. The events at the Winter X Games have remained more stable; only the big air event, during which athletes performed high jumps and tricks, has been taken off the initial schedule.

Like the summer games, the Winter X Games have traveled. The first event was held at Big Bear Lake Resort in California. After the first year the event moved to Crested Butte, Colorado, for two years and to Vermont for another two years. In 2002 the Winter X Games chose Aspen, Colorado, for their permanent base. This move represented a considerable shift in the values of winter sports because snowboarding had been forbidden on Aspen's slopes for many years.

Controversy

The X Games have not been without controversy, and the first event was largely ridiculed as a stunt designed to chase the dollars of Generation X. Critics doubted that an audience would tune in to watch such ridiculous sports as competitive climbing and compared the games with other made-for-television sporting events such as the Battle of the Network Stars, which pitted television stars against one another in various sports, including the celerity tug-of-war, and had been roundly panned in the 1970s and early 1980s. The criticism mirrored some of the comments that ESPN executives had heard when they launched the network in 1987: No one would watch except for a handful of sports junkies, who were not numerous enough to support a cable network. ESPN proved its critics wrong and continued to gamble.

Critics also denigrated the competitions that made up the X Games, arguing that bungee jumping and competitive

A street luge racer. Source: istock/ David Crockett.

X Games on the Moon?

As the X Games grow in popularity, one scientist at NASA, Dr. Tony Phillips, has an interesting venue idea.

The Moon would be a great place for X Games. Don't laugh. NASA is returning to the Moon, and where people go—especially adventurous people—sports follow.

The Moon's rugged terrain and low gravity are going to appeal to extreme athletes. Imagine what a Motocross Freestyler could do in ⅙ g. He revs his engine, tears up the ramp and soars into the sky—6 times higher and 6 times farther than usual. That's Big Air.

Dirt bikers would love it, too. Lunar impact craters provide natural racing turns and jumps. And there's plenty of moondust to cushion a hard landing. Of course, the track would need to be six times bigger than Earth tracks. Otherwise, in ⅙ g, the biker might fly.

Out there, the gear is going to be a little different. Moon bikes will look a bit weird: woven piano wire tires, exaggerated fenders, oversized handles, and a wide seat for big space bottoms.

Oh, and they'll be very quiet. Rev the engine and . . . well, that was no thrill at all!

The thrill comes in the jump—spinning gracefully through "the air" for what seems like eternity.

A perilous spray of moondust. Terrain hot enough to boil water. Breathtaking vacuum. What more could an X-athlete want?

Source: NASA. *Lunar X Games.* Retrieved February 1, 2007, from http://science.nasa.gov/headlines/y2006/04aug_xmoon.htm

shared when considering sports, and this absence caused many critics to disparage the validity of the entire event. Richard Sandomir of the *New York Times* rhetorically questioned if the games "presaged the fall of Western Civilization" and called them the "Psycho Olympics" (Sandomir 1995, B14). Robert E. Rinehart, in *Players All: Performances in Contemporary Sport* (1998), pointed out that ESPN explicitly tied extreme games to older, more established sports, constantly pointing out that the participants were professional athletes, just as if they were football or basketball players.

The first charge was undoubtedly true. ESPN was trying to tap into the Generation X market and was doing it well. Reviews of the games praised the network's coverage but in most cases continued to disparage the sports themselves. The coverage was fast and furious, not allowing for dead time. The interviews were snappy and brief, unlike those that many viewers were accustomed to on other sports programs. The network made a tremendous effort to cover the performances from all possible angles and experimented with placing cameras wherever it could, including on the helmets of competitors and on their equipment. All of this gave the games an MTV feel—television for the short attention span. The action was constant, and the attitude was "in your face," which is precisely why this representation of extreme sports appealed to younger viewers.

The second charge, that the games are not actual games as Americans had come to define them, was also true based on that definition. However, the games were an important point in evolution of the definition, for better or worse, of what constitutes a sport and an athlete. The athletes of extreme sports felt too constricted by the demands of more traditional sports such as football and basketball. Sports such as baseball, the traditional national pastime, which did allow for more individualism, lacks constant action and is therefore too slow moving (boring, in other words) to hold their attention. The Extreme Games, by giving these sports and athletes a national stage, helped to legitimize them and their vision of the meaning of sports.

Another common criticism is that almost as soon as the games had finished, the edgy sports that made up the program began to become just another corporate game. Most of the athletes who competed in extreme games came to them with varying degrees of suspicion or loathing for the corporate world, but as big sponsors began swarming, few could resist the chance to cash in, or sell out, depending on one's point of view. Accounts of the atmosphere at subsequent

climbing are not sports but rather just the pastimes of a bunch of disaffected outcasts. The lack of a ball or bat in the competitions ran counter to what most Americans considered sport. Furthermore, the absence of team competition ran counter to a deep cultural bias that most Americans

X Games often focused more on the "corporate fat cats" who swarmed to identify and brand the latest star than on what that athlete did on the halfpipe, terrain park, or jump. For example, Megan Kleinheinz, a snowboarder, remarked that, "All snowboarders say they're anticorporate, but they'd give their eyeteeth to get sponsored" (Morris 1998, ST1).

Part of the allure of extreme sports from the beginning, at least for many of the leaders in the various sports, had been the opportunity for self-promotion. New technologies such as cable television, the Internet, and inexpensive video recording equipment helped make such self-promotion possible. This allure also made many of these athletes ready to transform themselves from rebel to brand name. *Outside Magazine* mocked the attitude of athletes who play up their "radical attitudes for mercenary purposes" (Morris 1998, ST1). Critics among the communities that spawned the athletes were quick to point out any moves they considered to be selling out, and there was no shortage of targets.

Missy Giove, a star in mountain biking culture, embodied the extreme sports attitude through her tattooed and pierced appearance, her alternative lifestyle, and her frequent brushes with authority. Yet, rather than compete in the most visible event of her sport, she skipped the Winter X Games in 1998 because of conflicts between her sponsors and ESPN. Reportedly, her personal corporate sponsors, including the car maker Volvo and bicycle maker Cannondale, did not want their logos to be covered by ESPN's sponsors when she appeared in the games. Such behavior, which is easy to construe as selling out the sport to corporate interests, has made the X Games an easy target for purists in the various sports.

The lineup of corporate sponsors for the X Games also reinforced the image that extreme sports were being bought and paid for by corporate America. The largest sponsors for the original games included AT&T, Nike, General Motors, Chevrolet, Pontiac, Mountain Dew, and Taco Bell. These corporations and the current group, which includes Coke, Verizon, and Coors, gain what ESPN, in its online media kit, claims is unprecedented loyalty among eighteen-to-forty-nine-year-old male viewers, who have more than five hours of potential advertising exposure through the network each day. The network is in an enviable position with the X Games because it owns the concept and therefore does not have to compete with other networks for the rights to the telecast. The thrust of the marketing essentially is: If one wants to sell to the most prized demographic, the eighteen-to-forty-nine male group, one should go through ESPN.

The X Games have only helped the network increase its hold on this valued group.

When the games moved to San Diego for their third gathering in 1997, they also ran into protests from environmental groups, including the National Audubon Society. The groups sought a restraining order against the games over fears about the environmental impact on two endangered bird species, the California least tern and the western snowy plover. The games went on after the network and environmental groups reached a settlement, and they remained for two years in San Diego. The crowds set new records for the spectacle, with more than 200,000 each year.

Environmentalists, along with many others, were also upset when Travis Patrana, a freestyle motocross participant competing in his first X Games, jumped his motorcycle into San Francisco Bay. He forfeited his chances at winning the competition, and the network refused to run tape of his stunt. This apparent disconnect between the philosophy of extreme sports and the corporate need to smooth the sharp edges of the participants further fueled claims that the games had "gone corporate."

Despite the critics, the games continue as a central part of ESPN's sport package, and their popularity rivals or surpasses that of more mainstream sporting events such as the Olympic Games, at least in the most prized marketing demographics. In 2000 Nielsen ratings showed that 37 percent of U.S. teenage males tuned in to the games, numbers that the Olympics could not match. In 2004 the games were televised live for the first time to give viewers the same feel as the more venerable events.

The popularity of the games has also created more demand for extreme sports, both in traditional sporting venues and in the popular culture. The Winter Olympics, in an attempt to lure this younger audience to its telecasts, adopted snowboarding in 1998 as an official sport, in part because of the popularity of the X Games. In 1999 the Extreme Sports Channel, owned by the Extreme Group, a British corporation operating in the Netherlands, began broadcasting. Advertisers plaster the "extreme" label on everything from pickup trucks to soft drinks in an attempt to fit their products within the young, hip culture that accompanies these edgy sports. This process has also filtered into the popular culture, causing such venerable figures as Tarzan and James Bond to update their images, becoming more like the radical skateboarder or snowboarder to appeal to Generation X. In this change ESPN and the X Games have been on the leading edge, pulling the culture along with them.

What NeXt?

The X Games have brought extreme sports into a more mainstream position in the sporting world and raised the visibility of formerly fringe pastimes and their stars. ESPN's experiment has also increased the feeding frenzy of marketers seeking to capitalize on the popularity of these sports and to sell to the prized eighteen-to-thirty-four demographic. In the process the games and their coverage have broadened the definition of what constitutes a sport and an athlete in the United States and around the world.

Russ Crawford

Further Reading

Brown, P. L. (2000, August 13). This is extremely sporting. *New York Times*, WK2.

Donahue, B. (1998, March 11). For new sports, ESPN rules as the x-treme gatekeeper. *New York Times*, p. G8.

Elliot, S. (1996, June 21). The X Games: Going to extremes in an effort to tap a growing segment of sports. *New York Times*, D6.

ESPN ABC Sports. (n.d.). ESPN is man's best friend. Retrieved July 29, 2006, from http://mediakit.espn.go.com/index.aspx?id=138

Lair, K. (2004, August 1). The X Games just keep getting better with age: Extreme sports celebrate 10 years of action. *New York Times*, S1.

Morris, B. (1998, February 8). Extreme sport, extreme chic, extreme hype. *New York Times*, ST1.

Pedersen, P. M., & Kelly, M. L. (1999). *ESPN X Games: Commercialized extreme sports for the masses*. Retrieved August 7, 2006, from http://sptmgt.tamu.edu/espnx.htm.

Restraining order is sought against ESPN's X Games. (1997, May 29). *New York Times*, B13.

Rinehart, R. E. (1998). *Players all: Performances in contemporary sport*. Bloomington: Indiana University Press.

Ruibal, S. (2004, January 22). X Games taking a new track. *USA Today*. Retrieved July 29, 2006, from www.usatoday.com/sports/olympics/winter/2004-01-22-x-games-broadcast_x.htm

Sandomir, R. (1995, June 30). Most extreme part of extreme games is extreme coverage. *New York Times*, B14.

Index

Note: **Bold** entries and page numbers denote encyclopedia entries.

Note: **Bold** entries and page numbers
denote encyclopedia entries.

 **Index**

Note: **Bold** entries and page numbers
denote encyclopedia entries.

Note: **Bold** entries and page numbers denote encyclopedia entries.

Note: **Bold** entries and page numbers denote encyclopedia entries.

Note: **Bold** entries and page numbers
denote encyclopedia entries.

Note: **Bold** entries and page numbers denote encyclopedia entries.

Note: **Bold** entries and page numbers denote encyclopedia entries.